THE PROSPECT

Olwen Hufton is Professor of History at the European University Institute in Florence and in 1994–5 was co-director of a European Union forum on gender and the use of time. As the William Kenan Jr. Chair of European History and Women's History at Harvard University she was the first head and architect of the Women's Studies Program, as well as Senior Research Fellow at the Minda de Gunzburg Center for European Studies. She is a Corresponding Fellow of the British Academy, and the author of many books including *The Poor in Eighteenth-Century France*, which won the Wolfson prize for the best history book of 1975. In 1996, *The Prospect Before Her* won the Fawcett Prize for the most significant contribution to our understanding of women's lives and experience.

THE PROSPECT BEFORE HER

A HISTORY OF WOMEN
IN WESTERN EUROPE

VOLUME ONE
1500 – 1800

Olwen Hufton

FontanaPress
An Imprint of HarperCollinsPublishers

Fontana Press
an imprint of HarperCollins*Publishers*
77–85 Fulham Palace Road,
Hammersmith, London w6 8jb

Published by Fontana Press 1997
1 3 5 7 9 8 6 4 2

ISBN 000 686351 5

Photoset in Linotron Garamond No. 3 by
Rowland Phototypesetting Ltd, Bury St Edmunds, Suffolk

Printed in Great Britain by
Caledonian Book Manufacturing Ltd, Glasgow

For Caroline and Clare Eliza

CONTENTS

ILLUSTRATIONS

ACKNOWLEDGEMENTS

————◁○▷————

There are nine and sixty ways of constructing tribal lays
And − every − single − one − of − them − is − right!
RUDYARD KIPLING, 'IN THE NEOLITHIC AGE'

ANYONE rash enough to embark on an enterprise of this extent realizes as
the effort draws to a close that almost every single one of her friends who are
scholars in the field might have done the same thing somewhat differently.
There might have been a little more about sexuality, more about power, more
gender theory, more big names, if someone else had been the writer. *So be it.*
I have spent my professional life researching, writing and teaching about
comparative European social history and in the records concerned with survival
under adverse circumstances, with poverty, the relationships beween rich and
poor, the dynamics of communities and crime, so that this history of women
draws in the first place upon this intellectual baggage. It also, however,
owes a huge amount to friends whose work has so enriched and extended an
understanding of the many issues involved.

My first thanks are due to Patricia McNulty, in whose company I first
taught about some of the issues appearing here in the dim and distant sixties
and who read most of this script. Then comes Lyndal Roper whom I so much
admire and who drew my attention to lacunae and possibilities. Natalie Zemon
Davis, Joan Scott and Louise Tilly first invited me to talk about some of these
themes in America in 1974 when we were all new in the field of women's
history and their friendship has meant much to me. Angus MacKay and David
Higgs were unsparing in providing me with information in areas where I was
ignorant. My neighbour and fellow worker in the field Carolyn Williams was
always prepared to respond to my more abstruse questions and I never ceased
to be dazzled by her knowledge. In the course of writing this book a lot of
new friends were made. First the Dutch group, Lotte van de Pol, Rudolph
Dekker and Florence Koorn, and Herman Roodenberg, who have been
immensely generous in sharing their work and passing on to me developments
in the Netherlands. Then those made (or in the case of Simon Schama perpetuated) in the context of Harvard: Caroline Ford, Alex Owen, a host of brilliant
students some of whom were part of my writing gender history group and
will find in this book ideas we shared. I would pick out Deborah Cohen, Cara

Robertson, Paul Franklin and Michelle Jaffe, all of whom added in some way to this book, and Julie Pavlon who presided over my life and was very special.

This book, however, was to be finally written in Italy, while I was teaching at the European University Institute in Florence. This particular experience has been enriching in many ways. First I would like to thank the historians of the wider Florentine community, Sara Matthews Grieco, Gabriella Zarri and Giulia Calvi and the members of the Pentofillo group, who not only welcomed me into their midst but introduced me to developments in Italian women's history which has for me a stunning freshness and originality of direction. Secondly, valued colleagues helped, particularly John Brewer and Gérard Delille. Thirdly, I have encountered a new generation of European students in an institution which is providing a learning process for the faculty as well as the students. Of the early modernists, Silvia Evangelisti, Concepción Torres and Elisa Sampson should know that they made a fundamental impression on my knowledge of the function of religious orders. The memory of Agnes Hochberg, whose untimely death left us all diminished, will remain for ever green. My thanks must also go to Kathy Fabiani, who spent more hours over the Xerox machine than she probably cares to remember.

Finally, every book is a personal odyssey. This one was coincident with a death, that of my mother, the thorny path through adolescence of two beloved children – who were able by the end to make some contributions to this script – and aspects of the human condition which beset middle life. Brian Murphy and Beryl Williams were valued supports on both the personal and the intellectual level. New and esteemed friends – Ruth Harris and Iain Pears, Yota Kravaritou, Verena Stölke, Barbara MacLennan and Ruth Whiting of Bedales School, to whom I owe a great deal – enriched my life during the writing years. There was also birth. Olwen Dekker may have to go through life explaining her name, but her arrival in the summer of 1993 was very timely. It made me ponder further on continuities and changes and what remains in the lives of women of the world we are supposed to have lost. In addition, the event determined the title of this volume.

OLWEN HUFTON
SETTIGNANO, FLORENCE, FEBRUARY 1995

INTRODUCTION

The Limits of the Possible and Questions of Change

> I read it [history] a little as a duty; but it tells me nothing that does not either vex or weary me. The quarrels of popes and kings, with wars and pestilences in every page; the men all so good for nothing, and hardly any women at all, it is very tiresome; and yet I often think it odd that it should be so dull, for a great deal of it must be invention.
>
> CATHERINE MORLAND TO MR TILNEY, IN JANE AUSTEN, *NORTHANGER ABBEY*, BEGUN 1798

IN THE late 1950s Keith Thomas was rash enough to offer a series of lectures on seventeenth-century women to Oxford undergraduates. His colleagues found the subject bizarre and the students simply did not turn up to listen.[1] There were doubtless many good reasons. Oxford was virtually a male bastion at the time and the odds on getting a question about women in the final examination papers were probably a million to one against. Above all, however, the subject was perceived as neither relevant nor interesting.

Times have changed. The history of women as a field of enquiry emerged in the late sixties as an offshoot of the women's movement and the demands for civil rights. The conspicuous absence of women from the historical record, unless they belonged to a few small categories — queens, consorts, famous mistresses of yet more famous men, courtesans or saints — meant that history was unbalanced. Their absence was also seen in the sixties as pointing either to a grave sin of omission or to a flagrant suppression of the evidence, and hence to a distortion of the record by the historians of former times. Whether the omission was unconscious or deliberate, the result was the same: women, with a few notable exceptions, had been denied a history. Those anxious to develop women's consciousness cited the words of Simone de Beauvoir, who thought that this denial was the reason why women could have little pride in themselves.

Remedying this omission became an essential part of feminist historiography in the 1970s. Attempts were made to restore women to the historical record by focusing on their roles and experiences and by examining the effects of significant historical events like the Reformation or the growth of capitalism upon their lives. This spirit of enquiry was both vital and very productive. It inspired historians who were already working in the field of social history to re-examine their sources and to question the chronological framework upon which history was constructed. Did women have a Renaissance or an Enlightenment? It brought about the resurrection of sporadic earlier works like Alice Clark's *A Working Life of Women in the Seventeenth Century* (1919) or Lady Doris Stenton's *The Englishwoman in History* (1957), which were re-examined, reprinted and sold in numbers which far outstripped the original editions. Most importantly, perhaps, it inspired a new generation of young historians to seek out a specifically female experience in the past.

The affluent sixties and seventies were a period of burgeoning historical production. Social history was perhaps at the cutting edge of developments, under the joint stimulus of the *Annales* school and those interested in the dynamic of class formation. Family historians and demographers, historians of crime and of popular mentalities (that is, modes of understanding the physical and spiritual world, human destiny and social relationships), contributed to a growing body of knowledge and opened up new ways of looking at the past. Much of the early work in these fields had either ignored women or did not consider that they had any particular social role, outside the purely reproductive, to distinguish them from the record of men. Critics were initially suspicious of women's history as 'ghetto history'; it was accused of supplanting one imbalance by another, an activity which was directed towards discerning oppression, uncovering the injustices of the past to remedy those of the present, just as Marxist historiography was committed to finding class conflict. In spite of this criticism, the frontiers of knowledge about women in the past were pushed outwards, and in many fields of historical endeavour a deeper sensitivity to gender difference is now apparent.

Gender history, in which the particular responses of each of the two sexes and the interaction between them is given weight, has taken as much by sap as it has by storm.

Cultural history achieved a historiographical dominance in the eighties. A new generation of historians fell under the influence of the philosopher Michel Foucault, preoccupied with power relationships and the historical construction of codes of practice which defined right and wrong, normal and abnormal. Equally influential were anthropologists such as Lévi-Strauss, Clifford Geertz and the sociologist Norbert Elias, whose work on the meaning of ritual within the court society of Versailles and of the essence of the civilizing process – both published before the war – underwent a conspicuous revival.[2] None of these scholars saw sexual distinction as a primary concern; the total absence of women from Elias's narrative is not only striking but serves to date the work. But what they did do was to define and seek to understand 'culture'. Culture was broadly explained as a set of shared meanings, reflecting ingrained beliefs and determining ritual and practices and the expression of attitudes within a particular group. This group, which could be no larger than a guild or could comprehend an entire empire, was distinguished and demarcated from other groups by these shared meanings or beliefs. Within wider entities like a village or even a region, people's beliefs and attitudes could be conditioned or modified according to wealth or education, whether they belonged to ruling élites or to the illiterate masses. There was clearly a great tradition, or high culture, which could be differentiated from a little tradition, that of the *Volk*.[3] Acknowledging this distinction, the new cultural historians were quick to insist that the beliefs and attitudes implicit in both high and low culture would necessarily embody assumptions about the essence of manhood and womanhood, the male and the female. Each sex could, for example, be arbitrarily allocated certain attributes and roles: strength and valour belong to men, to make them warriors and hunters; tenderness and frailty to women, to make them nurturers and servants of men. Such attitudes would, furthermore, lay down constraints on what was fitting for each sex. Gender roles, it was argued, were constructed from beliefs, and lay at the core of any culture, determining in the case of each sex what was appropriate and what unfitting, the honourable and the shameful, the acceptable and the forbidden, the possible and that which was to be denied. In this kind of approach the Muslim veil, for example, could be a symbol and marker of an entire network of attitudes and beliefs about the proper role of women in their relationships with men within Islam. The sum of a culture was like a dance in which each generation, through a process of acculturation, learned steps according to his or her sex and class. The agents of that process of acculturation were parents and siblings; the church, the village, the peer group; other communities like guilds; the printed media, from chapbook and broadside (cheap literature available to the masses) to high literary culture. All these and innumerable other agencies contributed to the construction of class and gender roles. Both women and men were made, not born.

It followed, then, that for a developing generation dedicated to finding out about women in the past to understand the relative position of men and women in a given society, it was essential to perceive and interpret attitudes and beliefs pertaining to gender roles in text, language and visual representations. An extensive examination of such evidence would permit an understanding of the meaning of gender to that society and the messages that were conveyed to each ensuing generation.[4]

This approach has been particularly revelatory when applied to micro-history, that is, the close examination of small incidents or case histories so as to give not merely a narrative account but an interpretation of events by using psychoanalysis, psychology, semiotics and all the tools of social science. Micro-history has become one of the scholarly growth industries of our time and produced some very exciting reading. Natalie Zemon Davis, for example, in *The Return of Martin Guerre* (1983), examined a case in which an aberrant husband returned to find himself supplanted by an impostor; and she used the evidence of the resulting trial to ascertain the expectations which a particular culture, village society in sixteenth-century France, had of women and the opportunities it made available to them. Similarly, 'ego documents', that is, autobiographies and other personal testimonies (memoirs, letters, diaries, lawsuits and so on), some written by women and others embodying female voices, have been abundantly exploited to discern the impact of cultural constraints on the lives of individual women.[5]

To read and interpret a text like a lawsuit or a set of memoirs can shed immense light on how ideas on gender influenced an individual life or a particular event in the field of micro-history, but at the level of broader generalization such an exercise poses problems for the historian.

First, it has proved difficult to transfer this approach on to a broader canvas without straying into the realms of conjecture; for many social historians the attempt has carried the risk of over-speculation, the erection of the theoretical or 'generic' woman and man, versions of womanhood and manhood, at the expense of what was, as far as one can discern, the experience of real people.

Secondly, in some cases the search for gender attitudes, and the belief that individuals were made not born, have tended to discount biological differences between women and men and to insist on gender as a cultural construct alone. The English and American feminist movements have since the beginning of this century seen biological arguments as a way of denying women equality of opportunity and as an excuse for men not to share the traditional caring and nurturing tasks of women. In the twentieth century these arguments have much to recommend them, but they remain problematic. In the early modern period, biology has to count for something. No one, for example, could plough a five-inch furrow in a condition of advanced or even early pregnancy.

Thirdly, in attempting to understand the significance of rituals and cultural rules, insufficient attention has been given to the material constraints which determined the lives of the vast majority of people.

This book is about the interaction between beliefs about what was appropriate to men and to women and what occurred in the practices of everyday life. I wish to explore notions of womanhood and manhood and how such notions influenced the lives of people, as they were distinguished by wealth and geographical location, and to see how such notions and practices were modified by time. Above all, however, my aim is to integrate any experience that was defined by gender into the wider social and economic framework, a specific material world, and one in which ideas about gender were only one thread in an entire web of beliefs. The work draws upon more than two decades of writing devoted specifically to women and gender, upon a huge and ever expanding corpus of social history written with a sensitivity to the differing experience of women and men, and also upon a great deal of social, economic and cultural history which predates the pursuit of a specifically female experience.

The general social and economic history of early modern Europe has, in very broad terms, largely been written in two ways. The first stresses continuity with the medieval inheritance and accentuates the lack of fundamental change in the early modern period. The second has focused on change, whether economic (the rise of capitalism), political (the rise of the state) or socio-cultural (the construction of modern man, the making of the modern family), or on mentalities so as to pick out shifts in beliefs and attitudes (such as the waning of religious fervour). Change has been interpreted as either abrupt (the magic switch of industrialization) or gradualistic. To discern the origins of change in a given society has been proclaimed to be one of the worthiest endeavours open to the historian. It is, however, one of the most parlous. It can involve a search for a few seeds of a different strain in a field full of a traditional crop. It risks perpetrating the teleological fallacy by allowing the exceptional experience to override what was common. For these reasons, a cognizance of basic continuities in the lives of the many must be acknowledged.

Fernand Braudel has been in the forefront of the historians of continuity. His three-volume work on material civilization is not only a classic but a distillation of a huge corpus of knowledge sifted and interpreted so as to make understandable the physical constraints of the world in which people lived before industrialization.[6] When he described early modern Europe, Braudel began with an analysis of material existence and made reference to the structures of everyday life and the limits of the possible in what he saw to be an unchanging or immobile world. This approach was justified by his insistence that the life of every single individual, and his or her scope for action, were determined by the physical constraints imposed by geography, climate, technology and medical knowledge. He discerned in this world an almost total lack of change, which was particularly visible when he looked at agriculture, diet, the range of commodities available to most people, the imminence of disease and fear and the slow growth of population, with intermittent cutbacks due to famine and pestilence, which prevailed until the eighteenth century. Braudel's work was insufficiently nuanced. It presented an abbreviated version of economic man, one with a stomach rather than a mind, and he made almost no reference at all to women. Yet an acquaintance with the world he described is essential to an understanding of social relationships and the conditions of existence in the early modern period, because it accentuates the fundamental material and physical constraints which impeded change over a long period of time (*la longue durée*).

In Braudel's analysis, most Europeans between 1500 and 1800 looked directly or indirectly to the land for their livelihood. The best land was in the control of the wealthy and landed élites lived comfortably on agricultural rents and taxes paid by their tenants, the bulk of whom, along with small owner-occupiers, eked out an existence on the brink of poverty or at least were locked in a remorseless struggle for sufficiency and survival which many were doomed to lose. One bad harvest, or still worse a series such as characterized the 1690s in northern Europe (subsequently dubbed by historians 'the little ice age'), could see mortality outstripping the birthrate, as disease took its toll of the undernourished. In those Mediterranean societies which in the same decade experienced drought and swarms of locusts, the starving and the destitute flooded into the towns. The great cities of the plain of Languedoc, for example, became the burial ground for the mountain dwellers, men, women and children of remote villages in the Massif Central where food stocks were exhausted. The refugees, who were unwelcome everywhere, perished and left as sole witness of their plight their names and dates of death in the parish registers on their escape route.

In some regions, particularly the more barren uplands of central France, Alpine and Pyrenean regions or the Tuscan hills, the rural world consisted almost entirely of small owner-occupiers farming minuscule units often carved out of very marginal land. When the population grew in the sixteenth and eighteenth centuries, new land – though progressively less productive land – was brought under cultivation, or already frail sub-subsistence units were further subdivided. In other areas, the growth of cities, with their special demands for meat and dairy produce, encouraged switching from grain production to livestock, creating dependency on new outside sources of supply of grain. The extension of the vine over parts of the Mediterranean basin from the sixteenth century contributed also to the dependency of one part of Europe on another. European merchants reached out into the Baltic to find new sources of grain in exchange for wine, fish and salt.

But there was little that was new in the way Europeans farmed their land, and new crops were slow to make inroads into traditional planting rotations, though vegetables were increasing in variety. There was almost no technological breakthrough to enhance agricultural productivity throughout the period. The techniques illustrated in medieval Books of Hours were still being used by the sowers, reapers and gleaners painted by Millet in the mid-nineteenth century. The stooped figures of women bent double in the fields weeding for ten or twelve hours a day serve as a reminder that the work was backbreaking and took place in all weathers. Such work was a huge consumer of human strength and a generator of physical pain, varicose veins, rheumatism, arthritis and the prolapsed uterus.[7] Much of southern Europe lived with the recurrent problem of drought and smallholdings were frequently dependent on hand watering or the carrying of buckets of soil to sustain terraces. Most of this work was done by women and watering could occupy the farmer's wife for three to five hours a day in summer. Small wonder that Catholic prescriptive literature urged the pregnant woman to surrender as much of this kind of work as she could if she wished, as she must do as a Christian, to see a living baby.

Bread or some starchy substitute was the staple food. For most people ease was defined by having enough grain to provide everyone in the household with an appropriate daily bread ration (four to five pounds for an adult male, three for a woman, two for a child). 'Give us this day our daily bread' was an appeal utterly central to the lives of most Europeans and to their relationship with their deity. Vegetables were also important. Peas and beans were made into soup in the north-west. Root vegetables, carrots, swedes and turnips as well as cabbages, lent some variety. Round the Mediterranean a richer range of vegetables including tomatoes and aubergines was available, as well as more pungent flavours. Garlic was rubbed on hard bread, and olive oil was a considerable enrichment to the diet. Throughout Europe wine, cider or small beer, according to region, washed the meal down. The hedgerows yielded fruits. The forests were scoured for mushrooms.

Milk, cheese, eggs, butter and bacon or a little salted pork or blood sausages (black puddings) were the first luxuries most families ever knew, but they depended upon the ability to maintain livestock. Most families kept a few hens, a cow, a pig or a goat. The cow, in particular, frequently marked off the family that was fairly adequately nourished from the one that was not, but its presence was dependent on the availability of pasture. On the coast fish and shellfish and crustaceans (the food of the poor, as Jan Steen demonstrated in his *Lean Kitchen*), usually gathered by women and children at low tide, were a valued protein element. The salt herring produced by the Dutch converted the generality of the Republic's citizens into some of the best nourished of Europe and served as the basis of a lively export trade to both the Baltic and the Mediterranean. Cod, caught in North American waters, salted and dried, was also increasingly used on the continental Atlantic seaboard and in adjacent cities.

In the very poorest regions of north-west Europe which had enough water, the potato was by the eighteenth century beginning to make some inroads, and rice production was extending in the Po valley and even into parts of southern France (where it was associated, quite rightly, with malaria). In any one region, however, the variety of the diet was poor and ruled by the seasons. In these societies livestock was critical to the productivity of the soil. Apart from kelp on the coastlines, there was no fertilizer other than animal manure and for many families in the north-west there was no source of fuel other than animal turds picked up from the fields and dried, usually by women.

Such were the physical constraints of the world in which the *dramatis personae* of this volume lived, worked and reproduced themselves. Most of the energies of the European agrarian population, their working lives and the roles they assumed, were concentrated on the production of enough food to sustain life and sufficient fuel to keep warm in winter and to cook their food. To realize these goals frequently demanded abundant resourcefulness, and preoccupied both women and men throughout their lives. When survival was the sovereign imperative, a grim determinism ruled.

Diet and the availability of fuel for heating and cooking were significant markers distinguishing the rich from the poor. Daniel Defoe, writing in the 1720s about his extensive journeys throughout Britain, divided the people into seven categories. There were the great who lived 'profusely'; second, the rich who lived 'very plentifully'; third, the middle sort who lived well; fourth, the working trades who laboured but felt no want; fifth, the country people, farmers above all, who fared 'indifferently'; sixth came the poor who 'fare hard'; and last came the miserable that 'really pinch and suffer want'. Defoe thought that four-fifths of the population of Britain fell into categories four to seven and about a fifth into the last two, where poverty and misery overlapped and the transition from one to the other was easily made.[8]

Defoe's divisions serve well enough for any of the generations who are the concern either of Braudel's analysis or of this book. Most of the population of Europe depended on the state of the harvest and lived in anticipation of the worst. Fear of shortage and of being forced to pay high prices in the market was something shared by at least the bottom half of every European population. A wealthier segment, able to sell grain, traded on the profits of shortage, and at a time of rising population anyone who could muster a surplus did well. If the proportions of rich and poor in any population over the eighteenth century were relatively unchanged, this should not disguise social polarization. Those at the top had perhaps never had it so good, but the base of the social pyramid had broadened and the landless and those living precariously were in some regions much more numerous. The disappearance of famines and plagues and the beginning of population growth generated increased demands for food and work, reflected in higher prices and in wages which did not necessarily keep pace with inflation. The control of food supplies generated antagonisms. Farming families surrendered part of their produce to tax collectors, landlords and seigneurs who possessed rights in the land, and the conflicts engendered provided good business for lawyers. Such conflicts could also erupt into extensive civil strife, as in the German Peasant Wars of the 1520s and the peasant movement in the early stages of the French Revolution.

As well as living with hate and resentment, rural society, particularly at the lower levels, was rent by fear. Animal pestilence, such as murrain, was another kind of event which could destroy the long-term viability of a farming family's precarious livelihood. If the cow or goat or pig disappeared the household lost simultaneously its protein source, its fertilizer and the cash it could realize from fattening the animal's progeny. The fact that a beast which was seemingly healthy one day could sicken and die the next evoked fears that modern society can scarcely understand.

If harvest failures were highly discriminatory in their human consequences, disease was more egalitarian. The seventeenth century was the last real century of plague for Europe – thereafter outbreaks were confined to ports trading with the east – but other diseases, viral pneumonia, typhus, typhoid, and those which hit children such as measles, diphtheria, scarlet fever and chicken pox could descend upon a community in any one year and exact a collective toll beyond the power of medical knowledge to assuage. Smallpox was an especial scourge, if declining somewhat in virulence in north-western Europe in the eighteenth century. Few, even by then, were not blemished by the disease and an unscarred complexion was the first criterion of beauty. The commonest concealment made by the portrait painter anxious to please his or her client was the obliteration of such scars. The wealthy covered them in a thick white make-up which, being lead-based, was itself poisonous. Syphilis in a virulent form spread throughout the European continent in the aftermath of the Italian Wars at the end of the fifteenth century to assume less deadly aspects by the eighteenth century. Sores and pustules and noses eaten away by the ravages of sexually transmitted diseases were the hallmark of the veteran soldier or sailor or the whore plying her trade on the city street. Scurvy was the lot of many who did not have access to fresh food, and the bent, the bow-legged and the knock-kneed from rickets should be added to the gallery of deformations visible particularly in the north and north-west where fresh fruit and vegetables were seasonally circumscribed.

Nor was it only the poor who prayed for healthy 'straight' babies. The rich, in that they were better nourished and could flee the seat of plague and the unhealthiness of town life, were better placed to withstand the ravages of many diseases, but they could not buy immunity from fear. Fleas and polluted water are no respecters of persons. In rich and poor families alike, uncontrollable disease and physical disorder could rupture the unit. Mortality rates were highest in the first few months of life, and still high to the age of ten; anyone who survived this important birthday had a reasonable chance of making fifty. Even so, human life had a fragility both apparent and real. Until the eighteenth century population growth was usually followed by cutback, and when sustained growth began to be apparent it reflected in many countries a slight upward movement of the birthrate due to earlier marriage, rather than a fall in the deathrate.

Demographers of 'pre-industrial' or 'traditional' societies discern distinctive patterns of late marriage: 24–26 for women, 26–28 for men; the upper limits would reflect difficult times, since marriage depended on obtaining a farm or some other form of living. Such marriages produced roughly four to five children (excluding miscarriages and stillbirths), of whom enough would reach adulthood to ensure in normal times sluggish population growth. Patterns for the aristocracy were very different, since for most of the period the marriages of those family members designated able to marry took place earlier. The average family, then, was much smaller than in nineteenth-century industrial society, but for the bottom three-fifths of the population the nurturing of even a small brood demanded abundant ingenuity. It was common, for example, in the mountainous regions of Europe, such as the Alps, the Pyrenees, the Massif Central, the Alto Adige, the Tras os Montes, for the father of a family to absent himself for anything up to nine months a year in order to stretch the product of the holding further. Furthermore, and this was true across Europe, before the eldest children reached the age of marriage, one parent was likely to be dead.

To set against what he saw as the immobile world of the village, Braudel placed the city and town, which he saw as the only possible dynamic forces in early modern society. He pointed to a process of fitful commercial evolution in which certain cities – Florence and Venice in the fifteenth and sixteenth centuries, Antwerp and then Amsterdam and the Dutch cities in the seventeenth, London and the great Atlantic ports of England and France in the eighteenth – secured a temporary primacy and forced the pace of geographically restricted economic change. In spite of the lack of dynamism he found in the rural world, society as a whole generated some surplus wealth. This wealth, concentrated in the hands of the few, went in part into investment to sustain the base productive apparatus, but also into consumption and into sparing those who could afford it the efforts involved in supplying a house with water and basic services or, at more elevated social levels, in purchasing an affluent and leisured lifestyle. These developments nourished commercial evolution and urban growth by the production of goods and the distribution of imported commodities. The development of towns as commercial centres, and shifts caused by changing trade axes, created in Braudel's almost motionless Europe islands of activity and agencies of geographically limited change. Consuming society continued in the main to derive its wealth from the land, but there was a society of merchants, manufacturers and service trades which catered to its wishes. The towns grew as well in response to the demands of the countryside for goods it could not produce.

The movement of part of the rural population into the towns in search of work, the increasing complexity of commercial development and of the organs of government which were town-based, made the early modern city a considerable market for both basic and luxury foodstuffs. Demands could only be met by securing more food from the countryside, or extending the provisioning zone or, in some cases, by an international traffic. The countryside was hence drawn into change. Urban demands for luxury foodstuffs, meat and dairy products could, where the land was suitable, lead farmers away from grain into livestock production or into intensive mixed farming. If by 1800 most of Europe was untouched by such developments, the Netherlands from the sixteenth century, parts of Britain, France and Germany from the eighteenth, knew significant regional changes. From the seventeenth century, Holland was the entrepôt for Baltic grain to supply the grain deficits of many European regions. In the processes of change, wherever they were felt, some made fortunes but others lost out as landlords revoked common grazing rights to their own advantage or engrossed holdings in the name of increased output. Urban growth and commercial development modified, perhaps to a greater degree than Braudel was prepared to admit, the dominant narrative of continuity.

In the three centuries with which we are concerned, the kinds of goods that money could buy multiplied very considerably and as they did so they generated wealth and work. At the beginning of the period even in sturdy (or surplus-producing) peasant families most people came into the world on a straw mattress on the floor or on a communal bed shared by all the family. Their first view of their surroundings was of a room with unglazed windows and they took their first steps on an earth floor sometimes covered with rushes which might be renewed annually. They ate from wooden trenchers, sat on hard wooden furniture and wore clothes that were woven at home, roughly constructed and handed down the generations. They ate the same food that their fathers and mothers had eaten and lived with flies, rats and mice and in close proximity to livestock. Rooms were smoky and draughty in the winter. Water was fetched from a well, a spring or a river, and used sparingly for cooking and swilling pans and dairy utensils and yet more sparingly for washing the body and linen.

By the end of the period, however, the sturdy peasant as well as the urban middle classes and the gentry could satisfy whole series of new wants and cravings. Their dwellings were radically transformed. Stone and brick had replaced daub and wattle, rooms had gained in size and comfort, windows were glazed, and porcelain, metalware and a variety of textiles were available for furnishing and for personal adornment. Floors were flagged or of sanded wood and animals were banished to outhouses. More houses had books, pictures, prints and journals. Tea and chocolate and coffee and a wider variety of foods were available. Cleanliness at these levels of the population had reached a new level and fashion had come to stay as an ever-changing phenomenon dictating how the body should be presented to society. Silks and laces, muslins and fine woollens, printed cotton and flimsy fabrics meant to last no more than a season had made an appearance. Modish millinery which changed with the seasons was invented in the eighteenth century, corsetry and lingerie multiplied to achieve the perfect shape as fashion demanded.[9]

The changes were, of course, much more apparent at the top than at the bottom of society. Consuming society was not the same as producing society, and the degree to which the bottom half and more of the population failed to participate in new levels of consumption is conspicuous. Most Europeans, even by the end of the eighteenth century, rarely washed and the clothing on their backs was second- or third- or fourth-hand. Barefoot children, acceptable enough perhaps in sunny Mediterranean countries in summer, were common in the poorest agricultural regions, such as Ireland, the Highlands, the Massif Central, and visible in many of the towns and cities of north-western Europe which had poor immigrant communities. Small wonder that shoes were one of the articles most commonly filched from the market stall when immigrants made their way into the towns. Whatever the changes in the stately home and the urban bourgeois dwelling, the mud cabins and rat-infested, thatched hovels of the rural poor remained largely unchanged.

Early modern society might then be viewed as one in which continuity prevailed in the lives of the many, but it coexisted with patchy, gradual, regionally-distributed commercial evolution. This image is confirmed if, for example, we examine Dutch society in the seventeenth century. Here trade and commerce fuelled not only the fishing and ship-building industries, but domestic ones such as textile and porcelain production. Town life grew apace, drawing in the rural young who not only manned the trading vessels of the young Republic but also furnished casual labour and, in the case of young women, domestic service. The scale and affluence of bourgeois culture in Holland reached new dimensions.

A century later the initiatives for new developments had shifted to England. Here from the 1780s, at least in certain regions, a new 'age of manufactures' was in process of development. Falling well short of an industrial revolution, or a general social transformation in which the artisan's workshop was overtaken by the factory, this period saw some regionally distributed manufacturing growth on a domestic basis which drew in particular on the cheap labour of rural women and children for the production of new kinds of textiles. How many people's lives were affected by this development is a matter for speculation. Textile production may have tripled, but that does not mean a tripling of the labour force. Certainly agriculture maintained its dominance in the British economy until the middle decades of the nineteenth century, but in specific regions, not only in England but in France, the southern Netherlands and parts of Germany, some change was afoot.[10]

Clearly the population increase that occurred in the eighteenth century as a result of the disappearance of great pandemics of plague and the great subsistence crises that had marked earlier centuries resulted in a demand for new employment opportunities. Many of these, however, were not in industry but in the service sector. Those of middling rank and upwards who possessed the means sought first to make their own lives more comfortable. Ten to eleven per cent of the population of any major European city in the seventeenth and eighteenth centuries were servants employed in a variety of capacities but primarily to relieve those who employed them of drudgery. This service sector became larger over the same period and was increasingly the province of women. The multiplication of artefacts and the evolving fashion industry also generated work. Everywhere over this period towns and many cities were growing, sustained by a rural influx largely of the young, who came into service or apprenticeships, and also of the dispossessed of the countryside who came hoping somehow to tack together a livelihood. What is also clear is that the broadening of the base of the social pyramid occasioned by demographic growth made labour cheap, and the cheapest labour of all was female labour. It was a situation in which there were winners and losers and one in which the differences in material standard of living between those at the bottom and those in the middle and at the top were sharply defined.

A study of material civilization tells a great deal about a society, but far from everything. Missing from Braudel's narrative is the world of mentalities, and the relationship of this to material culture was not negligible. Other evolutionary changes have to be set alongside material development. Norbert Elias in *The Civilising Process* (1982) sought to define a mechanism whereby, starting from the French court of Louis XIV, a transformation of morals, comportment and a view on the world was effected. Over the succeeding two centuries a trickle-down effect occurred. The standards and codes of behaviour of the highest levels of society were adopted by the more modest. This emulation, along with an unquestioning submission to the authority of the state, were critical processes in 'the invention of modern man'.[11] For Elias and those who have developed many of his ideas, the transformation turned a 'savage', that is, someone violent and rough, prone to irascible acts unrestrained by law, someone who urinated and defecated in public, rarely washed, cared nothing for discretion, into someone conscious of rules of politeness and nicety, table manners, courtesy, sexual comportment, a respect for external standards as a calculated way of negotiating a system. Such was the transformation, for example, of the factional nobles of the Auvergne, whose savage acts of appropriation and murder were brought under control by trials and penalties instituted by the monarchy and known as Les Grands Jours d'Auvergne.

In this view, controlling rewards and pensions through the carefully articulated rituals of the court day at Versailles, the monarchy succeeded in taming the nobility. The sword and the armed retainer were removed from internal politics and the duel was used as a cleaner way of resolving points of honour among gentlemen. For social élites throughout Europe, who took their tone from the French court, the process meant the substitution of genteel pursuits, such as house building, music and literature, for boorish activities. The educated and the ambitious who were not noble soon came to see this as the road to advancement. The gentleman came to be defined as someone of refined tastes and the word 'politeness', borrowed from the French *politesse*, entered the English language.

Many would question whether Elias was correct in picking out Versailles as the genesis of a linear development from barbarity to civilization, while still wishing to retain the notion of an evolution of manners over time.[12] A cultivated, mannered court, such as was visible in many of the Italian Renaissance states, does not necessarily have much impact on a wider society; and if Versailles was somewhat larger than the court of a Medici or a d'Este, it is questionable whether without other contributory factors any change in manners or comportment could have occurred on any scale. Had Elias followed the history of the court lady, literate and cultivated as she was, from Christine de Pisan onwards and seen her lack of impact on the rest of womankind, he might well have modified his thesis. Furthermore, contemporaneously with Louis XIV, in the cities of the Dutch littoral there was a bourgeois culture which may have shunned the excesses of court manners but which certainly had a developed sense of appropriate behaviour. There is nothing 'uncivilized' about the tranquil settings of a Vermeer. The court was not then the only possible agency of change.

Several developments were in fact contemporaneous. The reduction of civil strife that was seen in the late seventeenth century (as opposed to international wars) reflected either the strengthening hand of monarchy (as in France) or the control of royal power through Parliament (as in England), but for the nobility it meant the opportunity to concentrate their energies elsewhere. The gentleman was a product of peace, not war, and the stately home could only supplant the castle when strife receded. More importantly than this, there were also other agencies at work intent upon effecting changes in the external and internal comportment of human beings. Both the Protestant reformers and the Catholic church were concerned with the imposition of standards of morality and decency of conduct. They were intent on control, each for their own confession. The revolution in manners described by Elias was concerned with external appearance and appropriate behaviour – the suppression of base and violent conduct – and the motivation for this change was the desire for social rewards, the perks of court society. The churches, however, aimed to go deeper. They sought to control minds as well as bodies. It mattered little to them how people conducted the externals of behaviour provided that they adhered to rules governing 'morality' and codes of belief in every sector of life; and the rewards they promised could not be collected in this world.

There was not much to choose between the standards that the Protestant and Catholic churches sought to apply, nor was there much difference in the success they enjoyed at least for the next two centuries.[13] They sought to transform the village priest or pastor from the lewd fornicator described by Le Roy Ladurie in *Montaillou* (1978) into a man of exemplary conduct with a new awareness that his role was to instruct his flock in the catechism and to inculcate in them orthodox beliefs and behaviour compatible with the ten commandments. The two churches struggled to control the rituals of life, including baptism and virtually indissoluble marriage, and to condemn adultery, violence and ignorance.

They did not necessarily make a total breach with the past. Indeed, their activities may merely have intensified what has been termed the birth of a 'guilt culture' in Christendom which had been in process since the Middle Ages.[14] The message they promoted was one of rigid adherence to a moral code in which the sins of the flesh or any kind of sexual deviance were punished by a reinvigorated concept of hell. This was embellished in the Catholic version by the intrusion of a sojourn in purgatory, a temporary hell even for the bulk of those who would one day be received into heaven. There was only one path to heaven and it demanded either sexual abstinence or a heterosexual, lifelong union in which the aim was the production of another generation of orthodox believers. The two churches put their influence behind a religion of suffering as a means of pleasing a deity who kept constant watch and missed nothing, and they insisted on the omnipresence of the Devil, a force for evil capable of manipulating any who wavered. The pursuit of the sexual deviant, and even more strikingly of the witch, was the corollary of their efforts. The female body was re-endorsed as the prime locus of vice. On the more positive side, though with a view to strengthening their own hand, they put their energies into a programme of education which achieved – patchily, perhaps, but with accelerating momentum – new levels of literacy. This in itself was potentially another agency of social transformation.

Again, we should not exaggerate the immediate impact of such initiatives. By 1800 about 65 per cent of French men and 35 per cent of women could sign their names. Probably many more could read. Britain, Holland and Scandinavia, and parts of Germany had outstripped these levels, while in Mediterranean Europe they were lower overall. The Latin-based education of upper-class men contrasted conspicuously with the rudiments of reading and writing that were made available to those of lesser social status and to women. However, it is clear that increasing numbers of Europeans – twice as many men as women – had the experience of a little schooling, and the ability to read gave access to ideas current in polite society. Roger Chartier has traced the way in which the court manual for the writing of polite letters, having first appeared in the seventeenth-century French court, appeared a hundred years later in books of popular instruction – even though by that time the formula was less respected in higher society. Quite ordinary folk knew that they had to negotiate a system and that they would do this most effectively if they copied the practices and conformed to the demands of courtesy prevalent among their betters.[15] Charity schools, established as a result of religious initiatives, not only sought to instil appropriate behaviour but twinned it with conformity to the newly enforced moral code. Along with pre-marital chastity, they urged that proper modes of address, more careful speech, cleanliness and care in apparel, eased a person's way through a system in which the stakes were always piled against the poor and those who lacked *savoir-faire*, and in which instant judgements were made by reference to personal appearance. It certainly paid to be nicely mannered when you turned up for a job as a servant in a comfortable home and it was to your advantage to know terms of respect in a law court (indeed, the criminal population of Newgate held mock trials to rehearse how to impress the judges).

Nothing is more difficult to estimate than the pace of change or for how great a percentage of the population continuity still predominated. What is clear is that over the three hundred years covered here a deep chasm opened up between the culture of the rich and comfortable (mannered society) and the rest, between the informed and the ignorant, between high and popular culture, and these differences were as conspicuous as the disparities in their material lives. In 1500 the intellectual baggage of the majority of European élites was close to that of their social inferiors. For example, that of the rural squire on the one hand, and the villagers about him on the other, contained common elements and attitudes, speech and beliefs. They knew the same stories, songs and bawdy jokes. Servants lived in close proximity, even to the extent of sharing the bedchamber of master and mistress. Young men accompanied the seigneur's son to war, where they shared the spoils of plunder and rape with a similar chance of contracting gangrene from an undressed wound or syphilis from a random sexual encounter.

Two centuries later a conspicuous distancing had occurred. The rough castle had been transformed into the stately home and the comportment of its occupants was drastically changed, separating master and mistress from servant and tenant. The lord no longer took his men to war and he was more likely to have a 'kept mistress'– a person who emerges in the late seventeenth and eighteenth centuries and who perhaps incarnates in her person increased commercialization and the veneer of the civilizing process – than to put his health at risk by unguarded sex with a common whore. The gentleman was marked out from the boor and even the *nouveau riche* had to work to be recognized as a gentleman, for social standing was no longer merely a question of distinctive clothing and the parade of wealth. The sumptuary legislation whereby many European societies, as late as the seventeenth century, had sought to insist on difference of degree by restricting the materials and jewels that could be sported by those who were not noble faded into insignificance. What now mattered were manners, education and *savoir-faire*. The distinction between the rural bumpkin and his innocent wife and that between the aspirant noble and the real McCoy became an important part of European humour. Molière's *Le Bourgeois Gentilhomme* (1670) is a monument to the second theme and Goldsmith's more endearing Tony Lumpkin who refuses to please his mother by forsaking the manners of his village friends is written by reference to the first. Wycherley's *The Country Wife* (1672) has an innocent, in the sense of naïve to the point of stupidity, spouse imported into the town where she joyously colludes in a polished urban adulterous relationship. Carlo Goldoni's comedies of manners of the 1740s managed to incorporate distinctions both between town and country and between classes which were infinitely nuanced. In *The Venetian Twins* the innocent, in the sense of unsophisticated and uninformed, unrefined man from Bergamo (the mountainous backlands) is distinguished from his refined and sophisticated twin from Venice who in turn is contrasted with the over-refined indeed 'effete' young blade from Rome. Audiences recognized and reacted gleefully to such stereotypes.

The culture of the élites did not remain static. Indeed the hegemony of Christian teaching, and its cornerstone the Bible, were increasingly challenged from the late seventeenth century by a learned minority who turned to science, empiricism and rationalism as the mainsprings of their thought. The inconsistency of Scripture, and the apparent lack of proof for the existence of external forces for good and evil, disturbed the convictions of a small, educated élite. The insistence that this world was the testing ground for the next and that hell and divine retribution awaited the aberrant were notions which were progressively weakened, modified or destroyed. Man need not be a passive agent of God's will but could be arbiter of his own destiny, able to question authority and contest arbitrary government as the work of man not God. Such a radical rethinking of the premises on which human existence was based carried with it implications for a reassessment of the respective roles of men and women. However, as a movement the Enlightenment was fully capable of replacing the authority of God by that of men. Moreover, its impact was initially socially confined. Indeed, Jean Delumeau has suggested the paradox of such a challenge occurring just as the strengthening of the hold of the Catholic church over the minds of the masses was reaching its peak and polarizing still further élite and popular culture.[16]

There are other narratives of continuity and change in the recent historiography of early modern Europe. In the 1970s Lawrence Stone argued that the early modern period was one of radical change in the ordering of human relationships in Britain. He posited a medieval world – one which continued in many ways into the seventeenth century – in which choice of spouse was denied and individual interests were subjected to those of the wider family. The relationships between parent and child were dictated by gloomy church teaching in which the infant was regarded as a vehicle of original sin to be chastised into right conduct, and infant mortality made parents reluctant to place any emotional investment in their offspring. In this view, a radical change by the end of the seventeenth century marked a transition from a society based on kin group allegiances, where personal predilections were subordinated in furtherance of the interests of the group, to one in which free choice of spouse and affective individualism (that is, the right to personal determination and enjoyment of the conjugal relationship) triumphed.[17]

This kind of argument meshes neatly with notions of change predicated on the emergence of a culture more receptive to the desirability of earthly rather than heavenly contentment and of a more 'civilized' society substituting domesticity for violence. It also interweaves itself with the growth of consumption. The more comfortable home was a *sine qua non* of the argument. Others, notably Phillippe Ariès, have urged an equally dramatic turnabout in the way parents viewed their infants, as evinced by the attack on wet-nursing and the emergence of a juvenile commodity market in the form of special clothing, toys and books. He pronounced the eighteenth century 'the century of the child'.[18]

The voices raised against these overarching interpretations of sudden change and gloomy readings of human relationships in earlier centuries were strident. Alan Macfarlane claimed that affective individualism was evident in England at least from the Middle Ages. Keith Wrightson challenged the interpretation as presenting too crude a view of the sixteenth century and for taking too little account of groups which, unlike the aristocracy, never managed their personal affairs by reference to dynastic considerations.[19] In the view of these and other historians, the concentration on change loses sight of continuities in the lives of the many which are more important. The reliability of the evidence permitting such grand themes to be discerned has also been widely questioned. The testimony of journals, correspondence, memoirs, in which the writer expresses a personal view or recounts a personal experience, only permits observation of a very limited social group, the literate. For the sixteenth and seventeenth centuries personal testimonies are rare, and those that exist frequently proffer contradictory evidence or are silent or fragmentary on emotional issues. Very few emanate from the pens of women.[20] Any changes that can be posited as emanating from a transition from a violent to a more domesticated lifestyle, based on such evidence, have to be largely confined to the aristocracy, and even here metamorphosis was far from absolute. The emotional and married lives of lesser folk remained largely unchanged.

Changes in the attitudes of parents to children have also been strenuously denied by means of a thorough evaluation of all the extant memoirs and journals. Simon Schama, who showed Dutch society in the Golden Age as a society in which a high value was placed on domestic virtues and on young children, pointed out that parental affection was meted out according to the standards of the day.[21] The child of the rich, laden with artefacts, is not necessarily more prized than the offspring of the more humble. Equally fundamentally, the automatic assumption that the harsh attitude towards parent–child relationships found in prescriptive texts issuing from reforming churchmen necessarily reflected real life, has been cogently questioned. Who can assess the potency of good advice?

All the narratives of continuity and change embody issues which are affected by gender. They raise questions such as: what were the roles played by women in traditional agricultural societies, and which women experienced change due to demographic growth and commercial development? Were the lives of these women more or less changed than those of men? What were the consequences of the 'long Reformations' which laid an iron grip on sexual relations and elected the body and the sexual act as the locus of sin? What were the effects of this 'guilt culture' on the lives of those individual women who could not or did not conform to the model? When did this iron hand relax its grip? Do we have a convincing history of motherhood or merely a series of black legends? Who acquired literacy and what were the consequences for women, distinguished by class, of acquiring it? How deep was the process of acculturation in respect of gender roles; was it modified over time, and if so, in what ways and for whom; which women challenged the premises on which it was based and why did they do so? How is persistence of the status quo in many areas of life for many women to be explained? What promoted and what impeded the development of alternative visions?

Much of the writing in women's history emanating from the Anglo-Saxon tradition since the sixties has been focused on change and, more specifically, on change for the worse. It is a saga of discontinuity or of 'descent from paradise'. The reason for the prevalence of this interpretation is perhaps that much has been written with a view to explaining the predicament of women in the twentieth century. Changes have been posited in economic status to describe a linear decline from a precapitalist Utopia in which women had dignity and independence, to a state of exploitation. Or the first century of the early modern period has been declared the golden age of patriarchy when fathers ruled, choice of spouse was denied, sexual aberrance was pursued, witches burned at the stake, the infanticidal mother condemned to death and church and state worked together to subdue womankind to patriarchal control. Both the Renaissance and the Reformation have been interpreted as periods in which control was assumed over 'women'.

The paradigm for the economic decline of women exists in the influential work of Alice Clark, a middle-class, university educated spinster writing in 1919 about the seventeenth-century Englishwoman. She compared the sturdy farmer's and artisan's wife whom she discovered through considerable archival work with the useless woman of later literature, conspicuous for her lack of meaningful activity, and she laid the responsibility for this metamorphosis at the feet of encroaching capitalism. She also idealized the working home of the seventeenth century, where she assumed husband and wife toiled as partners, and compared this situation with the later harshly severed world of work and home. Clark was in many ways writing the predicament of many of her contemporaries into the script. More dangerously, to advance her thesis of the serial decline from healthy activity to idleness or exploitation (depending on class) she had recourse to prescriptive literature and assumed that the ideology was strong enough to produce the reality.[22]

Recently, however, this kind of narrative has been challenged, both by medieval historians who have failed to locate the halcyon days of women's independence and high status, and by those who have both firmly shifted the effects of industrialization into specific regions and postponed until the mid-nineteenth century its impact as an agent of the separation of home and workplace.[23] Others have urged a qualitative improvement, an expansion rather than a reduction of the potential for development in the lives of middle- and upper-class women (a *prise de conscience* or the ability to find something of their own subjectivity) in the course of the period.[24] These debates are important to the business of understanding. They also serve to accentuate the futility of the search for a single narrative, a generic woman to represent all women.[25]

What follows is a history of the varying experiences of women, differentiated by geography and wealth over a long period, the world of the material constraints of Fernand Braudel and at the same time of those historians of culture and of commerce who have urged gradual and patchy evolution. The canvas for the study is deliberately very broad and involves most of western Europe because it is written in the belief that much is common ground. Special emphasis, however, is given to the experience of Britain and France – territories comprehending a third of all western European women – because most work has been done upon them. More recently, the Netherlands and Italy (particularly in the Renaissance), Germany, and latterly Spain and Portugal and Ireland, have made considerable advances in the field of gender history, making comparisons and contrasts possible. Material permitting the extension of this study to eastern Europe is at present lacking. Nor will the New World find much mention because the economic, demographic and religious framework of reference differed conspicuously from the European experience and would demand extensive analysis beyond the scope of this already long volume. During the three hundred years under review many changes occurred in different aspects of the lives of many Europeans. The Reformation, the Counter-Reformation, the early Enlightenment and changes attributable to demographic and economic growth, as well as to what Elias called the 'civilizing process', were all developments which could have a significant impact on the lives of both women and men.

It would be foolish to suggest that any single individual could do full justice to the volume of work which has emerged. What is offered here is one historian's attempt to provide an overview and an interpretation across national boundaries, to seek out both the common and the distinctive, the overriding continuities and the main agencies of change. The book seeks to distinguish between women, individually and collectively, and versions of womanhood, but also recognizes that ideas of womanhood may indeed contribute to determining the limits of what was possible to real women in early modern society. For this reason these ideas, subsequently to be tested, will be our point of departure. Put another way, the first task will be to examine the composition of the sauce deemed suitable for the goose, and how it differed from that deemed appropriate for the gander.

CHAPTER ONE

Constructing Woman

The picture speaks though it is mute.
ERASMUS AFTER HORACE, *ARS POETICA*

ON THE walls of every art gallery, in collections of prints and in the vast corpus of literature remaining from the early modern period are found representations of woman and man. Some are intended to instruct, some to warn, some to amuse, some to incite lust, some to invoke glorious deeds and provoke emulation. Few, if any, are neutral. They embody cultural assumptions; some confirm each other; some appear to contradict. None, of course, is a true reproduction of reality. Each is the product of a creative mind carrying a specific intellectual load. Where do we find a point of ingress into this huge body of imagery? How do we begin to define women and men? Most early modern writers would have elected to begin at what they thought was the beginning, with the creation of Adam and Eve and the fall of man.

The Brancacci chapel of Santa Maria del Carmine in Florence was sumptuously decorated in the fifteenth century by three of the great masters. The oldest, Masolino, incorporated a famous Adam and Eve. The naked figures are the epitome of physical perfection. They are endowed with youth, beauty and apparent innocence. The translucent whiteness of their skin is enhanced by dark green foliage. Above Eve, however, looms the agent of impending doom, the serpent. This serpent is no authentic reptile: she has the head of a woman, is a blonde and, as the recent restoration of the frescoes has shown, a blonde with blue eyeshadow and red carmine on her lips. She breathes out a faint stream of vapour which is directed towards Eve. We know the content of her words, but what the picture also seeks to impart is that the fall of man and the birth of original sin were the result of a female conspiracy, an all-woman event.

The rendering of the snake as a woman was not uncommon in contemporary iconography. Michelangelo was to choose the same interpretation for the Eve of the Sistine ceiling.[1] Furthermore, in choosing to make his temptress a blonde, Masolino was also expressing a male preference which is hundreds of years old in the west. Whereas the shape of the ideal woman has varied enormously over the centuries, oscillating between the corseted and the natural, the generous bosom and the flat chest, free-flowing locks and artificial curls, poets and painters – with a few noteworthy exceptions such as Shakespeare, who wrote sonnets to a dark lady, or French sixteenth-century poets who praised raven hair, or Titian who created a new colour for his beauties – have insisted that a truly beautiful woman's crowning glory should be her blond hair and her fair complexion.[2] Eve, as God's initial creation of woman, must by definition have been beautiful.

On the opposite wall of the Brancacci chapel, Masolino's associate, the more innovatory Masaccio, painted a powerful and tragic expulsion of the pair from the Garden of Eden. The current guidebook asks us to note the majesty and manliness of Adam in his grief, his upright carriage and the bent head that conceals his tears. Eve, on the other hand, is devastated. She cries out and her face is ugly and distorted in pain. Her body is shapeless, suggesting that she already carries man (generic) in her womb. She hides her breasts, for she has replaced naked innocence by the shame that comes with knowledge. She knows what she has done and it is too late. The expulsion from paradise is all her fault.[3]

To single out these particular frescoes as a point of departure for a consideration of representations of womanhood is neither totally arbitrary nor whimsical. Although they were a product of high culture, and may have been placed in the chapel to remind the Carmelites at prayer of the superiority of a celibate life, their subject-matter, the story of Adam and Eve in the Christo-Judaic interpretation of the origins of man and his wife and the story of their fall, was a common constituent of both élite and popular beliefs. Among the myths and legends pertaining to the nature of womanhood that of Eve was for many centuries the most powerful, and the version of the creation that appears in the book of Genesis might almost be said to be the foundation text for western European ideas on the essence of womanhood. It passed into painting and sculpture, appearing both in the cathedral and in the cruder carvings of the parish church. Women embroidered the story and it is found in every kind of literature from theological treatise to creative verse. It thus gave cultural homogeneity to a representation of the western European woman.

The creation of Eve followed that of Adam. She was made not in God's image but in that of man from a spare rib. Eve's betrayal of man, leading to the expulsion from the Garden of Eden, tainted mankind with original sin and resulted in man himself having to toil for his bread. It brought upon woman, however, extra punishments. Because *her* tongue had led man astray she must henceforward be under his governance and obedient to him. She must suffer pain in childbed and gloominess of disposition. Eve's contribution to notions of womanhood which stretched from biblical times and survived the medieval period intact, might be summarized as three traditions: that of woman as the agent of the Devil and as a temptress; that of woman as a heedless chatterbox, gossiping and garrulous, whose tongue needed to be kept under control; and that of woman as man's downfall, woman as scapegoat for his (or their joint) mistakes.

Western Europe at the beginning of the sixteenth century expressed unfaltering loyalty to a patriarchal Christian God and to a view of the world as his creation. The church educated the élites and hence governe¹ the transmission of literacy and higher learning, while from the pulpit it sought to control the minds of the masses. No organ was more powerful than the pulpit in reaching the people and shaping their ideas. Much of the message which the church strove to convey was overtly misogynistic. It not only incorporated a gloomy view of the world which presented earthly life as a passage through a vale of tears which was a testing ground for the life to come, but it also insisted that man was impeded in his heavenly aspirations by carnal relationships with woman. Such views were modified and softened by the acknowledgement that woman too had an immortal soul and was capable of obtaining salvation if certain rules were obeyed.

The degree of illiteracy shared by the priests and the masses at the beginning of the period ensured the immunity of the bulk of the populace from the finer points of theological debate, and pagan precepts and practices may still have coexisted with their Christian allegiance, but by 1650 this was much less the case. The emphasis of the Protestant Reformation on closer biblical knowledge for everyone and of the Catholic Counter-Reformation on a more intensive exposure of the flock to the teachings of the church propounded by a better educated clergy, made western Europeans progressively throughout the sixteenth and seventeenth centuries 'the people of a book'. Incorporated in that book were some dominant images of both women and men and very specific instructions for the comportment of the sexes. Biblical texts could be used by the reformers of both groups to urge the necessity of strong patriarchal control of the Christian family and the frailties of woman.[4]

Numerous women in the Bible could be drawn upon for representations of womanhood in text and image. If Eve dominates Genesis, Mary the mother of God opens the New Testament. Mary was the inverse of Eve. Virginal and innocent, she listened not to the Devil in the guise of the snake but to the angel of God. Hearing of God's intention, she spoke only to express total obedience to his will. The contrast is evident. Mary's characteristics were her spotless asexuality – when God placed his son within her womb he chose a woman who knew no other man; her silence – she speaks only three times in the gospels; and her suffering. She was, as the churchmen urged, alone of all her sex and no woman could aspire to be like her. She was not and never could be a model. But what other women could hope to do was to emulate individual traits such as her courtesy and her humility. She incarnated these aspects of behaviour which were appropriate to womanhood. From the late fifteenth century, the Dominicans promoted throughout Europe the cult of the rosary which presented Mary as an intercessor with the godhead on behalf of mankind and fostered also cults relating to Saint Anne, her mother. In part by their efforts, two centuries later depictions of an etherealized Mary, Queen of Heaven, were the commonest image of the Virgin in continental churches.[5]

To set against perfect Mary in the New Testament there was the flawed but redeemed Magdalen whose history and legend had by the beginning of the sixteenth century become quite indistinguishable. Created from a muddle of scriptural episodes in which a woman with seven devils is added to the whore who anointed the feet of the Saviour at the Pharisee's feast and who in turn is added to the Mary, sister of Lazarus, who listened to the words of Christ while her sister Martha did the cooking, this 'Magdalen' stood for the triumph of penitence as a means to salvation. The frailest, vainest, most errant of women could achieve redemption through devotion to Christ.

There are many other biblical stories of women providing both negative and positive characteristics. Some were known for their vanity, manipulation, deception and cunning: Jezebel and Delilah, Gomer, wife of Hosea, and the whore of Babylon, the Scarlet Woman of the Book

of Revelation. All of these used their sexuality to evil purposes. Their
fates could provide cautionary tales and they could be used to represent
womanhood at its worst. But there are also very positive images, heroic
women like Judith and Deborah who contrived to save Israel (albeit in
Judith's case through studiedly feminine guile which enabled her to
enter the tent of the Assyrian general and cut off his head). There is
also the repeated biblical imagery of the devout and sacrificing women
who wound swaddling bands and grave bands, gave their last mite to
the temple, listened readily to Christ's teaching, subsidized the disciples
and outnumbered men at the foot of the cross. Pontius Pilate's wife
was clearly the nobler partner, for God spoke to her through her subconscious in a dream. Then there is the industrious woman, the good
housewife of Proverbs 31, whose efforts ensure the wellbeing and wealth
of her husband and the comfort of her family by a dawn to dusk work
schedule conducted in silence. Such imagery is picked up in Christ's
parables where careful household management is likened to the
behaviour of the soul alert to salvation and conversely disorder of mind
is likened to an unswept house in which a negligent housewife dozes,
or a lack of preparedness to receive Christ is compared to a bridesmaid
whose lamp is not trimmed to welcome the bridegroom.[6]

To set alongside the stories are the injunctions, the rules which the
church adopted as a model for the conduct of women. Although Christ
surrounded himself with women, he did not choose them for teaching
work. Saint Paul, however, was fully explicit. Taking up the Genesis
story, he formulated the rules which were to be asserted from the
pulpit, from prescriptive literature and from the judge's bench in the
ecclesiastical courts for almost two millennia. These words constitute
yet another foundation text in the history of women.

I desire then that in every place the men should pray, lifting holy hands
without anger or quarrelling; also that women should adorn themselves
modestly and sensibly in seemly apparel, not with braided hair or gold
or pearls or costly attire but by good deeds, as befits women who profess
religion. Let a woman learn in silence with all submissiveness. I permit
no woman to teach or to have authority over men; she is to keep silent.
For Adam was formed first, then Eve; and Adam was not deceived, but
the woman was deceived and became a transgressor. Yet woman will be
saved through bearing children, if she continues in faith and love and
holiness, with modesty.[7]

Both Catholic and Protestant confessions attached great weight to the written text, but for the Catholic church this meant both Scripture and the traditions of the church which had subsequently been incorporated into theological writings. The Protestants stood by scriptural text alone. Some, particularly the Zwinglians, feared the visual image which they considered so powerful that the ignorant might take it as a substitute for the real thing. Such an error would lead to the worship of a graven image or the idolatry condemned in the commandments. To depict God, the Holy Family and the Saints was not only dangerous but a travesty, for no artist could know the truth. This point of view did not deny the efficacy of instructional prints to help people to right conduct, but artists must find other means such as classical figures to convey God's messages and not try to depict holy people. Or they must single out texts dealing with a generic woman whose virtues could be captured in visual imagery without running the risk of idolatry. French Huguenot printers favoured the wife of Hasdrubal, a Carthaginian general who killed herself and her children rather than swear allegiance to Rome. The favourite subject for Dutch sixteenth-century religious prints became the good housewife of Proverbs 31. She whose virtues are extolled, but who is nameless and uncontaminated by Eve's legend, could be used as an example for all women:

A good wife who can find?

She is far more precious than jewels.

The heart of her husband trusts in her, and he will have no lack of gain.

She does him good, and not harm, all the days of her life.

She seeks wool and flax, and works with willing hands.

She is like the ships of the merchant; she brings her food from afar.

She rises while it is yet night and provides food for her household and
     tasks for her maidens . . .

She looks well to the ways of her household, and does not eat the bread
     of idleness.

Her children rise up and call her blessed; her husband also, and he
     praises her:

'Many women have done excellently, but you surpass them all.'

Charm is deceitful, and beauty is vain, but a woman who fears the Lord
     is to be praised.

Give her of the fruit of her hands, and let her works praise her in the
     gates.[8]

For Catholic theologians pictures, as long as they conformed to church teaching, were fully acceptable and indeed to be promoted as a means of instructing the illiterate. To humanists such as Erasmus or for the Tridentine bureaucrat Paleotti, and for important Catholic theologians and administrators who sat at the Council of Trent in 1560, it was needful to control the content and presentation of biblical images, recognizing that they could help the ignorant to conceptualize heaven and its occupants. Beauty was a gift to the artist from God: while clinging to textual purity the artist could also draw on divine inspiration.[9] Above all, depictions should lift divine figures out of the realm of ordinary people. Mary, for example, should be presented as flawless in ethereal beauty as well as in soul. She enjoys eternal youth as the teenage mother of the heavenly infant. When Caravaggio painted a *Death of the Virgin* (1606) using an ordinary, worn-out, shabby woman he was accused of debasing her and making her look like a prostitute fished out of the Tiber. Totally obedient, virginal, unflawed, this woman had to be apart and perfect, alone of all her sex.

Protestant theologians argued that the medieval church had added too many speculative embellishments to the figures of Mary and Magdalen. The importance of the first had been exaggerated and the emphasis on divine motherhood had detracted from the role of the Saviour himself. A process of retrenchment should take place.[10] Magdalen must be eradicated almost completely. Even Catholic theologians were uncomfortably aware that she had been endowed over the millennia with a sexy history. She was the nearest the artist could come to the profane Venus within a religious context. Indeed, Titian went so far as to paint her nude: others covered her nakedness with her long, flowing hair. Many sought to make her religious ecstasy akin to sexual orgasm. In sixteenth-century Venice where, for a limited period, high-class prostitution of gifted women was the wonder of the civilized world and the delight of diplomats and kings, to be painted as and identified with Magdalen was apparently a frequent practice. Counter-Reformation theologians insisted on the cleaning up of such representations, but without much success. When, in 1674, Louis XIV abandoned Louise de la Vallière for Madame de Montespan, she was sent to a Carmelite convent in the rue Saint Jacques and her portrait was painted as a penitent Magdalen. Protestant tourists, products of a culture which had rejected this dubious papist concoction, flocked to view, intrigued by the possibilities implicit in the representation.[11]

At the beginning of the sixteenth century under the joint stimulus of the newly invented printing press, the Protestant Reformation and the Catholic Counter-Reformation, both laymen and theologians seized the pen which fed the presses. There streamed forth a mass of didactic and discursive literature – theological discourses, sermons, domestic conduct books, good advice books, theoretical works examining the roles of the sexes, law codes and commentaries, medical treatises and pseudo-scientific work examining sexual differences – and creative literature of all kinds which often drew upon fictional sexual relationships; at the more popular level there were broadsides, prints, woodcuts, and chapbooks and ballads. Literacy levels were very low and those of women generally lowest of all, although in the late medieval courts more women than men could read. Notwithstanding, both Protestant and Catholic recognized that the minds of men were swayed through the word and that salvation depended on understanding which came through the perusal of Scripture backed by good advice. At the core of this kind of writing was the conviction that the right domestic relationships were critical to the salvation of souls and the formation of the next generation of Christians.[12]

Whom did this literature reach? To whom was it read? How was it read? The good advice literature of the sixteenth century was written by men and not aimed specifically at women – unless at the aristocratic women who were able to read. Most of it was probably intended to be read aloud by the head of the family. It has one overriding purpose: to help both men and women towards the goal of every Christian, that is, eternal life, and hence to avoid damnation. It proffers representations of the perfect husband, wife, son and daughter and has as its point of departure the idea that each and every human being will one day be called to account for his or her conduct. The literature offers what it considers to be the key to success on this critical occasion when no lies can be told and no inadequacies concealed. It takes as a given that the household is a divinely ordered organization with one head, the husband, who has a right to expect the obedience of his wife and children. It employs the analogy of the first family, that of Adam and Eve, and draws the appropriate conclusion of the evils that can befall humankind if the proper order is not respected. In the literature, the good woman appears in four roles, as a daughter, a wife, a mother and a widow, and for each there is an appropriate form of conduct.[13]

There is very little difference between the books emanating from

Catholic and Protestant writers although in some Catholic works more consideration is given to the relationship between family members and a confessor-priest and arguably as well to the question of sex. There is more about the sexual act itself in the Catholic texts. In most works aimed at an audience outside the purely aristocratic, more emphasis is given to specific household tasks: indeed, one such work, Fray Luis de León's *La perfecta casada* (1583) has recently been hailed not merely as a spiritual guide but as a working manual for the domestic economy of the pre-industrial family.[14]

One enormously popular book aimed at women alone was the work of the Spanish humanist Juan Luis de Vives, *De Institutione Feminae Christianae* (1523), translated into English in 1540, into Italian in 1546 and reprinted in most European languages several times over the next centuries. Vives is solely concerned with spiritual attributes. Work is not mentioned in his pages – perhaps not surprisingly, since the book was initially written for Catherine of Aragon. It is divided into three sections devoted respectively to maidens, wives and widows. Maidenhood is a time for forming the right habits, prayer and piety, humility and obedience. The young girl must learn to control her tongue, for nothing so much condemns a maid as does idle gossiping and a shrewish tongue and nothing so much recommends her as silence and meekness. The chapter on what a wife should do at home is summarized in the quintessentially gloomy pronouncement that 'great sadness of behaviour and arrayment is required in a wife'. Throughout the work woman is presented as prone to triviality if left to her own devices but, with the right guidance from a careful and considerate husband, mindful of mutual self-interest, motivated by spiritual love and knowing his Christian duty to be the kind but firm governor of his wife, the couple can achieve the ideal of the godly life and eternal salvation.

The section on widows is very revelatory: here we see the humanist confronted with the problem of the woman alone who constituted a particular dilemma since, apart from her confessor, there was no obvious man to act as her guide and controller. Three of the chapters are devoted to the right behaviour of the woman towards her deceased husband. She is recommended to lead a quiet and cloistered life and if she goes out should be accompanied by 'some good and sad woman' (sad in the sense of serious, forswearing gaiety). Her thoughts should be constantly on her salvation and prayer her frequent recourse. She should, however, avoid the company of friars and priests. Vives is clearly worried either that she might lead them astray or that they may give her the wrong advice, or behave inappropriately in the confessional. Remarriage is discouraged. Vives' tone is firm but on the whole quite gentle. Salvation lies in the next world and a woman's life must be a perpetual struggle against her innate tendency to frivolity if she wishes to achieve it.

Sixty years later, Saint Francis of Sales wrote his *Introduction to the Devout Life* (1619), a work which was translated into several languages and which in the mid-twentieth century was still the devotional work most commonly recommended to Catholic women in France and England. He offered it to a court lady, Philothea, 'lover of God', representative of the aspiring Christian woman. Its sections in praise of matrimony, 'equally holy in rich and poor', define the state as 'the nursery of Christianity which replenishes the earth with faithful souls'. Husbands are enjoined to tolerate 'the weaknesses and infirmities of wives', but these are seen as being of a physical not a moral nature and should provoke 'no kind of disdain but rather a sweet and affectionate compassion'. The wife is recommended to devote to her husband 'a respectful love and full of reverence' and she is reminded that she was made from one of his ribs 'under his arm to show that she should be under the hand and guidance of her husband'.

The widow is again given special consideration. She should not remarry but should remain in chaste widowhood. The virtues proper for the exercise of a holy widow are perfect modesty, the renunciation of honours, ranks, assemblies, titles and all such vanities; serving the poor and the sick; comforting the afflicted; instructing girls in a devout life; and making herself a perfect pattern of all virtues to young women. Necessity and plainness should be the two ornaments of her dress; humility and charity the ornaments of her actions; courtesy and mildness the ornaments of her tongue. In short, the true widow is in the church a little March violet, who sends forth an incomparable sweetness by the odour of her devotion and keeps herself almost always concealed under the broad leaves of her lowliness, while her dark colour testifies to her mortification.[15]

Among the many Protestant analogues to the Catholic marriage manuals was Thomas Becon's *The Book of Matrimony* (c. 1562). This good advice book addresses many of the same themes found in Vives or Francis of Sales, but the tone is more pragmatic and the advice descends to the minutiae of everyday life. Although written by a Puritan it could easily be mistaken for a Catholic work, albeit one aimed at a lower level of the population than the great Catholic texts. The husband is enjoined to love his wife, to beget children and to live chastely. He has special obligations towards his wife because her salvation in large part is his responsibility. He should act as her guide, be her friend, provide for her, defend her and help her to see what is right. The wife must first serve her husband in subjection, be modest in her behaviour and demure in her apparel, careful in her speech to avoid gossip and remain silent where appropriate. In her management of the house she should be thrifty and punctual. The last injunction doubtless reflected the need in agricultural societies to get things done on time, and the whole echoes the wording of Saint Paul in the Epistle to Timothy and the image of the good housewife in Proverbs 31. Together with her husband she should bring up her children according to Christian standards and see to it that they find an occupation. The training of daughters and equipping them for Christian marriage must be her especial concern. If she fails in this particular duty, she carries a particularly heavy moral burden. Throughout the work both husband and wife are constantly urged to keep their eyes on the Last Judgement and its possible terrible consequences.

Much didactic literature was designed for the ears of the unmarried girl, that is for daughters and maidservants, and may have been intended to be read to them after household prayers. Becon himself compiled a *Catechism*, as well as his *Book of Matrimony*, designed for such purposes, which again could have emanated as much from a Catholic as a Protestant pen. He assigns the maid (that is, the unmarried girl who might or might not be a maidservant) nine duties, and elects those to which all writers of the day accorded priority. First, the maid must fear and serve God. Second, she must obey her parents. Third, she should never be idle, for out of sloth

> springeth all mischief, as pride . . . banketting, drunkenshype, whoredom, adoultry, vain communication, betraying of secrets, cursed speakings . . . and so to give themselves to honest and vertuous exercises, to spinning, to carding, to weaving, to sewing, to washing, to wringing, to sweeping, to scouring, to bruing, to bakinge and to all kinds of labors without exception, that become maides.[16]

Becon clearly did not identify reading and writing as a necessary occupation for girls. What preoccupied him above all was the list of horrible consequences, falling nothing short of moral destruction, attendant upon lack of virtuous occupation for women. In much the same vein, the maid's fourth concern must be the avoidance of 'vain spectacles, games, pastimes, playes, interludes' which might encourage the frivolous side of her nature and lead to conduct menacing her chastity. Again, the same destruction could ensue if the maid kept the company of 'lewd and wanton persons' which Becon warns her against in his fifth injunction. Sixth, he urges 'let her kepe silence for there is nothinge that doth so much commend . . . a maid, as silence'. Such a daunting obsession with the undesirability of the gossiping 'tongue ripe' woman, whose unguarded language led Adam astray, pervades all the literature of good advice.

Seventh, Becon instructs the maid, as a member of the more lustful sex, to suppress the carnal desires she will experience after the age of thirteen until she is ready for marriage. Almost inevitably there follows as the eighth injunction prohibitions relating to clothing and the presentation of the body. 'All honest and godly disposed maydes [should] content themselves with comely and semely apparel . . . according to the doctrine of the gospel.' Finally as the ninth counsel the girl, after she has made her marriage choice, must be sure to make her parents aware of her intent and seek their advice.

In this kind of literature, emanating from whatever confession, the young man, a future husband and father, is enjoined to cultivate certain virtues assiduously. They are fear of God, respect for parents, chastity, sobriety, the avoidance of bad company and anger, sound financial management and gravity of person. Self-discipline is enjoined upon the male no less than on the female. Though allusion is infrequently made to physical violence between the sexes, when it is mentioned it is condemned – except perhaps by some German writers. Man, it is urged, has upon his shoulders the huge responsibility of guidance and is accountable to God. Physical violence is the last recourse of a husband despairing over his wife's aberrance. The author of *A Godly Form of Householde Government*, which ran into five editions between 1598 and 1630, catches the spirit of the approach.

A wise husband and one that seeketh to live in quiet with his wife, must observe these three rules. Often to admonish: seldome to reproove and never to smite her. The husband is also to understand, that as God created the woman, not of the head and so equal in authority with her husband: so also he created her not of Adam's foot, that she might walk jointly with him, under the conduct and government of her head.[17]

The model of the Christian marriage in the truly godly society is thus conceptualized as a patriarchal power relationship in which the husband must constantly invigilate his wife's conduct and bring her to account, but he must do so in a kindly way. Tyranny is not the intent. The relationship should be one of harmony in which the male and female complement each other. He creates wealth, she saves; he seeks a living, she keeps house; he deals openly with the world, she keeps herself apart from all but a few; his virtue is enhanced by skill in discourse, hers by silence. While he may give, she must save; while he can apparently bedeck himself at will provided he wears the trousers, she is urged to be discreet in dress. He is accountable in the next world to God; she is accountable in the here and now to her husband. Above all, while he negotiates the household's external relationships, the orderliness of the inner household is her preserve. From a reading of this literature we can see that successful masculinity can be assessed by the creation of wealth and public renown in a hostile world, whereas the yardstick for the successful woman is an ordered domestic environment, a haven of tranquillity and good management where the right moral principles prevail.[18]

The commendation in Protestant literature of sobriety in dress for women contrasts markedly with the standard practice among the affluent in Mediterranean Europe. Although, even in Italy, clerics protested against sumptuousness in dress, clothes were an unrelinquishable marker of affluence. Excessive display portended vanity, in the minds of clerics, and they believed that the distance from vanity to moral laxity was slight. In the literature of good advice emanating from all creeds, chastity was exalted as the most important attribute of the virtuous woman whether maid, wife or widow. A woman's honour depended on the restriction of sexual intercourse to her husband's bed, whatever the circumstances. Furthermore, she should not give the least hint that she was interested in attracting the admiration of the opposite sex by immodest dress or indiscreet glances – in fact her reputation was best preserved by staying at home or only leaving it in proper company. A wandering or 'gadding' woman was on the brink of dishonour and that dishonour reflected upon her entire family.

The church in the Middle Ages had vaunted the celibate ideal as one far higher than the married state. As Saint Paul said, 'It is better to marry than to burn' – and better still, by implication, if spiritual progress is not impeded by sexual relationships. This was held to be true for both men and women. However, Luther's attack on the monastic life and what he saw as the realities of clerical celibacy, that is, clerical sexual laxity, laid the foundations of a Protestant tradition in which the married state represented, at least in theory, the highest attainment for both men and women. When God presented Eve to Adam, he 'solemnized the first marriage that ever was' and hence indicated that he saw marriage as man's natural state and celibacy as abnormal. From this it might be inferred that woman's status within marriage was somewhat enhanced because she no longer represented second best for her husband. However, Luther's view of womanhood was both gloomy and conservative. He saw women as specific reproductive vessels with inferior reasoning powers and a proclivity to succumb to temptation. He followed certain biblical texts closely, particularly Leviticus ('The Laws') and Saint Paul's Letters. Hence Luther's holy household was one of tight patriarchy where fathers ruled and the priest-confessor was eliminated as mediator.[19]

Although it continued to endorse celibacy as a high and indeed perhaps the higher ideal, the Catholic Counter-Reformation on the whole abandoned invidious comparisons between the religious and the secular life and presented both as holy. From the fifteenth century onwards, with the promotion of Saint Bernardino of Siena and the French mystic Jean Gerson (who much influenced the young Luther), the cult of Saint Joseph, the virtuous carpenter and earthly father who taught Christ his craft and saved the Virgin Mary from earthly infamy, was resurrected. The devotion, which had fallen into abeyance from the seventh century, was popularized in Spain by Saint Teresa of Avila and in eastern France by Saint Francis of Sales. In the traditions of the church, Saint Joseph was an old, that is asexual, husband who respected his wife's virgin status. However, his very presence in the raising of the Infant Christ symbolized God's approbation of the patriarchal family. The Holy Family was thus the model for every family in whatever confession, an earthly Trinity. As a cult within the Roman Catholic Church, it appears to have begun in the fifteenth and reached full development in the seventeenth century.

In the Catholic tradition the earthly father/patriarch could be held to account, by a confessor priest pending Judgement Day, for his conduct and that of his wife and he carried sins which had involved her. Though, for example, the Catholic Church condemned *coitus interruptus*, it exonerated the wife from the husband's sin. Thomas Sànchez, the Jesuit theologue, thought a wife should consent to *coitus interruptus* only if she was ignorant of her husband's intent to sin, but a century and a half later Alphonse de Liguria (1696–1767) said she must consent even if she knew his intent was to commit a sin and that confessors should not enquire about what happened in the conjugal bed but merely ask the woman if she had been obedient to her husband.[20] However, in areas where Catholicism was trying to hold ground against the encroachments of Protestantism, respect for patriarchal authority was modified. A husband who sinned in the eyes of the church by becoming a heretic should not be followed in his aberrance by his wife. On such occasions the good housewife of Proverbs 31 was unceremoniously dropped in favour of the strong or heroic women capable of assuming leadership in spite of their sexual frailties. Such leadership must still be confined to the home. When Mary Ward sought to found a woman's order to emulate the Jesuits and save Christendom, the papacy was frankly embarrassed. It could not associate the Roman church with gadding women.

The prescriptive literature clings closely to Scripture until the beginning of the eighteenth century. It reveals the preoccupation among theologians and moralists with making the people of the west 'the people of a book' and in so doing promotes the image of a woman with all the frailties of Eve but one who can be saved from excess by her husband or father. Her salvation lies partially outside herself. This literature defines the orderly or what should be. It lays burdens upon both women and men. Above all, it springs from the belief that while absolute perfection is probably impossible one must struggle to do the best one can.

Were there alternative versions of womanhood to the models provided by biblical text? Certainly, if it was the strongest, the Bible was not the only influence from the ancient world transmitting an interpretation of gender difference. The classical legacy, which slumbered during the Dark Ages to be resurrected during the Renaissance, owed nothing to the imprint of Christianity. In this legacy of myths and legends appeared Pandora, a pagan Eve, who opened a box forbidden to her and in so doing brought disaster to mankind. Much more significant, however, was that body of medical thought recorded by the ancient Greeks, who themselves drew upon ideas originating in Egypt and the Middle East, which was re-examined and promulgated during the Renaissance.

Renaissance thought gave a new emphasis to the importance of 'scientific' enquiry and turned its attention to experimental anatomy. New commentaries were made on the work of doctors and philosophers such as Aristotle, Hippocrates and Galen. The Greeks started from the premise that the creation of woman preceded that of man and that she was an imperfect version which was subsequently improved to become the male masterpiece. Woman's imperfection was argued by comparing her body to that of the male and assessing the contrasts which emerged. The female body was colder and wetter and her sex organs were internal rather than external. She lacked the physical strength of the male and so she was passive rather than active, a person for the home, not the political arena. She had, located within her body, a uterus and this was instrumental in the production of the next generation of human beings. But what role exactly did it play?[21]

The Greeks were not unanimous in their interpretation of the functions of this organ, although they recognized it to be clearly significant, and some of their confusion was transmitted to the post-Renaissance world. The revival of Greek science in the fifteenth century was largely due to the admiration of a new generation of medical thinkers for what they saw as the empiricism of the Greeks, who had not laboured under Christian prohibitions on the spilling of blood and the dissection of the cadaver. In spite of this deep admiration, the Greek approach to the female body was not absorbed without some modifications into the developing science of medicine and anatomy in the early modern period. The notion of woman as an 'imperfect' male was dropped; women were seen instead as a physical deviation from the male norm. Like the ancients, however, Renaissance doctors and their descendants interpreted the female body as differing in several critical ways from that of the male masterpiece. The first way was that woman had a different reproductive role and hence a body dissimilar to that of man; the second was that she had a different brain; the third that she had a contentious uterus. Difference did not mean simply specifically different organs but inferior attributes. To be hot and dry, larger and stronger, was better than to be colder and wetter, smaller and weaker. German, British and French anatomists of the eighteenth century interpreted the smaller female cranium as indicative of a smaller and inferior brain and the narrower female ribcage as an indication that women needed to breathe less vigorously to sustain a female lifestyle. The different body included a different brain, one that was smaller but also one which was a prey to irrationality. Here the issue became difficult to distinguish from the debate that raged over many centuries about the uterus.

The Greek words for uterus and for hysteria are the same. This connection was not accidental but embodied notions which were much older and which may have come out of Egypt several centuries before – to pinpoint the genesis of ideas in the ancient world is nearly impossible. The relationship between the uterus as an organ and the physical state of hysteria converted the uterus into something which determined the disposition of womankind. What made the uterus problematic was that it had a monthly cycle and hence related woman somehow to the moon (embodied in the word 'menstruation' is the notion 'month' which itself can be lunar). It could be argued that this lunar relationship exposed women to lunacy and irrationality because the moon might exercise an influence over woman's imagination and contribute to a lack of control over the passions. In other words, the uterus generated hysteria. It could also be argued that this special organ made woman prone to physical weakness and psychological as well as physiological disorders. Until the end of the seventeenth century the presence of the uterus was blamed for woman's irrational behaviour. It made her garrulous, lustful, lovesick, melancholic. In The Anatomy of Melancholy (1621), Robert Burton accentuated the physical nature of gloom. Woman was a physiological depressive. The uterus was also seen as hungry for sexual intercourse. The best-selling treatise on women's disorders written in the eighteenth century, Astruc's Traité des maladies des femmes (1761–5), a six-volume work which drew on ideas stretching back into classical times and which ran into multiple editions in all major European languages, argued that all women's psychological and physical infirmities which men did not have emanated from the uterus and that only healthy, that is regular, sexual relations could preserve a woman's fitness. All unmarried women and widows were in this reading prone to ill health. Indeed, for Astruc there are only three kinds of women and they are divided by menstrual pattern. The first have a normal monthly cycle, the second an over-heavy blood loss and the third one which is scanty to absent. All their psychological characteristics emanate from the extent of the flow.

In the late seventeenth century an Englishman, Thomas Willis, pioneered the science of neurology through his theory of the cerebral origins of hysteria. He too drew on classical antecedents, but interestingly on ones which had been allowed to slumber while attention had been concentrated on the uterus. At the same time new vigour was given to the debate on a topic which had been confusingly aired by the Renaissance revivalists of Greek science. Was the male or the female sex the essential one in generation?

Some Greek doctors and their Renaissance commentators had posited that the uterus did not belong to woman at all but was an independent entity floating in her body. The hunger of the uterus, it was alleged, made the woman lustful. She, it was held, gained in vigour through the procreative act whereas the male gave of his seed, an endeavour which wearied him. The Greeks, lacking the microscope, had not been able to distinguish between ova and sperm. Galen believed that each of the sexes produced a seed which came together to produce the child. However others made the male the generative sex and held that he placed his seed in the woman's body where it sought out the uterus. In this rendering, the seed was male property and woman's function was to provide the nurturing environment (the ground) where it could grow. Leonardo da Vinci, as he recorded in his notebooks, thought that the evident disproof of such a theory was that a black and a white parent formed a child with the traits of both, but there were many theories which could be summoned to explain the resemblance of the child to the mother while retaining the myth of the male as the solely generative sex.[22] Breast milk, for example, was believed to endow a child with both spiritual and physical characteristics.

The spirit of scientific enquiry generated by the Renaissance ensured that the debate did not remain static. Indeed, the human body was from this point on the intellectual agenda for study and commentary. However, it was not until the eighteenth century that a bisexual scheme of generation was formulated with any clarity. The distinction between ova and sperm accepted, seventeenth- and eighteenth-century thought concentrated on the question of whose part was the more essential? In this power struggle, the 'ovists' insisted that the female egg was the more critical. For the 'animalculists' the male sperm was what mattered and they held that it swam into the uterus or nest and banged a lid debarring access to any competitors.[23]

The study of the human skeleton during the eighteenth century, a time when a small proportion of intellectuals were challenging the authority of religion, encouraged a preoccupation with biology which progressively shifted the burden of the argument for woman's subordination to man away from Scripture towards 'nature'. However, until well into the nineteenth century, the two views co-existed. The possibilities involved in blending the two are pertinently revealed if we pursue views on menstruation, a specifically female attribute.

In the Book of Leviticus, a compilation of Judaic laws, the instruction to men is unambiguous. 'You shall not approach a woman to uncover her nakedness while she is unclean from menstruation' (chapter 18 verse 9). For Aristotle, woman's wetness and uncleanliness were synonymous. Galen believed that the blood discharged in menstruation fed the child in the womb and that scabs, pustules in the head, itches, fever and measles were all caused by corrupt menstrual blood with which the unborn child had been in contact. Pliny wrote that wine would turn sour if the shadow of a menstruating woman fell on it, that a dog would turn rabid from eating menstrual blood, and that a flourishing plant splashed by it would wither. The late medieval scholastic Duns Scotus added to Pliny's observations, 'It makes the man to whom it is administered lose his good sense and it makes him a leper.' In such a view, it becomes the perfect constituent of the witch's brew. Then in the 1560s the Flemish doctor Lievin Lennes suggested that intercourse during menstruation was responsible for monstrous births and deformed children.[24] This view certainly passed into the consciousness of literate élites throughout western Europe. It is found, for example, in Quillet's poem on the begetting of beautiful children, a preoccupation which taxed doctors and theologians in the late sixteenth century.

> Press not your Wives, the height'nd Lust incite
> The soul to try the pleasurable Fight,
> While the Blood monthly rushing from the Veins,
> The flowing Womb with foul Pollution stains . . .
> But if by chance the Seeds concurring fix,
> And with the impurer Dross of Nature mix,
> What a detested, miscreated Thing
> From such ill-suited Principles must spring?
> Foul leprous spots shall with his birth begin,
> Spread o'er his Body, and encrust his skin,
> For the same Poison which that Stream contains
> Transfer'd affects the forming Infant's Veins

> Inbred it fixes deep and radically reigns.
> For Natur's common Bosom, nothing exceeds . . .
> Ye husbands then such foul Embraces fly,
> And tho' provok'd the nauseous Bliss deny.[25]

Although by the end of the seventeenth century some of the more extreme views of Pliny were mocked in commentaries, menstrual blood was still associated with disease. For Astruc at the end of the eighteenth century, it is the agent of syphilis, the fluid of contagion. Yet the phenomenon was in some way related to procreation. It was therefore 'a natural disease' and for an adult woman not to menstruate when not pregnant was a sign of something abnormal. It meant that the blood was going instead to the brain, a sign of impending lunacy. A remedy for this condition was supposed to be bleeding in the foot in the waxing moon.

Herbals are full of concoctions to restore to women 'their flowers', in the sense of the scum of fermentation, or 'their courses'. Sometimes menstruation is here referred to as a 'natural purgation' – impurity was washed away each month. In all renderings, menstruation was something which marked woman's inferiority to man.

The works of the Greek medical men and those Renaissance and later scholars who drew upon their ideas make singularly depressing reading. However, just as within the Bible there existed positive images of exemplary women, so in the classical tradition, if not the one used by the doctors, there was another type of imagery which makes a striking contrast to that of the woman with the dirty and flawed body. There were the beautiful, Aphrodite/Venus-type women for whose love war was fought; the gods themselves were prepared to assume animal or other forms to rape or seduce them. The medieval chivalric code which placed woman on a pedestal, etherealized her and made her love and esteem the reward of the gallant warrior drew on these classical notions as well as on the cult of the Virgin. The Renaissance celebrated the physical perfection of both men and women and the potential of human existence. It captured the physical beauty of real women using the models of antiquity. It also endorsed woman as the repository of certain indispensable attributes. Kindness, tenderness, caring and comfort were symbolized in the word *caritas*, itself represented by a woman.

Beauty and kindness have never been considered negligible attributes. Furthermore, both the classical and the biblical traditions incorporated certain women remarkable for their moral strength in physical frailty. Lucretia, chaste unto death, Antigone, Andromache, Penelope, Cornelia, mother of the Gracchi, Lysistrata, the Sabine women who imposed peace on warring nations, were all examples of classical heroines who could be set alongside Deborah and Judith. They were women of courage, but of a particular type of courage which mostly manifested itself in endurance, in holding on to their perception of the good, remaining loyal, pure and inflexible in the face of hardship and temptation. Lucretia, in particular, was a model for both Catholics and Protestants. No biblical woman died in defence of her reputation, so she filled an important void. The triumph of the classical heroines was the greater because they were handicapped by their physical weakness. These women were rivalled in virtue only by the early female Christian martyrs and those later saints who showed exemplary and unwavering fortitude when persecuted by men whose physical strength far outstripped their own.[26]

Perhaps the strong imagery peddled from the pulpit, delivered at school and read within the literate family of what was the ideal rather than the norm helped formulate the opposite, the disorderly, the unruled or unruly. This person, a woman fully in control of a weak husband who abnegates his patriarchal role, plays a major part in treatises and sermons but yet more insistently in satire, comedy, poetry, story and, thanks above all to the Dutch, in visual imagery. The comic, but at the same time threatening potential of this figure, who can undermine and subvert the accepted moral order and make nonsense of the sombre authority of priests and theologians, is obvious. Which of Chaucer's pilgrims has gained greater popularity than the Wife of Bath? Who flouted the rules of modesty and chastity, or the notion of a wife ruled by her husband, more than this earthy, lusty, five-times-married 'gadding' woman who used the pilgrimage to expand her adventures but who above all else wanted to be loved by her husband? The invention of the printing press gave the unruly woman a vigorous and pervasive existence in word and picture. Since monogamous marriage was at the heart of the western European social system, something most men and women experienced, it was also the key to western humour. The contrast between ideal marriage and real life afforded scope for irony, parody, satire, and had a resonance in the minds of all who heard or read or viewed it. It purported to disclose what was, rather than what should be.

The attributes shown to be those of the disorderly woman in a world whose standards are turned upside down are those most declaimed against by the moralists, so they bear witness to the pervasiveness of stock biblical and biological precepts. Her attributes are usually seven. First, she has a shrewish and uncontrollable tongue which is her main weapon in the defeat of her husband. Secondly, she is lustful and unchaste in her search for sexual gratification: even the Devil will do as a sleeping partner. Thirdly, she is profligate and particularly given to extravagance in apparel. Fourth, she is vain and in her love of self will stop at nothing. Fifth, she will intrigue with other women or will sway the minds of the men who are her creatures to overthrow male authority. Sixth, her greed knows no bounds, and seventh, she has a penchant for strong drink from which follows all manner of further undesirable behaviour. In this literature the women are evil or at best wanton, and the men are fools, defeated by female bad temper or female wiles. The men are also emasculated by their wives. In German imagery they are presented as lions without claws, or as those who have surrendered the right to wear the trousers to women.[27]

This kind of representation appears to have been most vigorous in north-western Europe, in British, Dutch, German and French literature and prints. Dunbar's *Two Maryit Women* (c. 1508) and *The Schole-house of Women* (c. 1510) adopt the technique of taking a woman, in the second instance a widow of much vaunted experience, and letting her own words betray and condemn her. The widow, for example, advises unhappy wives, whose woes are listed to include their husband's meanness with money and indifference to sex, to console themselves and to make an intolerable life tolerable through lusty sexual relationships with 'othir bachilleris blumying in youth' which they can secure by seductive apparel. Between 1560 and 1570 appeared a spate of satirical poems dependent upon the stock image of a wanton, disorderly married woman. Their titles convey the content: *The proude Wyves paternoster*, *An hundred poyntes of evil huswifrye*, *A commyssion unto all those whose wyves be thayre masters*, *A Shrewde and Curste Wyfe lapped in Morrellskin*. The last-named denotes not only how a woman can dissimulate and be other than what she appears to be but also draws conclusions as to the need for control by the husband. Embodied in work dedicated to other issues, the disorderly woman intent upon the fall of good men nowhere took form more cogently than in Thomas Dekker's *The Bachelors' Banquet* (1603). Here rational man is destroyed by the effect of woman's irrational humours.

This erosion of the rational and well-intentioned male by a super-stitious and ignorant wife given to extravagance and gossip with her friends constituted the kernel of Hieronymous Sweerts's *De Tien Vermak-elijkheden des Houweljks* (1684, translated as *The Ten Pleasures of Marriage*) and *De Biegt der Gertrouwde* (*The Marriage Trap*, 1679), which included a set of prints illustrating each stage of the disintegration of a marriage. These works were international successes. The new wife indulges her taste for finery and the entertainment of her friends. When she is slow to become pregnant, the house is filled with the smell of boiling herbs, either potions to promote her own fertility or intended to pervade the entire atmosphere to make both parties potent. Once pregnant, she belongs not to the husband but to the women of her family and friends, the gossips who will attend the birth. Thereafter, the house is full of drying nappies and baby linen. The denouement of Sweerts's plot is that the husband becomes alienated from his own home which he gradu-ally cedes to his wife and to a monstrous regiment of women.[28] The story is meant to amuse but there is no doubt that an alarm bell is ringing. The clear implication is that the husband should have done something to reassert his position and to regain control of the home which he is financing.

The Dutch were adept at lending both textual and visual form to the contrast between the ruled and the unruled home. At one level in genre painting they extolled the joys of domesticity summarized by a clean, orderly woman, quietly nursing or instructing her children, or spinning when the chores (symbolized by a sweeping brush) are done. Here the shining cleanliness of the environment underlines the point that order, physical and spiritual, depend upon woman's fulfilling a particular domestic role. However, let her fail in her duty and chaos ensues. In *The Dissolute Household* (1688) Jan Steen, who mastered the technique of letting the observer draw his or her own morals, shows a home where the mistress slumps over the dining table after a heavy meal and too much drink. Her children are stealing money from her pocket, the servant is behaving wantonly with a musician and the family linen is about to disappear. The husband has turned his back on this spectacle of depravity and his leg rests in the lap of a whore whom he has presumably invited in because his wife is unconscious. A dog scav-enges good roast meat left casually available and gambling cards litter the floor. Vanitas symbols abound, including the monkey (representing trickery and salaciousness) and the clock to recall the shortness of life's time span. The household is doomed to destruction and above the sinful scene hovers a basket containing the beggar's crutch and bowl. [29]

How is this scene to be interpreted? Steen revelled in ambiguity and in taxing his audience's mind. Is the master of the house responsible for not controlling his wife's intake of drink? Or are we to blame the lady herself for her lack of vigilance? She is, after all, responsible for household management. Would she, if at all alert, permit the desecration of the household by the introduction of a whore? If she were an adequate wife would her husband turn elsewhere, and what about this example to the maid and to the children? Neither party is innocent, but the lady's dozing, passive as it may seem to be, is at the heart of the matter.

Another variant on the dominance of the unruly woman was to present the helplessness of men when surrounded by a female conspiracy. 'Who rules Holland?' ran a riddle of the 1640s. The answer was 'the Devil'. Then came the explanation for this apparent absurdity. Amsterdam rules Holland; the burgomaster rules Amsterdam, but he is ruled by his wife and she is ruled by the maid and the maid, you may be sure, is ruled by the Devil. [30] From this dominance absurdities and dangers could flow. The conniving maidservant has a long literary history which perhaps reached its apogee in the eighteenth century in the hands of Sheridan, Carlo Goldoni in Venice, and Beaumarchais in Paris. Some plots pivoted on the collusion of mistress and maid: women unite across class boundaries to undermine the allegedly dominant male. In others the man must buy the support of the maidservant, who is suborned by gold to help him win his suit. Critical to an appreciation of the imagery is that women are capable of low animal cunning and that the power of men is apparent rather than real.

It is obvious that literary works devoted to the paradox of disorderly/ orderly women had much the same intention. They reinforced the belief in the desirability of male government of women, and of paternal authority within the confines of the home. The implication is that, although many aspects of the norm are generally not observed, this is the standard, God-ordained model of a household to which every family should aspire.

The range of possibilities for a male–female relationship did not of course end here. There are examples, perhaps sufficient to constitute a subgenre of the western literary tradition, in which the theme of woman as someone who is as clever as man and sometimes cleverer is allowed to surface and gives the plot its dynamic. Under such circumstances the woman steps into a male role and fills it with honour. On the English stage women's parts were of course played by boys until after the mid-seventeenth century, and cross-dressing may have either obscured or emphasized the issue. Thus Portia, wearing a lawyer's gown, outsmarts the wily Jew and appropriates an understanding of true justice, accepting the letter of the Venetian contract by granting Shylock his pound of flesh but denying him Christian blood. Viola in male garb can court Olivia in a Twelfth Night romp and not be found wanting. However, the reversal is transitory to cope with exigent circumstances and, the need passed, the heroine reassumes her female form and hands back authority to her lover/husband. The honourable woman is frequently made a victim of the irrationality, jealousy or tyranny of husband or father and responds rationally with suffering. Elsewhere, as in the tragedies of Corneille or Racine, the woman can assume the mantle of family honour when the men are annihilated. She can remind men of their duty and impel them towards actions from which she as a woman is debarred. Her courage can contrast with their vacillation and she can make sacrifices even unto death. In recognizing the limitations imposed on her sex and the obligations that must fall to men she becomes the spokesperson for duty. Tragedy enhances woman in her relations with man just as comedy seeks to ridicule her. High culture abounds with examples of women who influence men, for good or ill, and of men who struggle to achieve their approbation. A jealous husband will kill in anger – and regret it – but he should not stoop to lesser physical violence. The shrew is tamed by words, by hunger, by deprivation of sleep and by her growing realization of the constraints on her sex, but not by beating. Petruchio is an agent of the civilizing process.

How do the representations of women and their relationships with men trickle down into popular culture? One way of assessing this process is from analyses of the first printed *livres bleus*, the books carried in the pedlars' packs which circulated in seventeenth- and eighteenth-century France, and the chapbooks, 'small books and pleasant histories' which were similarly hawked through Britain.[31] They were intended to be read aloud, in tavern or farmstead or at evening meetings for entertainment, by someone who had the pence to buy and the ability to read, and were mostly written by men, though they may have been stories traditionally told by women. There are national differences between the contents. The British books were more concerned with religion and there were more popular heroes and heroines than there were in the

French collections which drew more conspicuously upon stories of the great and the famous, of high society. Both kinds of work revelled in burlesque and farce. The attitude towards women found in the French works can be summarized in the phrase *l'honneur de la femme est d'être inférieure*. She also appears in the guise of a source of wealth for the man who knows how to play the system.

In the Occitan fairy-tale *Jean l'Ont Pris*, for example, which was written down in 1745 but drew on much older traditions which find echoes elsewhere in southern and central Europe, the hero, an orphaned beggar boy, has his first financial break when he finds a store of money under his dying grandmother's mattress. He builds up his wealth further by marrying, in return for a large sum of money from her impregnator, a rejected and disease-ridden (also recognizably Protestant) pregnant woman whose early death is anticipated. He then moves on to marry the woman he really loves, whose dowry he increases by making her pregnant so that her father is anxious to be rid of her. He knows her love for him and she connives at her loss of chastity. The women in such tales are passive but co-operative. Their wealth can make a man but action must be left to him.[32]

The English tradition finds women more assertive, though within bounds. Let us take the example of *Long Meg of Westminster*, a 'pleasant story' of 1582.[33] She is a migrant from Lancashire in London in search of a job as a servant, a strapping wench who can take on a man in a fight and win. Since she fights fair the men respect her and she wanders around London at night in men's clothing with a sword which she uses to protect the poor and suffering. After a series of adventures in which she finds herself in the army, where her bravery earns her a life pension, she marries a soldier and even when he administers blows she shows herself the submissive wife. In her words: 'Whatever I have done to others, it behoveth me to be Obedient to you and never shall it be said, though I Cudgel a Knave that wrongs me, that Long Meg shall be her Husband's Master.' The sympathy of the audience is thus preserved and circumstances are once more made the modifier of what is appropriate. In low culture tales of blows between couples are common. However, ultimate submission of wife to husband is a *sine qua non* and co-operation between the two is the guarantee of their standing in the community.

Fairy tales and those in chapbooks had their roots in popular culture. From the late seventeenth century, however, they were collected, refined and put into gracious prose, in some instances by French salon women, making them fit for consumption by the upper classes. They commanded a special place in the acculturation process of the young and were part of a shared heritage of the élite and the humble. Both cultures, then, agreed on the fundamental principles of the relationships between men and women. Deviation from the norm is permissible under certain circumstances, but the norm is preserved intact. The household has its proper head in the male. If he is absent through death or personal misadventure or just on business, he has a natural replacement. If he is unjust or tyrannical the woman has a right to use strategies against him. The beautiful blondes of Italian fairy stories who grow beastly bodily hair to ward off a lusting widowed father might be relevant,[34] like the lives of medieval saints who are saved by miraculous means from pagan marital tyranny leaving the principle of obedience intact. The usual recommended way to deal with tyranny was suffering. In Vives' *Linguae Latinae Exercitatio* (1539), a work in dialogue form perhaps intended for older schoolboys, there exists a model house. In the dining room are hung three pictures. The first is of Griselda from the *Decameron*, who bore all the humiliations imposed upon her by her husband to test her patience and obedience. The second is of Saint Godelieve of Flanders, strangled in spite of her immaculate behaviour by her tyrannical husband, and made a saint in recognition of her suffering and the miracles associated with her tomb. The third is of Catherine of Aragon (1485–1536), the newly dead and wronged wife of Henry VIII, who never departed from the path of the dutiful wife. The placing of such pictures in the dining room where the family gathered about a table whose offerings testified to the efficiency of housewife or housekeeper might remind the wife of where her duties lay.[35]

How do such representations relate to the lives of real men and women? They are cultural artefacts and embody imagery designed to reflect and to confirm stereotypical roles. They pass value judgements on both women and men, leaving neither spared from criticism. They aim to instruct. They reflect shame and honour codes integral to the society but show how they can be modified in the workings of everyday life. They can be counted among agencies which are striving to promote what is widely considered to be the best way to achieve salvation, a better hereafter. But they remain fictional, products of the imagination. There are, also, other representations of women and men to be found in a study of ecclesiastical, written and customary law. Law, as Montesquieu urged, is also a product of a civilization, a cultural artefact. It imposes constraints designed to realize certain ends or to promote what a particular society perceives as needful to achieve social order and organization.

The notions of gender embodied in law are, of course, capable of placing a direct restriction on the way in which individuals live out their lives, since laws are backed by force or customary procedures which proclaim alternative action invalid. We must *ab initio* insist that a considerable chasm often existed between the letter of the law and its practice, but such a recognition still leaves the law as a basic framework of reference intact. European law could take many forms, written or customary, ecclesiastical or secular, criminal or civil. However, whatever the diversity of form, the representations of womanhood and manhood, and the different forms they assumed, were likely to be much the same since church and state were virtually unanimous in the norms they sought to promote.

The Roman Catholic Church was built upon the Roman Empire, the widest empire that Europe had known. The Romans were responsible for a body of written laws whose influence was reflected wherever the Romans had maintained a strong presence, as in Italy, Spain, Portugal and France south of the Loire. Roman law had also a strong influence on canon law, of which marriage law was a part.[36] North-western Europe, including France north of the Loire, England and the Netherlands, were areas of customary law; but in both areas of Roman (or written) law and of customary law, a person's legal status depended on gender. Women were recognized and categorized as daughters, wives (above all) and to a degree as mothers; men were classed as sons and then as heads of households, as husbands and as fathers. To husband and father fell responsibility for the conduct of those seen to be his dependants. In Spain and Italy women were virtually debarred from a physical presence in the courts and husband, father, kinsman or lawyer had to speak for them. In areas of customary law they had a legal identity. Even so, before the 1790s throughout western Europe a husband could be called upon to answer for the conduct of his wife if she was shown to be guilty. This might not in extreme cases preserve her from punishment, but if her husband was a party to her misdemeanours the blame and the punishment could fall in whole or in part upon him. If she stole property her husband was liable for its restitution. If she stole in his company, his was the greater crime. A married woman could say almost anything in public against an individual or a group and as a 'silly' or irrational woman would not be punished, but if her husband was present when she made such utterances then the charge of slander was incurred by him.

Blackstone thought that English law lifted too much from the shoulders of women and the tendency of eighteenth-century criminal reformers was to urge that some of the distinctions between husband and wife before the criminal law be removed. The price a woman paid for reduced liability was that, since her husband carried the responsibility, it was deemed right that he was the first judge of his wife. He could expect from her conformity to certain standards such as keeping to her house and restraining her tongue and if she did not conform then he had powers of correction. The euphemism *correction modérée* (moderate chastisement, which included beating within acknowledged boundaries) was seen as his affair. This correction should not assume disproportionate levels. In north-western Europe judicial structures existed which allowed the beaten wife to call her husband to account and cease his violence.

Traditionally, common or customary laws recognized that a husband might need a little assistance in controlling the unruly woman, particularly the one with an unbridled tongue. The 'scold' (she whose vicious tongue harmed her man, her neighbours and by extension good moral order in the community) was technically liable in England to be ducked in the public pond. But the possession of a community ducking school, like the presence of a pillory, was intended as a deterrent, a reminder of what might happen if a person overstepped the mark, rather than as an indication of common practice.

The model wife at law, then, was in the first instance obedient. For this reason, the murder of a husband far exceeded in gravity wife murder. In English law, it was classed as petty treason, because the male head of household filled within the family the role of the king within the realm and parricide was equated with the destruction of sovereign power and the subversion of a God-ordained order in the household, the primary social unit. If the law gave some protection to the woman whose husband led her astray it came down very hard indeed on the woman who murdered her husband. Two of the last women to be burned at the stake in England in the eighteenth century (they had already been strangled) had been found guilty of poisoning their husbands. Poisoning implied malice aforethought and it clearly violated the trust that every man had to place in his wife when he sat down to his dinner.

The situation of the wife-murderer was radically different, particularly where cumulative violence had overstepped the usual boundaries.

Both the Catholic and the Protestant churches condemned immorality in the form of adultery in both sexes. During periods of stringent application of Christian moral codes such as in sixteenth-century Protestant Germany, England during the Puritan period or Holland in the Golden Age, adulterous husbands could indeed be brought to court and prosecuted. However, the situation was complicated by the existence of a double standard of conduct. The home was the primary unit in which the legitimate progeny of a couple were sheltered and that progeny were the natural heirs to the father's property. They were his seed. An adulterous woman threatened the principles on which the perpetuation of property was based. An adulterous man left his home unscathed unless he sought to bring his concubine into the house.

Such perceptions found themselves expressed in direct form in countries with criminal codes based on Roman law where a woman taken in adultery by her husband could be killed by him on the spot without his incurring the charge of murder. In the case of Spain, he could restrain himself and choose the means whereby she should die after a judicial hearing.[37] Neither option was open to a woman. In the ecclesiastical courts to which Catholic women had recourse to gain separation from an adulterous husband and the restitution of property which might allow them to reconstitute a livelihood, the plaintiffs could find themselves denied their suit unless they could show aggravating factors such as the introduction of a concubine into the conjugal home, violence to the point of endangering life or bestial practices. Even then, however brutal or adulterous he might be, the abused wife could not claim custody of her children. The father was seen as the generative sex and the children as his property.

The law also confirmed the idea of woman as the more lustful sex. This perception had particular application to adult rape victims – the law took a sterner view of the abused child. Under most European codes, a woman could not claim that rape was responsible for her pregnancy since her very impregnation was held to demonstrate her active consent (it was 'assumed' that no conception took place without pleasure). There was no question of the criminal law applying a universal standard to men and women.[38]

The position of women in civil law, whether written or customary, was subject to variations based on social status. The critical areas in which women might be disadvantaged were the transmission of property and the negotiation of credit. In all countries which had known the influence of feudalism (that is, France, England, parts of Germany and Italy), the principle of primogeniture operated and the transmission of the noble fief or landed estate was through the legitimate male line. The justification for this was that, while not precluding the inheritance of land by women in default of a male heir, the fief was designed to provide the income to fulfil military obligations. The marriage of a noble heiress and the absorption of the fief and its management into a male patrimony was a serious preoccupation of the crown, and until the mid-seventeenth century the monarchy in England could use rights of wardship over an orphaned heiress to arrange her marriage as a way of rewarding a royal client. Laws respecting the division of property did not dissolve with the breakdown of feudal structures. Indeed, throughout western Europe many aristocrats entailed (that is, secured with legal backing the transmission of their estates through a single male heir, usually the eldest son) in order to preserve the wealth or standing of their clan. At the same time, they sought to provide for their other children through monetary bequests or offices in church or state. A daughter was given a dowry on marriage, usually a sum of money or goods, and thereafter renounced all claims on her father's estate.

At other social levels most fathers certainly tried to see that all their children had some assets, though how effectively they could do so depended on the extent of their resources and the demands made upon them.[39] However, whatever the distribution, the property which a woman took into marriage — whether in money, goods or land — passed into the management of her husband. He absorbed it, administered it and paid any taxes due on it. If he did a bad job and misused her funds, a woman could have difficulty in protecting her property against his ineptitude or profligacy. She could not reclaim her input unless he died or a separation was agreed upon and she had technically no voice in its disposal although suits were on occasion undertaken, usually with the collusion of the wider family, to protect her property against the ravages of a drunken wastrel. Such efforts could meet with little success if the assets had been dissipated.

So the law conceived of a universal woman, one under the protection of her father or husband, but it was capable of seeing at least two circumstances in which women might need some help. The ecclesiastical courts took breach of promise seriously, particularly when the promise was endorsed by the community and the woman was pregnant. The civil courts in areas of written law generally gave the widow the right to repossess her dowry before other claims were made on the estate. These were moments when there was clearly no strong male figure to protect her. Otherwise, the law resigned every married woman into the care of her husband.

To the semi-responsible being of whom the husband was the first judge who appears in law codes and custom, and to the model endorsed by the church of the obedient wife seeking salvation through a godly husband, must be added a further woman, woman the worker or economic woman, she who had to sell her labour in the marketplace. This woman causes problems. The good conduct literature emphasized the work women should do to conform to the model of the good housewife, but this work is within the home or the confines of the property. *La perfecta casada* of Fray Luis de León, drawing on the imagery of Proverbs 31, shows that the couple are financially dependent on each other's labours in the home and in their fields and that this is a God-ordained complementarity. The complementary role must be the wife's first concern. If he needs her to lead the horse while he ploughs, she must obey. If she neglects to help him she falls short as a wife. However, the marketplace where labour outside the home had to be sold was a public space which does not give recognition to such work. Socio-economic woman at this point perforce crossed a psychological boundary. In early modern Italy, a man who could not maintain his wife and daughters within the home counted for little in community esteem. Both the man and his daughters were deemed *di poca* (worth little) – even though they might work unremittingly under his roof for wages he negotiated without loss of status to himself. In Europe north of the Loire, honour was on the side of work, but the position of woman in the workforce remained very different from that of men. Why should this be so?

It was not until the nineteenth century that a clearly formulated discussion of the female worker and the female wage took place. When it did, however, it drew on assumptions which were hundreds of years old. In 1808, Jean Baptiste Say, who occupied the first chair of political economy in France, explained that a man's wage had to sustain man the worker and provide for the reproduction of the labour force. His wages must then include subsistence costs for a wife and children, his natural dependants. Say's economic person, in the full sense, was a married man with two children competing with other such men in the labour market. A woman, however, was considered to be a dependant. When she entered the market for a job she already had a roof above her head and someone to defray the costs of heating and perhaps providing her with food. Since she did not need wage levels to provide her total subsistence she was prepared to work for lower wages. A woman who needed to be self-sufficient and therefore to receive a higher remuneration was unnatural or abnormal. Being in the minority, and unable to compete with women 'in the natural state' (under the economic protection of a man) she could not affect female wage levels.[40]

Embodied in Say's explanation – one which in every way conformed to market practice – is an obvious principle: that economic man is a family man and his demands lift wage levels for all men, even bachelors. Economic woman is also a family woman, but her demands depress wage levels for all women to the point where they do not permit an independent existence to the spinster – the abnormal woman. The text encapsulates tersely the spinster predicament.

Say's explanation of differential wage levels could be used to justify a 'law of unequal exchange' which prevailed between male and female labour in the marketplace.[41]

This 'law of unequal exchange' established the value attached to certain goods and services. If work could be performed by women it carried a lower remuneration than if it was deemed men's work. The cost of labour was embodied in the goods or services produced. The degree of skill attached to work has no relevance to these concepts. Lace-making or embroidery or the painting of porcelain are not unskilled, quite the reverse, but they can be done by women and hence command women's, that is low, wages. Work as well as the worker was linked to gender in the marketplace. Put another way, a man seen doing women's work for wages had lowered the price of his labour and was on dishonourable terrain.

The models of female and male which received expression in holy text and the institutions of church and state, in the law and in custom and in the workings of the marketplace, sought to define the scope of action of both men and women. They might be summarized by reference to one of the commonest mass images in north-western Europe from the sixteenth to the nineteenth century, the ladder of life produced in particular abundance by the Dutch but appearing almost everywhere as part of the pedlar's pack to be stuck on the walls of the humblest cottage. The ladder ascends and then descends. Each rung represents a phase in the life cycle and demonstrates behaviour thought appropriate to the men and women at that stage. The female passes through life as child, adolescent girl at her orisons, betrothed maiden, bride, mother and grandmother. After maternity she ages fast but her life cycle is summarized in the reproductive process. If the woman is seen at work it is sewing or embroidering beside the cradle, the image of domesticity. The male has infinitely more varied roles. He might be a soldier, a lawyer, a sage. He ages more gradually. Indeed, he is frequently quite spry to the end when he is carried off, as is his partner, by the angels whose vigilance over their life conduct has been constant, to appear before the tribunal of the Last Judgement.[42]

The ladder of life depicts what is seen as essential and appropriate, that which is God-ordained, the universal to which each man and woman should aspire. The extent of the sales of such an image indicates that it was one available to high and low, the farmer's wife, the maidservant, the farmhands, the child growing into adolescence. How did they read it? Did they compare their parents with the ageing figures? Did they see it as a likely trajectory for themselves? For every child who fixed his or her eyes on the ascending and descending image and was taught about the possible and the appropriate, the rules of the game, another factor intruded, that of actual experience. What follows is an attempt to construct some of that experience and show how it might reflect or modify the imagery.

CHAPTER TWO

—◁◦▷—

The Strategic Plan: Marriage as Goal

There is more to marriage than four legs in a bed.
OLD ENGLISH PROVERB

Who marries for love without money hath good nights but
sorry mornings.
PLINY, BUT TRANSLATED INTO ALL EUROPEAN LANGUAGES

Consider my dear girl that you have no portions and
endeavour to supply the deficiencies of fortune by mind. You
cannot expect to marry in such a manner as neither of you
shall have occasion to work and none but a fool will take
a wife whose bread has to be earned solely by his labour
and who will contribute nothing towards it herself.
ELIZA HAYWOOD, A PRESENT FOR A SERVING MAID, 1743

THE LITERATURE of good advice placed marriage at the centre
in the lives of women and men, except, in Catholic thinking,
for those intending to dedicate themselves to God in the
religious life. The view was generally endorsed by European society and
monogamous marriage was seen as the institution at the heart of the
social system, a position it had occupied for so long that the memory
of man ran not to the contrary. In the sixteenth century the reformers
of both religious camps sought to take control of this all-important
institution. Until that time the marital relationship had been created
by a promise or oath (the most solemn act possible by individuals in
medieval society) made in front of witnesses: now the aim was to make
it invalid unless performed in church, in conformity with a set of
rules about consanguinity and after fulfilment of other criteria (the
announcement of banns or the granting of special licences, and so on).

Without such control, the churches' dominance over the lives of individuals could be no more than partial. The family was the cradle of Christians and the guarantor of biblical morality.

Secular authorities were also far from indifferent to the making of marriage. For the French monarchy in the sixteenth century the marriages of the great and the powerful were accompanied by such massive transferences of wealth and family alliances that significant power bases were created which could shake monarchical power. For the English in the mid-eighteenth century, the clandestine marriage was to be deplored because the lack of publicity which surrounded it meant that the couple had only a fragile commitment and fathers could escape into the blue leaving behind them children dependent on public funds (a concern far from dead in the 1990s). The desirability of the proper ordering of monogamous marriage, with the family suitably controlled by patriarchal authority, was nowhere in dispute.[1]

Few Europeans could ignore the importance of marriage in their lives. It mattered to both men and women, signifying their entrance to the adult community. It was, moreover, a step which once taken was almost impossible to undo. 'Look before you leap' could not be over-emphasized by one generation to another. One's spouse was one's life companion and the marriage step was intended as one of finality. As the nineteenth-century novelist concluded, it was the denouement of the human drama: 'Reader, I married him.'

In a world predicated on the subordinate role of women, to live outside marriage and the family was almost inconceivable. In Catholic countries, those dowered by their families might enter a cloister or, more generally, the presence of a family with resources to maintain one in spinsterhood might to a degree modify the generalization. For men too, matrimony represented a desirable state. The support, succour and sustenance achieved by the matrimonial bond recommended the marriage partnership to most people. What was sought in marriage might vary according to social class. In violent medieval societies the high nobility had used marriage as a means of building up support networks to be called upon in times of civil strife and to promote dynastic interests. This use of the matrimonial bond had been and continued in the early modern period to be yet more refined into a commercial union, one based on wealth guaranteeing an extravagant lifestyle, but which could also give prestige and political, if no longer military, strength as well as ensuring that property passed to one's progeny. At the other end of the social scale, marriage was more overtly about economic survival and the rearing of children within a stable and solid unit. A wife's services, at this level of the population, were as critical to the survival of a man as vice versa. She complemented his labours; the pair had mutual interests to promote. If at one end of the social spectrum marriage was economic and political, at the other end it was overwhelmingly economic.

Most Europeans were farmers, and, as William Cobbett was to say, 'a bare glance at the thing shows, that a farmer above all men living, can never carry on his affairs without a wife'.[2] In towns and cities, characterized by small workshops which were organized into guilds, particularly strong in Germany and a crescent descending into northern Italy, full mastership of a guild could depend not only on fulfilling the requirements of apprenticeship and being able to purchase entry, but on having a wife. Marriage was seen as a sign of maturity and the preparedness to assume responsibilities. A workshop needed the artisan's wife to ensure that it was properly run and its morality impeccable.[3]

These were not the only reasons pushing couples to marry. In sickness especially, each was vitally dependent upon the other. The unmarried were pitied and deemed inadequate unless rich and male, and even they were seen as placing their lives at risk. To be seriously ill and unattended by a wife or daughter was a state to be avoided at all costs, for only close female relatives could be truly dedicated to a man's preservation. Servants were known for their trickery and if they thought they had the prospect of a small legacy for devoted service had a vested interest in accelerating the master's exit by neglect at the critical juncture. Even Samuel Pepys's cousin, who made something of a cult of bachelorhood, could not face the prospect of existence when the devoted spinster sister who had been his housekeeper died. She had lifted from his shoulders the burden of seeing that he was not robbed by tradesmen and servants and had been ready with the cup of posset when he was sick. Find me a widow, he instructed Pepys, between thirty and forty, without children and with a fortune. One who in addition would not make great demands upon his time and who was sober in her habits.[4]

To be old and alone without the support of children was yet another situation to be avoided if at all possible. For the rich the perpetuation of name and property mattered; for the poorer the prospect of unaided debility and the loss of the physical strength needed to gain a living were obvious fears. Such a profound appreciation of the realities and

fragility of life made marriage a state to be undertaken wherever possible. To all these considerations, the sixteenth-century reformers were
to add salvation. For a woman marriage and childbearing were the road
to eternity and she should not forget it.

For both sexes, the goal was not merely marriage but the right
marriage, joining the worthy couple in a 'fitting match', an instructive
concept in which appropriateness was the criterion. An appropriate
union was one in which wealth and status, religious affiliation and age,
as well as less easily defined attributes such as temperament and moral
qualities, were seen to be approximately consonant. In a 'fitting match',
rich and poor, noble and commoner (unless with good reason), Jew and
Gentile, Catholic and Protestant, old and young were not brought
together. Canon law forbade marriage within degrees of consanguinity:
parents could not marry their children, nor brothers sisters, and cousins
to the fourth degree were also excluded from the marriage pool. Even
adoptive parents could not marry the children they had adopted.
The church was afraid of incest and hence of mortal sin and guarded
against it.

However, the Catholic rich could always get a permission or dispen-
sation for which they paid dearly to Rome. As the Spanish Jesuit Thomas
Sànchez tells us, in his enormous *Disputationum de Sancto Matrimonii
Sacramento* which ran into more than a dozen printings between 1602
and 1669, the prohibitions on the marriages of cousins or uncles and
nieces could dissolve under certain circumstances. These included those
areas where the marriage pool was very small or where a woman could
not command a dowry to marry within her social class. A woman over
twenty-five should be allowed to marry within the degrees if she had
no other prospects and was menaced with living alone and hence losing
her honour (in practice this category was used to reinforce other considerations). A widow with children to educate who received an offer within
her or her husband's family should be allowed to go ahead in the interests
of the children. In an honourable family, in terms of wealth or blood,
threatened with the extinction of the name, such a marriage should be
accepted. No less a person than the great humanist Erasmus thought
that the story of Lot, who had intercourse with his daughters, illustrated
the need of a man to prevent his line from dying out. Perhaps most
important of all to the Roman church, where Catholics had difficulty
in finding other Catholics, marrying within degrees of consanguinity
was acceptable. Many rich Catholic families, however, anxious to keep

money within their clan and preserve their standing in the community, regularly sought dispensations even when their line was not threatened. Certain families from the great urban patriciates, like the Gozzadini in Bologna, intermarried legitimate and illegitimate children of the same house. In Italy, Portugal and northern France, dispensations for marriages within unacceptable degrees were frequently sought by those who could pay the fee.[5]

In all countries, unequal and unfitting matches might take place, but they represented, as it were, a failure in the system of values and as such their doom was regarded as probably inevitable. Such matches could then be used in evidence to those contemplating similar folly. Sometimes the rules were waived, for example by the old and famous who were particularly prone to pick out the young, beautiful and, it was hoped, fertile. Or purely practical considerations could interpose themselves. Where, as in sixteenth-century Germany, an artisan's widow could offer a younger man entry to a guild, condemnation of the December–May match seems to have evaporated. Here, however, we are not dealing with a first marriage, nor perhaps usually with women beyond childbearing years.

There were fitting unions for all sectors of society, although the concept petered out at the bottom of the social scale. Implicit in the notion of 'fitting' was that of economic strength adequate to sustain the couple according to standards which varied from the aristocratic to what was hoped would be sufficient to guarantee the survival of a family. The resourceless couple might share an equality of penury, but a marriage between them could not have the approbation of the wider society – particularly a Protestant society – for it would certainly result in pauperdom and the fruits of the match would become a charge on the community. Not to have anything at all at the outset of a marriage, as opposed to having a little, was probably unusual. On the other hand, commentators in all countries on the reasons for the growth of poverty pointed to those who married on the *idea* rather than the actuality of a sufficiency and whose resources were inadequate for the sustenance of a family. In short, the notion of what was 'fitting' embodied a concept of responsibility for the future: it implied a life plan, a strategy. The couple needed, at the most basic level, to be perceived as able to support themselves and temperamentally suited, that is, they should get on together affectionately and be conscious of mutual interests. At the highest social levels they should also be of the same 'degree'.[6]

For rich and poor alike, preparation for the married state meant serious long-term planning, if not from infancy, at least from childhood or early adolescence. Young women could be roughly divided into those whose parents or family would give them a dowry, that is, provide a sum of money, and those who had to seek such financial means for themselves. The head of a noble house and father of a family had to consider the implications arising for the house out of the number and sex of the surviving children. In the case of daughters, a considerable financial outflow would have to be taken into account, a planned surrender of assets in whole or in part to occur on marriage. The dowry became increasingly formalized in the sixteenth and seventeenth centuries and continued to be so as the mark of a more stable and a more commercially evolved society. Women became the bearers of liquid wealth, clothes, jewels, furnishings and above all money, wealth regarded as the guarantee of suitable status for the bride over her entire life. The trend of dowry levels was increasingly upwards for the great landed classes, and this remorseless rise may have reflected more than inflation. Two further considerations should be taken into account. The first is that the development of the courts made the cost of maintaining a presence in court circles increasingly expensive, while the appurtenances of nobility from the newly built stately home to its contents became increasingly varied and costly. Fashion, too, made inroads into the purse. The second is that the wealthy bourgeoisie, in an attempt to gain social status, were prepared to use the marriage of a daughter as a means of securing connections with the great families and hence competed with the old houses in this respect. The size of the dowry or marriage portion was itself a marker of social status.[7]

The increase in the size of dowries was uneven over nations. It was much less apparent in the eighteenth century, for example, among the Scottish peerage than among the English, who were closer in this respect to the noble families of France and Spain. Indeed, in Spain legislation at the end of the eighteenth century tried to prevent the dowry exceeding twelve times the annual income of the head of the bride's house.[8] The escalation was apparent in most countries from the opening decades of the seventeenth century and had different results in different contexts. In Britain it meant a huge rise in the number of aristocratic spinsters: one-third of the daughters of the Scottish aristocracy could not expect to marry. In France it led to an apparent restriction of the noble birthrate. The number of children born to a French peer fell from four to two from the sixteenth to the eighteenth centuries and the French female aristocrat had finished childbearing by the age of twenty-five.[9] The dowry everywhere created inequalities among the daughters of wealthy families. In Italy and Spain the level of the dowry filled the convents. Three-quarters of the female children of the Milanese aristocracy, for example, before 1650 would be sent to the convent. In other Italian cities it might be a more modest third. These proportions fell a little in the late seventeenth century and still further in the eighteenth century as the convent incurred the hostility of Enlightenment rulers such as Leopold of Tuscany.[10] In England, even in the medieval period, the convent was never a major absorber of single women,[11] and there was more preparedness on the part of aristocratic fathers to countenance the marriage of a younger daughter to someone of yeoman stock. To marry out of caste was more shameful for both a Spanish and an Italian noble family, a loss of honour which was not readily accepted, and here the convent was a very acceptable substitute.

The family strategy of the noble was, then, determined by the numbers of daughters to be married and the standing of the family. The marriage of even one daughter in a way to dignify the name could cause some of the great houses to part with as much as a third of their assets. The father of an upper-class family had perforce as his family grew up to give a great deal of thought to how he was going to raise the money to dispose of his children well and, if he had a large family, to find ways of reducing the drain on family wealth – the church or, in the case of sons, military, court or ambassadorial service. The mother had to occupy herself with the education of her daughters so that they could be ready for their launching. In the sixteenth century, in England and France, parents often sent their female children into another noble house (against payment) to learn the business of running such an establishment, needlework skills and suitable accomplishments and at the same time to build up contacts with a view to marriage. The civil wars of the mid-seventeenth century ruptured this process. Protestant girls of the higher social echelons were often taught at home. Their education was directed towards the acquisition of social skills, singing, dancing, an attractive appearance, the right manners, delicate needlework, as well as to basic literacy. By the eighteenth century in Protestant Europe, the governess was in the ascendant and the French language and rudiments of more authentically academic subjects were more obvious. French and some Italian girls were sent to convent boarding schools where they were kept rigorously segregated from society. The idea was that a young girl could be readily contaminated by the world and must keep her innocence. However, such innocence did not imply ignorance of her future. She was intended as the mistress of a noble house and the perpetuator of a dynasty. She had to keep her eyes on the prize.

The weighty business transactions needing years of advance planning which preceded the establishment of an aristocratic marriage were obviously not replicated lower down the social scale. Even so, a great deal of thought had to be given to the settlement of children. For sons the key to success was increasingly education, so that they could aspire to openings in church, state and growing overseas empires which would provide for them independently of family funds. This was in marked contrast to the experience of daughters, for whom parental funds were necessary both to establish a good match and to provide some income to see them through life. Where such assets were lacking, spinsterhood was a distinct possibility. Endogamy was remarkably frequent within middle-class professional groups: clergymen married clergymen's daughters, lawyers' sons married lawyers' daughters and so on. Business relationships were cemented and money changed hands – albeit somewhat less of it – to establish a fitting match. Middle-class parents kept a close watch on their daughters. Most were educated at home by their mothers and the contacts they formed were liable to come under maternal scrutiny. The proof of their vigilance is the almost total absence of women from this social group from lists of unmarried mothers or those who became pregnant before marriage took place.

Most Europeans in this period were farmers and the bulk of these smallholders, farm labourers or cottars. The proportion of the population that was town-based was growing, perhaps reaching 10 to 15 per cent of the whole by 1800, but the dominant employment sector was agriculture. There were some industrial towns and villages and more and more industrial outwork had crept into many villages, but most girls were born of farming stock and aspired to become farmers' wives. This aspiration dominated their life-view and demanded serious forward planning. The farmer's wife would be expected when the moment for marriage came to be able to bring assets in money, cattle or kind to help towards the renting and stocking of a farm. The future husband would be expected to have some assets which would put a roof above their heads and pay whatever was required for a lease or to have some expectations from his parents. The two funds were rarely equal and his might be twice as large as hers. She would also be expected to possess certain skills which would contribute to a joint family economy – keeping and tending livestock and poultry, dairy work like milking and cheesemaking, preserving and pickling, as well as spinning or whatever ancillary cottage industry was available within the region. There was some national and regional variation on who brought what into a marriage and the degree of independence of the couple, but some assets in money, kind or competence were expected.

At the very bottom of the social scale a wife's input could mean no more than a bed, a cow or household utensils. In Roman law the principle *nullum sine dote fiat conjugium iuxta possibilitatem* (let no marriage be formed without a dowry as is possible) meant that if the bride's family did not pay to the groom what they had promised (usually when the pair were betrothed), the marriage could not take place and any previous understandings were nullified. This was not a principle of Tridentine thinking, which sought to establish the public religious ceremony as the only valid way of getting married and hence regarded the monetary aspects of the step as less relevant. Even so, in areas of Roman law financial considerations were usually honoured before the religious ceremony; and so entrenched was the notion of no marriage without a dowry in Europe south of the Loire that many of those without such means did not bother to marry but might form a free union. Furthermore, there are examples of brides in both Spain and southern France being shown the door or treated as village paupers when their fathers failed to honour dowry agreements. The Council of Trent, which sought to reform public morality, tried to oblige the parochial clergy to report adulterous relationships to the bishop and empowered him after a warning to expel the woman, but this kind of prohibition was ignored in Spain and neither the diocesan courts nor usually the Inquisition sought to enforce the recommendations. In Italy the reformers were only marginally more successful and those imbued with the Tridentine spirit placed considerable emphasis on raising charitable funds to procure dowries for poor girls so that they would be able to marry.[12]

North of the Loire and throughout north-western Europe the principle *dote qui veut* held sway. Many couples did not make a formal settlement at marriage because they had very little. However, not having funds to bring to marriage did not mean that a dowry or some monetary equivalent was not seen as desirable. Those with no resources at all were at the very bottom of a social pile. Some perforce sought to marry with nothing or very little, but unless they had a working skill much in demand, such couples were at risk of being a social charge and in Britain the community could seek to oppose such marriages or settlement in the parish. In Germany, too, such couples were regarded with apprehension.[13]

The dowry, in money or kind, might come from a number of sources. Ideally, and if a young couple at the outset of marriage were to be people with a comfortable stock of assets behind them, the parents would contribute to a settlement. Others, perhaps the majority, were very dependent on their own initiatives. Thirdly, here and there and with little consistency as to size and frequency, charities existed for the dowering of poor girls. This was an approved direction for private charitable initiatives and for municipal resources in both Catholic and Protestant societies. However, they were at their most considerable in Catholic Europe and perhaps in Italy in particular. During the sixteenth century, in Florence and other major Tuscan cities, there was a shift away from donations and bequests to nunneries to the establishment of dowry funds. This new priority perhaps reflected a belief that nunneries were already well endowed and that the dowry fund represented a more pressing social need for a broader social spectrum.[14] Such funds were intended as charitable initiatives, but *Monte delle dote* also functioned as dowry banks in which families could invest so as to guarantee an annuity to a daughter. One great advantage of this practice was that the capital could not be touched by the husband. Erasmus's considerable wealth, left to the city of Basle, was divided into a *Stiftung* for the support of scholarship and a huge endowment to provide dowries for unmarried girls. Rome, the city par excellence of the dowry fund, by the eighteenth century endowed 2000 girls a year. In Protestant countries the charities dealt with very limited numbers.

A fourth source of income for a bride, not strictly a dowry but funds to launch a marriage, came from relatives and the community rallying to help a young couple deemed worthy of help through the traditional giving associated with the wedding feast. This could be an important source for British brides.[15]

The dowry or assets that a young woman could command, coupled with the resources of her partner at the time of marriage, were of critical importance in an agricultural society. Some husbands might ultimately inherit some land or assets, but many would look to rent and had limited hopes of improving their position as the years passed. On setting up, livestock and seed were purchased and the linen and cloth which would probably have to see the family through much of its lifetime were carefully stored. The replacement of cattle and textile commodities as the years went by would be desirable. A cow or a pig would be intended to reproduce itself and these were carefully prized. If the family in difficult agricultural years, or through personal misfortune, lost or parted with these assets, then the tenuous boundary separating sufficiency from hardship or destitution had been crossed and, at such a time, poor relief was not to be assumed. Indeed, where voluntary charity rather than institutionalized relief was the norm, as in Catholic Europe, it could be nonexistent.

The importance of having something behind one at marriage was therefore generally acknowledged to be considerable. It was for this reason that young men were urged to disregard the beautiful for those with means. Every young girl was made aware that such were the rules of the game and that physical attraction, while not to be discounted, was of secondary importance. To love, care for, feel affection towards your partner, were obviously important considerations, but so was having something to your name. The acquisition of means was therefore a goal towards which the young must work. For girls, this vision of the future, or life plan, was made apparent to them from childhood. It was an intrinsic part of social conditioning. They had to know the rules of the life game.

A young girl was endowed with a very clear idea of what her survival strategy must be. If her main dowry source was to be her father and she lived at home, then she worked and acquired skills which contributed to her long-term worth within her own home. If it was not, then she had to plan for a period of work outside her home but with a distinct target in mind – the accumulation of a dowry, a 'nest-egg', a *pécule* (little hoard). Parents had to make their daughters cognizant of the sovereign imperative of assets throughout their educative process, not merely schooling but the skills which were taught at home.

In some instances, future planning began in infancy. The job of the mother was perceived to be to give her daughter as many survival skills as possible and ideally to start her on the path of capital accumulation. This could be done in many ways. The choice of godparents was important because they could provide contacts. Indeed, in Brittany it was not unusual for the seigneur's wife to act as godparent to every girl-child in the village, which drew her into the business of helping in the search for work by providing references. Even at humble levels, all over Europe, godparents frequently endowed a child with a couple of hens or a 'peppermint' pig, the runt of a litter which could be fattened by the mother and the beast sold. "Tis many a girl made her fortune from the egg money' ran an Irish proverb, referring to these small economies which might at the end of the day build up an asset. Two lambs could constitute the laying down of a flock if grazing land was available. At a lesser level, wool picked up from hedgerows could be used to spin thread or serve as stuffing for quilts. A girl's sewing efforts were meant to be part of her hope chest or bottom drawer.

Picturesque and doubtless executed in hope, these small endeavours would not necessarily make very much and unless her family could augment them or there was enough work at home in which to engage her profitably, then the girl must look to, or have found for her, outside paid employment. This was a step apparently taken much more reluctantly in Italy and perhaps also in Spain and Portugal, where codes of honour dictated that a woman could only exist in an honourable state within her own home. To leave it, and poverty dictated that many should take such a step (certainly large numbers of eleven-year-old Spanish girls left home to live as largely unpaid servants in the houses of relatives or city contacts), meant crossing a dividing line between the respectable and the state of dubious reputation. Elsewhere, and this was true throughout France as well as in Britain, Scandinavia, Holland and Germany, honour was on the side of work. If a girl needed to labour to build up skills and assets outside the home, that fact alone did not constitute a disreputable state. In most instances it was quite the reverse and viewed as normal.

Many parents in north-western Europe saw their daughters leave home at twelve to fourteen and begin to labour on their own account to lay the foundations of their own future. If a girl was the eldest child and her mother was dead, or sick, or ailing, then her father might keep her at home as a mother substitute for the rest, but to do so was to place her future at risk unless he could endow her. For many families the departure of a daughter may have meant real hardship in personal and practical terms, for a twelve-year-old girl in this society was no longer deemed a child and her assistance on a smallholding or in indus-trial outwork could be important. Notwithstanding, her best future hopes depended upon leaving. Her brothers would not necessarily face the same fate. If the holding was sufficient to keep them in work and needed a pair of hands, they might stay at home. They would then expect in due course, if their father was the owner, to take over the land or receive some settlement. If they too had to leave home to work on another farm, or entered an apprenticeship in town, they did so two years later than their sisters. The reasons for this age disparity may relate to the need for boys in agricultural work to have developed the physical strength needful for heavier tasks before leaving home, or the desire by their families to retain a pair of male hands as long as possible. Whatever the reason, the girls went first and more of them went than did boys.

At this point we need to note the difference in the aims of male and female. The female saw her work as a source of capital accumulation which would terminate on marriage. She might at the end of this initial spell take pride in the skills she had developed and which she might, indeed, subsequently put to use, but the sovereign imperative was money and goods. The man or boy who went to work on another farm also hoped for monetary gain which would one day help him to run his own farm. If he worked on the family holding, however, he had nothing but his keep from his parents. An apprenticeship in town would provide him with a life skill, but the apprenticeship would yield him no money and his mastership would have to be purchased. Whatever he did, however, his search was for work which would enable him to earn a living throughout his life. His identity as farmer or as worker could be firmly fixed. The death of a brother or relative might cause the apprentice weaver who had left his village for the town to rethink his plan and return to the fields, but whatever he did, he thought in the long term.

The choice of work for a twelve-year-old was very limited. No one expected that a young girl should sally off into the totally unknown without an address in her head and people who knew that she was coming. Her limited skills, her age and prevalent ideas on women and their labour all contributed to the narrowness of the options before her. She could not earn enough to support herself in independence and so someone must both put a roof above her head and serve as father substitute.

Answering the needs of the young country girl was domestic service, comprehended in a very broad sense to include the farm servant, the

range of servants to be found in more substantial houses and in tradesmen's shops, and the maid of all work in very modest establishments.
The range of work had a common element, residence and the form of
payment, which was made as a lump sum when the girl left her
employer. The fact that such a range existed should not suggest that
any one girl could choose at the outset the category to insert herself
into. Everything depended on what was available, on what her mother,
sisters, cousins, aunts, godparents, family and community contacts
could provide. Something, too, depended upon her background. Family
and kin and the local community could all be actively involved in the
search to find work for her. The reputation of her family was critical.
What might she have learned at home or at school? How strong was
she and how did she look? Was she clean and neat? What was the
character of her mother? All these considerations would be particularly
important if a substantial residence was to receive her.[16]

Perhaps most country girls hoped in the first instance that a local
farm would receive them, and certainly local job resources were exhausted before looking further afield. A local job meant proximity to home
for rare days off. The local farm servant might marry someone in the
neighbourhood and would certainly gain the kind of experience that
would benefit a farmer's wife in the years to come. Here she might
learn, in addition to cleaning and scouring pots and pans, skills such
as pickling, malting, salting, preserving by smoking, drying, storing
in grease or brine, working in the byres milking cows and goats and in
the hen yard, hoeing vegetables, laying potatoes, weeding, haymaking –
all depending on the nature of the regional economy. In Tuscany even
by the late eighteenth century, the more considerable the farming establishment in which she worked, the more prestige the girl enjoyed. The
Ospedale degli Innocenti, whose patrons included the local aristocracy,
tried to place their girls on *mezzadria*, middling-sized farms where the
farmer's wife could teach the girls a range of skills. The more learned,
the better one's prospect as a wife. In poorer areas, particularly where
there was a shortage of water, a servant girl could spend much of the
agricultural year carrying buckets to upland terraces or to cattle. This
kind of work was identified as women's work, but it did not endow her
with skills. It pushed her to the bottom of the working status pile.

At the outset of her working life, a girl could command very little
in the way of remuneration, but she would hope to progress in skills
and as she did so could command higher wages, if necessary by moving.

A distinct servant hierarchy was recognized, for example, by an assessment of wages made by justices in Rutland in 1563:

> A chief woman servant being a cook and can bake, brew, make white bread and malt and able to oversee other servants may have as her wages by the year 20 shillings and for her livery 6s 8d . . . [one who cannot] dress meat, bake, brew and make malt of the better sort may have for her wages by the year 18s and for her livery 5s . . . a simple woman servant which cannot but do outworks and drudgery may have for her wages by the year 12s and for her livery 4s.[17]

Rutland was an area of arable farms. Where there were large dairy farms in north-western Europe, the skilled dairymaid was counted among the most valuable of farm servants. A farmer could make good profits from butter and cheese and both needed careful preparation. Furthermore, cleanliness had to prevail in the dairy, otherwise curdling could ruin everything. There was no change in the nature of dairying between 1500 and 1800 and so the descriptions of the dairymaid's work in the farming treatises that peppered the eighteenth century probably serve for the entire period and modify the cosy pastoral image of the dairymaid that appears in Dutch and other pastoral landscapes and idylls:

> She may be known by her red plump arms and hands and clumsy fingers: for in most great farms they are forced to milk their cows abroad, a great part of the year; I may say, almost all the year even in frosts and snows, while their fingers are ready to freeze in the action: and sometimes while they stand in dirt and water . . . and indeed, it may be justly said of these, that their work is never done; for where twenty and thirty cows are kept, they must begin at about four o'clock [PM] in the summer to milk and at the same hour next morning: and between these times they have enough to do, to scald and scour their utensils and make butter and cheese; and thus are constantly employed throughout the year. A good dairymaid is a very valuable servant; I mean one that readily rises betimes; is skilful and diligent in making the best butter and cheese; is cleanly in the performance of it, making the most of her milk and doing all in her power to promote her master's interest.[18]

The lot of the Flemish maid who dealt with stall-fed cattle may have been somewhat easier in winter, since she was spared the long walks into the fields, but the difference was merely one of degree.

Milking and dairying were valuable to the employer, but women's wage levels did not approach those of the male labourer in husbandry. What it did do was to establish a relationship between women and the exploitation of the cow which was very important. For the most marginal of farming families, the cow, where grazing could be obtained, represented the best source of fat and protein for home consumption and ideally for wider sale. In most countries it was perhaps the first thing bought from a bride's assets on marriage. In Ireland dowries were counted in cows.[19] Skill in dairying was therefore the single most valuable talent a farmer's wife could command.

After a few years in her first and perhaps most lowly job, and in order to improve her situation as she progressed in skill, the farm servant in Britain might hear of a better opening in the vicinity, perhaps caused by a girl's leaving to marry, or she might take her career into her own hands and proceed at the relevant time of year to a hiring fair, usually held at Martinmas (11 November). There, farm servants of all kinds brandished the tools of their trade and wore a distinctive garb to attract a would-be employer. Cooks wore brightly coloured aprons and carried a large spoon, milkmaids a stool. After work had been obtained and wages agreed by a bargaining process which many employers decried, a little 'earnest' or 'fastening' money exchanged hands (sometimes also known as 'God's penny'). Then the newly employed of both sexes turned the day into a holiday. The public space of the fair and the market was open to women as much as it was to men.[20]

The fairs were not an absolute guarantee of work. William Marshall in the harsh 1790s reported that many farm servants were tramping around villages in search of work.[21] A girl who found a good place might be advised to hold on to it and it is clear from memoirs and diaries that many servants stayed in one position for years and counted themselves fortunate to be able to do so.

The problem was that outside the great dairying regions of Britain, the Netherlands, Flanders and north and western France, where male and female servants existed in just about equal proportions, the demand for resident female labour appears to have been slight and in some areas may have been decreasing at least in percentage terms of all the available jobs. Population growth which characterized the eighteenth century meant that more women were looking for work. Engrossment of commons and smallholdings to form large arable farms in areas of 'capitalist' farming, and elsewhere the proliferation of smallholdings in poor areas such as the Massif Central or the Alpine and Pyrenean regions, to the point where they could not sustain a family let alone a servant, were factors contributing to the dwindling possibilities of farm work for the young girl. In parts of England there was also a growing preference for cheap, non-resident male labour which did not need servicing by a resident servant. On small farms of, say, under forty acres, the farmer's wife or daughter could cook for the male hands and in areas of great arable farms the employment of women was restricted to a couple of girls or a cook to feed the men. It was, however, precisely these areas where the smallholder's and the day labourer's daughters needed work, for the resources of her family were likely to be slender. This girl, from childhood, had to see her future in different terms.

Theoretically, for this girl, there existed a number of possibilities. First, there might be work in the larger village, town or city as a domestic servant, a complex categorization. Secondly, she could stay at home, if some cottage industry existed which afforded her the prospect of long-term employment. This second alternative was certainly growing in Britain, the Netherlands, France and Germany from the late seventeenth century, when manufacturers were reaching out into the country to locate cheap labour. The impact of such a work possibility on the life plan of the young girl could be considerable. Thirdly, she might live or have contacts in a region where cottage industry was coupled with farm service and where farmers would take on a girl providing they could profit from the industrial work she did. This was not uncommon in Brittany, where flax spinning was done at certain periods of the year, and in Bas Languedoc where in the late seventeenth century the developing woollen industry serving the Levant created a demand for carders and spinners. However, when the flax harvest failed or when slump occurred in the Levant trade, the women would be unceremoniously dismissed because, without the industrial income, the farmer could not afford to keep them on.

Another possibility was to join an urban workshop as resident industrial employee. The emphasis had to be on the residence given. In most European towns where employment in textile production existed, female labour was remunerated at very low levels and without subsidized or shared accommodation would not permit survival, let alone the accumu-

lation of any surplus. In the silk industry in Lyons, for example, the
heavy demand for female labour to unwind cocoons, prepare shuttles
and serve at the looms led manufacturers to seek to fix a cheap and
constant labour supply by drawing upon girls from the hilly regions to
the north and west of the city. This was not a common pattern elsewhere, however. More industries, like the production of lace at Le Puy
or in Bruges and Malines, had workers' dormitories run by religious
women where girls could contract with merchants for piece work. Sometimes the girls themselves could form small clusters in a kind of informal
dormitory situation and women would bring in their younger sisters.
This seems to have been possible in Honiton in Devon, where, during
the eighteenth century, wages in lace-making for a skilled worker were
relatively high and subsidized accommodation to attract workers was
available in the town.[22] Most of these workers had left by their late
twenties.

The existence of different work possibilities did not mean that each
girl had a dazzling array of options before her. Indeed, the reverse was
true. For most there can have been no element of choice at all. Everything depended on family contact and the traditions of the village and
what was available within a radius of twenty to thirty miles. Local jobs
were filled to saturation before young girls at the start of their working
lives moved further afield, and when they did so they moved along
well-established routes, most probably had an address to go to, or had
kinsfolk and neighbours' daughters in the vicinity. Sometimes, in Spain,
the village priest could have a line of contact to a particular city and
would serve as a referee for a servant girl to a family. Young girls were
not pioneers: all must have departed into what was for them the
unknown with considerable apprehension. There is some evidence to
suggest that some followed migratory flows established by male seasonal
migrants. Once such flows had been established, however, they became
self-perpetuating as they were replicated by new generations of girls.
Hence Galician girls came to predominate in the domestic service sector
in Madrid. Girls from the Southern Massif came to Montpellier and the
cities of the Mediterranean littoral, and Paris had clusters of Picard and
Norman girls.[23]

It is possible to find villages where the outflow could be in several
directions, and different patterns for males and females could exist as
they did in the Limousin and the Creuze where men were drawn into
navvying and building work in Catalonia for anything from three to

five years. However, it is not clear whether such young men were at the start of their working lives or more advanced in years seeking to bolster their incomes and maintain their smallholdings, rather like the Sicilian or Turkish *Gastarbeiter* of our times. What is clear is that they were not followed by their sisters. We can say that if more women than men moved from their native villages – simply because agriculture could retain men more easily – they did not move as far. The move to capital cities was, in particular, one only taken by young girls when they knew where they were going. A detailed study on the prostitution registers of early modern Amsterdam demonstrates that girls from contiguous villages who formed the bulk of the Amsterdam servant class and who came to the city through contacts were conspicuously under-represented. Those who came in their twenties by boat from the northern provinces, on the other hand, are highly visible. The girl who was forced to venture into the unknown or even the relatively unknown and who hence broke with traditional paths and was without contacts was the one at risk.

These migrations exist from at least the late Middle Ages in all parts of Europe.[24] In many cities (London, Venice, Madrid) agencies of women acting as go-betweens for servant and employer existed, but many of these were suspected of complicity in the vice trade. Custom and contacts were the guarantors of safety. By the end of the eighteenth century, demographic pressure on areas of smallholders and a regionally specific absence of local work were multiplying the number of risk-takers.

Domestic service was by far the largest category of female employment Europe-wide until after the First World War. Although the proportion of adolescent girls who went into this kind of work is not known, what is clear is that the numbers of women involved were growing. Urban censuses show that country girls in service accounted for about 13 per cent of the total population of any city north of the Loire in the pre-industrial period and the feminization of the service sector was apparent from the mid- to late seventeenth century, although in Mediterranean Europe it was less marked until the nineteenth century. By 1806, one person in eleven in Britain was in service and women outnumbered men by eight to one. The same was largely true elsewhere, as can be discerned from household listings. Sixteenth-century Geneva, seventeenth-century Würzburg, Dijon in 1764, for example, conform to the same pattern. Seventeenth-century Amsterdam had even greater proportions of these young women immigrants.

The population of the pre-industrial city was predominantly female and weighted in favour of young women in the age group 13–26. A proportion of these would, at the end of a period of service, return to their villages with their accumulated earnings, a fact which has to be inferred from the sudden shrinkage of the numbers of women in their late twenties in the towns. It is impossible to be precise about how many used the city merely for the initial earning phase of their lives and hoped then to return home. Observers believed that smallholding societies produced the greatest number of young people who returned home because the possibility of setting up house on modest means lured them back to their native villages. Areas of large farms, on the other hand, were likely to drive away the labourers' daughters in perpetuity and convert them into townswomen. Probably a great deal depended upon who they met in the town and what contacts were retained with their place of origin. With certainty, one can say that the twelve- or fourteen-year-old girl had before her a service stint of a further twelve to fourteen years, her lifespan over again. This was the time it took to save up for her dowry or to realize that she could not amass much more. During inflationary periods, when rents rose and prices were high, the young might have to prolong this period of earning and postpone marriage.

The demand for domestic servants was considerable and the range of work was almost infinite. 'There is scarce any general name of a calling that contains under it such different kinds of persons, as this of a servant' (Richard Mayo, *A Present for Servants*, 1693). The first luxury that any family permitted itself was the services of a girl, a maid of all work, to take on the drudgery involved in carrying water – a major time and energy consumer – and coal or wood, going to market, or performing laundry services. As sections of the European population increased in wealth through trade and industry and the production of surplus food-stuffs, so the demand for servants grew, while the increasing population, and consequent regional impoverishment, provided an abundant supply.

The world of service embraced a whole series of gradations and, in many instances, degradations. Aristocratic households at the highest level like those of the Dukes of Marlborough or the Earls of Lonsdale or the Dukes of Orleans, counted their servants in hundreds. Most noble households, however, employed between six and thirty servants; the gentry and higher mercantile sectors of the population between six and twelve; a modest professional household could have three or four. Parson Woodforde in the last quarter of the eighteenth century on a stipend of £300 a year kept five: a farming man, a footman, a yard boy, an upper maid who did the cooking and an under maid who took care of the dairy. This clergyman's household was sustained in part by someone running a farm and the dairy produce was sold. The line between town and country was far from rigid and many town houses had enough land attached to keep poultry and livestock for the family table. A moderately substantial artisan like Henry Coward, ironmonger and grocer, who had an apprentice and employed a journeyman, kept two maidservants in 1684, 'one to wait on her mistress who minded little but her own ease' and the other who did the kitchen work.[25] Generally, where men were employed by the household, the mistress of the house had at least one girl to help her. However, the commonest pattern in cities – even Amsterdam in the seventeenth century which has left a strong visual legacy of the servant world – was the one- or two-servant household.

The feminization of domestic service north of the Loire reflected labour costs and the nature of the work. The cheapest servant anyone could employ was a woman, therefore the work had attached to it levels of pay deemed appropriate to women. The process of feminization in Britain may have been accelerated by a tax on male servants imposed in 1777.[26] However, the phenomenon was general and there does not appear to have been any competition from men in the low-paid branches of the service sector.

The hierarchy of servants in an aristocratic household shows that it was possible for service to have a career structure. This structure became increasingly complex as society 'increased in civility', its demands became more sophisticated, and both the aristocracy and middle classes increased in affluence. Service was the growth sector par excellence. In the stately home, batteries of cooks and footmen, butlers, valets, coachmen, equerries, ladies' maids, nursery maids, upstairs maids, laundry maids, scullery maids, pantry maids each had a role to play in the running of the great house. The enterprise had to be run with precision and order and morality clearly respected. For this reason, English stately homes by the eighteenth century employed a housekeeper to oversee the work and conduct of the women and to keep an eye on harmonious but not too close relationships. Cooks who skimped on the servants' food to line their own pockets could then be reported. In such houses the wage levels of the various grades of servants varied considerably. In Britain in 1800, ladies' maids, companions and housekeepers earned between ten and twenty pounds per annum; female cooks between seven and fifteen pounds; housemaids between four and ten pounds and kitchen scrubs as little as two. The maid of all work in the house of a marginally modest family, or the tradesman's domestic skivvy, could earn three or four pounds a year: the girl or scrub who cleaned the floors of public buildings or worked in a tavern as barmaid or waitress was likely to make two.[27]

The world of service was therefore complex and the point of entry probably the single most critical factor. There was no automatic process of promotion from one gradation to the next and probably the best that most girls could hope for was that they went to a post in a one-servant household vacated by a relative or family contact, in a household that was kindly, respectable and unlikely to default on their wages when the time for collection came. Wages were paid when a servant left a situation and although this could help a girl to save it could also expose her to the unreliability of her employer. In many posts, physical stamina was a priority since carrying coal, wood and water and tending fires and ovens was heavy work. Lighting and tending fires, and bringing in water for cooking and cleaning, were probably the commonest household tasks ceded by the housewife when a family took on a maid. Cooking was also extremely labour-intensive in the days when meat was roasted or broiled over an open fire using gridirons or spits operated by pulleys.

In large households, scullery or kitchen maids were at the bottom of the servant hierarchy and worked full-time at a complex routine of tending fires and turning spits and cleaning up the messes generated as well as washing dishes. From the seventeenth century, porcelain tableware, rather than the wooden or pewter platters or trenchers which were cleaned with a piece of bread, appeared in ever larger numbers of households, and had to be washed by the kitchen maid. She was first to rise in the morning, because nothing could be done before the fire was lit and the kettles boiled.

Laundry services were also complex and became increasingly so over the period. In the seventeenth century baths were infrequently taken. Public bath houses were closed when plague was a threat and the women who had worked in them, who were rated as prostitutes, sought work elsewhere. There was something of a cult of bodily filth. It was believed that the body produced fluids that were needful to good health and which should not be washed away but merely sponged to remove odour.[28] James I never washed more than his fingers and graphic descriptions exist of the stench of the French king Henri IV. However, clean linen was seen as eminently necessary for the respectable and affluent. This was worn under top garments which were heavy, constructed to last and not intended to be washed. The starched ruffle and the lace collar and cuffs, however, were the gleaming embellishment that marked out the rich. They were faithfully captured to the last lace stitch by portraitists.[29] Behind the production of these ruffs was a maid who knew the secrets of Dutch starching and how to use a 'poking' stick to crimp a ruffle. Over the eighteenth century, garments became lighter and the introduction of cottons increased laundry work, as did the increasing complexity of ladies' underwear when drawers and silk and boned corsetry replaced leather stays and flannel petticoats which were hardly ever washed.[30]

Many urban households employed the service of a laundry woman who came once a month to do the 'buck', the washing of sheets and heavier articles. Or there were laundry establishments where laundry maids were employed. In other households laundry was the work of the maid. Houses with their own well or with a pump for running water, common in Britain and the Netherlands, were more likely to do the wash at home. In France, laundry for all but the most aristocratic households was taken to the washplace and in some villages this meant the river where stones were used to pound the material. It was carried heavy and dripping from the river, to be dried on lines or spread over hedgerows. Like the milkmaid, the laundry maid was celebrated for her muscle power.

The business of ironing and folding the laundry was no less onerous. Ironing needed a heavy, dry, flat iron heated near the fire but kept out of contact with the coals lest it should blacken the linen. Several irons were used at a time and were replaced as they cooled: 'dashing about with the smoothing iron' referred to the rapidity with which a maid had to move between the fire and her work. Linen was a valuable and highly prized asset which marked out the family of standing. In many instances, it came as part of a dowry at the outset of marriage and lasted throughout life and even throughout generations. Iron mould (or rust) on linen immediately devalued it so that great care had to be taken. Lace also needed special tending, for it was both valuable and delicate. After washing (always on its own) it was frequently stiffened by being dipped in milk and left to dry out. The servants who did this kind of work were dealing with valued commodities.

The onerous work of cleaning, cooking and washing was performed by the general run of domestics, but in the most affluent houses there were also servants to attend the persons in the nursery and the boudoir and others more publicly attending in the dining room, at the front door and in the street. In such houses the specialist servant dealt with tradesmen, shopped in the market and ran errands. The degree of specialization helped in the formulation of a professional identity. A good and competent servant knew exactly the worth of her services.

If a girl entered her first job by recommendation, she gained a better one by references stating experience and competence, or in a large household was promoted on the strength of her record. Large houses in the cities tended to recruit girls from their rural estates. When a girl was 'recommended' by a relative she would be brought to see the mistress of the house or the housekeeper, usually by the recommending party or bringing a letter of recommendation with her. She would then be judged on her speech and appearance, samples of her needlework skills and what the relative could insist had been her moral and religious upbringing. In Britain and the Netherlands by the eighteenth century, basic literacy was also required for work in the better establishments for levels above that of kitchen maid. This cannot have been the case in France and Mediterranean countries where literacy levels were lower.

In the sixteenth and seventeenth centuries the mistress of a solid house might see to it personally that her maidservants acquired basic reading skills and developed their needlework, but a century later the demand for the better jobs was so intense, and popular levels of literacy so much greater, that this aspect of the mistress's role diminished. In any case, the high aristocracy had never thus involved themselves. A good housekeeper assumed responsibilities previously left to the mistress, kept an eye on the development of the servant within the system and could encourage a young girl to develop herself 'for her preferment'. She was the future referee for the girl[31]. She also seems to have been a figure specific to north-western Europe; in Mediterranean societies a male steward was still employed.

Many of the educational initiatives which took place throughout north-western Europe under the impetus of the Reformation and the Catholic Counter-Reformation were designed to turn young girls into good servants. The English charity school, for example, which emerged at the end of the seventeenth century and burgeoned in the eighteenth, had the upper end of service in mind for its pupils. This was seen as advantageous both to pupils and to those who founded the schools, merchants' wives and members of society who were the employing classes. The philosophy behind the construction of the ideal maidservant was that her employers and ultimately her husband wanted the same thing: sober, industrious, thrifty, obedient, competent women who appeared clean and neat and made the right impression. The girl who could present herself as the product of such an establishment, with needlework skills attested to in sampler or specimen darn, with her hair neatly tucked under her cap, her apron cleanly starched and the appropriate 'yes ma'am' at her command was on the way to success. Moreover, she had the right references. Compare her situation with that of the Irish immigrant to London who knocked at the door of a would-be employer, covered in lice, having been weeks on the road with no more salubrious record behind her than that of a cabin where pigs scavenged on the open floor and chickens' droppings fell from the rafters. Mrs Patrick Savage of County Down, who had greater aspirations than income and purchased her service as cheaply as possible, bemoaned having to have recourse to girls who did not know what a smoothing iron was and who came down the stairs backwards, breaking china as they went, because their only experience was of the ladder to the rafters. She had problems with theft, and several women who helped themselves to any alcohol that was left on the sideboard.[32]

It was probably advantageous everywhere for the servant to get out of the single-servant household if she could do so, for the maid of all work was really a drudge. The chances of doing so, however, were not high and were limited not merely by competence, but by the competition for the better posts which increased conspicuously in the late seventeenth and eighteenth centuries. In England and Holland advertisements in newspapers for better servants, that is, specialist servants such as cooks and chambermaids, were not only restricted to those who could read them but were also initially dependent upon application in handwriting accompanied by references. Even so, competition was intense. The Revd Mr Trusler in 1786 alleged that one advertisement would bring applications from 'scores' of applicants. Thirty years earlier, the magistrate Sir John Fielding said of London that 'there is always . . . an amazing number of women servants out of place'. He then proceeded to identify them as 'those of a higher nature, such as chambermaids whose numbers far exceed the places they stand candidates for . . .' Jonas Hanway, another reliable commentator, thought that a single advertisement for the post of female cook would bring a hundred applicants. Yet at the other end of the servant spectrum, Fielding noted the lack of 'the useful housewifery servant commonly called maids of all work' who were insufficient in quantity to meet the needs of the capital.[33] Other observers and tract writers bemoaned the quality of the material offering itself for service at the bottom. Such girls were not 'nicely got' but were the issue of parents lacking the means to provide them with the education necessary to read 'virtuous books' or which would teach them how to behave in 'a proper and decent manner'. Many would steal food or abuse the family property. From the servant's point of view, there were many hard jobs and ungrateful, carping mistresses. In some houses there was a rapid turnover of staff, perhaps accelerated when servants saw their job had no prospects.[34]

Commentators throughout the entire period were rarely objective and constantly harked back to a past of which they in all probability had no real experience. Eighteenth-century critics in fact pointed less to a dearth of womanpower than to what they considered to be a shortage of the right kind of servants to serve the modest household. From the point of view of the servants themselves, the problem was the lack of higher servant places.

There were many reasons for the competition for superior positions, of which the most pressing was the higher wage followed perhaps by the improved conditions of service at the top. At the bottom the job was backbreaking. The calculations of Richardson's Pamela on how she as a pretty, chaste and nicely mannered girl could negotiate herself through levels of servanthood, picking up her mistress's cast-off clothing and securing perks such as 'reading time', all the time wisely hoarding her wages and looking to have reliable employers, embody a few literary embellishments, but they certainly reflect the ideals of the higher end of service. Every servant girl knew that if she could rise in the servant hierarchy she could not only put away more but could come by valuable experience which would serve her throughout her life. The laundry maid could set up a laundry or serve as a freelance washerwoman. The talents of the cook were never lost.

Observers and those who wrote learned tracts upon the girl in service would expatiate on the uselessness of the lady's maid whose training left her totally unequipped for a useful role after marriage. In such works, men were urged to beware women whose talents were a knowledge of luxury and affectations and who aped their betters by wearing their mistress's cast-off finery. Such women were suspected of every artifice and dissimulation. Fashion put a premium on the French lady's maid, who was held to be particularly adept at turning a great lady's appearance to best advantage. The French maid is found in many of the more fashionable houses in European cities, though she was emphatically a luxury only the upper crust could afford and how many of them were truly French is never easy to say. Needless to state, the position of lady's maid was much sought after. She had reached the acme of her profession. She in no way identified herself with the wench who cleaned the kitchen floor.

Servant mobility was directly related to the demands of affluent society. Furthermore, progression to upper levels was denied to those who began at the bottom when women of higher social class took the better jobs. This process became increasingly manifest from the late seventeenth century. The lack of professional outlets for middle-class women who had some education but whose families could not provide dowries for them – the case with many clergymen's daughters – meant that the upper class of the servant hierarchy, that of housekeeper, companion and to some degree lady's maid, became one of the few sources of employment for these women. Housekeepers in Britain were invariably drawn from widows and older women of middle-class origin. In Catholic Europe, too, the reforms of Trent caused bishops to demand that the housekeepers of clergymen should be older and respectable women so as to preserve the reputation for chastity of the parish priest. The French capitular clergy frequently looked to a genteel but impoverished widowed relative to manage their houses in just the same way as did the canons of British cathedral closes.

Changing fashion, and in particular the demands for skilled hairdressers and the French-speaking ladies' maids, to a degree also curtailed the aspirations of those who did not possess these talents. There were 'schools' in cities that taught hairdressing. As the natural styles and simple ringlets of the seventeenth century were replaced by the more elaborate coiffures of the eighteenth, and the use of wigs and hairpieces and powdering also demanded new expertise, hairdressing became a prized skill. Modest businessmen purchased such courses for their daughters confident that a post as lady's maid would be the return on their investment.[35]

A study of domestic service in Madrid beginning in the eighteenth century provides some interesting comparisons and contrasts with the British, Dutch, German and French situation. Most jobs were found

by personal contact but from the mid-eighteenth century a daily publication called *Diario Noticioso, Curioso-Erudito y Comercial público, y Econ-
ómico* carried daily advertisements placed by aspirant servants and
wet-nurses. At the beginning only about 20 per cent of the servants
were women and this publication would suggest that the feminization
of service did not occur until the second half of the nineteenth century.
However, most did not use this means and at the bottom end of service
the very young girl lived for her keep alone in working-class families.
They used her for water porterage and as general skivvy. What is
apparent is that forms of payment varied very considerably. All servants
were fed and most expected to be able to profit from the sale of a little
food. Many received cast-off clothing which was also sold for profit. In
difficult times (1766–77) many servants who advertised their availability declared a willingness to work for their keep alone, but they
expected some wages in better times when food was less costly. Within
many households, even quite modest ones, the maidservant would
expect perks like the dripping from meat to sell to street vendors for
candles. In short, there were a few pickings to make a little money. At
more exalted levels *peynar* (to dress hair) always carried its price.[36]

   Taken overall, the world of solid service was not regarded as
demeaning or as one in which employer and servant lived in antagonism.
It was filled by women who had a clear aim in view and pride as they
advanced towards attaining their goal. It was service in tavern or petty
tradesman's shop which was despised. Here the maidservant could find
herself sleeping in a cupboard or in a corner of the kitchen. She was at
risk from the advances of apprentice, journeyman or master – probably
in that order – and was vulnerable to dismissal or loss of wages if
her employer's financial situation deteriorated. Whatever her efforts or
personal probity, she was exposed to multiple hazards beyond her control. Success was to be measured in continuity of employment, which
meant a modest sum after twelve to fourteen years' labour. When her
energy began to decline, employers lost interest. One thing alone is
clear, that most rural girls had no alternatives to domestic work and
where other options did exist, they offered even less security.

Among these alternatives, in certain highly specialized regions, was
industrial work. A great deal of diversity is encapsulated in what has
been called 'proto-industrialization', that is, the manufacture of goods
during the intermediary period between production in the artisan's

workshop and the establishment of the factory system. The first Age of Manufactures, generated by a growing consumer society, turned for a workforce to the cheap labour of women and children in the countryside. Work, whether the complete process or a part of the manufacturing procedure, was 'put out' to the cottage. Or as an alternative model in some regions, as at Lyons where silk was produced or at Honiton where lace was made, cheap labour was drawn into the town for, it would appear, a very specific period of a woman's life, that before marriage. Work 'put out' kept a girl living at home. She was spared the severance from her family occasioned by domestic service and this was a very positive attraction. Her earnings, however, might be retained by her family rather than used to accumulate a capital sum. This did not matter if she hoped to marry a local man who was himself part smallholder, part industrial worker, because the capital sum needed to set up house was much less and the couple would depend on the work of their hands in industry. They occupied a distinctive slot in the transition from an agrarian to an industrial economy and in the decline of a dependence on having some monetary assets at the outset of marriage. If, however, the industry was town-based, and drew in cheap rural labour on a residential basis, then this was much nearer to the traditional life plan of the country girl. She needed a roof above her head so that she could save her wages.

Most regions of Europe had some local industrial initiatives, although they could be very slight, and most of these only offered work at certain times of the year to married women and children. There were, however, a number of textile industries with markets which transcended the purely local and in some cases were international. These were centred in towns but drew, particularly during phases of buoyant growth, on rural labour some of which, to ensure a manufacturer continuity of production, would be housed and fed by the employer. Examples of this kind of industry are the silk manufacture at Lyons, Nîmes and Tours and the cities of northern Italy, such as Bologna; the production of lace in France and the Low Countries and Britain; the stocking industry of the English Midlands; and some production of woollen cloth in Britain, France and Spain. Such industries could pull in young girls and offer them the potential of saving for marriage away from home.

Silk, manufactured to a high quality, is a costly cloth. In the sixteenth and seventeenth centuries, Italy probably produced the most extensive range of furnishing and clothing products, but by the eighteenth century

Lyons was Europe's silk capital. The work was done in small workshops under the direct supervision of the manufacturer. Female labour was required to empty cocoons and reel the thread, to assist at the loom as draw-girl (the one who raised selected warp threads so as to permit the insertion of multicoloured threads to create a repeating pattern or isolated motifs). Upon the deftness of the draw-girl depended the speed and accuracy with which a pattern could be achieved. She was continually on her feet and the job was for an energetic young person. Women were also 'pattern readers', bawling out the intervals for the distribution of particular threads. The work of men was largely to set up the warp, throw the shuttle and ensure the evenness of the material. Every workshop therefore included a minimum of three or four women and a male apprentice in addition to the master. In larger establishments the ratio of women to men was something of the order of five or six to one.

The women involved were drawn not from the city of Lyons, unless they were the master's daughters, but from the mountainous villages of the Forez, Besse and Bugey and parts of the Dauphiné. They were known as silk-maker's servants because they lived in (often sleeping under the looms) and like domestic servants they were paid on an annual basis or when they left the employment of the master. Like servants they started in their early teens and expected to work for about fifteen years before having saved enough to embark on matrimony.

The conditions of work were among the worst anywhere. Cocoons were unwound by plunging them into bowls of very hot water to melt the sericin which bound the cocoon together and then the reeler amalgamated the filament with that from another or several cocoons and gave the thread a slight twist as it was put on a reel. The atmosphere was therefore constantly damp and the working area restricted since the loom took up most of the space. Tuberculosis was rife in the workshops and mortality rates high. Death was perhaps the commonest cause of worker replacement. The silk industry simply ate up human labour and one position could be filled in two or three years by three or four girls, often related, who simply stepped in when the predecessor died. Whatever the conditions of labour, and whatever the vicissitudes of an industry which was dependent upon the dictates of fashion and hence prone to slumps in which the female labour force could find itself out of work and on the streets, it continued to pull in the daughters of smallholders. Some survived deprivation and the burning up of their physical strength to emerge with dowries healthy enough to purchase his mastership for the apprentice they chose as husband – which could include their own master's son.[37]

The woollen industry based on the Languedoc towns of Lodève and Clermont was organized in much the same way. Needing about four or five times as many spinners and carders as weavers, it looked to a pool of female labour from the barren hills of the Massif Central. Many of the women who came had brothers who worked on the grape harvest at the appropriate season and hence maintained some contact with their native villages to which some, after fourteen years of labour, might return. The money they brought with them would constitute a significant inflow of urban capital into the countryside.[38]

The lace industry, too, though it generally required some philanthropic assistance, could be so organized that a frail sum to constitute a dowry for the working girl might be raised after twelve to fourteen years of labour. At Le Puy in the Massif Central, and in the cities of the southern Netherlands, convents or local associations of philanthropic women ran lace-makers' dormitories where shelter and the costs of lighting and some heating were provided free to the girls, though they had to pay for their food. The profits of their labour which came from selling their work to lace merchants, could then largely be hoarded. Although this was an industry which paid its workers some of the lowest recorded wages, in spite of the skill involved, it could be made to produce the much desired dowry.[39]

For a girl to get a dowry for herself, it must be emphasized, she needed to leave home and the step was one which must have entailed conspicuous emotional hardship for both the young girl and her family even if we suppose her employers kindly (which emphatically all were not). Many girls, though perhaps not a majority, if forced to travel far might not see one or both of their parents again. There could, however, in certain specialized regions, be industrial developments affording opportunities to the young of both sexes which permitted them to forgo the need for a capital sum, to stay at home and to labour with their families. Endowed with a skill, and confident that the work they did would furnish them with enough to live on through life, young couples could marry in their villages and perhaps live in extended family groups. The dowry gave way to a trousseau of a bed, sheets and utensils.

The industry in which the couple were involved had to be in a phase of buoyant expansion with apparently good long-term prospects. The characteristic pattern of proto-industrial development based on the cottage workshop and the family which looked in part to agriculture and in part to industrial labour was notoriously volatile. Industries were born and died and there was no certainty that one industry would be replaced by another. However, in its expansive phase a manufacture could offer relative prosperity and the ability for young people to remain in their place of birth. Textile production was particularly demanding of female labour and indeed could require the services of anything from four to eleven women to keep a weaver working non-stop. Where such work existed women jumped at the opportunity, preferring textile work in their own homes, however monotonous, to carrying water or hoeing in inclement weather. The demand for male agricultural labour was not diminished. Indeed, farmers had then to compete with the industrial employers and this could push up male agricultural wages as well. Young people could marry earlier, since they did not need to save up to hire and stock a farm. Such was the pattern at Terling in Essex and Shepshed in Nottinghamshire, where there existed an extensive stocking industry in the seventeenth century, or at Auffray, Elbeuf and Darnetal in Normandy in the eighteenth to cite but a few of innumerable examples.[40] But what happened when such industry took a downward turn? Quite simply, one or two generations of young people could be caught in a poverty trap. After fifty to a hundred years of relative prosperity, the traditions of looking for work outside the parish had been lost and they hung on hoping for an end to the slump. They became dependent upon the charity of the large landowners. For this reason, a considerable landowner like the Duke of Rutland resisted the extension of the stocking industry on his estates, preferring that the young should leave the parish and marry later than those of neighbouring villages where the young stayed and contracted earlier marriages on the strength of the income from their work. Although they were denied the prosperity of the good times, when slump came His Grace had fewer paupers on his hands. He could and did also boast that he had done his tenants a good turn.

In spite of the duke and others of his kind the numbers of women who looked to industry for a livelihood was growing and many of these had made a permanent severance with older, migratory traditions of their villages. These industries were established in certain regions and shifts occurred with the ebb and flow of fashion and with the introduction of cotton and the technological inventions (for women above all the spinning jenny) which proceeded apace from the 1780s. Taken overall, the rural female industrial worker represented a minority of all women workers, but in some parts of England she was becoming the dominant model and she also had a clearly defined existence in particular regions of Northern Ireland, France, Germany and wherever industry reached into the countryside.

Another woman who had largely abandoned the notion of a dowry was the working girl of urban origin. This was more generally true of towns north of the Loire. In areas of Roman law, the dowry remained a more entrenched consideration even in the towns. Like the girl of the textile villages, the working woman of the towns considered a skill and the prospect of continuing gainful activity after marriage, along with a bottom drawer of sheets and towels and a bed (a trousseau rather than a dowry), as the main requisites for marriage. This woman did not leave home to find work but either worked from home or in her parents' home which could be a shop or workshop. If no opportunities existed within the family or its wider networks then she might be driven to seek an opening in the marketplace. But at no stage did she compete with the country girl for the lower levels of domestic service.

How do we account for such a difference in outlook? First, the dowry in cash or kind makes more sense in a rural context as a key to survival. It enables the purchase of livestock, the stocking of a farm which gains in viability through the input of capital. In Roman law countries where there could be greater disparity between the ages of partners a dowry was also seen as the guarantee of some funds for a widow. Added to this, the town girl was the legatee of different job possibilities. These of course depended upon her family and upon the local economy. She was prepared, probably because she saw little alternative, to run the risk that a time might come when she had no capital reserves beyond her job skills.

In many cities and towns, industry and commerce were organized on a guild basis. Indeed, studies of Reformation German cities (Augsburg, Nuremberg, Nordlingen) see the guilds as the overarching social organization of the working classes.[41] The guild hierarchies and the patriarchal family workshop provided a context in which the father (master of the workshop and head of household), the mother (master's wife and helpmate), the son (apprentice guaranteed the mastership after training), the daughter (likely to marry a journeyman), all had their allotted place. The guilds laid down the terms of production and were responsible for restrictive controls enforced by municipal law to protect the interests of their members and to guarantee quality of production. They were, very generally, strongest in Germany, some of the Flemish cities and those of northern Italy and Spain, and weakest in Britain. However, conspicuous differences existed in the strength of types of guilds to enforce their control and stop work slipping from them. By the 1770s, in France, Spain and Tuscany, they were also under attack from Enlightenment reformers and did not emerge unscathed. Added to this, the production of new articles of consumption, new textiles, confectionery, fan-making, mantua-making, porcelain production and so on, grew up outside guild control.

At the beginning of the period there were artificers' guilds (usually wealthy), building trades (generally much poorer), guilds for food, cloth and clothes production (some of which like the haberdashers could be weak), glaziers, tanners, shoemakers and leather workers, and those offering very specialist services like printers and printmakers or cabinet makers. Not all of these provided work for women. Building work often went on outside the framework of any workshop. The shoemaker was generally very poor and worked alone. Tanneries were not places where women were found, as a detailed study of the Santa Croce region of Florence revealed.

In the context of the family business, however, it was expected that the master's wife would be aided by her daughter in managing the workshop, providing food for apprentices and journeymen, doing the books, running errands and vending the finished goods. What else a daughter could do depended on the nature of the work and what was permitted by the guild. The main guardians of workshop practice were not the masters themselves but journeymen anxious to ensure a future for themselves in a particular branch of production. They were prepared to countenance, for example, in the case of butchers the production of sausages and black puddings by wives and daughters, or in the case of silk weavers reeling and ancillary services at the loom. Confectioners' wives and daughters could make chocolates and decorate pastries. No one contested the right of wives and daughters to work in a shop or at a stall leased in the name of the husband and father. The tendency of a master in an occupation where there was scope for the employment of his daughter – particularly if he had no sons – may have been to familiarize her with the techniques of the trade. At the humblest levels, where the master in question did not employ journeymen and where any apprentices kept quiet, then the master's daughter unofficially may have done much work without incurring opposition from the guild. However, if the fact should be revealed, the offending master could receive a reprimand and his daughter's services would have to be sacrificed. Complaints were more common in periods of economic strain, particularly when the labour supply was overabundant and rising prices outstripped wages. In easy times, journeymen were less anxious and might permit without complaint some infiltration by women into what they saw as their sphere of activity. However, come the hard times and two kinds of women could find themselves ousted from employment or suddenly curtailed in what they might do. The first were those outside the workshops who had poached territory and the second were the master's women. Fierce battles, for example, were waged in the guild records of Geneva in the eighteenth century as journeymen clockmakers insisted that the masters' daughters restrain their activities to engraving watch cases and making limited parts. Under no account, it was insisted, should they assemble anything.[42]

Even when the guilds began to lose much of their power, and governments moved against restrictive practices in favour of a *laissez-faire* economy, women existed as workers most easily in those areas which had never been subjected to guild domination and hence marked out as male preserves. These were usually areas where the needle and goods of moderate worth were in question. In the course of the eighteenth century, the development of millinery, loose garments such as the mantua, and an increasingly complex world of undergarments opened up new prospects for women outside the domination of the guilds. This was for working women the most striking aspect of the growth in the economy. Both drapers and hatters initally contested the production of hats and bonnets by women, but the ephemerality of fashion demanded the finished product be of relatively modest cost and they simply ceded the territory because the profits were marginal. Millinery became women's work. It was an area of production into which an urban girl could go on some kind of apprenticeship basis. However, it was recognized that to set up in production she would need a capital sum of about £300. As a milliner working for someone else, the wages she could command were slight and millinery became a pauper craft.[43]

With work in the needle trades came derisory levels of remuneration. The seamstresses and makers of stays and bodices, of bone lace and embroidery, of lingerie and shawls, of gloves and bonnets and lace caps, and all those who provided the paraphernalia of a girl on a swing in a *fête galante* were townswomen. Progressively, as the eighteenth century advanced, the dressmaker took over from the tailor, who clung to his monopoly of outer garments for men and to riding habits – both of which were relatively immune to fashion changes and used heavier and more expensive cloth. The tailors abandoned claims to making dresses and mantuas to the dressmaker and even royalty found it more appropriate to employ a woman than a man, thus giving a sign to the rest of society. A dressmaker might not have a formal apprenticeship, but she would certainly spend a couple of years in a workshop, though on a nonresident basis, while she learned her craft and her parents would in all likelihood have to pay for this period or at least accept that she would not be paid. Even when experienced, very few, unless patronized by the high aristocracy, made a comfortable living.

Where she could not count on a father's workshop to absorb her, then a town girl was likely to follow her mother's occupation or that of an aunt. Laundress produced laundress; seamstress generated seamstresses. Chocolate-maker mothers and aunts trained daughters and cousins. Tavern and café keepers' daughters helped their mothers run the business. Indeed, the tendency of urban families to absorb their female children into a work pattern may explain the relatively small number of recorded formal apprenticeships for women. Female orphans were the only girls for whom such assurances of steady employment were usually sought. Even when this was the case, as among the orphans of Geneva where girls were apprenticed to mercers or to the makers of watch chains, the step was not seen as securing the girl a long-term future livelihood. The orphanages of Bristol and the Ospedale degli Innocenti in Florence shared a common scepticism about any work for a girl that was not offered on the basis of residence in an honest family, the acquisition of skills and the prospect of an accumulated sum, however small, at the end of the employment.

A girl's own family was seen as the best and most secure employer she could have in a town context – in some instances the direct opposite of the rural situation where the girl needed to bring town capital back to her village. A good urban mother would strive to her utmost to acquire and make the furnishings for a bed, kitchen utensils and linen necessary to establish her daughter. It was hoped that the skills and resources she imparted to her would be the means to help her negotiate life after marriage and it is clear that many daughters of women with small businesses, particularly taverns or drinkshops, *buveries* or *guinguettes* or *bettole*, would in fact one day take over from their mothers.

In many instances what an urban mother could impart were skills which would do no more than contribute to a marginal existence. In sixteenth-century Norwich little girls were taught by their mothers to spin while their brothers perhaps went to school. Spinning was a pauper craft, or one which was ancillary to a male wage. In early nineteenth-century Bruges female children were taught by their mothers to make lace. No one thought it appropriate to teach little boys to do so for this was women's work and would not sustain manly survival.[44]

Defined by the status of her family, by the limited job potential for women in the workplace, and by a concept of female labour predicated on a notion of woman as future wife, a woman's working life was thus designed to equip her for a single future, marriage. Over the three hundred years examined here job potential increased, but low wages permitted no alternative visions. As she approached her mid-twenties, it was possible to assess the extent to which a woman had achieved her target and how rosy were her prospects of forming a viable partnership. No matter how assiduous her forward planning, everything depended on good fortune in negotiating the system. The setbacks were legion. They ranged from the insolvency of employers to personal sickness, industrial slump or to succumbing to a man whose intentions did not involve matrimony.

Some pressures might come from her own family. It could be hard to resist messages that help was needed at home because of sickness or difficult times. When a mother died, the eldest daughter, whether in service or not, might be recalled and unless her father remarried her period of capital accumulation was curtailed.

Perhaps most to be feared were periods of unemployment, when both maidservants and industrial employees had to cut into their reserves. Employers had little compunction about showing a girl the door when times worsened for them, and mistresses could lose patience with a girl whose temperament they found irksome or whose standards fell below their expectations. Silk workers in Lyons who had travelled a long way from Alpine villages could not contemplate a return home at such times. They hung on, hoping that the slump would be of short duration and that if they had picked up their back wages they could survive without totally consuming them. Some, as the money became scarce, slept in the brick kilns at night. Predictably, it was at such moments that the descent into prostitution could take place.

Another major fear for the working girl was falling ill. Her physical strength had to be sustained for her to realize her goal. No one thought it their business to keep an invalid beyond a week or even a few days and even then much depended on the nature of the complaint. The French Hôtels Dieu would, if they had the space, usually receive sick servants and the young girls would come with their bundles of scanty possessions which they would leave with the *gardienne* or portress. They knew that their places would be rapidly filled by others and that if they recovered they would, in all probability, have to find a new employer even if they were barely convalescent. Some had scant hope of recovery. In the archives of the Hôtel Dieu of Lyons remain to this day some little notebooks, the property of servants to the silk manufacturers, in which they recorded what was owing to them and what they had expended on clothing during their employment. But they had contracted tuberculosis in the hot, steamy atmosphere of the silk workshops and as the disease advanced had no option but to stop work. Leaving their clothes and shoes to the guardian at the hospital to be collected by their relatives if they did not recover, and either the money they had brought with them or the record of the employer's debts, they spent their remaining hours in a shared bed in the huge wards. If their relatives heard about their death and picked up what was owing to them, they did not take the little notebooks which remain to this day as the last poignant testimony to the failure of the best laid schemes.[45]

Other diseases offered more chance of recovery than did tuberculosis but left the potential dowry depleted through loss of work time. Among the worst things that could befall the maidservant was to suffer an accident which left her physically disabled. For either sex from the working classes, to be disabled was to be a liability to someone, and in the *sauve qui peut* world of service it meant dismissal, whoever may have been responsible for the accident. The young person with scurvy, rickets, impetigo, visible boils and sores that could be taken for congenital syphilis was not precluded from obtaining work, but it would be of the lowest and the least reliable kind. These were the uncomfortable facts about the world of service and what could stand between moderate success and total failure.

We must suppose that for most young women in the first phase of their working life some problem would occur that might limit their aspirations and economies. The hope had to be that something would remain and that earning capacity and opportunities were not radically curtailed. Every story of a working life for both men and women was fraught with difficulties. Both needed sustained physical strength and those dependent on industry had to fear recession. During the worst periods of unemployment, however, women were more at risk than men and the lack of commitment to them by employers – in contrast to apprenticeship indentures – made them particularly vulnerable.

Occasionally we encounter minor mysteries which prompt speculation of a kind which throws light on the young girl's efforts to raise money. In the late eighteenth century, Thomas Furber of Nantwich engaged a young woman named Martha for the annual sum of £2 17s 6d. She was a maid of all work. Over the year he advanced her £1 10s and provided her with a pair of shoes, a pair of stockings, a shift, a handkerchief and a bottle of tincture of myrrh (the commonest panacea for toothache) costing sixpence. At the end of the year she was overdrawn on her wages by two shillings, but because she was a good, industrious, honest and sober girl, Furber overlooked the debt.

Where had the money gone? It might have been spent on clothes beyond the necessaries provided. Since she had hardly any time off and was not a drinker, the scope for spending money on pure entertainment was small. There is no suggestion that Martha was providing for an illegitimate child at nurse: the sum would not have been adequate and Furber might have been less eulogistic about her good character. Perhaps she was sending money home to help a member of the family. Perhaps Furber did not give her enough to eat and she bought food when she could. Perhaps the aching tooth had to be pulled or she had some other physical condition demanding remedies. Two things are clear. The first is that one did not have to be profligate to spend a pound and ten shillings over twelve months. The second is that Martha was at the beginning of her life in service. If this was a deficit year she might hope to do better as she got older and became more experienced. Clearly she could not stay with Furber but must hope for a better job.[46]

Any dowry at all raised by a woman from her own efforts without parental subvention constitutes a success story, a triumph over pitfalls innumerable. The time taken to realize the wherewithal to buy a cow or pig, a bed and a bit of basic household furniture and cooking equipment, bedding and a little linen, could be anything up to twelve years of uninterrupted service. Before all her assets had been mobilized, however, but in full command of a concept of her commercial worth, the working woman began to consider her prospects. Who might she marry and what kind of livelihood might the couple make together? She was by now in her early to mid-twenties and the time had come to advance in the planning strategy.

CHAPTER THREE

Finding a Partner, or Questions of Choice

What is the difference in matrimonial affairs, between the
mercenary and the prudent move? Where does discretion
end, and avarice begin?

JANE AUSTEN, PRIDE AND PREJUDICE, 1813

IN 1640, Jan Steen depicted an old man, a 'greybeard' offering a
gold ring to a young girl. 'The greybeard' was a stock theatrical
character of a ridiculous, randy old man, familiar to many, and
indeed still used as a stereotype by Rousseau a century or so later when
he wished to discuss the follies of age and the inappropriateness of an
'uneven match'. In Steen's picture, the girl is seated and to her left is
a young man with his hand on her lap, an explicitly familiar and physical
gesture. Through an open door we glimpse an old woman, the girl's
mother, gleefully carrying away a money bag. Steen has trapped a
moment of tension, a turning point in the girl's life, when a choice
must be made between age, riches and lust on the one hand and youth,
virility and love on the other. On the wall behind the girl a ladder of life
hangs from a nail and it serves to remind the viewer of the importance of
the moment. If the wrong choice is made, the girl's life could be
ruined.[1]

There are few representations which present in so economical a
manner the problems surrounding the issue of choice and who should
make it. The questions are posed and the viewer is left to draw his or
her conclusions. Is this mother the fit person to chose the girl's husband
or will she not think beyond the old man's money bags? Is the young
woman capable of the right preference and does she have the power to
exercise it? In whose hands does her fate lie?

A debate on who should choose a life partner, the parents or the
aspirant husband or bride, took place at different times in different

national contexts and among different social groups. At the beginning
of the sixteenth century all European aristocracies generally considered
matrimony to be too important an issue to be left to the young and
family or clan were involved in the construction of an alliance. The
Council of Trent in the decree *Tametsi* (1563), which sought to bring
marriage under ecclesiastical control, declared that the church abhorred
unions lacking parental consent but refused, once they had been solemnized in church, to proclaim them null and void. For this reason,
Trent was not accepted by the French monarchy. The important Ordonnance of Blois (1579), which endorsed some aspects of the Tridentine
reform, turned its face against marriages without parental consent,
declaring them null under civil law, and was followed by a corpus of
regulations including the stipulation that a son could not have freedom
of action until he was thirty.[2] In 1697, Louis XIV laid down that a
parish priest could only marry a resident of his parish (six years constituting residence). If the spouse was from elsewhere letters of clearance
should be given by the priest of the parish of origin. This familiarity
with the contracting parties, it was hoped, would make clandestine or
bigamous marriage almost impossible. Theoretically, clandestine marriage became a capital offence. Furthermore, marriages involving a
minor made without the consent of a parent could be annulled by civil
courts on the grounds of abduction (*rapts de séduction*), carrying heavy
penalties. Although some voices in France by 1730 were urging more
weight be given to the choice of the interested parties, generally speaking, throughout this period, the French state endorsed parental choice.
A child who it was feared was yielding to passion and in danger of
trying to escape parental prohibitions on his choice of partner could
until the 1780s be imprisoned for a short cautionary period under a
lettre de cachet. During this period of incarceration it was hoped that he
(or sometimes she) would see sense.[3]

The French legislation, it should be stressed, was concerned above
all with the conduct of the aristocracy, seeking to preserve the status quo
against Tridentine changes. The legislation did not *ipso facto* preclude a
future bride or groom's preference for a particular partner being heeded
by the parents. What the legislation demonstrates above all else is that
a great deal of money, effort, prestige and power could be involved in
a marriage and that parents must have a considerable voice in partner
selection.

The legislation could, of course, be called upon by members of all classes. Young people from the country labouring on their own account in the towns were supposed to alert their parents to their intentions and secure their approval, and the parochial clergy worked hard to see that this was done. However, many couples intending to marry as they approached their thirties were already orphans and distance limited the intervention which parents might have wished to exert. It could be virtually impossible to control the actions of people who had worked for themselves and whose parents could settle nothing upon them. The legislation in France rarely impeded working couples who were already in their mid- to late twenties, who had left their home and place of birth in their teens, and had lived and worked for several years in the parish where they intended to marry. In fact control diminished, in most countries, the lower one descended the social scale.[4]

In Spain and Italy hostility to *Tametsi* was less overt than in France.[5] This did not mean that a free choice was guaranteed to those intending to marry. Far from it. The aristocracies and patriciates kept as close a control of their daughters as they could effectively manage by virtual confinement to the house except for weekly mass or parentally organized events, and exercised as tight a supervision as possible over the people with whom their nubile daughters came into contact. They betrothed them when they were young and could marry them at twelve, the age of consent. Secluded and with no experience, a young girl reared to anticipate a certain destiny could find opposing parental authority hard, indeed impossible. The clergy might ascertain that the bride was willing to marry the intended partner, but perhaps few probed very closely. Occasional rescues did occur. No less a person than Saint Teresa of Avila told the story of an incident among the high aristocracy of six-teenth-century Valladolid, where the eight-year-old Casilda de Padilla, the only family member who remained when her elder brother and sister opted for the religious life, was betrothed to her uncle. This union would have maintained land within the family and prevented the line dying out, thus getting over the prohibition on marriage within degrees of consanguinity. The child was sent to live with her uncle for several months of the year, 'when she had been with her *esposo* (betrothed) during the day, to her great contentment, and loving him more fully than her years required, she would fall into a great sadness seeing how the day had ended, as all those to come must do'. She ran away to a convent and in spite of a royal warrant to have her returned, on her twelfth birthday she chose the religious life. In Casilda's case, choice meant not to marry the man selected by her family and to find her freedom in the convent. The story shows the limits of the options and we might question whether the church would have been so quick to protect her if she had not declared her preference for the religious life; but it also shows that clerical intervention could overthrow parental influence.[6]

The best-laid family schemes could go awry. Runaway marriages, if perhaps never numerous, are documented and once they had taken place, the church would not declare them invalid. Or parents could find their hands forced by children who broke the rules. In 1542, Leonor, eldest daughter of the lord of Castril, married one Diego de Pisa, son of a royal judge. Her family protested that she could have had a much better match and mourned the wedding, but claimed that Diego had dishonoured her and had gained access to their house in a clandestine courtship. It seems unlikely that this pair had done more than see each other alone – private contact being the great thief of female honour – but clearly, whatever contact they had had determined that the wedding must go ahead.[7]

The degree to which the control of relationships within the Spanish and Italian aristocracies and patriciates was modified in the eighteenth century is not easy to appreciate. The power of the Italian patrician family over its daughters during the sixteenth century could be described as absolute. Who was to marry and who was to enter the cloister was not a decision made by the young girl. In Venice by the end of the eighteenth century, however, there were fewer forced vocations. Choice had expanded to permit young girls the possibility of *not* entering a convent. This did not mean that they could choose who to marry, merely that there was some relaxation in the system.

There was also more mercantile wealth which could undermine caste boundaries as evinced by the common lament that this was happening and more were marrying lower down the social scale. In addition, among educated élites in France, Italy and Spain, there was a growing knowledge of the arguments on behalf of freedom of choice and which extolled the virtues of companionate marriage occurring in north-western Europe. All this may have provoked panic. In Spain in 1776 there was a tightening of the marriage laws in which parental consent to the marriage of minors was made a sine qua non. In 1803 the age of majority was made 25 for men and 23 for women. The instigators of the first laws blamed a spate of runaway marriages, but perhaps what we are seeing is a tightening of family control in face of any liberalization of the times. It put the Spanish theoretically in line with the situation in France and emphasized that the élites of Mediterranean Europe intended much closer supervision of the young than was usual in England and Holland.[8]

In Protestant societies an evolution of attitudes was more marked. The reformers of the sixteenth century were explicit on the need for parental consent. In England the Convocation of Canterbury in 1604 stated that this should be required up to the age of 21. How much choice was allowed by parents depended very much upon class, partner availability and the peacefulness of the times. Generally, and under circumstances where family or civil disasters did not intrude, marriages, it was hoped, would find the consent of both parents and the contracting parties. From the mid-seventeenth century, theoretical debates on the question of marriage became increasingly insistent on the merits of the freedom of choice for the partners. From the 1680s the marriage contract was abundantly used by philosophers such as John Locke as an analogy for the social contract made between subject and ruler when a social organization was initiated. In any power relationship, if tyranny was to be avoided, the full consent of the contracting parties was imperative.[9]

The change in the tone of discussion did not, of course, lead to an immediate fundamental change in the mores of the aristocracy. However, the response of the reading public to Samuel Richardson's best-selling novel *Clarissa* (1747), which took on the fashionable theme of choice, was unambiguous. The heroine is a poor little rich girl, an heiress from the gentry, whose parents seek to force her into an unsuitable match and who in desperation runs away with a cad, Lovelace, who rapes her. When Clarissa chooses death rather than marry her seducer, because she knows what sort of a man he is, her role as heroine is assured. She has the right priorities: death as the solution to loss of virtue, but death under circumstances which condemn her parents and her rapist. Shocked by the callous indifference and tyranny of her greedy parents, who sought to inflict a life of misery upon her by the imposition of a man of their choice, society applauded her decisions whilst lamenting her death. Johnson and Boswell concurred that parents should limit their intervention to good advice.

A new generation of women writers elected choice as their dominant theme. Two points are being made. The first is that the decision about whom to marry should be made by the contracting parties and the second that they should do this with extreme care and with close reference to character as well as to material considerations. From the late seventeenth century, particularly when the woman writer was at work, issued a stream of good advice suggesting what those wishing to marry should look for and how they should proceed. As Aphra Behn put it in a text that drew heavily on the ideas of the Dutch Hieronymous Sweerts:

> Search not after great riches but for one of your own degree, for the rich are insulting, self-conceited and proud. Admire no outward beauty; because they are proud of their beauty and imagine themselves to be goddessess . . . Shun those who are much lesser than yourself. For when a mean one finds herself promoted by a great match, she is much prouder and self-conceited than one of good extraction . . . Follow the advice of understanding friends. For to be wise and in love was not given to the gods themselves.[10]

Most girls from solid upper- and middle-class families were prepared to accept the advice of family and friends. Musing on her marriage to a dull professor at Göttingen, Caroline Michaelis commented in 1781 on how she had been led into a match, as were other German girls of her class and temperament:

> My brother gave me in marriage to the man he had marked out for me since childhood, his best friend who loved me from that time. In this marriage I fulfilled the wishes of my family, my friends, and his, and for a long time my heart was in agreement with them. Guided by these powerful motives I made my choice.[11]

Some eighteenth-century writers, among them Dr John Gregory and Dr James Fordyce (the latter wrote the famous *Sermons* which Jane Austen's tedious and ill-favoured Mr Collins read to the Bennet sisters), thought that the discussion had gone too far. It had resulted in girls becoming too finicky and losing sight of the fact that their benign qualities as wives could transform a boorish and coarse man into one of sensibility.[12] However, even this literature assumes that women do not proceed without exercising some choice.

While most eighteenth-century good advice literature emanating from Britain and Holland places an emphasis on the desirability of choice for the contracting partners, it still urges that their choice should be made by reference to the good counsel of others. The literature is opposed to tyranny, as evil in the home as in the wider society, but it is on the side of sense, reason and therefore the merits of good counsel. Choice had, in short, boundaries of the appropriate.

A consciousness of an evolution in attitudes on the printed page should neither lead us into a view of sixteenth-century marriage as one predicated on parental choice alone nor into one of seventeenth- and eighteenth-century marriage as a condition of which only the young were the arbiters. Money continued to matter. For the great families of Europe in all countries a marriage was the culmination of a long process involving the efforts of the parents, their families, their wider kin, their friends and the bride and groom. The higher one went up the social scale the more people were involved. The mediating services of friends and relations were used to secure the right introductions and to find out the approximate worth of the potential partners. Where the views of the bride and groom were taken into consideration, they were only one of the factors – though they could be critical.[13]

How was the selection of a marriage partner then made? In families with both sons and daughters, the marriage of the heir was important in determining the fate of other family members, both sisters and brothers, but was particularly crucial for sisters. The heir of a noble house was, or should be, in pursuit of as great a sum as he could attract for the dowry of his bride. Most money exchanged hands when the daughter of a new noble or a rich banking or mercantile family formed an alliance with a scion of an old house, because the step marked the upgrading of her family in social esteem. The input of the groom's family was in part measured in terms of family status, so in terms of liquid wealth it would usually be much less than that of the bride. It was the exchange of millions for a title. Even when this was not the case and the couple were of equal status, the bride would still be the provider of liquid assets surrendered in whole or instalments for the duration of the marriage. The groom would be guaranteed his inheritance, which would be spelt out, and his family would engage enough of the groom's inheritance to ensure the couple the appropriate standard of living. None of the groom's property was lost to the house although enough might be engaged to guarantee reimbursement to the bride of her input in case of widowhood. The influx of the bride's liquid wealth into her new family would, however, be used, as were the dowries of all first sons' brides, by the husband's family to settle the groom's sisters, or a proportion of them. The money therefore circulated, one bride's dowry being made to work for others. Clearly a great deal of pressure could be put on an elder son to marry money if there were daughters to establish.

Younger members of a large family, if they were to secure some endowment, had to wait. They were under less pressure to make a decision, which could be both an advantage and a disadvantage. If they were under less pressure to make an early choice, they could have much less in the way of resources with which to attract a husband, but at least their marriages would have less consequence for the other members of the family. However, truly prestigious families did not without very special reasons marry their daughters into families of lesser social standing even if they had condoned or encouraged that of a son to someone of less standing who had money. The English gentry were more flexible than their continental counterparts in that they more freely intermarried with yeoman and upper mercantile stock. Perhaps as many as a third of British brides from the aristocracy and gentry would marry somewhat, but not too far, down the social scale.[14] Continental aristocratic families were more aware that daughter disposal indelibly marked the standing of the bride's family. Better an unmarried daughter at home or in the cloister than a record of social failure.

In Britain, under the laws of strict settlement, a father had to regulate with the heir of his choice, who was usually the eldest son, the settlement of the inheritance. The settlement was usually made on marriage and meant the passing of the estate in its entirety in due course – usually on the death of the father – to the heir. Even when the heir came into this inheritance, his control of it was emphatically limited. The income from the estate had to provide the agreed income to the widow of the former incumbent (his mother or stepmother), dowries for sisters and sums to settle younger brothers in suitable positions and to support any family spinsters who might remain.

It is not fully clear how many husbands of well-endowed brides made a fortune from marriage. Everything depended on how many other women had to be settled out of the bride's capital input. If the husband should prove short-lived, and if the funds had been used to establish daughters or to pay family debts, then a family's predicament could be very difficult. What is clear is that if the system was not played carefully by a family with several family members to marry, the house could see itself diminished in both wealth and prestige. Dowry litigation by widows seeking to repossess their due against families protesting their inability to pay at that moment was a very common phenomenon, most particularly in Italy and Mediterranean Europe.

A great deal of difference, then, marked the approach of the aristocratic houses to the marriage of the eldest son and daughter from that of the younger scions. The family with only one or two children to dispose of could also contemplate the marriage business with far less anxiety than could the more numerous family. It was perhaps for this reason that the French higher aristocracy became more careful to limit the numbers of their offspring.

Ideally, though many refused to co-operate, the male heir with brothers and sisters should move while young to establish himself. If he lingered the younger children could find themselves in an anomalous situation, not knowing what exactly would be apportioned to them. If he moved smartly, however, and married to financial advantage, they were the real beneficiaries. There must have been a great deal of family pressure on an eldest son to contract a match which would help out his siblings and the house in general. Lady Pilkington was both furious and dismayed when her eldest son clung to the joys of bachelorhood as he approached his thirties. The third Duke of Hamilton, who had three daughters to marry and was waiting for the tocher (dowry) of his heir's bride, was impatient with his son's dilatory approach to choosing a wife. 'Before long your sister Susan will be married which brings payment of tochers fast upon me and which should be your part by bringing in a good portion rather than being a charge to me.'[15]

The evidence suggests, in fact, that although fathers could place a great deal of pressure on their sons to marry, they were careful not to go too far. Were they as liberal with their daughters? The question is almost impossible to answer: the evidence is very varied and circumstances were different for each family and, indeed, very often for each child. In the great houses the eldest female child could generally, though not invariably, expect the most substantial dowry. The rule, frequently broken, which seems to have pertained through much of Europe, was that if there was only one daughter she should have at least the same sum as her mother had had. The logic here may have been that wealth brought into the family by one generation was offset by the next taking it out. Some mothers may have already died by the time of the daughter's marriage, thus liberating the securities intended to provide a widow with funds. Every family had to make calculations: if there was more than one daughter, then the family had to decide where to put its money. Generally, and presupposing a male heir, the greater the number of daughters, the less the younger ones could expect in the way of a dowry and this could be a serious impediment in the search for a husband. To be the fourth or fifth daughter, of no matter how wealthy a line, could make spinsterhood a real threat. If there was no male heir, and hence no influx of vital capital, then sometimes in Catholic Europe the elder girls were sent to a convent and the youngest child was the one to be married, allowing the family to hold on to its wealth as long as possible. Certainly this situation pertained amongst patrician families in Venice.

To suffer from a physical impediment, to be sickly or low in the pecking order, made spinsterhood or the convent a possibility. However, aunts or godmothers who had been widowed and who had gained control of their assets could help to settle a godchild or a favourite niece and hence might cause prospects of spinsterhood to recede. Bishops, cardinals and abbots were also known to siphon off some of the profits from their benefices to help out both nieces and nephews. The well-favoured or family beauty might find herself receiving an advantageous offer from a man who did not have sisters to settle, or who was prepared to accept less than his status might have earned because he was arbiter of his own destiny. Such an event could alter the opportunities of a particular family member and cause a fourth or fifth child to pre-empt her sisters in the marriage line.

The marriage which was arranged between Sir Ralph Verney and Mary Blacknall in 1631 took place when she was thirteen and he a few years older. An orphan and an heiress, she went to live in her husband's house with his sisters while he completed his education. Mary was never confronted with choice, though she had no aversion to Ralph and a deep and lasting affection developed betwen them. Ralph was not a successful manager of money and made some unwise investments which affected the position of his sisters. Margaret's portion had been partly composed of the jointure of a widowed aunt, but was diminished by her brother's management. She was in her twenties before she found what she deemed a suitable match, in exchange for a hundred pounds in cash and a promise of a thousand to come. The match was not a happy one and eventually broke up. Margaret settled then for a jointure of a hundred pounds per annum. Her younger sisters fared worse rather than better. Sir Ralph was eager to marry them off from their early teens, but Mary's dowry had also been mismanaged by being put out at interest to one Sir Martin Leicester who had fallen behind in his payments. Mary was aware 'that my position is bad by that reason that I cannot enjoy that which my father gave me [that is, her portion].' With little more than an annuity of fifty pounds a year offered by her brother until Leicester paid up, she was prepared to contemplate marriage to someone her inferior, but she reconsidered and it was not until she was in her late twenties that she found someone to her liking and of similar background. Her sister Elizabeth who had been a wild teenager and was actually discovered on a male servant's knee – thereafter she was sent to boarding school – also experienced problems arising from insufficient funds to back her desire to marry. None of the Verney sisters appears to have experienced smooth marital negotiations nor a happy outcome.[16]

In the sixteenth and seventeenth centuries, across western Europe, aristocratic women could still be described as lineage pawns and kings were interested and involved in the partnerships which were constructed. Similarly, kings' ministers in order to enhance their own influence at court could embark on a strategy to ally daughters and nieces with those they thought would bolster their political weight. This is one reason why the monarchy and the aristocracy in France consistently refused freedom of choice for the contracting parties. Richelieu not only cemented his position with the marriage of his nieces but came to rely on their efforts to promote his construction of a power base through family alliances.[17] Madame d'Aiguillon was particularly assiduous in her efforts on his behalf, although not invariably successful. She arranged for her eldest nephew, who would inherit a dukedom, to marry Mademoiselle de Chevreuse, who would bring both wealth and the support of three powerful families, the Lorraine, the de Rohan and the de Luynes, into the match. Her nephew, however, fell for Madame de Pons, widow of the Maréchal d'Albret, older than he was and known as *la laide Hélène*, and succeeded in marrying her. His younger brother also escaped his aunt's machinations by marrying a woman of neither great fortune nor great name, and the last foiled her entirely by joining a religious order. 'My nephews go from bad to worse,' moaned Madame d'Aiguillon.[18]

Cardinal Mazarin was apparently more successful. His nieces were endowed – perhaps out of state revenues – and alliances made with top nobles and the world of finance.[19] Mazarin, a foreign outsider, albeit one with the ear of the Queen Regent, thus sought to integrate himself with those who could easily have become his critics. It is clear from an examination of the disposal of the relatives of these two cardinals that whereas nephews could resist or foil the ambitions of families, nieces and daughters were easier to manipulate.

The cessation of civil and religious wars and the widespread social and political dislocation attendant upon the Thirty Years War, which had lent a particular intensity to alliances between noble houses, reduced some of the pressures on the already powerful nobility to cement their strength through the marriage bed. Nevertheless, marriage was too obviously an entrée to greater power to be ignored by the ambitious. The eighteen-year-old Duc de Saint-Simon, ambitious for the ear of King Louis XIV, perceived that the Duc de Beauvilliers, *premier gentilhomme de la Chambre du Roi, chef du Conseil Royal des Finances, Ministre d'Etat* – a man of influence – had seven daughters. He asked for the hand of the eldest, who was fourteen, but the duke said that she had expressed a wish to enter a convent and he thought that the youngest four would do the same. Another was severely handicapped. Saint-Simon immediately pressed for the one left and was not deterred when her father said that he could not settle much on her. He admitted that it was her family he wished to marry. The duke politely refused his offer, even though the match would have been financially advantageous for his twelve-year-old.[20] Saint-Simon's position is instructive. He had no sisters and therefore his family would not see an exodus of funds to marry them well. On the other hand, he felt that this left him without close and powerful allies and that, above all, was what his marriage should achieve even if his bride brought him no dowry. In the event he was remarkably successful. His wife Gabrielle de Lorges brought him the support he needed as well as a close companionship.

Marriage remained the expression of success and the means by which money was transferred between noble clans and was brought under the control of many old noble houses by a process of diffusion. What they had to offer was an ancient lineage and often political power, as well as the prestige of an honourable past. This last attribute had only a real marketable worth at the moment of marriage. It did not of itself generate new wealth. That precious commodity was to be found elsewhere in the possession of newer, parvenu, even non-noble financial and mercantile families. The daughters (not the sons) of these new houses, if they were appropriately endowed, could exchange wealth for coats of arms. Their less illustrious names would be surrendered and lost and the beneficiary was the antique dynasty.[21]

On any ballroom floor in the stately home, by the end of the eighteenth century, were young women in white ballgowns who knew exactly where they stood in a particular pecking order and for many their status was problematic. If the wishes of the young (otherwise known as romantic love) could be factored into any particular choice, the sobering fact was that marriage cost more for a girl's family than it had ever cost before. Hence on the dance floor were many young women who were likely to end up disappointed in their search and who would be urged by their parents to accept an offer they would not have contemplated if money had been a less important consideration. There were also those with little money and good looks hoping that a gentleman of means who was not worried by the prospect of providing for sisters would find them attractive and that money would then be no impediment to choice. For even if hard economics mattered, affection was insidious and could upset the formulated plans of parents. It was the human factor, the variable that could modify the best laid schemes.[22]

There were of course many different levels of high society. There were court and country families, the former embracing dukes and peers and the latter a provincial nobility. In France, for example, there was Parisian marriage, or marriage negotiated through the Versailles nexus, and provincial marriage, which was a no less complex, though somewhat lowlier, affair. The wealthy *noblesse de race* (that is, of ancient lineage) who wished to maintain the éclat of their house, to acquire pensions and sinecures that would extend their powers and enhance their revenues, to secure bishoprics or offices for a son and to ensure that they were not outstripped in such exercises by other families, perceived little alternative to a presence at court – one which could be very expensive to maintain. Versailles was so arranged as to absorb the nobility in its functions and rituals. However, for many, the price they paid for the effort to have the ear of the king, or his ministers, or those who held the patronage key to important positions, such as the keeper of the *feuille des bénéfices* (a book in which bishoprics and their occupants were recorded and a pecking order for the acquisition of the best established), could be boredom relieved by gambling, intrigue and sexual dalliance.

The tone of the court varied from the overtly lax to the relatively austere. Much depended on the monarch and his wife or mistress. The transition from Madame de la Vallière and Madame de Montespan to

Madame de Maintenon, a woman of unflinchingly high principles, lifted the moral tone of Versailles, but new depths were fathomed during the reign of Louis XV when the monarch's own conduct contributed to the general atmosphere of permissiveness and intrigue. The dangers of life at court for the reputation of a young girl could hence be very considerable. To avoid such risks, and ever bearing in mind the need for even the richest and most distinguished girls to have a chaste and unsullied reputation at the outset of marriage, many of the great houses conducted negotiations between the parents and indeed relatives and co-opted 'brokers' at court while the intended bride was at home in the provinces or in an exclusive convent boarding school in Paris where the grille separated her from the contamination of the outside world. When proceedings advanced, suitable occasions had to be arranged, such as dinner parties and chaperoned soirées where the intended could gain some knowledge of each other. What was aimed at was consent on the part of all interested parties.[23]

The brides were very young. Indeed, the greater the fortune they possessed, the younger their age on marriage. Most were in their late teens. They were largely convent educated since from the middle of the seventeenth century the monarchy, led by Madame de Maintenon, and the church, in the form of a new group of women's religious orders, turned themselves to the promotion of a schooling in religious orthodoxy for the daughters of the aristocracy in the company of their peers as the most suitable preparation for life.[24] Paris had forty-three such convents by the end of the eighteenth century. The most prestigious were St Cyr (the foundation of Madame de Maintenon herself) and L'Abbaye aux Bois, where the daughters of the Choiseul, Montmorency, Chatillon and Talleyrand families rubbed shoulders. Louis XV's own daughters were educated at Fontevrault, the pinnacle of educational élitism from which they emerged indelibly pious. The educational standards of these establishments were quite high. St Cyr demanded 140 years of noble ancestry before permitting entry, but charged lower fees than the others. At school the girls formed contacts and may have been unconscious purveyors of the attributes of their friends through letters and journals to their families.

News that Lucy Dillon was ready to marry roused considerable interest. The daughter of a maréchal de France, niece of the Archbishop of Narbonne, who was likely to be generous in her direction, and a political asset to whoever married her, she was as well the heiress of her grandmother. Her husband would have advantages at court because she would occupy a role as *dame du palais* next to the queen, as her mother had done. The suitors were named to her and she considered their attributes. She rejected the Vicomte de Fleury as thick-witted, Espérance de L'Aigle as insufficiently illustrious and far from her equal in name, but agreed to meet, as someone potentially suitable, Frédéric de la Tour du Pin, son of the governor of Provence and cousin of the Archbishop of Auch. Her aunt arranged an ostensibly accidental meeting for them in the parlour of the Abbey of Penthemont, where they would officially be visiting the abbess (also a relative). She advised Lucy to be there at eleven wearing her most becoming gown and with ornaments in her hair. With written and verbal attestations, this 'surprise meeting' and then meetings over dinner with the young man, supervised of course by her relatives, with intermediaries then negotiating the settlements and sureties, she agreed to marry him. Her parents and his met to sign the official documents as to the settlements and only after that did the two parties meet alone. They were betrothed and the marriage was prepared. Lucy's was perhaps model behaviour and a taste of some of the sagacity that was to preserve her through the Revolution. She proceeded cautiously. She took advice. She considered her own destiny, but she followed the cautious rituals incumbent upon someone who knew her wealth and position and who wished to be secure in her choice, a choice that befitted her rank and station.[25]

The aunt who had arranged the first meeting had herself consented to the initiation of a match with the Marquis de Créquy, more than ten years her senior, having seen him through the convent grille in the company of a nun. She approved of his conversation on this occasion, had seen written character references, and before the marriage went through the rituals of viewing and listening while the parents negotiated the business side of the arrangement.[26]

At the court were also found the wealthy financiers who kept the world of Versailles afloat. The French nobility was not a closed caste but could be penetrated by money according to certain established rules. The person in question must purchase *noblesse* or rank, usually through a venal office that carried noble status; he must live nobly, that is, backed by land and rents as well as the financial or commercial assets that made his aspirations possible. His arrival would be marked through the disposal of his daughters in marriage. The process whereby titles were exchanged for millions can be plotted by reference to the marriages of the daughters of these wealthy financiers. In the eighteenth century, for example, the daughters and granddaughters of Crozat, the *receveur général* (who advanced money against revenues from taxation for the appropriate cut), entered ducal families and those of the high aristocracy by marriages with the Evreux, the La Tour d'Auvergne, the Montmorency, the Broglie, the Béthune, the La Tour du Pin and the Biron. All these could be classed among the top twenty aristocratic houses of the realm. The daughters of Olivier de Senozan, *receveur du clergé* (he managed the accounts of the huge assets controlled corporately by the French clergy), married into the houses of Montmorency and of Lamoignon. The daughter of another *receveur général*, Fillon de Villemur, married the Comte de Houdetot and the daughter of Jean Joseph Laborde, the court banker, the Comte de Noailles. The examples are endless and make the same points. Old families could not wait to get their hands on money. The daughters were under considerable pressure to assist the social ascent of their newly established financial families and some may have allowed a coat of arms to replace other personal predilections. They were dazzled by status. This is not to say that they proceeded with no knowledge of the man they were to marry, but if love ever existed it must have followed, not preceded, choice.[27]

The sons of the newly ennobled houses had to proceed differently and very cautiously. They had purchased for them offices which drew a line under their base ancestry. Some did not marry until middle age, when time had lent a little more lustre to their names.

Such a man was Jean Samuel Depont, son of an ennobled merchant who had bought him an office in the Parlement de Paris and had secured for himself a top administrative position as Intendant of the Généralité of Moulins by the time he was in his forties. He had been lucky in his twenties in building up some influential contacts which included the members of the salon of the Marquise de Montesson. Once established as an intendant, he sought to contract an alliance with Marie Madeleine l'Escureuil de la Touche, still in her teens but with expectations as the daughter of a financier – one not quite at the same level as the Crozat, but very substantial. Her father saw Depont as a solid match which would link his financial house to one of administration where there were always profits to be made from lending money. He put into this marriage 240,000 livres against Depont's advance on his inheritance of 180,000, plus his income from his office and a house he already owned. The father's investment in his daughter equalled a third of his wealth. For

Depont it was a good match and he may have been made aware of the girl's existence through the Marquise de Montesson herself. Certainly the early stages of introductions or viewings were invariably in the hands of women. In turn the new Madame Depont was to help Madame de Montesson's niece, Madame de Genlis, to find a suitable match for her daughter. The Depont marriage contract was signed in the presence of the king, a prestigious but costly procedure, and witnessed at Versailles by illustrious members of the high aristocracy, of the world of finance and from the salons.[28]

The marriage was hardly a love match, but it was one between an able forty-year-old and a sensible teenager based on abundant good counsel and limited personal knowledge. They were a 'successful' couple with a beautiful new house in the Marais and they operated in almost the best circles. Their only daughter, however, was to make a less than successful marriage, complicated perhaps by the times. In 1788 she married a scion of the house of Fontanges, a marquis, but one whose title was not accompanied by great means. The marriage broker may have been the Bishop of Metz who was known to both families. For the title of marquise, Mademoiselle Depont had provided for her 250,000 livres (about the same as her mother had had), but the husband's input was slight. Depont was wise enough to retain the capital sum and pay interest on it to the couple — perhaps not trusting the financial acumen of his new son-in-law who was an infantry captain. The marriage broke up at the time of the Revolution, when the husband became an émigré. We cannot know what the story would have been in less troubled times, but it bears the hallmark of a marriage wherein a wealthy young girl, an only daughter, was herself attracted to a young aristocrat and persuaded her parents, with her father less than fully convinced, that this was the right step.

Throughout western Europe, kin and contacts were mobilized to facilitate the expansion of the range of contacts. Madame de Cadillac, of a noteworthy Toulousain provincial noble family, gives an adequate summary of the kind of preliminaries involved in matchmaking in the mid-eighteenth century:

There is a question of marriage for my son. Some mutual friends have proposed this young lady and M. de Cadillac has replied evasively. Here is a young lady of very good birth. She is a Duras and her mother is a Larochefoucauld [obviously a minor branch as this was a ducal name].

She is nineteen years old, has 150,000 livres in coin. She has one brother
. . . who has a regiment which is with the Army of Flanders. The father
is 86 years old [obviously someone who took a younger wife] and has
40,000 livres income [again someone prepared to sink about a third of
his resources on his daughter]. He has land in the Saintonge and a
domaine near Cadillac . . . Marshal Duras [the head of the Duras house]
likes this old man and his family very much and takes care of their
advancement. It is he who said that the girl was not rich enough to
marry at Paris and that she must establish herself in the provinces.[29]

Involved in this preliminary testing of the water are friends who have
an idea of the girl's commercial worth, the precise details of her lineage
being common knowledge. The relationship of her branch of the family
to the marshal matters very much. He is in a position of influence at
court from which further honours and emoluments might issue. However, he is not prepared to provide the wherewithal to turn Mademoiselle
Duras's marriage into an expensive court affair. She is designated by
her house to be destined for a substantial provincial noble. At this point
in the game, Madame de Cadillac does not really know whether the
Duras house is interested in her son. If she gives a cautious expression
of interest, they might confirm whether this is in fact the case. If it is,
Madame de Cadillac, her friends and relatives must mobilize themselves
to organize dinners, dances and outings where the young people can
meet under supervised conditions, carefully watched by the exclusive
society of which they will be one day a part.

Madame de Cadillac is an invaluable source of information showing
how provincial noble society participated in the business of forming an
alliance. She explains, unconsciously but clearly, how relatives or friends
of young prospective brides and grooms 'leaked' information about the
prospects of the young woman or man in question. In the case of the
young woman, she tells us, her financial assets were always overvalued.
This had the effect of arousing greater interest in her than if the truth
had been known. Then, it was hoped, a prospective husband would be
attracted by her temperament, looks and talents. When her actual
monetary worth was revealed, he or his family might be prepared to
accept the lower sum once the variables of attraction and affection were
introduced into the situation; but once the initial negotiations had
begun it was dishonourable to lie about money.

This 'leakage' of information which allowed for some exaggeration seems to have taken place over most of western Europe. In Tudor England, both court and country marriages were frequently negotiated by widowed mothers who drove hard bargains. In some instances (Margaret, Countess of Bath, Bess of Hardwicke and many more) women contracting second or even third marriages for themselves had as one of the conditions the marriage of their daughter to the heir of their future husband.[30] Grandmothers, godmothers and aunts could also be caught up in the search for suitable husbands and could arrange visits and introductions. By the eighteenth century, the London season had institutionalized rituals in which the young and aristocratic could be exposed publicly but relatively safely. In the eighteenth century, the development of Bath and other spas, and later Brighton, created wider opportunities for structured social intercourse in which prosperous families, both gentry and upper middle class, could meet under supervision and contacts be formed.

At the higher social levels, women were very important in the early stages of the formation of relationships. The fifteenth-century humanist Alberti had intimated this to be the case in Renaissance Florence:

> When by the urging and counsel of their elders and of the whole family, young men have arrived at the point of marriage, their mothers and other female relatives and friends, who have known the virgins of the neighbourhood from earliest childhood and know the way their upbringing has formed them, should select all the well born and well brought up girls and present the list to the new groom to be.[31]

This text summarizes effective practice throughout all the countries we are concerned with, as well as showing that grooms might have some choice in the matter where brides had little or none. Mothers, aunts, godmothers and trusted friends exchanged letters which conveyed news of prospective partners and at social events ranging from mass to dinner parties and dances chaperoned and presented their girls. The older generation of women sat around the dance floor and watched while they conveyed and picked up information. They approved or disapproved of particular individuals, counselled on the appropriate behaviour of their charges and schemed for the right introductions. 'Word' circulated about the size of a dowry, the importance of relatives and the possibilities of an inheritance.[32] When serious negotiations began, however (though important widows constitute exceptions), the women usually had to cede to the men and the father of a prospective husband or his kinsman or even the man himself – particularly if his parents were dead or he had entered into his estate – had to negotiate with the father of the prospective bride or with her kinsmen if the father was dead. That was man's work. Rumour was at once replaced by reality.

In the provinces there existed networks of solid families who enjoyed a quiet affluence far from the capitals. High rentals and food prices brought an ever-increasing prosperity to this section of the population in the eighteenth century. With investments in land, government stock, and on the Continent in offices, this section of the population was remarkably endogamous. The French nobles of the parlements (*de robe*) intermarried and thus consolidated their standing in the courts and in the locality. This nobility or gentry was copied in its behaviour by the substantial middle classes, merchants, solid farmers, lawyers, clergymen (in Protestant countries) and doctors. Again, and for very practical reasons, there was considerable intermarriage among professional groups. Marriage, it was hoped, would cement business relations or perhaps bring two already large farms together one day. In seventeenth-century London and Amsterdam merchant and burgher families are known to have fostered relationships by inviting family contacts and their families to dine so that young people could have supervised opportunities to become acquainted. Families and friends contrived to arrange occasions – dinners, dances, musical entertainments, Twelfth Night festivals and picnics – where contact could be reinforced. Throughout the early modern period, parents placed emphasis on musical accomplishments, if only singing, because a girl's performance might be one way of presenting her in an engaging manner. Carrying a piece of competent needlework might be another: it was not for nothing that seventeenth-century Dutch burghers had their daughters painted with some evidence of such needlework skills beside them, and the presence of a lute or spinet in sixteenth- and seventeenth-century Italian and Dutch works also betokened 'womanly accomplishments'.

Obviously, the behaviour of these social groups bore more than a slight affinity to that of the highest classes, even if a more egalitarian distribution of parental assets among children prevailed. But did a freer choice operate at these social levels? There is evidence to support both replies in England and Holland. Edward Coke, the father of English liberties in his struggle against the absolutist tendencies of the Stuarts, tied his daughter to the bedpost and whipped her until she agreed to the match he had arranged for her with a member of the Duke of Buckingham's family. The marriage was a disaster.[33] Alice Thornton in the mid-seventeenth century married in accordance with her mother's request although it was contrary to her own inclinations. The same was true of Mrs Delaney more than fifty years later. Both were deeply resentful of their parents. On the other hand, Lucy Hutchinson, who described her courtship by Colonel Hutchinson as equal to that of a French romance, had previously resisted all pressure from her mother and friends and marked their displeasure 'that she refused so many offers which they thought advantageous enough.' Thomas Blundell accepted the refusal of his daughter Molly to undertake a match that he had recommended with gracious resignation:

> I have long since told her that I would not compel her to marry, much less to marry one she could not love and so to make her miserable as long as she lives, so to leave her entirely to please herself . . . All I require is that he be a gentleman of a competent estate, one of good character and a catholic.[34]

This kind of attitude is abundantly documented even for the harsher seventeenth century and it leaves the impression that English parents were, generally if not invariably, concerned that their children's marriages should be based on affection, with due emphasis as well on substance, and that this willingness increased in the later part of the period. However, there is no doubt that girls reared in closely confined circumstances under the watchful eye of their parents could be subjected to moral pressures from family and friends not to let a particular opportunity pass. Spinsterhood was a threat and it was one which the middle classes knew as well as the aristocracy. The dilemma of Charlotte Lucas in Jane Austen's *Pride and Prejudice* – celibacy or Mr Collins – would have been recognized by many women who could expect little financial support from their parents.

Parental influence perhaps bore a direct relationship to the amount of money they would put into a match, and whether their children were living at home. Parental constraint could be limited to a withholding of funds or severance of contact. In Amsterdam there existed from the seventeenth century a specialist firm of lawyers to whom a young couple of age (twenty-five for a man, twenty for a woman), and who could afford the fees, could appeal if parental consent were withheld. In contrast, at rural Twente in the Netherlands parents seem to have maintained the right to withhold assent even from adult children as late as the eighteenth century.[35]

Literature and society gossip abounded with stories of young people who eloped, flouting parental authority. It would appear that at most social levels parents wanted to maintain contact with their children, and when a son or daughter married without their consent, most expressed sorrow but few allowed retribution to go much further.

For the farmer's daughter, reared in a particular area and whose family had a close knowledge of the sons of neighbours, choice was geographically circumscribed. Those who lived at home and never left the neighbourhood where they were born, married into families known to their parents and relatives. In English villages up to 80 per cent found a spouse from within a ten-mile radius and the same seems to have been true in most of rural Europe. Initiatives seem to have been left to the groom or his family. The girl's father had to be asked for his permission to court and later to marry his daughter. The young man would have to list his expectations and he would expect the father of the girl to retail hers. At this point in time, the future bride's role seems passive, but mothers were known to help or hinder the promotion of a young man's suit and discussion between mother and daughter may have also been a preliminary to determining how a father responded to advances from a young man. However, at all levels of society the norm was for initiatives and discussions to be the work of the men of the families.

In Ireland from the sixteenth century a woman's dowry was counted almost entirely in the number of cows she could provide. Chieftain families settled for eighty cows and even more, gentry for forty, a Limerick fisherman, Thomas Heyrie, in the 1590s accepted a dowry with his wife of 'three cows and three heifers, 21 sheep, a brass pan worth forty shillings, two pairs of sheets a bushel of beare [winter barley] and three shillings in money'.[36] At the bottom level one cow and a bed or bedding persisted as the commonest Irish dowry. These were the kind of details that were revealed when a father heard and accepted a proposal from a young man and was satisfied that the man in question had some substance on which the young couple could establish themselves.

The woman who had been an upper farm servant and who had suffered no interruptions in her period of labour would have little trouble in her middle twenties in finding a male farm worker (in France a *valet de ferme*) whose efforts equalled her own; depending on the availability of a holding – not in the conditions of the late eighteenth century to be taken for granted – they could proceed to marriage. Even if the woman had as a girl left the country for the town, she was not necessarily precluded from returning home with her little sum and settling down as a smallholder's wife, just as many country boys who had served an urban apprenticeship hoped to return home and be farmers. Certain smallholding societies were chronically dependent upon this influx of capital when the young returned from their urban labours. To take an example, in a mountain village like Massat in the Pyrénées Ariégoises, holdings were very small. There was virtually no such thing as a substantial farm and absolutely no demand for resident labour. Farming families who lived in the village were dependent on seasonal migration for survival, particularly winter movements into Spanish cities. The young left in their teens to become servants in Toulouse, but they did not lose the urge to return to their native village.[37] That urge might spring from family loyalty or from more mundane considerations such as an alliance with someone who might one day own a patch of land through inheritance. In these smallholding societies, the relationship with the land was often the crucial factor and the ownership of a few terraced strips constantly under the threat of erosion from the intemperate climate could appear to offer the young couple greater security than anything available in the town.

The return of the children of Massat to their snow-clad hills was in direct contrast to the strategy of another group of servant girls and apprentices in Toulouse who had come into that city at the age of twelve or fourteen. These were from the Lauragais, an area of large farms which used seasonal but not much resident labour. Some of these farms were owned by large *parlementaire* families who held high office in the great provincial law court of Languedoc and who imported girls to work as servants in their Toulouse houses, but many more came into the city for lowlier jobs. There was no hope of renting a farm back in their native villages, so the young men and also the young women had made a severance with their place of origin. Capital cities throughout Europe drew in these youngsters. Indeed, they may have been the bulk of the better servant sector. The question was, whom would they chose to marry?

A percentage of servant marriages may have been to other servants (though by the end of the period it must have been small, given the preponderance of women in service). The demand for married servants was low and the couple who intended to remain all their lives in service probably had to wait for an opening. Affluent ecclesiastics preferred to employ a married couple to avoid rumours of scandalous behaviour, and substantial noble and bourgeois households were often relieved enough to retain the services of specialist servants known to be honest. However, the demand was not great.

Some servant girls married tradesmen who often came to the back door delivering commissions. Or they married into the most numerous artisan or apprentice group in the area where they lived. In the Santa Croce area of Florence, for example, the dominant male employment was tanning and, not surprisingly, most maidservants married tanners. Since such girls did not live at home parental assent was not regarded as a sine qua non. By the age of twenty-four, when most girls were contemplating matrimony within the next year or so, many were already orphaned. There is plenty of evidence from city records of couples making their own choices. In London, for example, at the beginning of the seventeenth century, a Hertfordshire girl, daughter of a modest farmer unable to provide her with a dowry, spoke thus:

> Her said father doth not yet know of this entended marriage but when he shall understand thereof he will be verie glad of it because it is for her preferment (her father being but a very poor man and having more children is not able to give mutch at marriage with her).[38]

Many servants were, of course, in households where the head exercised a degree of patriarchal control and expected to be consulted, if not about who the woman intended to marry at least about when. As long as the girl remained in his service his consent had to be sought. However, since the job usually entailed resignation on marriage and the payment of her accumulated wages, the servant would give her notice to leave and need no longer ask the employer's permission. Between departure and marriage she would move in with her intended husband or his relatives or friends. During such a phase the husband-to-be assumed a protective role. The case of Sybil Powell in 1607 follows a typical pattern. She was the twenty-year-old daughter of a Worcestershire husbandman who had died five years earlier. She was thus described by a gentleman of St Martin's Ludgate:

> The mother of the said Sybil Powell is a poor woman and not able to bestow any portion upon her and therefore has left her to her own disposition. And that the said Sybil has inhabited in and about London for the most part these past seven years . . . and was servant to him [Edward Pye] about four years . . . and is now out of service, remaining at the house of one Henry Lackland of St Sepulchre, turner and brother of the said Richard [the groom] who placed her there about three weeks since and maintains her at his own cost until such a time as they shall be married conveniently.[39]

These were women who, far from their family of origin, had undertaken marriage according to their own choice, and where such a distance prevailed this looks to have been the dominant pattern. One could not in any society at any time arrange marriages for people of 24-plus who had laboured for twelve or more years to support themselves. Such couples were old enough to be capable of mature judgements. The literature of good advice counselled writing home to tell one's parents of the character and assets of the intended partner as in the model letter of 1653 'From a young woman in service, to her mother in the country, to ask her advice whether she should marry her master's apprentice'. But at this time only a small proportion of working girls could write and we cannot know how many of their parents could read. Distance imposed independence.

What then shaped choice of partner at these social levels? Clearly some physical attraction and compatibility of disposition were deemed important by those who have left diaries commenting on their election of spouse. Astrologers were frequently consulted to endorse the choice of a partner and to ascertain whether any double dealing was taking place. Popular ballads abounded with paeans to the trim figure and the bright eyes, even if physical attraction was presented in popular aphorisms as a will o' the wisp. In these societies, the man or woman who was not pock-marked and suffering from vitamin deficiency diseases, congenital defects or industrial malformations counted as handsome. A girl without varicose veins by her mid-twenties was deemed unusual in Franche Comté. Beauty, it should be remembered, is in the eye of the beholder.[40]

Attraction and affection, however, had to coexist with the prospect of sufficiency. A girl who was known to have been saving steadily for several years and was well esteemed by her employers, one who was also good-tempered and agreeable, could be an irresistible proposition for a young man. Such a girl could afford to be choosy. Money had a way of rendering even the plain and otherwise disadvantaged more attractive. With a small dowry even the mother of an illegitimate child could find a husband, as the Ospedale degli Innocenti in Florence knew well. This institution was a central distribution centre of dowries for foundling girls throughout Tuscany and it is worthy of note that whatever the premium on chastity attached by the church to sexual relations, it did not necessarily withhold funds from a woman who married someone other than the father of her child. The Soccorso of Bologna, inaugurated by the impeccably rigid and authoritarian Cardinal Paleotti, recognized that even whoring was justifiable in the cause of accumulating a dowry; and the prostitute was helped to take action against clients who would not pay and hence kept her on the streets longer than was needful. These were standards which churchmen outside Italy would not have accepted, but they show how money could triumph over shame.[41]

The evidence, then, would suggest that in much of Europe until the twentieth century, wealth played a vital part in determining who married whom. For many of the landless in areas of Roman law, where the bride had no dowry there was no formal marriage – though clearly free unions were not uncommon. Girls with means, on the other hand, need never lack a husband. The purse triumphed over the heart. The prior of Sennely en Sologne in 1700 commented on the practices of his parishioners:

> They get married out of financial interest rather than any other inclination. Most of them when looking for a bride only ask how many sheep she can bring in marriage. Women and girls who have lost their honour are not precluded from the search. It is a daily occurrence to see a man take a wretched bride, pregnant by someone else and adopt the child for a modest sum.[42]

Sennely en Sologne was a parish of the most abject poverty and the parish priest was observing behaviour which he considered both lax and based on values which he as an educated man and a Catholic found hard to accept. Had he lived in a more affluent area, he might have been less despairing. Indeed, the gloomiest views of matrimony continued throughout the period to be held by clerics. Other sources attest less grudgingly to the joys of courtship.

Most young people, wherever they lived in western Europe, sought to bring their marriage plans together in their mid-twenties. Roger Lowe, an apprentice mercer, felt he was approaching the time for marriage in 1663 when he saw reasonable prospects of the mastership and a livelihood. However, he waited five years to wed Emm Potter, whom he met in the company of friends and relatives in an alehouse during Ashton Wakes in 1664. His courtship of Emm consisted of walks and drinks in the company of friends as well as escorting her to weddings and funerals. At the latter he also met her parents. Emm waited, however, before making up her mind.[43]

It seems to have been common for a man or woman to have a clear view of their prospects before courtship began. The future husband had to have the expectation of a farm; the urban apprentice had to wait to finish his apprenticeship; the industrial worker might have to raise the means to purchase or hire machinery and rent premises. However, that did not stop many from having someone in view. Chance obviously played its part in determining the contacts made, but the wider community mobilized itself to facilitate encounters for the young in circumstances, if less formal, certainly reminiscent of opportunities arranged by the upper classes. One practice, the evening get-together, *veillée* or working bee, brought old and young together and allowed the unmarried the opportunity for contact under supervision. Above all in France, the *veillée* was an evening work session carried out in particular farmsteads or cottages in which neighbours gathered and shared the cost of heat and light. Everyone was engaged in an activity, even if it was only cracking nuts for oil or putting pins on paper to fill a pedlar's tray. In the nuclear village or the small town this kind of working session could be a nightly event in winter. It was the scene of chapbook reading and story-telling, of ballad or hymn singing, while needles clicked and the old discussed the conduct of seigneur, priest and tax agent. For the young, those living at home, servants or apprentices, this could be the occasion to become acquainted, to exchange looks and smiles, and to share a bench, a common task and conversation. In more sparsely populated areas, *veillées* were less frequent and had to be arranged occasionally by hiring a barn. Then they were predominantly for entertainment: indeed, the element of sociability was paramount in Italy, where dancing and jollification ruled. Still, however, they were occasions for everybody and the young were exposed to each other while the older and wiser kept an indulgent eye on their behaviour.

In some regions, like the lace-making centres of the Pays de Velay, or certain German villages, the *veillée* or *Spinnstube* was an exclusively female function to help increase the output of work and the men, for whom little domestic employment existed, sought distraction elsewhere. The lines between male and female sociability were drawn much more firmly and church or the Sunday afternoon readings of saints' lives and pious works held during the winter were the only regular means of contact, however distant.

The German *Spinnstube* belongs emphatically in the tradition of European working bees, but it bore some imprint of the cleansing hand of the Reformation. The events were held by the unmarried of the village, mostly the women, who engaged in spinning or knitting against a background of music or story-telling, but they were visited for a part of the time by the unmarried men – hence the attempts at suppression by the church, which wanted closer moral policing. A totally desexualized gathering of working women alone was perhaps the church's goal. Priests and magistrates appealed to parents to exert control over their daughters. Enlightenment observers in the eighteenth century praised the linking of work and sociability. In fact, it was impossible to eliminate sensuality and boisterousness among the unmarried at the *Spinnstube*. The young women of each village appreciated that the gathering was a part of sociability, contact and linkage to the marriage market. Even when men were excluded, the girls talked of matrimony, the deeds of men, and helped a bride-to-be, once the marriage was in sight, to gather a trousseau.[44]

Where the *veillée* or its equivalent took place infrequently, then religious festivals, processions and dances assumed a preponderant part in helping promote contact between the young. In most instances, the young men arranged their own entertainments for these festivals. The young bachelors of the parish elected a leader (*le chef*) to be a kind of master of ceremonies. They also chose one of their number to bang the drum and hired a fife player, arranged the procession which initiated the proceedings and set up the local tavern keeper to provide drink in the outside setting. The dancing that followed the procession was the high spot.

Sometimes, as a preliminary to the festival's events, the leader initiated *dônages* or pairing procedures. He pronounced, usually as a result of drawing lots, *je dône Pierre à Marie*. This could oblige the young woman in question to no more than a dance or a number of dances. If it was known that Marie touched Pierre's fancy, then a little conspiracy could be undertaken to promote the outcome of the *dônage*.[45]

Youth groups in southern France met every Sunday evening throughout the period. Sometimes they were all-male gatherings, which might come together to arrange brief dances. Sometimes they were bolder in organization. In Burgundy, for example, at the beginning of winter the village bachelors met after Twelfth Night to divide up the parish girls among themselves. Lots might be drawn, but usually an element of amicable bartering and exchange occurred. Once the choice or selection had been made there was no changing, and the couple met for public events organized by the group until the year was up.

The Counter-Reformation church throughout France tried to break up the youth groups, whose activities clerics regarded as verging on the permissive. They deplored the dancing as lascivious and the drinking as dangerous for the chastity of the women. They were not successful. The young had their rituals, rites of passage, and this had to be recognized.

A variant on these practices in the Protestant Netherlands were the festivals where the young would orchestrate an evening's entertainment using the services of a professional broker, who would move among the village young and negotiate a temporary match. In Schagen on *kermis* day the eligible young would line up in the church square and a regulating official, perhaps chosen for the day, would weed out those too old, those too young, or outsiders from other villages who were intruding. Then pairing off would begin and the young man had to pay for his companion's cakes and ale for the occasion.[46]

Like their Catholic counterparts, this did not please the Calvinist clergy. They too condemned dancing as unseemly. The Synod of Gorinchem in 1652 objected to 'ill-considered outings by young people' and in particular to goose-pulling tournaments where girls could fall over, showing more of their anatomy than was deemed modest. In 1644 the Synod of The Hague made extravagant claims that libertine practices among the young meant that scarcely four in forty came to marriage 'with decent conduct'. The standards of these Protestant clerics were perhaps very high and what they meant by decent conduct is almost impossible to discern. At the time they were voicing these complaints illegitimacy levels had apparently never been lower. Mid-seventeenth century Protestantism in Britain, Germany and the Netherlands would seem to have asserted a tight control over the sexual behaviour of the rural masses which disintegrated by the end of the seventeenth century in Britain and in the eighteenth century in Holland. In 1801 a reprint of seven colloquies made by a priest of Emmerich, which drew on an earlier Brabantine work, censured rural parents for their tolerance. They had too casual an attitude towards evening visits of young men to the house, and they allowed the two sexes to work in proximity in the fields. Dancing and drinking accompanied weddings, and even funerals were used as matchmaking opportunities. The priest sought to impose on the masses the stricter control over courting found in more exemplary bourgeois households.[47]

In towns and cities, fairs, wakes and festivals took the place of the *veillées* and *kermesses*. Most young workers had a few hours off on a Sunday afternoon although they had no entitlement to this. They seized the opportunity to dress up, to wear a clean cap, a scrap of lace on the bodice, and shoes rather than clogs. Thus arrayed, they sallied forth on the walk or the *promenade*, a set itinerary known to all the young of the town.[48]

No one ever went alone. Girls went with fellow servants or workers, apprentices with their workmates. On the walk their paths crossed and they accosted one another. Girls saw boys from their native villages and exchanged news. The grocer's boy who delivered to the back door could now address the maidservant who took in the goods. Badinage and laughter enlivened the worst weather. Sometimes the walk was merely along the main street. Sometimes it was a tour of certain public buildings or public parks. In larger cities there were several walks and certain trades or immigrant communities had preferences. In time groups broke up into couples, but it could be several weeks or months into a relationship before two people were actually seen walking together apart from their friends, and the date at which this separating out occurred would be noted by the friends of both parties as the first visible sign of the beginning of a courtship. This was not only of interest to the entire community. If anything should later go wrong between the two, and the girl find herself, say, abandoned and pregnant, then how the courts and the community viewed the conduct of the young man depended partially on the longevity of the relationship and his known behaviour towards her.

As a development from this pairing, the young man would be seen buying a drink or a small luxury like a pie, sweetmeats or sugared almonds for the girl. These manifestations were also noted by the peer group. If the relationship were to develop further a few small presents might change hands, but they would be of a rigorously practical nature. Knitting needles, a packet of pins or needles, or a lace bobbin bearing the couple's initials were more likely gifts than combs and ribbons unless it was a festival. Letters with expressions of affection were very acceptable and a special genre of model love letters existed in both English and French. To have a written token of affection of this kind showed seriousness of intent. Eventually, the couple might take to more secluded walks away from the group in the woods or on the ramparts.[49]

In Mediterranean towns and villages, walking with one's relatives had a particular part to play in sociability patterns. Along with attending mass, walking perhaps constituted the only opportunity the young had to view each other. The tendency in such societies to seek young brides, who in Sicily, for example, would not have left the parental home and would not be expected to furnish their own dowry, meant that relatives carefully mediated whatever association might occur. Once an approach had been made to parents and accepted by them, and tokens exchanged which all could inspect, older village women might act as chaperones and keep a distance – though not permitting the couple to pass from view – while they walked and talked and built up some knowledge of each other. Such at any rate was the situation for girls from well-ordered families.

The period of courtship was also a period of serious future planning. It was the time for assessing how successful either party had been in fulfilling their strategic plan and what this earning period of their life could now contribute to the next step on the ladder of life. What have we (the couple) got in hand? What can we count on to come to us from parents, from our own efforts? If we work another couple of years before marriage will this enhance our economic strength? What potential for leasing a farm exists in our village? Do we have the means to stock it? Can the bride provide a bed and blankets, textiles to see us through, kitchen utensils, a cow? The urban working-class couple had a different range of questions. For the apprentice, did the marriage offer the prospect of purchasing the mastership? For the female servant, do I go back home to my village with my earnings? What prospects lie there for me? Or what kind of joint livelihood can my intended husband and I make in the town? Am I eligible for help through a dowry fund? Should my father or widowed mother make an application on my behalf or as an orphan do I have to do it myself? Will the parish priest help me to do this? Will he back my application or write it for me? In what terms should I present my future husband to the foundation?

Considerable personal variations obviously intruded in all these questions. Increasingly in the face of industrial development changes were occurring in some regions of Europe. If a putting-out system existed, another question might be: would spinning as a source of income serve to make marriage viable with less capital resources? If industrial work for both parties existed, could they marry without further delay? Answers to these questions depended on how viable an industry was regarded in the long term or in the second instance on whether work for men existed outside guild regulation. Silk weaving in Lyons, for example, required an apprenticeship and entry rates to guilds were high. In contrast, cotton production in north-west England imposed few restraints.

Good advice literature counselled the maidservant to think carefully at this juncture and perhaps put her money into a little business to preserve her in widowhood. Clerics and commentators frequently bemoaned the lack of foresight, the failure of couples to calculate and make provision for future hardship. Certainly, the precariousness of the future family economy is striking for those who fell into Defoe's bottom three categories, or belonged to perhaps the bottom fifth of the French population, or somewhat more than that of Tuscany or Ireland. Optimism prevailed if industrial slump or reduced harvest was not on the doorstep. If either was present, then the couple waited for normality to return. They lived in hope.

In settled communities, family, clan and peer group could encourage a particular match. Evidence suggests that in many rural societies, in parts of England, Scotland, France and Germany, the promise of marriage, widely known about in the community, continued to be taken very seriously. Once it had been given, and without waiting for the church ceremony, there was less strictness in the invigilation of the young couple and there were customs (bundling, night-courting) in which they (often in the company of other couples gathered for the same purpose) were left alone together all night with the promise (helped by a few layers of clothes) not to let petting advance too far. In some north European villages the pregnancy of the bride before marriage may have proved the fertility of the union. However, taken overall, it is patent that pre-marital pregnancies probably reflect a serious relationship which went too far rather than a general sanction of sexual relations outside marriage. It is very clear that in Tuscany, after the new laws emanating from Trent, a number of court cases demonstrated that the promise (before the church ceremony) had been the signal for carnal relations. The new legislation permitted a few men to wriggle out of a relationship they now regretted. The Catholic church after 1563 appears to have had considerable difficulties in driving home to the masses (not the élites) that the church sacrament, not the customary public promise, was the more serious affair and the only guarantee of matrimony. It tried, however, to insist that betrothal should take place with marriage in view and hence precede the marriage by no more than a year so as not to strain the instincts of the contracting parties too far.

Tradition and difference in adaptation to the new regulations of the reformers doubtless go some way to explain the huge differences between levels of pre-marital pregnancies over the sixteenth and seventeenth centuries. The English situation, where most ambiguity reigned in the sixteenth century and the church was slower to assert a control of matrimony, shows that about a fifth of rural children were conceived, though not born, out of wedlock. Numbers fell in the seventeenth century. In France there was considerable difference between region and region, but again the trend is downwards as the grip of the clergy tightened in the seventeenth century. The German and Dutch reformed clergy also waged an unremitting and not always successful battle against custom.

Some left with bastards on their hands may have been girls of rural origin who carried belief in 'the promise' into the more fluid relationships of the towns. Certainly the growth of cities, accompanied by the numbers of young people in precarious urban jobs, seems to have multiplied the numbers of infants deemed illegitimate by the priests who kept parish registers. Up to 17 per cent of all births in certain French cities by the end of the old regime were outside marriage and some of these were doubtless the product of unions which were not casual but where the parties concerned had few resources and were not prepared to spend their precious money on church endorsement. In short, from London to Seville, clerical control receded in the city where the best ordered plans tended to disintegrate.[50]

In Britain up to 1750 the average age at marriage was about twenty-six, falling to just over twenty-three by 1800. In France the age oscillated between twenty-two and twenty-four during the seventeenth century and had risen by the end of the old regime to over twenty-six. In both countries the average husband was two years older than the average wife. The couple belonged then largely to the same age group and uneven matches, in terms of age, were unusual. In Germany, according to Michael Mitterauer, the remarriage of an artisan's widow who could hand on the mastership, or of a woman with a farm, to a younger man could lead to a greater gap in age distribution between spouses.[51]

Most statistics reflect above all the behaviour of the rural masses, who constituted the bulk of the population, and their oscillations reflect the hardness or ease of the times. In the aftermath of plague there would always be a rash of marriages and remarriages as households which had lost one partner reconstituted themselves. More people would then experience matrimony. On the other hand, demographic growth could mean rising rentals, engrossment of holdings and hence fewer farms available for lease, and dearer food. Couples would have to wait longer and save longer. Hence the contrasting experience of France and Britain in the eighteenth century reveals more than anything else the strains experienced in the French countryside as population grew without a concomitant economic expansion to support it. Dutch evidence suggests that in Holland, too, the prosperity of the seventeenth century favoured earlier marriage, but that in the more difficult agrarian conditions and industrial depression experienced by the Republic in the eighteenth century marriages took place later and there were more who never married at all.[52]

The north-western marriage pattern contrasts with that in Mediterranean lands, though the contrasts are reduced over the period. In the fifteenth century in Italy and Spain, the age differential between partners could be as much as fifteen years, with the girls marrying at fourteen and the men at twenty-nine.[53] The range narrowed over the next two centuries with the women marrying later. Such a system may have ensured the chastity of the bride upon marriage but it was also tailor-made to produce widows, and the age differential may also have contributed to a relationship between husband and wife which was less egalitarian in terms of experience of the world than that prevailing in the north-west. However, by the end of the period, the age differential was much the same as in the north-west of Europe.

Once the business of finding a partner was accomplished and the prospect of marriage was in sight, assets mobilized, betrothal promises exchanged, the solidity and prospects of the couple were known to all. The couple from Massat whose only assets after a decade of labour on the part of both parties was the rental of a small farm and a dancing bear which he could lead around the towns and villages in winter to rake together a few sous to send back home, and the aristocratic lady whose dowry included money, jewels, furniture and clothes, faced predictably different futures. Wealth may not have guaranteed either happiness or satisfaction, but poverty generated a whole Pandora's box of problems which could menace the long-term viability of a union.

CHAPTER FOUR

On Being a Wife

Jack Sprat could eat no fat
His wife could eat no lean
And so between the two of them
They licked the platter clean.
OLD ENGLISH NURSERY RHYME

The *Lichstuben* (collective working bees) of the married women are more seldom, because the time is just not enough for them, and during the evenings they still have many tasks in the house, the care of the children, etc. When these tasks are finished, they then take their rest in order to build up new energy for the next day. Also the jealousy of the men when their faithful partners leave the four walls, causes them to look askance at the possibility.
ANON, DIE LICHSTUBE, 1587

ON THE ladder of life the married state occupied a special rung at the top and the wedding ceremony was a critical rite of passage. Church, state, kin and community all had a stake in this important event.

If the first strove to regulate marriage through a public and publicized church ceremony proclaiming the legitimacy of any future offspring, kin and community transformed the event into something which marked the standing of the couple and indicated just where they belonged in the social order. Surrounding a union were celebratory rituals. Where such did not exist or were very perfunctory, the very lack of social display proclaimed the precariousness of the new unit. Poverty did not rule out a church marriage, legitimized in the eyes of God, but it might cost too much in terms of fees and community expectations. Hence, at the bottom of the social scale in England, clandestine marriages (performed by some kind of priest but with lower fees and without banns and rituals) continued until 1753 when they were made illegal under Hardwicke's Marriage Act. Thereafter, an incalculable proportion of the English poor joined their counterparts in continental Europe and simply formed free unions.

The churches sought to shift attention from the celebratory rituals which could cost families dear to the church ceremony – in the case of Catholics pronounced one of the seven sacraments. All churches wanted solemnity, a recognition of the gravity of the occasion as well as publicity. The exchange of rings, symbol and marker of marriage, was endorsed as fitting.[1] The churches were set against street weddings and, even if they succeeded in getting the pair into church, railed remorselessly against traditions in which the groom appeared inebriated at the altar.[2] German Protestant reformers went so far as to refuse to conduct a marriage under these conditions. Notwithstanding efforts to instil gravity, the wedding was a mixture of the sacred and the joyously celebratory, even profane, an expression of family and community involvement.

Weddings broke down into a number of categories with considerable overlap. There were those financed by family and kin, those provided by family and kin with some input by the guests, and those where the guests paid to share the feast. Absolutely central to many village weddings was the esteem in which the bride was held. In certain parts of England, Wales, Lutheran Germany and German-speaking Switzerland, communities mobilized themselves to contribute to the new household and celebrations through the 'brideswain' or its equivalent.

In Yorkshire tradition had it that the wedding was preceded by a bidding or brideswain wherein the wife-to-be sat spinning in a wagon which was dragged round the village. Neighbours and kin threw coins or the cart was loaded with furniture and utensils, new or old with some wear left in them, which would help the couple to set up house. In Cumberland, before the wedding day the groom's family invited neighbours and kin for 'various passtimes' – a social evening, no less – which involved a collection of money. Depending on the wealth of the kin, anything from a few to a hundred pounds could be raised. A similar practice existed in Glamorganshire, where days before the wedding a simple repast of plain and fruit bread, butter and cheese and ale was offered by the bride's parents or kin and then a collection plate was passed round. Relatives might be expected to give five shillings and friends a shilling and the collection could add up to £25, almost as much as the dowry or the bride's savings. Catherine Hutton described the economics of a wedding feast in eighteenth-century Glamorgan which sought to minimize expenditure for the bride's family and help the couple at the same time. A marriage could take place for four shillings, three for the vicar and one for the clerk. Afterwards 'the more the better' went to the public house and paid a shilling for dinner and sixpence for tea. If the father of the bride could afford it he paid for the meal himself and then all the collected sum went to the bride; if not, the costs were deducted and the residue presented to her. In this way everyone helped.[3] In Lutheran Germany a bridal cart, in which the bride sat wreathed in flowers, circulated the village or small town bearing all the wedding gifts and crowned by the linen prepared collectively for the marriage by the unmarried women in her age cohort and by the bride herself. The linen was a symbol not only of the bride's industry but of the esteem of her contemporaries and, as well as providing an exercise in ostentatious display, the intent was to raise more giving.

Everyone dressed up as finely as they could for the wedding feast. Smart clothes could be hired, in Italian cities from the Jews who made a speciality of offering expensive materials and costume jewellery. Indeed wherever Jewish communities existed, they seem to have been involved in the loan of finery and 'glad rags'. For wealthy families everywhere the costs could be very high. Thousands of *gulden*, *livres*, and pounds were expended on an aristocratic wedding. An English gentry family probably spent up to £200, a yeoman or solid farmer up to £50 and a labouring family somewhere between five shillings and five pounds.[4] Many spent more than they could afford in an attempt to raise the social standing of the bride's family as well as that of the couple.

The most expensive occasions in Europe were probably those at Versailles where enormous fees were given to clergy and scribes and musicians even before the clothes and the banquets were taken into account. The marriage of Lucy Dillon extended over several days. The contract was signed in the presence of the king, the royal family and the court. There then followed several days in which lavish presents were offered to the bride by relatives of both families and by friends and courtiers. The husband endowed her with a large basket containing precious jewellery, lace, ribbons, gloves, hats and clothes. The Princesse de Hernin's present was a table laden with a Sèvres tea service and there were many of equal worth. Then came the day of the religious ceremony conducted by the Archbishop of Toulouse, with the bishops of Langue-doc, the Archbishop of Paris, several ministers of the crown, generals and about sixty other guests. The Minister of War gave the new husband a month's leave from his military duties. After the service in the chapel at Montfermeil, all the women present, according to age and degree of relationship to the bride, kissed her and she for her part undertook a distribution of expensive souvenirs: fans for the ladies, epaulettes for the military men, hatbands for the prelates. Then the great feast began and the bride, in white silk covered in Brussels lace, presided over the four-hour banquet. Outside, the servants had a feast too and after the formal dinner Lucy went out to them while they drank her health. Over the next few days spent with her husband, she practised the curtsey and chose what she would wear when presented at court as a married woman, Madame de Gouvernet, Marquise de la Tour du Pin.[5]

Each step in this elaborate series of rituals established the young aristocratic couple in the society of which they were a part. Two clans were united. Everything appropriate to their rank had been carried out.

In towns where the guilds were strong they were caught up in the marriages of their members. A master should be married and therefore the step could be a rite of passage between the state of journeyman and that of master. In Augsburg the eve of the wedding was marked by a drinking party where master and journeymen rubbed shoulders, but at the wedding feast itself the masters sat separately and later only danced with their wives, while the young men processed separately and sat together and danced with as many young women as possible. This was an opportunity for making acquaintances that could not be neglected.[6]

The role of the bride during the wedding could in general be described as passive. She was led by the friends of the groom to the church, she was given away by her father, she was joined in matrimony, and finally she was bedded. She promised to honour and to obey and she was placed under the protection of her husband. However, the positive participation of brides in the biddings and brideswains and the rituals of the feast in north-western Europe served to make the figure of the new wife more authoritative. She was mistress of the feast. The presents in money and kind were put into her hands. She provided the appurtenances of the new dwelling, if not the dwelling itself, and she could proudly demonstrate her contribution. She had 'something to show'. These furnishings and any livestock were a testimony to her input into the marriage, markers of her substance and her identity as wife.

In contrast to wedding feasts in which plenty ruled, and the bride took pride in her trousseau and linen, was the marriage described in the Occitan tale about the rise of Jean l'Ont Pris told by the Abbé Fabre in 1745. The opening scene depicts a beggar's feast of baked birds and hedgehogs with berries and stolen fruit, provided by the family of the bride for guests drawn from the dregs of society. A wedding of this kind could probably never have taken place, since the couple in the story could not even have afforded the cost of the church ceremony. Rather the tale is a satire, an aping of the manners of the propertied by the propertyless, and told to inform the reader of exactly where the hero's parents stood in the village hierarchy.[7] Instead of this fictional feast of hastily raked together free food, a penniless, dowryless or virtually resourceless pair might celebrate their union with a few drinks or simply not bother. The French historian Pierre Chaunu posited that it was at the lower levels of society that free choice of spouse existed, but such a statement ignores the dreadful fragility of the unions of the very poor. This level of the population was illiterate and has left little testimony as to how a union in which both were without means was conducted.

A number of memoirs, of an unusual kind because they emanate from women who became literate later in life within a convent, shed light on some of the difficulties that could be involved in a marriage with great age disparity even – perhaps there more than anywhere else – at the very bottom of the social scale. A sixteenth-century Spanish nun who found her way to Mexico tells us how she lost her father as a young girl and her mother at fourteen. Even before her mother died, as the youngest in a family of limited resources, her kin had valued her little and put her out on the hillsides, barefoot, in all weathers to guard the flock. However, after her mother's death she was promptly negotiated in marriage to a man of seventy, also a farmer. No one seems to have consulted her and she records no wedding ceremony in church or outside, no celebratory gifts. It may well be that the girl herself did not protest because she feared the violence of her kin if she should refuse and knew she had nowhere else to go. Her family did not part with a dowry and her new husband's family may have been interested in her for her physical strength, because she was of child-bearing age, and to satisfy the sexual urges of the old man. That he had such urges is fully apparent. The young girl found herself a drudge by day and subject to the physical demands of a toothless and repellent husband by night. She tells us that she preserved her sanity by closing her eyes and thinking of the relationship of the blessed Virgin with Saint Joseph – also an old man and one whose cult was more popular in Spain than elsewhere. 'Widowed' in a short space of time, without children and still in her teens, she had no claims whatsoever on her husband's family who simply sent her back to her kin. She now knew she was at risk. Her family had no use for her and might attempt a repetition of her previous marriage to spare themselves her keep. She had nowhere to go and turned to an aunt who pitied her and took her to a convent which was finally persuaded to take her as a servant.[8]

This is a tale from which many inferences can be drawn. One is that outside the dowry system in countries of Roman law, there was little dignity for women. With a dowry this woman could have had a husband on terms of respect. Without it she was a slave. Another inference is that the girl was entirely at the mercy of her kin and simply had no conception of life outside her village or any notion that if she ran away anyone would feed her. Uneducated, though not unintelligent as her poetry was to show, she demonstrates the predicament of the lowest level of women in rural Mediterranean society without a father to support them, without a dowry and unable to speak for themselves.

Very generally and with many exceptions, the totally resourceless were likely to shift from country to town; and unions with frail financial backing were more likely to be urban than rural. There were many reasons for this. In areas where charity was a secular community concern, pressure could be placed on the resourceless not to contract a union which would multiply the numbers of those on the list of claimants. Secondly, it was easier to tack together a livelihood and to find marginal accommodation in the town than in the village. Thirdly, those who had sought out the town for work in adolescence but who had failed to accumulate much in the way of reserves, were likely to stay there. What after all could the village offer them? Free unions were hence far commoner in the cities than elsewhere and clerical pressure to marry was feeble among the packed lodging houses and the shifting, volatile, marginal classes who could never afford the conformity church, state and community would have liked to impose.

The dominant pattern in north-western Europe, and less commonly in Mediterranean France and in some southern cities, was for the couple to set up house, 'settle down', *s'établir* (establish themselves), *casarse* (house themselves) – there is an instructive concept of this kind in all European languages. Two concepts were involved here. First it was customary for the couple to form an independent household with one head and one mistress. They had their own hearth (*Rauch* [smoke] or *feu*) and the mistress of this household took orders from no one except her husband. Although the notion of settling down varied according to the social group to which one belonged, it implied commitment to each other and conformity to norms of behaviour appropriate to married people. Wives should not behave coquettishly and neither party should seek to attract the opposite sex. The place where a couple settled was where they would rear their family and where they belonged in every sense. The rich might have a place in the capital or near the court as well as a country estate, and many of the poorest elements in society were dependent on seasonal migration, but they would for the most part return. Permanent expatriation was for the young and single. Once a couple had settled down, they had roots in a community.

In most of Mediterranean Europe, though with some exceptions, the single household/family unit was less usual.[9] At the beginning of the sixteenth century in Italy the norm was for a woman to be married in her teens to a man ten to fifteen years her senior and often such a bride entered a household where multi-generational occupancy was the norm. She lived in the company of her in-laws and took directions from them, and the couple was subservient to the head of the family who could be the husband's father, his elder brother or, on occasion, his widowed mother. The young bride was not, at this stage of her life, mistress of the house in any way. Over time, the age of brides rose and that of husbands fell somewhat, though upper-class girls continued to marry very young. Some of these young brides had a very limited knowledge of the man they married. They entered their new household as virtual strangers to a situation over which they had little control.

Evidence based on lawsuits, and reinforced by travellers' observations, suggests that the Mediterranean woman was more homebound than her British, Dutch or French counterpart and that the extended family could place a severe curb on a wife's efforts to seek protection from a brutal husband by leaving the home.[10]

However, in more congenial circumstances the extended family could help the young girl by taking from her shoulders some of the responsibilities of her new role and placing her in a virtual community of women to share experiences. The situation depended, inevitably, on the family itself. There are, moreover, areas where the new husband came to live with the bride's family, as in the Alto Minho in Portugal, leaving only to set up an independent household in the vicinity. Here inheritance of land and wealth was (and is) at least as much through the women as the men. Landless or resourceless women had no means to marry, though they might form irregular unions and were interested in having children to help them beg or later to help support them by their work. Those with the prospect of an inheritance, however, and with some means to marry, remained in a supportive community of their own relatives. This was, however, an area where there was considerable emigration of men to the New World, which may have enhanced the strength of women in the community.[11]

To generalize about the quality of marriage across cultures and classes, time and space, taxes the capacity of any historian and fierce debates have raged. The strong patriarchal model vaunted by prescriptive literature emanating from church and state can look somewhat different when applied to the real-life experience of some individual couples, 'marriage in action'. Furthermore, generalization about trends in emotional experience, the development of more affectionate relationships over time, can become ensnared in conflicting evidence. To look across cultures, and particularly to bear in mind differences between areas of customary and areas of Roman law, suggests that patriarchal control had a more conspicuous endorsement in the latter. This control was reinforced by the strength and inflexibility of the dowry system and its intermeshing with shame and honour codes: no honour without financial means. The closer circumscription of the honourable woman's activities in the home also strengthened the intensity of patriarchal control.

However, marriage was a partnership and the need to make it work and to recognize mutual interests was intrinsic to the undertaking across cultures. When marriages broke down and separation suits were instigated before the ecclesiastical courts it became apparent that both women and men had similar expectations of respect, consideration and affection. Of course many were disappointed and the greater freedom of action enjoyed both by men of means and by those prepared to cut the traces and disappear into the military or the navy meant there were more embittered, abused and discontented wives than husbands. It was certainly much easier for men to take pleasure outside marriage. Clearly, there were good and bad marriages, compromise choices and those wrecked by unforeseeable disasters. What can be pursued are the experiences of the institution in different contexts and an overall view of the survival strategies involved in marriages distinguished by class and region over time. Above all, we can examine the partnership element in marriage, the wife's role and the meaning of the complementarity[12] praised in the good conduct literature.

Complementarity in marriage can be discerned at all levels of the population, but it meant something very different at the top than at the bottom. A number of specialized studies exist on Tudor and Stuart courts and although the classic studies of Versailles omit gender as a critical determinant in court behaviour, any familiarity with Saint-Simon's observations of Louis XIV's court permits comparisons to be drawn. A court wife was dedicated to the promotion of the interests of her husband and their joint families, whose bonds the couple epitomized. In practical terms, this meant seeking to increase the wealth, power and prestige of their house by gaining access to the bounty of the crown (rewards, gifts, pensions, offices, sinecures at royal disposition). In sixteenth-century England, the wife at court nurtured contacts: she proffered appropriate gifts such as deer or fine wines to the monarch or his chief ministers or supporters, in order to win long-term or immediate advantages.[13] Thomas Cromwell or Cardinal Mazarin were almost equally showered with gifts, but the assiduous lady intent on fostering good relationships for her house could distribute tokens quite widely. Lady Lisle, for example, sent Thomas Cromwell deer and presents such as cheese and wild fowl; to Sir William Fitzwilliam, French wine; to the Earl of Sussex (married to her niece, but Lady Lisle judged that he would be able to help in placing her two elder daughters in advantageous positions at court) she again sent French wine. He received it 'wondrous thankfully' and delivered his gratitude by helping to secure Anne, the eldest daughter, a post as maid in waiting to the queen. To the Duchess of Suffolk she sent both wine and a pet dog and in return the duchess claimed herself ready to 'acquit' the pleasure Lady Lisle had given her. The Countess of Rutland received numerous gifts and promised 'if there be any pleasure that my lord or I can do for your ladyship here or elsewhere, ye shall have the same'. Later the countess received one of the Lisle daughters into her household.

Some wives reported political developments at court to husbands absent on the king's business. Henry VIII's cousin Elizabeth, Countess of Kildare, had no hesitation in defending her husband's actions to the monarch. The Countess of Worcester, whose husband was under criticism for his activities in Glamorgan, wrote in his support to Thomas Cromwell, who received numerous letters as well in the late 1530s from women defending their husbands' behaviour during the crises surrounding the Pilgrimage of Grace.[14] There are examples of assiduous women like Lady Bray who saved their husbands from the Tower.

Above all, wives laboured to promote good relations which could lead to marriage alliances for their children and offices for their husbands. While neither bestowing nor receiving patronage on their own account, they were a significant element in patronage networks, critical to the process of soliciting and facilitating the bounties which were intrinsic to this system.

Every queen had her attendants, ladies in waiting, maids of honour, ladies of the bedchamber. When a queen rather than a king was head of state such women became a key to favours and the vehicle through which petitions were made to the monarch. The women themselves were not highly paid by the queen out of the funds of the wardrobe, but there were profits to be made. Elizabeth I cynically encouraged the women who waited upon her to take large fees for presenting petitions from individuals so that the ladies would have enough money to gamble with her. She would enquire how much the lady in question had received from the petitioner and if she did not consider the amount sufficiently large would refuse the petition.[15] Between the deaths of Elizabeth I and of Queen Anne the power structure in English politics shifted very considerably and proximity to the monarch lost much of its political value. Financial rewards also diminished. Even so, Sarah Marlborough received an annual stipend of £5600 for her services to the queen, a small sum perhaps in the aggregate income of the Marlboroughs, but by no means trivial. Furthermore, for many years the Marlboroughs were strengthened by the widespread knowledge of their favour with Her Majesty.[16]

The memoirs of the Duc de Saint-Simon are highly informative about the role of women in the world of Versailles.[17] He was convinced that a wife could very considerably enhance the career of her husband and offers two striking examples of women who did this very successfully: one who achieved success through virtue, discretion and amiability and concentrated her efforts on securing the approbation of the king's wife, Madame de Maintenon, and one who did it through the king's bed but succeeded in turning the position of mistress into that of friend. The first, Madame Voysin, enjoyed an intelligence which far outstripped that of her boring (*dur et sec*) husband who was Intendant of Hainaut. She knew how to entertain, converse and, above all, how to make people aware that she considered them and their rank without being obsequious. During the siege of Namur she entertained Madame de Maintenon and turned the entire household over to the lady and her attendants, herself acting as discreet manager behind the scenes. Sensing that her guest had not brought enough warm clothes she provided cloaks and, when Madame de Maintenon sought her presence, demonstrated wit and charm so that within a short time and in no way due to his efforts, Voysin became a *conseiller d'état* and Madame Voysin was brought to Versailles where she never intruded upon Madame de Maintenon and always waited to be summoned. She took care to entertain with great care and astuteness anyone who could help her husband. Her efforts got him the Ministry of War (1709), which he almost squandered by some unguarded remarks which reached the ear of the king. His wife smoothed the troubled waters and Voysin continued to receive court favours. In Saint-Simon's view he was totally unworthy of his wife and insufficiently grateful for her efforts.

The second example was the Princesse de Soubise, as great a lady in her own right since she was a Rohan Chabot. After her marriage into a distinguished if far from affluent branch of the family, she came to court and attracted the attention of the king. The affair was carefully managed and her husband was pliable, keeping himself in Paris while his wife was at Versailles. It turned out much to his financial and social advantage: he ended up *duc et pair*. Even when she no longer occupied the royal bed, the princess's letters and requests went straight to the king, though she always took care to tell Madame de Maintenon what she was doing. The children, who were arguably fathered by the king, were also her concern. Saint-Simon recounts the monetary gifts, rents and finally the palace (Hôtel Guise) which she acquired for the Soubises subsidized by royal money. For him the princess was to be admired because of her dedication to the interests of her house.

Saint-Simon was capable of praising those whom he deemed to have promoted dynastic interests however they might have done so. What the Princesse de Soubise felt for her husband could not be categorized as romantic love, but there was certainly solid affection and respect in the partnership which outlasted her physical relationship with the king. She had no doubt where her interests lay. Sexual dalliance, if not threatening to the honour of the husband's house, was to be countenanced. Saint-Simon himself contracted a marriage at the age of twenty out of pure political interest with one of the daughters of the Maréchal de Lorges, Gabrielle. What was undertaken for clearly political motives (he wanted to marry into the right family), became very clearly a love match. He was to write her praise in fulsome terms: 'avec qui j'espérais le bonheur de ma vie, qui depuis l'a fait tout entier . .' (with whom I hoped to find happiness and who fulfilled all my expectations) and he left instructions that her coffin should be riveted to his to express the indissolubility of their marital bond.

It would seem that in court circles it was fashionable in the presence of others to affect a certain indifference towards one's spouse.[18] This was an essential part of civilized behaviour, *le mariage à la mode*. The fashionable language of Paris and London and Madrid would suggest that indifference of one married partner to the other was the norm and was part of the civilizing process parodied by Molière. Montesquieu was to write of Parisian society that a man in love with his wife was one so dull that he could not be loved by any other, and Hogarth's *Marriage à la mode* (1731) leaves little to the imagination on the subject of the deteriorating relationship of the aristocratic couple seeking distraction outside marriage. In 1762, Geneviève de Malboissière wrote to her friend Adelaide Malboissière about a mutual acquaintance.

Imagine, M. de Flavigny is still in love with his wife. What a lasting passion after ten months of marriage living together in proximity. They will be an example for posterity.[19]

However, it should be recognized that what the European aristocracies knew how to do to perfection was to distinguish between long-term affection, esteem and family interest and the short-term passion conducted within the ephemerality of the court. No group, unless it was the very poor, so held in contempt the rules laid down in prescriptive literature concerning marital chastity than the European aristocracies. Certainly, the infidelity of the husband was most generally tolerated but, having produced the legitimate line, great court ladies, or a proportion of them, also engaged in amorous encounters. Illegitimate children fathered by the husband were frequently acknowledged, aided and integrated into families. Little distinguished in this respect the Gozzadinis of sixteenth-century Bologna from the Lennoxes (the family of the Duke of Richmond) in the eighteenth. While acknowledging the greater scope for affectionate and companionate relationships in the more peaceful context of the late seventeenth and eighteenth centuries, we should acknowledge that many of the nobility, and particularly the men, took some of their pleasures outside marriage. The affectionate life had liberal boundaries.

The king's conduct lent the tone to much of this behaviour. Kings' mistresses, whose presence depended on the king's favour, were predominantly interested in lining their own pockets and forwarding those who might help to perpetuate their position. They were at the core of political intrigue and gave a kind of sanction to aristocratic laxity. Many of these women were ephemeral. Those who were not tended to have gained ascendancy in the king's later years when his sexual appetites were waning and his need for real companionship and an appreciation of the problems of being a king were paramount. Louis XIV secretly married Madame de Maintenon, looking for essentially the same attributes that an increasingly infirm Henry VIII sought in Katherine Parr. He admired her piety and her honesty yet, unlike the English king, he did not give her the official title of queen. Madame de Pompadour managed to hold on to the title of *maîtresse en titre* while a series of lesser women came and went – in some instances at her bidding – because she had an unscrupulousness and manipulative cleverness capable of managing the lazy and lascivious Louis XV and she succeeded in converting the relationship into a friendship. Friendship was not an easy thing for monarchs to find. Few royal mistresses, if any, achieved the ascendancy of de Pompadour.

The life of the provincial nobility was less exposed to temptations and free from the remorseless search for favours from the king. Montesquieu contrasts the wholesomeness of life in the Bordelais with life at Versailles. He admired his mother for her astute household management and the solidity of her devotion to his father and the family. She, like most mistresses of a large establishment, busied herself with the supervision of servants, with household budgets and the maintenance of important family and local contacts. Some of these could be political. English local politics were based on ties fostered among the local landowners and the lady of the house was at the nexus of the business of hospitality as well as that of planning for the next generation. The term *noblesse oblige*, reduced to practical terms, usually meant some involvement by the lady of the house in the misfortunes of the tenantry.

It was expected that the lady of the manor would visit the manse or co-operate with the parish priest to help maintain certain moral standards in the village. It was due to the initiatives of many such women that groups of lay women or congregations of religious women or some acting on an individual basis were brought into the villages to cope with problems arising from poverty and sickness or for the better instruction of the young. The seigneur's wife could set a tone of moral order.

In the sixteenth and seventeenth centuries, when aristocratic marriages consolidated alliances between clans for mutual support, the lifestyle of women was deeply affected by the violence of the times. Individual memoirs and letters reveal women left for long periods in charge of estates while their husbands were at war or involved in property litigation in the capital or provincial city. In normal times, the husband's main preoccupation included the management of his estates, helped by a bailiff or steward, and the extension of the family's wealth by augmentation of the estate, by investment, by office holding and so on, while his wife was concerned with overseeing the house, with hospitality and with raising the children aided by the appropriate personnel. Involvement in government administration at the national or the local level could increase the need to entertain and to maintain local contacts. In abnormal times, when the husband had to be absent his wife simply assumed his role. She was the natural substitute. Wives levied rents, sanctioned and sometimes oversaw the sale of produce and involved themselves in the maintenance of the estate. When, in the midst of the English Civil War, the Norfolk gentleman Thomas Knyvett told his wife, 'I know I cannot have a better steward then thyselfe to manage our affaiers', he voiced the opinion of similar husbands kept away from home by the exigencies of politics. The couple had a community of interests.[20]

For many, these were tragic times and diaries and correspondence reveal personal suffering as a result of separation. Lady Fanshawe described how her husband was obliged by military orders to leave her when she was weakened by a difficult delivery and when both knew that the baby was so feeble it could not survive. She wrote:

It was the first time we had parted a day since we were married, he was extremely afflicted even to tears, though passion was against his nature. But the sense of leaving me with a dying child, which did die two days after, in the garrison town, extreme weak, and very poor, were such circumstances as he could not bear with . . . And, for my part, it cost me dear, that I was ten weeks before I could go alone.[21]

Others found themselves petitioning for the release of their husbands from prison after military defeat or contesting orders for the sequestration of family property. Several royalist husbands subsequently described how their wives had managed to preserve the body of the estate largely intact. In a few extreme cases, some wives were forced into the struggle themselves and defended their besieged homes.[22] Such activities were not confined to mainland Britain and they could be on either side of a struggle. In the Irish rebellion of the 1640s, for example, Lady Forbes resisted a nine-month siege in which she gave refuge to all the tenantry and offered the same to 200 Protestants from the neighbouring area. She furnished the castle with ammunition and victuals and then hung on until the only food left was dried cow hides. She surrendered only on the promise of safe convoy for all the inhabitants of the castle. Lady Luke Fitzgerald won English respect for her defence of the castle of Tregroghan. Perhaps Lady Elizabeth Dowdall, however, secured greatest renown when she defended Kilfenny Castle in Limerick. After a month's siege and numerous attempts to storm the castle, she claimed that her men had killed more than 200 assailants.[23]

As in the French religious wars, the Fronde and the Thirty Years War, where individual aristocratic women could be forced into similar roles, these conflicts saw no long-term change in the position of women. Courageous as they might be under particular circumstances, letters and memoirs reveal that wives were filled with anxieties and preoccupied not only with the defence of property but with the absence of husbands and sons at war and their safety. For most the aim was to protect children and the wider household from disruption. They represented the desire to preserve normality in abnormal times.

The strife which peppered much of Europe in the sixteenth and the first half of the seventeenth century receded in the later seventeenth and eighteenth centuries. From then on, if we set aside the period of the French Revolution, most of the aristocracy could expect to die in their beds. Even so, when crisis came for the French aristocracy during the Revolution, the wives of *émigrés*, those who fled the country because they feared arrest and trial for supporting the monarchy, were in many instances active in preserving the patrimony from sequestration. They initiated divorce proceedings and went on to claim their stake in the property as innocent victims of their husband's perfidy in abandoning them and betraying the French state.[24] A detailed study of how much noble property was thus preserved remains to be made but if, as has been shown, the old French nobility emerged at the Restoration still controlling massive holdings of land and wealth, women as directors of family strategy were in large part responsible.[25]

In the eighteenth century, both the nobility and the gentry were involved in creating country residences for themselves. The business of negotiating with architects and planners was usually left to the husband, but interior furnishings and the comfort of the completed house lay in large part with the mistress. The family had more space. Servants' quarters were more clearly delineated. Taste reposed not only in architectural proportions but in colours and textures. Paintings, including portraits of master and mistress and their progeny, were indicators of affluence. So were porcelain and silverware, artefacts which bore witness to the taste and standing of the couple and were most likely to be the choice of the lady of the house. In the same way her clothing, that of her children and of the servants bore witness to her husband's status. To read Mrs Delaney as she comments on materials and teacups, draperies and needlework in the houses she visits is to catch a glimpse of the importance of such articles in the business of gaining respect during the early days of the consumer society.[26]

Middle-class marriage demonstrated the complementarity of the couple in a similar way. The man's role was making money and conducting business; the woman's, however, extended far beyond saving and careful household management. The bookkeeping side of many businesses was, right through our period, very often the work of the wife, in spite of Defoe's lament that this practice was fast disappearing. Sixteenth-century records speak of 'the casting of accounts' as the work of wives and daughters of businessmen. When Nicolas de Maes chose to paint the world's commerce, he took as a symbol an old woman with a heap of papers, a pair of spectacles and a huge bunch of keys, dozing slightly on the job yet in control of the movement of fleets and the warehousing of assets. Some manufacturers' wives received the consignments from outworkers (who frequently sent their wives to make deliveries).[27] Doctors and veterinary surgeons also used their womenfolk to keep the books, record the debts and manage the repayment of credit. Mr Thrale the brewer, who could well afford the services of a clerk, left the bookkeeping to his talented wife and was well advised to do so as she had a far better business head than he did. He did not allow her into the kitchen because, very unusually, he was interested in good food and liked to do the ordering of it himself.[28]

When merchants had to travel on business far from home, then local transactions, including new business, were left in the hands of the wife, although probably depending on her age and expertise. Most of the evidence that we have of such businesswomen is drawn from north-western Europe. The German couple Magdalena and Balthasar in six-teenth-century Nuremberg provide an example of the couple as a business team. He had to travel across Europe in pursuit of his business interests and, given the difficulties of transport, such an enterprise was risky and cut Balthasar off from his home. He maintained close contact with the family through a voluminous correspondence and was deeply anxious to have news of the children as well as what was happening on the business front.[29]

The English clergyman's wife is one of the middle-class women of the past about whom the most is known, if only because clergymen tended to keep diaries. When clerical celibacy was abandoned at the Reformation, to be married amounted to a statement that one was a good Protestant pastor, but the first wives were in a deeply ambiguous position. Society had great difficulty in adjusting to the new situation – indeed, so hostile was popular opinion that an act was needful in 1553 to insist that the children of married clergymen were legitimate and their wives had a right to dower. When Mary Tudor succeeded her Protestant brother, Edward VI, many clergy wives fled into exile and some were repudiated by their husbands. Others knew loneliness and fear. Margaret Cranmer, wife of the archbishop who went to the stake, was of German origin and the daughter and sister of sincere Protestant reformers. She spent Mary's reign in exile, returning to England when Elizabeth came to the throne, and tried to repossess a little of her husband's attainted (confiscated) property. She subsequently married twice, first a Protestant bookseller of some wealth and note and sub-sequently a younger man, Bartholomew Scott, who turned out to have married her for her money and did not respect the marriage contract which provided her with a separate income and for the education of Cranmer's son.[30]

Margaret Cranmer was a figure made tragic by the times in which she lived. Elizabeth I, though a Protestant, was averse to married clergy and administered some crushing snubs to the wives of bishops. The famous words directed at Archbishop Parker's wife who had accorded her some hospitality: 'Madam I may not call you; mistress I am ashamed to call you; but yet I thank you', were an unambiguous indication to the unfortunate woman that her marital status was not acknowledged by the queen. We cannot know how many wives reached the levels of devotion of the wife of William Mompesson, vicar of Eyam, the celebrated plague village in Derbyshire in 1666. She refused to accompany her children to safety and stayed with him to help and support him in his efforts to seal off the village and thus restrict contagion. She paid for this effort with her life. His eloquent tribute to their mutual devotion is laid out in Eyam church for posterity to read.

Within a century the status of the clergyman's wife was conspicuously changed. By 1700 she was well on the way to becoming the kind of wife we recognize in the diaries of the eighteenth century. Very often the daughter of a clergyman herself, she had become a very distinct personage in both village and town life and was regarded as the acme of respectability. Her history remains largely to be written.[31]

The role of the parson's wife was not only to lift any domestic responsibility from her husband's shoulders, leaving him in his study to write his sermons, nor merely to teach an above average sized family their letters, but to serve as a model wife in the community, visit the sick and suffering poor, give advice to village women and, in towns, sit on the boards of orphanages and institutions dedicated to good works. She also had to be able to offer hospitality. Many clergymen were younger sons or relatives of the lord of the manor who owned the living. This could be a comfortable one, but others were poorly endowed and promotion to canon or bishop depended on patronage from the higher clergy. The clergyman and his wife were judged as a team. Not all, of course, performed the role to perfection and some were content with a perfunctory commitment. Others were remarkably energetic. Susannah Wesley, mother of the evangelical John and eighteen others, held together an unwieldy household on next to no money, educated her children at home while they were small, did parish work and constantly wrote letters and paid visits to higher clerics to bail her incompetent husband out of debt while he sat in his study and wrote bad poetry. Her strength was exemplary.[32]

In summary, the business of complementarity, or smoothing the path by promoting the right public image of private solidarity, careful management or moral strength, was the job of the professional man's wife. The fitting management of the household defined its standing in the community. Apparent harmony in domestic relations mattered. To be quiet and content was how society judged a successful marriage.

For the majority of Europeans who looked to a living from the land the most usual designation of a married woman was that of 'farmer's wife' and this term covered a vast social spectrum. At the very top, particularly in periods of buoyant agricultural prices, surplus producing farmers were the recipients of new wealth and the image of the farmer's wife bedecked in new finery, her corpulent body squeezed into a corset, as a purchaser of new consumer goods and with new airs and graces was the delight of eighteenth-century caricaturists. Critics posited a new idleness in this figure as the eighteenth century wore on, and a tendency to distance herself from the business of the farmyard. Much of the critical literature, however, is designed to show the rich fleecing the poor and the effects of the polarization of wealth. Objectivity is at a low premium. The larger the farm, the greater the likelihood that the farmer himself was a business manager rather than a tiller of the earth by his own hands. Similarly, his wife was an organizer. She supervised the kitchen and the meals that were provided for the farm hands. She ruled the dairy and could in her own right be responsible for business negotiations concerned with the sale of products. She could give orders to men as well as to the dairymaids and kitchen helper.[33]

The term 'farmer's wife' carried with it the notion of particular kinds of work recognized as essential to the efficient running of a farm: hence the reluctance to grant a lease to the unmarried.

The farmer expected his wife to be a worker. Failure to have her full support services was seen as a just cause for marital grievance. The husband angered by his wife's dereliction of duty could find a voice in the German Lutheran village courts, which sought to preserve marriage by an early resolution of causes of friction. The court of Neckarhausen, for example, in the eighteenth century defined inadequate wives by their failure to lead the horse pulling the plough while her husband followed or by their spending time which should have been spent on the couple's own land in helping relatives. Idleness meant a failure to perform essential services.[34] The farmer's wife generally tended livestock, particularly chickens and pigs (the *basse cour*), grew vegetables, did dairy work, kept bees, preserved and pickled, helped prepare goods for sale and perhaps took them to market, lent a hand at harvest and during haymaking, and exploited gleaning rights or the use of commons where such existed. Obviously her work varied according to the nature of the local economy and the size of the farm. In some regions it was possible for women to work as well in rural industry, in casual labour on larger farms during busy periods or, at the very bottom of the scale, on the roads, carting stones. Country women, however, were not usually seen as generators of cash but as providers of vital support services. This assumption needs explanation.

It is almost impossible to disentangle a wife's financial input into a family economy, even when she was engaged in industrial employment. In some instances where the putting-out system prevailed and all family members were engaged in textile production, the husband was paid a composite sum. Where the wife worked at spinning or lace-making she was a piece-worker. Though the daily wages of the full-time worker can be discerned, the married woman who laboured in her own home slotted such work in between other tasks, feeding and tending livestock, carrying water, gathering fuel, growing vegetables and so on. She may never have realized the full daily wage for textile work because of other demands on her time. At the end of the eighteenth century in England specimen family budgets of those dependent on the work of their hands became fashionable. These budgets, however, were usually conceived in terms of cash inflow to the family as a whole and left out of consideration the contribution in services and kind which woman's labour produced. Howitt, in his *Rural Life of England* (1840), asked a rhetorical question:

> Who does not know what sums are made by cottagers and small occupiers of the produce of their gardens and orchards, by carefully looking after it and some one of the family bringing it to market and standing with it themselves?[35]

The answer to this question was clearly everyone knows and that the work usually fell to the farmer's wife. In areas of mixed farming involving grain, cattle and vegetables, dairying and the lifting, packing and selling of vegetables at market were her concern. Jan Siberechts (1627–1703) painted this division of labour to perfection in his *Ferme de Maraîchers* (The Market Garden) where all the visible characters involved in the despatch of the vegetables are women, or his *Cour de Ferme* (Farmyard) which is centrally occupied by women with livestock, vegetables

021499

and one who has the time to delouse a child. In Brittany, a lease form called *domaine congéable* was usually fulfilled by the husband growing grain and paying a money rent and taxes and the wife tending livestock and running a vegetable garden, spinning flax and from this endeavour paying the 'small dues' in kind, fruit and vegetables and poultry, attached to the lease.

The lower on the social scale, the more important the wife's monetary input. In one of the mixed mining-farming villages of the Midlands and north Wales, the case of Richard Milward, his wife Jane and their six children was thus described in the late eighteenth century: 'The management of the ground is in good measure left to his wife Jane (although) her husband always assists in digging after his hours of ordinary labour (in the pit).'[36] In thirteen years their scrap of ground yielded good crops of potatoes, peas and cabbages which she sold in Shrewsbury. She kept a pig and used its droppings for manure along with what she and the children could scrape off the roads. Without Jane's efforts, a family of six children would have been reduced to pauperdom.

What Jane and her kind were doing was adding occasional sums to the family budget and working a smallholding that went some way to feeding a family while the collier's wages paid the rent and taxes and other necessities. Generally, a married woman did not appear in the paid agricultural labour force unless she was at the bottom of the social scale and then her work was seasonal. It had to be weighed against what she would lose if she neglected work at home. She did not take on any more than was strictly necessary to keep her family warm and fed and out of debt. Throughout this period, the presence of a large number of married women in the agricultural waged labour force was a sure sign of hard times, of low male wages, of a slump in local rural industry, or bad harvests which could severely reduce the viability of many precarious subsistence units. At such times, they would willingly take on hoeing and weeding for the larger farmers for wages well below those paid to men – indeed in difficult times there was never enough work to go round.

The introduction of heavier tools for haymaking and threshing held down the demand for women's labour towards the end of the eighteenth century. In better times, too, women were conspicuously absent and winter hoeing of vegetables was particularly shunned. No matter how unpleasant the conditions of cottage industry, it was better than a field in inclement weather. At the bottom levels of the rural population, life was a remorseless struggle against poverty, of foraging for food and animal droppings, saving every scrap of fat for soup and lighting, spending long hours weeding and gleaning, filching firewood, feeding rabbits and pigs with greens and roots gathered from the hedgerows, making candles out of pork grease or cracking nuts for oil – the list is endless and the work unremitting.[37]

A married woman could not choose how to use her time when poverty was staring the couple in the face. Sheer need could force her into the labour force or to take on extra textile work and, as J. B. Say pointed out, it was the price of married women's labour which tended to determine wage levels for all women. As someone with a roof over her head and some support from a husband, she was prepared to accept low wages. In fact married women constituted the cheapest form of exploitable labour available to an entrepreneur, especially for spinning and sewing outwork. The demand for spinners always outstripped that for weavers because it never took less than four women to keep one weaver occupied. The women could be engaged on behalf of urban weavers while their husbands continued in agricultural work. However, in a few specialized regions such as the North Riding of Yorkshire which produced worsteds, and around Barcelona, Rouen and Troyes where the cotton industry was developing apace in the eighteenth century, industry progressively became the dominant preoccupation of both sexes and reduced the dependence on agriculture. Cottage rents rose to reflect not the value of the land but the potential for industrial income in the area. Husband, wife, children and relatives could all labour together.[38] As long as the industry continued in a buoyant phase, a new prosperity could be enjoyed.

There was no guarantee, however, that industry would seek out all poor areas or that cottage industry would continue undisturbed, without feeling the pinch of a slump. Indeed, the way of living of any family could be dramatically changed, virtually overnight, by any one of a number of situations. Poor harvests, for example, could see a reversal in the kind of jobs performed by husband and wife. Richard Jones, as a small boy living in Ruthin in Wales in the late eighteenth century, described how in a terrible harvest his mother said to his father:

I'll make a bargain with thee; I'll see to food for us and both the children all winter if thou, in addition to looking after the horse, the cattle and

pigs, wilt do the churning, wash up, make the beds and clean the house.
I'll make the butter myself. 'How wilt thou manage?' asked my father.
'I will knit', said she. 'We have wool if thou wilt card it, I'll spin'. The
bargain was struck; my father did the housework in addition to the work
on the farm and my mother knitted . . . and so it was (that) she kept
us alive until the next harvest.[39]

This text is worthy of note. The family concerned was not poor in the
strict sense, since it had capital assets which included livestock. However, the principal grain harvest had failed and money had to be found
to buy the staple to see the family through to the next harvest, recognizing that the father's labours would be needed in the spring on the land.
In the meantime, the farmer became the farmer's wife. He assumed the
womanly jobs of milking and mucking out and feeding, churning,
washing and housework and carding wool which his wife had usually
done. This left her free to expand her knitting activities which previously
were only a part-time endeavour. She kept control of the butter-making,
however, since this was skilled work and the butter was intended for
market. For this period of time she provided the money to buy grain
and he did the rest.

The reverse situation could occur where the sudden contraction of
industry, stripping the area of its usual ancillary source of income, left
women looking around for some means to plug the gap. They might
try a return to the agricultural labour force, weeding and hoeing. Spinners were always laid off before weavers and the rural force before the
women of the towns. This could leave rural outworkers in difficulties.
In the hard winter of 1789 women in the regions of Elbeuf and Darnetal
in Normandy simply marched themselves and their children around the
larger farms to ask for work or to beg.[40]

Huge regional differences became still more considerable in the
second half of the eighteenth century as industrial development, particularly in textiles, settled in specialized regions, ones often with a poor
agriculture or a largely pastoral base. However, to set against regions
of industrial change are those where economic development lagged conspicuously behind population growth.

In mountainous and remote areas where the terrain was difficult and
communications poor, industrial activity was rarely highly developed.
The Maremma Toscana, the Massif Central, the Alps, the Pyrenees, the
Welsh interior, most of southern Ireland, the Tras os Montes or Alto

Minho in Portugal or Galicia in Spain constitute a few examples of areas of smallholders in many cases precluded from industrial outwork. The holdings, however, were rarely sufficient to sustain a family throughout the year and so these regions developed significant patterns of migration in which the roles of the respective partners could vary from the traditional in striking ways.

Generally the men were the expatriates and married women remained behind with the children. This was not an invariable pattern, however. The Savoyard family on the move during the winter, when the men were teachers and story-tellers and their wives and young children strung along behind to share whatever there was to be had, or the Welsh women and children who walked from Wales to Kent to pick soft fruit and vegetables to carry into Covent Garden during the summer season, or the gangs of Scottish Highlands women who joined their husbands to do summer work on Lowland estates, constitute some of the innumerable exceptions to the norm.

The aim of the migrant was ideally to accumulate a small surplus which could be brought back home and used as the ready cash with which to pay either the rent on the farm or royal taxes. Many migrants, however, could hope to do little more than keep themselves alive during their absence. Their wives and children, then left behind, could consume what was left of the previous year's crops. *Manger hors de la région* (for the adult male to eat outside the region) was the summary way of describing this customary practice in France.[41]

Migratory patterns were subject to considerable variation. Some left in the spring after the sowing or when the potatoes were laid, and returned in late summer for the harvest. Some left after the harvest for a winter stay in a city which during the cold months needed coal- or wood-carriers and then returned in spring. Some farmers did both. They were tinkers in the winter and chimney sweeps in the summer. Back in the Auvergne they were farmers. They did the heavy work, identified as men's work, demanding muscle and shoulder power in turning the earth.

Dependence upon an income from migration meant that the farmer's wife was for many months the farmer. She assumed total responsibility for running the holding in the absence of the husband and almost certainly had the power to contract debt in the husband's absence, in some cases on the strength of his remittances. The women of the Rouergue, for example, saw their husbands leave in summer after the grain harvest to work on the grape harvest of the Mediterranean littoral. If they were lucky they would also get work stretching into November to harvest the olives and perhaps as well to do some pruning work on the vines. The women back home gathered the chestnut crop and the last vegetables. They picked nuts, which they would crack and crush during the winter months for oil. They planted winter cabbages and they arranged for the sale of grain to pay the Michaelmas taxes.

Those women of the Auvergne who saw their husbands depart twice did much the same work after their husbands had left for the cities in September. This was not an exodus likely to realize much money, but it would help spin out resources at home. If the grain stock ran low during the winter the farmer's wife borrowed, promising that her husband would pay on his return. In a bad year, if he had made little or if the grain had run out early, then more borrowing would have to be done when he did return to ensure the spring sowing. He would do the ploughing but everything else was left to the women. In the regions around Thiers where pins were produced the women made papers of pins for peddling around the villages in the summer months. In other villages they made up sulphurous purgatives which were also part of the pedlar's pack. In addition they did all the weeding, cattle tending, decision-making and borrowing. When the intrepid traveller Arthur Young visited the Auvergne in the late 1780s he marvelled at the fact that he only saw women doing the farm work and assumed the men were loafing at home. Other travellers commented on the industriousness of the women. Le Grand D'Aussy, for example, blamed male sloth for the fact that the women were seen first and last in the fields and thought they clearly went to bed later than did their husbands. What he may have been pointing to was a popular method of reducing the risks of conception, or he may have been wrongly interpreting the visual evidence before him. For several months of the year, only women and men too old to carry loads or walk the long distances remained behind in these villages. If the worst happened and the grain stocks ran out, it would be the women who marched the young and old into the towns of Riom and Thiers and hammered on the door of the poor institution to request admission.[42]

In Ireland the spread of the potato to Munster made it easier for women to manage while their husbands were away. It was a crop designed for migratory practices. Though some of the laying and lifting may have been done by men when they returned from their wanderings, the tasks could also be done by women, and between these two events the plants needed next to no effort on anyone's part. The men left for London and other cities of Britain, confident that they could cadge a lift home out of the poor rates. Meantime, the women at home ran the holding, milked the cow and gathered the weeds that fed it and the pig, cut and carried turf and raised their families, waiting for their menfolk to return with the money that might pay the rent. Once more, travellers pointed to the celebrated industry of the Irish wife and condemned the idleness of their husbands.[43]

Communities where the husband was frequently absent appear to have had a number of common characteristics. First, the women were not only capable of the business of survival under very adverse circumstances but they were indelibly pious. They clearly relied very heavily on the sociability provided by the church and the comfort of prayer while their menfolk were absent. Secondly, the women were renowned for industry and virtue while the men were held to be quarrelsome and dishonest. No immigrant had a worse reputation than the Auvergnat in Paris, unless it was the Irishman in London or Glasgow. Similarly, when the couples were reunited the women seem to have valued their menfolk beyond the ordinary. Alone among Frenchwomen, the evidence would suggest, the Auvergnat mothers did not count their daughters as their children, only numbering their sons. Irish women reputedly 'cockled' their returning husbands and their male children. Some of this reporting may not be objective. Yet it is easy to see how the dynamic of homes and villages was altered by the return of the seasonal migrant and how all hopes were pinned on his initiatives. It was always deemed easier to be the ones left behind. Back at the farm the wife kept the holding together, but he was the farmer, she was the farmer's wife.

In Pyrenean villages, husband, wife and children travelled down the mountains to the earlier harvests of the valleys and then returned home to their own crops. Come the autumn, however, many of the men left to peddle wares in the Ebro valley or to serve as tinkers there, mending pots and pans. The pedlars' packs included combs carved from the horns of sheep by the men and, yet more valuable, woollen stockings knitted by their wives the previous winter. The region round Lourdes, long before the advent of Saint Bernadette, produced carved religious objects which sold well in the Spanish cities. From the eastern Pyrenees there descended a stream of men in October to work on the olive oil harvest and then several went south to Barcelona, which throughout the seventeenth and eighteenth centuries seems to have had a heavy demand for casual workers and navvies in the winter. If the harvest back home had been sufficient to maintain the rest of the family until spring came, the other members stayed put. If, however, times were particularly hard, before the snows descended the women marched the children into Toulouse to beg on the steps of Saint Sernin. Many of the women had been in domestic service in the city as girls, so they knew better-off families who might give them a little food. They also had friends and relatives who had gone there as adolescents and had stayed on as brides to tradesmen and labourers. The women who made the winter journey back to the city to beg could look to these for some help or even shelter. Some of their contacts had perhaps fallen into the ranks of criminals and prostitutes. When the police conducted a purge on the prostitute population of the city in the 1780s it was these temporary immigrants who rallied to attack the building in which they had been incarcerated. The *filles de joie* may have been an important constituent in the process whereby these mountain families survived hard times.[44]

One constituent of the economy of expedients could be wet-nursing. In poor regions which were close to large cities, fostering city children (foundlings or children of the artisan classes) could be a common part of the family income of less substantial farming families. Wealthier children could also be put out to nurse for more money to slightly more affluent rural wet-nurses. In Italy a contract was made between the father of the nursling and the husband of the wet-nurse, who was paid for his wife's milk. By the Revolution nurses in France were paid direct. In Spain and southern Italy wet-nurses were drawn into the city. Along with the maidservants, those arriving in Madrid (usually from Galicia) advertised their services and the age (ideally no more than ten weeks) of their milk. They expected to be very well fed by their employers and at the end of about eighteen months accumulated enough wages to go back to their husbands and purchase a cow. Ten or so months later they might repeat this process.[45] Because the cow represented the difference between tolerable and intolerable poverty, it could be said that mother's milk was the key to survival for the entire family.

The expedient economy was infinitely varied. Moreover, the number of families who had to look to makeshifts of one kind or another to see them through the year was growing in the eighteenth century all over Europe as the population expanded, a growth as conspicuous in the

German village of Neckarhausen as in the scattered hamlets of the
Auvergne or the Alto Adige. In tacking together marginal resources,
women were critical.

The term 'farmer's wife' was clearly an umbrella covering a range of
activities and significant differences in where the burden of the work
lay and the relative viability of the farming enterprise. Married women's
work in the towns has largely been described by reference to the guilds.
As we have seen, these were at their strongest in Germany and in a
crescent stretching down into northern Italy, but they also had a significant presence elsewhere, though one weakened very conspicuously by
1700. Historians of early modern Germany take the artisan's workshop
as the model for the Protestant holy household with its head, the master,
in full control of a male hierarchy of journeymen and apprentices, aided
by his wife who performed ancillary services, catered to the demands
of the enterprise in terms of food, drink and lodgings, perhaps did the
books and was often involved in selling the finished product.[46] The
demands on a wife in any particular enterprise could vary very considerably, being greatest perhaps in those where manufactory and home were
the same and least in those where the work was done outside the
workshop, as in the case of the building trades, or where the enterprise
was small, a virtual pauper craft, affording next to no scope for wifely
involvement.

   Censuses carried out in France in 1794 and 1797 show that the
majority of carters, farriers, wheelwrights, smiths, building workers,
gardeners, shoe and clog makers and tanners did not employ their wives,
who were likely to be involved in textile piece-work.[47] Furthermore,
individual guilds embraced members who differed very considerably in
the scale and hence the wealth of their enterprises. Among the master
silk weavers or manufacturers of Lyons or Seville, for example, are
found a limited number of extremely wealthy individuals who lived
very comfortably; their wives probably made no contribution to the
finances of the household, beyond the capital input from their dowries,
and may never have set foot in the business premises. The same was
clearly true of the very wealthy goldsmiths and silversmiths of London
or the Italian cities, or the more substantial apothecaries.[48] Involvement
by a wife in the business seems to have been greatest in guilds concerned
with food production and distribution and in those modest enterprises
where the couple lived over the shop or workshop, where the wife was

clearly part of a working team. Whatever she did had to be flexible, so
that it could be combined with the bearing and rearing of children. If
the enterprise prospered a great deal could be shifted on to the shoulders
of servants. Someone, however, had to cook, shop at the market, carry
water for domestic and perhaps work needs and administer to the home-
based enterprise; and for many artisans' wives the job fell to them and
conditioned how they lived their lives. Wet-nursing agencies such as
the *bureau de placement* in Paris show that the wives of producers of cooked
meats (*rôtisseurs, charcutiers*), but not butchers, bakers, confectioners and
restaurant keepers, were their main clientele and clearly those who had
to weigh the costs of nursing a child and raising a toddler against their
input into the family business.[49]

Any study of the artisan's wife must begin with the recognition of
differing degrees of input according to the nature and scale of the
enterprise, where that enterprise was located, and differences over time.
A world of difference separated the working world of Augsburg, Nuremberg or Strasbourg in the sixteenth century from that of eighteenth-
century Paris or London. Textile production, in particular, knew
significant changes over the three hundred years considered here. The
introduction of new cloths tended to take place *outside* the conservative
guild structure, which could be very slow to adapt to the changing
tastes of the consumer – indeed, in the long run these changes helped
erode and impoverish the guilds.[50] Bearing in mind the vicissitudes of
guild evolution, the differences between time and place, we can examine
the guild member's wife in an early modern city such as Augsburg or
Nuremberg or Geneva and see the complementarity of male and female
labours less in the sharing of the productive process (generally the men
control the making or assembling of the artefact) than in the purchase
or preparation of raw materials (spinning for the weaver, mixing glue
or paint, melting beeswax and so on), in decoration (engraving, embel-
lishing confectionery, sewing on buttons, embroidering motifs), and in
organization. As long as the guild system lasted anywhere and involved
the full panoply of journeymen and apprentices, the servicing of the
needs of the workshop was the wife's concern. Apprentices could be
remarkably aspersive when they considered the master's wife fell down
on the job. Henry Coward said that the wife of the ironmonger to
whom he was apprenticed left everything to a maidservant, so the
standards of the establishment were low; Ménétra, as a journeyman
glazier in late eighteenth-century France, inveighed against masters'

wives who served the men and boys indifferent food on chipped plates. Arguably, the Great Cat Massacre, in which the apprentices of a Parisian printer massacred the pampered pets of the master's wife who were better fed and nurtured than they were, would not have occurred had she properly fulfilled what was considered to be her job.[51]

The organization of meals might only be one aspect of the business that fell to the master's wife. Deciding who ran errands, delivered orders to the back doors of substantial houses, fetched new supplies of raw materials when they ran out, could all be aspects of a wife's working day. Specific productions could generate work that the masters themselves, engaged in manly tasks, did not want. The butcher, for example, busy at the slaughterhouse or in cutting up carcasses, would not concern himself with tasks such as making sausages, smoking meat or pickling in brine. These all needed prompt attention, but since they were not the valuable parts of the butchery business and were work for the kitchen as opposed to the butcher's premises, they were fitting for women. Above all, where the retail outlet was the market stall rather than the master's shop, the master's wife presided.

Clearly the nature of the business determined whether the market stall or the shop was the outlet. Large or valuable artefacts were not sold through the market. Furniture, for example, particularly fine furniture, was discussed with a client, commissioned by him or her and delivered direct from the workshop. The public did not encounter the master's wife during the transaction. Many towns, through borough custom, guild regulation or municipal laws, prevented women from trading in their own right. In early modern Oxford, for example, only free men of the borough or their widows were permitted to do so. However, if the actual vendor was a married woman operating in the name of her husband the laws were not breached. Most commonly, throughout Europe market stalls were leased by men who were the nominal traders, but the actual work of selling was done by women.[52]

The visual evidence of the past has left us a remarkable impression of the omnipresence of women as market traders. Dutch genre painting, for example, abounds with fishwives and vegetable sellers enticing the customers in markets and on quays. The fishwife dealt with the small customer while the fishmonger negotiated with the fisherman for his catch. The lines for the activities of the respective partners were in fact laid down by the guilds, but each depended on the other for the profits that sustained the family. A glance around the markets of western

Europe might reveal some interesting variations on the range of goods on sale, but the preponderance of women as sellers is everywhere remarkable. In the markets of Augsburg and all the German cities, as in those of Lisbon and Manchester, butchers' wives sat selling sausages and black puddings. Nearby were stationed potters' wives surrounded by cooking vessels and chamber pots. Theft charges laid by shoemakers' wives show that they sat with pairs of shoes for sale. In hot weather the wives of *limonadiers* sold drinks and there were trays of sweetmeats and pies over which a woman presided. They rubbed shoulders with country women vending vegetables and fruit, eggs and their home-made butter and cheese. Women also had an important role to play in the sale of grain and bread.

Theoretically, from the sixteenth century there existed a complex series of laws aimed at regulating the sale of grain. Producers were supposed to bring all they had for sale into a specific market. The traffic, however, increasingly fell into the hands of middlemen and women, mostly from the towns, who negotiated with farmers or bought an entire crop, having seen only a sample, outside the official markets. They then undertook the retail sale of the grain in the markets, creaming off a part of the profits. Women who sold flour in the Paris market seem to have belonged to 'seed and corn' families.[53] Their husbands were merchants and middlemen, even millers, but they were the ones who were in direct contact with the small consumer. In the special bread market of Bruges the bakers' wives sold the huge loaves which their husbands had baked at dawn, while in the Terreiro de Paco in Lisbon, in 1699, sat thirty-one licensed female bread sellers including five with a very extensive business (*medideiras ponderosas*) and these women controlled and made good profits from the sale of bread in this important square. In times of rising bread prices when the consumers protested over the cost of this vital commodity, such women sellers were frequently the first who had to confront the discontented housewife. Contention was never very far away from the early modern market, which was a microcosm of married women's activity and the most public space in early modern society.

The investment made by the master's wife, sometimes in terms of capital, sometimes in terms of labour, into the family business should not be underestimated. Nor should the dynastic element in guild society be overlooked. Where masters did not have a son to inherit their business, a daughter's marriage to a journeyman could give an artisan the prospect of an inheritance. If a son was to inherit, daughters trained in aspects of servicing a particular trade might marry within it, but perhaps more married out.

The silk industry in Lyons provides an excellent example of inter-family relationships in some of the workshops. The weavers of Lyons had to pay an entry fee to the guild of over 200 livres. This was a large sum of money which the apprentice could not find from his own labours. Even the son of the master might turn his attention to the little hoard of the successful draw-girl, the immigrant from the barren hills of the Besse or the Bugey, in order to finance the mastership for him. He would, of course, be in competition for her favours with any other apprentices in the vicinity.[54]

The master's daughter (one who had also worked in the silk business as a girl, not the child of the more affluent manufacturers) frequently married out of the industry. She could not look to a cash dowry nearly so attractive as that of her sister worker from the countryside and so she could not offer her prospective husband the same prospect of advancing into mastership. This is not to say that she would abandon the industry on marriage. If she married someone whose work did not demand her services, then she might well return to her father or brother's establishment as a worker or do some piece-work in her own home. If she did this, however, she would receive a wage, whereas the new master's wife would find her services unremunerated. The latter would find herself organizing new silk reelers and draw-girls — perhaps her relatives from her native village — supplying food and lodging to the personnel and doing jobs as they arose within the workshop. For much of the next twelve years she would be pregnant but forced to put her children out to nurse because of the unsuitable environment of the workshop for child-rearing. Few women would find themselves more consumed by the physical toil which their work patterns imposed upon them.[55]

A workshop like the silk workshops at Lyons could be composed of several members of three families, his and hers and theirs. The labour they employed could be made up of his sisters and her female relatives or connections come down from the hills in addition to outsiders, depending on the scope of the enterprise. The resident family and the immigrants slept in the same close premises, shared the same food and the same working hours and often the same sociability patterns. The children of the employers might be sent to contacts of their employees or of the wife herself for nursing and then return to work in the silk workshop. A guild structure was not needed to have a family enterprise. Textile villages like Terling or Shepshed in the English Midlands housed manufacturers of commodities like stockings which were not guild-based but based on a family model of production.

There were also textile industries involving a purely female force. A lace-maker, for example, could continue her work after marriage, if only part-time, as long as the husband's business did not make too many demands on her. In the cities of Bruges, Brussels, Ghent and Mechlin lace-making provided employment for some of the most highly skilled women in Europe who sat at work from dawn to dusk, out of doors when the weather permitted because the cleaner air preserved the colour of the lace. Entire streets were given over to the production and the area reverberated with lace chants. After dark the women gathered together in specific cottages to share the costs of lighting. The 1814 censuses suggest their husbands to have been craftsmen, journeymen and unskilled workers. Spriggers and flowerers who embroidered muslin in Ulster again worked in informal groups to share costs and also to keep each other at work by encouragement and sociability.

These women's industries were often organized from top to bottom by women. The merchants who negotiated with the workers for the sale of the finished product and supplied them with raw materials were frequently married women who had a small amount of capital. The women either brought the work to them, or in the case of the lace industry in the Pays de Velay (much of which was conducted in remote villages) the urban merchant women of Le Puy and Lyons employed *leveuses*, women who collected work from the villages and travelled to the town. Small-scale mercantile activity of this kind by women – particularly married women – also marked productions such as linen manufacture in Belfast and Brittany where trade was again done at the back door, with the merchant receiving goods brought to her by the workers who could be from the surrounding area. One of these merchants in Belfast was Mary McCracken, sister of the Irish patriot.[56]

The literature of good advice urged the maidservant to put her dowry into a nice little business or commerce which would tide her over any problems that might occur should her husband fall sick or should she be left a widow with children to support. The advice was sound, though it could hardly apply to the tradesman's wife who was her husband's working partner and had her assets bound up in his business. If, however, her husband's job offered her no scope for gainful activity the advice was well worth taking; exactly how it could be followed was subject to limitations imposed by guild regulations and restrictions and to immense regional variation.

Every successful maidservant who had experience of preparing food, and in particular she who had worked on the premises of pork butchers and piemakers, confectioners and chocolate makers, was capable of turning such experience to her advantage. However, unless married to someone in one of these occupations, she could only exploit her talents to the full in an area where guild control was weak or ambiguous. She had to fill a space which the guild did not seek to occupy.

For example, in any town or city were women who sold cooked meals to their working neighbours or to the prisons. The families of prisoners were obliged to supply their relatives with food while they were awaiting trial and usually contracted with a married woman working from home to deliver hot food, or bread, cheese and small beer. Many workshops also were supplied in this way when the master's wife, daughter or maidservant could not cope with the extra work. In much the same line of business were women who ran taverns in which victuals were sold along with ale or wine. This kind of enterprise, tavern, drink shop, *buverie* or *guinguette*, was ideal for the woman whose husband operated in an area which afforded her little scope for making money. Equally, the profits from such a small commerce were unlikely to support two adults. French policemen, for example, were notoriously underpaid, so their wives topped up their income by running taverns. Ironically, the tavern, if perhaps not one run by a policeman's wife, was usually the place where thieves disposed of their loot and the products of poaching. The police were supposed to see that licensing laws were respected, and they could protect their wives' businesses by harsher regulation of any competitors. The shop was often the home and whatever the keeper sold was a profit.[57] Tavern-keepers' daughters frequently married someone in the building trades, because such labour was hired from the tavern. There was little the plumber's or roofmender's wife could do to assist her husband, but her experience in the drink trade fitted her to operate such a business on her own account and left her buttressed in the event of widowhood. She might in any case inherit an establishment from her mother or take over a rental when she died or retired.

Other maidservants who could branch out into their own little business on marriage were those who had experience in laundry work.

Taverns and restaurants, hospitals and private individuals all had the need of such services and many women could find work by building up a list of clients whom they visited once a month to help them with the family 'buck', sheets and table linen, shirts and whatever the establishment produced in the way of heavy washing.

Another possible direction for the woman whose husband did not need her services and which was compatible with rearing a family was the job of *concièrge* or lodging-house keeper. In most cities there were virtual ghettoes of immigrants from particular regions likely to seek out lodgings run by relatives who had established themselves in the town. The time to undertake such an enterprise was just after marriage when the couple would be likely to have a few resources to invest.

Women whose work was part of their maternal or paternal legacy clearly took their skill into marriage and continued as before. So did those who had had some kind of apprenticeship to dressmaking, millinery or staymaking. There was an immense amount of needlework – always chronically underpaid – which could be carried on from home and was paid by the piece. Making shirts and lingerie, handkerchiefs and trimmings were the kinds of work available to the needlewoman, though demand varied with the times. These were areas of activity which the male guilds rarely contested; nor, in the main, did men enter that other great female preserve, the second-hand clothes trade.

This business was one of the most considerable in early modern Europe. Most people did not buy new clothes or did so only at very special periods in their lives. Clothes were, at least until the late eighteenth century, carefully handed down from parent to child, aunt to niece and so on. Italian women from the higher classes were defined by their clothes and garments were highly valued pieces of property. Some of the first wills made by Englishwomen in the sixteenth century as *femmes covertes* bequeathed favourite garments, lace and pieces of jewellery. The clothes of the dead which were unsuitable for the next generation were sold. Servants expected the hand-me-downs of their employers and indeed counted on these as extra income. Children who had begun their lives in linen which had previously served as shirts or petticoats progressed, as they grew, into garments which were cut down, mended, had the weaker parts removed and if there was any wear left in them they were either handed down to brothers and sisters or sold for a few pence. By the nineteenth century the second-hand clothes market of Glasgow, Paddy's market, had become the centre of an export trade in which the cast-offs of Scotland were despatched in weekly cargoes to Ireland. At the centre of much of the business throughout Europe was the *revendeuse*, the reseller of clothes and artefacts.[58]

In Venice the Jewish traders controlled the wealthy part of the trade, which dealt in cloth of gold, laces and embroideries and sumptuous draperies for the embellishment not only of people but of houses. Outside the ghetto, however, there were Christian women involved in the recycling of humbler commodities. In some towns they were organized in a guild, but the business was very fluid and traders came and went. Anxious to control theft, the police force of Paris under the control of a formidable organizer named Le Noir, instituted a system of licensing the main women involved.[59] They were believed to be linked with the criminal underworld and the 268 women who appeared on the list were visited regularly by the police and expected to hand over a proportion of their suppliers whom they suspected of dealing in stolen goods. The importance attributed by Le Noir to this business is significant. Most people in early modern society owned few consumer artefacts and clothing constituted an important part of their assets. Clothes were perhaps the most commonly stolen goods across the length and breadth of the Continent.

Dress also precisely marked social status. At the beginning of the period most countries had sumptuary laws restricting the use of certain materials bought new to certain classes of people. Purchasing goods second-hand meant that silks and velvets and cloth of gold could be worn without, it was claimed, violating the legislation. Certain members of society had a special need of finery. Lawsuits concerning prostitutes reveal many to have been in debt to the brothel madame or the modiste for their flamboyant clothes. Many more were circulated through the second-hand clothes dealer. Venetian prostitutes in particular needed an array of silks and pearls and high-heeled red shoes and cloaks to advertise their status as courtesans. There was a subculture in which second-hand finery circulated, and from at least the 1580s, the authorities believed that if the sale of second-hand finery to prostitutes could be cleaned up, the growth of the vice trade could be stemmed.[60]

Spanish satire revelled in the nobleman who parted first with his undergarments and then with his decent doublet and finally with his cloak so as to keep up appearances until the last moment. John Gay's Mistress Trapes, with her trunks of satins and laces filched from the upper classes, was the hub of a society of crooks and prostitutes. She was capable of transforming the criminally disreputable into the apparently aristocratic. It needed merely the 'aping of manners' to make the metamorphosis complete. But if the second-hand clothes dealer has a literary identity linking her to the underworld, for ordinary people she was an essential trader. She did not need premises but could operate from home with a little storage space. Clients communicated their wants to her and she would endeavour to oblige them over the ensuing weeks. She knew how to look at a garment and see how it could be made over for a client. The women of Paddy's market and the Barras in Glasgow might arrive at the beginning of a particular day with no more than a small bundle of goods. Other women would then arrive, some with goods to exchange, others in search of a bargain, and they would soon be surrounded. It was the perfect business for a woman because it needed little capital, could be practised when convenient, and did not, except in times of real crisis, face competition from men. Europe was largely clad, setting aside the outer garments of the affluent, by these women.

Women at the lower levels of society were remarkably adaptable over the issue of work. Widows who remarried into a different category of business from that of their former husband could transfer their selling skills to another commodity. Seamstresses could pass from shirtmaking to the production of lingerie or the making over of second-hand clothing. Many urban women from the poorest groups were multi-occupational, with no one source of revenue affording them very much. Those who sold a few commodities on market day might sew gloves or shoes when they had the opportunity and the time on other days. When the looms of the Spitalfields silk workers were still and the industry was in slump the reelers made fireworks at home or sewed condoms for a Mrs Phelps who had the equivalent of a mail order firm throughout Europe and may or may not have been a woman. Elderly women of repute and experience could be *Kindbetthelferinnen*, helpers in childbed, who tended the mother until the midwife appeared or assisted her by pummelling the mother's back or preparing drinks if labour was long and arduous. Other women might acquire a shroud and would wash and help to lay out the dead, wrapping the bodies of the poor in the shroud which was removed after the relatives had paid their last respects, washed and stored until the next time. In London a small group of elderly matrons kept the Bills of Mortality. They visited the homes of the dead and recorded the likely cause of death according to a limited number of categories. The job was regarded as risky, because of the fear of contagion, and the women in question were not people of education, let alone medical learning, though historical theses about the incidence of disease have been extrapolated from their records. They belonged to a large and indefinable category of women who took what they could as a source of income and adapted it to their life patterns and the rearing of their children.

There were others reputed to have knowledge of cures and herbs to deal with sickness, or to serve as aphrodisiacs or cures for lovesickness. Straddling a boundary between fortune tellers and cunning folk who dealt in a kind of white magic, such women hardly made a living out of their practices but rather used them as part of an 'economy of expedients' – a term meant to imply reliance upon a multiplicity of small income sources. Women, whether in town or country, could be at the centre of an entire family economy in which they, their husbands and children knotted together perhaps a dozen activities which carried them somehow, precariously, through the year. These activities could cover any range of minor tasks, cleaning, carrying wood, water or coal, running errands, tending the sick or wet- or dry-nursing, doing outwork to supply seasonal events like carnival, vending pies or cooking for neighbours, sitting on a street corner with a few small objects for sale, or running a dame school whose purpose was more to keep children safely out of the way of working parents than to impart knowledge.

They might also comprehend nurturing a special relationship with church or civil authorities so that a family was known as worthy but needing of relief, or in Catholic countries exploiting a relationship with a better-off household which might part with left-over food to the children of the poor on a regular basis. The families who were the recipients of such aid had to be known for their virtue and in particular that of the mother. There were of course poor families who absorbed into their economy more nefarious practices such as pimping and procuring and prostitution itself – though that depended on age – as well as distributing and fencing stolen goods.

For many women, work was never done. They may have sat outside their houses and chatted with neighbours but in their hands was needlework, knitting, crochet, lace, nutcrackers and so on. If the male head of the household fell ill or disappeared, then the wife's labours had to be expanded to cover the resulting deficit in the family economy. Adjustments were constantly being made.

The lower classes, dependent upon a multiplicity of expedients to produce enough to sustain a family, were of course condemned to a remorseless struggle to make ends meet and poor lists make abundantly evident the plight of families reduced to want by the death, disappearance or incapacity of the male breadwinner. The consequences of a system which insisted that women should work but not have a professional or career mentality produced then, as it still does, innumerable victims when the ideal family model crumbled. A society without birth control, in which the salvation of women was predicated on the production of children, allowed women little vision of independence. Their identity was constructed not on professional status, but on wifehood and motherhood and both entailed work. By the end of the eighteenth century a working-class woman in the cities and towns could spend up to two hours a day queueing for water and carrying the pails home as well as provisioning her family in the market. If less committed to domestic cleanliness than twentieth-century women, she was expected to keep the home swept, chamber pots emptied, mattresses turned. Housework had a different meaning. Mediterranean women waged a continuing battle against lice and insects and bedbugs were everywhere a menace and had to be dealt with even if never eliminated. Simple meals could demand abundant ingenuity, and keeping the fire fuelled was another time-consuming task. We have no time budgets for early modern society but little reason to assume that a woman's day had the routine quality of the male worker's. She balanced the household's imperatives and shifted her efforts as exigencies dictated. She did not make for the hostelry at the end of the day, if she wished to maintain her reputation, but she might open the window, shout to her neighbour and look out upon the world.

Once married, as Restif de la Bretonne so pertinently remarked, the days of dancing were over: from now on the wife's music was the cry of the children, her dancing walking with them, her conversation, responding to their chatter.[61]

CHAPTER FIVE

Motherhood

> The Fountaine of parents duties is Love . . . Herin
> appeareth the wise providence of God, who by nature hath
> so fixed love in the hearts of parents, as if there be any in
> whom it aboundeth not, he is counted unnaturall.
>
> W. GOUGE, OF DOMESTICAL DUTIES, 1622, 498–9

CHRISTIAN marriage presupposed the birth of offspring. For church, state and the wider society, it was also the most effective guarantee that children would be provided with a sheltering environment designed to ensure that a woman was not left to rear her family alone or a man allowed to escape from the responsibility of maintaining his offspring. To beget children was the duty of the Christian couple and the responsibility of the citizen. It represented the destiny of humankind. As an eighteenth-century Catholic manual stated, in a view that might have issued from any confession:

> After the consummation of holy matrimony comes its precious fruit, children. Married people, having received the gracious gift of fecundity from God, *one which he withholds from some* [my italics], must render him thanks in all humility every time a child is born. They must ask of him grace and the sanctification of their parenthood through the Christian education they will bestow upon their progeny.[1]

Children also represented the perpetuation of property and perhaps it was hoped that, after pain and sacrifice, they would be the consolation and protection of parents in a violent and troubled world. For women, however, they represented something more. Defined as vessels for the reproduction of the species, for married women not to have children carried with it connotations of failure and inadequacy. To be barren was a judgement of God. In all European societies the blame for a failure to produce offspring was, almost without exception, laid at the feet of women. The French recognized a state of male impotence leading possibly to annulment and another, called picturesquely *le nouement de l'aiguillette* (the knotting of the castrating ligament), but this was attributed to having been bewitched or subjected to a neighbour's curse which could be lifted.[2] The English recognized a condition crudely known as 'brewer's droop', a failure of male performance in bed caused by over-indulgence in alcohol. However, under most conditions, the woman was blamed for a sin or offence in the eyes of God which had caused him to render her infertile. She carried the stigma of shame and she was also denied salvation, though this was more strenuously enunciated in Catholic writings.

Memoirs and diaries attest to the grief and sense of inadequacy that infertility could provoke in women and the degree to which it could become a cause for self-reproach and an obsessive examination of one's conduct in the eyes of God. Even those who recognized that they were not entirely – if at all – to blame, could be caught in a dilemma.

When Isabella de Moerloose of the region of Ghent married a local pastor in 1689, he was already about seventy and she only in her twenties. It was an unequal match in terms of age but also in terms of class since she had been a governess to his children. The pastor was sexually active (indeed, his earliest intentions towards Isabella were of a strictly dishonourable variety), but he was perhaps reluctant to jeopardize the inheritance of his existing family: he tried by *coitus interruptus* and oral sex to avoid making Isabella pregnant, all the while boasting to his friends in her presence of her appetite for him. Isabella, embarrassed, ashamed and unhappy, did not know where to turn. To discuss her husband's conduct in bed would be improper and disloyal. A young wife, like any other, must show herself anxious to support her husband and not denigrate him in public. He was a man of standing in the local community. Yet she was uncomfortably aware that the neighbours were talking and that, given that he had fathered children by his former wife, she was regarded as totally responsible for her failure to conceive. Her breaking-point came when a young neighbour who was about to marry came to ask her for her nappy drying sticks. These were strong sticks collected before matrimony by every young bride in anticipation of the next event. The neighbour frankly, and with perhaps a touch of malice, pointed out to Isabella that since she was barren she had no need of her sticks. Isabella burst into tears. For the first time she gave vent to her pent-up rage and sorrow, which she told the girl was divine punishment for having married an old husband who had cheated her and stripped her of her natural role in life. When she later wrote her life story, after his death and after some less than successful attempts to construct herself a life as a teacher and member of a Protestant sect, it was clear that her failure to become a mother was the pain she felt most keenly.[3]

When the newly married couple were bedded on their wedding night, local custom often involved fertility rites. In the Pyrenees the couple were given leek soup – a vegetable very generally believed to have aphrodisiac qualities; in Burgundy their nightcap was mulled wine spiced with a special concoction of herbs; in Brittany the brew was of milk, eggs and herbs. Onions and eggs were very widely allotted powers of aiding conception. The various brews were administered by the young people celebrating the wedding.[4]

If the bride was not already pregnant, it was expected that she would be within weeks or a few months. If conception was slow to occur, local customs, many of them rooted in pagan times, others based on the advice of neighbours and relatives, would determine what the would-be mother should do. Very rarely did the recipes and rituals involve the man. Often they were of a transparently phallic nature and involved touching, rubbing or performing a physical rite believed to induce conception, such as rubbing the stomach against the statue of a saint or a menhir or a designated old tree or prostrating the entire body on a holy tomb in a church. At Romarantin in France, for example, local women who wanted to conceive would lie on top of the prone figure of Saint Guerlichon in the Abbey of Bourg Dieu. Figures of the parturient Virgin, which had some popularity in the fifteenth century, also drew a lot of women; the abandonment of this kind of statue may reflect Counter-Reformation anxiety that the statues were themselves being endowed with magic properties. Throughout Europe, the keyhole of the church door would seem to have offered some hope to the women who were prepared to stick their finger through it and to accompany the act with a fervent prayer. When the clappers fell out of the church bell at Mende in central France, women appropriated them as a recourse for the barren, who must touch or grasp them and utter a prayer or incantation.

Some of the prayers were directed towards certain saints associated with childbed. In the sixteenth century Saint Margaret of Antioch topped the list, followed by Saint Nicolas in northern Europe. They were joined by Saint Anne and ultimately outstripped by the Virgin herself. Grottoes and springs where the barren could drink the waters were places of common recourse Sometimes the holy water was carried away and made into a *tisane* with herbs or even scratchings from a special statue or stone. The dust or scrapings from statues of the Virgin were regarded as having magic properties which would help in conception.[5] Pilgrimages were also made, sometimes to places where the Christian and the pagan tradition rubbed shoulders.

In Provence, for example, Gréoux les Bains was a sanctuary of Notre Dame des Oeufs (literally, Our Lady of the Eggs) built on an earlier site of pagan worship. Here a despairing woman could perform a ritual in which the pagan element dominated. She should go there with an egg in either hand. One she must eat and one she must bury in the sanctuary. She should then return on 8 September and uncover her buried egg. Prayers to Our Lady accompanied this ritual and it had to be accomplished in full before pregnancy could ensue.[6]

At Saint Germain en Laye, the monks claimed they possessed the authentic girdle of Saint Margaret of Antioch, and this relic was of course a place of pilgrimage for Parisian women of all classes.[7] Wherever the hand of Protestantism was felt, recourse to relics and to nominally religious customs which savoured too overtly of pagan practice was condemned and eliminated, but Protestantism could not eradicate the belief or hope that taking certain waters, herbal mixtures, or eggs, leeks and onions, while performing particular incantations or acts, could lift the curse of barrenness. The church might recommend nothing but prayer and proper conduct, but the despairing woman had recourse to a rich legacy of superstitions which afforded her solace and hope while she waited.

For the literate there were manuals written by theologians and doctors which have certain common themes. Intercourse is a serious business which should not take place too frequently lest the uterus become wet and slippery and impede the seed in its search for a firm hold. A woman should lie on her right side after intercourse to encourage the conception of a boy. (Male children were associated with all things right; some believed the male seed came from the right testicle and the female from the left.) Above all, the woman must lie still for at least half an hour after copulation lest she should expel the seed. As late as the eighteenth century, in England, *Aristotle's Masterpiece* explained to the couple the best way to conceive in terms which were indistinguishable from many seventeenth-century French confessional manuals; they were given authority by spurious attribution to the classical scholar.

Once a first conception was achieved, a new set of worries intruded. Would mother and child survive the birth? How many times would the wife be pregnant, and how many pregnancies would produce living issue? To the individual couple these were real questions, but unanswerable by any but the deity. His will was the determinant. Historical demographers can contemplate with coolness statistics which cover the highly emotional and charged experiences of real life. They tell us, for example, that the advanced age at marriage characteristic of early modern society north of the Loire obviously curtailed family size by limiting the reproductive period. The average number of children born to a French rural family was between four and five. In England it may have been somewhat less during difficult economic periods when the age at marriage rose. Averages conceal class differences and differences in child-rearing practices. The aristocracy and the middle classes, who married younger, generally had much larger families – sometimes twice the national norm – although by the eighteenth century the French aristocracy were limiting the numbers of births. Those sections of the population which put their children out to nurse had much larger numbers of children born to them than those in which breast-feeding was standard practice. Noble women were therefore likely to spend much of their married life pregnant and so were more exposed to death in childbed. For working women, all kinds of factors determined their reproductive record. Seasonal migration, or mortality crises arising from harvest failure (common in late seventeenth-century France and Mediterranean Europe), the dislocation attendant upon plague, for example, all had their part to play in shaping the record. However, one safe generalization is that unless they were part of a family economy where the presence of a young child on the premises was detrimental to production – as in the case of the silk workers at Lyons, who used wet-nurses and so were rapidly re-impregnated – working women only spent a relatively small part of their married lives pregnant though they might have a 'sucking child'.[8]

If some women were pregnant on marriage, more became so within the first year. If this pregnancy was followed by a live birth, a further two years could elapse before another baby was born. Demographers explain this interval by reference to prolonged lactation, feeding on demand, without a substantial pap substitute to reduce that demand. It is also possible that the long intervals between births were due to miscarriages produced by poor diet and hard labour. Sexual taboos, such as abstinence from intercourse during the breast-feeding period lest the activity curdle the milk, or the conscious avoidance of sexual union practised in many different ways at differing social levels, may also have helped to prolong the intervals between births. Madame de Sévigné, in seventeenth-century France, urged upon her daughter after three pregnancies in quick succession, the desirability of having her maid sleep in the same room to depress the sexual urges of the Comte de Grignan. The upper classes increasingly enjoyed the advantages of separate bedchambers and the availability of the paid mistress. Lower down the social scale, keeping children in the marital bed and ensuring the husband had fallen asleep before the wife joined him may have been ways used by a woman to lessen the prospects of pregnancy. Women may not have known much about the mechanism of their bodies, but married women were fully aware of what made them pregnant.

It is also acknowledged that at most levels of society there existed some knowledge of contraceptive practices and techniques. Sponges tied on ribbons suspended from the waist and soaked in vinegar or *eau de vie* were certainly known at the French court. *Coitus interruptus* was, however, probably the commonest method – widely condemned by both Protestant and Catholic divines as 'unnatural', the sin of Onan, so that even prostitutes in court insisted, to win the judge's favour, that they never let a man's seed go to waste through such an unnatural practice. One seventeenth-century British wife complained that:

> her husband did not deal with her in as befitted a married man and . . .
> what seed should be sown in right fine ground he spent about the outward
> part of her body and with that threatened that if she were with child he
> would slit the gut out of her body.[9]

There were also abortifacients, knowledge of which was passed on from one generation of women to another. Herbals recommended not only potions to abate the lust of men, which could be purchased at fairs or prepared from garden plants which included hemlock, vervein, woodbine, camphor, cannabis, dill, female fern, honeysuckle and so on, but an astonishing range of herbs and fomentations to bring on women's

1. Masalino da Panicale, *Adam and Eve in the Earthly Paradise and the Temptation* (1423).

2. Masaccio, *The Expulsion from Paradise* (1423).

The Eve legend had the authority of biblical text. Succumbing to temptation through her gullibility, Eve's words of persuasion led man astray and to the expulsion of both from Paradise. As punishment she and all woman-kind were made subject to male governance and enjoined to silence.

For the Counter-Reformation church, the Virgin could not be represented as an ordinary woman and Caravaggio's picture was rejected by its patron. Progressively, an etherialised Mary, alone of all her sex, became the dominant version.

3. Caravaggio, *Death of the Virgin* (1606).

4. Philippe de Champaigne (1602–1674), *The Assumption of the Virgin*.

5. Titian, *Mary Magdalen* (*c*.1531–5). Mary Magdalen, saint and sinner, afforded many painters, such as Titian, the opportunity to depict an explicitly sexy woman. He doubtless used a prostitute as model and many courtesans were painted as Magdalen.

6. Titian (1485–1576), *Tarquin and Lucrezia*. Lucrezia who died as no biblical heroine did, in defense of her reputation, occupied an important place in both Catholic and Protestant iconography to accentuate the overarching significance of female chastity.

7. Jan Steen, *The Dissolute Household* (1668). Steen's negligent housewife lies behind the moral collapse of the family. Here whoring, theft, gambling and waste attend a woman in a drunken stupor.

8. Sixteenth-century German woodcut. The viewer may be amused by the trouser wearing woman flogging her man but the image, an intrinsic part of western humour, is intended as a warning against the chaos attending the subversion of gender roles.

Siberechts summarises neatly the range of women's work in dairying, rearing livestock and growing vegetables. A child, deloused by an older woman, indicates the integration of work and child care.

9. Jan Siberechts, *La Cour de la Ferme* (1664).

10. Jan Siberechts, *La Ferme des Maraîchers* (1664).

The one servant household was the norm in seventeenth-century Amsterdam. De Maes's virtuous young servant sits in a simple but spotless kitchen plucking fowl but the growth in consumption multiplied a maid's tasks and silverware, for example, needed careful maintenance in a status conscious household.

12. André Bouys, *La Recureuse* (1737).

13. Jean-Siméon Chardin, *The Washerwoman* (1733). From the seventeenth century even modest houses used a washerwoman for heavy household linen. She was known for her muscle power and capacity to lift dripping burdens and heavy irons.

14. Antoine Raspal, *Sewing Workshop in Arles* (late eighteenth century). The seamstress, often apprenticed and in a workshop is an eighteenth-century development and this reflects the ephemeral nature of fashion, lighter cloths and the cheapness of her labour. Hers was a pauper's craft.

15. Adriaen van Ostade,
The Fish Vendor (1672).

Women traders were
ubiquitous in market and
street and the fishwives of
northern Europe were
famous disseminators of
rumour and dissent. Some
women peddled goods made
by their husbands. The
seller of brooms and cut
logs counted amongst poor
marginal traders.

16. Godfried Schalcken,
Woman Selling Herring
(1672).

'courses' – a euphemism carrying several connotations. Of these, which included possets of wormwood, saffron and hyssop, the most likely to work if taken in the right quantities before the pregnancy was far advanced were ergot (still used to bring on an overdue birth), penny royal (still used in Lancashire in the depression) and savin, celebrated in popular proverbs and known to be used as an abortifacient in Norfolk in the twentieth century. Midwives were thought to be versed in preparing these concoctions, as were whores. Some of them work by poisoning the foetus. It was also popularly believed that strong liquor and bleeding the feet would terminate a pregnancy and a woman who had had recourse to such practices was likely to be charged with infanticide and found guilty.

However, demographers urge that such practices, though they modified the pattern of births within particular families, did not alter overall birthrates and that they were used not to free women from having children at all but from too many children. Knowledge of how and when these 'spécifiques' or recipes were taken belongs to a world of women's experience which historians have been scarcely able to fathom. We may tentatively suggest that, while we know that barrenness was regarded as a curse, an overabundance of living children was seen by couples with inadequate resources as something less than a blessing.

Once conception had occurred, the mother-to-be was advised to watch her conduct carefully. Carrying heavy burdens, dancing and any energetic behaviour outside the home must be avoided. This advice could not be followed by those who had to labour in the fields. The Catholic mother was clearly instructed that she carried the responsibility for the life of a being who could not secure entry to the kingdom of heaven without baptism. Even without this grim reminder, pregnancy was regarded as a difficult event for the mother and apprehension about the impending delivery was great. *Femme grosse a un pied dans la fosse* (a pregnant woman has one foot in the grave) ran a French proverb which reflected a general consensus. But there were other problems to be feared as well as the death of the mother.[10]

Paramount among these was the birth of an abnormal child, a 'monster'. Current wisdom attributed the birth of the mentally and physically handicapped to one of two reasons. The first was that the couple had sinned in the eyes of God, which made the deformity of the child the responsibility of both parents since the seed was the father's contribution. The second was the experience of the pregnant woman. Her imagination (irrationality, lunacy) could inflict irreparable damage upon the foetus. The linking of the monthly cycle of menstruation with the moon rendered her particularly prone, during these difficult months, to fantasies which could have a dire impact upon the unborn child. As late as 1745, and bearing some imprint of the Enlightenment, appeared a tract entitled *Lettres sur le pouvoir de l'imagination des femmes enceintes* which sought to apply logic and physical explanations to the apparent irrationalities of which pregnant women were deemed capable. In fact a debate on monstrous births seems to have raged among medical men and theologians throughout the period, pivoting on the question of why some children were born normal and others not.[11]

The experts recommended that women should avoid fixing their gaze on the abnormal in whatever form it came – dwarfs, cripples (beggars with sores and deformities followed pregnant women, knowing that they would be bought off), ugly crones, hags and cretins, toads and nasty creatures. Contemplation of, or shock inflicted by, any of these and innumerable other phenomena could have a disastrous effect as they fed the pregnant woman's imagination. Nor should the pregnant woman gaze at the moon – a sure way to give birth to an idiot. Women were recommended to spend as much of their pregnancy as possible in the home and to focus their attention on objects worthy of contemplation. Catholic theologians following the Council of Trent advised contemplation of a picture of the Holy Family, especially of the child. The body of the perfect baby Jesus and his sinless merciful mother could, if studied assiduously with the appropriate prayers, help to produce an unflawed reproduction of the model, man in God's image, and at the same time an easy and uncomplicated birth. This study was better done at home than in church since even the ritual of the mass contained hazards when subjected to the volatile and deadly imagination of the pregnant woman. Although she must fulfil her spiritual obligations, she was advised to close her eyes at the moment when the priest placed the stola about his neck. Absorbed into the imagination of the mother, contemplation of this act could eventuate in the child's being strangled at birth by the umbilical cord (*placenta previa*).[12]

Protestant divines scorned the idolatry implicit in pictures of the Holy Family – although virtuous images promoting reflection were not discouraged – and placed emphasis on prayer alone. However, the belief in Protestant virtue and that God favoured his elect endorsed the notion of the abnormal child as a reflection of divine displeasure, one of the wages of sin, or as the result of the conduct of the mother in pregnancy. Either way, it left the mother racked by apprehension. Had she and her husband had intercourse when menstruation was not fully over? Had she been scared by a rat? Had she been overlooked by a crone who might be a witch?

Responsible parents therefore examined their conduct both before and during pregnancy lest it should affect the wellbeing of mother and baby. The tension is revealed in letters and memoirs. Lady Bridgewater in the mid-seventeenth century prayed that her child might be 'borne without deformity, so that I and its father may not be punisht for our sinnes, in the deformity of our babe'. And 'Notwithstanding all my fears,' wrote Elizabeth Turner in 1670, 'it was free from blemish . . . (It was) a goodly, lovely babe.'[13]

The birth itself was the time of greatest anxieties and these were well founded. Normal childbirth, that is, the unproblematic delivery of a child at term, with the baby presenting itself in the standard position in the birth canal, unentangled in the umbilical cord, would seem to have been only slightly more dangerous in the early modern period than it is today. Problems arose with any complication. A premature birth occasioned by the rupturing of the waters, a breech birth or other abnormal presentation, a multiple delivery or a ceasing of contractions so that the baby might suffocate in the birth canal were the kind of events to be feared. Most parturient women had their first child in the second half of their twenties. Many were undernourished or badly nourished. Rickets, which was common, could complicate the birthing process. There was no real antenatal care. Some women knew that the baby they were carrying was already dead. Many who had no other option worked in the fields until the very last moment.

In Britain, on average, probably about 25 women in a thousand died in childbed in the sixteenth and seventeenth centuries (in comparison with something like 0.12 per thousand in our times). The rate for France was at times perhaps higher, reaching 40 per thousand. A mother with a stillborn child was four or five times more likely to die than the one who produced a living child. Mothers, then, had every reason to worry. Everyone must have known someone who had died in giving birth. Experience of unproblematic deliveries did not necessarily lift anxiety. Alice Thornton described the birth of her fifth child, a breech birth.

The child staied in the birth, and come crosse with his feet first . . . at which time I was upon the racke in bearing my child with such exquisite torment, as if each limbe weare divided from other, for the space of two houres; when . . . being speechless and breathlesse, I was . . . in great mercy delivered.[14]

On this occasion the mother emerged with her life but the child, after the prolonged labour, was half-suffocated and lived only half an hour. Alice's pain produced nothing.

At all levels of society, relatives, friends and neighbours came to help the mother during her labour before the midwife arrived, or (in the case of most villages) the local wise woman who did the job for little or no payment. If the woman's mother was alive and did not live too far away, then her place was at her daughter's side. Indeed, for her not to be there (if she lived relatively close) was regarded as utterly abnormal. In 1576, Sir John Maxwell of Pollock in Scotland roundly blamed his mother-in-law, Lady Cunningham, for her failure to attend his wife's confinement. Furthermore, he insisted that her absence had distressed his wife so much that she had failed to conceive again for another six years. Everyone knew, he insisted, that it was 'the custom that either the daughter is with the parents at the time of her birth or the mother with her'.[15] Although Saint Anne was clearly not there when the Virgin gave birth, depictions of the birth of the Virgin herself are populated with women helpers, as well as Saint Erementia, the alleged mother of Saint Anne, or Saint Elizabeth, attesting to the public character of the birthing process. The role of the visitors was to sustain the mother until her pains became more frequent and the birth was imminent. This was women's business and perhaps the main way in which female sociability and solidarity expressed itself. The women, as a group, had a collective experience of childbed.

There was nothing to accelerate a labour. As the Countess of Warwick recounted when she went to help her niece:

My Lady Barringtons being in labor . . . I stayde with her all night she having a most terable sharpe labor I was excidingly afraide of her and with much earnestness and many teares begde a safe delivery for her.[16]

The women who came to help knew the comfort of rituals. Catholic women had a Marian girdle placed on their heaving stomachs and special prayers were recommended by the church:

> Oh Mother of the holiest one of holies who approached nearest to his divine perfection and so became mother to such a son, obtain for me by your Grace . . . the favour to let me suffer with patience the pain which overwhelms me and let me be delivered from this ill. Have compassion upon me. I cannot hold out without your help.[17]

Support and encouragement at this time, though parodied in satirical literature and prints, were the best that could be done in a society lacking pain-killing drugs.

In every noble household and in the lowliest cottage, a birth was a collective drama and the room of the birth was living theatre. At the village level it was an event shared by a good proportion of the village who brought their collective wisdom emanating from their experience to fortify the mother in her travail. *Kindbetthelferinnen* appear in every village society. Indeed, a lonely, unattended birth was abnormal and even suspicious.

A large number of theories have been elaborated about midwives in early modern Europe. Indeed, the midwife has been central to the thesis of a serial decline in the position of women over the period since, it is alleged, women progressively had to cede ground to the male midwife and so were 'pushed out' of the oldest profession available to them. Recent close empirical research has revealed such an interpretation to be over-hasty and crude.[18] There was no single midwife to represent all midwives. Indeed, geography, accessibility to reasonable roads and communications, the wealth of the mother, the size of the community in which she lived (whether a substantial town or a tiny village), as well as family traditions, religious persuasion and other cultural considerations combined to determine what was available to the parturient mother. In Germany, Holland and England there were midwives licensed by the municipalities. In Germany they appear to have been very poorly paid, but the lowness of the fees does not necessarily reflect an attempt to prevent midwives becoming too wealthy. Rather, it points to a kind of 'moral economy', whereby the authorities guaranteed a cheap service to all who needed it. Fees, like the price of bread, could not be left to market forces since this would expose the poor. The wealthy were not obliged to use the municipal system. In Holland, some midwives seem to have had great social standing in the community and enjoyed a good, though not sumptuous livelihood. In England there seem to have been many more unlicensed than licensed midwives, since licenses cost money.

The use of a male midwife claiming superior scientific expertise grew among those who could afford his services in the second half of the eighteenth century, but the huge majority of women continued to be delivered by other women; at the very bottom of the social scale there were women who performed such services in exchange for poor relief and so were not paid by their clients. Substantial Englishwomen could choose their midwives with care and some Quaker women whose skill, probity and education in the art of midwifery became legendary were sought out and could clearly pick and choose their clients. There was a tendency to choose a midwife of the family's religious affiliation, which broke down in the case of choosing the Quaker women; families were probably most concerned to avoid Catholic midwives who might baptize an innocent babe in the wrong faith or exact a confession from a dying mother.

In France, Louis XIV's hiring of a male midwife to deliver Madame de la Vallière may have set a fashion among the court nobility, but only by the end of the eighteenth century, in Paris and among the well off, had the practice become established. The government's efforts to lift the standards of midwifery in France by sponsoring courses from Madame de Coudray, a pioneer in obstetric medicine, revealed how much work was in the hands of women and how the quality of midwifery varied from village to village.

Throughout Europe the licensed or established midwife in a community was a person of good repute who could be called upon to appear in court and give evidence in infanticide cases on whether or not the accused woman had given birth. In Catholic societies she bore the responsibility of baptizing a puny infant lest it should die before the priest arrived, and of recognizing a mother's need for extreme unction. In the eyes of the Catholic church her moral standing was as important as her competence. The priest did not license the midwife, but his approbation could be important, particularly if she was paid from parish funds. The fact that the church disapproved of the intrusion of men into the birthing process may explain why male midwives did not make much progress in Mediterranean societies during this period, although a struggle for the more important clientele was afoot in the capitals from the late eighteenth century.

How capable was the female midwife? There is no simple answer since standards varied, but in towns and larger villages she was usually a woman of experience or training and certain urban women have left an impressive record of competence. One Dutch woman, Catharina Schrader, left a remarkable set of memoirs recording her experience over more than fifty years and about four thousand deliveries. The widow of a surgeon, who may have endowed her with some anatomical knowledge above the run of midwives, she was inherently suspicious of medical men when it came to the delicate business of bringing babies into the world. She believed them too rough and too crude, too ready to pronounce the baby dead when it failed to suck on a finger, or to lop off limbs when the labour was an abnormal presentation and so slow that it stretched over as much as two or three days. She saw the practices of surgeons as murderous both for mother and child. Although she knew that certain conditions – notably *placenta previa*, the dreaded entanglement in the cord – meant that the baby was probably dead and that saving the mother was the main task, she grieved over infant deaths and every case was special to her. Her memoirs reveal that she worked tirelessly during very unsocial hours, travelling through snowstorm and flood over a large circuit for half a century, though the pressures of the job caused her to curtail her activities. She was a professional whose strength was patience and experience. These had taught her to manipulate the position of the unborn child to help the mother. Confronted with a difficult presentation she would try to facilitate the baby's exit by manual skill. She was extremely versatile in the ways she helped women to a more comfortable birthing position, using a stool for some, encouraging others to lie on their sides so she could pummel their backs and yet others to lie on their backs. She could not save everyone but when she died in 1746, hers was an impressive record.

Literate and informed, Catharina Schrader was a highly esteemed member of the Dokkum community, and her work made her a comfortable income – to be compared with that of a village schoolmaster. Her descriptions of her work contrast strongly with records from other sources. Those French towns which requested the presence of Madame de Coudray to teach local women frequently commented on the ignorance of existing practitioners and painted some gloomy pictures which may have been an exaggeration of the real state of affairs. The village midwife

was presented as untrained and ignorant, capable when nature arranged
an easy delivery but incompetent when presented with the least abnormality. Limbs were lopped off whenever the presentation was irregular,
and a suspension of contractions meant the certain death of both mother
and infant. Certainly most commentators are insistent that the critical
factor in the mother's survival was a normal presentation – head first –
and a labour lasting hours rather than days. Any other birth was
described in the eighteenth century as abnormal or *contre nature*.

Medical thought Europe-wide, until the end of the seventeenth century, insisted that the baby itself determined the way the birth proceeded. This view changed by the end of the eighteenth century when
more were prepared to attribute the birth mechanism to the uterus
itself. The use of forceps was becoming increasingly common in towns
by the end of the period, but the consequences were not usually satisfac-
tory and the child's head could be damaged. Some early forceps were
merely water squirting devices to baptize the child likely to be dead
on exit. A caesarian section was usually only performed on a dead
mother. Some surgeons, deeming that mother and child were both
likely to die unless action were taken, performed this operation at the
almost certain risk of immediate death for the mother if the father of
the child gave his permission, but few babies survived the process either.
When the child died as well as the mother, it was often replaced in
her belly for the purposes of burial. At the end of the eighteenth century
it was estimated that there was one caesarean section for every 3445
births in Britain. These figures may have perhaps a spurious accuracy.
What happened in most of Europe is not known. The Catholic church
would not sanction any intervention that threatened the life of either
party. Evidence suggests, however, that midwives and surgeons would
consult the father and aim to preserve the mother. Midwives were always
suspected by churchmen of neglecting Christian principles and many
were at loggerheads with the local priest.[19]

A birth could have four possible outcomes: a living mother and child;
a dead baby; a dead mother; a dead mother and child. If the first was
the most numerous experience, the other categories were directly known
to all.

In large households, the birth occurred in a warm, darkened room
with a blazing fire, plenty of bowls of water and a lot of women relatives
and friends as well as the midwife. We shall suppose the outcome
happy, like the birth described in a seventeenth-century French

poem by Angot de Lespeyronnière, *La Lucine ou la femme en couches* (1610):

> One runs to the mother the other to the sister's house
> One gets water to revive the mother
> The father is distressed in waiting
> He reads the life and death of St Marguerite
> Then activity intensifies
> The awaited fruit is delivered in good state
> One says 'it's a son' the other 'a daughter'
> The other says, 'he has hair', 'he's the image of his father'
> The other judges the performance of the mother
> A thousand discourses of pregnancy, children, wetnurses, milk, successful
>   deliveries
> They boil a pot full of marvels, herbs, roses
> Then they show the new born
> Look he is his own master
> Look how he moves
> Smile little darling, dear little boychild
> There there it's only wind . . .
> Papa come close, my son will kiss you
> He's of your making and look how he understands
> And how beautifully he cries . . .
> 'Come close' say the women 'take his hand.
> You'll sleep alone tonight
> Kiss your wife She is distressed
> Your sport has caused all this discomfort
> Men are lucky they have only pleasure
> They can follow their whims whilst their poor wives
> Lose body and soul to please them.'[20]

The water in which the newborn baby was washed was in some European societies — there are instances from both Portugal and Italy — regarded as symbolic. That which had washed a girl was tipped over the ashes in the hearth to keep her at home: that used for a boy was taken to the door and thrown outside to indicate that he must deal with the world. In many French villages it was believed that the umbilical cord of a girl should be tied and cut as close as possible to her stomach while that of the boy was accorded a couple of inches. In Brittany the large church bell announced the birth of a boy, the smaller that of a girl, or three peals announced a boy and one a girl.[21]

The birth and attendant rituals over, some of the women relatives might stay on to cheer the mother during the ensuing uncomfortable days while she awaited the arrival of her milk. Villagers called, bringing cakes or eggs for the mother. Visual satire on the childbed chamber in the aftermath of the birth usually showed a blazing fire before which linen was drying and the helpers were in such a state of inebriation that the baby was neglected to the point of letting it fall in the fire. *Les Caquets de l'Accouchée* was an early seventeenth-century literary collection of so-called tales, social observations and witticisms which allegedly sustained one high-born mother during these days. The tales were the creation of a male imagination concerning events involving mysteries they imperfectly understood and mistrusted, but the idea is to impart the notion of amusement to accompany fear and subsequent relief. The childbed helpers were 'gossips', women who perhaps knew something intimate about every man in the village, revealed during the hours when they sought to distract the mother; and she too disclosed information. For those living on farms and in small farm cottages, the birth over, the women helpers retired to look in later. For the majority of women, exhaustion and a living child were the result. It was appropriate to rejoice and be thankful.

The midwife in Catholic countries was expected to baptize the infant if he or she was in the least frail, lest it should fade without a Christian identity and hence be ineligible for Christian burial. Modest families, having chosen godparents in advance, simply carried the child to the church for baptism and to have the necessary entry placed in the parish register. This was a very important religious and civil act, recording entry both into a society of Christians and into a particular community, a record of identification which would be carried through life. To have been born in a particular parish was information demanded to establish eligibility for poor law relief in England; it was information demanded by law courts; in Catholic countries priests were obliged to check with the priest of the parish of origin before marrying anyone from outside their own community. The registration located a person and made him or her an insider in that particular environment.

On the occasion of the baptism, the godfather, usually a close relative or dear friend – for the job carried with it obligations to help and protect the child if the parents died – bought sugared almonds for the godmother and the midwife and handed out a few coins to the children of the parish to celebrate the entry of a new community member into their ranks. It was an occasion for generosity and rejoicing. 'Wetting the baby's head' in Lancashire referred not merely to the cross of baptism administered from the font but to the drinks purchased afterwards by the father and godfather for neighbours in the alehouse.[22]

The mother was not always present at the baptism. In Catholic countries she must wait forty days before a purification ceremony, including prayers to the Virgin, allowed her to re-enter the community of the faithful, a reminder that although she had given a new Christian to the world, her baby was tainted with original sin. Anglican mothers underwent a 'churching', a somewhat modified ceremony of purification. Wealthy families (particularly for the first births) turned the baptism into an event and waited until the mother had recovered. Relatives travelled considerable distances to acknowledge a new member of a house or clan.

But what happened if the child had been stillborn or died before baptism? The mother had laboured in vain and her bruises and tears were likely to be more, not less, considerable. The death of her infant did not stop the milk rising in her breasts. She had failed, and the event might be interpreted as a punishment for her sins. To the physical suffering was added another consideration. To Catholics death without baptism condemned the infant's soul to wander in limbo, a belief which may have been reinforced by late medieval clerics anxious to instil into families the importance of infant baptism though not officially sanctioned by the church until the end of the eighteenth century. Limbo was neither heaven nor hell but an uncomfortable nothingness in which the unshriven wandered, returning to haunt the living. To avoid this fate for their children, some mothers in France, Switzerland, Germany, Austria, the southern Netherlands and Italy had recourse to attempts to resuscitate the baby by miraculous means.

If the little corpse could be made by a miracle to show some signs of life, the merest fluttering of an eyelid, a change of colour from waxen blue to white, a drop of urine, then the child could be pronounced to have shown signs of life, could be quickly baptized, and was spared limbo. The mother could at least then rest in the knowledge that its spirit was not debarred from eternal life nor from eventual reunification with her in paradise.

Hence the *sanctuaires à répit* (literally, shrines for respite or resuscitation) to which the Catholic masses had recourse with their little dead babies to pray for a miracle, a momentary sign of life, obtained by intercession of a saint or the Virgin. Such places are first recorded in the fourteenth century and they flourished throughout the early modern period even though the Catholic church itself was hostile to them: they were denounced both by clerics who promoted Tridentine reform and later by eighteenth-century sceptics as an expression of superstition. They were categorically condemned by Pope Benedict XIV in the mid-eighteenth century. In fact the church had very little control over them. They belonged to the distraught mother and father and to the midwife anxious to help them gain relief. Midwives would insist that the child brought to the shrine had gained in warmth, had emitted urine or sobbed for an instant, and many priests found themselves, under the insistence of the mother in a state of distress, conducting a baptism even when they themselves were in doubt that the child had ever shown a sign of life.[23]

The Abbé Thiers, *curé* of a parish in the Perche at the end of the seventeenth century, denounced the shrines as 'a false, pernicious cult and a travesty of the sacred'. The women, however, were far from docile to the dictates of the priest, who found himself forced to admit signs of life he had not seen while refusing to use the word 'resurrection'. Often the women to whom the unwilling priest yielded had prayed for three or four days, fasting before the altar of the shrine on which the baby's corpse lay. One priest recorded the joy of a woman who had misunderstood his response. After a four-day vigil he told her to take the rotting body away and she carried it to the nearest officiating priest and told him that the other priest had seen signs of life.[24]

The Protestant tradition did not admit limbo which, lacking scriptural authentication, was seen as a papist invention. At the popular level in England where, as elsewhere, baptism was regarded as a magical rite giving protection, attempts by Protestants to change baptismal rites caused a great deal of anguish. In the late seventeenth century Protestant parents in Béarn actually preferred Catholic baptism to the ceremony performed by their pastors. The unbaptized child was not accorded a place in the parish cemetery, a source of considerable distress to parents. Having never been part of the Christian community, the baby could have no part in eternal life. As late as the 1780s, Parson Woodforde recorded his personal sorrow when he had to explain to parents that such children could not be buried in a family vault. Many historians have urged that parents were indifferent to the death of infants, or at most accepted it stoically and with resignation. Certainly such stoicism was urged upon them by theologians. God's will had to be done. Men were urged, in particular, that this was appropriate. However, women's memoirs and diaries, their personal testimonies and the evidence of the *sanctuaires*, suggest that they were not spared grief. The large number of Protestant treatises extolling stoicism in the face of infant loss is perhaps a pointer to parental resistance. An infant's death may have been God's will but they cared. A further pointer as to how a mother was perceived to feel for her baby is given by the beliefs held in specific regions concerning maternal death when the infant survived.

In Alsace, for example, it was believed that such a woman should be buried with a sturdy pair of shoes in her coffin since the road from eternity is long and she would need them to return every night for one month to ensure that her baby was fed. A variant is found in Provence, where when the mother died before the cleansing mass, the godmother came to her room with a pair of shoes, took up the child and said, 'Mother, the mass is going to begin, you must get up and walk.' The party had then to leave and if the floorboards creaked the mother was following. She was watching over her child.

The survival of birth was the first obstacle. If the child could get through the next few months it stood a good chance of surviving infancy. Many women's diaries are filled with appeals to God and the saints to preserve their sick infants and intense anguish over fevers. The death of a baptized child could still cause much anguish. Anne Bathurst had a mystical vision of her 'two little children, died one at fourteen weeks, the other at fourteen days end' ascending to heaven. Contemporary religious thought denied the propriety of grieving for the baptized child who would be received among the saints, because innocent, and whose death was the will of God.[25]

If more fathers than mothers were able to maintain a stoical exterior when confronted with infant death, this is not to suggest that grief was a female monopoly or that it could be allowed to consume the bereaved in perpetuity. Some sought to externalize sorrow by recording the event on tombstone or in painting. Sir Thomas Aston on 2 June 1635 found himself a widower when his wife died in childbed with a stillborn child. He commissioned a painting from John Souch in which appeared the living and the dead body of his wife, the cradle crowned by a skull and draped in black. The bereaved husband and the small son – who was himself to die two years later – wear mourning and the child grasps a criss-cross staff, a reminder of death and resurrection. What is caught is grief, helped by structured mourning.[26]

It is possible that the proximity to death through child-bearing helped to lock many women into a particular religious intensity. It reminded them that both they and their children had a tenuous hold on life.

The aristocracies of Europe aspired to reproduce a living male heir. Many, and it is difficult to be more precise, failed to do so. Some women prayed, as did Lady Mordaunt: 'If it be thy blessed will let it be a boy'.[27] The expression of a preference for the male sex is most commonly found when families had one or more living daughters. Two French queens, on hearing that they had given birth to a girl, clasped the child to their bosom and consoled themselves that they now had a companion, belonging to them and not to the state. When, in 1602, Marie de Medici bore two daughters in succession, King Henri IV consoled her and 'said that God knew well what was best for them, that it was necessary to make alliances with Spain and England'.[28]

Several aristocrats, like Madame de Sévigné, were obviously disappointed when their first living child was a girl, but rapidly adjusted to the situation. Her daughter adjusted to a female firstborn perhaps less easily. A large number of daughters was worrying, but the situation could resolve itself with subsequent births. Even so, men like Sir Philip Monceaux, who fathered nine living daughters, were distinctly depressed at the news of another female birth. Where would the money come from to establish them? Girls took money from the family. With boys there was always the chance of the generation of some new wealth.

This question could trouble the middle classes as much as it did the aristocracy. At the end of the eighteenth century, a Mrs Weeton chided her mariner husband for his lack of enthusiasm for their new-born daughter, to which he replied that his love for the child was unquestionable but what might become of her? A son might go to sea or join the East India Company, but a daughter's future must be a constant worry.[29] Agricultural societies always tended to value male labour more highly than they did female because of the need for physical strength. Sexual preference, however, perhaps receded in industrial towns and villages where there were good prospects of female labour generating income within the home.

Taken overall, children were referred to as comforts and blessings, *onnozele schapen* (little lambkins), chickens and doves, pigeons, and they were given affectionate diminutives like nursling, darling, *dochterchen*.

Most women in the early modern period breast-fed their own children, something we would never guess from the tirades against wet-nursing that began in the late seventeenth century and continued throughout the eighteenth. Those who did not do so belonged, as already noted, to aristocratic families and city élites, to those of some urban middle classes, to parents who could afford to put a baby out to nurse and who lived in the capital cities which were regarded as unhealthy, and to some industrial families. Foundlings from the local hospitals were also put out to nurse. Taken overall, it is to be doubted whether more than about four per cent of children were fed by someone other than their own mothers. However, as much as a tenth of the children born in Paris were put out to nurse by the mid-eighteenth century, a number much inflated by the considerable number of rural foundlings despatched to the capital. The silk workers of Lyons, though not other workers in the city, also sent their children out to nurse in the barren regions of the Besse and the Bugey simply because the workshops, with vats of boiling water for softening the silk cocoons, were physically dangerous for a young child and the mother was occupied full-time with the running of the business. Couples who had businesses such as shops and restaurants, or food-producing concerns where the mother's attention was engaged full-time, were also likely to put a child out to nurse.

In Britain the capital was the most considerable producer of nurslings to be sent into the country. The aristocracy and to a degree the middle classes also used wet-nurses. Both Jane Austen and Samuel Johnson, for example, were put out to nurse. In other societies, such as the Dutch Republic, much less use was made of wet-nurses. In Italy the practice was confined to the aristocracy, the comfortably off citizens of larger cities and the foundling hospitals. Generally, comfortable families expected to find a wet-nurse no more than a few miles from the city so that the parents could visit regularly. Michelangelo's family sent him to Settignano, within comfortable visiting distance from Florence; Samuel Johnson's mother used deliberately to leave behind some small article so that she had an excuse for going back sooner. The Austen family had a nurse so near that a visit to the wet-nurse constituted a Sunday walk.

The practice mystifies a modern reader and has been used to argue the indifference of parents to children. However, it becomes more understandable if we consider the beliefs and conditions of the times. In the fifteenth and sixteenth centuries wet-nursing was encouraged rather than the reverse. City life was considered, and indeed rightly so, to be unhealthy, and upper-class women were thought to produce inferior milk – the tight lacing of bodices may have made this a reality. There were also taboos on sexual intercourse as long as lactation continued (it was believed that the milk was weakened). It was held that lactation impeded the recovery of the high-born mother from the weakening effects of childbirth.

The available artificial substitutes for mother's milk were usually nothing more than a starchy pap of boiled barley or wheat, sometimes sweetened with honey or sugar, into which a cloth was dipped which the infant then sucked. Animals' milk was not deemed appropriate because it was believed that milk had the capacity to convey attributes. Use of cow's or goat's milk carried with it considerable risks, notably the bestialization of the recipient, and popular horror stories dwelt on the characteristics of children abandoned in the forest and suckled by a boar or a pig. True, there were success stories of children suckled on goat's milk directly from the teat of the goat, but this was usually as a result of losing the nurse.

It was therefore considered that the best start in life for an upper-class child was provided by a country woman who was a superior milk producer. Ideally, she was in her mid- to late twenties, had box-shaped breasts, a milk supply of the right consistency in super-abundance and good health as judged by her complexion and her teeth. This woman had proved her capacity as a milk source by having successfully nurtured and weaned her own child, a practice which did not bode well for that infant; perhaps it was passed to a relative in return for a share of the profits. She promised the parents to lead a life of sexual abstinence while she was selling her milk and she lost her job the moment she had to admit that she was pregnant. She was supposed to be a woman of upright life and good principles. The French aristocracy would have nothing to do with wet-nurses who had red hair since this was believed to be the product of the parents' having had sexual intercourse during menstruation and such a person was of suspect morals. The wet-nurse should also be a married woman because one who had borne bastards could be of dubious probity and the milk might carry her lax moral attributes.[30]

Such requirements, of course, represent the ideal and it is impossible to compare the ideal with the reality. In the case of the wealthiest families, a wet-nurse had to be on standby at the birth and it was regarded as totally irresponsible not to have this person ready and waiting. Royal wet-nurses, women of some standing, were brought to the palace. A proportion of nurses were brought into, and remained in, the child's home. How many is not known although it was advised by some seventeenth-century Englishwomen 'so you may see the ordering of it yourselfe and feede the nurse at your own trencher'. Such scanty evidence as exists suggests that the aristocratic women who used wet-nurses throughout the period were very concerned for the credentials of the nurse. She usually came to a family through the recommendation of one of its members and indeed was frequently sought out by the relatives of the mother. Obviously she had to be hired before the child was born and there is some evidence that the choice was confirmed by the father and an inspection made of the nurse's body. Those with skin diseases or other obvious malady were then disqualified. Parents who delayed over finding a suitable nurse were deemed negligent and to be putting the baby at risk.[31]

Where the nurse did not move in with the family, as was undoubtedly the case with less illustrious infants, then affluent parents were concerned to know what kind of home their child was going to. They did not despatch it to a pauper's hovel and, without exaggerating the cleanliness and comfort of the home in which the child would pass his infancy, it was at least a modest farmer's dwelling in which the wife led a comfortable enough existence to be able to sit down and nurse a child. The Florentine bourgeoisie and the prestigious Ospedale degli Innocenti, which had aristocratic patronage and paid good rates, used much the same kinds of people, the wives of farmers holding *mezzadria*, who belonged to the more substantial peasantry (the Ospedale only used poorer women if times were hard and child abandonment increased). It might be noted that the husband of the wet-nurse did all the legal contract work, laying down the terms for the use of his wife's milk and nursery services. The homes of such couples were in marked contrast to the hovels of the Morvan into which Parisian foundling children were summarily despatched.

Until the later seventeenth century, the forces enjoining wet-nursing for social élites appear stronger than voices of dissent. Yet from the early sixteenth century onwards, humanists, some clergymen and medical opinion sought strenuously to promote breast-feeding by the natural mother. The debate does not seem to have met with any sympathetic response from upper-class parents until the 1690s and even then, no real shift in actual practice except among certain individuals has been detected. In Britain the argument for maternal breast-feeding was advanced as part of a movement to promote the regeneration of the British aristocracy, deemed in the context of the Stuart courts to be particularly prone to degeneracy and loose living. The character was shaped by milk the infant had ingested and the manner in which the child was reared, so a degenerate élite could be blamed on milk from a dubious source. Doctors added to this the notion of disease transmitted through polluted milk. The burgeoning natural law school progressively insisted upon the natural desirability of maternal breast-feeding and urged that not to feed one's own child would result in death and unnatural consequences. The Dutch middle classes in the mid-seventeenth century would seem to have been fully persuaded that breast milk was the best expression of a mother's love and that no real mother should trust another to do her job. The nursing mother was not only a common subject for the painter but was extolled in verse. Jacob Cats in *Moeder* thus addressed all young mothers:

> Employ O young wife, your precious gifts
> Give the noble suck to refresh your little fruit
> There is nothing an upright man would rather see
> Than his dear wife bid the child to the teat
> This bosom that you carry, so swollen up with life
> So finely wrought, as if 't were ivory orbs.[32]

The French aristocracy perhaps needed more convincing. However, the philosophers of the eighteenth century, reaching a high spot with Rousseau (who addressed his breastfeeding theories to womankind while, by his own admission, consigning his own children to whatever wet-nursing services the Parisian foundling hospital could provide), placed the natural argument first and as a further inducement assured the mother that she could expect a newly tender relationship with her child.

Individual aristocratic and, perhaps even more, educated middle-class women were won over to the arguments. In letters and journals a

number of them attested to their conversion to the theories of the
philosophers, though some, like Madame Roland, were frankly disappointed to find that the tender closeness to their children, promised
as a reward of their efforts, did not persist into adolescence. However,
the majority of women from these social categories do not seem to have
experienced radical conversion. There is much evidence to suggest that
a discredited wet-nurse rather than academic argument determined practice in individual cases.

The custom was always fraught with problems and certainly the
wet-nursed child seems to have been more at risk than the maternally
nursed counterpart. One of the few reliable statistics available to support
this suggestion is that one in five noble boys in England died in infancy
in comparison with the national norm of one in seven. The nurse's
circumstances could change. She could become pregnant or be shown
to have neglected a child. The eighteenth century was marked by an
increasing social polarization, the enrichment of elements of rural society
and the immiseration of the many. The surplus-producing farmer had
never been better off. In addition, the penetration of rural industry into
the countryside made a steadier form of income and activity available
to many women. Wet-nursing had never been popular and the result
was that the supply side of the business moved decidedly down the
social scale. At the same time a great chasm was opening up in terms
of hygiene between the classes. Among the upper class, a new obsession
with personal hygiene developed and cleanliness in the nursery and more
frequent bathing of the infant became a sine qua non of child care.
These considerations may have accelerated a trend among upper- and
middle-class families to keep their children at home. The increasing
use of cow's milk diluted with boiled water, rather than a starchy pap,
was probably a greater breakthrough in the preservation of the aristocratic child than the treatises of the *philosophes*. If a suitable resident
nurse could not be found, or if she proved unsuitable, this substitute
for maternal milk could be administered by a dry nurse in the child's
own nursery.

The volume of pediatric advice in all languages increased rapidly
from the mid-seventeenth century and in England some of it was written
by women. The nursing mother should watch her diet and forgo rich,
fatty and acidic food and alcohol in favour of fresh meat and poultry,
milk, cheese and vegetables. A controlled nursery regimen of meals,
baths – for English boys in cold water – and walks in all weather was

promoted. The nursing mother should avoid strenuous labour which could reduce her milk supply and get plenty of rest. The household should accommodate itself to her needs. This kind of advice manual, available to the literate and hence the better off, accentuated the difference between different levels of society.[33] The farmer's wife, for whom a nursling was one part of her daily routine, was unlikely to be able to concentrate wholly on the child to the neglect of other work.

A world of difference separated the wet-nurses of the middle and upper classes from those that working women and most of the foundling hospitals could afford. The demand for cheap wet-nursing grew with the increase of foundlings and the development of commercial city life. That said, it looks as if the demand by London shrank in the period while that of Paris and Lyons grew. Paris had a *bureau de placement*, an agency for the placement of babies, accepted from the parents or the midwife and picked up by the wet-nurse herself and conveyed back to her home in Normandy or Picardy. The efficacy of the arrangement depended more than anything else upon the speed with which surrogate mother and baby were brought together, but the death toll among these children does not seem to have been conspicuously higher than that among children in the city who were not put out to nurse.[34] Of those picked up alive by the wet-nurse, the survival rate seems to have been 75 per cent.

This was in stark contrast to the necrology of the foundlings left to the Hôtel Dieu and the children sent from Lyons into the hills of the Besse and the Bugey. In the first case, the children were delivered by *meneurs* who strapped them into paniers on the sides of donkeys and stilled their cries with wine or eau de vie on a soaked rag. The dead were thrown out en route.[35] It could be days before the children got to a nurse and when they did she was usually someone from a very poor social level, since a foundling was a risky speculation and believed to be a potential source of syphilis for the nurse. In the case of Lyons, unless a family had a personal contact in the surrounding villages to whom the children could be sent, wet-nurses were found by touts who scoured the villages and brought in women who picked up the babies. There was no real check on whether they were feeding more than one or in what conditions the children were kept. A concerned official, M. Prost du Royer, estimated that 6000 babies left Lyons each year and only 2000 returned, and those in poor physical shape. However, his closely examined sample was limited to 22 children of whom two-thirds died. [36] (Three-quarters of children raised in Lyons would seem to have reached the age of five.) The ones who returned from the wet-nurse came home with rickets and other vitamin deficiency diseases. Birth mothers physically attacked the women who returned their children, claiming they had been ruined for life by physical deformities and diseases they had picked up in the nurse's hovel. No one, not even Prost du Royer, however, suggested that a woman giving birth to a child on a silkmaker's premises could bring up her baby herself. Her labours helped to sustain a working unit and included older children dependent upon their parents for their daily bread. He was concerned that the provisions for caring for children at nurse should be improved.

From classical times until well into the seventeenth century children were swaddled during the first few weeks of life, since it was widely believed that the infant body emerged from the womb unformed and that binding it so as to immobilize the limbs in a kind of package helped the baby to grow straight. Aristotle, Plato and Galen had all put their authority behind this practice. It may well be that rickets was an obsession in early modern society and that mothers wanted to guard against knock-knees and bow-legs. The practice also had the advantage of keeping the child warm and it imitated the close, confined space of the womb. The infant with its limbs bound in linen bandages and then the whole wrapped around with extra material was then carried about by its mother or inserted in a narrow cradle in which movement was impossible. The linen was changed in many cases no more than twice a day. The urine of breast-fed children does not smell until the addition of more solid foods or animal milk and the practice of swaddling probably rarely extended beyond eight weeks. Even so, the critics of swaddling who emerged in the seventeenth century vaunted natural movement and commented remorselessly upon faecal odour.

Lanolin and olive oil were widely used to coat a baby's buttocks. Nappy rash is perhaps unusual in breastfed children, though once pap is used to supplement the diet, unless the baby is frequently changed and cleaned, it could be a problem. In Teniers' picture of *The Quack*, a mother relieves her baby whose bottom is spotted with unmistakable nappy rash with an ointment from the quack's pack. It suggests the problem to have been common even to the Dutch mother whose standards of cleanliness – viewed on a European scale – would seem to have been high.

Even upper-class children were not washed much before the end of the seventeenth century and it could be argued that no section of the population embodied to such a degree the deliberate cult of bodily filth which flourished in early modern Europe. According to this orthodoxy, corporal fluids were deemed healthy to the body and so were infrequently removed. The sponge was commoner than the bath. Even the children of the élite in the seventeenth century may not have experienced immersion in water before their second or third year. Consider the record of Louis XIII. Born on 27 September 1601, his encounters with water or any cleansing process were as follows:

11 November 1601 – his head rubbed for the first time;

17 November 1601 – scalp and forehead rubbed with butter and almond oil, cradle cap extensive;

4 July 1602 – head combed for the first time;

3 October 1606 – (he was five years old) his legs were washed for the first time in tepid water;

2 August 1608 – (he was almost seven years old) bathed for the first time with Madame, his sister.

This schedule was written down and officially approved and was carefully presided over by a doctor. The royal body was always seen as special.[37]

Cradle cap was popularly believed to be a protection for the cranium, and was not generally removed until the soft part of the child's skull had closed over. In the Auvergne, even in the mid-eighteenth century, children were several years old before this crust was picked off. In Britain and Holland, it was gently removed from the infant's head by rubbing with a little butter.[38]

The belief in the need to preserve the body's fluids was replaced within the upper class from the late seventeenth century onwards by a concern for personal cleanliness and doctors extolled the virtues of the tepid bath for the young child to be followed by the cold bath for the developing boy. How much of the rigorous regimen recommended by doctors was actually carried out is not easy to say. The literary vogue for classical examples and the belief that manliness was the product of austerity and discomfort – epitomized by the cold bath and a plain diet – may not have been put into practice. However, what is clear is that élite babies in north-western Europe became cleaner and that swaddling was abandoned.

Lower down the social scale, change occurred more slowly. While women worked in the fields or in the *basse cour*, the baby was either left behind or laid on hay or straw while the mother worked. Traditions of leaving the baby unwashed were hard to dislodge. Tending the child conformed to honoured practices such as allowing none but the mother to bite the child's nails – the standard way of cutting until the advent of fine scissors – lest the child should become a thief. (Nail pairings were considered to have properties which could be used for black magic.)

Demand feeding was perhaps the norm among the lower classes, though the child had to be accommodated within working routines. If left behind, while the mother worked in the fields, an elderly relative or another older child could keep watch and bring it to the mother at her place of work. In summer it could be taken to the field and placed in the shade with an older child as invigilator. The place for a very young baby was believed to be the arms of mother or nurse. The baby's cries were to make its wants known and to secure its proximity to the mother. For this reason the best place for a child to sleep was popularly deemed to be in the mother's bed where she could save it from the terrible dreams that shattered infant repose and caused it to wail in the night. Doctors and theologians railed remorselessly against this practice. It was believed to be at the root of death by 'overlying', the stifling of the child in the parental bed. Parish priests demanded that the baby be placed in a cradle and asserted that if this was not done, the parents were failing in their duty.

Deaths from overlying may well have been the cot deaths of the past. It is now seriously doubted that a child can be suffocated in this way and cot death remains a mystery. However, throughout this period, if a child was put to bed in apparent health and failed to live until morning, its death was blamed on the mother and faulty maternal practice. Coroners' inquests on infant deaths accepted overlying as an accidental death but often chided the parents, even if they protested that they had kept the infant in a cradle, demanding that they be more vigilant in future. It does not appear that such warnings reduced the practice. The baby should be at its mother's side so that it could be comforted and brought to the breast. Its cries stilled by food, the rest of the family could sleep.

Weaning probably did not occur until eighteen months although by that time other nutritional elements had been brought into the child's diet. Bread, sometimes boiled and sweetened with honey, custards, and then crusts for helping the teeth through were gradually introduced.

The actual time of weaning varied according to the health of the mother, the size of the child and also family and local practice. Doctors recommended lactation up to, but not beyond, eighteen months and thought that some mothers went on too long, thus 'cockling' or 'cockering' their children. There was, however, enough popular lore to encourage postponing weaning until the summer months were over. The reasons for doing this may have been imperfectly understood by women but it was an old wives' recommendation with some sense informing it.

The biggest killer of children who survived the hazards of birth was summer diarrhoea, no doubt caused by the microbes that swarmed in the child's germ-laden environment. The excrement of hens was dropped on the farmhouse floor and piles of manure lay near the back door. Houseflies and bluebottles must have been ubiquitous. Babies would have been particularly at risk from these factors and although women associated the disease with the month rather than the physical conditions about them, they regarded weaning at this juncture as risky.

Several diarists from the upper classes, whose houses must have been distinctly cleaner than the average farm, record losing a child at this stage. Antoine Froissard, for example, in the 1530s provides a good example of post-weaning deaths. His family lost two children through weaning precipitated by the pregnancy of the mother which began about a year after the previous birth. The story demonstrates that lactation did not always guarantee infertility and that church injunctions to avoid intercourse during the breast-feeding period were not invariably respected.[39]

Popular belief, again to the annoyance of doctors, thought that the weight of a child mattered. *Il n'y a rien de plus beau que la graisse sous la peau* (there is nothing more beautiful than a little fat under the skin) ran a French proverb, expressing a widely held belief. Again, it is possible that the parents rather than the doctors got it right, since the child with a few reserves could survive better the fevers and diseases of childhood without growing too weak.

There were few professional groups more misogynistic than doctors. Perhaps this prejudice originated in their classical training, but it surfaced above all when recommending child care. In their view, mothers 'cockered' their children, spoiled them with excess and forgot the important lessons of Sparta, that the way to produce the healthy ideal citizen was through austerity and an exposure to the elements. John Locke, whose *Essay on Human Understanding* (1690) was a milestone in western political thought, was also a doctor with views on child care. He thought that small boys should be reared after weaning on small beer and bread, with cold baths and regular exercise and with leaky shoes. Any modern nutritionist or parent would recognize the folly of much of that advice: this so-called expert's recommendations would leave the child prone to vitamin deficiency diseases and with stunted growth as well as a permanent cold. Sure enough, a bewildered parent was subsequently to register dismay when having insisted on such a regime for a son, the child was weak and sickly.[40]

The printed herbal was a compilation of old wives' cures: aniseed and fennel boiled in water for wind, gentiane for thrush and sores, poppy tea to quieten a fretful baby, camomile to ensure peaceful sleep, pyrethrum for worms. Gordon's cordial with its opiate base was by the end of the eighteenth century making inroads as a way to induce babies to sleep, but this was a commercial product coming not from the herbals of the past but from the growing business of the apothecary, an early intrusion of commercial practice into infant rearing.

What we would today call infant training was fairly rudimentary. Children were not encouraged to crawl but were stood in little walking frames made of wicker so that they could feel their feet on the ground and were supported until their muscles strengthened. In rooms with open fires, the child needed protection from accidents.[41] Cooking pots and trivets surrounded the fireplace and could be dangerous if the mother's back was turned unless the child's mobility was restricted. Even in upper-class nurseries, crawling was held to delay the time when the child would walk. To allow the child to crawl was to allow mankind to adopt animal practices by going on all fours. Children had strings attached to their clothes so that their mothers could lead them, as if on reins, when they began to walk. When the first independent steps were made, the strings were severed – an important rite of passage in which mothers recorded their pride.

Toilet training was more of an urban phenomenon than one which concerned country dwellers. National practice may have varied as well as the differing expectations of class. A multiplicity of Dutch and English prints reveal the young child using a chamber pot. The French, however, were thought somewhat remiss in this direction by the more northern parts of Europe. Madame Roland's wet-nurse merely directed her to a corner of the garden which was generally used by the family. Even so, a French rural mother was decried by the neighbours if she let a child defecate unrestrainedly in the house and gave it no toilet training whatsoever. This was regarded as child neglect, as was clear evidence that the child was over lousy. A line was drawn here. Both fleas and body lice were associated with the young but a mother should see to it that they were controlled as far as possible. The simple description *moederstag* – mother's work – under a Dutch seventeenth-century painting refers unobliquely to a woman combing and taking the lice from her child's hair.[42] This was a symbol of the good mother removing the noxious and controlling the child's mind. However, most children lived on farms in proximity to animals and slept on straw which allowed fleas to circulate without impediment. If we add to this that as winter approached children in Britain from even solid farming families had their chests larded with goose grease and were stitched into their clothes so that they could not take them off and catch cold, then the association of children with lice becomes understandable. Spanish mothers could spend several hours a day on removing lice. Upper-class children were kept cleaner because they had more linen which was more frequently laundered. Even so, many young aristocratic children in the eighteenth century had their hair cut very short in an attempt to minimize the problem of hair lice.

Worms were another frequent problem. The gut of one eighteenth-century French farmer, when dissected on death, was found to contain no less than 39 different varieties. Most were picked up from proximity to animals. Animal excrement on dry earth and unwashed or inadequately washed food were an abundant source of threadworms. Tape worms were present in inadequately prepared pork. All could be picked up under the fingernails. Even the aristocracy were not immune and the prosperous brewer's wife Mrs Thrale worried incessantly about her daughter Queenie's worms which caused the child severe discomfort. Most of the infestations were probably of threadworms which caused no more than itching, but even these if left untreated (by something like pyrethrum which is reasonably effective), and if the child in question was weak and debilitated and unable to take in nourishment, could become a major problem.

The herbal and collective wisdom could cope with the simple maladies of childhood. Fevers, high temperatures and croup were more disturbing. This could be the point at which the doctor was called, though what he could do to relieve the situation was minimal. Nor was there much help against the killer epidemics which could take a particularly heavy toll of the very young. At such times, death became a collective experience in a parish. Smallpox, diphtheria, scarlet fever and typhoid were not endemic in communities, but a sudden visitation could decimate whole families. Of these, smallpox was receding in face of medical progress by the end of the period, though it remained a deadly and dreaded visitor.

There was nothing automatic about a visitation from such a killer in the lifetime of any particular child. Child mortality statistics reveal that these deadly diseases usually lagged a little behind the toll exacted by the birth process and loss of life within the first year. The perils of weaning, in the form of the ubiquitous summer diarrhoea at eighteen months, could be acute. Food shortages due to harvest failure or deteriorating economic circumstances could weaken the resistance of the young from impoverished families to complaints such as measles and chicken pox, mumps and whooping cough. Confronted with such maladies in childhood, the upper-class child had a considerable advantage over the poor one.[43]

Indeed, if the upper- or middle-class child survived its early infancy, its hold on life was certainly stronger than that of the children of the poor. Better nourished and relatively isolated from the germ-infested environment of the farm cottage or the urban tenement, these children stood a good chance of surviving childhood and adolescence, unless they were sent to a boarding establishment where mortality rates were extraordinarily high.

Did attitudes towards children change in any way over the three hundred years studied here? Lawrence Stone and the historians of affective individualism have argued that before the eighteenth century, baptized by Phillippe Ariès as the 'century of the child', there was much indifference to children by parents promoted by a stoical acceptance of death and a pessimistic view of their chances of survival. Others, notably Elizabeth Badinter, have gone further and insisted that 'mothering' is an invention of capitalism and that the wet-nursing sought by the rich for their offspring and the statistics of child abandonment by the poor point to a lack of emotional involvement with offspring.[44] Such views have been both softened and modified by closer analysis which takes account of the circumstances of individual families across class. The gloomy recommendations of sin-obsessed clerics and doctors critical of 'mothering' practices, characteristic of both Protestant and Catholic societies, did not invariably reflect real-life situations. Of course there were neglected and unwanted children as there still are. However, the evidence of memoirs and autobiographies, of letters and memorabilia like child portraits, suggests that children were wanted, valued and cherished according to the standards of the day and the possibilities open to individual families right throughout the period. What can look like indifference to the outside observer might, in the conditions of the times or under socio-economic imperatives specific to a certain class, be the best way of dealing with a particular situation.[45]

With this recognition in mind, the phenomenon of child abandonment becomes more intelligible. It should be seen as not only the practice of a tiny minority but one effectively confined to those cities (and their rural hinterland) which had foundling hospitals. This meant the Italian cities and some in Spain and Portugal, though they spread to Paris in the seventeenth century and to London and some German and Scandinavian cities by the eighteenth. The hospitals of many French cities were in fact receiving foundlings by the beginning of the eighteenth century, though not equipped to do so. In the fifteenth century, Italian institutions seem to have been used primarily for the illegitimate offspring of the patriciates, but thereafter many of them were increasingly taking in legitimate children whose families could not afford to rear them, perhaps because they threatened the mother's earning capacity. It has been argued in the Italian case that abandonment gradually became integrated into the 'expedient' economy (or family survival strategy) of the working populations of certain cities. In so far as the evidence exists, it would seem that such children were the third or fourth offspring whose survival could only be at the expense of the other living children. An increasing proportion of these foundlings were reclaimed by their parents when they became capable of earning their own living so that, for example, while only 6 per cent were reclaimed in the sixteenth century in Florence, 72 per cent were reclaimed in the eighteenth; in Rome the proportions were 19 per cent in the seventeenth century and 39 per cent in the eighteenth. The northern European pattern suggests that while poverty may have impelled abandonment, illegitimacy remained a significant factor. Moreover, the percentages of reappropriation were much smaller.[46]

In the sixteenth and seventeenth centuries, civil strife could on occasion cut off parents from children. Aristocratic parents were conscious that they could die leaving their children orphaned and vulnerable not merely to loneliness but perhaps to the intrusive hand of monarchs and nobles interested in the disposal of a noble fief or estate. For such reasons, both boys and girls were sent as young teenagers to live with relatives or acquaintances who could introduce them to a broader society, or in the case of girls teach them more effective household management. Such an education was purchased. Godparents were kept in close touch with a child's progress and were expected to help and promote the child's interests, particularly if one or both parents died. Indeed the fragility of human life as well as the hardness of the times contributed to a strong parental anxiety to ensure the future of their children and this could include the efforts made to arrange marriage. If a young girl was orphaned, she could be received into the home of her future husband and protected by his parents. If she was an heiress, she was also protected from the intrusion of the king who could seek to appropriate her property through wardship rights.[47]

Autobiographies and journals from these troubled times reflect largely the behaviour of the upper classes and are mostly written by men. Many embody anxieties about the physical wellbeing of their children. Those written by women are more concerned with the minutiae of everyday life and the daily traumas that could affect their families. They reveal anxieties and worries, but also pride and pleasure in the progress of their children. The correspondence of Balthasar and Magdalena from sixteenth-century Nuremberg demonstrates concerns with which any modern parent could readily identify. Their son was not an assiduous or ideal student. His parents had many anxieties. His mother worried about his health and whether he was keeping warm when absent from home and both parents were concerned about his lack of commitment to his studies.[48]

Parents might be under instructions from clerics to reprimand the faults of their children severely as a way of breaking the spirit. The child in all religious confessions was seen as having been conceived and born in sin. Punishment for error and unremitting verbal strictures, a sparse diet and avoidance of petting, made up the collective message which churchmen sought to impart. To discipline the child through corporal punishment and moral strictures was seen as the positive obligation of the parent. How much of the severe message was integrated into the conduct of parents is much less easy to determine. Though many parents, both male and female, do record beating their offspring, nothing suggests that it was more than an occasional practice and the degree of the beating is almost impossible to ascertain. This was not flogging and the modern parent who has not smacked a child may well be in a minority. Furthermore, beating is almost never recorded as having been administered to girls and was very infrequently done by the mother.

Parents could be under extreme pressure from the churchmen to watch their children carefully for signs of evil behaviour. The mother of Isabella de Moerloose in the mid-sixteenth century was such a woman and her reactions are worthy of note, since she provides a rare instance of a mother who did beat her child and that child a girl.

Her baby was a matter of anxiety from birth because she was born with a caul over her head. Some regarded this as a sign of good luck but others were more apprehensive. It was not a normal birth and though the baby was good and healthy and a first child, the mother was not entirely easy. The priest, her confessor, cautioned her to keep watch lest manifestations of evil appeared. When the little girl oscillated between bouts of intense shyness and intense volubility, he told the mother something was wrong and that she should be beaten. The mother heeded the advice at least occasionally – enough to imprint the event on Isabella's memory. However, when her confessor recommended that she shut the child in a dark room for several days to stifle the devil, she drew a line. She could not inflict such suffering on her child. Isabella blamed her mother in later life for listening to the priest at all and making her unhappy. However, she had broken with the Catholic faith while her mother had been devout and was clearly terrified that her eldest child might be a witch; chastisement was the only solution open to her.[49]

In any country, there are few testimonies to suggest that the beating of the child by its parents was a common occurrence in spite of the alleged experts in child rearing. Even in the sixteenth century, when times were violent, there surfaces a great deal of evidence of joy at the spectacle of the child's development, the babbling, the first words, the initial independent steps, 'their stammering, their little angers, their innocence, their imperfections, their necessities, are so many little emanations of joy and comfort.'[50]

The Dutch have left the most considerable visual testimony to the mixture of anxiety, care, according to the norms of the day, and enjoyment parents derived from the young. A Dutch print shows that nightmare is likened to the snatching of a baby by death from a cradle. Little girls and boys are cleaned and given food, taught to say their prayers and cherished, this mostly by their mothers, and they are also enjoyed. Saint Nicolas's feast is the time for indulgence of the well-behaved. Gingerbread men and spinning tops, pipes and drums are bestowed. In the general revelry of Twelfth Night, an infant toddling 'king' is stood on an upturned bucket and pronounced to 'rule' the feast. Throughout Europe this feast of the three kings was a time for giving gifts to the young. Even if it was not until the eighteenth century that the commercialization of present-giving to children developed on a large scale among the better-off classes, long before the advent of rocking horses and special card games, fancy bread, oranges, and sweetmeats were treats for children at fairs and on public holidays for all classes throughout the early modern period. It would seem that adult enjoyment was always enhanced by the presence of children at these times.

Dolls would appear to have been regarded, at least from the seventeenth century, as appropriate toys for little girls. Their appropriateness may have pivoted on the scope they gave for emulation of the maternal role. Dutch prints show the dollmaker's stall to have been patronized by both mothers and daughters and that there were dolls for all purses. Dutch Protestant divines tried to stop their sale in 1663 on the grounds that they encouraged idolatry and there followed a 'battle of the dolls' which turned out to be a victory for the young consumer. Many seventeenth-century dolls were dressed in a miniature version of adult clothing – as indeed were children at this time – but little by little, the doll became more overtly a baby to be tended by the small girl as her mother nursed her sibling. Pedlars sold crude wooden dolls with painted faces and without clothes which for a few pence could lighten any little girl's heart while confirming her female status. It was an important part of the socialization process: tops and little boats for boys, dolls for girls.[51]

In the eighteenth century the commercial revolution identified the affluent child as a consumer. The cult of domesticity that permeated the writings of the *philosophes* extolled the joys of family life, but how much real influence they had on the conduct of families is no easier to ascertain than that of the gloomy forebodings of the clerical establishment. The child with a nursery of toys is not necessarily more cherished than the one with a peg doll.

On more certain ground, at all levels of society the parents, and the mother in particular, were responsible for the socialization of the young child. What a mother told her child, and especially her daughters, was part of a shaping process, acculturation, bestowing a view of the world. There are few pointers to the content of this process. Isabella de Moerloose described some of the tales her mother told her. She was instructed never to go near canals in the dark lest an ogre seize her and suffocate her by sticking a large ball in her mouth. Later in life when her pastor husband tried to have oral sex with her she realized the significance of this tale. She was also told about the blood carriage driven in dark nights by the agents of the queen of England who bathed in the blood of children. Isabella, like all the children of the canals, was being instructed in the necessity of going home from her play promptly before dark and avoiding possible encounters with deviance. The Englishman Reginald Scot, the philosopher Jean Bodin and later John Locke and Lavater believed that parents were responsible for creating in the minds of their children visions of witches and evil spirits which were transmitted through an inheritance of folk-tales. Certainly the cursing old woman who made children into pies and the folly of wandering abroad and poking one's nose into the unknown were a significant part of the prohibitions and fears that one generation passed on to another.[52]

Some of these stories were picked up as part of the fabric of everyday life On every farm there were believed to be spirits at work who needed appeasing if milk was not to turn sour or dough refuse to rise: pucks, trolls, Joan the Wads and mischievous little personages who must be humoured and placated by a saucer of milk. Mothers in Catholic countries tied *scapulaires* on their children to keep them safe. The child in the cradle was committed to the care of Saint Denis (*saint des nids*). Breton children were shown menhirs crowned with crucifixes and told of evil spirits tamed by Christianity. The blending of the religious with the profane was, as every priest knew, learned in childhood.[53] The guilt and fear cultures of the dominant religious orthodoxies were instilled before reason was developed.

Above all, mothers taught their children about the process of survival in their particular world and their particular social class: 'This is how we do things: this is how we think.' Obviously here there were huge differences, but there were also common elements. On the reputation of the mother that of the daughter depended. A witch would beget a witch, a whore a whore (a witch's or a whore's get). The concept of 'like mother like daughter' exists in all languages long before the fictional marquis in Laclos' *Les Liaisons dangereuses* (1782) cynically explained that a woman would do anything she believed her mother had done before her – in this case consent to illicit sex. Whatever skills a mother had she must impart them to her child. In addition, the mother was without doubt in most cases the major influence in inculcating a notion of gender roles into her daughter. She knew what women should know and did what women should do.

Her female role was not the only one to be transmitted. Ideas relative to social status and in some cases ethnic or religious identity, and what these meant in the practical observances of everyday life, had to be conveyed to the next generation. Amsterdam, some German cities, Venice, a few Italian towns as well as Spain and Portugal before the great persecutions, had Jewish communities, some living in ghettoes reserved for them. Debarred from public religious life, but with the tasks of perpetuating rituals within the home, Jewish mothers had also to impart to their daughters the logic of menstrual taboos, the need for contact with members of their own communities, Jewish specialness and its implications for women. Glückel of Hameln (1646–1724) left a series of memoirs in which her account of her daughters (and their husbands whose advice she takes as a widow) reveals the intensity of mother–daughter relationships continuing throughout life as she, and in turn they, helped each other in negotiating their social world.[54]

For upper-class women aided by a battery of nurserymaids and governesses, dancing masters and teachers of French, this guidance might not have extended beyond overseeing an educational routine in which a young girl was taught to know her status in life and given accomplishments which would show her off to the full, like fine needle-work and singing. She would also be made aware of appropriate behaviour, never to exceed the bounds of modesty and always to err on the side of understatement. She learned from her mother the skills of household management, enhancing the internal appearance of the home, planning dinner parties and other social events. When she came 'out' in her late teens, her apparent social innocence was intended to be a mask cloaking a carefully inculcated scale of values. Her mother would be the yardstick against which she was measured. Any inappropriate behaviour would reflect on her upbringing.

Lower down the social scale the business of being a woman was learned in the course of more practical business: cooking, cleaning, working, appearing at the washplace. A daughter's place was for her first years beside her mother. She fed the hens and gathered weeds to feed rabbits and goats. She learned to crack nuts for oil and to turn

over turds drying for fuel. If living in a fishing village she went down
to the strand with her and trawled rock pools or fetched home kelp for
fertilizer or even for soup. Together mother and child plundered the
hedgerows and picked up fallen fruit, gathered mushrooms or wild
herbs which lent taste to soups whose content might not be much more
than a little stale bread and a piece of salted pork fat. The child collected
sticks for kindling – it is not for nothing that the good child in fairy
stories parted with her bundle in charity to help a poor old woman –
gathered acorns for fuel and for pigs, and grass and leaves for rabbits.

Each season had its rituals of things that needed doing if the household was to survive. Hence, from the corners of Dutch genre paintings
little girls in particular watch their mothers pluck chickens, bake bread,
make pancakes over a blazing fire, peel and core apples, chop onions,
lay the table and sweep the floor. They stand by her side as she breast-
feeds the baby ready to get her anything she should request. In due
course the infant will pass to the charge of her sister. Special occasions,
Christmas, Twelfth Night, Easter, demanded special culinary efforts.
If her mother spun wool or cotton, this was a technique she acquired
early. The earliest mother and daughter pictures are usually of the
Virgin and Saint Anne. Frequently Saint Anne is shown teaching the
Virgin to read. Then in the sixteenth century as her cult develops,
the mother winds wool which the Virgin knits or sews. The implicit
symbolism is that the raw material, the means to achieve perfection, is
something conveyed by the mother to the daughter.

Above all, their physical proximity and the invigilation of the daughter by the mother is seen as critical. The 'industrious mother' passes on
needlework and spinning skills. These skills were those of the home,
the proper place of mother and daughter.

What was also included in the socialization of the female child by
her mother was a set of social relations with the priest and other members
of the local community. There were those owed deference who might
be useful one day. There were those who might help if the family fell
on hard times. In parts of France, the priest divided up the poor of the
village and the mothers of impoverished families took their children to
a certain house every day for a drink of milk and a bit of bread or for
household scraps to make into soup. Linkages were encouraged between
the virtuous poor family and those who were better off. Such knowledge
allowed the giver to know that the beneficiaries of charity were worthy.
In this assessment of virtue the character of the mother was critical.

The good mother did not encourage idleness and her children did not grow into thieves.

There were other members of the community who might help a girl later in life to 'find a place'. In this instance, 'place' refers to a residential job but the word far exceeded this meaning. To 'know one's place' did not imply that one was at the lowest level of society but rather had a consciousness of where one belonged in a particular society, not only in economic and professional terms but also those of age, sex, and family connection. When Richard Gough wrote *A History of Myddle* in 1701, he began by describing the occupants of the village with reference to pews in church, allotted to particular families. Each member of the community had a visible place every Sunday linking that person to a clan. It was more or less the same everywhere. In Languedoc, for example, the seigneur and his family had the front pew and were served first at communion and then ranked behind them came village notables. Linkage to a particular family was like a label signifying honesty or dishonesty, virtue or lack of virtue, meanness or generosity, honour or shame. Sometimes the church congregation was divided not only by family but by sex; but whatever the pattern, while a boy sat next to his father, a young girl sat next to her mother. This was her place. Her mother spoke for her. She was her voice and her window on the outside world.

If a mother was literate, a qualification which applied to under a third of French women although well over that mark among Dutch and English women by the end of the period, then she saw to it that a child knew her letters. There is no evidence of a literate mother with an illiterate child. Some may have performed this task of teaching themselves, others used available village schooling and those who could afford it used the governess or convent boarding school.

The education of a daughter was not viewed as the same thing as that of a son. For the generality of the population a girl's first teacher in survival skills was her mother. Further education was less concerned with literacy than with additional vocational skills. Sons were, however, less the concern of their mother's guiding hand and when they went to school the aim was much more the learning of letters.

The availability of village schools varied enormously according to country, locality and even from village to village. At the lowest level the English dame school, like its Dutch counterpart, was little more than a childminding service where a little literacy might be dispensed by a widow or other matron who sat with her spinning wheel or her knitting and regarded her job as to keep children out of mischief while their parents worked. All this activity was perhaps only a small part of her income. Some English village schools and certainly charity schools aimed higher. Religious instruction with knowledge of biblical texts, reading and writing and arithmetic, sewing at several levels – plain and embroidery – were what a girl might come by in the charity school. It was probably through such establishments and by maternal efforts that literacy thresholds were crossed in Britain.[55]

In France some schools run by religious orders only operated during the dead season.[56] All taught the catechism, for the aim was to make good Catholics. Some taught reading, but not invariably writing, and some were vocational – they taught spinning and sewing or lace-making. In the Pays de Velay, for example, women known as *béates* ran a school, of a kind, which operated as a childminding service for the young while their mothers worked at home with their lace bobbins, but as the children grew older the *béate* taught the girls to make lace as well as teaching them the catechism and to *manuscrire* or read contracts and documents. The boys had no place in such establishments once childhood had passed so that the separation of male and female during adolescence was almost absolute. In her teens a competent lace-maker might be recommended by the *béate* for a place in one of the dormitories in Le Puy itself, where the girls were given free shelter and helped to save the proceeds of their work towards a dowry.

Whether charity school or *petite école*, a girl's education further conditioned her to a particular role and endorsed the value judgements of the society of which she was a part. If she continued to live with her family, she waited on the men who had been at work in the fields and she helped with the cooking and the sewing. Society had a vision of what was appropriate for her and to reach outside that vision was almost impossible, given her education and her opportunities.

When and if, as was common, a point of severance with her family came, then the joint contribution of mother and school to a girl's qualifications (in French *formation*, in Spanish *gobierno* or discipline) were brought to the fore in the search for a place. As the door of the farm closed behind the girl, she made her first steps towards adult life. The wheel had come full circle. The strategic plan was under way for her adult future as wife and mother.

How much contact was maintained with families after the severance occurred is not easy to say. The potential for contact clearly varied with literacy and how far a girl had to travel to get work. If it was only a matter of a few miles, then a visit on half-holidays, or a meeting on market days when a rural mother might bring goods into the town for sale, were probably the main possibilities for contact. Seasonal labourers from the Rouergue who descended from the hills to work on the grape harvests of Languedoc called off to visit their sisters in service in Montpellier or Lodève or to see those who worked as spinners in the textile industry of Clermont de Lodève, and brought with them news as well as taking it back home. Without the ability to write a letter, such contacts could only be infrequent. Severance was the sharpest the lower one got down the social scale, perhaps more than anything else because of the illiteracy factor.

For middle-class society, the separation of mother and daughter was infrequent, unless the girl went to a boarding school when contacts were maintained by letter and by visits as journals and correspondence show. While sons left for school, college or university, most daughters remained behind as company for mothers and siblings. They represented continuity in the household until the moment of marriage came.

Modern sociologists consider the relationship between mother and daughter the strongest of family ties in western culture. Something of this strength in traditional societies perhaps came from the closeness of those tied to a domestic environment, where the mother was the example and first teacher and counsellor in how to negotiate the system. As long as she lived, she would be her daughter's natural recourse for advice and a presence in childbed and sickness. Even in those regions characterized by heavy female migration, mothers who might never see their daughters again strove to put away a bit from the eggs or the sale of milk or rabbits to help with the dowry. They waited anxiously for news.

Working-class women in the towns, and middle-class women from both town and country, probably had the most sustained contacts with their daughters and most conspicuously shaped their life strategies. Poorer rural families parted from their children in adolescence, and even if contact was maintained their influence diminished. For the aristocracy, if Lady Mary Wortley Montagu is to be believed, the reverse was true. Whereas babies and young children could be left to the nurse, and girls to the governess – who of course needed observing to make sure that she did her job properly – there came a point in the mid-teens when they needed presenting to society, chaperoning, instructing in appropriate behaviour and to have entertainments arranged for them as part of the rituals involved in announcing that they were on the marriage market. The absence of upper- and middle-class girls from the illegitimacy statistics throughout Europe attests to the success of maternal vigilance.

For a mother's ultimate job was to advance or maximize her daughter's marital prospects, whatever these might be. Her success was for most social classes the production of a virtuous, hard-working, thrifty and chaste daughter, as near as possible to the model stated in the prescriptive literature but one possessing enough *savoir-faire* to negotiate the system. Women were perhaps aware that their own chances of seeing their children reach adulthood were not high and that education as they understood it could not be deferred. The orphaned child, particularly the orphaned female child, was perceived to be a tragic figure: the stepmother was someone who favoured her own children over those of her second husband. The plight of Cinderella struck a chord familiar to all who listened and most of the listeners must have known that fairy godmothers were few and far between.

CHAPTER SIX

◁◦▷

Widowhood

That Lady Russell, of steady age and character, and
extremely well provided for, should have no thought of a
second marriage, needs no apology to the public, which is
rather apt to be unreasonably discontented when a woman
does marry again, than when she does *not*; but Sir Walter's
continuing in singleness requires explanation.

JANE AUSTEN, PERSUASION, 1818, CHAPTER 1

Rise and stand up
And tackle your plough team!
Plough a five inch furrow.
Look at me, my treasure,
With no-body to help me
When I go reaping or cutting!
Who will do my business at market?
Who will go to the Hill of the Mass.
As you lie stretched from now on
Och ochón.

TRADITIONAL IRISH KEENING SONG

Death makes me poore.

THOMAS DEKKER, THE SHOEMAKER'S HOLIDAY, C. 1598

T HE HAZARDS of childbed made a cull, if one which has been
somewhat exaggerated, of women in their late twenties and
early thirties. Their partners at all social levels, widowers who
were still young, would have little difficulty in replicating the married
state. It was as if the first marriage, however strategically planned, had
never taken place.[1]

If there were more widowers than widows from these early years of marriage, the young widow was not an uncommon personage. Heiresses and women of wealth still of marriageable age with years of childbearing ahead were repossessed and renegotiated in a new alliance by their families of origin. In Italian patrician circles this even held true if they had had children. For all women from all social classes who were widowed before they were thirty and had no more than one or two children, remarriage was likely. Although convention demanded that she wait a little longer than a widower before retying the knot, between 60 and 80 per cent of these young women – the higher figures marking periods of high employment or the years immediately following an outbreak of plague – would find a new partner and begin again as if the first marriage had never occurred.[2]

Such a woman was not encumbered by large numbers of children and the assets she had brought into her first marriage were still largely intact. Indeed, in some instances her new husband could benefit in a number of ways (taking over guild membership, or the lease of a flourishing holding, for example). This young, remarrying widow is to be distinguished from the one in an older age group. In many cases, only if she was in control of substantial assets through the repossession of her dower, and perhaps advantages under her first husband's will such as, in Germany, entry to a guild, could the older widow hope to find a new partner. The older she was, the less her chances of remarriage. Only about 20 per cent of women over forty could hope to make a new match and the numbers who remarried after fifty are negligible in all societies and at all times.

The reasons are perhaps obvious. If a woman had several children by a first marriage, they could complicate her situation in several ways. Either they had to be maintained out of such means as she possessed, or their claims to her late husband's property could restrict her freedom of action. Equally clearly, once the menopause loomed and there was little chance of issue, marriage was not generally undertaken. The marriage of an older woman to a younger man was not unknown and on occasion could be to the young man's financial benefit, but it was one that the contracting parties felt they had to justify. William Lily, for example, a twenty-six-year-old servant in Elizabethan London, described his marriage with his mistress, several years his senior, in the following terms:

My mistress who had been married twice to old men was now resolved to be cozened no more . . . she was of a brown ruddy complexion . . . plain . . . no education. She had many suitors, old men whom she declined; some gentlemen of decayed fortunes whom she liked not . . . By my fellow servants she was frequently heard to say she cared not if she married a man that would love her so he had never a penny . . . The disproportion of years and fortune being so great betwixt us . . . However, all her talk was of a husband.

He proposed and, though hardly in love, he clearly felt affection for her and the six years before her death were ones of contentment. She left him £1000, of which he used £530 to buy thirteen houses in the Strand and with this collateral got £500 in dowry from a new wife when he married eight months after the death of the first. Society could appreciate the logic of both the old wife and the new husband.[3]

Women in early modern society, in general, lived longer than men – if not by very much – even taking into account the hazards of childbed and the arduousness of work and reproduction. Marriages lasted on average about sixteen to twenty years, depending on the times, and the female was the likelier survivor. Since she was also the partner less likely to remarry, any society was apt to carry a far greater proportion of widows than it did of widowers.

The bereaved husband's chances of finding a replacement for his dead wife, no matter the age at which she had died or the number of children born to the initial marriage, were very high indeed. The new partner, with important exceptions made for the upper classes, for certain artisanal groups, and for the working population of the largest cities, was likely to be chosen from the single women of the parish. Whatever sadness a man experienced at the death of a young spouse, a farmer or an artisan simply had to find a replacement. He could not run a farm or a business alone. Those who were more affluent, and intent on perpetuating a lineage, had to resign their grief and start again. In seventeenth-century Germany 80 per cent of all widowed men found new wives within a year of widowhood, but only 40 per cent of widows found new husbands. In eighteenth-century Norway, over 60 per cent of male cottars would remarry but only 30 per cent of cottar widows. The lowest northern statistic comes from Denmark where, taking the entire age range in the seventeenth century, only 25 per cent of men and 22 per cent of women among the peasant population appear to have married for a second time.[4] However, such numbers appear high for women compared to the record of Mediterranean Europe. In eighteenth-century Tuscany, for example, remarriage among the popular classes was almost entirely a male affair.[5] There were many unmarried men: because of the restricted amount of available land and inheritance practices, the eldest son usually married, but not his brothers. If his wife died he took another and in over 80 per cent of instances he chose a bride who had never been married, for sound financial reasons. The widower's family held on to his first wife's dowry in the name of the children and he took another single woman with means behind her on whom no other children could exert a claim.

The behaviour of rural society would appear to have been in contrast with that of the more fluid large cities characterized by heavy rural immigration and dependent upon this flow to maintain the level of population. Pre-industrial cities were killers of both men and women. It followed that the bereaved of either sex, if they had some means, could find remarriage easier than in the country. Furthermore, the cities themselves may have served as a pole of attraction to the widowed who wished to remarry.

There were many more social pressures impelling a man towards speedy remarriage than a woman. Even at quite lowly social levels, men were considered demeaned by being seen doing women's work – particularly housework and washing. They were not accustomed to tending children and the services performed by a wife on the farm or in the workshop were not easily replaced by waged labour. Honour demanded that a man find a new wife to perform these tasks. A man from higher social levels had to think of the perpetuation of property.

Honour made different demands on women than on men. A woman's first task after her husband's death was to demonstrate to society that she venerated his memory. She was shamed in the eyes of the community if she did not provide him with a proper funeral and demonstrate distress. Over the sixteenth and seventeenth century mourning clothes and ceremonies everywhere seem to have become more complicated, but the most elaborate rituals for the honouring of the dead husband emanate from Mediterranean Europe: in Italy complex rules governed the widow's dress, deportment and position in the funeral cortège. Ecclesiastics in Ireland, Britain and France, however, expressed concern at the inroads the funeral rites could make into the widow's funds at a time when she had to face all kinds of other financial demands. The

Bishop of Cashel, for example, in the 1670s waxed eloquent on the follies of the Irish wake which cost far more than the wedding feast and where the widow was financing, though she could ill afford to do so, a conspicuous form of village entertainment.[6]

The widower was allowed to be more parsimonious and more helpless in the arrangement of a feast, which was after all women's work. Whereas, throughout most of Europe, it was deemed dishonourable for a widow to remarry within a year, it was perfectly respectable for a man to remarry within three to six months. These periods of restraint could be reduced still further in the aftermath of plague: indeed, in such times both men and women found remarriage much easier, particularly in devastated cities.

The Catholic church was to be counted among the influences restraining a woman from remarriage. It hallowed widowhood and although remarriage in church was permitted, nuptial benediction was withheld from those concerned. Furthermore, it did not advise women to remarry and many confessors may have exerted pressure on wealthy widows not to do so, for throughout the seventeenth century the church was becoming progressively more interested both in the widow's energies and in the funds she might command. The widow who had repossessed her dowry was a source of wealth simultaneously troubling and challenging. The stance of the Catholic church was not replicated by the Protestant confessions, for whom marriage was a desirable state for all women; though it was in practice recognized that this applied to women of childbearing age. The elderly widow could be left in the care of children enjoined by Scripture to remember their duty.

The widow was, then, a familiar and to a degree acceptable member of society whom all acknowledged should be recognized, and provided she behaved as society deemed appropriate, she was accorded a measure of respect. She had married, as convention insisted she should, but God had taken her partner, a personal tragedy for which she was in no way to blame. However, in a world whose value system was predicated upon female subordination to a male head of a household, and where female earning power was indeed limited, widows at all social levels posed particular problems. These were women alone, some in command of money and assets, others so poor without a man to support them that they might threaten public morality or make demands on the public purse.

Something of the apprehension with which the widow was regarded is found in prescriptive, medical and creative literature. In all good conduct books dedicated to defining exemplary behaviour, the subject of widowhood receives some treatment. The widow in differing guises also appears in creative literature – in plays and novels and in fairy-tales. Among the model letters of the seventeenth and eighteenth centuries can be found letters of good advice to widows about to contract marriages with unsuitable young men to the detriment of the progeny of the previous marriage. Such interpretations of widowhood reduce themselves to certain common themes. Most could be subsumed under the generic title of male fears about the unattached female — particularly one who might deprive the offspring of the first marriage of what was rightfully theirs.[7] At the end of the period, however, novels written by women, of which Jane Austen was the mistress, provide a very different version. Here the widow is seen as very much dependent upon the provisions made for her by both her late husband and her father, and as someone who could be locked in very serious financial problems unbecoming to her class.

Theologians and moralists dealt with the widow as if she was part of a homogeneous group. The aim of much prescriptive writing was to contain a woman who had experienced sex and hence had had her libido aroused. Now her husband was not there to control her, her ungoverned lust was seen as a threat. The widow is recommended to live a life of chastity dedicated to honouring the memory of her deceased partner. Vives was insistent that, of all women, the widow should be the one most dedicated to privacy. He criticized confessors who might encourage widows to lead an over-public life. Some theologians thought they should be encouraged to enter religious houses. In Italian convents the ecclesiastical hierarchy insisted upon the separation of the virgins and the widows, lest those who had had no knowledge of the carnal state should learn about what exactly went on in the matrimonial bed, and thus blemish their innocence or experience lustful thoughts. The convents themselves were not enthusiastic about admitting widows, whom they saw as a potentially critical, querulous and therefore disruptive element.[8]

The implications of medical writing on the widow are also that, having had her sexual appetite whetted, she was an aroused and lusty force and hence predatory, needing a male replacement. This image is absorbed into the interpretations made by playwrights and novelists. Les Liaisons dangereuses (1782) has as the architect of disaster and tragedy a wealthy widow who has the money and the leisure to manipulate her lovers and plot the downfall of the chaste woman. Goldoni's *The Artful Widow* (1748) and Mrs Malaprop in Sheridan's *The Rivals* (1775) provide comic facets of the worldly wise and sexually rampant uncontrolled widow. In *The Beggar's Opera* (1728), Polly Peachum is told by her parents to snap up Macheath as she will soon be a wealthy widow, the state every woman hopes for on matrimony; here John Gay drew upon a stereotypical assumption in this comedy of manners in which the poor are accredited with the reasoning of the rich.

Defoe hit a more sombre note. When Roxana is widowed with children and faces starvation, she clings to the maxim "Tis better to whore than to starve', dumps her children on their grandparents and becomes a kept woman. Her only income is from her sexuality. The novelist presents the reader with a predicament. Roxana is an impoverished widow. What else could she do? The plight here outlined is the lack of adequate resources, but there is more than a shade of criticism of one who takes the obvious way out.

The widow as distressed gentlewoman, this time of unimpeachable morality, finds complex and sympathetic rendering in the works of the women novelists of the eighteenth century. The mistress of the art of knowing exactly what could in quite arbitrary fashion threaten a woman's livelihood and marital prospects was Jane Austen, who created in *Sense and Sensibility* (1811) two heroines whose problems emanated from their dependence on a woman, the widow of a man whose estate was left to a son by a previous marriage and who had merely recommended to his son that he 'provide' for his stepmother and stepsisters. Lacking an income guaranteed at law, and in face of a breach of a verbal promise, the widow had only the most slender of means.

Here is a view of widowhood which touches on the essential problems and summarizes the arbitrary nature of the state. It underscores a simple point. A woman at the outset of matrimony needed to have whatever assets she brought with her into marriage, and whatever her husband agreed to settle on her, *clearly embodied in a legal document*, the settlement. The husband's last testament should then be fully explicit in making further provision for her and detailing clearly the position of the children. He should also state whether the mother was to be executrix or joint executrix of the will. These two legal documents, more than anything else, make clear the widow's position and protect her. Jane

Austen's perception should inform all studies of widowhood: the point of departure is a consideration of her position in law.

In the first instance it must be assumed that the wealthy drew up settlements on the eve of marriage. In countries of both Roman and customary law the widow had a right to whatever she brought into marriage (the dowry) or, by agreement, she had a right to the income or usufruct of this sum. She could also claim the clothes, jewels and furniture she brought with her and whatever her husband had settled on her at marriage, a third or a half of what they had communally owned (that is, had come to own after the marriage) and anything else the husband cared to bestow upon her in his will provided it did not cut across other legal obligations entailing his property. This was the common ground.

It was normal in areas where customary law prevailed for the widow to be seen as the natural guardian of the progeny until they were of age. Usually, under the terms of his will, the husband of considerable means would appoint a member of his kin as joint guardian to oversee the interests of the children, but the rights of the wife to live in the conjugal home until the heir was of age, and thereafter to have provision made for her, were regarded as the norm. In the event of her remarriage she did not lose custody of the children, but a careful husband, anxious to protect their interests, would appoint a guardian drawn from his kin to see to it that the wife took no more than was her due and did not cut into the income from property intended for the issue of the match. Clearly she lost the right to inhabit the conjugal home. This concern that a remarrying widow might jeopardize the inheritance of the rightful heir caused many anxieties. Indeed, the French were anxious to ensure that this weak link in the chain of property disposal through the legitimate line was somewhat strengthened. For this reason, in the late sixteenth century a corpus of legislation emerged to restrict the gifts that a widow with children could bestow on a second husband.[9]

Beginning with the law of Francis II in 1560, widows (assumed to be sought in second marriage for their wealth rather than their persons and blinded by their folly) were restrained from lavishing extravagant gifts on their new partner 'to the desolation of good families and consequently the diminution of the strength of the state'.[10] The state was far from disinterested in the transference of wealth from noble house to noble house at a time when nobles formed factional alliances against the king. The body of legislation which was enacted was made to apply to all levels of society, though clearly its application *de facto* only applied to those with means. When a man died his property and that held in common with his wife was sealed off and valued within five weeks of his death so that the widow could not assume direct control of anything that was not hers.[11] If she remarried, a French widow lost her rights to guardianship of her children unless her husband's kin sanctioned the continuation, and they had the right to exact guarantees from the new husband to respect the rights of the heirs. The English and Dutch situations were less clear and much depended on the husband's will. Frequently, where the widow was given control of property and children, some rights were rescinded in the event of her remarriage.[12]

In Italy the widow was due nothing more than her own property. She was not regarded as the natural guardian of the children of the marriage, although in his will the husband could give her some rights of guardianship. She had married into a family and that family, her husband's, had the right to reclaim his property and to manage it on behalf of the heirs. The husband could cut across some of these rulings in his will by naming his wife *donna et madonna* of his patrimony as long as she remained unmarried. This provision gave the widow enjoyment of the full usufruct of all that was left and the right to live in the marital home with the children. Should he also specify that she should have total freedom from being called to account for the management of the usufruct, her power was greatly increased. By proclaiming her *donna et madonna* the family was spared having to repay the dowry and she and her children could be kept together. The husband could, however, totally ignore a young wife in his will, so that on his death she was either forced to leave the conjugal home and to surrender her children, having repossessed her dowry, or she was whisked away after the funeral by her own family. Such an omission from the will might reflect the position of a husband who considered his wife too young and inexperienced for the management of their affairs. Or the husband could merely allot to her the custody of the younger and usually female chidren. In short, the widow was utterly dependent on the framing of the will and if she remarried considerable complications could arise. Even the *donna et madonna* who had fully enjoyed the confidence of her husband then lost the custody of her children. Furthermore, she needed to repossess her dowry – a source of endless litigation. Rather than repay a dowry, a family might wish to hold on to the widowed mother. Should she, however, decide to remarry and repossess her assets, her severance from her first husband's family could be abrupt and total. The children were left behind with the relatives of their father who managed their property until the heir came into possession and made provision for the dowries and settlements of the siblings. This situation could convert the remarrying widow into the 'cruel mother' of Renaissance writing who had 'abandoned' her children. In fact she had no legal alternative if she wished or was obliged to remarry. Roman law sought to protect the heir in terms of property, not affection, and it apparently held motherhood to have very little worth.[13]

Progressively, over the seventeenth and eighteenth centuries, some of the potential harshness of the law was in practice modified by an increasing tendency on the part of husbands to leave wills expressing a wish for the mother to have greater control over the future care of her children – on occasion, by the eighteenth century, even if they remarried. Venetian widows, for example, seem to have had increasingly developed powers of initiative. Elsewhere the Magistrati dei Pupilli or delle Vedove e Pupilli (courts of widows and minors) which assumed guardianship of the children on behalf of the state, but had the powers to place the rearing of them in the mother's care and secure for her the income from the estate of the dead father to do so, became the recourse of the woman who wanted to hold on to her children. Indeed, it is now suggested that these courts may have been the most important institutions in Italy in promoting a concept of a value of the maternal against the dominant notions of patriarchal control. Furthermore, over the seventeenth century, legislation was enacted permitting widows who wished to remarry to reappropriate their dowries in cash more speedily. The position of the remarrying widow, however, remained deeply problematic.[14]

In areas of Roman law the repayment of the widow's dowry took precedence over any debts on the husband's estate, but in areas of customary law this only applied if a separate settlement to that effect had been made on marriage. When a written dowry settlement recorded by a notary had not been made, a husband's testament was the only formal record of what the widow should enjoy on his death and what should be the rights of the heir. This fact would seem to have been widely appreciated where there was even the smallest piece of land or cottage to bestow. Some sixteenth- and seventeenth-century English farmers appear, for example, to have been remarkably scrupulous about leaving such a document to safeguard the wellbeing of their wives as far as they could do so. The widow was usually left the holding to rear any children until the majority of the eldest son, after which she was usually guaranteed houseroom and a small acreage of land on which to support herself which should be tilled by the son. The amount of houseroom was defined with great care. For example, Grace Meade of Orwell in East Anglia was left the right to use the small parlour in the house inherited by her son in 1585 'with free egresse and regresse to the same' (this did not mean a separate entrance, but to be allowed access to her room and to the fire to cook undisturbed). She got four acres of land which her son was to plough for her and a load of hay a year along with a few cows and sheep and a plough team. All this was only as long as she remained unmarried.[15] A constant refrain in the wills of married men is that the decision to remarry breaks any claim the widow might have on the property which both have worked. Or, if she does remarry, her new husband must guarantee to perform his duties towards the offspring of the marriage. Hence, when Thomas Adam died in 1592, he left his house and freehold to his wife, Margaret, only until his son John was 21 and the will stated that if she remarried, 'he that shall mary hyr before he dothe contract matrimony with hir shalbe bound to my brother . . . Robert Adam to perform . . . all such legacies as she is charged with by . . . this my will.' Some childless men did not begrudge their wives taking their property into a second marriage, but tied the land in such a way that it should revert to nephews or greatnephews when she died, not go to the issue of the new marriage.[16]

Some of these simple wills attest to great thought by the husband. A landless labourer named Robert Salmon, also a native of East Anglia, who had only a cottage to bequeath, was clearly worried that his wife and their surviving daughter might not get on well together after he was gone. He left the cottage to his daughter on the following condition:

> Rose my wife, a bedroom in my kitchen with the easement of the fire there . . . and if my said wife Rose and Agnes Salmon my daughter cannot agree for the kitchen then I will my said daughter . . . at her costs and charges shall build her a little house on the backside of the kitchen with a chimney in it. And if so, my said wife shall depart from the kitchen into the little house before mentioned.[17]

The testament was the only bridle that a man in areas of customary law could effectively place on his wife to protect his heirs. Otherwise the progeny could suffer real loss. In 1759 a Norwegian priest remarked about a woman with sons approaching adulthood: 'the remarriage of the mother caused much hurt to her children. I tried to stop this marriage as she is over fifty and is going to her ruin.' Confronted with an intended marriage between an older widow and a manservant, he commented: 'Marriage between old widows and young servants I feel to be almost sodomy and therefore I try to stop it as much as possible.'[18]

The widow with possessions which she enjoyed without restriction was of course particularly attractive as a prospect in times of rising population when holdings were difficult to come by.

In any situation, it was impossible for a widow to be richer by the death of her husband than she was during his lifetime. What she did secure in many cases was greater autonomy, though this could be limited by the conditions of the husband's will. In fact, any individual widow could be vastly different from the next, which is why we find them falling into the contrasting categories of 'merry' and 'distressed'. The first, free from marital constraint and in possession of assets they themselves managed, could worry their relatives as to what they would do with this wealth. At the other end of the social spectrum, the widow who inherited her husband's debts,[19] had little or no dowry (or in north-western Europe one that was not properly recorded by a legal settlement) and was dependent on the work of her hands to keep herself and her children was an insistent presence on lists of paupers. The state of widowhood was arbitrary and subject to immense individual variation. There were rich and poor widows, old and young, women who lost their partners in time of plague which, in the aftermath, produced a very active marriage market. There were widows of guild masters who could offer a journeyman the entrée to the mastership at a reduced rate. There were widows encumbered by children. There were, in Italy, widows cut off from their children and ones who were severed from the source of income they had enjoyed with their husbands because their husband's families had repossessed the commerce which was the basis of their livelihood on behalf of the heir.

There were those whose experience of matrimony had been such that the death of a spouse opened up liberating vistas. Such vistas themselves varied. For Mrs Delaney it meant freedom from a boring aged husband and the ability to eschew remarriage and become the doyenne of London etiquette.[20] For Madame de la Peltrie it meant the repossession of her dowry and the means to finance herself and a handful of others to join Mère Marie de l'Incarnation in Canada, there to christianize the Indians. For Madame du Deffand widowhood allowed her to develop her salon life. However, the merry widow may have been the exception. For the majority, widowhood brought problems and a change in lifestyle. Certainly, new decisions had to be made.

Probably all widows faced a number of major questions almost immediately. What is my financial state and how will I manage? Can I continue to live in my old home? In Italy the question, what is now my relationship with my children? could be important. Rural widows had to consider the problems attached to the working of the land their husbands might have left them to manage until their heirs came of age. The widow of an artisan had to find out whether the guilds would allow her to continue production in her husband's name. Other widows had to assess how great a stake they now had in the business in which they might have worked as hard as their husbands. The question, should I and can I remarry? may soon have passed through the widow's mind, as well as, do I wish to do so? For the widow dependent on the work of her hands the loss of a husband must have had nightmarish dimensions and some of the strategies she would have to use to survive must have immediately been rehearsed in her mind. Many of these questions were obviously interlinked.

The well-dowered aristocratic bride whose family had settled considerable resources upon her and who had children by the marriage could be left by her husband in a managerial position of his assets pending, perhaps, the coming of age of the heir. Even then, the mother could be left with rights in the estate – particularly if she only took the interest on the cash she had paid in as her dowry – and she could still be left as one of the managers of the assets of other children. Such women could end up matriarchs with huge responsibility for the wellbeing of the family.

Maddalena Nerli of Florence, for example, widowed in 1605 at forty-three, was named by her husband as guardian of their five living children and manager of their wealth. There was no question of repaying her dowry because she continued to live within the family. Over the next few years she married off three of their daughters appropriately, and at some expense, and her sons entered careers, one in the army and one as an ambassador for the Medici. The wealth streaming out of the family

during these years of daughters' marriages and settling the sons was
large and Maddalena took a small apartment, leasing out the Tornabuoni
palace in Florence to increase her revenues and cut costs. She took
care of the running of town and country properties, loans and debts,
sharecroppers' contracts, orders for draining and ploughing land, as well
as the purchase and sale of livestock. At the age of sixty-three she
became sole guardian of her daughter's children when their father died.
Their mother was sick, so the father had not left the custody of the
children to her. He named five guardians in addition to the grandmother, but the other four, for various reasons, renounced their obligations, leaving the children in Maddalena's care. The eldest of the girls
in this new family was in turn to die a widow and her children, all
boys, were also allocated to the care of their great-grandmother, now
seventy-six, who placed them in a seminary school.

Maddalena was in every sense of the word what the Florentines were
to call a *donna di governo*, a matriarch making decisions at all levels.
Her sons died unmarried before her.[21] The *libro di famiglia* (family log)
she kept suggests that such responsibility was not what she would have
chosen. She managed well, but expenses were heavy and, living on fixed
assets, she was constantly beset by administrative problems to sustain
the honour of the family. She died well respected.

This kind of figure can be found in most national contexts though
they are not numerous; many women, like Maddalena, did not want
the responsibility that running an estate entailed and were relieved
enough to hand over when the heir was of age. Sometimes, as in the
case of the van Lockhorst family in the Netherlands,[22] the widow handed
over but watched the heirs administering her property, that is the assets
which guaranteed an income on her dowry and settlement. This was
done amicably and in the consciousness that both parties could profit.
The mother, widowed in 1617, oversaw all accounts of the properties
managed by her sons but let them invest her wealth, which they did
very advantageously and with her knowledge. She took their advice. In
other cases, the heir could smart somewhat under the widow's tutelage.
Dame Juliana Ker, a formidable Scots dowager, insisted on retaining
for herself a corner of all her late husband's properties in the form of
lodgings as well as her jointure. She was fully explicit on this point
when she handed over to her son, George, the house of East Mains of
Polwarth in 1634. She would maintain the low chamber 'which I will
keep for my own use and pleasure and will keep the key thereof and

have my bed and coffer therin, to come there when I please . . . which, I trow, will be sooner nor you believe.' This was followed by the brisk reminder, lest he should protest, 'Do not storm at this nor think it comes from any other, for of my conscience it does come of no living creature but myself only who will not for nobody denude myself altogether of some house to come where I please.'

George was clearly powerless against his mother, whether or not her claims would have held up in a law court.[23]

The larger the estates of the marriage partnership, the better the widow's chances of recovering what was her due and of re-establishing herself very comfortably as arbiter of her own destiny. A. P. W. Malcolmson's study of the Ulster heiress in the eighteenth century suggests that a number of families owning estates were in some trouble over the claims of dowagers to the repayment of dower and that this retarded the marriages of the next generation. At a lesser level, where the backing of land to secure the wife's assets did not exist, widows could find that the wise management they had anticipated from their husbands had not in fact occurred, or the uncertainties of the times had eaten into their assets. In the troubled Civil War period in Britain a lot of women saw their assets shrink and, though their marriage settlements were confirmed in law, full repayment could not be made through little fault of their dead husbands. In the early part of the following century the collapse of John Law's 'Mississippi scheme' had implications for those women whose husbands had chosen to invest their funds in his company in anticipation of huge speculative profits.

Generally, the more a bride's family sought to influence the way her money was managed, the better her state in widowhood. The increasing reliability of government stock and the development of the Bank of England, as well as secure investments like *rentes sur le clergé de France*, or lending to municipal councils, or to the tax farmers of Languedoc, helped to improve a woman's prospects of a safe income on the death of her husband. However, many widows must have watched with trepidation the dilapidation of their funds by the injudicious management of their husbands. Furthermore, however clearly laid down were the rules of what must return to the woman on widowhood, families could contest those rights.

The wealthy matriarchs and managers of their husbands' estates were those widows whose independence frightened other members of the house or clan. They were seen as women with the power to reduce the

income of the progeny from the first marriage if they should remarry.
They had secured financial control of their input in the match and if
they also had management of the property of the heirs the result could
be very disadvantageous for the children of previous marriages. Dutch
law in 1659 tried to lay down: 'A man or woman who remarries while
children of the previous marriage still live . . . is obliged to provide
for children (a) child's share . . . or in the case of many children, a
child's portion' (Groot Utrecht's Placaat boek, 1729, 1.469). The most
striking examples are found in areas of customary law. Agnes van Reede
tot Drakesteyn, married in 1636 to Reynout van Tuyl van Serooks-
kerken, lord of Rynhuisen, might be a case in point.[24] The property of
Rynhuisen was sold within three days of Agnes's second marriage in
1657, thus reducing the estates of four children by her first marriage.
The most conspicuous English example is that provided by Bess of
Hardwicke, who possessed a very small dowry – £25 – but had a
beautiful face and real intelligence. In the 1530s she attracted a young
noble, Robert Barlow, who settled a generous jointure on her at marriage and died within months of the event. In 1547 she married a
widower, William Cavendish, a large landowner in Derbyshire, and
when he died in 1557 she shared the estate with his and their issue.
Two years later she married another widower who died after six years
without direct heir bequeathing all to his 'dear Bess'. Eight years later
she contracted a further marriage to George Talbot, Earl of Shrewsbury
and one of the richest men in England, and married two of her daughters
to his younger sons (thus astutely keeping dowry money within the
group in the manner of Italian patrician families). Not only did she
embark on the construction of Chatsworth but also the rebuilding of
Hardwicke Hall, her parents' home. The heir of the Earl of Shrewsbury
believed his house much impoverished by 'dear Bess', who had used
the income from the estate to improve the condition of her clan and
had denied the Talbots the income they might have expected from large
dowries from their brides.[25]

The case of Bess of Hardwicke indicates some of the power which a
determined, many times widowed woman could exercise. The absence
of legislation to curtail the widow's activities may explain why English
and Dutch prescriptive literature continued to worry about the widow
and what she might do with the income from rights, privileges and
investments pending the majority of the heir.

*

How did widowhood affect the farmer's wife? Again there are conspicuous differences if we look at those countries where inheritance by the widow in the lifetime of the heir was the norm and those where the control of the husband's property returned to his family for management and exploitation pending the heir's majority. Throughout France as a whole, between 10 and 15 per cent of farms had a woman as the nominal head and it was her name which appeared on the tax rolls. However, many of these women appear to have been doing a holding job until they handed over to a son. Within a few years the name of the widow as householder disappears and that of a son takes her place.

If the farm was held on lease, as in the case of the Breton *domaine congéable*, in Britain or in Lower Saxony, the widow had the right to maintain the lease until it expired whether or not she had able-bodied sons to help her. At this point, a number of hard practical considerations confronted her. Manpower had been lost. Could it be replaced without endangering the profitability of the farm? Kinsmen might step in to help with the heavy work of ploughing and harvesting, but almost certainly some work would have to be done by paid labour. In communities of small owner-occupiers, too, the predicament of the woman faced with the loss of a pair of hands could be difficult. If the farm was a small one, a subsistence or sub-subsistence unit as in the Auvergne or the Rouergue, and the family had depended on extra efforts by the father as seasonal migrant or industrial worker in the dead season, the losses from these sources would also have to be weighed in the balance.[26]

No farmer's widow improved on her situation by the loss of a husband unless she was able to remarry and carry the assets from her previous husband into the next marriage. A critical revenue-generating source had been lost, his labour, and the profit margins on the holding were hence reduced. If the farm was large, the losses could be sustained more easily than in the case of a subsistence unit. The wife of a solid landowner or tenant farmer on a long lease could be a model for 'Lady Bustle', celebrated by Samuel Johnson in *The Rambler* as the woman who, on her husband's death, put on a pair of sturdy boots, hitched up her skirts and sallied forth in the dawn hours to give the farmhands precise instructions for the day. Then she returned to 'woman's work' about the farm, organizing the servants in the preparation of food and feeding poultry and supervising dairy work. She was a businesswoman and took on the sale of crops. Indeed, her only conspicuous sacrifice was that of leisure. Johnson made his readers aware that Lady Bustle was doing two jobs: the one she had had before her husband died and the one of supervision that he had previously done. She did not, as he had tended to do, waste time chatting to other farmers about the weather and she was sparing on the time allotted to the purchase of finery. However, it is very clear that she took on management, not labour. Her husband had not himself followed the plough and nor did she.[27] Her situation is to be contrasted with that of the widow on the subsistence unit who had to redouble her physical efforts as well as continue her own work. Hence the Scandinavian proverb: 'A badly run farm either lacks a woman or is run by a woman', which referred specifically to farms where the only male labour was a hired 'hand'.

If the farm was held on a short-term lease – nine years being the commonest tenancy in the smallholding areas of France – then it was questionable whether the owner would renew it when the time came. In Scandinavia, refusal was automatic and the cottar widow faced eviction after the next harvest.

In France, widows with sons who had married and occupied adjacent farms, or were working on others, might after the funeral contract *actes d'avancement de succession* with them in which they put the holding into the hands of their children against a specified livelihood. These agreements had the force of law behind them if either should default. Where industry had penetrated the countryside, some tried to hold on, abandoning the land to the heir against a small consideration, perhaps a room and some food or the means to rent a cottage with a vegetable plot, working at lace or like craft and perhaps pasturing a goat or a pig on the common. It afforded some scope to the widow who tried to stay near her relations and a large number, if not always a majority, managed to occupy a corner of a son or daughter's dwelling and make something from industrial efforts, if not enough to have an independent existence. Sometimes a number of them would cluster together in particular villages and share some of the costs of rent and fuel. The lace-making area of the Pays de Velay penetrated far into the hills, but there were distinct lace trails between certain villages which were visited by lace merchants or their representatives, and it is in those villages that most widows clustered, sometimes accounting for between 16 and 20 per cent of all householders. Such women lived a marginal and precarious existence.[28]

Throughout north-western Europe, the Europe of long, cold, damp winters, we find rural widows appearing before the manorial courts for stealing firewood or illegally pasturing their animals on someone else's land. Frequently they were without kin or with kin too poor to help them. They lived on the fringes of hamlets facing a bleak old age as their forces diminished and they became progressively more dependent upon the goodwill of the community – which could run out. Some of them will appear again in this narrative, condemned as witches. In England, where poor relief was dependent on rights of settlement, there was perhaps the greatest incentive for these marginal widows to stay put so that they could qualify. Even so, many gravitated towards towns which might afford prospects both of remarriage and of work.

The available evidence suggests that throughout Europe about one in five of all those widows reported to be maintaining a farming household belonged in the upper income bracket, one or two were moderately comfortable, two or three were either poor or destitute and dependent on kin. This figure cannot include those who had abandoned the farming community altogether and made for the towns, so it gives an optimistic view of the rural widow.[29]

The urban widow fell into many categories and the town could attract both poor rural widows and also women who thought they had a better chance of remarriage in the city and who had relatives who might harbour them. These were not necessarily women totally lacking in resources but ones who for sound reasons – there were too many obstacles to continuing a farming or commercial livelihood without their husbands – chose to seek out the town. Many widows found a new husband in London. More generally for indigenous urban widows, their status depended on the assets they had taken into marriage, the wise management of their husbands, and testaments that left them to run their husbands' business where this was possible. There were many instances where the widow was either precluded from continuing or found it impossible to do so.

Most towns of over 4000 people had professional groups of doctors, apothecaries, lawyers, notaries and, in Protestant societies, clergymen. All these categories tended to marry within the group. A good professional practice would see the widow comfortably endowed with a house and an income from investments, but precluded from stepping into her husband's shoes since she simply did not have the training. The widows of professional men appear conspicuously among the French *rentier* groups (that is, those living on investments). It may well be that *rentes* or annuities were seen as the best guarantee for the widow after her husband's death.

In the case of apothecaries who owned a shop, the widow might advertise business as usual and employ a qualified man to mix medicine even if she sometimes did this herself. The widows of doctors and surgeons could not step into their husband's practice, but there was the widespread belief that the wife of the deceased or his heirs had some stake in the lists of patients and that anyone who assumed the patients of the former doctor was expected to pay into his estate.

Clergymen's widows were in a very particular situation. In Protestant countries there existed, at least from the seventeenth century, special charities to help the clergyman's widow construct a livelihood for herself. Though there were handsome livings which permitted the incumbent a surplus from which savings could be made and settled on the widow and children, there were many more where a free house and a modest stipend were the only income and these disappeared when the clergyman died. However, there was some expectation that, wherever possible, the new incumbent of the living should be chosen from unmarried clergymen and that he should marry the former pastor's widow. Or, and perhaps more frequently in England, the newly widowed woman might be recommended as housekeeper to the senior capitular clergy whose houses graced cathedral squares. They were also seen as eminently suited to become matrons of orphanages and charity schools where such posts existed. Very frequently, in default of such outlets, the impoverished clergyman's widow could be thrown back on her family of origin for support.

Offices were a form of property and the incumbent had to be a man. The wives of most top level office holders had no claim on the proceeds of the husband's office unless, pending the transmission to an heir, such an office was leased out. Generally it was part of the husband's patrimony, but if purchased after marriage, or if her assets had been used in the purchase, then the widow had a stake in its sale. The term office holding is a very broad one. At the bottom it could refer to people like jailers and janitors, inspectors, guards, poorhouse, bridewell and hospital officials, all jobs which might have been purchased or acquired through patronage. Some of these offices were never actually filled by their owner – he used the services of his wife. Indeed, such posts often required that the applicant or incumbent be married.

Running a jail in England, for example, was not regarded as full-time work for a man. He was expected to have some other source of income because he had to lay out money to feed and house prisoners left to his care and then recoup it from the Quarter Sessions. Until the end of the eighteenth century a likely source of revenue was the sale of ale to the prisoners, usually on the jailer's premises. A second source of income was hemp beating. This was done by the prisoners, the jailer providing the raw material, negotiating the sale and paying the prisoners a token wage. Often his wife supervised the business aspects of both the brewing and the industrial work as well as buying food for the inmates.

What could happen when the jailer of an important prison died is shown in a letter from Eliza Prince, widow of John Prince, late keeper of the House of Correction at Abingdon, to the Quarter Sessions:

That your petitioner is left in very distressful circumstances with a family of eighte children, the eldest of which being a daughter of only 14 years old and three of them have natural infirmities which will probably render them incapable of gaining their livelihood.

That your petitioner's husband and his father and grandfather have been Keepers of the House of Correction at Abingdon for a great many years and your petitioner has a brother and a brother in law very well qualified and willing to assist her in the future management of that prison and she can find sufficient security if required for her faithful discharge of the office of Bridewell keeper.

Your petitioner therefore humbly prays to be continued in the office of Keeper of the House of Correction that she may be thereby able to provide bread for her family which must otherwise be unavoidably thrown on the parish for maintenance.[30]

This letter was written by a very astute woman whose understanding of the system is unquestionable. She based her claim to the job on the grounds that there was a long family stake in it but, knowing this to be insufficient, she stresses the presence of able-bodied men to assist her and then threatens that without the job numerous children will be thrown on the parish for support. She had other weapons to deploy if the petition was not granted. She had been doing the job with the help of her brother for several months following her husband's death and there had been no incident to suggest that she was not performing the role competently. Her husband had died in very suspicious circumstances, having been found murdered – it was thought by a prisoner or someone who bore a grudge – and she might have thrown in that the poorhouse at Abingdon was run by a widow.

The petition was granted and we find her asking for a turnkey to the prison some five years later. Others in her position were given a year to find a husband who could do the job or to guarantee the justices that she had a prospective husband in mind. Between 1688 and 1775, just over a quarter of British jails had a widow as keeper.

If the widow's ability to manage the jail had been in question, the justices at the Quarter Sessions, daunted by the prospect of eight children to be supported by the parish, might have offered some concession which would have guaranteed an income. Many Houses of Correction employed matrons to oversee women, particularly when they were 'lying in', or sick. Charities in Britain intended for helping particular sectors of the indigent or orphaned were almost always administered by women employed by a board of governors which could itself, like those of Haarlem, be composed of Regentesses. These would chose respectable women to do the business of tending the children. Women were generally prepared to deal only with other women and usually elected the respectable matron as the effective liaison between help and the recipient. Towards the end of the period when charities directed themselves towards improving the lot of prisoners the role of the matron expanded considerably. In Catholic France, this kind of work was in the hands of religious congregations, themselves often founded by widows. In Italy associations to help the poor and women in specific situations such as *malmaritate* (unsatisfactory marriages) were again directed by widows.

For the working population in the towns and cities of France, Germany, the Netherlands and England, the relationship between women and the guilds was perhaps the critical determinant in deciding the widow's fate. In many artisans' enterprises, the wife knew how to run a workshop. She was mistress of some of the skills and she certainly knew all about bookkeeping. Her ability to continue to run the business, however, depended not only upon the work itself and whether she could do it but whether the guild would allow her to continue in production. Would the guild for example let her carry on in her husband's name and replace his labours by employing journeymen? Would it insist that to continue she should marry a journeyman who would then be given master status? Above all, would it allow her to keep on, and if need be replace, apprentices, who were the cheapest form of labour? Thirdly, when her husband's accounts had been settled as they must be upon his death, would enough capital remain for her to continue in business?

The replies to questions relating to her abilities were relatively straightforward. Women could bake and brew, cook and dress meat, run a print shop, but they could not for example work in the building trades as masons or carpenters (though they could organize the business and carry loads on the building site), nor usually as tanners or smiths or in cabinet-making. Very often, however, the wives of such workmen had a working role independent of that of their husband, like running a tavern or some form of domestic industry. For them the pivotal question then became how far this income source could be stretched to provide the main livelihood for the bereaved family. For those who had worked with their husbands in his workshop, their ability to proceed depended on whether there were sons to inherit the business and whether they felt capable or wanted to go on with it.

The issue of repayment of debt was generally experienced and was probably the first of the widow's worries. When the male head of a household died, his creditors moved immediately to demand payment of all outstanding bills. At the same time, a resident maidservant or employees other than apprentices, who were a special case, also asked for payment of their back wages. These demands on top of the funeral expenses could be sufficient in themselves to explain why some widows did not have the wherewithal to continue. Many found themselves at this point forced to sell the stock of the business at a loss because they needed to raise ready cash to acquit debts. Often they had to decide on priorities.[31] Indeed, there are many cases of maidservants who found the wages owing to them were cut because the husband's creditors were paid off in preference to the weakest and most vulnerable of the employees, and the least likely to take the widow to court. Since many artisans' widows in areas of customary law had no formally laid-down dowry they could be left totally unprotected and without assets. For this reason alone perhaps over 50 per cent of urban widows, whether in Stuart Salisbury or Oxford, were not living in the marital home a year after their husband's death, and two years after his death still more would have left, some doubtless to remarry.

By far the most complex set of questions, however, related to the guilds. These, generally speaking, had a very ambivalent attitude towards widows. On the positive side, the masters genuinely wanted protection for their own relatives and one of the advantages of belonging to a guild was the knowledge that some security should be provided. The master's son was usually guaranteed an apprenticeship and entry to the guild at reduced rates. Frequently a master's widow who married a journeyman could obtain guild status for her new husband. The guilds had interests of another kind to pursue, however. First, they were supposed to exist to guarantee quality and uniform standards in trading practices. The widow had not done an official apprenticeship and hence goods manufactured or services performed by her could not be the product of a formally inducted skill. The members of the guild also had considerable personal interests in restricting the numbers of producers of a particular commodity so as to stop the market from being glutted and keep up prices and wages. The two ways in which they did this were to limit the number of journeymen, qualified workers, passing into the guild, either through entry fees or by making them wait for a place; and to assume a hard stance towards widows so that the number of workshops would be reduced and the business of the dead master would be placed elsewhere.

Ideally, and an action which would reconcile the interests of the guild with the survival of the widow, her remarriage to a journeyman of the guild who could be guaranteed entry to the mastership was to be encouraged. This move held the situation at par and, in order to help bring it about, some guilds waived mastership fees for the marrying journeyman; that could be a card in the widow's hand.

Some guilds recognized that the widow should be allowed to continue to practise in her husband's name but sought to impose restrictions on how this might be done. These restrictions varied not only from one type of enterprise to another, but from place to place and century to century. At any one time what was going on in Augsburg could differ from the practice of Strasbourg, or Oxford from Abingdon. However, the kinds of limitations they sought to impose could be summarized as follows. First, they could insist that she continue in business for no longer than a month until the work in hand was finished. To make this a little less harsh they might allow the widow to carry the right of mastership to any journeyman of the trade she elected to marry within a stipulated interval of up to two years. Or they could allow her to continue, but they would insist that certain functions be carried out by journeymen.

Sometimes this made good sense. Printing widows in Britain and the Netherlands, for example, were allowed to continue only if they had a journeyman to pull the press, a heavy job which if not done properly gave a poor print face. Sometimes, however, convention intruded to determine what was seemly. The undertaker's widow could not be a visible presence at a man's funeral. A man's death had to be presided over by men.

Some guilds would limit the widow's operations by restricting the number of journeymen she could employ. Perhaps worst of all, they could preclude her from negotiating new apprenticeships and insist that she transfer the current apprentices to a new master for the remaining years of their indenture. This was as good as telling the widow to stop business immediately. The reasons given for such a step were that as training could only be done by a master, both apprentices and journeymen who acted under the direction of a woman would be deemed inadequate workers and disadvantaged in their pursuit of preferment. However, given that most apprentices were actually trained by journeymen, what could be afoot here is a thinly disguised attempt to edge a widow out of production. The justification for such steps was usually couched in terms of skills transmitted, but reinforced by reference to a value system in which the head had to be a man. When the dismemberment of a fairly considerable workshop was at stake, or the reduction of a large to a smaller enterprise, lurking in the background was the conviction that the proper unit of production was that of the married man with a wife and children and that women did not need as much to survive.[32]

The normal response to the widow was not such a hard line but rather minor actions limiting the scale of the enterprise by restricting the numbers of journeymen and apprentices a woman could employ. However in hard times, when markets were glutted and masters and journeymen were feeling the pinch, both existing widows and newly widowed women could find themselves the sudden target of newly restrictive guild legislation. Or new conditions could suddenly be imposed such as the demand on the widow to pay the equivalent sum to the price of the mastership or there could be a prohibition on her doing business at certain fairs or in certain commodities. At the Restoration of Charles II, printing in Britain fell on hard times after the boom which polemical tracts and devotional literature had enjoyed during the Civil War and Interregnum. At this juncture the Stationers' Company in London simply struck the poorest printing houses, all of which were run by widows, off the list of licensed operators. Other more substantial widow printers survived. This kind of draconian activity was not common, but the widow could rarely rest entirely easy and to continue in business often meant flagrantly ignoring the restrictions placed upon her. If discovered she could find herself before the municipal courts or jurisdiction and called upon to defend herself. Those waiting to report her infractions were most commonly journeymen and other masters' wives. It is from the litigation that frequently ensued that we learn most about the problems of the master's widow determined to stay in business.

Some trades had greater demands than others for journeymen or apprentice labour. Metal workers, for example, needed assistance. They could not work alone. It would seem that some widows would try to keep a business going until the convenanted labour was finished. Then, unless there was a son to inherit, the widow would simply depart. Sometimes a daughter would be likely to marry a journeyman in the not too distant future and this would encourage the widow to try to hold on until she could hand over to her son-in-law.

Lawsuits inevitably concern cases involving tension; the success stories never came to court. In Reformation Augsburg, for example, the widow Apollonia Mair ran a successful tannery (very unusual for a woman), so well that she petitioned the Municipal Council for a central trade shop. Her son ran another shop, so she was not merely keeping a business going until he was ready to enter the mastership. The official civic glazier was also a widow from 1535 to 1539. However, to set against these success stories, the goldsmiths' guild on the grounds of the prestige of their craft denied widows the right to carry on business in their dead husbands' names. When the widow of Joachim Nitlin petitioned to be allowed to continue his workshop during the Imperial Diet she was smartly told that she lacked the requisite skills, could not by reason of her sex control the journeymen, was young and not poor – hence to be classed as a future wife. In this case, the message being delivered was that she should get on with the business of finding a husband.[33]

In other cases there was a real fear among guild masters and journey-men that any widow could subvert the skill of a trade by marrying a journeyman of insufficient experience who would then secure free admission to the mastership. To reduce this threat, many guilds tried to insist that the journeyman who married a widow should be banned from buying and selling until he had acquired a stipulated number of years' experience.

Probably women nestled most comfortably within guilds where the chief preoccupation was the preparation of food. This seems to have been the case in Oxford, in Germany and in many French cities, but there were exceptions. If the butchers' guild of Augsburg allowed the widow to make sausages, it banned her from the slaughterhouse. In many German towns even the limited business of sausage manufacture could only be conducted from the home and not from the meat market in the town centres. Where widows were allowed to sell fresh meat, they were restricted to particular cuts and again they were kept out of the main market. At Memmingen, widows had to choose between selling sausages and selling fresh meat; they could not do both.[34]

Most common infractions of guild and city regulations involved door-to-door selling by widows and their children. Some German town councils allowed very poor widows to peddle 'if they did it with modesty and decorum'. This probably meant away from the main market centres. Sometimes, as a concession to widowhood and to mark a Christian festival by manifest charity and succour for the poor, widows were allowed to sell special Christmas sausages which the butchers were not allowed to offer.[35]

A relatively uncontested area of butchery was the use of innards and tripe and cow-heels. Bladders were used for sausage skins, suet for dripping, and cow-heels when boiled yielded a sticky substance used by gluemakers as well as for thick soups. Unpleasant to handle and odoriferous when less than fresh, this was an area of the business which brought scant remuneration but was thought appropriate for widows who monopolized the job in Strasbourg and other towns.

Most cities throughout north-western Europe permitted the baker's widow to continue in production as long as she paid guild fees to the company and did not remarry. Many such widows opted to specialize in small fancy breads and pastries and pretzels. The reasons for this choice could be purely practical, reflecting the predilection of a woman who wanted to do her own work without employing a journeyman and to retail it through trays and stalls staffed by her children, or such constraints could be imposed upon her by the guild itself. Again, German bakers' guilds frequently – though not invariably – gave widows a monopoly over making of Christmas biscuits (*Lebkuchen*). However, a man's livelihood had to be protected. Hence in 1616 when the widow of a pastry baker in Strasbourg sought permission to make egg bread with yeast, since she was weak, poor, encumbered with children and her egg bread was popular, she was denied lest 'others would take this as an example, and great disorder would be the result'.[36]

In the sixteenth and seventeenth centuries clothing guilds were even less tractable in Germany and both tailors and mercers kept a very tight control over the making of outer garments and the retail sale of fabrics. Seamstresses, some of whom might have their own very weak guild, were debarred from making outer garments. In times of real hardship the tailors could contest even the making of shirts and linen clothing. However lingerie-making in general was so poorly paid that men were unlikely to stay with it when given any alternative.[37]

Inroads into the fabrication of outer clothing by women did not come until the adoption of the mantua in the eighteenth century. This was a frock coat of loose construction made from light cloth which, it could be argued, was capable of being constructed by a seamstress and did not need tailoring. Some female mantua makers did run apprenticeship schemes and the work was relatively uncontested by men; because of the level of remuneration it was identified as women's work. The eighteenth century certainly saw the rise of the dressmaker and her encroachment into areas where the tailor had previously had a monopoly, and this was a trend encouraged by the queens of Britain and France who increasingly used the services of a dressmaker.

Many English guilds and in particular tailors' guilds, like the one at Oxford, were very weak and their members poor. Tailoring was never regarded as a virile trade and may always have attracted the relatively puny for apprenticeship. To undertake litigation as business crept out-side its influence and passed into the hands of women was not easy for the tailors. Furthermore, common law did not prevent a woman from producing goods. The restriction was one introduced by the borough in which a guild was registered. Hence, in towns without borough statute and guild regulations women gradually began to make serious inroads into the production of clothing. The tailor's widow who remained in Oxford might find herself subjected to demands for guild fees or quarterage from the borough, but if she moved the short distance to Banbury she could operate more freely. Such practical considerations may have led to widows clustering along with spinsters in areas where guilds were weak or where there was no guild control. With or without the guilds, however, dependence upon the needle alone was a sure recipe for impoverishment.[38]

There would appear to have been greater possibilities in north-western Europe for widows carrying on some part of their family commerce than there were in Italy. A study of Bologna in the eighteenth century, for example, reveals that at one point only 44 widows were actually in control of the commercial premises previously owned by their husbands. This was perhaps less the effect of guild control than because the business was claimed by the husband's kin in the name of his children. Bitter litigation could ensue, when the widow saw the business declining and she was totally unable to protect the interests of her children.

The highest proportions of widows in any given population are usually found in cities and in particular towns. It was usual, throughout Europe, for widows to constitute about 12 per cent of the heads of urban families – somewhat less in England, where laws of settlement as a qualification for poor relief may have held down the numbers of widowed women likely to migrate to towns to something more like 9 per cent. However, merely counting heads of households could mask the real numbers of widows in certain cities. Rome, above all, but also some of the more considerable Italian cities, Seville and southern Spanish cities, may at any one time have had twice as many widows who were not heads of family and who were clustering together to sustain a livelihood or living in a room in the dwelling of the son or a daughter. Several factors combined to make these great Mediterranean cities widow-capitals. First, the disparity between the age of women and men at marriage enhanced the likelihood of widowhood for many. Secondly, the difficulty experienced by women in these countries of Roman law in inheriting a rural patrimony, or indeed a commercial enterprise which had previously been the family's livelihood, against the claims of kin to protect the interests of the progeny appears to have been much greater than in north-western Europe. Women who had reclaimed their small dowry assets were pushed into a move to the city and the attempt to rent a room,[39] hoping to find some casual work which would help them to exist.

The urban widow, then, could be in any one of a number of circumstances. She could be an artisan's widow, one indigenous to the town, with supportive kin groups or a family of grown children to help her, or one who had nothing but young children who were a continual drain on her purse. She could be the widow of a casual labourer who had always had difficulty in making ends meet. She could be an immigrant from the surrounding area in good or feeble health. She could be young and hopeful that she would have the chance to remarry in the town, or old and helpless looking for charity. Some distinctions need also to be made between the possibilities available in north-western Europe and those in the south.

Rome stands out as a particular widow centre. As the locus of much Counter-Reformation institutional charity, widows from the papal states were drawn there; in some streets around the Piazza Navona, the heart of the baroque city, the heads of households in some of the side streets of artisans' workshops and lodging houses were over a third widows. Most had young children, particularly girls, and without doubt the charitable dowries helped to attract them to the city in the hope of ultimately settling their daughters. Most lived in one or two rooms, sharing a yard and a pump, and some of them cleaned for the other tenants or for the landlord as a means of paying the rent. Many had relatives in the nearby streets and once a daughter or a son had settled in the city, kin networks formed.[40] At the bottom of the social scale, and this was as true of a city like Bologna, they clustered in particular houses and shared a room or facilities. The markets provided other cleaning and selling work and also the many churches and public places offered, if all else failed, the opportunity for begging. One source of work which seems to have outstripped all others as the recourse of the poor widow was selling drinks in *bettole* (little refreshment stands like the French *guinguettes*) which were permitted to sell a more limited supply of drinks and food than the *osterie* or taverns.

The density of the widow population around the Piazza Navona suggests there must have been a great deal of sociability and interdependence among them as well as help from kin. Scrubbing, cleaning, nursing, sewing, cooking for working neighbours and, when all else failed, begging and appeals to charity were the recourse of the widow. This was not just in affluent Mediterranean cities. An analysis of the population of Carrick-on-Suir in Ireland in 1799, for example,[41] reveals that widows accounted for one-fifth of the total adult female population above the age of twenty. Almost one house in three contained at least one widow. The huge majority of them were poor and illiterate, sharing rooms or parts of houses with other families or other widows to whom they were not apparently related. They outnumbered the widowers in the town by four to one.

The key to the situation may be twofold. The men of the area could migrate to the Newfoundland fisheries or join the army or the navy. Carrick, however, had a manufacture of woollen cloth which appears to have been the means of supporting even the oldest of the women, at an admittedly penurious level, and this may have made the little town a magnet.

The success stories among them are of women who inherited sturdy businesses from their husbands. These included Mary Cahill, aged seventy, who continued a business for the production and marketing of cloth, Catherine McEniry, also a cloth dealer, and Honora Hayes, aged 56, who combined the business of dyer and corn dealer. Ellen Russell, who kept a shop in the main street, inherited a good business in 1789 but by 1806 was in Clonmel jail for debt. The rest of the widows made something by carding, spinning, working as charwomen and washerwomen, bread women, beer sellers and in the needle trades, but at least half of them were underemployed, periodically unemployed, or in some way dependent upon community and family. Yet only 5 per cent were living totally on public charity. Something in Carrick kept the clustering widows alive in poverty. They perhaps exploited vegetable plots and had access to cheap fish and other help in kind through their kin and through supporting each other. Widows' networks appear to have existed at all levels of the population.[42]

Societies which produced large numbers of sailors tended also to produce large numbers of widows, of whom we may suppose a proportion to have been abandoned wives. In Honiton in Devon, a community where many of the men were sailors or fisherfolk, the lace industry in the eighteenth and nineteenth centuries generated enough for women to live on if they formed small groups of four or five to share light and heat, combine shopping at the market and help each other cope with problems arising from sickness or child care. In Seville and Amsterdam, both cities producing large quantities of sailors – indeed, over the seventeenth century it is thought that over a million Dutch sailors perished on the East Indiamen, or at least did not return home – perhaps as much as a quarter of all households were headed by widows. The Venetian ambassador described Seville in 1525 as a city 'in the hands of women' because so many men had left for the New World. Legislation in fact prohibited married men from being permanent expatriates, but there was little effort to ensure that such laws were respected and certainly there was no prohibition on matrimony for sailors, and nothing to stop merchants who intended to return from leaving their homes for long periods.[43]

The ambassador was referring to the large numbers of women visible in the urban economy. What he reported has much applicability to

Italian and Dutch ports – even his own Venice, had he chosen to look more carefully. Of the large numbers who were widows, everything depended upon the wealth and the type of business they had inherited from their husbands. Those who lost husbands with business assets in South America were not precluded from continuing to draw income from these sources, but a male relative or a paid employee had to do the actual work of buying, selling, investing in cargoes and so on. Some had made such investments as wives, again using a male intermediary, and they merely went on as they had done before. They continued to run the shops that sold silks, silver and gold buttons and fine linen. They ran market stalls and sold fish, tripe and dairy products. Seville's main industrial base, however, was the silk industry and the silk workers' guild imposed very stringent restrictions on the master weaver's widow. Although both men and women were admitted as weavers, a widow could only continue to operate her husband's full business for one year after his death. Thereafter, her work had to be submitted to the guild for inspection and if deemed adequate, she might continue in business but must reduce her workshop to one loom – deemed sufficient to support her – and the only apprentices she might take on were her own children.

Such stipulations must have been ruinous for the widow. The profits she could make were very reduced and almost certainly precluded her from buying raw material on her own account or weaving anything but the simplest cloths. The smallest ripple in the industry's performance would see her in financial difficulties and in no time she would be just one of the 3000 female piece workers in silk who worked at exploitative rates for the masters.[44] There was nothing unusual in such a situation. In Bologna at the same time, the clientele of the For, the archiepiscopal court which dealt with unlicensed prostitutes, included many young widows, or widows with young daughters, who were silk reelers and weavers but who had to rent the loom they used and found that this reduced the income from their work to a sub-subsistence level. Some claimed that illicit sex with the owner of the loom was one way to reduce the costs of the rental, others that what they could earn from weaving would only keep them in food and that someone else had to provide the rent of a room large enough to accommodate a loom.[45]

The situation could be both tragic and ironic for the master silk-maker's widow. If, as at Lyons, she had invested her accumulated earnings as a draw-girl into the purchase of the mastership for her husband,

and now saw the business dramatically reduced or her capacities to produce at all challenged, she faced immediate or imminent hardship. Whenever an industry went into slump the first businesses to go were the small ones, and many of these, where they had been allowed to continue, were run by widows. A slump or disappearance of an industry could result in severe problems for those even partially dependent upon this source of revenue. In sixteenth-century Abingdon, for example, widows lost the spinning associated with the cloth trade in that town and new depths of immiseration were reached.[46] Later in the sixteenth century the development of malting in the area was very lucrative for a widow with capital to invest; even with no more than a few pounds she could buy barley and malt it in her fireplace. In Hertfordshire, not many miles away, some widows secured a small but regular income by malt-making. Others invested in larger amounts of barley and had the malting done by commercial masters and a few owned malt houses and kilns – the legacy of their husbands, perhaps.

Malt-making, however, was not a labour intensive concern and provided scant work for women and children with no capital at all. Within a hundred years – not within any particular widow's lifetime – new industries like processing hemp had crept into Abingdon, but there was nothing ineluctable about such developments. Gradually, in addition, Abingdon became a considerable port on the Thames and with that came an extension of the catering industry to supply the bargemen and travellers, ideal work for the widow. In the interim, however, many widows were simply thrown on poor relief. Even where this was relatively generous, as in eighteenth-century England, it produced only a half or a third of what was needed to feed, keep warm and shelter a single person.[47]

The widow such as the sailor's widow who was at the bottom of the social pile in an area lacking in a viable industrial outlet was in fact thrown back upon that economy of expedients, those marginal sources of income which were combined to eke out a precarious livelihood: begging and structured relief, selling – even if it was only stolen firewood or dubious potions to allay lovesickness and pain – prostitution and procuring, smuggling salt (in Brittany and Flanders), and fortune telling. Above all, the widow had to hope that her relatives would help her, particularly if she had children to rear.

To be the child of a widow in straitened circumstances could be disastrous for a daughter unless, as in Rome, there were charitable dowry funds to help her. Lists of paupers reveal that the widow was much more likely to live with her unmarried daughter than with her son.[48] In Italy this may reflect her lack of custody over her son but a widow–daughter relationship is commonly also found in north-western Europe and here it may well be that the widow sent her son away for some kind of apprenticeship but kept her daughter so that the two of them could make the slender resources they had go a little further. In such circumstances the daughter was unlikely to be able to save for marriage, and this factor seems to have increased the likelihood of spinsterhood at this level of society. On the other hand, if the daughter married, she was likely to end up sheltering her mother.

The prostitution records of Seville and Bologna show that the poverty of the widowed mother living with her daughter could turn the daughter into a whore and the mother into a procuress. The poor widow perforce trod a dangerous line between minimum sufficiency and destitution.[49]

The poor relief lists of seventeenth- and eighteenth-century towns attest to the predicament of the widows, who along with abandoned wives could account for a third or more of the recipients. The highest levels are found in Spain, where in the Catalan assessments of 1780–1800 widows account for half of those receiving alms.[50] Society in general had no difficulty in placing them among the deserving poor and according them a right to whatever scant assistance was available, but their best support remained their kin. If she had a son or a son-in-law, a married niece, a sister whose husband was prepared to shelter her or speak for her, then a woman on very slender resources could hold together a frail livelihood. However, many were not so fortunate. In Italy and Spain in the early modern period, the resourceless old, even those with kin, were unceremoniously abandoned or, as in Flanders, simply auctioned by the community to those who would shelter them as cheaply as possible.[51]

At the bottom of the social scale widowhood must have seemed a grim spectre. When English good advice literature, with a pragmatism unparalleled elsewhere, counselled the maidservant on marriage to purchase a shop or business with the money she had earned, knowing the odds on widowhood were high, the priorities were appropriate. The shop was always there, a buttress against the plight of the widow who sent her son to market with their remaining cow and saw him return with a bean which was allegedly magic.

CHAPTER SEVEN

Of Difference, of Shame and of Abuse

10 Jahr, kindischer Art
20 Jahr ein Jungfrau zart,
30 Jahr im Haus die Frau
40 Jahr ein Matron genau
50 Jahr eine Grossmutter
60 Jahr ein Alters Schuder
70 Jahr alt ungestalt
80 Jahr wust und erkalt.

JOHANN FISCHART, STUFENLEITER, 1578

[At ten a child, at twenty a maid, at thirty a wife, at forty
a matron, at fifty a grandmother, at sixty age-worn, at
seventy deformed, at eighty confused and grown cold.]

TO BE A daughter, a wife, a mother and in time perhaps a
widow were seen as normal steps in an unfolding life pattern,
one celebrated in print and verse. But what happened if in the
years between twenty and thirty a woman did not find, have found for
her, or want to find, a male partner? The historical record does not
readily yield information on those who deviated from the model.
Demographers identify a 'never married person' as someone over fifty
who died celibate. It is true that marriage for the first time over the
age of forty was not unknown, but in normal times (defined by the
absence of plague or other killers and with perhaps some exception made
for the largest cities) it was relatively rare, so that these assumptions by
demographers probably result in an under-recording of the true incidence of permanent spinsters in the population.[1] Nor do demographic
statistics allow for free unions. Most of them were compiled by looking
in detail at the experience of villages and there is good reason to believe
that the unmarried frequently migrated to the towns in search of work.

However, they give an approximate idea of the numbers in question. In France, for example, of those born between 1660 and 1664, 7 per cent would not marry: this would fall to 6.6 per cent for those born in 1690–91, rising to 8.5 per cent for the generation born in 1720–24 and reaching 14.5 per cent by the end of the century. The British pattern shows a high point of celibacy among those born in the 1670s. Of those born in 1671, 16–18 per cent would not marry, but by the second half of the eighteenth century this figure would have fallen to 5 per cent, thereafter rising to between 7 and 10 per cent by the end of the century. The standard explanation for these ebbs and flows is linked to real wage performance. Drastically condensed, the conclusion drawn is that permanent celibacy diminishes in times of rising real wages and the same conditions lower the age at marriage. As an illustration, the French record in the eighteenth century points to falling real wages at a time when England was experiencing buoyant economic growth. Put another way, in difficult times when economic growth lagged behind population growth, there were more spinsters because conditions precluded a proportion of the young from saving enough to lease and stock a farm, or such a farm was not available. The unmarried man had options that were not generally open to women, such as the army, the navy, seasonal migration or temporary expatriation. Since female wages were not generally calculated with an independent existence in mind, any fall meant that more spinsters had to survive in ever more difficult circumstances.[2]

Little class-specific demography has been done, but analyses of the British and Scottish peerage suggest that, while aristocratic spinsterhood was low in the seventeenth century, it rose dramatically in the eighteenth century to about 25 per cent and 30 per cent respectively and these levels were maintained.[3] Among such women it is possible to find individuals like Louisa Stuart who positively chose the single state. In English Catholic gentry families, for whom the marriage pool was small, a high percentage of daughters opted for the conventual life in continental Europe.

If an influential set of historians has urged that the eighteenth century saw more love going into marriage, the growing number of aristocratic spinsters bore witness to the fact that more money was going into it as well. What the unmarried daughters could expect was to be kept in comfort from the family estate and to share a modest dwelling, perhaps the dower house, at a requisite distance from the newly embellished main house. Such women might accompany aunts and nieces on their travels, serve as chaperones for young girls in the family and tend the aged in their dotage. They were literate and sometimes articulate and are found in philanthropic initiatives and on the subscription lists of booksellers. Some count among a growing number of unmarried critics of a system which absorbed their brothers into the church, the law, imperial service and politics and left them with very limited horizons.

The place for the well-born spinster in Catholic Europe was tradition-ally the convent. By the mid-eighteenth century the life of a religious was less commonly adopted in France and Italy and choice, however limited, between the convent and spinsterhood may have been acknowledged.[4]

High numbers of spinsters were also found in middle-class families, though a systematic study has not been attempted. Anglican clergy-men's families, for example, were large and it would appear to have been normal to marry no more than a couple of daughters per generation (usually to other clergymen), leaving the rest to serve as housekeepers, governesses, ladies' companions or simply to stay at home to tend aged parents. The church made considerable provision for clergymen's sons to have Oxford scholarships which brought them within sight of a clerical living, but it did nothing for the daughters. Those who remained at home could be left some guarantee of a livelihood out of family funds, but it was frequently very precarious, and many, like Jane Austen, were dependent on the goodwill of relatives for any comfort in their lives. Literate and frequently used to living in houses which had books and journals, the clergyman's daughter was likely to try to edge her way into teaching or even into print.[5]

Lower down the social scale, the older unmarried woman who was in possession of a sound physique could still be absorbed into maid service. Some households preferred an older and more responsible woman, and some family businesses could make use of the accounting skills and knowledge of daughters who had acquired these in their youth. However, where these did not exist, low female wages which precluded an independent existence clearly taxed the ingenuity of a whole range of industrial workers – spinners, lace-makers, silkworkers, glove stitchers and those who sought to make a living from the needle trades. One solution might be 'spinster clustering', grouping together in twos or threes or even more (just as widows sometimes did) to share rental and heating and lighting costs, and to minimize the time spent at market, or queuing for the household's water, or delivering work to manufacturers. Clustering is found in cities like Lyons which had a strong industrial base, and in towns and villages which had industrial outwork, but rarely in purely agricultural villages. In Lyons groups of spinsters jointly rented garrets which were icy in winter and stifling in summer. They apparently found this way of life more acceptable than sleeping under the loom as they had done in their youth as *servantes chez les ouvriers en soie*.6 Clustering was not of course confined to the lower orders. One very middle-class establishment at Montcollier House in Belfast, for example, consisted of two widows, Mrs Wilson and Mrs Mackey, and three spinster sisters, the Misses Bland, who pooled their limited resources to cover housekeeping and to maintain a genteel image. These clusters were family substitutes in sickness.[7]

It is possible that the extension of a religious life without enclosure in service of the community, which was seen in the seventeenth and eighteenth centuries in France, soaked up some of the spinster surplus from a broad sector of the population. Nevertheless, early modern Europe still had a large number of single women dependent upon a makeshift economy and upon relationships with family and friends, who lived in fear of a descent into ill-health or old age. One demographic constant is the failure of spinsters to live as long as married women.

The physically handicapped were perhaps the most likely to remain unwed. Traditional societies not only interpreted abnormalities as a reflection of the sin of the parents, but in the case of a deformed woman also saw them as likely to restrict her from labouring efficiently in the fields and as reducing her capacity to produce healthy babies. Even in better-off society in Catholic Europe, the handicapped and the ill-favoured were seen as natural nuns. The convent would shelter them when they were too weak to do much other than pray.[8]

What of those who did not want to enter into a heterosexual union? Was it possible for women to live in a homosexual relationship? The question is virtually impossible to answer. We have no idea of the relations between the widows and spinsters who clustered in towns. What we do know is that, unlike male homosexuality which spasmodically provoked group hangings or executions, female homosexuality manifested itself infrequently and less explicitly before the law. Lesbianism as a term is a nineteenth-century invention. In the early modern period, there was no recognized sex without a penis. This is not to say that sexual relationships between women did not exist, but that the evidence that would enable us to discern and categorize them is ambiguous or lacking. If an action is not defined then it is not punishable in itself, though it might be and indeed was in some instances, possible to find other means to convert the action into a crime.[9]

What is clear is that there was a tradition of female transvestism in the period, of trouser-wearing women who adopted male roles in their working lives.[10] More than 50 such women have been discovered in Britain and 155 in the Netherlands. These are not impressive numbers, but since the women in question were only caught when wounded or ill or when discovered squatting down to urinate, there may have been many more. Such trouser-wearing women fled from traditional female occupations – they are frequently described as 'splintering the distaff' – and they usually enlisted in the army or the navy. Their particular incidence in the Netherlands may indicate the greater possibilities for such activities in a country where mercenary troops were constantly being raised and where the East Indiamen had such demands for manpower that those who enlisted were not scrutinized too carefully. About 50 per cent of those with known origins did not come from the Republic but from the wider German hinterland and most who recorded a previous job had been servants, seamstresses and pedlars, precarious livelihoods. Either these women were averse to female work, or felt themselves drawn to men's work, or needed more money. Until they were discovered many acquitted themselves well. Sixteen out of the fifty-odd known British cross-dressers were soldiers or sailors and some of the former received pensions. A few were maintained in the ranks as soldiers after discovery, but the navy sent them back home although without criminal proceedings. A small subsection of the Dutch contingent used the ploy to secure a cheap passage to the East Indies where they hoped to marry as women. Most, however, clearly rejected their female past and a handful passed into legend for personal bravery. Whatever the toll on their emotional lives and the fear of discovery, they had not let the male side down.

A line must be drawn between these trouser-wearers, of whose sexual exploits nothing is known, and a very small number (five English and a few more Dutch) who dressed as men, led male working lives and 'married' women, in some instances more than one. These women usually came before the magistrates charged with fraud, a serious offence, and were in almost all cases brought before the courts by their 'wives' who wished to annul the union. The accusers would emphasize how they had been duped and how the 'husband' had delayed the issue of congress. Some of these relationships, however, had lasted several years and we must assume either that the 'wife' had neglected to proceed against her partner through shame or ignorance, or that she had colluded in the relationship and only brought the matter before the authorities due to a disagreement in which she could produce the trump card. An examination would of course take place to see whether the private parts of the 'husband' were in fact those of a woman. In an important treatise of 1700, Luigi Maria Sinistrati defined a sexual condition called tribady, in which one woman was able to penetrate another by means of an exceptionally developed clitoris, and he enjoined careful examination to see if this had occurred.[11] A number of isolated cases were tried under the rubric of sodomy, which could carry the death penalty. The crime of sodomy could be extended to the notion of 'unnatural practices' (any that secured disapproval). If a false penis or allegations of abnormal clitoral development were in question, such a charge could be made. By the eighteenth century in Holland, if not in Germany, the term was narrowing to imply anal copulation by men.[12]

Neither in England nor in Holland did punishment for women accused of such offences usually extend beyond prohibition of any rep-etition of the activity, in the first place, and, in Holland, banishment from the province or in England a short prison sentence. A second offence in Holland could secure a banishment penalty of as much as twenty years. However in Germany a case in 1721 tried under the heading of sodomy was followed by the death sentence[13] and there is earlier pictorial evidence intimating that there may have been other cases.

The imputation of 'immodest acts' within their walls could haunt convents and they were quick to clamp down on irregularities. How many such cases might have existed in this guilt culture is difficult to ascertain. The case analysed by Judith Brown of an Italian nun who in 1600 seduced another nun into sexual contact shows how difficult Europeans found the notion of sex without a penis.[14] In Britain a rumour of this kind of activity could close a school. In the case of Woods and Pirie versus Helen Cumming Gordon in 1811, a libel case against Gordon for spreading the rumour that two teachers who ran a school immodestly slept together, resulted in a victory for the two teachers.

The defence cited a lengthy list of literary, not real, cases as evidence for such practices among women. In giving his verdict, the judge noted that: 'I have very little doubt that in all ages and countries women have enjoyed this mode of pleasure seeking.' The two unmarried teachers were dependent on the school for their livelihood. Implicitly their class and their spinster status may have raised issues in the judge's mind that he had no wish to contemplate.[15]

Spinsters, trouser-wearing women and those who sought a partnership with another woman clearly did not proceed in the orthodox manner up the ordained ladder of life. For those who sought to progress according to the established rules there were many who encountered impediments. Incidents such as a slip in virtue (sexually defined to mean loss of chastity) might transform the honourable woman into the shameful, the virtuous into the sinful, and cause such a person's life to deviate from the respected norms. Honour was constructed above all on female chastity, but that did not mean that all females were chaste. It was also predicated upon the dutiful and caring protection of the woman by a strong male figure, but that did not mean that all males were dutiful, caring and conscientious about this version of their purpose in life. It followed that the life of any woman or man could be punctuated, disrupted or even destroyed by failures of one or the other sex to conform to the norms imposed upon them by the requirements of society. The woman who was pregnant outside wedlock, the one who looked to illicit sex for a livelihood, the rape victim, the unmarried couple living together, the beaten and abused wife, the one who saw her livelihood disappear as her husband dissipated their joint earnings on drink or on another woman, or the loveless, carping wife who made her husband's life a misery or the one who made him a laughing stock in his community by her drinking or her lewd behaviour or her neglect of their children – all these were real-life situations and their problems were intrinsically connected to the failure, sometimes through no fault of their own, to conform to the models Christian Europe espoused.

The Reformation and the Counter-Reformation, backed by the state, struggled to make public, regularized, Christian marriage the norm for the Christian and the citizen and thereafter to hold couples within an indissoluble bond. To further their design, given the frailties of human nature, penalties had to be invented and enforced for those who did not conform and the existing judicial structure had to be activated to cope with those who infringed the rules. The patriarchal family needed to be backed by the force of law.

The centrality of marriage to the social framework, and above all its virtual indissolubility, obviously imposed particular strains on the less than perfect union. The church, in insisting upon marriage as a permanent bond and backing this with the force of law, the spirit encapsulated in the phrase 'till death us do part', condemned an ill-defined number of couples to live out their lives in an unremitting hell. Some couples could separate by private agreement, but this did not leave them free to remarry. Marriages could be annulled under specific circumstances. In Catholic and some Calvinist societies, certainly in France, Scotland and Geneva, these included male impotence — as long as it could be demonstrated — which was justified on the grounds that as the bearing of children was the salvation of woman, to be cut off from this possibility was to be denied eternal life (this biblical injunction seems to have been ignored in England). Annulment was also possible for a couple who found that they had married within unacceptable degrees of consanguinity, as long as this discovery postdated the matrimonial act. Separation for a specific number of weeks, months or years or even in perpetuity could be obtained, the last most generally only in the event of the adultery of the wife or if her life was endangered by violence on the part of the husband. A husband's adultery would only lead to perpetual separation if he forced upon his wife humiliation such as bringing his concubine into the matrimonial home.[16]

In Catholic Europe separation from bed and board did not mean that the wronged partner was free to remarry. The church set its face resolutely against the notion that marriage could be repeated. The Calvinist church was a little less adamant in its attitude. Under certain circumstances — which almost reduced themselves to the adultery of the wife — remarriage was possible, although the number of cases in which it was accepted was usually very small. In Calvinist Geneva the court complained in 1600 of its unfair reputation for 'rupturing marriages easily'.[17] In fact it averaged less than one a year throughout its existence until 1750. In Scotland, again, between 1658 and 1707, only thirty-five couples obtained divorce and over 50 per cent of these really had grounds for annulment. Nineteen suits were inaugurated by wives and included cases of impotence; sixteen were brought by the husbands. Though the discontented partners emanated from a broad social spectrum (from the peerage to the middle classes) the step was quite costly.[18]

In England from the late seventeenth century an ambiguous situation existed in which an aristocratic husband could institute a Private Act of Parliament under which an adulterous wife could be divorced, allowing him to remarry. The church courts lost interest in adultery during the closing decades of the seventeenth century, and about the same time in Britain the offence of 'criminal conversation' came into being. Here, a civil action could be brought by a husband charging another man with adulterous intimacy with his wife and claiming monetary compensation; successful cases were inevitably followed by divorce since the fact of adultery had been proved. In Lawrence Stone's view, the 'crim con' facility ushered in a development in the official disintegration of élite marriage. However, such a recognition does not seriously erode the principle of the virtual indissolubility of marriage for all but a handful of those with the means to buy their way out of the system.[19]

At the very bottom of the social scale in Britain there existed a practice, at least from the eighteenth century, about which claims have been made on very sparse evidence – that of wife sale. In some public place, such as a market or tavern, someone who the wife would probably have known would pay over a small sum of money to the husband, maybe no more than a few shillings to buy drinks so that the exchange was advertised publicly. Such agreements, of course, did not have the approbation of church or state.[20]

From 1792 in France, though modified during the Napoleonic period, divorce followed by remarriage was available to all social classes, a situation which to the British epitomized the descent of liberty into licence. However, those who took advantage of this situation were usually women (outnumbering men by something like three to one) who had some prospect of reconstructing an economically viable life outside marriage.

The doggedness with which early modern society clung to monogamy sanctioned by the church is to be explained above all by religious conviction. These were societies intent on salvation and intrinsic to that process was marital fidelity and the shunning of adultery. God had sanctioned the first marriage in the persons of Adam and Eve and Jesus Christ had endorsed the institution by his presence at the wedding of Cana, where he had even performed a miracle to ensure the flow of wine. No man should put asunder what God had joined together. The wife who complained to her confessor of her husband's treatment was advised to accept her suffering and see it in the same light as Christ's ascent to Calvary. She should pray for her husband to change, but should accept God's will. Indeed, one Italian guide, F. Bartolini's *Esercitio Spirituale per ogni giorno di Quaresima sopra la passione e morte di Giesù Christo* (1563), written by a Jesuit confessor in late sixteenth-century Bologna and recommended to an aristocratic woman locked in a difficult relationship with her husband, had as frontispiece a woman toiling behind Christ on the road to Calvary.[21]

As long as Europeans did not falter in their commitment to heavenly, rather than earthly, happiness as laid down in Scripture, the ascendancy of this view of marriage was guaranteed. Given their lack of control over their property, the threat of the loss of their children and their incapacity to live independently by the work of their hands, a high tolerance level of marital violence and sexual infidelity was demanded of the pious Christian wife. There was no obvious alternative to the living hell of their marriage. For men, with possibilities for dalliance outside marriage and their greater physical strength, which gave them the edge in altercation, obviously there was little incentive to alter the status quo. However, there was an obvious relationship between commitment to religious doctrine and the refusal to admit the necessity of divorce. The further a society went along the road to religious indifference, as the case of Revolutionary France demonstrates, the more conspicuous its lack of commitment to the indissolubility of the marriage vows.

To examine the dissent surrounding marriage, or even a small part of it, we must turn to a particular kind of historical document, the judicial records emanating from a wide variety of ecclesiastical, civil and criminal courts. The ecclesiastical courts dealt with straightforward infractions of marriage promises, bastardy suits and requests for separation or, in the Calvinist case, divorce. However, their range of penological discretion was limited. Those in search of compensation had to seek out the civil courts, and when sexual or marital offences were really serious, the affair was for the criminal courts. Ecclesiastical courts could debar offenders from sacraments and demand penance, but they could not pronounce the death penalty. Collectively, these archives could be called the archives of abuse and discontent and, in the case of those emanating from the criminal courts dealing with issues such as infanticide, rape and spouse murder, the archives of sexual, social and marital disaster. They are textually graphic and rich. They vary in quantity and quality and we can have no idea whatsoever of whether they convey the true extent of any particular problem or merely the tip of an iceberg. In short, they can be used qualitatively but not quantitatively. Furthermore, with very few exceptions, they permit only a snapshot view of the problems of a particular individual at a given moment and give us no notion of what happened after the verdict was passed, action taken or the case dismissed. What was the subsequent history of the woman who claimed breach of promise or brought a paternity suit against her lover? What were her positions in the community and in her family, her long-term marriage prospects, the fate of the 'illicit fruit'? We cannot know for certain. As Foucault said, such records offer us 'lives condensed in a few lines, a few pages, misfortunes and adventures impossible to count reduced to a small pool of words.'[22]

As well as the judicial archives there are private agreements between the contending parties which take place outside the control of the courts but are often backed by legal documents, notarial agreements. The litigation surrounding breach of promise or paternity suits was very often undertaken with monetary compensation in mind. This compensation could redress at least in part the status of the woman who had given her favours to one she thought an earnest suitor, or pay for her confinement and the care of illegitimate progeny. A married couple whose marriage had irretrievably broken down and who had sufficient resources to live separately could arrive at an amicable private settlement of the kind that permitted separation but not remarriage. This was the mode of agreement arrived at between Lady Mary Wortley Montagu and her husband; she spent her later life travelling around southern Europe. However, before such agreements could be concluded it was needful for the husband to surrender whatever assets the wife had brought with her into marriage and agreement had also to be reached on control of, or access to, the children. Such arrangements depended upon the co-operation of the parties concerned and could not be defended in law.

All European laws before the Napoleonic occupations were jungles of varying density. Marriage law was often an amalgam of canon law, which laid down the rules of marriage, and customary law, which had jurisdiction over matters arising from debt and credit. There was immense scope for the involvement of lawyers.

The volume of litigation relating to marriage increases substantially, in some instances from the end of the seventeenth century and in others from the late eighteenth. In all countries, Catholic as well as Protestant, the eighteenth century also witnesses the rise of the lawyer skilled in arguing the case for separation and for the monetary arrangements which should accompany it. One reason for the emergence of these 'experts' may be a recognition that there are methods of finding a way through the system while preserving it intact for the many. Or the development can be attributed to a weakening of church authority, or to the acquisition by both men and women of some consciousness of the 'wrongness' of their situation and to the cognizance that only experts (men) can negotiate the labyrinth of the law. The development is revealed in the language of both ecclesiastical and civil courts, which is both manipulative and reductive. Barristers and even clerks of court develop a rhetoric and special formulas, the one to persuade judge and perhaps jury, the second to provide a record embodying locutions acceptable to evolving notions of what is appropriate. Litigation develops a kind of culture. The contending parties are out to prove their case or deny allegations. They mould 'truth' to suit their purposes or they lie to promote their case. Opposing fictions are bandied about. Or the judge or prosecutor formulates questions which shape how the case is put and determined. The testimony of witnesses becomes subject to the interpretation of the judge or lawyer who controls the outcome through questions employing words, embellished by rendering and innuendo. Language is sovereign, language in this context is power.

Judge, prosecutors and, where they exist, jurors, are all men. They have never been beaten or abused nor themselves experienced an unwanted pregnancy. This is not to say that they are incapable of dispensing justice as they understand it or that they do not attempt to be fair. They see themselves as guardians of moral order; and moral order is best maintained when the weak have a measure of protection and when the community does not have to bear the charges of individual misdemeanours. They approach accuser and accused with an assumption of a particular God-ordained order (which it is their job to interpret and maintain) in which women are under the control of husband or father who is their initial judge. They also have notions of what is appropriate to womanhood. A woman's character, if her allegations against a man are to carry even a measure of plausibility, should be unflawed. Unfortunately many of those who came before the judges did so in a position of weakness. They had been impregnated, abused, raped or beaten. They were patently flawed and hence they were on trial as well as the men they accused.

The judges were also the legatees of the double standards applied by society as a whole. An adulterous woman was far more to be condemned than an adulterous man who made sure his dalliance was outside the home. A man had a right to beat his wife if she deserved it and whether or not she did so was determined by the decisions of the judge according to criteria of what was proper to either sex in his view. All courts were tolerant of male drunkenness leading to debauchery, violence and the dissipation of the household's resources, unless thresholds were crossed like the selling of the conjugal bed. However, let a woman drink to the point of urinating in her clothes and a very different view was taken. Her character was destroyed.

The case histories of the courts embody a mixture of the true and the false, assessed according to criteria which were not always, perhaps rarely, neutral; none the less, they are the only extensive testimony to the fragility and vulnerability of a woman's predicament in societies which used female chastity as a marker of worth and denied women the right to self-sufficiency through labour. They also show women as helpless victims within marriage. True there are also wronged men – one for approximately every six women in the French ecclesiastical courts and one for every three women in the divorce courts of the Revolution – and it is clearly impossible to assess the relative suffering of the respective partners in the 'unquiet' marriages of traditional society. The English evidence from Private Acts of Parliament and the 'crim con' cases by its very nature focuses on the infidelity of the wife. Otherwise, the great majority of plaintiffs in the ecclesiastical courts are female, as are the victims of sexual offences and spouse murder in the criminal courts.

The issues before the ecclesiastical courts break down into two broad categories with subsections: pre-marital (breach of promise, impregnation) and post-marital (annulment, separation, abuse, adultery, bestiality), with a third possible section for scandalous behaviour – to include free unions – and defamation of character. In the criminal courts, infanticide can perhaps be seen as the most serious extension of the effects of pre-marital sex and spouse murder the most serious outcome of the disintegration of a marriage.

The most considerable volume of cases coming before the English and French ecclesiastical courts in the seventeenth and eighteenth centuries related not to the breakdown of marriage but to breach of promise. During the seventeenth century any breach of promise in France had to come before the ecclesiastical courts. In countries of Roman law such cases also included issues arising from the failure of the father of the bride or groom to conclude a notarial act registering the claims of one or the other party to a dowry or a son's legitimate claim on the estate of the father. The bulk of cases in all countries, whether Protestant or Catholic, related to the lowest levels of society. Most of the women in those cases which came before the ecclesiastical court of Cambrai, for example, were textile workers or servants and this would seem also to have been the English model; and many of the relationships broke down through poverty which caused the young man in question to draw back and perhaps wish to leave the village to look for work elsewhere.

When defloration was involved many of the families were out for compensation and when it looked as if the girl had proved her case against her seducer monetary settlements of some kind could take place out of court. Many of the cases are couched in terms which make the circumstances of the defloration tantamount to rape. This was an offence, however, which could be taken to a criminal court because if proven (and the accent is very much on the 'if') it could entail the death penalty.

The issue of rape raised questions concerning the appropriateness of the conduct of the woman involved and about the essence of womanhood rather than merely the offence of the man. It raised the spectre of woman as the more lustful sex, tempting man to his fate, and the view of woman as properly anchored in the private not the public sphere. If she left that sphere to set foot in an unguarded place, should she be considered guilty of courting her fate? These were not the only teasing questions and ambiguities called into account in the criminal courts when it came to adjudging the issue.

Like infanticide, rape doubtless had a huge 'hidden figure', that is, was subject to chronic under-reporting. Even in our own times criminologists suspect that over 95 per cent of sexual offences go unreported. In early modern times, when sexual chastity was more highly prized and women feared either a devaluation of their status in the marriage market or parental ire if they should reveal what had happened – particularly if they had strayed from home or placed themselves in compromising circumstances – this tendency must have been very strong. There also existed the very real fear that the problem, if reported, would lead to a scrutiny of the relationship between the victim and the offender: the least evidence that encouragement had been given, evidence that could be easily fabricated by the alleged rapist's friends, nullified the girl's chances of redress. Worst of all, if rape should be followed by pregnancy, it was widely believed and accepted in the courts that a rape had not occurred, for the woman's pleasure was a sine qua non of conception.

In British law in the early modern period, rape was defined as 'the unlawful and carnal knowledge of any woman above the age of ten years against her will, or of a woman child of ten years (or under) with her will or against her will'. The penalty, if the case was proved, was hanging. Until 1576 the age of consent was twelve years. At the Old Bailey and the London Sessions between 1730 and 1830, 294 cases of rape and child molestation were presented (almost three per year) and of these 57 (about one-fifth) were for the abuse of girls under ten and 28 of the accused were hanged.[23] This proportion should not be regarded as in any way indicative of the real picture. Confidence in a successful prosecution may have led parents to report child molestation more readily than women would report instances of rape in which their characters were on trial. The cases reveal some horrifying details. Some of the children may have had venereal disease and this may reflect the belief that an infected man could heal himself by sex with a virgin. Packed lodging houses with shared beds may have multiplied the risks for children in the capital.[24]

In Essex between 1620 and 1680 there was a rape case about once every two years and of them about a fifth ended in a hanging. The men who ended on the gallows had raped a child or a woman of a higher social class with whom they were not acquainted and the case had been reported almost immediately.[25] Justice Hale, commenting on a number of allegedly 'malicious' rape cases in Sussex in the 1660s, remarked that:

It is true that rape is a most detestable crime and therefore ought severely to be punished with death, but it must be remembered, that it is an accusation easy to be made and hard to be proved, and harder to be defended by the party accused tho 'never so innocent'.[26]

In fact, the party accused could be virtually sure of acquittal provided he steered clear of children, knew his victim, who was of the same class as himself, and as long as she was too frightened to report him within the ensuing five days. After that short period, the charge of rape became 'stale' and juries were instructed that they could not listen to it. The refusal to listen to a case that was more than a week old was common to all European countries.[27]

The girls most likely to find charges of rape rebutted were working girls. The circumstances in which the alleged offence occurred reflected the total lack of privacy they experienced in their working lives. As servants, for example, they frequently slept in corners of the kitchen or in cupboards. As both servants and resident industrial workers, they were also regularly sent into the street to perform errands. Some of the young girls who clustered together in the cellars of the Flemish cities and did industrial work were also a prey for the man who delivered the raw materials. In any garrison town, and this was true Europe-wide, the military with time on their hands lounged around taverns and pursued the young maidservant when she appeared in the streets. Sometimes undesirable acquaintances were made and once she knew the person concerned, however briefly, then it could be argued that the girl had given encouragement and foreplay had become something more serious.

Women who worked in taverns or who were known to have friends among the military or who strayed 'heedlessly' abroad were unlikely to get much of a hearing in court. In Mediterranean courts charges by girls who were not kept in close confinement and under the supervision of their parents were not taken seriously. The girl who worked outside her father's house was at risk. He was a failure and she was potentially worth little. In such instances, the rape of a working-class girl was almost a non-offence in the criminal courts.[28]

However, a quite different attitude was taken towards the man who raped a woman of higher social standing, particularly if he did so in the confines of her own home. Let us take the instance of a man of lower social class who raped someone from a family of greater wealth with a view to pushing up the sum of money that would be settled on a deflowered daughter. (In the fairy-tale *Jean L'Ont Pris* this is exactly what the hero does, but the girl is anxious to marry him and connives at her defloration.) The question was, where did seduction end and rape begin? The young man's defence in court would certainly be that he loved the girl and wanted to marry her as quickly as possible and that the girl had colluded. Such was the case of a clerk of a Gascon wine merchant, charged with raping the merchant's daughter Catherine in the mid-eighteenth century. She and her family, however, denied that there was any question of marriage and the young man was hanged.

Had he raped the servant, he would almost certainly have been acquitted of any charges.[29]

It is difficult to assess what Catherine's plight would have been after the rape and what kind of a husband could now be found for her. Intercourse across social boundaries may have left a girl more tainted than if she had had sex with someone of her own class. The upper and middle classes kept a strict eye on their daughters, and with some success. Slights on female honour had to be resolved by a public apology and in some cases money. However, if an upper-class girl found herself deflowered by one of her own class, if not of her own wealth, then compromise was advised. Society viewed with resignation a girl who was soiled merchandise marrying the man who had thus devalued her, and not only in Mediterranean Europe. The Irish abduction societies, unparalleled elsewhere, depended on the valuation, by society in general and the woman and her family in particular, of a compromised and/or deflowered heiress. A 'squireen', as the almost penniless sons of minor gentry were known, would identify an heiress — defined modestly as anyone with a dowry of over £1000 — and abduct her. When she had lost her reputation, marriage and an income for the adventurer followed. The abduction of an heiress corresponded with a certain macho lifestyle among the young of both Dublin and Belfast society.[30] A scholarly study of the phenomenon in Ulster suggests that the income to be made in this way was not great and might easily have been equalled by seeking a career — but that would have meant work. While the upper classes and the British government were anxious to stop the practice the former were not prepared to stand out against it in the case of their own families until two heiresses, the Misses Kennedy, refused to marry their abductors and denounced them before the courts. The young men were condemned to death. At this point the populace rallied against the women, who were hounded and victimized, while the young men, dead of course, were deified as brave and romantic. In the popular view, the young women should have handed over their money and turned them into husbands.[31] Everyone knows that a good woman can create a good man even from wild material.

An increasing proportion of breach of promise cases which came before the ecclesiastical courts were accompanied by claims for the support of a bastard. Most of the women in question from the lower orders of society claimed that they had been led into permitting sexual intercourse by the 'good hope' of marriage. For some it was clearly a case of bad luck. Their intended spouse had died, had been pressganged into the navy or was in the army and had been called away. Some of the women had been in situations where they were sexually exploited, the most common being domestic service in laxly regulated households. The apprentice was as likely to be the impregnator as the master, indeed in many instances more so, but he was also more likely to have to marry the girl, whereas the master could escape with a payment to her. Indeed, in the records of the ecclesiastical courts of Cambrai, there are masters who impregnated three maids in succession but who succeeded in nego-tiating marriages for the young women with third parties. One seducer, for example, offloaded the pregnant maid on a certain Adrian Malice, orphan (and presumably penniless), for the sum of a hundred florins and a complete new set of clothes.[32]

The community and the court were on the side of the young woman if she had ceded her virtue within a context which demonstrated that the pair were intent on matrimony. The honour of the family depended upon that knowledge, and if it was properly established and some child support was obtained then a case study of Languedoc in the eighteenth century would suggest that such daughters were for the most part sheltered by their families and were not precluded from a later marriage. Whether they could hope for a husband of the same social status is not clear. Where the girl had not behaved modestly and the alleged impregnator could muster other men to claim they had enjoyed her favours, then the family was shamed and some showed the girl the door. When, for example, his daughter was abandoned by her lover and a baby was born, Antoine Leopold Fenzy drove the unfortunate girl from the house with a stick, 'declaring she had dishonoured the family by the birth of an illegitimate child'.[33] Some judges, and there are good Breton instances, deplored the characters of the men who claimed they had all slept with the woman and imposed the costs of the birth and the upkeep of the child on the lot of them on the grounds that they should mend their ways, but this was an unusual procedure.

Shame caused many pregnant girls to leave their villages and try to make for the anonymity of the town. In England where parishes were very concerned that the upkeep of a bastard should not be a charge upon them, anyone who harboured a travelling pregnant woman could theoretically find himself brought to court and charged as was John Pike before the ecclesiastical court of Little Bedwyn in Wiltshire in 1610 'for harbouring a stranger in his house that came to him from

Gloucester great with child . . . We desire that the said Pike and the woman concerned may be cited in court that the father of the child may be known and the parish discharged.'[34]

Martin Ingram has pursued the experience of thirty-nine 'travelling' pregnant women in Wiltshire between 1615 and 1629 whose places of origin are clear. Most came from adjacent counties, one from Montgomeryshire in Wales, one from beyond Somerset (Devon?). One was en route to London, another for Taunton. Sixteen were from within Wiltshire itself but only four were within the parish where they had conceived the child.

Intense misery surrounds these stories of wandering women. Each was looking for someone to 'stand her friend in her moment of misery' and local officialdom was only too ready to move her on. Some of those reported for sheltering them had done so for cash. Some were owners of alehouses. A Hankerton carrier charged three shillings and fourpence per week in 1615 for harbouring a pregnant woman (at a time when a labourer's wages were about a shilling) and a Malmesbury innkeeper charged twice that amount in 1627. The women here cannot have been resourceless. Sometimes kin were called on to help and aunts in particular, who had settled at some distance from their relatives, might help in a time of crisis. Even so, in 1610, Anne Frie of Broad Hinton told the magistrates that when she had found 'a walking woman . . . in travail of child in the open street' she took her in 'for womanhood's sake'.[35]

The numbers of cases against harbourers are few, however, and it seems likely that most unmarried pregnant women and their families and shelterers never appeared before the courts. The stringency of the law was in fact not totally respected. However, at most social levels the bearing of a bastard carried with it shame and suffering and placed the friendless and those lacking in kin support in a precarious position.

The private suffering of women impregnated and alone can perhaps be best appreciated by an examination of the records of the criminal courts and the specific subcategory of murder, infanticide. This category of criminal behaviour has been examined in some detail for early modern Holland, parts of Germany, England, Belgium and France.[36]

In the mid-sixteenth century in France and some seventy years later in England stringent laws were enacted against infanticide and in all north-western European societies harsh legislation was either reinforced or re-enacted in the wake of the two Reformations. These laws have been presented as a manifestation of the tightening hand of patriarchy against women living outside marriage. Contemporaries would have argued somewhat differently, that the laws expressed concern for the child dying without Christian baptism. The mother had the option during pregnancy of revealing the father who was liable for the support of the child so that it did not become a burden for the parish. The harshness of the punishment was fully in the spirit of what has been called pre-Beccarian justice, that is, one which knew that it could only bring to court a small percentage of offenders and took the line that deterrence by occasional harsh example was the best way of holding down the incidence of a particular offence.*

It is only in this subcategory of violent crime – infanticide – that in Britain, France and the Netherlands women outnumber men, for very obvious reasons. Infanticide is a crime which accounts for about 30 per cent of murders in the parlement of Paris and in that of Toulouse in the seventeenth century, but only about 12 per cent in the eighteenth. The British evidence is very patchy. In Surrey, for example, between 1663 and 1802, the crime accounted for 34 out of 318 murders or about 12 per cent of the whole. In Essex, 84 women stood trial for infanticide between 1620 and 1680 and this accounts for about 20 per cent of all homicide cases. Other regional evidence for Britain (paralleled by evidence from Belgium and Holland but not as clearly in Germany)[37] confirms the trend of a fall in numbers in the eighteenth century. Very generally, we can think of infanticide as constituting about 10 per cent of all murders and hence a very small part of court activity. Are we to suppose that fewer babies were murdered by their mothers as the eighteenth century progressed, or that the crime was less frequently reported?

It has to be acknowledged that the murder of a new-born baby was a very hard crime to detect and to prove under most circumstances. The woman who neglected her baby to the point of starvation, who claimed that it had suffocated in its cradle, or who put it out to a nurse who did not have enough breast milk to feed it, did not in the eyes of the law commit infanticide. A married woman, particularly one who

---

* This notion of justice, criticized in the second half of the eighteenth century by the father of modern penology, Cesare Beccaria, was gradually replaced in Revolutionary and nineteenth-century law reform by the principle of a punishment proportionate to the crime irrespective of the number of prosecutions.

had living children, could do all these things and not incur a charge even though her neighbours might suspect her; if called upon to supply a character reference for her in the event of another offence, such as the death of an older child, they might refer to her neglect. No one was particularly interested in following up infanticidal nursing. One official in Rennes in the eighteenth century was an exception to this rule and discovered that two women had in the space of a week reported the deaths of several children who were their responsibility and who had been put out to nurse with them either by poor families or by single women against a low fee. The women clearly did not have breast milk to feed them. However, they could not be prosecuted under existing law. The city of Rennes in fact provides a second pointer to a practice which may have been much more extensive than court evidence would suggest. After the fire of 1721, an extensive rebuilding programme was undertaken which necessitated the digging of new drains and the replacement of old ones. One old drain alone yielded about eighty skeletons of infants who had died in the first hours of life.[38] No one had appeared before a court charged with any of these deaths. Were they children born in legitimate wedlock or the offspring of unmarried mothers? The question must remain undecided.

Who then was charged with infanticide? The answer is everywhere the same and reflected the state of the law and the assumptions made by the law as well as practical considerations relating to who was likely to get caught and who felt that she needed to dispose of her child in this way.

In France, the letter of the law was that of 1556 in which the mother of an illegitimate child was obliged to declare and register her pregnancy and at the same time reveal the name of the father of the child. The purpose of the law was allegedly twofold, to prevent infanticide and also to make sure that someone should finance a living child. Failure to register the pregnancy did not *ipso facto* incur the death penalty if the woman had a living child delivered in full public knowledge by a midwife or responsible person. The official parish midwife was supposed to ask the name of the father while the parturient woman was at the height of her labour pains, this being the moment when she was likeliest to tell all. In the event of a secret birth and the discovery of a dead child, however, the failure to register her condition was taken as evidence of intent of concealment and proof of intent to kill. Further evidence, such as that of a stillbirth, did not need to be taken into account. Enlighten-

ment thought in the eighteenth century deemed this legislation over-
harsh, but it remained in force until the Revolution and those prosecuted
under it were found guilty in about 70–80 per cent of cases.[39]

In Britain, there was something of a swing in attitudes towards the
crime over the period. The issue of the bastard child likely to be killed
by its mother was actively debated by the Jacobean parliaments in
1606–7 and again in 1610. Not until 1624, however, did there appear
the 'Act to prevent the murthering of bastard children' which was the
basis of legislation relating to infanticides until 1803, its very name
revealing a prejudgement on who the victims were likely to be:

> Many lewd women that have been delivered of Bastard Children, to
> avoyed their shame and escape punishment, doe secretlie bury or conceal
> the Death of their Children and after if the said child be found dead the
> said women do alleadge that the said child was born dead: whereas if it
> falleth out sometimes (although hardlie is it to be proved) that the said
> Child or Children were murthered by the said women their lewd mothers
> or by their assent or procurement.[40]

The letter of the law presupposed that the mother of a dead illegitimate
child who had delivered in secret was a murderess. It accepted the proof
of one witness prepared to state that the child had been born alive. The
toughest period of application of the law, when it appears that 30–40
per cent of the few women who were caught and prosecuted were given
the death penalty, appears to have been in the decades following the
enactment of the legislation. Indeed, in Essex between 1630 and 1639
eleven of the twelve women brought to trial for the offence were hanged
compared with four out of eighteen between 1670 and 1679 – admittedly the laxest years following the Restoration. The period of severe
application of the letter of the law was therefore very short.[41]

From the closing decades of the seventeenth century, judges began
to deal with women charged with infanticide much more leniently.
Many were uncomfortable that the Jacobean statute reflected a much
more continental approach, presuming the guilt of the accused. They
were also uncomfortable about the reliability of the evidence used to
show that a baby had ever lived. This evidence was largely a test to see
if the child's lungs had ever contained air by floating them in a bucket of
water. Innocence was proven if the lungs sank. The test was definitively
rejected as having no validity by the Scottish surgeon William Hunter

in 1783 (subsequently published as *On the uncertainty of the signs of murder in the case of bastard children* [1812]), and judges were clearly relieved at no longer having to have recourse to this practice. Forty-six women were tried for infanticide and acquitted at the Old Bailey in the eighteenth century. The evidence used to secure acquittal was the demonstration that the mother had not in fact concealed her pregnancy and could show that she had in her possession some child's linen to cope with the arrival of the child or that the event was known about. Midwives were called upon to declare whether or not in their view the child had ever lived and they usually denied that it had done so thus confirming the mother's story. One Surrey judge clearly believed himself more enlightened than the jurymen and actually instructed them to believe the mother's story, and in the same court one judge accepted a plea of temporary insanity from the mother. To have a child already living and to show that she was a reasonably caring mother by feeding and clothing it warmly and attempting to control the lice was also seen as evidence that a woman would not murder a baby.[42]

On the Continent, more conspicuously than in England, judges were very concerned with how the mother had dealt with the body of the child. One Dutch mother told the judge with tears in her eyes that she had given birth to a baby – as the neighbours suspected from her bulk – but that it was dead and that she had placed it carefully in a box and buried it. So distressed had she been that she had dug it up twice to ascertain that it was really dead. She was acquitted. Conversely, studies of infanticide cases in Belgium and France show that to bury the little body in the farm dungheap or to mix it and the afterbirth into the pig swill where it would be eaten by the animals was a sign of guilt, a lack of real respect for human life for which the mother paid with her own.[43]

Though no jurisdiction provides a large sample of infanticidal mothers, their attributes across Europe appear to have had everything in common. In part this emanated from the letter of the law which presumed the infanticidal mother to be unmarried, a bastard bearer. The insistence upon the criterion of concealment, above all, reflected this belief. A married woman did not need to conceal her condition. In fact, if she was really poor and her residence in a parish established, she could get much more from poor law and charitable resources by actually flaunting it. Secondly, a woman who lived in her own home – particularly on an isolated farm – as opposed to being an employee in someone else's, enjoyed a greater advantage in any attempts to conceal

her state in that she might be able to count on the help of her relatives
who might even dispose of the child for her. Thirdly, family help in
the form of providing a little extra in the way of a dowry to secure a
match, if the real father would not marry her, eliminated another group
of women. Fourthly, a woman whose family had economic resources
and wished to purchase anonymity, could use one of the numerous
'lying-in' establishments which enjoyed a twilight existence in most
European cities and in early modern England even in rural areas which
lay outside an official parish boundary and thus escaped inspection. Such
was the one at Stratfield Leys outside Oxford where the Stuart courtesans
went to have their babies delivered and have them put out to nurse.

These facts meant that the woman accused of infanticide was a particular kind of person, a spinster or widow, usually in her mid- to late
twenties and from the lower classes. The commonest occupation cited
at the trials was that of maidservant or former maidservant. She murdered her child at the moment of birth, usually by strangulation or
suffocation so that its cries were never heard. Or it was drowned in a
river or thrown down a well, or bled to death because the umbilical
cord was not tied. The mother gave birth to the child alone, either in her
garret or in an outhouse or stables away from the rest of the household, or
sometimes it took place in the open air. The descriptions have a starkness
to them: 'elle a accouché au bord d'une vigne . . . près d'une rivière
. . . (she gave birth near a vineyard . . . near a river)'. Details such as
how she stifled her own cries or separated the child from herself or how
she avoided getting her clothes stained with blood which would give
her away are rarely given. What does emerge, albeit interstitially, is
that the girl is an outsider to the community. She is away from her
family.[44]

Domestic service was of course the largest single category of female
labour, but it was also the kind of job that carried with it certain
conditions. Firstly, revelation of the girl's pregnancy would almost
certainly mean dismissal even if the impregnator was the master of the
house. There were few prospects for re-employment in domestic service
for a woman carrying a baby around; to take it to the foundling hospital
would make the event public and some payment would be demanded
for the support of the child. She could try to deposit the child anonymously, but a girl carrying a bundle and perhaps walking several miles
to one of these institutions could be readily spotted. In Britain revelation
of her pregnancy would involve questions about the father and judge-

ments on her behaviour and if she failed to give information she could be sent back to the parish of her birth to spare the parish where she had been impregnated the cost of supporting her and her child. She would not only be shamed in the place of her birth but might not have a family there any longer to help her. She might become the centre of legal squabbles about which parish should support the child.

If she could hide the pregnancy, however, and if after unsuccessful attempts to provoke a miscarriage – always supposing she knew about them or could find someone who did – she could keep the birth quiet, then she might retain her job, keep whatever family she had in ignorance and not cut into her past earnings which were her possibility of marriage one day. Some maidservants attested to the collusion of the mistress in trying to provoke an abortion (usually by bleeding in the feet and drinking strong liquor). These may be cases where the impregnator was the employer, as in a conspicuous percentage of German infanticide cases.[15] In France, however, he is less likely to be the father of the child than the fellow servant or apprentice, according to the declarations of the women who were prepared to name their impregnator, although we do not know how many were telling the truth. By the time a Frenchwoman came to court charged with infanticide, she was already a law breaker for not having denounced her seducer; and having chosen silence at the critical juncture she now had to bear the charge of infanticide alone.

Economic factors were rarely mentioned in British trials but French servants, perhaps recognizing the inevitability of conviction, could be more explicit: 'comment voulez vous que je gagne ma vie et celle de cette enfant?' (how do you expect me to earn my living and keep a child?)' The question was never answered.

To some degree, the murdered child was the victim of the law of unequal worth which kept women's earning power low. It was also the victim of being born to a servant, whose type of work excluded the possibility of rearing a child. In some cases the murdered baby was a product of the shame involved in giving birth to a bastard where there was no family to come to the woman's support. The politicians of the Constituent Assembly in 1790–91 insisted that the last cause was the most important, but in fact the second might be the most pressing contributory factor. Textile workers in Flemish cities, for example, were significantly less represented in infanticide statistics than servants although they were apparently heavier producers of illegitimate children, suggesting either that their work made keeping a child easier than did life in service or that they were women living in free unions. Many of these were also living far from home.[46]

Denunciation of a suspected infanticidal mother came from three sources. First, it was made by fellow servants; second, by a suspicious employer; and lastly, particularly in the case of widows, by neighbours. The justifications for reporting the case were 'secrecy', that the child had had a pagan death (without baptism), or the denouncers claimed to be disgusted by promiscuous behaviour. Employers would alert the parish priest who would call in the midwife to examine the girl's breasts to see if they had milk in them and then officials would demand to know where was the body?

When the Jacobean statute was repealed in England in 1803 it was not followed by a rise in the numbers of reported cases of infanticide. In France, when the crime was devalued as part of an archaic and primitive law code at the time of the Revolution, the numbers of reported cases escalated and continued to do so throughout the nineteenth century. Yet if the numbers rose, the typical accused mother remained the same.

Under canon law carnal relations outside marriage constituted fornication. The Council of Trent was fully explicit. At its twenty-fourth session it stipulated that those living in a state of concubinage, whatever their social status, should, after having been warned three times by the authorities of the place in which they were living, expect excommunication. Women were faced in addition with a public beating. Excommunication was also the threat which theoretically hung over the head of those who behaved scandalously in England; and the couple engaged in a liaison could be reported and brought before the Dutch consistory courts where the woman was deemed technically a whore.

In fact, excommunication was rarely used as a punishment in cases of scandalous behaviour. The couple conducting a liaison probably generally escaped the attention of the ecclesiastical courts unless an illegitimate child, or allegations of *mauvaise vie* (literally an evil lifestyle, which usually meant promiscuity or prostitution), drew attention to them. Many of those who were liable for prosecution under this ruling were in fact living together because one party was already married or because consanguinity made marriage impossible. If they were both outsiders to the parish the local priest might not be aware that the couple were not married unless he was alerted by the conduct of one or both parties.

It usually took the birth of a number of illegitimate children to draw attention to an irregular union. Added to this, in towns, and particularly in countries of Roman law where concubinage was very common, clerical assiduity in this respect was fairly minimal. Even in the diocese of Cambrai there was a marked difference between the pursuit of the adulterous couple from the village and those from the town. Furthermore, the punishment rarely exceeded public penance before the parish priest in the full view of the congregation.[47]

In Calvinist Geneva, adulterous couples could theoretically be banished from the town. In fact this happened rarely. Men escaped pursuit almost entirely and only the aberrant woman was at risk. In England during the stern application of Puritan principles both parties could be called upon to appear barefoot and bareheaded in church carrying a candle. In France when the existence of an adulterous couple was confronted, only the woman seems to have been singled out for attention. In what was probably the most severe case of this kind in the diocese of Cambrai, in the eighteenth century, Adrienne Baudour, mother of four children all by different fathers and about to give birth to a fifth, had to appear in church before six dignitaries to hear her sins read out, go down on her knees and ask forgiveness and promise to amend her ways, and recite five decades of the rosary daily throughout the year.[48] In all, about fifty cases of this kind came before the diocesan court of Cambrai between 1710 and 1770 and almost none of them involved townspeople.

In a large city such as Paris, the parochial clergy tried to involve the civil authorities in cases where they clearly felt that they could not get the offending party into church and in any case something more than a public apology was needed. In the case of Marie Anne Bassin (1777) who had a fruit stall in the rue des Deux Ponts and was the wife of a thief serving ten years in the galleys for stealing lead, the curé of the Ile St-Louis said that she had lived since the departure of her husband in flagrant libertinage with Etienne Chair, a Protestant and wine merchant in a shop adjacent to her business. She admitted to three children by him in as many years and had two more by different fathers. One of these children was in an orphanage. On top of all this her house was resorted to by the prostitutes of the neighbourhood who paid her for the use of her premises for their illicit commerce. The curé declared that the neighbourhood was scandalized by her conduct. The commissaire was not spurred to severe action. He was prepared to give her a month's warning to change her ways given 'that she has a business to run and that moreover she is the landlady of the premises where she lives'. Which part of her ways she had to change is not clear. Perhaps the commissaire thought she should cease to make her premises available for brothel purposes; perhaps she should cease to frequent the bed of Etienne Chair. At any rate the commissaire did not think that the disruption occasioned to tenants by expelling the landlady was a warrantable price to pay for stopping her activities.[49]

At such a level of the population, where the husband was absent for whatever reason, from prison to desertion, the situation of a woman alone was recognized as likely to lead to irregular conduct. The line between liaison and prostitution in the furnished rooms and teeming lodging houses of the cities was a fine one. Virtually resourceless widows, abandoned wives, women working for poverty wages, fell into relationships of an impermanent kind which helped them to stay alive and which they perhaps hoped to prolong. At Bologna the concern was less to stop these relations than to ensure that the parties had never been married (and hence were guilty of fornication rather than adultery) and that if prostitution was an income source, the licence fees to practise had been paid.[50]

The judges of the ecclesiastical courts gave more attention to cases concerning marital annulment or breakdown than they did to the problems surrounding the formation of marriage or the establishment of paternity cases. Cases involving marital breakdown were on the whole more complex and those who sought to terminate their marriages, or at least to alter the behaviour of a spouse by a period of separation, were drawn from a broad social spectrum. There was some difference in the workings of ecclesiastical courts or village courts in different national contexts. In Protestant Germany, as evinced by the courts of Neckarhausen, and in Switzerland, for example, it appears that local courts dealt with matrimonial disputes at any early stage of matrimony, possibly to prevent a significant deterioration over time. Catholic courts dealt with such matters rather later, perhaps because the parish priest was assumed powerful enough to deal with early difficulties. Another difference which merits further study is the absence of certain issues, for example, male impotence as a ground for annulment in English (but not Scottish) ecclesiastical courts in contrast to French ones. Was it that God's will was given a different emphasis in a British context, or that children within wedlock were not seen as a woman's only path to salvation? Where contrasts can be drawn between a Catholic and a Protestant court (Constance/Basle), the Catholic court between 1550 and 1610 saw 95 cases of impotence in comparison with 7 in the Protestant. However, more divorces for adultery occurred in the Protestant court.[51] The French ecclesiastical courts demanded a report by four men, two surgeons and two doctors, to be made after one or two examinations of the husband, who usually denied the charge. The case was only really clear-cut and the female plaintiff on secure ground if the reproductive equipment of the male was patently inadequate and could have never functioned nor be presumed to function in the future. This was empirical evidence and the matter could be speedily resolved within weeks. Hence Marie Marguerite Bonchet 'noticed within days of living with her husband that he could not consummate the marriage because he had a natural deficiency, one which could not be overcome precluding him from the act of procreation and making him a eunuch.' The husband Jean Ghislain Thésin denied the charge and alleged 'a carnal relationship with his wife a hundred times . . . he had already been married to a woman for four years and three months without her complaining . . . his second wife sought a pretext to separate from her husband whether he was capable or not.' The matter was firmly resolved by the medical group. 'We have examined the generative organs . . . and in light of the smallness of the testicles and their lack of requisite form, we declare the said Jean Ghislain Thésin impotent.' A second examination came to the same conclusion and Marie Marguerite was a free woman.[52] However, had Thésin's testicles been larger and less obviously defective, the case could have been more problematic. She would have had to show that no union had ever taken place. The only means to do this would be by an unruptured hymen which a midwife could be called upon to attest. Even if this was shown to be the case, the male was given two more chances extending perhaps over four to six years from the start of the marriage. If the husband insisted, as most did, that the wife was a liar and that she had a defective character, was one who wandered from the house, took pleasures outside the home and was totally uninterested in fulfilling her conjugal sexual role, then the affair could drag on for years. Thus Estienne Bouter, who had the satisfaction of being proclaimed by the judges un homme entier (a complete man), declared that his wife had taken an aversion to him and 'had already left him twice and had taken with her all she wanted from the house including gold rings.' The woman in question countered with what she saw to be the evidence of her lack of progeny and her need to think of her future given that she was not truly married, and so it went on.[53]

The reluctance of men to accept impotence as a long-term problem reflects their social definition. It was an absence of manhood – *vice de construction* – bringing shame upon them. It branded them as unnatural 'monsters', the product of parental or personal sin. The lawyers who initiated the case of wives who were anxious to insist on the impotence of their partners usually advanced the case that the woman was denied her natural means to salvation and invoked the words of Saint Paul, *she shall be saved in childbearing* (I Timothy 2:15), laying upon the judges the onus of possibly withholding eternal life from an innocent party. When the husband was conspicuously older than the woman he had married (an unequal match), then the lawyers pointed to the innocence of the bride and her martyrization when subjected to the efforts of her impotent spouse.[54]

The women denied the possibility of their own infertility and this for churchmen was of course a problem. Who was to blame for the non-production of progeny, given that offspring were a grace which the Lord withheld from some? The infertility of the wife was not seen as a cause for annulment unless it could be argued, and a midwife prove it, that she had never menstruated (*le défaut de puberté*). In the rare instances that this is cited, the marriage had usually taken place when the bride was young and under parental pressure and the parents were heavily censured by the judge.

Bigamy was also a cause for annulment. This was more frequent in Britain than in France, perhaps because of the insistence by the Catholic clergy on the Continent on checking the credentials of the contracting parties before performing marriage; but even in France it may have been an occurrence in the more fluid relationships of the town. Given the high rates of mobility, relatively poor communications and the relative casualness of the English clergy, particularly in conducting a clandestine marriage, regarding the need for any supporting documents, it was possible for the propertyless to leave their wives, settle elsewhere and marry again. We cannot know whether it was a common practice or not simply because the number of cases that surfaced was small and successful bigamists went undisturbed.

On annulment, the parties could go their separate ways and the wife could repossess her dowry, if she had had one, and try her luck again.

The impotent husband, however, was prohibited from attempting to contract a further union.

Separation from bed and board was less finite. The couples who came before the courts had no chance of starting again and in France, for the most part, they would only get temporary respite from their problems. The evidence suggests that a bad marriage was a disaster from the beginning and although the couples who came before the courts usually did not have many children, they waited for anything from three to five years before trying to make an escape. Eighty per cent of the women who came before the ecclesiastical courts cited violence as the reason and entered a plea that their lives were in danger. In Cambrai in the mid-eighteenth century, the degree of violence described was impressive. There was no point in coming before the courts at all if it had not reached life-threatening dimensions. Their lawyers helped them to describe how over the years of their marriage, verbal violence in which the wife had been the target of insults (predominantly sexual or bestial) and public lack of respect, behaviour seen in high as well as in low society, had been followed by physical assault. Each description makes harrowing reading. The Seigneur of Rinsart, grand bailli d'Avesnes (a judge), had pursued his wife on several occasions with a sword and a pistol which he had fired, an axe which he used to break down the door of her room and a burning torch. Her wounds were impressive and she was able to show them in court.[55] P. J. Lemaire broke his wife's arm, beat her with a horsewhip, threw her to the ground and kicked her, leaving her senseless with bleeding head-wounds. Along with blows went threats of death (reinforcing the notion of life-threatening violence). Marguerite Hallot, wife of a merchant, claimed her husband had on several occasions put a knife to her throat and fired a gun in her direction, telling her that she should prepare for death. The neighbours had responded to her screams and could be called to attest to the violence of the scene. Isabelle Dubus, married to a 'gentleman' (Sieur Daniel de Boudry, ecuyer), claimed that her husband had made four attempts to strangle her and that she had been saved by the servants.[56]

The women insisted that they had given their husbands no cause to beat them – that is, they recognized the right of a man to correct his aberrant wife, but insisted upon their innocence. Many dwelt on marital violence during their pregnancies. Hence Julie Josephe Lemaire reproached her husband in court for repeated violence while she was in labour which his beatings had precipitated and the child was born dead.[57] Often violence seems to have been primed by drunkenness. Jeanne Bourdon claimed that her husband came home drunk more often than not and that when he did so he was violent towards her, the children and the servants and would drive them all from the house and bang the door in their faces (debarring a wife from the matrimonial home) and he threatened in the hearing of all to break her arms and legs (life-threatening violence).[58]

The invention of distillation in the seventeenth century and the circulation of spirits which accompanied the commercial revolution in the eighteenth and went on growing, along with drink-related violence, throughout the nineteenth century was perhaps the main guarantor that 'the civilizing process' did not secure benefits for a large number of wives from all social classes. There was some complaint by husbands of their wives' drinking habits, but the worst offences which resulted were dirty and unkempt clothes (the wife was a slut) and a neglected house and children. No drunken wife threatened her husband's life. Some dissipated the housekeeping money, but far more husbands dissipated their wives' possessions. To buy drink, Antoine Cordier 'even sold his wife's gold necklace and her wedding ring'.[59]

Complaints of violence outstripped marital infidelity, which was the second complaint of women seeking separation. This may reflect the fact that separation was more likely to be successful in dealing with life-threatening violence than for infidelity which occurred outside the home. Jeanne Thérèse Delvaut declared she could no longer tolerate the relationship her husband had with two women by whom he had two children and when she found out about this she could not bear to let him near her.[60] Nor, happily for her, did Anne Terin allow her husband to have intercourse, because she knew that he spent the night in brothels and had venereal disease which she — along with the woman who did the laundry — had spotted.[61] A subsection of marital infidelity was familiarity with the servants within the home. Particularly humiliated were those wives whose husbands slept with the maid and brought her to dine at the table saying they preferred her to the mistress. A certain Jean Baptiste Coquerelle had told his wife that he preferred the maid to her and 'he intended to go live with her and that he would kill his wife and stick his dagger in her all over her body'.[62] Prima facie this would seem to have been a good case for the plaintiff, marital infidelity within the home and life-threatening words.

Judges were less impressed by complaints brought by wives which involved the withholding of housekeeping money so that the mistress of the house was humiliated in front of the servants. They were relatively unmoved by complaints against men who lived off their wives' money having dissipated their own. Marie Thérèse Bernard, daughter of a substantial goldsmith and with means she had brought into marriage, complained that her husband mismanaged her funds and that he had let the business she owned decline disastrously and for eighteen years had not lifted a finger, all the while keeping a fancy horse in the stable. Debts surrounded the household. From the archives of discontent and abuse of the diocese of Cambrai we might conclude that the worst marital prospect was an army officer with expensive tastes, a disinclination for work or business, with a pistol in the drawer and an expensive horse in the stable.

The women made their case and the husbands responded by claiming that it was all a pack of lies and that their wives and the servants were not to be trusted. Servants and neighbours were uttering 'calomnies atroces, impostures'. At this point the parish priest was called in to serve as character reference. He need only be brief:

> The plaintiff is an honourable woman who has good cause to complain of the debauched and drunken conduct of her husband and is fully justified in her request.[63]

A woman who did not have the support of the parish priest might as well not bother to initiate a suit. He knew how long she had suffered, and length of suffering definitely mattered to these courts. He would not be on her side if she met infidelity with infidelity. Between 1710 and 1791 out of 416 cases initiated, 345 got temporary or permanent separation from their spouses. The success rate for women plaintiffs was about 85 per cent. However, looked at more closely, unless violence to the point of threatening life was in question, temporary rather than life separation was the norm and upper-class women almost never succeeded in getting permanent separation for debauchery and dissipation of the wife's property by the husband. The adulterous husband was told to mend his ways during the period of separation in which the income on his wife's property must be paid. The adulterous wife could be assigned to a convent for two years pending reconciliation. If she had produced a bastard, then permanent separation might be accorded. The number of cases is small. Under no circumstances did separation permit remarriage.

In Paris there existed a form of justice independent of the courts to which the women of the working class *quartiers* had frequent recourse. The women who appeared before the *lieutenant de police* would lay down a complaint against their husbands and provide witnesses of social standing, notably the parish priest. What they wanted was the incarceration of a violent or adulterous spouse by *lettre de cachet* for a short correctional spell, a period perhaps no longer than a few months, at public expense. Such *lettres* were abolished in the 1780s because they were alleged to be the tool of an arbitrary government and they have been represented as a means whereby husbands could silence their wives. In fact, in Paris, more women used them against their husbands than vice versa and most used them to be temporarily relieved of a violent or drunken spouse.[64]

The women who laid their complaints did not attest to a single or even a simple beating but to reiterated offences compounded by other misdeeds which they had suffered over several years. The typical maltreated wife who elicited a *lettre de cachet* had usually suffered for a minimum of ten years and had drawn her case to the attention of the *lieutenant de police* some years earlier. He rarely acted in response to the first complaint. She could provide witnesses to attest to her worthiness. She was industrious and virtuous. She did not frequent the café bar and she was devoted to her children. She could show that she had brought a dowry into the marriage and that dowry had frequently been put into a small business. Not only was her husband violent towards her but he was frequently a drunkard and consequently an irregular worker or a wastrel. When his wife tried to make him see the error of his ways and the dissipation of their joint livelihood he responded with physical force and the neighbours were frequently witnesses of the results.

A clinching issue for the *lieutenant de police*, however, in deciding whether to grant the wife's plea was whether the husband had misbehaved in other ways. Selling the matrimonial bed was an important indication of his wickedness and counted for more than a beating. Other substantial indicators of his depravity were resorting to violence in order to drive his wife out of the matrimonial home and then introducing his concubine. The *lieutenant* also gave some weight to evidence suggesting that an entire family was being reduced to pauperdom.

If the women who thus lodged complaints belonged to the working class it was to a distinct subsection. They ran small shops or businesses and they had some hope if the wastrel violent husband was taken from their lives – however temporarily – of reconstructing an independent livelihood. Conspicuously under-represented in the complaints that came before the *lieutenant général de police* were working women who had no economic viability without a man to support them and their children.

Far less numerous than complaints of wives against husbands are the reverse. When men sought to have their wives corrected by a short spell of incarceration they complained that their wives were guilty of four things simultaneously: of drunkenness as a result of frequenting taverns; of wandering abroad (gadding); of wasting the housekeeping; and of neglecting the children. The man reinforced his complaints by stating he put his wages or the housekeeping money into the hands of his wife and she dissipated them. He never, according to his account, had recourse to violence.[65]

The aim of this form of justice was to preserve marriage by demonstrating official disapprobation and bringing shame upon the aberrant party. In other parts of Europe the same spirit is manifest but involved a much earlier intrusion. In Neckarhausen in the eighteenth century, a case of marital dispute came before the village court (*Kirchenkonvent*) roughly once a year. Twice as many cases were brought by women as by men.[66] The court was not concerned with life-threatening violence but with morality and proper conduct of married people. The pastor played an important role as mediator before matters got to court. Most of the cases were brought by women in the early years of marriage (age 27–30) in contrast to the long-standing issues which came before the French and Spanish courts. Abusive language, violence and drinking constitute the bulk of the charges brought against husbands, and violence consisted of punches, slaps, blows with a fist or club, but rarely kicking. A husband had the right to chastise his wife but there were limits to what he could do without risking court action. In 1742, Anna Hentzler reported a quarrel with her husband which had provoked a beating. Claiming she was sick, she had refused to lead the horse in the field her husband was ploughing. He hit her with a stick and when she left to tell the pastor he threatened her with a rope. At the hearing it was revealed that Anna gave help to her sister in another village and this was used against her. The court judged that she had deserved her beating. In 1747 a fight between Agnes Spiedel and her husband Hans Berg came before the court. This was a second marriage for Agnes and her stepson had found a sum of money which she claimed she had saved before her marriage, but the husband said it contained coins minted since and so he had beaten her with a sword while the stepson held

her. The husband also claimed that she had been master of the purse
for too long. The sentence was four hours in jail for the husband because
he had used a sword, but two hours were meted out to the wife because
she had given provocation and also cause for complaint. She had sought
to deceive and to arrogate herself the role of the husband. The verdict
would seem to reflect a very specific requirement for a model of wifely
behaviour.[67]

The separation suits of Wiltshire in the seventeenth century seem to
have involved couples whose finances were floundering: we find the
emphatically 'decayed' gentleman who clings to his wife for economic
reasons, all the while hating her and ill-treating her.[68] The women
become increasingly desperate to save themselves physically and to salvage their property, or at least some of it, with the aid of kinsmen.
Unofficial separation could lead to prosecution, but how often couples
ran this risk is not clear. Among the couples who lived 'unquiet' lives
in former times physical violence may have been common. To lend
statistical precision to such a statement is as difficult as it is when
dealing with the present. Wife-beating was a private affair which took
place largely in the home and if the neighbours or servants were privy
to the dispute they did not necessarily intervene. Wives and husbands
were judged by their neighbours and not unless violence was perceived
to be at life-threatening level and only if the wife was seen as the
innocent victim, not as a scold or shrew, was intervention likely. If the
wife abused her husband's confidence, called him names behind his back
which devalued him in the eyes of the community, and questioned his
authority within the home, then neighbours approved a degree of violence. If she committed a misdemeanour outside the home and he was
present or knew about it, then the husband was party to her crime
unless he could separate himself from it by the 'correction' (verbal or
physical) of his wife.

If he did not do so then the offence gained in gravity. A man, for
example, was expected to exercise control over a woman – particularly
over her tongue – and slanderous remarks gained in seriousness if the
husband was present. He could be made accountable, at some cost, for
her utterances. Similarly, both British common law and French codes
and customary law recognized the right of a man to restrict his wife's
movements and keep her within the confines of the house. Economic
development, however, particularly in north-western Europe, in Holland and Britain, drove a coach and horses through the notion of woman

confined to the home as more and more women played an active role in the urban economy. Significantly, it was in these countries that judicial opinion moved more and more against the wife-beater. Notwithstanding this gradual trend, it continued to be popularly believed throughout the eighteenth century and beyond that a man had some right to correct his wife by force.

English common law enabled the Englishwoman to 'pray the peace' against her husband, that is, she could put him on a kind of good behaviour parole and if he violated that stronger action could be taken. Very few women took advantage of this – perhaps no more than one or two a year in any jurisdiction – and when they did so the level of violence involved was high and far exceeded mere blows. At Easter in 1790 a Dorset woman, Mary Jefferies, prayed the peace against her husband Bernard. He had not only threatened to beat her with a rope until the breath left her, but had a record of thrashing her regularly and had assaulted her with a block of wood causing her to flee her home. The flight of Mary from the conjugal dwelling and her fear of returning was widely endorsed. Six months later in the same jurisdiction, Jane Lanning accused her man Isaac of repeated violence towards her. He dragged her by the hair and when she fell to the ground kicked her. The next year, again in Dorset, two women claimed violence against them by their husbands and threats of death. Then a year elapsed before May Dymford prayed the peace against her husband Nicolas, a man known to be violent and who not only beat her but had dragged her around by her hair so often that she was now prone to fits.[69]

In any jurisdiction such cases are not more numerous and they tell the same sort of story. In England as in France, the once beaten wife did not have recourse to justice and nor did the mildly beaten one. The cases of the women were almost invariably accepted by the justices who took sureties from the husband. Few cases appear again, but that may be because the woman would suffer want if the husband was sent to a bridewell or given a punishment that curtailed the family income. Husbands in court never denied beating their wives but played down the degree of violence and cited provocation – the nagging wife who would have tried the patience of a saint, and who can still appear in the vocabulary of the British judge.

A major problem for the beaten wife was the reconstitution of some kind of livelihood if she left her husband. For this reason, in France, only those with some hope of repossessing a dowry or protecting a small business had any long-term prospects of life away from a bully. At most social levels women clung to their marriages as long as was humanly possible, even where the husband was involved in an adulterous relationship. Recent studies of defamation suits in English ecclesiastical courts in the sixteenth and seventeenth centuries reveal that a wronged wife – or one who suspected that her husband's thoughts were roving – turned in the first instance against the woman who had become the focus of his desires, publicly insulting her as a whore, someone who led other women's men astray, an Eve or Jezebel who dragged down the neighbourhood. The recourse to a stereotype which insists upon a woman as the real guilty party helped, of course, to preserve the legitimate union. It also shows that traditional notions of womanhood were as much part of women's mentalities as of men's. The targets of their insults replied in kind, vehemently anxious to preserve some standing in the community.[70] By the eighteenth century, however, more poor women came before the courts who did want separation from a violent or adulterous spouse but had nothing to repossess. Perhaps, and this must be speculative, they hoped to secure for themselves more favoured treatment from the poor law.

At the other end of the social scale in England changes were also occurring. The decline of the ecclesiastical courts in the eighteenth century, the growing uninterest of justices of the peace in adultery or immorality unless a bastard child threatened to be a cost to the poor rates, meant something of a decriminalization of sexual relations outside marriage. This decline was accompanied by an increase in the number of civil 'crim con' cases aiming to establish that a wife's lover had trespassed on the property of the husband (her body belonging to him) and that the husband therefore had a right to damages. The wife was not allowed to speak in her defence in court and neither were the plaintiffs or the defendant: the entire case was conducted by lawyers. The husband usually won his case and the wife's lover could be reduced to virtual paupery by the extent of the damages incurred. The civil action could then be followed by a Private Act of Parliament granting divorce and the parties could remarry.

The numbers of such cases should not be exaggerated. Before the 1760s there appear to have been fewer than twenty per decade and even in the abnormal peak of the 1790s only about seventy per decade.[71] The cases have all the interest of the sex scandals of the affluent and socially distinguished of our day and because some noteworthy names were involved at all levels, including those of the increasingly specialized and wealthy lawyers, they got a lot of publicity. The sensational sex trial developed into a literary genre. It also became a favoured leisure time spectator activity. It was frequently suspected that all parties colluded, or that at least there was complicity between the wife and the husband who received the damages as a way of lining his or their joint pockets. The dubious standards of comportment of the wealthy highlighted several double standards: the rich could do what the poor could not by way of obtaining divorce; the conduct of women was seemingly on trial but not that of men, because a woman who caught her husband with another woman in his bed could not initiate such actions; dalliance was converted not into sin but into adventure and gallantry. A French commentator in 1815 comprehended to perfection the hypocrisies involved:

> This criminal conversation is not prosecuted *criminally*, but produces only a civil suit for the recovery of damages, estimated in money. The jury determines the amount of these damages, by the degree of union and conjugal happiness existing before the criminal conversation which destroyed it, and by the rank and fortune of the parties. The smallest appearance of negligence or connivance on the part of the husband deprives him of all remedy against the seducer, who owes him nothing if he only took what was of no value to him, and which he guarded so ill. I have heard of £10,000 sterling awarded in some cases . . . The husband pockets the money without shame, because he has the laugh on his side, and in the world ridicule alone produces shame. A divorce is generally granted by Act of Parliament in these cases, and marriage generally takes place between the lovers. The publicity which such prosecutions necessarily occasion, and all the details and proof of the intrigue, are highly indelicate and scandalous. The testimony, for example of servants, of young chambermaids brought into open court to tell, in the face of the public, all they have seen, heard or guessed at, is another sort of prostitution more indecent than the first. Morals are far from being purified by this process: but the substantial infringement is prevented. This sort of chastity resembles the probity of certain persons who are sufficiently honest not to be hanged.[72]

The infrequency of the action itself reveals that this way out was seen as one in which certain people would lose public face and perhaps the support of friends if they adopted it. The price in these terms was too high to pay.

No Catholic country offered this means to escape and try again. In the ecclesiastical courts of early modern Andalusia over 50 per cent of the cases that were brought for separation cited beating and cruelty as a main cause and a further 20 per cent as an ancillary cause. The women who brought the suits were from middle to upper social levels. Doña Teresa de Pareja of Lucena was told, for example, by the vicar-general who dismissed her case: 'Cousin bear these beatings patiently since it is the Lord our God who has given you this cross to bear.' Some found that the initiation of a suit increased the propensity to violence and some 117 of 178 women appearing before the Andalusian court were sheltering with relatives while others had taken refuge in convents. Doña Francisca Paola Serrano, a clerk's wife, found that this was not enough. 'Now that it has become public in this town that I have gone to court my husband has persecuted me and I have had to leave town and go into hiding.'[73]

The most considerable problem that the women in this area seemed to have faced was actually getting out of the house to make a petition. It was clearly very difficult for women from this level of society to move freely; apart from Mass and a visit to the confessor, they were expected to remain behind closed doors. Unless relatives closely interested themselves in their plight, they could do little.

Violence between the couple could of course escalate into murder. Generally women figure inconspicuously in homicide statistics as murderers. Between 1663 and 1802 in Surrey, for example, women were charged with 37 out of 284 murders (approximately 1:7). Some of these charges were later reduced to manslaughter. The ratio appears to hold good for most of western Europe. Most murders by men were committed outside the home in workplace or tavern brawl, whereas most of those committed by women occurred in the home. Notwithstanding, the pattern in north-western Europe is one where the husband was two to three times as likely as his wife to commit spouse murder. It is impossible to generalize about Mediterranean Europe, but in rural Languedoc the ratios were reversed. Here more wives murdered their husbands.[74]

When spouse murder occurred, it was usually the culmination of a violent domestic quarrel in which farm or kitchen tools had been used. Poisoning was rare. Although it was believed to be a woman's crime and to have occurred more frequently than the records would suggest because difficult to prove, court evidence suggests that there were no more than a couple of cases a year in Languedoc and under one a year in any British jurisdiction. The murder of a drunken man by his wife as he slept is hardly documented. Women were anxious to show that what they had done they had done in the heat of a brawl, in anger and for self-protection. Only then would they escape the homicide charge. The very rudimentary nature of investigating police forces precluded very close examination of the evidence for their claim.

Where a wife was convicted of spouse murder, and premeditation could be shown, the most usual grounds were the desire to repossess her dowry and to remarry. This motive appears to be the commonest one for spouse murders by rural wives in Languedoc. The legal principle 'let there be no marriage without a dowry' often entailed deep resentment by a wife that her husband was misusing her and her property and that his removal would allow her to repossess what was her own. Where a man murdered his wife we are faced as well with acts of violence which exceeded normal limits.

In Languedoc, and this may be a Mediterranean pattern, dowry disputes also figure among cases of premeditated murder and they apply to all levels of society. A joiner of Auch, for example, 'quarrelled with and beat his wife who had not brought with her her promised dowry'. They arranged to separate, but he then plunged a knife into her stomach. Another woman from nearby was found floating in the millpond having been strangled. The neighbours knew who had done it. Her husband and his family had been outraged that the woman's father had not paid the dowry in full and they had made her a stranger in the house, forcing her to beg her bread.[75]

Murder of this kind is not found in Britain or Holland or even in France north of the Loire. This may reflect the 'dote qui veut' principle which existed in customary law or the premature emancipation of working-class couples in north-western Europe from a parent donated dowry. In these countries there may have been both resentment and disappointment if a promised dowry fell below expectations, and this may have got the marriage off to a bad start and been subsumed into a mounting toll of resentments, but whatever conflict was generated, it did not degenerate into murder.

Although this has to be an impressionistic conclusion, since the domestic violence that ended before the courts was doubtless merely the tip of an iceberg, it looks as if British and Dutch women were less exposed to the extremes of marital violence (such a statement must be relative) than were their Mediterranean counterparts. In circulating more freely outside the home and hence having greater contact with each other, in being able to bring a lawsuit to court themselves, and perhaps lacking the figure of the father confessor who sanctified female suffering, their tolerance levels may have been lower and expectations higher. We do not find the mayor of a British or Dutch or northern French town expressing himself as did the mayor of Castelsarrazin to the magistrates of Toulouse in 1783.[76] He asked for the public execution and breaking on the wheel of a wife-beater from his town whose wife had died as a result of his brutality. He urged a public example to act as deterrent and to spare him the solicitations of wives from households where beatings were a regular occurrence.

The enactment of divorce during the French Revolution meant that for the first time all classes could seek redress on an equal basis. An examination of the cases reveals few surprises. Seventy per cent were sought by women and from all social classes, but a third at least of all cases were abandoned with the suggestion that the couple had tried to start again. Desertion over several years, marital violence, drunkenness and adultery are the major categories into which the plaintiff's case could fall. More urban women than rural, more women who could earn their own living than those whose livelihood was bound up with that of their husband, and many who had not seen their first husband for so long that they wished to regularize a longstanding union appear in the records. It is easy to build up from the Revolutionary archives of discontent and abuse an image of what women expected from marriage. They do not expect an adulterous husband. They make no mention of romantic love but a great deal of their wish to be treated *maritalement* (as wives), that is, to participate, to be consulted, to be treated with respect and not like a servant, to be given the housekeeping money without having to beg for every small amount, to be treated with consideration in pregnancy, never to have unnatural sex forced upon them and never to be the victim of a husband's drunken anger. The husband for his part expected his wife not to be idle, to be clean and keep her children in good order, and not to spend time in taverns or away from the house so as to set the neighbours talking. Both wanted a serene household and felt abused if this was lacking.[77]

*

No one will ever be able to say what percentage of the households of the past failed to conform to these basic criteria. In 1701, Richard Gough, of yeoman stock, decided to spend his leisure hours in writing down the family history of the occupants of each pew in the parish church of his native Myddle, a prosperous little Shropshire village. In so doing he compiled a precious miscellany, remarkable because it viewed a community on aggregate at least over two generations, and it looked back to times when religious conviction of sexual rectitude was strong. Whereas memoirs detail personal experience and individual joys and misfortunes, and judicial archives focus on disaster, the *History of Myddle* retails the family fortunes of the many, viewed of course from outside and reduced to bare essentials and embodying a little gossip. So far it is the only work of its kind discovered.

There were few closed doors in Myddle. Gough makes it apparent that the strengths and weaknesses of each occupant of the parish, which was remarkably endogamous, were known to the neighbours who were often kin.

He was an educated, tolerant, loving husband who did his best for his sons, though his daughters for unrevealed reasons remained spinsters at home and looked after their father after his wife's death. Gough had absorbed the value system of his time, but he was not a misogynist and he aimed, not always successfully, at objectivity. There is no evidence of black legends pertaining to the nature of womanhood, though there are many relatively gentle stereotypes such as conniving maidservants, astute widows and light or lewd women. He does not fail to comment on the relative attributes of each partner in a marriage and he makes it clear that there were more inadequate husbands in Myddle than inadequate wives.

Gough starts from the premise that the family has an obligation towards all its members, including responsibility to see to it that profligate husbands – of whom there are many in this account – do not dissipate the portions of their wives and that if these are backed by land then it is the job of the family to step in before the property guaranteeing the wife's support is lost. Although Gough is sparing on personal tragedy, he retails as commonplace situations in which many wives brought land and money into marriage only to find it lost by idle or unfortunate husbands. For Gough, this is almost a fact of life and he indicates that most of the couples concerned survive, if in a poorer state.

Those who do not have the support of their families – interpreted in the sense of the broad kin group – are many in Myddle. Some suffer more than others. Consider the fate of the orphaned Elinor Buttry, left to the guardianship of one John Hussey with a portion of £100. Covetous of her money, Hussey arranged her marriage to his son Richard while the couple were under the age of consent and Elinor, although she had doubts which she expressed to neighbours, when the time came to endorse the match did not refuse.

> She consented to the marriage, butt proved a bad wife, for shee soone became too familiar with William Tyler, her next neighbour (a person of the most debauched morals of any that were then in the parish) that shee gott soe bad a report as was not to be endured by her husband and when he reprooved her in friendly terms . . . this Elinor upbraided her husband in such opprobiouse termse, that beeing not able to live in peace with her, hee left her . . . Hee gave his wife her £100 portion, and shee went to Lytle Drayton, where she kept an alehouse, and Wm. Tyler went often to visit her and at last had a child by her whom they called Nell Hussey.[78]

For Gough the blame for this affair falls on the shoulders of John Hussey for his greed. He is opposed to arranged marriages, but if they occur then families must help to preserve them. This is the logic behind his description of the unhappy life of one of his own kinsfolk, Anne Baker:

> She was a lovely, handsome woman, and was marryed (more to please her father than herselfe) to a neighbouring gentleman of a good, (butt of a decaying) estate. Shee had one son by him, and then left him, and went away with a Captaine, who promised to take her over to Ireland butt hee left her at Chester . . . Shee made some shift to come to Newton from Chester, and my great grandfather . . . sent my grandfather to Sweeney to make up the breach, which was done by giving a second portion. Shee returned again to her husband, but dyed not long after.[79]

This is not a happy tale and in fact shows the predicament of a woman of some means but caught in an unhappy marriage. To take her back, as a fallen woman, the husband has to be paid by her family.

Gough firmly believes that a good woman can bring an aberrant male to good behaviour and that conversely a light, drunken or lewd woman is the ruin of husband and issue – particularly her daughters. Consider the Downton family, where a hunchback and idle son has an advantageous match arranged for him by his father:

> During her lifetime this Samuell lived in good fashion. Hee had one son by her named Thomas and four daughters. She dyed before her children were brought up to maturity. He hired a servant maide to looke to his children. Shee was but a young girle of obscure parentage, but somewhat faire. Hee married the servant which his children were much trouble at. And therefore his son left him . . . the daughters all left him as soone as they were able for service. Hee quickly contracted more debts than hee was able to pay. Hee sold the lands hee had by his first wife but this tenement he could not sell (beeing settled at his first marriage) . . . hee . . . left Alderton and went to Cockshutt where he kept an alehouse and had great custom – perhaps for his wife's sake whom the people there called white Leggs because she commonly went without stockings.[80]

Bare legs were a sure sign of lust. After giving birth to four children the couple ran out of money and fled by night, leaving the children to the care of the parish. Samuel begged a living and his wife sold pins and laces from door to door, finally leaving her husband for a pedlar. Samuel came back home where his son occupied the tenement and was maintained by him until death. However, the tragedy of this family saga was not at an end:

> Thomas Downton, by his parsimonious living . . . was in a condition to live well; but unexpectedly married a wife with nothing. Her name is Judith – shee was brought up all her lifetime as a servant in some ale house or other, and she proved such a drunken woman as hath scarce beene hearde of, she spent her husband's estate so fast that it seemed incredible.[81]

He died and Judith was reduced to pauperdom.

There are nevertheless plenty of stories to show that however virtuous the wife she was not protected from a profligate husband. Edward Muckleton, a gentleman, was fortunate enough to marry an heiress with a good estate. She had all the virtues:

> Shee was a provident housekeeper, if not too parsimonious, but hee proved not a carefull husband for hee sold part of his wife's lands . . .

and they say his wife never consented to it, however (though some suites have been brought concerning it yet) it was never recovered.[82]

Edward's son Rowland was three times married, the first time to a wife who did little; the second time was to a woman of 'masculine spirit' who quarrelled with him and the couple came to blows wherein she lost an eye. When she died he married a widow and they had children but clearly they were not happy and ended their days each in the house of a different child.[83]

Gough's Myddle was not without contented marriages but it had many more where the couples rubbed along – and, indeed, they had little alternative but to do so. The main enemies to contented matrimony are drinking, usually, though not invariably, by the husband, and debt through lack of careful management, also usually on the husband's part; idleness contributes to debt. The abuse of women's property rights within marriage follows.

Gough also indicates the degree to which money could redress loss of honour or reputation. The case of Elizabeth Astley, a midwife of 'very great accompt in her time' and married to one Richard, an excellent cook, in great demand at the time of the Assizes, might serve as a case in point. In youth as a servant to Sir Richard Lea she had been impregnated by him and given birth to a bastard daughter. Sir Richard recognized his obligations and settled upon the child a tenement worth about £10 per annum for as long as she lived. This was the equivalent of a dowry of about £200. As long as she was a child, the mother and her new husband enjoyed the revenue.[84] The other bastard children of Myddle are less fortunate and one is abused by the man who impregnated her mother.

Myddle has only one truly wicked woman, Elizabeth Onslow, who wished to be quit of her husband, a peaceable man, and had recourse to poisoning. By dint of the support she received from her father's family she escaped the death penalty but, condemned by the parish as a bad lot, she had difficulty in finding another husband and ended up with a cattle thief who perished on the gallows. The community view was that his wife should have perished with him.[85]

The women of Myddle are dependent upon husbands who are wise managers and deal with them honestly, upon relatives who step in to protect their interests, and upon accepting their lot. No one lives easily in isolation in this society and it is clear that many inadequate marriages are sustained through living in the place one has always lived in and the presence of neighbours and kin. Let women take to ale or lewdness and they merit marital correction and community opprobrium. Gough believes that the place of the woman is in the home and that the wife should not be of a 'masculine spirit', which seems to mean that she should not seek to tell her husband his business: nor should she have a sharp tongue – a sure way to drive him to the alehouse. However, he assumes that when they are left to widowhood or misfortune, they will lay aside any pretence at dependence and will cope. Moreover, he accepts that some women in fact 'rule', particularly remarrying widows with means behind them.

Contentedness rather than happiness is for Gough the best recommendation of a marriage, but it is not an attribute he acknowledges to exist widely. There are several 'unquiet' households and in the situations he describes 'resignation' and a large degree of resilience would seem to have been the predominant marks of the marriages. He does not describe the tensions surrounding going 'broake'; he makes few allusions to marital violence except of the extreme variety; and when women die in childbed his eye is always on how the children fare under the next marriage. Myddle is in fact a chronicle of an imperfect world in which the price of life membership for women is the acceptance of traditional roles which expose them to the managerial mistakes and character defects of the men they marry. For their part, the men are victims of their wives' temperaments. The women rule the interior of the home and can decide whether the house is peaceful or not. Above all, he shows that the women of Myddle did not live in isolation from each other. The saga of any marriage in Myddle was an open secret and a man's reputation could be rapidly destroyed by rumours disseminated by women.

How typical was Myddle? We cannot know, but some of Gough's observations have wider applicability. First, in a village, aberrance was more widely known and tongues wagged more quickly. Both men and women had their reputations in the community to consider. There were close agencies of social control in the form of the vicar or priest, the lord of the manor, who might also be justice of the peace, the employer and the kin group. The holy household which was the dream of both Catholic and Protestant reformers was never perhaps the norm. The energies of those who punished domestic aberrance were soon abated and moral crime was soon more readily punishable, if it was punished at all, when committed by a woman than by a man. The lack of protection for a woman who was the recipient of physical violence is a universal constant. The process of disintegration or deceleration in reforming zeal, manifest from the late seventeenth century, occurred more swiftly in town than in country. The aberrants of Myddle often leave their village and make for the town, where authority had more on its mind than private morality, for there public temptations posed a constant threat to private morality. How effective was reforming zeal when confronted with these manifestations of public vice? How could the town be brought into conformity with biblical diktat so that the holy household could dwell in a holy city?

CHAPTER EIGHT

◈

Kept Mistresses and Common Strumpets

Vice came in always at the door of necessity, not at the
door of inclination.

DANIEL DEFOE, MOLL FLANDERS 1721

THE ARCHIVES of the ecclesiastical courts, with their histories
of broken or disrupted lives, bear witness to the problems of
individuals and couples in their sexual relationships. From its
inception the Christian church set itself, with differing degrees of
emphasis, against sex outside marriage. Fornication, defined as intercourse between unmarried persons, and adultery, intercourse between
parties of whom one or both was already married, were both accounted
sinful. To commit either offence was technically to be in a state of
mortal sin.

Adultery, however, was taken more seriously by the ecclesiastical
courts than fornication. *Thou shalt not commit adultery* was one of the ten
commandments and refers to both sexes. In practice, as we have seen,
a double standard operated: the adulterous woman, who threatened the
legitimacy of progeny, was seen as more culpable than the adulterous
man, whose dalliance outside marriage did not threaten the home.
Fornication, too, weighed more heavily on women than on men. The
records of the courts, both before and after the Reformation, show that,
whatever the intentions of the reformers, in most instances a double
standard again prevailed. Deflowered woman was devalued as a moral
and social entity and, if her impregnator did not marry her, another
man would expect monetary compensation for taking her as his wife.
Frequently, in this process, she lost social status. The male fornicator
might carry some moral shame, but he could readily put his past behind
him. He did not suffer devaluation and his sin did not cloud his
future.

The stance of the pre-Reformation church on fornication, although theologically clear, was in practice ambivalent. The writings and behaviour of several distinguished Fathers of the Church, including Saint Augustine, indicated that even the holiest of men, instruments of God himself, could at certain stages of their lives have indulged their sexual urges without jeopardizing their long-term salvation. Penitence could atone for sin. When in the sixteenth century the Spanish Inquisition sought to make more explicit the church's official condemnation of fornication there was widespread ignorance that such activity was a sin in the same category as adultery.[1]

In late medieval society it was widely accepted that unmarried men would want to prove their manhood by sexual activity. Women from the higher social classes were carefully invigilated with a view to precluding pre-marital activity. Who, then, would serve as pre-marriage partner to the sexually active male? This dilemma was resolved by positing a figure, the 'fallen' or 'common' woman, the prostitute, and she existed as a personage with a defined social purpose in pre-Reformation society. It was assumed she was a woman from the lower classes, who had been deflowered, had lost her honour, and had had her sexual appetite whetted so that she would fornicate again. In many cities there existed a licensed municipal brothel, or in certain areas private brothels, where professional prostitutes could ply their trade. The notion was that their activities would be carefully circumscribed.[2]

The advantages of having a licensed brothel, or alternatively a pool of registered prostitutes operating in an area restricted to certain streets, were both moral and economic, and as such were actively promoted by the Dominicans in the late fifteenth century. The moral argument was simply that a limited number of women could serve a large number of men. Such women had already fallen, and hence were not in a state of grace. Their activities freed other honest women from harassment and helped them to retain their virtue; thus whores helped to preserve the moral order. Furthermore, because fallen women were contained in specified locations, woman as temptress was neutralized. Her services had to be sought out by those embarking on sinful practices. Licensed brothels were forbidden to allow entry to married men, a stipulation which could readily be disregarded. The client was also assumed to be a hot-blooded young man or a travelling person, sailor, merchant or soldier.

The women contained therein were also assumed to be unwed. As the Dominican preacher Johannnes Flakenberg stated when he advised the city of Crakow to establish a municipal brothel: 'In Christendom, common women are tolerated by the Holy Church in order to prevent worse evils.' In an important work by Fray Francisco Farfán called *Tres libros contra el pecrecado de la simple fornicación* (1585), the friar distinguished very carefully between fornication and adultery, simple fornication being an act which, though a mortal sin, did harm to none other than the perpetrator, if the woman involved in the act was already a common or fallen woman.

> The brothel in the city then, is like the stable or latrine in the house. Because just as the city keeps itself clean, by providing a separate place where filth and dung are gathered, so neither less nor more, acts the brothel; where the filth and ugliness of the flesh are gathered like the garbage and dung of the city.[3]

The dung in this text is the woman, not defined otherwise than by the adjectives 'fallen' and 'common', meaning available to all but the particular property of none.

The licensed brothel of the pre-Reformation city could, as in the case of Ulm, make some allowance for the ultimate salvation of the women's souls by allowing them a weekly visit to church to light a candle and pray, though they were not allowed to receive the sacraments.[4] They could also make an annual confession. Other towns were less tolerant in this respect. There exists a letter of 1501 from a group of women enclosed in the brothel at Carmona in Spain, which was surrounded by a moat so that the 'brothel father', who leased the establishment from the municipal council, could monitor those who came and went. They claimed that they had not been let out of the brothel for two or three years and were treated worse than slaves at the hands of infidels. The women were prevented from going to church to confess and were particularly worried that Easter was approaching and that they had not cleansed their consciences of their sins. They asked to go to Cuenca, knowing that they would not be allowed into the local church. The council had not let the women out in case they plied their trade outside the brothel, but in so doing had cut them off from the solace of religious forgiveness, one of the few pointers we have to the low regard in which the council held this branch of its paid employees and the unhappy state of the women who worked there.[5]

A licensed brothel also brought in fees to the council that leased it, and in those Italian cities where licensed prostitutes operated the councils profited from the sale of permits to the women in question. What the councils did with the money is not clear. Perhaps the income was used for policing services, to see that the restrictive legislation was observed. Certainly it was a reservoir of funds which could be channelled for useful purposes.

Licensed brothels, which were standard practice elsewhere, did not exist in Britain, Scandinavia and the Netherlands (although the bishop of Winchester laid down conditions confining the prostitutes of the stews of Southwark to the brothel without any right of exit). Restriction to defined areas and distinctive dress were also obligatory for prostitutes in Italian cities. Scarlet or bright yellow clothing made the woman obvious so that she could be moved on if she strayed out of the official limits. This provision also helped men to know what sort of woman they were approaching. The official recognition given to prostitution in Mediterranean cultures may reflect the high demand from men who did not marry until their late twenties, but who sought sexual gratification long before; the large numbers of clerics who were, of course, unwed and might fall into the sin of sodomy – one far worse than fornication – if women were not available; and the careful invigilation of women of higher social status.

Demographic growth in the sixteenth century increased the numbers of women alone or in marginal situations. Added to this, in certain cities there were not only large numbers of clerics but, in the ports, sailors and during the Italian wars vast numbers of soldiers representing all the contending nations who teemed into Italy. They were accompanied, inevitably, by camp followers. The demand for commercial sex was substantial and the supply was also abundant. Many women used prostitution to gain money for a dowry to help buy them a marriage. This recourse was recognized as common in Italy. In Spain, where there was a continuous outflow of sailors to the New World, the imbalance between the numbers of resident women and of men in the ports was marked, and hence there was a pool of poor, unmarried women or widows for recruits to the vice trade.

When the persecutions of *conversos* (Christians with Jewish ancestry) began, a flood of poor women left Spain to settle in Rome. The reasons for this strange migration from a zone where Christians were persecutors to the very core of Christianity are mysterious. The women who fled settled in the same poor areas as the immigrant widows (see Chapter Six), where they formed groups and lived partly on casual work and partly on prostitution. They were to be the dramatis personae of an early novel which had a prostitute for heroine, *La Lozana Andaluza* (1528) written by a syphilitic priest named Delgado. He set his story in 1527, the date of the fall and the sack of Rome, and made Lozana a symbol and metaphor for the debasement of the city itself.

In the eyes of Protestant reformers, too, Rome was a harlot. She was referred to as the Scarlet Woman of the Book of Revelation, the Whore of Babylon, the mother of whores. Lax priests, the tolerance of sexual vice, luxury and corruption were added to the tales of rape and pillage by the invading or defending armies. The availability of commercial sex in the capital of Christendom as well as the longest living legacy of these wars, the spreading of syphilis across Europe, contributed to the building up of Rome's unsavoury reputation abroad.

Sixteenth-century Italians, for their part, might have elected Venice as the capital of whoredom, because it was in this city in the early sixteenth century that there emerged a culture ceding a prominent place to the courtesan.[6]

The Italian Renaissance celebrated the possibility for educated men to realize their full intellectual and physical potential, to feast on the beautiful, to expand their mental horizons by drawing not merely on the heritage of Christian thought, but upon a classical legacy in which whore, concubine, and the beautiful boy all had a part to play. Physical and spiritual love, profane and sacred love, were inextricably interknit and the pleasures of the flesh were extolled. Philosophers, notably Aretino, drawing upon this classical legacy, laid claim to a man's right to savour of an earthly physical experience analogous to divine ecstasy.[7]

The courtesan, a woman of some education, usually with musical gifts and with physical beauty and refined tastes, as well as one who excelled in the erotic arts, became a stereotype in sixteenth-century Venetian culture and the same figure had a presence in Rome and the larger Italian cities when the ravages of the Italian wars receded. In spite of much scholarly attention, relatively little is known of their social origins and training. In some instances, daughters may have learned the rules of the game from their mothers. Questions such as how long a woman could remain a courtesan after her beauty faded and she became, in the words of the famous courtesan and poet Veronica Franco, 'a yellowing pearl', or how solid a fortune could be amassed, remain unanswered. A courtesan was clearly not a prostitute (*meretrice*) since she did not solicit her clients; they visited her and provided her with a residence and clothes and jewels. Prostitution was technically illegal. But was there any mobility between prostitute and courtesan groups? Did the former ever become the latter and vice versa? It is easy to conceive of a courtesan on the way down turning prostitute, but nothing is yet known of this mobility. What was the relationship between the courtesan and the acting profession? Is it any more than accident that the rise of the prima donna in the *commedia dell'arte* coincides with the heyday of the courtesan? The courtesan's independence and wealth have been much vaunted, but the evidence so far reveals a chronic dependence on her protectors who could use the woman as a convenient sexual toy for the enjoyment of their friends but demonstrate little loyalty to her in her later years.

It was this latter consideration that made Veronica Franco think in terms of setting up a charitable home in which such women could spend their last days. She has left a record of the pains and pleasures of the courtesan's life, one dependent above all on the maintenance of her appearance. These talented women were a tourist attraction, the first recourse of a King of France when in 1593 he visited the Pearl of the Adriatic. They were painted, fêted, celebrated, but became vulnerable when past their prime.[8]

Although they certainly did not disappear, their open, public acknowledgement was curtailed by the purifying hand of the Counter-Reformation. Even so, they contributed quite powerfully to the identity of Italy as a godless, 'Catholic' society in which the Christian prohibition on fornication was ignored. A correlation was made between the Catholic church, headed by the Pope of Rome or Antichrist, and sexual laxity. When the Protestant reformers, beginning in Germany in the 1520s, moved against the Roman church, the brunt of their attack focused on corruption, the departure from the authority of Scripture, and the sale of indulgences, which obliterated or reduced penalties for sin; but in all these issues was caught up, in a far from silent subtext, the further issue of extramarital sex. As Protestantism evolved, the avowed aim of godly society became a public commitment by the ruling establishment to chaste sexual relationships. Protestant identity was constructed upon the moral superiority derived from the belief that Protestants were more seriously committed to this end than Catholics. The Protestant fornicator could not buy his way out of his guilt by penitence, and the absolution of the priest after confession was without meaning. Mary Magdalen was a figure of Catholic legend lacking true scriptural authenticity. The fallen woman was an agent of the devil and the licensed brothel a marker of the godless society.

The texts on which the reformists chose to focus were the ten commandments, the assurance that no adulterer (to include the fornicator) might enter the kingdom of heaven and 'the wages of sin are death'. Among 'the people of a book' certain texts were favoured and Christ's association with formerly immoral women was overlooked in favour of uncompromising Old Testament prohibitions. As states assumed the colours of the dominant religious confession, sexual behaviour, including the issue of prostitution, became politicized.[9] Protestants moved forward in the inexorable belief that immorality at all levels must be extirpated in the godly state and that prostitution was the product of papistry. In some German cities a number of brothels had been abolished on the eve of the Reformation, having attracted public criticism. Then, led by Luther, Protestant reformers not only closed the municipal brothels but gave the official prostitutes dowries and left future offending fornicators, both male and female, at least theoretically liable to persecution by the secular authority.

Catholic reformers, on the other hand, while they clung to the ideals of chastity and insisted that the sexual offender was in a state of mortal sin, held on to the belief in redemption for every penitent Magdalen. However, that penitence must be absolute and made readily available. A woman, fallen or common, poor or homeless, on the streets, would obviously choose whoredom rather than salvation. Something must be done to help her to forsake her evil ways and follow the road to salvation. The Catholic reformers were not passive when charged with encouraging lax moral behaviour, but they would not forsake the notion of ultimate salvation through penitence. They also had to remedy the image of themselves as immoral by extirpating sexual permissiveness among the ecclesiastical hierarchy. Individuals, conspicuous among them Carlo Borromeo, Archbishop of Milan and cardinal and Counter-Reformation saint par excellence, and Gabriele Paleotti, Archbishop of Bologna, cardinal and missionary bureaucrat, as well as substantial numbers of lesser men and women inspired by confessors and theologians, laboured to construct both institutions of refuge and retrieval for fallen women and means of increasing the dowry funds of working girls.[10] Such funds were seen as the way to a purer society.

A sense of the differing approaches of Protestant and Catholic reformers promotes an understanding of some of the differences in the evidence on prostitution available from one country to another. In areas of Protestant confession, most of the evidence comes from law courts, and we see the prostitute through the prism of the judge and the persecuting authorities. She emerges as a criminal. In few Protestant states, however, was there a sustained effort to punish fornication as a criminal offence. Holland and Geneva constituted the most outstanding exceptions, and even there the momentum of persecution was lost in the eighteenth century.

In Catholic countries, the institutions such as retreats and asylums provide a body of evidence of a very different kind. Those who administered them usually aimed at the rescue of a particular sort of prostitute at a particular juncture in her life. These institutions sometimes predated the Counter-Reformation, but had a most active existence in the sixteenth and seventeenth centuries. Even in Catholic countries, however, municipal authorities could take actions designed to reduce the activities of prostitutes and seek to enforce them through the courts.

The licensed brothel had generally disappeared everywhere by the late seventeenth century. The most populous Catholic country, France, saw only a token development of rescue institutions (*repenties*) and *la police des moeurs* (moral policing) passed progressively into the hands of a state police force, reorganized by Louis XIV. Paramount among the concerns of the French police was the reduction of syphilis among the military, and legislation against prostitution was enacted in 1713, 1724, 1734, 1776 and 1777. From 1767 the army was prepared to pay for the incarceration of infected women in prisons, known as *dépôts de mendicité*. The frequent repetition of laws suggests their lack of observance. In France it is clear that religious ideals and state punitive action were designed to co-exist.

On the Protestant side, attitudes in England oscillated considerably. The stews were attacked under Henry VIII and some closed, though never permanently. The Puritan period saw a greater effort placed on moral policing, but from 1660 at least until the 1690s general laxity ruled. In the 1690s a number of Societies for the Reformation of Manners were established to promote private initiatives to bring prostitutes before the courts, by paying the costs of the lawsuits and the expenses of those who denounced the activities of lewd women. However, these repressive private initiatives were not invariably welcomed by judges and the beginning of the eighteenth century was to see something of a softening in attitudes towards the prostitute. A Magdalen Hospital was founded in 1758 on Nonconformist initiative very much in the spirit of the continental institutions of penitence and retrieval.

Why did this Protestant country adopt a Catholic approach, and Catholic countries use the police and the courts with increasing frequency? If something can be attributed in Britain to a preparedness to admit that misfortune had set the fallen woman on her course, more may reflect the recognition that both the hard line of the early Protestant reformers, designed to eradicate prostitution through punishment, and the softer approach of the Catholic reformers, aiming at reducing the phenomenon and making penitence available to the seeker, had failed. In desperation, each turned to the policies the other had rejected. Except for very limited periods of religious or moral fervour, the police were too weak and uninterested, or simply too corrupt, to pursue prostitutes actively. Often their situation at law was deeply ambiguous. In England, in the words of Blackstone, they were 'scarce, if at all within the description of any statute now in being', and were prosecuted only when they troubled the king's highways, or when charged with another felony such as theft. Whatever the high moral tone periodically assumed by reformers, the state of the prostitute in law could make action virtually impossible. Prostitution grew exponentially with the expansion of the population, the growth of cities and of commerce, and the concentration in towns of poor women whose earning power was severely limited. By 1800 it was not Rome and Venice which were the capitals of whoredom, but London, Paris and Amsterdam. The whore was a seemingly ineluctable and indestructible element in city life, persisting in spite of religious zealots and developing police forces.

The very different kinds of available evidence, and the chronological shifts and oscillations in approaches to the 'problem' manifested in different countries, make a comparative study of prostitution at first glance difficult. Certain questions can readily be answered, such as when and where was the issue of prostitution debated, by whom, and with what end in view? How active were authorities in implementing their policies? What was the perceived degree of responsibility of the two sexes for committing extramarital sex? Which prostitutes appeared before the courts? How was the offence punished? How was the prostitute explained? Was she seen as the product of sin alone or the product of poverty? Were the legislator, the magistrate, the ecclesiastical reformer, and the fiction writer at one, or did they differ in their approaches to her? These are easier questions to answer than who were the real whores, and why were they there? To what extent did the conditions imposed on women – that is, limited earning power, reliance on at least partial support by a man, shame and honour codes which devalued the fallen woman – actually contribute towards the creation of prostitutes, and can we locate prostitution within the life cycle of certain groups of women?

Certainly, we are ill-informed about how prostitutes themselves viewed their condition. Most could not write, and 99 per cent of the evidence reflects the attitudes of men as legislators, magistrates, ecclesiastics and philanthropists. Indeed, apart from the observations of nuns who ran pious associations in Italy, Spain and France, the poetry of Veronica Franco, and the racy memoirs of a few illustrious mistresses, there is little surviving testimony from women. True, the prostitute speaks in court, and her testimony could in some instances (in Amsterdam especially) be cogent, but the questions are put to her by a lawyer or judge intent on processing her case in the shortest possible time, and with relatively little interest in allowing for mitigating circumstances. When she replies it is generally to save herself rather than to respect the truth. Of the several hundred prostitutes who appear in the charge books of St James's in London between 1733 and 1739, many give false names, the favourite being Miss Nobody.[11] In France, women who were brought before the prévôtal court had been rounded up by the police in certain taverns and no further proof of their guilt was needed. The court was one from which there was no appeal. Everything conspired to suppress the true version of their stories.

A further impediment to getting at the real prostitute is the literary evidence. The whore excited the literary imagination, not least because sex sold print. The prostitute heroines or central figures of the early novel (Celestina, Courasche, Moll Flanders, Fanny Hill, Manon Lescaut) are part of a male fantasy, all of them bigger and stronger than the men who enjoy them. Their dispositions are cheerful and they thoroughly enjoy all their sexual activity. They court their fall. Courasche, the brainchild of von Grimmelshausen in the *Simplicissimus* series, is even described as enjoying being ravished by an entire regiment in a few short hours, though she later feels humiliated. In the course of her career, Courasche, alumna of the Thirty Years War, makes several adjustments as her looks deteriorate with age and her consorts move down the scale, from colonel to lieutenant, to captain to simple mercenary and finally to gipsy. All the men she encounters are weaker than she and meet their deaths while she survives: indeed, in associating with her they seem to court their doom. Manon Lescaut, who is finally sentenced to transportation, sallies forth with her lover without a hint that she might die of yellow fever. Moll Flanders triumphs over five husbands and at least five pregnancies and settles down to respectable middle age. There are no musings on the syphilitic prostitute dying insane or on children born blind: Courasche contracts venereal disease, but it mysteriously disappears in the course of the novel. Most of the literary whores even escape pregnancy (Defoe's are the exception). Courasche is sterile. Indeed, it was very generally believed, and was confirmed by medical thought, that prostitutes were barren since too much semen made the womb slippery and inhospitable. All the women in question are obsessed with money. Most of them succeed through commercial sex in putting something aside, so that they do not die in poverty. The literary whore corresponds to the image her clientele may have wanted her to have. She is lusty, healthy, invincible, and economically well-off.

The same refusal to see prostitution other than as an exotic, exuberant force is found in visual imagery, for example in Titian's erotic Venuses, and as strikingly in the 'Merry Companies' and brothel scenes which constitute a substantial subsection of seventeenth-century Dutch genre painting. These bear witness to some of the ambivalent attitudes towards extramarital sex prevalent even in that Protestant country which most actively pursued the prostitute at law. The women are joyful, rowdy, flirtatious, lustful, handsome and well-dressed. The services of the more exquisitely robed are negotiated by a madame. The poorer contemplate their drunken clientele with a mixture of philosophy, resignation and greed. They serve the soldiers, captains with coins in their hands or common soldiers slumped over their booze, but never, it would appear, the navy. Who bought these pictures? Where did they hang them? What do they reveal of the subconscious condition of the world of the worthy Dutch burgher? What is their relation to reality? Such questions have yet to be answered. Perhaps, as images, they were not generally intended to provoke reflection. In the Mauritshuis in The Hague, however, hangs a small picture by a woman, Judith Leyster's *The Proposition*. A woman, very modestly attired, bends over her sewing. A man by her side proffers a gold coin. The moment of tension trapped in the work is perhaps that in which a woman, currently virtuous and eminently industrious, ponders upon the choice between modesty, poverty and industry, and a sexual relationship with a wealthy man. It provokes, without answering, the question, what might cause a good woman to fall?

Hogarth's *Harlot's Progress* reveals the disastrous disintegration of a girl who comes to London and is pounced on by a procuress. Thus begins a career as a kept mistress, which declines through common strumpet, Newgate napper and finally corpse. This progression was very much how the fall of the country girl was interpreted in the eighteenth century but, minus the death scene, can be found two centuries earlier in the *Provveditori alla Sanità* (1542) of Venice, for example, which decries the activities of procuresses.

> There are diabolical persons who at the instigation of the devil are continually watching to seduce and lead astray poor orphans and girls who are forced to beg their living in the city, or even poor servant girls who are on their way to lodge with our nobles and citizens by offering to clothe them and be their mistresses, with many other blandishments. Once they have fallen into the hands of these bawds (*rufiarie*) they hire them chemises, headdress, stockings, shoes, dresses, cloakes and capes and by means of this the bawds keep them at their mercy and live off the earnings of their girls who can never free themselves and are constrained of necessity to commit wicked sins and become accustomed to these meretricious vices. This is the most potent reason for the infinite number of prostitutes now in the city and increasing daily.[12]

The agency of 'the fall' was not generally in the forefront of the reformers' minds in sixteenth-century Europe. They started from the image of a fallen woman whose state was to be explained by moral turpitude. She was, like Eve, the architect of her own demise. She had yielded to the weakness and imperfections implicit in womanhood and her lusty voracious appetite for sex dragged man down with her into sin. Enshrined in Scripture were denunciations of particular women: Gomer, the adulterous wife of the all-suffering Hosea; Salome, whose sexually titillating dance earned for her the head of John the Baptist on a plate;

the Scarlet Woman and her ilk. All showed that woman had within her the potential for immense evil through her sexuality and vanity. No socio-economic analysis of the prostitute was thought needful. To have fallen was enough for Protestant theologians and administrators and the causes of the fall were not deemed worthy of pursuit.

In adopting an adamantly hostile attitude to fornication, Luther and Calvin saw the fornicator, male or female, as an equal sinner debarred from the kingdom of heaven. The establishment of a Lutheran or Calvinist ruling class entailed the closure of municipal brothels, with compensation to the licensee and dowry payments to the girls *in situ*, even a new set of clothing, in exchange for the abandonment of their evil ways. Lutheran and Calvinist states also put their authority behind punitive legislation designed to punish both the prostitute and her clients. Luther at least identified some of the economic problems of the woman alone in offering such women cash payments to extricate themselves from the trade. Indeed, there are many parallels between his approach to the prostitute and to the nun. Marriage was woman's natural destiny and it was merely a case of reinserting women, corrupted by papist practice, into a conventional role and enacting a future legislation of a punitive kind against anyone who sought to make a livelihood by sinful means.[13]

The compensation plans applied only to women in the municipal brothels, not to any freelance operators nor to any future woman who found herself without alternative livelihood. Calvinist Geneva and Holland formulated comprehensive measures whereby the fornicator could be denounced and punished. Travellers recounted with amazement how husbands, reported by their wives for using a prostitute, could be dragged before a church councillor, admonished, and debarred from communion. In Amsterdam, sailors who returned to their wives with syphilis could be banned from the marital bed, or the marriage could be annulled. Whores could be severely punished by short- or long-term imprisonment in the new *Spinhuis*, a house of correction and a penological model for Europe. Here loose women were conditioned to a harsh work discipline so that they could return both chastened and reformed to Calvinist society.

Yet equal treatment for the prostitute and her client was more conspicuous in theory than in implementation. Even when the authorities began making an onslaught on the male fornicator, as in Augsburg, their energies in this direction soon abated. Unless the man was actually

caught *in flagrante delicto* in bed with a woman who was not his wife —
and such capture implied a police raid – then proof of guilt was difficult
to obtain. A man caught in the company of a whore could always claim
he had been accosted by the woman and that he did not know what
she was. Moreover, the magistracy, unless confronted with a wife who
had caught, or feared she was about to contract, syphilis from her
husband's activities, was on the whole prepared to accept the man's
story. In no society in early modern Europe were the police numerous,
and they could scarcely contain theft or disturbance of the peace of the
city. Their attack on illicit sex therefore tended to be targeted quite
deliberately. Their technique was to round up girls from certain taverns,
or they raided premises known to be brothels. The Amsterdam police
in particular learned there was money to be made from turning a blind
eye to the house which handed over thieves or paid a bribe. With the
development of police forces in the capital cities came a symbiotic
relationship between police and prostitute. The bawdy house increasingly gave information to the police on criminals, particularly thieves,
if it wished to survive.

The balance between Catholic and Protestant states in northern and
central Europe was decided by military conflict and entailed the raising
and movement of armies on an unprecedented scale. The armies
were accompanied by a vast number of women camp followers, in
addition to wives, who performed domestic services for the military,
washing, sewing, perhaps even tending wounds. The rank and file
could not afford to maintain wives, so the presence of an army always
disrupted the sex life of any community even in peacetime. The
military were the main clientele of the prostitute in many garrison
towns. They were also responsible for the sexual harassment of servant
girls, or the rape of women foolhardy enough to set foot in the
wrong quarters. The officers were always willing to transfer a man
facing a paternity charge. In time of war, rape replaced seduction
as armies went on the march. The context of Courasche is probably
quite authentic.

In Holland, the raising of mercenary troops and the arrival in port
of several thousands of sailors with money in their pockets obviously
created a strong demand for sexual activity, which had to exist within
a culture explicitly dedicated to moral rectitude. Something of the
duality of attitude in the Dutch Republic is revealed in a work, published in 1681 in Amsterdam, entitled *Amsterdamsche Hoerdom*, which

drew on the tradition of the Italian courtesan's book of the sixteenth century, or on a similar publication in Heidelberg in the seventeenth century. It was emulated and indeed became a fashionable genre in the eighteenth century both by the *Filles du Palais Royale*, a frequently published compendium or Parisian directory which catalogued the local whores and was intended for tourists, and by Harris's *List of Covent Garden Ladies, or Men of Pleasure's Kalendar*, which appeared, annually updated, between 1760 and 1793 and which gives minute factual descriptions of 'fine, bouncing, crummy wenches'.

The Amsterdam work, however, is not just a list of whores. It claimed to be outraged at the fact that Maria or Judith or Ulriche, each with certain physical endowments, offered certain specialist sexual activities at an address which could be found without difficulty. The work encapsulated some of the dilemmas of the Calvinist mentality which had set itself against fornication and which closed its municipal brothels, but which was fully cognizant that commercial sex existed in its midst (literally in its midst, for there was no special red light district in early modern Amsterdam). Furthermore, as Mandeville pointed out, with all those sailors in port, some commercial sex was essential to safeguard decent women. Yet such an admission could not be made openly, so Amsterdam ran an egregiously high punishment rate of prostitutes. The sailors, backbone of the country, and the military, defending Protestantism, escaped this 'justice'. They were the valiant men, engaged in useful work.

In England under Henry VIII, legislation against the common strumpet had resulted in the closing of the Southwark stews. In the late sixteenth and first half of the seventeenth centuries, Puritanism ensured that the prostitute operated in a different and difficult environment. As a major issue for debate, however, it came to the fore in the 1690s, a difficult period in economic terms which seems to have seen a conspicuous female surplus in many major European cities. The debate is coincident with what we might call post-Stuart critique. The Restoration court had been remarkable for its moral laxity, its flirtations with popery and a continuing hard line towards Puritan survivals. In the aftermath of the Glorious Revolution, nonconformity mobilized itself for an attack on social corruption whose genesis was firmly located

during the last two reigns, when the court did all they could to bring in Popery amongst us, a dissolute practise (i.e. fornication) was not only

indulg'd but became almost a necessary qualification for any man that
would have the Prince's favour.[14]

The debate was couched only in moral terms, but it had practical
manifestations. A Society for Promoting a Reformation of Manners in
the City of London and Suburbs set itself to bring the prostitute to
court and published an annual blacklist. By 1705, 7995 people, including 830 that year, had been named, and prosecuted and convicted as
'keepers of Houses of Bawdy disorders, or as whores, night walkers,
etc. And who have been sentenced by the magistrates and as the law
directs, and have been accordingly punished (many of them divers times)
either by Carting, Whipping, etc.' It generated a fiery and discursive
literature. A publisher named James Orne saw that sex was profitable
when put into words. In 1696 he published the first issue of *The Night
Walker or Evening Rambles in search after Lewd women with The Conferences
Held with them* etc. 'to be published monthly, 'til a discovery be made
of all the chief prostitutes in England from the pensionary Miss, down
to the Common Strumpet'.

Every evening 'the night walker' sallied forth, picked up a whore,
questioned and lectured her, and hoped for repentance. There is nothing
salacious in his pages; anyone who bought them for titillating information would be disappointed. The gentleman in question had an
overwhelming confidence in his oratorical talents and his first volume
shows him exercising every prejudice to the full. He notes his elected
whore's garb (love of luxury) and her hatred of 'work'. He moves straight
into threats of eternal damnation, and soon finds what he has been
looking for, a papist:

> To this (threat) she replied with impudence enough that such bugbears
> might well frighten us who were Protestants but for her part she was a
> Roman Catholic, and could be absolved when she pleased, and have the
> Eucharist brought on her death bed, which was a never-failing viaticum.
> I answered her that I thought the church of Rome might properly enough
> be called the Mother of Harlots in a literal sense, seeing by her doctrines
> and pardons people were encouraged to lead loose lives, adding Absolu-
> tions of their priests were mere cheats which would stand in no stead at
> the bar of God and therefore advised her to have recourse to the word
> of God where she would find that he would judge whore-mongers and
> adulterers. She told me that she saw most of us Protestants as much

addicted to that practise as Roman Catholics and if they look up to it
as so dangerous, how came it that we did not punish it more severely
in those of our own religion?[15]

The lists of the Societies for the Reformation of Manners of the 1690s
reveal that most prostitutes who were apprehended were British-born.
A hundred years on, two-thirds of the London female population were
born outside the capital, and an increasing proportion of prostitutes
were of north country or Irish origin. Orne's prostitutes do not usually
relate how they become whores – though one thought she was going
into 'service' and discovered her employer was a procuress. The tenor
of this type of discourse was to insist upon greater repression through
the punishment of the supply side of the business, but to allow some
opportunity of amendment.

Yet within the debate other issues were surfacing. When Bernard
Mandeville published *A Modest Defence of Public Stews* (1724) he covered
familiar ground, but added a few new touches. Mandeville, permanently
tongue in cheek, was perhaps pushing voguish argument to its logical
conclusions. He posited the licensing of bawdy houses in which certain
women, fallen because of the failure of their moral education, could
serve a dual purpose. The first (an attitude with venerable antecedents)
was the protection of the virtuous woman – Mandeville does in fact
acknowledge a positively predatory male – but his second purpose is to
keep venereal disease in check. In large part sin has receded from the
discourse. He asserts the view that the notion of sin is useful only as a
guidance for a young and gullible female. In the last analysis, he says,
illicit sex is inevitable. Least harm will be done to society if it is
contained within the brothel, the 'bog house', where diseased prostitutes
will be quickly removed by the madame anxious to retain the confidence
of her clientele (the use of the term 'bog house' reminds us of the
frequent pre-Reformation 'dung and sewage' imagery of the brothel).
For Mandeville the whore is a woman who is not schooled in honour
by a sound moral education aimed at protecting her from her true self.
What is her true self? She is someone endowed by nature with a set of
genital organs over-alert for coitus. With medical precision he describes
these organs, concluding:

Now it is hard that so many alert members, which can exert themselves
in such a lively manner on this occasion (coitus), should be at all other

times in a state of perfect tranquility: for besides that experience teaches us to the contrary, this handsome disposition would be entirely useless if nature had not provided a prior titillation, *to provoke women* first to enter upon action: and all our late discoveries, in Anatomy, can find no other use for the Clitoris, but to whet the female desire by its frequent erection.[16]

If Mandeville intended to provoke strident protests, he was successful. His medical evidence was not countered, but the notion of the 'papist' bawdy house was fiercely opposed. Interestingly, that one set of women should be immolated to preserve another set engendered a violent response. This debate gave new momentum to a questioning on the origins of whoredom, which moved from the simple notion of a quintessentially predatory Eve to that of the economically disadvantaged woman whose fall is the work of an upper-class male. After her seduction she is then abused by those who can afford to pay for commercial sex.

The persuasion among Nonconformist observers was that the prostitute came from the common sort, or was a respectable girl orphaned, or betrayed and abused. Such attitudes accorded well with the conventions of the novel. Famous procuresses like Mother Needham, waiting to pounce on the innocent country girl as she stepped off the wagon into London, passed into lore. Yet the girls who actually did the falling continued to be endowed in both creative and didactic literature with two attributes: the first is idleness, or at least an aversion to 'work' (meaning needlework), the second is a penchant for luxury. Both belong with the Seven Deadly Sins and in medieval iconography are frequently personified by women. The women are also seen as ignorant and gullible, and both attributes emanate from a defective moral education. By concentrating on these character defects, the English Nonconformist conscience found it possible to attack whoredom in two ways, one old, the other a new departure. The old way was preventive: the daughters of the poor must be soundly educated in virtue (the charity school, no less, with its emphasis on cleanliness, godliness, industry and morality). The sermons of the early Methodists transmit a world in which thrift and chastity are enjoined as the most desirable attributes for the daughters of the poor along with the shunning of alcohol which can only lead to poverty, idleness and lack of virtue. The second was reformative. It sought either punishment or reform. Here emerged the philanthropic spirit that endowed London with its Magdalen Hospital, in some part a copy of the institutions of Catholic Europe founded over a century before. Like them, its mission was rescue and retraining and, like them, it was too small to assume responsibility for more than a very few.

Who was the type of prostitute that the Magdalen Hospital and the Catholic *repenties* thought might be retrievable? She was ordinarily a young girl of good or honest family who had fallen into unfortunate circumstances, and who felt a genuine revulsion for what she was doing or had done. In 1799, when the London Magdalen Hospital was not in a healthy financial state (even at the beginning it had a mere 122 subscribers, of whom only 16 were women), a compact little publication appeared, entitled *Magdalen, or History of the First Penitent Prostitute received into the Charitable Asylum* by the Revd William Dodd. In epistolary form, it tells the tale of the orphaned teenage daughter of a clergyman (point one, an impeccable family lineage emanating from the Church of England not that of Rome) placed in a gentry family household. There the son of the house pays her attention, impregnates her, and suggests setting her up in an independent establishment (point two, an aristocratic seducer). 'Vanity, which had so long worked in my heart', the girl writes 'began to grow perceptible' (point three, the characteristic female frailty, love of luxury). She gives birth to a son and her lover continues to pay her attention, but after two years his affection cools and he seeks an embassy abroad (point four, he has an escape route from sin and can carry on his philanderings in foreign parts). She has a hundred pounds and some clothes, but her lover has left with the rent in arrears and so she is evicted by the landlord. On the street with her son, a woman offers her assistance and promises her work (enter the capitalist exploiter figure), but she finds herself in a dirty disorderly house and appeals by letter to her sister and then with her help to the Magdalen. In short, and point five, she makes her bid for redemption having been a pensionary miss, a kept woman, and *before* becoming a common strumpet, a street-walker. Hence an appeal was made to the British establishment by conforming to the images that the establishment had of the fallen woman, whose fall was attributable to misfortune and the unsportsmanlike behaviour of one of its own sons. Clearly the Revd Mr Dodd saw nothing to be gained from presenting the case of the girl who had committed the offence with her social equal. Protestant tolerance, or rather in many instances conditional compassion, depended on the act of fornication being one where the man's social status was distinctly higher than that of the woman. Who

she was when she fell, and how she fell, were the essence of the problem. Economic considerations were allowed to co-exist with moral
ones.

How different was the Catholic record? There is no single model that
can be advanced as typical. Post-Tridentine reformers were genuinely
sensitive to charges of moral laxity and inspired by humane, charitable
initiatives, but there was no central direction. A few developments can
be discerned by examining the work of bishops, philanthropists, and
municipal councils acting under pressure from the ecclesiastical hierarchy, and the efforts of the Spanish Inquisition. First, by about 1620
the municipal licensed brothels in Catholic cities (in Germany first)
had been closed. This suggests some turning away from the view that
prostitution was a necessary evil to preserve honest women. Such closures
ran counter to the advice of doctors, who thought the licensed brothel
a way to contain syphilis. There was active promotion of the penitential
aspect of Mary Magdalen. In Italy an attempt was made to bolster
dowry funds, and in large cities institutions of penitence were founded,
to rescue either the newly fallen girl or the prostitute who wished to
extricate herself from her trade.[17] Some effort was made by the Spanish
Inquisition to impress on men that the act of fornication, not just
adultery, was a mortal sin. Between 1559 and 1648 in Spain, 174
people, of whom 87 per cent were men, were punished under the
rubric 'simple fornication' – sexual intercourse where both partners were
unmarried. Most of the offenders came from the lowest levels of society,
and were reported for having trivialized extramarital intercourse as long
as both parties were unmarried. The Inquisition's clear intent was to
drive home to the aberrant the gravity of their behaviour in the eyes of
God.[18]

In the Nueva Recopilación of laws, made under Philip II, a scale of
punishment was laid down against pimps and brothel owners, who
exploited women and lived on immoral earnings. These were bad
enough, but there also existed a man 'so vile that he pimps his own
wife', or receives payment for allowing married women to commit
adultery in his house. Spanish Jesuit preachers gave a new emphasis to
the culpability of men in creating a vice trade. Their evidence to support
this was that brothels existed to service men. There was no parallel
institution to service the allegedly more lustful woman.[19]

The test of laws and exhortations was whether they had any effect;
whether, for example, the legislation of Philip II was used against the

pimp. The evidence would suggest rarely and with little result. More effective perhaps were the efforts of the Jesuits, who were active throughout Italy and Spain in the sixteenth and seventeenth centuries promoting new institutions, both of dowry funds and of places of penitence. They saw the two as working together to reclaim fallen women.

Some of the newly formed Italian, Spanish and French confraternities and sisterhoods which existed to raise money to give girls a dowry, required an applicant to present a curriculum vitae and that of the young man she hoped to marry. Some provided funding through Monte de Maritaggio, institutions which existed in parts of Italy. Rome, Florence and Venice had reasonably well endowed charitable funds, which they bestowed on a set number of local, honest, legitimate virgins from the city and in some instances on women who had conceived or born an illegitimate child but who had the chance of making an honest match and who were known to have reformed their ways. Most of the city funds excluded servants or girls who did manual work such as hoeing vegetables and who did not live with their own families. These institutions did not want to be flooded by demands from crowds of immigrant girls who came into towns looking for work. If possible, however, they wished to prevent the descent into prostitution. If it occurred an escape route must be found.

The penitent prostitute, or the daughters of prostitutes, or widows without family support, or deserted wives (considered a particularly vulnerable sector of society in sixteenth-century Spain) were seen as demanding consideration. Some appreciation of the problems these women faced through limited earning potential was shown in the debates of the confraternities, which financed institutions enclosing penitent prostitutes prepared to accept a strict discipline if not religious vows.[20] Indeed, the demands were such that, according to Veronica Franco, the leading Venetian courtesan, they deterred many. She wanted an institution where penitent women could live with their children, an idea which apparently found Jesuit support and may have been behind the founding in 1577 of the Casa del Soccorso in Venice, an institution temporarily helping the abandoned family. Before this, in Rome in 1520, Leo X founded an institution which placed reformed prostitutes under the rule of Saint Augustine. Venice followed suit with a rule which was gradually followed by non-prostitutes who could not afford husbands nor the dowry to enter a convent (again the linkage between prostitute and nun, both outside the family, becomes apparent). In

1522 there emerged at Milan a Retiro Ospizio di S. Valera for the assistance of Milan's syphilitic prostitutes who refused to retire. The aim here was simply to get them off the streets and the Senate ordered that anyone who tried to leave would be visibly branded, which would cut them off from plying their trade. Little by little this institution became a last-stage hospital for those with tertiary syphilis, a final recourse for the woman who had spent her life on the streets and who was now so diseased that death was imminent.

Many Counter-Reformation foundations changed the penitent prostitute into a nun or her replica. In Rome, for example, the refuge of Santa Marta founded in the 1540s was for former prostitutes dedicated to a life of penitential prayer and sewing. These were Magdalens who had chosen the path of Martha. In 1563, Carlo Borromeo founded a convent in Rome for former prostitutes prepared to turn nuns, and by 1598 it had fifty religious. Several women who helped administer these houses were drawn from former penitent prostitutes themselves.[21]

The situation in Catholic countries gave scope to some original initiatives. In Seville, for example, in the late sixteenth century, the Jesuits founded a *casa pia* for penitent prostitutes. Finding that the institution had only a limited appeal, one of the fathers persuaded a wealthy woman to whom he was father confessor to provide dowries of forty ducats apiece to each penitent prostitute who could after a short spell in the home negotiate an honest marriage. The numbers at any one time in the institution shot up from two to forty: if they could become wives they were eager to repent.[22] More conscious still of the realities of the situation was the approach adopted by Paleotti in Bologna. Not only did the Cardinal Archbishop encourage donations to a dowry fund but he also recognized that there was simply not enough money to dower all the women who had to turn to prostitution to earn a living and who came not only from the city but the surrounding country to lay claims to such funds. Without actually giving encouragement to prostitution as a means of dowry accumulation, he took the line that it was perfectly legitimate for prostitutes whose clients refused to pay them to sue them before the For Episcopal, a court of Bologna. The logic was that the withholding of their fees prolonged the length of time they would have to do such work. The male fornicator should pay both the woman and the legal costs. Bologna, under his guidance, continued to license prostitutes (all unmarried) and to punish freelance operators and adulterers. Fines from these as well as the licence fees were used to finance the asylum where prostitutes who had accumulated enough funds to marry could pass a penitential period, like Mary Magdalen in the desert, and could then be released unblemished, marry and be reintegrated into society.[23]

Paleotti's logic is impressive. He neither approved nor blamed, but simply regretted the presence of young women, with no other resources than their bodies, who were driven to Bologna in search of work. He was prepared to countenance anything that might help them to a better future, demonstrating a pragmatism and a realism which has yet to be identified elsewhere among sixteenth-century reformers, Catholic or Protestant. But the problem with the dowry funds and the refuges was that both were too small. Without the attraction of a dowry fund the penitentiaries offered little long-term hope to a prostitute. Progressively, throughout the seventeenth century, they came to be seen as of little effect in curtailing the problem of prostitution, and support for this kind of provision declined.

The refuges and penitentiaries for prostitutes that sprang up in the sixteenth and seventeenth centuries in continental Europe had a very clear idea of why prostitution existed. The Compagnie du Saint Sacrement in Lyons, for example, gave three reasons for the presence of illicit sexual traffic. They began with the trading aspect of the city, which meant that people with money were constantly passing through. Secondly, the military in permanent garrison were a perpetual source of corruption, and their pay was so low that they could not afford to marry. Third, the practice was fed by 'the slump in manufacturing which causes numerous young girls to fall into wretched prostitution and through this they help to feed their families'.[24] Here, temporary unemployment explains recourse to prostitution, suggesting that it was a temporary expedient.

In Protestant countries there was a greater reluctance to admit economic need, although by the eighteenth century it was accepted as *one* of the factors in the fall of woman. Administrators, particularly magistrates, possessed evidence that more lay behind the problem than a love of luxury. Fielding (and indeed Adam Smith) recognized that Irish girls who came to London were too dirty to secure respectable posts in decent households and therefore became scrubs or tavern girls, keeping themselves and sometimes relatives alive on the products of whoring to supplement their legitimate work. Sixty per cent of London prostitutes were immigrants, but it would appear mainly from the north. They were, in short, amateur rather than professional prostitutes driven by poverty.[25]

By the eighteenth century, in all European languages, there was a huge repertoire of terms to describe the prostitute: kept mistress, harlot, whore, lewd woman, pensionary miss, strumpet, night walker, street walker, Newgate Napper, Bridewell worker, lady of pleasure, lady of the town, moll, dolly mop, doxy, bawd; *fille* or *femme de mauvaise vie*, *fille de joie*, *libertine*, *prostituée*, *putaine*, *fille débauchée*, *fille galante*, *grizette*, etc.[26] Some of these terms were old, some invented for the century; some indicated a different level of involvement; some indicated the point of view of the commentator; some were kind terms and some were pejorative.

All of the women concerned committed the same moral sin, but some were much more likely to attract the attention of the police than were others. The *lieutenant de police* of Paris, Le Noir, in 1768 laid down carefully for his men where they should target their repressive efforts. Debauched women, in his analysis, could be categorized in three ways: the first group consisted of kept mistresses (*filles ou femmes entretenues*) of wealthy men; the second was composed of brothel women controlled by a madame; and the third was of freelance street-walkers. The first need not concern the police: the second could be invigilated at a distance through the madame. She would not want to fall foul of the law and would not allow rowdy behaviour to scandalize her neighbourhood, nor retain girls known to have venereal disease. The third category should be watched by the police. These were the unregulated women who caused scandal to neighbourhoods, accosted men in taverns where their presence produced rowdiness and disorder, and disseminated disease. These, then, are the prostitutes of the police files and hence not necessarily a real reflection of the overall composition of the prostitute population; the rest can only be pursued through the more impressionistic evidence of journals and memoirs.[27]

Taking all the evidence available, Erica Marie Benabou states that in eighteenth-century Paris approximately one adult woman in thirteen looked to prostitution for a whole or part of her income.[28] Perhaps with London as a possible contender, Paris contained the widest range of prostitutes in Europe, as Rome had done 200 years earlier. The top of the profession looked to a wealthy, frequently aristocratic clientele, married or unmarried, who associated keeping beautiful mistresses with social standing and who were considered provincial if they did not. The

Balais Balais. ⬥ A Paris Chez Joullain

17. Edme Bouchardon,
'Balais, balais' from *Etudes
Prises dans les bas peuple ou
les cris de Paris* (1737).

Cotterets. ⬥ A Paris Chez Joullain

18. Edme Bouchardon,
'Cotterets' from *Etudes Prises
dans les bas peuple ou les cris de
Paris* (1737).

19. ABOVE LEFT: Jean Honoré
Fragonard (1732–1806), *The Furtive Kiss*.

20. LEFT: Lucas Cranach (1472–1553),
The Ill-Matched Couple. The uneven match
involves a foolish old man and a greedy
young woman. The joining of hands
symbolises a union but the woman reaches
out for gold. The horns on the wall portend
the groom's conversion to cuckold.

21. ABOVE: Jacob Jordaens (1592–
1678), *Portrait of a Young Married
Couple*. Jordaens's young couple, equal
in age and wealth, are models of
the appropriate.

22. Lorenzo Lotto, *Messer Masilio e la sua sposa* (1523). The splendour of the Renaissance wedding is caught by Lorenzo Lotto. Hands are joined: the husband holds the ring and the wife's red robe and jewels, part of her dowry, establish the standing both of the new union and the families brought together.

23. Arthur Devis, *Robert Gwillym of Atherton and his Family* (1749). Property and matrimony are indissoluble and Arthur Devis's *ouevre* attests to the desire of the wealthy to express this in pictorial form. Here a house, inherited by the wife has been embellished by the husband to form an imposing new residence made the focal point of the picture.

24. Albrecht Dürer (1471–1528), *Birth of the Virgin*. Childbed was a collective event for female family, kin and neighbours as well as the midwife and childbed helpers. A lone birth was suspicious. The birth of the Virgin was the religious subject which allowed the sociability surrounding birth to be fully captured by the artist.

25. A Christian couple are duty bound to discipline and impose right conduct upon their children, principles frequently reflected in a depiction of the orderly family meal where the children's hands are neatly joined for grace. The artist of this painting dated 1627 is unknown.

26. RIGHT: Marguerite Gérard, *Motherhood* (1795–1800). In the late eighteenth century, the mother/child relationship in visual art becomes increasingly warm. Gerard's aristocratic tender mother who has not sent her child away to nurse receives a wet kiss and a tactile pinch.

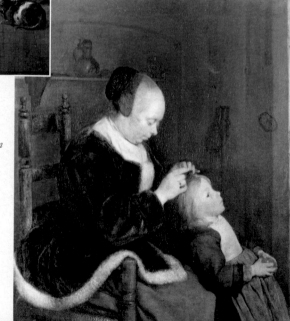

A mother must impart moral values to her daughter and her authority is expressed in the combing of hair and the destruction of lice. A girl becomes a virtuous wife and mother through example and watching her mother at work be it preparing food, ironing or caring for other children.

28. Jacob Duck, *A Woman Ironing* (c.1640).

27. Gerard Ter Borch, *Woman Combing the Hair of her Child* (1650).

29. ABOVE: Pieter Gerritsz van Roestraten, *A Woman Making Pancakes* (c. 1670).

30. Nicolaes Maes, *A Woman Peeling Parsnips* (1655).

31. Painting from the school of Caravaggio, (early seventeenth century) *The Virgin and Saint Anne*. In Catholic iconography St Anne represents working maternity, grooming and inculcating discipline in the future mother of God. Here the saint appears in worthy matron's garb, winds wool and supervises her daughter's work.

king himself, aided by Madame de Pompadour, was presented with a range of young teenagers, some of them aristocratic but more of middling rank, for his own personal use. At the other end of the spectrum were the street-walkers who provided sexual services for the changing, volatile floating population of immigrant labourers without their womenfolk, soldiers on leave with very little pay, or market traders of Les Halles.

The Parisian prostitute populace of 20,000 or more could be seen as ranging downwards from the 'kept mistress', including the *femmes galantes* of the theatre world, whose stars were inevitably 'protected' by an interested male figure. These women at any one time might service a number of men, although their keepers were not necessarily aware of the range of their activities. They usually began their careers in their teens and were the daughters of artisans, perhaps shopgirls, *marchandes de modes* or hairdressers. Frequently they embarked on their careers after a pact made between their parents and their initial protectors. O'Murphy the artisan *savetier* (soap maker), for example, had traded two of his beautiful daughters with aristocratic clients in return for monetary payment before his wife negotiated the services of the fourteen-year-old Louise in the direction of the monarchy. The girls (for they could scarcely at that age be called women) could expect the rental of an apartment to be paid, and furnishings, clothing and a cash consideration provided in addition. We can only speculate on how long was spent with any one gentleman, the motives for ending the arrangement and what happened next. Some seem to have parted company on pregnancy. How many of these women continued into their thirties in this way of life is not clear. The O'Murphy girls all found husbands in their early twenties, the well-endowed Louise marrying an army officer. A few became so celebrated that they foreshadowed the nineteenth-century demi-monde of ballet dancers and opera girls. How many later became brothel whores is not known.

There was no direct automatic descent from kept mistress to common strumpet. If the woman in question picked up a tidy little sum from her protector, she was not precluded from marriage. The police were certainly not interested in this level of the trade, unless a young aristocrat threatened his patrimony by infatuation with a particular woman – whereupon the police could, at the family's instigation and expense, become suddenly threatening. Taken overall, in Benabou's reckoning, the *femmes galantes* perhaps constituted something in the range of

8 per cent of all whores. These were women who used their bodies
for real profit, luxurious consumption and personal indulgence. Their
high earning days, however, depended on the maintenance of their
looks.

Beneath them were the brothel women, *femmes de mauvaise vie, filles
publiques*. However, there were brothels and brothels. They ranged in
police parlance from the clean, discreet, discerning (in the Faubourg
Saint-Honoré) to the bawdy (Saint Denis and Beaubourg adjacent to
Les Halles) and were treated accordingly. As for the women in them,
their age and physical attributes determined the quality of the establishment in which they might serve. Most of them had crossed over from the
needle trades, having been dressmakers, *ouvriers en linge*, stay-makers,
glove-makers and so on. They entered the brothel by direct negotiation
with the madame. She was perhaps someone who had been in the
profession herself, though, particularly in the more up-market establishments, she was no elderly hag. The police noted and gave tacit approval
to the discreet and businesslike houses which gave no trouble. They
were hostile to the women who actively lured girls into their houses,
and anyone who reported the use of children could be sure to bring the
police down upon a particular establishment. Probably most of the
women in these establishments had had sexual experience before they
entered.

The most disreputable houses which drew in a rowdy clientele and
which sent girls out to pick up men on the streets were a more obvious
target for police interest. Yet beneath the brothels, and perhaps more
numerous, were the girls, mostly immigrants and again usually seamstresses, laundresses and street sellers (not servants) who may have used
prostitution as an ancillary income to other employment. Women of
this class rented a room and paid the owner up to 50 per cent of their
profits every time they brought home a client. Such women were likely
to frequent markets and taverns and 'known' areas where customers
could be found. Every year in the closing decades of the old regime,
about 700 women and girls were arrested and usually given short sentences at the Salpêtrière. Two-thirds of those arrested were not Paris-
born. They were less likely to be brothel girls than freelance
street-walkers and what is conspicuous is their progressively lower age
(under twenty) as the century advanced. Their dossiers do not tell us
whether they intended to return to their village one day. Many declared
they were between jobs; some claimed lack of work; many were recidi-

vists; 87 per cent were single, but the police admitted they would only arrest a married woman if she was denounced by her husband.

The Parisian scene does not appear vastly different from that in London where there was again a distinct geography of whoredom. The expensive brothels were in St James's where the madames paid the girls a portion of their profits or a set wage. The theatre world of Drury Lane attracted high and low. Southwark and St Giles and Billingsgate probably had the lowest end of the trade. Police records are sparing in giving arrested women's professions, but it seems from random statements that they were milliners, mantua makers, haberdashers, needleworkers, charwomen, market women and tavern workers. Although Defoe said many were servants between jobs, the evidence does not support this, but suggests they were casual workers or in the needle trades. Many did not operate even from their lodgings. In the days before street lamps there were many dark alleys, as James Boswell knew, where an encounter could be effected and consummation could be had for a few pence, whereas in a lodging house it might cost one shilling and sixpence.[29]

How different was the situation in Paris and London in the eighteenth century from that prevalent in seventeenth-century Amsterdam, or in Counter-Reformation Rome, or in Reformation Augsburg?

The activities of the police in seventeenth-century Amsterdam[30] analysed by Lotte van de Pol show that commercial sex was most actively prosecuted in the 1690s, but that repressive vigour diminished conspicuously after 1710. The egregiously high levels of the 1690s may reflect general immiseration, increasing business during the period leading up to and comprehending the War of the Spanish Succession, or it may reflect the increased potential of soliciting after dark following the introduction of street lighting into Amsterdam. The decline after 1710 may be nothing more than an expression of defeat by the police, or it may reflect a reduction in business when the grand armies raised in Holland were disbanded and commercial traffic passed into a less buoyant phase. The women arrested in the period 1660–1720 were, as to 60 per cent and over, industrial workers by trade – knitters, spinners, silk workers, pin makers and seamstresses – followed by 20 per cent in service or charwomen (*schoonmaakster*) and 5 per cent were hawkers. Thereafter the number of textile workers diminished and servants and seamstresses form the bulk of the entries in the *confessieboek*. The women picked up for soliciting under street lamps, in *musicos*, or in the brothels

where they took their clients (Dutch prostitutes sought out their customers and took them back to the brothel, though they may also have
had visiting clients) were asked in court about their work skills, 'what
they were trained in', during the seventeenth century. After 1710 this
question was dropped and enquiry was made into 'how they made a
living'. The textile workers of the late seventeenth century did not
hesitate to spell out to the judges: 'Knitters (silk workers, pin-makers,
seamstresses etc.) can't make a living.' In the same period such domestic
workers who appeared did so because of the dubious and disreputable
nature of the households and taverns where they lived.

A majority of the offenders came from outside Amsterdam, and
disproportionately over-represented were those who arrived by sea from
the north Netherlands and Germany. They came in the same boats that
brought naval recruits for the East Indiamen into the capital. Prostitute
and clientele arguably arrived together, and the fate of one was perhaps
not as terrible as that of the other, given the mortality rates of sailors.
It may well be, though it is never expressly stated, that many had lived
at least in part by prostitution in their place of origin. The skippers of
the ferrying vessels may have been in collusion with the brothel madames
and given the girls their addresses. Perhaps the woman arriving in
Amsterdam intending to join the vice trade needed do nothing more
than ask a sailor on arrival where to go. Some may have already lost
their virginity to an army or navy recruit. When, or if, pressed by a
questioning magistrate, each of them would produce a story of seduction
and betrayal ending with a piece of home-made philosophy, or a rhetorical question: 'What could I do? Life had to go on.'

In eighteenth-century Amsterdam the dominant professional group
recruited to the vice trade was that of maidservant (15 per cent of the
total, as in Paris). More people had servants in the eighteenth century
than before. The job was very insecure, lending itself to abuse at the
bottom, and the term 'servant' may have increasingly been used with
a lack of precision to cover casual cleaning work or tavern service. In
substantial houses, so little free time was allowed to a servant that
prostitution was hardly a possibility. Before a magistrate, every woman
had an interest in casting a positive light on her working life. Her best
chance was to say that she could not earn enough from her work, that
it had temporarily dried up or, in default of work, that she was between
jobs. Implicitly, the women asked the magistrate: 'Is it not better to
whore than to starve?'

The penalties for whoring were periods of correctional training in the institution called the *Spinhuis*, though spinning was not the only textile activity that was undertaken. The idea was that idle, luxury-loving women should have habits of industry instilled into them through learning a textile trade. The *Spinhuis* was a tourist attraction in the seventeenth century. However, there is a certain irony in the election of such work as the solution to loose living. The same irony is manifest if we look at what the London Magdalen sought to teach penitent prostitutes. When it was founded in 1758 it was stated as axiomatic that the penitent should be taught a skill.

> The articles for the employment of those women may be, to make their own cloaths, both linen and woolen, to knit their stockings from the new materials, spinning the thread and making the cloth. To make bone lace, black-lace, artificial flowers, children's toys, spinning fine thread, also woolen yarn, winding silk, embroidery. All branches of millinary. Making Women and Children's shoes, mantuas, stays, coats cauls for wigs, weaving hair for perruques, Knitting Hose and Stockings. Making Leathern and silken gloves. Making garters. Drawing Patterns. Making Soldier's cloaths and seamen's slops. Making carpets after the Turkey manner . . . or whatever employment their several abilities and Genius leads to.[31]

Every one of these employments would be listed in directories as those from which the prostitute population was recruited. The *Spinhuis* and the Magdalen were in effect training penitents to resume their positions in society in jobs which would ensure they would probably return to the streets, if they were still young enough.

Even in normal times the women who were dependent on the work of their hands would find ancillary evening work. There were London silk workers who also made fireworks; Scottish knitters who also gathered and dried kelp; women cooked or performed services for others as well as working at a stipulated trade. The economy of the working class was always one of multiple expedients, and into this expedient economy prostitution or procuring could obtrude. This is not to say that every hungry woman shirtmaker who found herself out of work automatically prostituted herself — merely that, for some, supplementary or substitute income could be and was acquired in this way. The weight of existing evidence suggests the *commonest* prostitute type throughout the early

modern period was an amateur who owed a proportion of her income
to prostitution.

Sometimes prostitution was a temporary recourse in periods of
unemployment, like the cessation of the silk manufacture at Lyons when
servantes were simply shown the door and prostituted themselves from
the brick kilns where they gathered for warmth at night. During bad
phases in the lace industry women from Belgium made their way to
the Dutch ports. They were spared the humiliation of whoring in their
own towns and at the same time sought out a place where there was a
buoyant demand for commercial sex.

Lyndal Roper notes that of the women accused of prostitution in
sixteenth-century Augsburg, many did spinning or sewing when they
could get it. For example one woman, Anna Stodkler, had begun as a
needleworker to order in the employment of Hans Eggenberger who
then began to employ her as a prostitute and paid her without distinction for the two tasks. Another, Anna Linmaer, made veils and fine
handkerchiefs, looked after her children, worked at the public baths
with her husband, and made something as a prostitute when the
occasion presented itself. Margret Hofschneider fitted in sexual
assignments while on errands for her mistress. Some were healers or
practised pharmacy.[32]

The integration of prostitution within a general economy of work –
if one could get it – and the recourse to commercial sex in times of
difficulty or after a day's consignment of sewing or other labour, continued to be common throughout the period. Even the procuress can
be integrated into the economy of expedients. Some were tavern keepers;
others kept a brothel while running another business like a drink shop
or an eating house. Many servants on marriage set up as lodging-house
keepers and were paid if they allowed their premises to be used for
sexual encounters. The women, not their husbands, appear to have been
the ones who agreed the terms with a tenant and it was easy for the
landlady or concierge to turn a blind eye, for a consideration, to fornication on her premises. In sixteenth-century Augsburg, if it could be
shown that the woman had sent out for wine for the couple involved,
she could be accused of collusion. The very mention of such activity
suggests another way of cutting into the profits of the trade. Some
laundresses allowed their employees to bring clients into the shop where
the ironing was done, but expected a cut of the proceeds. In Amsterdam
bordeel and *musicos* where the girl picked up her client were separated,

and the tavern keepers could also share in the profits of the trade by recommending girls.

So there was a whole hinterland of people depending on the prostitute for support. They made demands on the profits of her business. The madame, the brothel servant in the better houses, pimp (more rarely in this period than in the nineteenth century), *marchande de modes*, the shopkeeper who supplied the prostitute with the clothes necessary to play the game against credit and expected reimbursement, tavern keeper, concierge, were the main dependants, other than the women's own families. The prostitutes of sixteenth-century Venice, of seventeenth-century Amsterdam and of eighteenth-century Paris were all heavily in debt for the clothes they wore. The cost of hiring a lace fichu in Amsterdam exceeded the income from a day's spinning or knitting. Venetian women needed high-heeled red shoes which were the marks of their trade, fake jewellery and glitter as well as bright clothing because all these were expected by their clientele.[33]

It has been argued that in 1526 there were 4900 prostitutes in Rome, an estimate based on tax lists and censuses, although the word 'prostitute' is not found on these lists. Their presence can only be inferred by adding the women given single classical names and no surnames to women whose Christian names were not followed by a surname but a place of origin, such as Teresa de Córdoba, to all the washerwomen, shirtmakers and needleworkers and all the women living in the same house in the above categories. The technique is justified on the grounds that other censuses put the letter M (*meretri*) against such women's names and that the woman worker without a husband was a likely prostitute.[34]

Angus Mackay effectively argues that the location of amateur prostitution in particular jobs led in sixteenth-century Rome and Spain to an entire sexual language: the unspun wool on the distaff (the breasts), the work of the pimp to collect wool (for the prostitute to spin), 'note how the prostitute is taught her skills and how tow is spun.' (The sexual act carried out by a whore is the spinning of tow, not of fine wool.) He notes certain Spanish proverbs: 'An old woman has been a prostitute or a procuress or a *mesonera* (a poor tavern keeper).' 'Prostitute in the Spring, procuress in Autumn, *beata* in old age.' In this second proverb prostitution is confined to women on the right side of forty, procuring to an older, experienced age group, while for an old woman there is nothing left but piety, begging at church doors with her rosary beads.[35]

In Jacques Callot's prints of the Thirty Years War the process is given pictorial form. The young women are camp followers and whores; the middle-aged are some kind of petty traders (at that point Courasche became a huckster); but the old are simply beggars festooned in rosary beads.

It is of course amateur or casual prostitution which lends itself most readily to the notion of the expedient economy, and it is impossible to say whether sexual services or needlework constituted the bulk of any one individual's income. The small proportion of prostitutes at the top of the profession were well provided for; the better brothels offered a reasonable livelihood servicing four or five clients a day; but for the simple street-walker forced to part with half her proceeds to the lodging-house keeper or use public places, there was little gain to be had. One of the girls of Augsburg stated she needed fifteen or sixteen men in the course of a night's work to survive.

The suggestion has been made that in the course of the eighteenth century, at least in Paris, prostitution professionalized itself, that is to say, became concentrated in the brothel as a full-time activity for the practitioner. Such a statement is impossible to prove. There were certainly more brothels, particularly in London and Paris, at the end of the period than at the beginning, but were there fewer part-time prostitutes? It seems unlikely. Furthermore, it is clear from the ages of the arrested women that it was unusual to practise after thirty. It may then have been for many a recourse in difficult times which ceased to be available once they had lost their physical attraction. Or those who had done well as kept mistresses or madames picked up their profits and left. Syphilis, visible in sores and in the salivation which revealed that mercury had been taken as a treatment, doubtless also curtailed the activities of many.

It is clear that throughout the period, with possible exception made for some Spanish cities, and here the evidence can be contradictory, the vice trade was in the hands of women. They ran the brothels and the powerful pimp figure was not a feature of the structure of the trade in commercial sex, although it is clear that some women, like Lozana, used teenage boys to make customers aware of their services. In so far as women were casual workers and as long as they could keep out of very pressing debts, then it can perhaps be argued that they had more control over their own lives than at a later date.

The prostitute has been represented as a subversive, an independent woman living away from her family, who flouted the rules of patriarchal society. Certainly she broke the rules. In so doing she provided reformers with a conspicuous example of woman as the eternal repository of weakness and original sin. She was hence a preserver of traditional versions of womanhood. She also, perhaps, helped to sustain traditional family structures by offering some escape to men trapped in difficult marriages. Familiarity with the clientele of the courts who dealt with prostitutes does not, however, encourage a view of them as independent. Indeed, the last word should perhaps be given to Lozana, the widowed Spanish *converso* shirtmaker driven into Rome by the persecution of the Inquisition. Perhaps she was real, perhaps only the creation of the syphilitic cleric Delgado, but her language is authentic enough as she muses:

> I don't know, but I am amazed at how many of the poor women who have served in Rome can survive. And what have they gained? Some have broken limbs, others are worn out and have nothing . . . some have no noses . . . (a sign of syphilis), others are beatas, or washerwomen or inn servants, or go betweens or procuresses. Still others spin but can't earn enough to live on.

Lozana identified the problem: it was one of *survival*. She knew that the profits of either shirtmaking or prostitution would not keep a woman alive for very long in a struggle in which the odds were stacked against the woman alone, but that as long as she had youth and some physical attraction, prostitution was a recourse and a resource which could not be neglected. This was the harsh reality that defeated the reformers' aspirations to a sexually pure society.

——————◄◦►——————

CHAPTER NINE

Women and the Devil

Since witches are usually old women of melancholic nature
and small brains (women who get easily depressed and
have little trust in God), there is no doubt that the devil
easily affects and deceives their minds by illusions and
apparitions that so bewilder them that they confess to
actions that they are very far from having committed.

JOHANN WIER, DE PRAESTIGIIS DAEMONUM, 1563

T HE DESIRE to regulate marriage, to promote chastity within
marriage, to outlaw sexual irregularity or relations outside marriage, are concepts far from alien to twentieth-century thought
even if the regulatory apparatus constructed in the sixteenth century
has been conspicuously modified. The reformers' concerns are, in
essence, central to our understanding. In one major respect, however,
the intellectual climate of the early modern period differs from our
experience: that is, it contained the notion of a world in which the
Devil, demons and evil spirits were omnipresent.

In regard to extramarital sex, the reformers elected the body as the
locus of sin. Furthermore, they were also legatees and perpetuators of
the belief that the human body was a vehicle for spiritual evil since it
was fully permeable by the Devil or evil spirits who could take possession
and assert their will. This facility, if it may be so termed, accorded
with the belief common to all Christians that the body and the soul
were separate entities and that the second was the part that would count
when it came to the final judgement which meted out eternal life or
eternal damnation. Lyndal Roper has spoken of a 'theology of the body'
and suggested that this was particularly central to Roman Catholic
thought, which believed in religious ecstasy, in the conversion of bread
and wine into body and blood, in the efficacy of the image to arouse

passion and in the celibacy of the priesthood to achieve nearness to God, as well as in demonic possession.[1] However, the last belief was also a part of Protestant thinking. Scripture showed that Christ himself had cast out devils and in one instance these had actually been transferred into a herd of pigs. What the new Protestant churches were not prepared to concede was the ability of a priest to assume Christ's role and to exorcize the possessed. Indeed, they believed that this celibate tool of the Pope of Rome could himself be an agent of the Devil and the act of exorcism as practised by the Roman Catholic Church was an instance of collusion in which the Devil's agent could make evil spirits perform. Incantations and rituals, the summoning of Mary and the saints and the physical rites performed by the priest over the body of the possessed in front of credulous crowds in this view allied the performing priest with sorcerers, wizards and witches in a grisly diabolic tragicomedy.[2]

The Devil, however fictional, has to be conceded a large part in the history of the two Reformations, and by extension in the history of women, because his alleged influence created a number of personages, among them the possessed, the heretic and the witch. There was considerable lack of clarity in the relationship between these three and they could easily overlap. Technically, the first was an innocent victim suddenly occupied by demons who contested the physical space of the body. The second adopted false views at the instigation of the Devil and was dangerous to others, and the third became the Devil's agent intent on harm on an extended scale. However, in some areas initially lost to and then regained by the Catholic church, exorcism of women possessed of Protestant devils became a great propaganda exercise reasserting the triumph of Rome over Protestant heresy and enhancing the public reputation of the exorcist – if not necessarily his standing among his colleagues. The Jesuit Peter Canisius in Augsburg in the 1570s carried out some notable expulsions of Protestant devils from the Fugger women, while Ignatius Loyola, legatee of the scepticism of Erasmus on the subject of exorcism, remained unimpressed.[3] In France after the 'miracle of Laon', a piece of theatre in which a sixteen-year-old girl, Nicole Obry, was exorcized of Huguenot devils in the cathedral, the practice of exorcism became a weapon in the religious conflict of the ensuing decades. One Marthe Brossier was exorcized several times after the Edict of Nantes allegedly secured peace between the warring factions. Exorcism meant control of the devils but not necessarily their expulsion, so the act could be repeated, and garrulous devils could speak through the mouth of the one possessed individual several times to show they were Huguenot. The possessed girl would writhe and turn, her tongue loll and eyes roll, parts of her body could be exposed and the whole incident could be made, in Sarah Ferber's words, into a kind of Punch and Judy show of dominance and submission; the possessed clearly developed a relationship with her cleric sponsor who used her to effect on successive occasions.[4]

The 'demoniacs' offering themselves for exorcism in these great spectacles were invariably women and they were usually young. Though not numerous, some gained great renown. Marthe Brossier, for example, travelled France and afforded the credulous spectacles of Protestant devils torturing her body until she finally incurred the disapprobation of university theological faculties. Allegedly she ended her life sustained by alms. The Catholic church was not itself in agreement over the efficacy of exorcism and the numbers of critics grew over the seventeenth century. But why were the demoniacs usually women? Eve, with her propensity to listen to the Devil and her gullibility, can be summoned as part explanation. In addition woman's alleged lack of rationality, her lack of self-governance and her empty mind left a convenient space for evil spirits. At once symbol and metaphor for ignorance and folly, she could be manipulated in the name of the True Faith by the priest-cum-Svengali who also gained fame from his expertise. We can only speculate on the baser instincts involved in the spectacle of a young girl writhing and exposing parts of her body.

Women in general, individually and collectively, were regarded as at risk. The collective possession of the nuns of Loudun showed the Devil capable of penetrating the convent wall and that diabolical possession could exist without a hint of Protestant heresy. Once allegations of witches began to affect a given area, demonic possession could spread to embrace the very young of both sexes as well as adult men and women, as it did at Zuggaramurdi in the Basque provinces between 1609 and 1614. On such an occasion, the line between possession and witchcraft, as opposed to possession and heresy, became difficult to discern, since the witch became the Devil's agent to effect evil and evil spirits were in the air.[5] Moreover, the fact that Protestants did not believe in exorcism did not mean that they did not believe in possession or release from possession. The issue was over priestly authority, not the active penetration of the body by the Devil.

The demoniac's essential innocence marked her off from those who colluded in or evoked evil or supernatural powers deliberately. The Devil and powers for evil (theoretically the same) were perceived as immensely complex. The witch, or Devil's agent, was the product of an amalgam of popular beliefs and involute theories emanating from the pens of scholars, theologians and lawyers.

In Thomas Dekker's *The Witch of Edmonton* (1621) a fictive witch muses on how this label came to be attached to her.

> Some call me witch,
> And being ignorant of myself, they go
> About to teach me how to be one; urging
> That my bad tongue (by their bad language made so)
> Forespeaks their cattle, doth bewitch their corn,
> Themselves, their servants, and their babes at nurse.
> This they enforce upon me; and in part
> Make me to credit it.

Dekker's witch is worthy of contemplation. Although the creation of an author famed for satires involving women who wore the trousers and flouted the rules, she is subjected to a powerful and not unsympathetic psychological analysis and made the product of a belief system, a complex process in which characteristics are attributed to her. Thus 'taught', she assimilates her ascribed role and comes to believe that her curses and invocations of the Devil can destroy cattle and crops and human beings.

Witches in this rendering were constructed from without, but they ultimately colluded in the process. The members of a community elect the label 'witch' for someone they mistrust, credit her with evil powers and convince her that she is indeed what they say she is. What made this collusion possible was a common, deeply ingrained set of beliefs, in magic, evil and in the ability of the Devil to win disciples to do his work. This set of ingrained beliefs co-existed with another set, of which Dekker showed himself in other plays also aware, of beliefs on the nature of womanhood and the particular relationship of this cultural figment with the chief architect of evil, the Devil.

Some of the most distinguished historians and anthropologists of our time have dedicated a great deal of effort to locating witchcraft within its social, political and religious environment, and have emphasized the complexity of the issues.[6] Some have given most attention to an identification of the alleged witch and her real persecutors or those who accused her in court. Others have emphasized the continuity of popular belief concerning the forces of evil which predated and postdated the period of persecution. They have concentrated on the discontinuity of élite attitudes towards the acknowledgement of powerful pagan occult forces and hence have shifted attention away from the witch to her persecutors. Others, in the process of presenting regional or national monographs, have discussed whether Catholic or Protestant secular and religious authorities differed in their approaches, and why certain areas produced more witch panics and trials than did others and what might trigger off such events. A series of feminist historians have used the witch to argue a sexual power struggle in which 'powerful' women healers and others were crushed by men because of their standing in the community. Much of this work has not relied on empirical evidence. Very recently, however, particular case studies of trials, micro-histories using gender as an analytical tool and essaying methods of psychoanalysis, have widened and enriched the discussion.[7] The debate on the witch is not closed.

To do justice to all the important work which has appeared is beyond the scope of this chapter and any attempt at synthesis is open to the accusation of over-simplification. No one, in fact, can offer a total explanation for phenomena lying in the realms of psycho-history. The most substantial historical reality is the alleged witch herself and her recorded fate before the courts, along with the concurrent theoretical debates and pronouncements of the persecuting establishment.

Belief in an evil force is probably as old as the history of humankind and certainly predates the witchcraft craze. Such a force was capable of malevolence at several levels. The most minor and trivial were events like the unexpected turning of milk, the spoiling of cheese, the presence of weevils in salt beef, the failure of dough to rise. Such troubles were frequently attributed to 'little people', fairies, Puck, Joan the Wad, leprechauns and trolls, whose humours needed respecting and whose mischief was the basis of popular lore. Such activity was to be lamented but accepted as an everyday hazard. At a more major level, however, an evil force could engender total individual or collective disaster. Disease, whether confined to a single person or experienced by a community in the form of a sudden deadly epidemic such as plague, was the most obvious of these. Cattle could lose their milk, or be collectively struck by murrain. Crops could be devastated by hailstorms, drought, mildew or locusts. A baby could be glowing and healthy one day, dead in its crib the next. To cope with the world in which they lived, peasants disposed of a whole range of folk beliefs and panaceas. At their most practical was a herbal remedy to administer to a disease. There were incantations and rituals, pilgrimages and visits to shrines to invoke 'saints', whose origins were in some cases pre-Christian, or to grottoes with waters to bathe afflicted limbs or ailing members of cattle, statues or rocks which could be touched, kissed or scratched and the dust drunk in a potion to promote a desired end. Such phenomena existed in profusion.

The medieval church had sought to substitute for these practices the power of prayer to its own pantheon of sanctity, but not with any degree of success. In default, it had reconciled itself at the popular level to a marriage with pagan beliefs, crowning menhirs (pagan holy stones) with crosses and incorporating local primitive beliefs in grottoes and shrines into the Christian tradition. In addition it dealt abundantly in the 'miraculous', with *scapulaires* to hang round the neck to ward off evil, girdles to help in childbirth, special prayers, incantations and ritual to cope with a variety of eventualities and a whole pantheon of saints and holy phenomena as a recourse for the afflicted. The conversion of bread and wine into body and blood was a 'magic' or 'miraculous' event performed daily by every priest. The populace believed the host itself possessed magical properties to assist in the war against evil and ill fortune; where magic ended and the miraculous began was far from clear.[8]

The pervasiveness of popular beliefs in an evil force was accompanied by one in which certain people, 'wise' or 'cunning' folk, were accredited with special knowledge of how to cope with a particular eventuality. They might dispose of herbal or other like knowledge or claim they knew incantations, or mystic instructions which the afflicted must carry out if their sickness was to be assuaged. In societies which had neither a veterinary surgeon nor much medical assistance, such people had a power we can only surmise. English historians have estimated that no one in fifteenth-century England lived more than ten miles from a cunning man or woman. One or the other was the first natural resource of people who were victims of the germ-laden world in which they lived.

Society, then, acknowledged a range of people with special knowledge, but the extent of that knowledge was not necessarily confined to the purely medicinal. Eventualities might occur, aspirations exist of a purely innocuous nature, such as the desire of a young girl to win a particular husband, of a woman to be fertile, of a man or woman to gain the favour of a certain individual, provoking a desire to invoke some supernatural aid by spell or by potion. At least from classical times there were women in the cities who dealt in love potions and fertility potions and who are the ancestors of Celestina-type women who were still to be found in medieval and early modern Europe.* Or there were people who could divine the future. The use of this kind of knowledge implied a desire to manipulate, to change or merely improve someone's life, through knowledge which could make contact with a force ordinary mortals could not touch. Such 'white' magic stayed on the right side of a line demarcating the force for good (subjectively determined) from the power to do evil. The title 'cunning folk' could be extended to those reputedly adept in coping with sick cattle and there were indeed farm servant women who were more readily employed because recognized as knowing remedies to cure cows and pigs of disorders. Wise women of the villages, childbed helpers thought to know a trick or two to help in the case of a difficult delivery, are also placed in this broad generic group. These special gifts or skills were remunerated, if not very highly, and these women were often old (the most experienced) or poor.

In most instances this kind of skill or knowledge could be subsumed in that complex amalgam of small activities which made up the economy of many poor households in the past. Rarely did it represent a full-time activity. Some may have been suspected of charlatanry. However, this was a society almost helpless in the face of disease. If a single cow could represent the difference between autonomy and dependence on charity, its threatened loss demanded action. A potion or incantation could always be worth a try. It was in this knowledge that every winter in poor areas of the Auvergne or the Pyrenees packages of mystic ingredients (sulphur etc.) were made to fill pedlars' trays with magic cures of all kinds. There were those for toothache and worms and boils and carbuncles and those for cattle. If nature remedied the situation the

---

* Celestina was a celebrated character in a Spanish play or novel of 1499, first prostitute, then procuress, who gave aphrodisiac potions for clients to take or administer to objects of their desire.

purchaser had lost little; if it did not then the pedlar had long moved on. The failure of the cure might provoke individual resentment, but the strategies were also accompanied by Christian prayer to specific saints, the use of holy water, recourse to relics, novenas and so on. Together, all such strategies constituted a package of hope for a reversal of fortune, or a manipulation of the course of events.

Not all the practitioners fell into the category of 'cunning folk'. The Renaissance had generated an interest among the learned in alchemy and all kinds of scientific 'magic'. In parts of northern Italy in the sixteenth century there existed priests who dabbled in white magic, potions and astrological consultations.

If some people knew how to invoke a force for good, perhaps they, or others, could also invoke one for evil? 'Black' magic implied the recognition that someone had a key to unlocking this force with malice. They, or their agents, could then turn against an innocent individual or community. The person in possession of this key was the witch (either male or female). The line between cunning folk and sorcerer was one which pivoted on degrees of knowledge and differences of intent.[9]

To lend this degree of clarity to the mass of primitive beliefs which were part of the thought process of 99 per cent of any society in the early modern period is doubtless to over-simplify, but it helps us to appreciate the popular bedrock upon which the belief in the witch reposed. It also allows the delineation of three personages − cunning folk, sorceress dealing in potions or gazing in crystal balls, and malevolent witch − who could be combined in one individual. There were webs of relationships linking the demoniac, heretic and witch on the one hand and cunning folk (healer), magician (sorcerer, crystal ball gazer, seller of potions) and witch on the other, and all the webs crossed. An age-old belief in the supernatural was located in a new phase of religious change and in particular social and economic circumstances. Demographic growth produced pressures on food supplies: pestilence and local shortage also combined to multiply the poor. 'The beggar', in Eileen Power's graphic phrase 'leapt into literature', and many of the beggars were very poor women lacking male support and forced on to the margins of the community.

To generate a witch persecution, however, in which individuals were marked out, prosecuted and convicted for collusion with the Devil, needed something more than poverty and a bedrock of popular beliefs. It needed establishment sanction and, indeed, very often some active promotion. The establishment had two branches, ecclesiastical and lay, but there was a relationship between them. The successful ruler was capable of imposing a dominant religious orthodoxy upon his subjects. Where this supreme orthodoxy did not pertain, vulnerability to witch panics was peculiarly intense. Between 1560 and 1660 it is estimated that about 100,000 witches were condemned, of whom about 30,000 were from Germany with a particular emphasis on small states with a troubled religious record. Persecutions were most intense in the frontier regions of heresy, that is, where two confessions met. Parts of Germany, Switzerland, France (particularly, it would seem, a belt running from Flanders to Lorraine) seem to have had the highest numbers in about three waves of repression. Scotland, England, northern Italy, Spain and Portugal were also affected. In Spain, the struggle against the witch paled beside the drive to eliminate Jews, *conversos* and Moors in the great racist purity of blood movement. Ireland knew no witch-hunts at all, perhaps because of the fragmented clan system; by the time the English occupation was effected, England had abandoned witch-persecution and was concentrating upon other evils of popery. When the French abandoned witchcraft persecution in the 1690s they turned immediately to more active repression of Protestantism, culminating in the Revocation of the Edict of Nantes. Viewing the situation overall, peaks of persecution were reached in the mid-fifteenth century, troughs occurred in the first half of the sixteenth century. Depending on the region, at any time from 1590 to 1690 the figures could suddenly shoot up and then subside without perfect correlation elsewhere. Then, beginning in France in 1682, legislation against witches enacted in the sixteenth century was repealed. The establishment, if not the populace, had lost interest in persecution.[10]

Witch persecutions, then, were geographically and chronologically circumscribed. If most Europeans believed in witches, most did not see a witch prosecuted in their village during their lifetime. However, in certain areas and at certain times, witch-hunts could be peculiarly intense and there was always the possibility that a plausible offender would be found.

The belief in witches still troubled several societies into the nine-teenth century. In England, Methodist communities with a heavy pre-ponderance of women were particularly infected. John Wesley believed fervently in witches, to the ridicule of Hogarth. As late as 1819 a witchcraft scare at Portland in Dorset divided the Methodists: the Revd

Francis Derry interrogated each church member and those who believed in witches were expelled from the society. Fifty or more of those thus expelled then founded a separate chapel. On this occasion, to quell the witchcraft scare, the secular authorities arrested individuals who had incited the local inhabitants to belief in black magic and to take action against 'witches' (old women, in this instance) who had 'overlooked' (seen or touched) their cattle or children with positively harmful results.[11] It is plain that the ultimate demise of the witchcraft phenomena as manifest before the courts depended on changing establishment attitudes and the infiltration of Enlightenment rationalism and scepticism among the educated classes. Elite culture and popular culture were radically severed by the end of the seventeenth century.

The Catholic church's acknowledgement and condemnation of witchcraft grew out of its continued battle against heresy which marked the late Middle Ages. This battle is manifest in a number of papal bulls culminating with the *Summis desiderantes affectibus* of Innocent VII (1484). For most of the fifteenth century the essence of witchcraft was not the damage done to other people, but its heretical character. Witches were allied with Cathars, Waldenses, and Béguines who, it was alleged, broke the traditions of the church, and the witches were defined as those who practised Devil worship or treated evil with respect. As the fifteenth century progressed, however, two works, the *Formicarius* (*c.*1437) of Johannes Nider and the *Malleus Maleficarum* (1486) of two German Dominicans, Krämer and Sprenger, took witchcraft theory much further. The first gave women a role in Devil sects as makers of potions and stealers of children, who were subsequently eaten or made into ointments which gave supernatural powers to the wearers. The second accentuated still further women's roles. The credulity of women, based on the preparedness of Eve to listen to the snake, their inability to keep silent and hence their habit of dragging others into their conspiracies, their insatiable lust which could prompt them even to accept the Devil as a lover, and their susceptibility to passion (hysteria) which made them vengeful, were all attributes which converted them into helpmates of the Devil.

Through women and their potions the Devil could inspire love or hate, render people impotent or incapable of sexual intercourse, or even cause them to believe they had been castrated. Witches could also change men into animals, possess them with devils, make them sicken and die, cause floods and hailstorms and fly mysteriously through the air. The two German Dominicans added a self-congratulatory postscript: 'Blessed be the most high who has so far preserved the male sex from such crime'.

The sexual obsessions of the friars are obvious to the twentieth-century reader, but many of their observations on the nature of witchcraft fit into established legends. They distilled many extant versions of the witch into one. The authors of *Malleus* also recommended a way for dealing with the witch. A denunciation or even a rumour could open a case and evidence might be accepted from children or personal enemies of the accused. In Roman law the judge was for certain crimes de facto prosecutor and the witch was subjected to an inquisitorial procedure in which she did not necessarily have the right to defend herself. Torture could be used to extract a confession, but the witch's failure to confess did not necessarily proclaim her innocence since this could be interpreted as a manifestation of the Devil's power.

The *Malleus* was very influential and served as inspiration for a spate of *Teufelbücher* (works about the Devil) which streamed from the early printing presses, particularly thick on the ground in Germany. Over the next twenty or thirty years, prints and woodcuts proliferated, some illustrating demonological treatises like Ulrich Molitor's *De Lamiis* (1489). The Freiburg drawings (1515–16) of Hans Baldung Grien were endlessly copied and his later paintings, notably *The Weather Witches* (1523) in which the female nude is portrayed in unambiguously pornographic pose, were influential in disseminating a corporal notion of the witch. In his drawings a relentless misogyny, pornography, fear and crude humour coexist. Pots of ointment made of infant flesh and other scatological ingredients to permit flight, hints of masturbation, sexual positions, desecration of the rosary, exist pell-mell. Delusion, corruptibility and the Devil's business are made one in the naked female flesh. *The Three Witches* (1514) in which a young witch peers at the viewer from between her legs with her buttocks set for anal sex and which has as a caption *Der Cor Capein ein gut Jahr* (Happy New Year to the Priest) is not easy to interpret. Is it intended to remind the priest of the omnipresence of evil and hence his job in the New Year? Or is it intended to indicate the collusion of the priest in evil?[12] Whatever the answer, Germany more than any other country would seem to have had a visual education in the evils of the female witch and the printing presses must be numbered among the forces promoting these beliefs. The relevant question is how the visual and literary imagery corresponded or failed to correspond with those actually accused of being witches.

The *Malleus*, a German production from the upper Rhineland (later a great centre of witch manufacture), went into several editions and translations although no theologian used it unquestioningly after 1520. Indeed, the Spanish Inquisition rejected many of its definitions. It was not translated into English until the modern period. Several of the issues it raised were subsequently deemed debateable, such as the interesting questions could witches fly and did they have sexual relations with the Devil? However, it formed the crude base from which several generations of lawyers, theologians and scholars subsequently refined witchcraft theory.[13] Writings on the theme proliferated and were debated in seminary, university and manor house. By 1580, when the great French lawyer Jean Bodin wrote his *Demonomanie*, he was able to present a fifteen-point schema. A witch was one guilty of any of the following crimes: a denial of God, cursing him, worshipping the Devil, dedicating children to him, murdering unbaptized children, pledging the unborn to Satan, telling others of the cult, honouring the Devil's oaths, incest, murdering men and little children to make broth, eating human flesh and drinking blood; killing people by spells and poison, killing cattle, causing infertility and famine, having sexual relations with the Devil. The Devil was always male, but was not necessarily perceived as a man. In fifteenth-century Spain he was depicted as a goat. Before 1645 in Essex, he appeared as a cat or a ferret.

Luther and Calvin ceded little to developing Catholic orthodoxy on the witch and her works. Luther's views on witches are found in his *Commentary on the Epistle to the Galatians*. If anything, his interests shifted away from the witch as a product of heresy towards the pact between the witch as an individual and the Devil. In Geneva the emphasis on heresy remained high, and the pact was an expression of that heresy. The emphasis on the pact made a tardy entry into northern Europe, including England, although the idea that the witch turned to the Devil for support and renounced God was not in doubt. The Elizabethan witch was a heretic but she was not usually said to be in direct contact with Satan. However, Keith Thomas found reference to an oral compact between the English witch and the Devil by 1612, and in the 1640s reference to a written covenant, and there are almost exact parallels of such a development throughout northern Europe.[14]

Catholic and Protestant orthodoxy alike condemned the convicted witch to death for collusion with the Devil. In northern Europe the emphasis was determined by actual *maleficium* or evidence of injury, and degrees of injury were taken into consideration in determining the length of prison sentence or whether the death penalty should be imposed. The latter was not used for lesser injury. This distinction was considered lax by zealots who wanted death for all witches.

In short, with the few distinctions of degree, we can say that throughout sixteenth- and early seventeenth-century Christendom it was heresy *not* to believe in witches. Witchcraft sermons were preached from the pulpit so that evolving witchcraft theory was openly disseminated. Tracts and treatises multiplied. If the aim was to deter the activity, the information also had the effect of introducing a wide populace to complex notions which began to alter their notion of the standard witch. Children in particular were inducted in a fear that witches could be after them, like Baba Yaga, interested in their flesh for consumption or their bodies for service. Children grew into men and women and carried their fears with them. In fact the religious establishment manufactured a 'model' witch and in continental Europe an inquisitorial procedure, backed by torture, framed questions (and hence answers) to conform to that model. In some areas the standard model witch created by the establishment begins to emerge quite distinctly in the legal dossiers. Furthermore, from the mid-fourteenth century the religious establishment was prepared to accept and to expect that the witch would usually be female. Secular authorities, who in fact handled most witchcraft trials, were intent on orthodoxy within their realms and they followed the church's instructions.

Culturally sixteenth-century élites concurred with the repression of the witch. Increasingly literate and tutored in church doctrine, they absorbed the debates of the day. They were also receptive, thanks to the Renaissance revival of Greek science and learning, to a misogynistic view of the female character which complemented the scriptural images of Eve, such as Aristotelian views of woman as 'botched' male, colder and therefore more compliant to the cold Devil than was the warmer man. The view of woman's physical composition gave a quasi-scientific explanation to the witchcraft phenomenon. Eve the tempted was inherently amenable to the Devil's influence. When he tempted her, rather than Adam, he knew what he was doing.

If the religious and civil establishments put into motion a witchcraft persecution, its momentum was sustained from below. Indeed, so intense was popular response that the hierarchy could only with difficulty contain it. Under a fifth of those accused of witchcraft by their neighbours in England were hanged. French, Belgian, German and Basque court judges recoiled before the volume of popular denunciations and sought to weed out fact from fiction.[15] If élites feared the witch, and there is evidence to show that many educated individuals did so, they perhaps located her in rural ignorance, poverty and squalor, not among themselves, either sister, wife, widowed mother or neighbour. When the masses accused a witch, on the other hand, they did so through imminent fear and rumour about someone in their community of whom they were apprehensive and whom they interpreted as having power to harm them. Unlike the prosecuting establishment, the populace wanted to prevent evils which the alleged witch might commit and looked to the courts to rescue them. The failure of the courts to accept fear alone, without evidence of either *maleficium* or on the Continent a confession or pact with the Devil, meant that some communities felt themselves still exposed to the witch. Occasionally in France doubting judges acted against their better judgement to preserve peace in the community.[16]

The blend of the scriptural, Renaissance science and misogynistic traditions emerges quite clearly when clerics and lawyers actually addressed themselves to the question of the sex of witches. When one Richard Barnard, a minister at Batcombe in Somerset, wrote *A Guide to Grand Jurymen about the Trial of Witches* in 1627, he stated:

There are more women witches than men and it may be for these reasons:-
First Satan his setting on these rather than men, since his unhappie outset and prevailing on Eve. Secondly, there more credulous nature, and apt to be misled and deceived. Thirdly, for that they are more superstitious and being displeased, more malicious, and so herein more fit instruments of the Devil. Fourthly, they are more tongue ripe, and less able to hide what they know from others: and therefore in this respect, are more ready to teachers of witchcraft to others, and to leave it to children, servants, or to some others than men. Fifthly and lastly, where they think they can command they are more proud in their rule, and more busy in setting such on worke whom they may command, than men, and therefore the Devil laboureth most to make them witches; because they, upon every light displeasure, will set him worke . . . which women will be ready enough to doe.

The instruction makes apparent how the differing elements in the cultural value system combined to create a model witch. The first four come directly from the *Malleus* – the first is also purely biblical; the second and third repose on the view of the lack of reason in the physical composition, but also reflect some of the observations of great medieval churchmen such as Aquinas who thus sought to devalue female commitment to Christianity; the fourth picks up the Pauline injunction to silence and the tradition of the scold, the nagging wife, but also savours of neo-Platonic science; and the fifth one may be no more than the Revd Mr Barnard's private conviction.

The British historian and anthropologist Alan Macfarlane has insisted that it was the attributes of the witch rather than the attributes of her sex which condemned her, as evinced by the fact that about a fifth of British witches were men. Yet there can be no doubt that witchcraft philosophy encouraged the expectation of witchcraft as a female not a male attribute. Notice, for example, how easily Thomas Ady in 1656 slips into the female when he alleges that a person when hurt assumes himself to be bewitched.

> For saith he, such an old man or woman came lately to my door and desired some relief, and I denied it and God forgive me, my heart did rise against *her* at that time, my mind gave me *she* looked like a witch and presently my Child, my Wife, my Self, my Horse . . . was thus and thus handled [my italics].[17]

A poor beggar at the door was three times likelier to be a woman than a man. Moreover, witchcraft was regarded as transmissible by matrilinear inheritance. A mother passed the knowledge on to a daughter – the witch's get (offspring) of Scottish parlance – though not necessarily to a son. Everything contrived to make women dominate in the witch statistics of most jurisdictions.

When we turn from theory to what actually happened in manorial and ecclesiastical courts, important national and regional differences are visible. In areas of Roman law torture could be used to elicit a confession. Words could be put into the witch's mouth. The judge was inquisitor. In areas of customary law individual denunciation was the rule and the judge had no special inquisitorial powers, nor was torture used. Hence in England and the Netherlands those accused of witchcraft appear with few trappings.[18] Here is a simpler, more prosaic witch; one who could not fly or mysteriously transport herself to a hidden place for a coven or witches' sabbath. If she had familiars they were usually straight out of the farmyard, cat or dog, rat or toad, but not a crimson or blue toad specially bedecked for evil intent. Her alleged involvement with the Devil pivoted on the belief of her accusers that she could summon him to perform a malicious deed (*maleficium*) and may also have rested on allegations of a pact with the Devil symbolized by a 'mark' such as an extra nipple or a patch insensitive to 'pricking'. However, the assertion of sexual orgies with the Devil, knowledge of the coldness of his body and details of grotesque fertility rites are almost unknown to the English courts. Here the witch trial was that of someone who was alleged to have committed *maleficium*, an evil deed, and had fallen foul of her neighbours, who sought to rid themselves of her presence by converting her into an enemy of God.

Such a figure exists in continental Europe as well, but could be outnumbered during phases of 'witch panics' in which mass denunciations occurred and 'possession' by the Devil on a large scale affecting village children (more rarely adults) was claimed.

The question 'who were the witches?' is most easily answered for Britain. Here the witch was a poor (though in Scotland perhaps a little less poor) old woman (average age 60) who had in some ways fallen foul of her neighbours and who had had recourse to a curse, a means of invoking the Devil which had been followed by misfortune falling upon the accursed. The first time such an utterance fell from her lips with alleged evil consequences witchcraft was not established, but the incident passed into village memory to be used as confirmatory evidence on another occasion. The line between cursing and 'scolding' (a malicious tongue) was a fine one. Their 'chief fault' wrote Reginald Scot of witches 'is that they are scolds',[19] meaning that their tongues were the means whereby the suspicion of being a witch was aroused. If charged and acquitted of sorcery on a particular occasion, the suspicions of the community were not necessarily allayed but passed into the bank of folk memory until the next time the woman's invocations were followed by disaster. In the interim she would be watched and debarred from public places.

After a woman was slandered as a witch at Devizes in 1653, local bakers refused to bake her dough (the association of witchery with bread that did not rise continued in Lancashire lore until the nineteenth century). Goodie Gilnot, similarly defamed in Kent in 1641, said, 'if she be esteemed such a kind of creature everybody will be afraid of her, and nobody set her a-work, in as much as she will be utterly undone'. Sarah Liffen of Great Yarmouth in 1719 'was so forlorn and wretched a person as she labour'd under the imputation of being a witch, and the youth and other rude folks in the town . . . did often insult and affront her as she walk'd out her own house.' (The last case suggests a distancing on the part of the lawyers from the conduct of the towns-people in favour of the woman in question.) Once a woman has acquired the reputation of being a witch she need no longer open her mouth. A glance became sufficent to transmit a curse. She 'overlooked' cattle or children and they fell sick: she 'overlooked' a haystack and it burst into flames during the night.[20]

As well as being old and poor, in Britain two-thirds of the women accused were either widowed or spinsters. They might have children, but the majority were seeking to eke out a living *on their own*. They hence fell outside patriarchal protection or, perhaps equally pertinently, their situation of semi-dependence on the community exposed them to the imputation of witchcraft. Some were in receipt of poor relief; others were illegally pasturing a goat or other livestock, others arousing their neighbours' ire through thefts of fruit or firewood. The phenomenon is hence related to the predicament of women alone. If married they had impecunious or disabled husbands. It should also perhaps be related to the economy of expedients. Those who uttered curses were likely to be physically powerless, economically disadvantaged women, trapped in a particular situation. Such women sought alms and were refused by a wealthier neighbour who subsequently suffered a misfortune. Or they were women found in situations technically on the wrong side of the law wishing to deter legal action. When a woman uttered a curse it was in furtherance either of a request – give me or I will do the following – or to express anger at refusal, or to prevent reprisals for an illegal action in which she had been apprehended. The curse viewed in this light lent power to the otherwise relatively powerless. For those tacking together a precarious livelihood it might have allowed them to pasture a cow or goat illegally or to steal a little hay without action. The efficacy of a curse depends on a belief system and belief in witches in itself may have helped some women to survive. This may explain why many Scottish widows, charged outside the courts with being witches by those who had been cursed, returned 'Ye say that I am'.[21]

In a period when witchcraft persecutions were to be feared, such a rejoinder seems at least foolish. Yet the odds on a prosecution for witchcraft occurring in one parish more than a couple of times in a century were low, and immediate survival may have been deemed much more important. Some Scottish women accused of witchcraft had lived with the reputation long enough to have titles. Walker the Witch was active in Inverkeithing in 1631; Janet Taylor at Stirling in 1634 responded to the title of the 'Witch of Monza'. Deafness could contribute to the reputation since it produced odd behaviour. The woman tried as Deiff Meg in Berwick in 1634 had had a longstanding reputation for oddity of which she was, for obvious reasons, unaware. Others, calculating on lending a degree of fear to their curses, used the preface 'If I be a witch then . . .'. Such insouciance, as it may seem, to the possible penalties for witchcraft either argues for the need to relieve pressing economic imperatives by the inculcation of fear, with a disregard for the imminence of such punishment, or it suggests a conviction that the Devil would look after his own. Of those Scottish women who confessed to a pact with the Devil (in many instances under torture, so it is impossible to estimate how many of them were really convinced they were witches), the Devil made them a single promise: *that they should not want*. How many poor women alone must have lived with the perpetual fear of want in mind?

It is perhaps significant that the witch phase is coincident with attempts to change or reform traditional charitable practice throughout Europe. Voluntary alms-giving, the recommended recourse of the Catholic church buttressed by alms from ecclesiastical revenues, was under demographic pressure and economic change. European states faced with the problem sought to define the deserving and undeserving poor. In the case of England the poor became the responsibility of the parish which was authorized to levy a local rate through which the domiciled poor could be aided. However, parishes responded with varying degrees of commitment. The poor were the burden of their neighbours. Help was grudgingly given. Furthermore, the Protestant ethic, particularly in its Calvinist and Puritan forms, associated prosperity with godliness and misfortune with sin. Keith Thomas relates how a female sectary admitted during the Interregnum that she fell into a religious depression when she saw her neighbours enjoy greater prosperity than she did, for it could only mean they prayed at home with greater assiduity. The careful line drawn between deserving and undeserving poor and the obligation to Christian charity coexisted with the belief that to be poor was a judgement from the Almighty: the poor had only themselves to blame for their idleness and improvidence. A failure to put their trust in God through the medium of prayer was responsible for their predicament. In Nicolas de Maes' paintings of old women alone, some sit with a spinning wheel; one with eyes closed in silent prayer before a loaf and a herring. Virtue is rewarded by sufficiency. But where did this leave the poor woman who could spin all day and not earn enough for her upkeep and for whom a regular loaf and herring and a roof above her head were not assured?

A close look at individual witches reveals the precariousness of their lives. However, this was not readily perceivable to their accusers. They interpreted the witch as a power-figure able to harm at will, who held the community to a terrible ransom. Isabella de Moerloose reveals with frightening clarity how a belief in witches influenced her relationship with her mother who feared her child (born with a caul) was under the influence of the Devil and perhaps a witch in the making. Encouraged by the parish priest she beat and closely watched the child, fearful of manifestations of devilry and with a view to protecting her daughter from the Devil's agents.[22] That individuals and communities feared the witch and acted against her as a measure of self-protection we can have little doubt. That their fear was enhanced by individual or collective guilt following a mean or thoughtless action, a denial of charity or failure to overlook a misdemeanour, is equally apparent. The putative witch's only ally was the belief in the eternal quality of evil, that to harm her was to invite reprisal by the Devil, but this was not an infallible shield. Hence, the witch represented a social conundrum: she was there because society believed her to be there, and because it believed in her powers she had a measure of power.

On the other hand, we cannot know how consciously an individual came to believe she was a witch and how far she was the product of her own beliefs or of exterior pressures which may have persuaded her she had some power. The women who screamed curses, the 'tongue-ripe', the scolds, were perhaps reacting as positively as they could against their poverty and sense of social worth. Christian charity had proved frail support: the Devil perhaps could do no worse.

Such an approach must perforce be speculative, because the thought processes of those who lived with hunger and cold are not obvious and yield themselves with difficulty to the historian. Yet 'He promised I should nae want . . .', 'Je ne manquerai de rien . . .', the phrase occurs in every European language in the mouths of the women who confessed collusion with the Devil and could almost be interpreted as the last hopeful straw to be clutched at by the drowning. It has to be viewed in the context of a society which saw poverty as a judgement, in which those who in normal times had something lived in perpetual fear of those who had nothing, and where those who trod the line between poverty and destitution were perpetually apprehensive of the force of disaster which seemed attributable to supernatural powers.

Poverty perhaps also bred its own kind of defiance – known in Scotland as *smeddum*, the propensity to answer back, the refusal of deference. The classic case of a Scottish witch trial was perhaps that of Janet MacMurdoch (probably a widow since her husband, James Hendrie, is never mentioned), a subtenant of the laird of Broughtone. Her first trouble in 1665 was with his baron-baillie for non-payment of rent. When he impounded livestock she 'promised him an evil turn' and he shortly afterwards lost a cow and a calf. When challenged with causing the event she promised him worse, and soon after, his child died of sweating sickness. John Murray, a bonnet laird (owner-occupier), had caused Janet to fall 'by one accidental twitch of the foot' (a euphemism for kicking her violently?), and five or six weeks later two of his calves turned mad and died. Robert Brown alleged that in 1668 he had turned Janet's cattle off his grass where they were illegally pasturing and she told him he should not have so many cattle of his own to eat his grass. Within a year he had lost fifteen. Another landowner had impounded some of her livestock for illegal pasturing: the next day his child died in a peat bog. William Gordon, another substantial farmer, also lost cattle after chasing Janet's stock off his land. The woman employing Janet's daughter accused her of using her mother's devilish tricks, only to be visited by Janet who asked 'why called you me and my daughter witches, for you shall have something better to think on'. Her husband fell ill within the fortnight and after Janet came to the house and was given food and drink he suddenly grew better. The critical issue came in 1667 when an altercation occurred between Janet and Jean Sprot. This time Jean had let her cow steal some of Janet's grass. The cow sickened and died. Jean's husband then caught Janet in his barnyard on the sabbath with a sheaf of corn. He reproved her (for working on the sabbath) and she 'bade the divill pyk out his eyn'. The following week he contracted a disease and died, after Janet had refused to come to the house to remove the curse and restore his health. Janet when accused did not defend herself, though she accused Jean Sprot: 'she was a witch as well as herself'.[23]

Janet was obviously a problem to the community. Behind in her rent, with insufficient grazing, she had an undesirable habit of borrowing and not returning. She was not coping with running her holding. She was ill-tempered. Most of her accusers had higher social status than she – though Jean Sprot, who turned her in, was probably equally badly off, 'a witch as well as herself'. Above all, Janet was aggressive and defiant, perhaps making an 'ego prop out of the label of witch'. Not only had she lost the sympathy of her superiors but of the community as a whole. That loss of sympathy was probably critical in determining the bringing of this old woman to court. Though the norm was for the witch to be accused by those slightly higher than herself in the social scale, to be accused by an exalted social personage *alone* would probably not secure conviction. Villages could be split when the slightly more affluent in times of misery found themselves apprehensive of the have-nots.[24]

Janet MacMurdoch's case involved no graphic details of trips on broomsticks or references to sexual intercourse with the Devil. She did not deny the charges and conviction followed swiftly. The starkness of her trial contrasts strikingly with that of Jeannette Clerc, a farmer's wife from a village near Geneva, charged in 1539 with much the same deeds as Janet. She was declared responsible for the death of a neighbour's cow; a horse went mad because she bit it; two oxen refused to work after she quarrelled with the owner; two people were poisoned, one by an apple Jeannette gave her and another by a meal she cooked for her – both recovered. The critical issue, however, was the death of a relative of her husband when Jeannette threw a powder given to her by the Devil into his face. Two weeks of intense interrogations by lawyers with an intellectual baggage stuffed with witchcraft theory resulted in a confession from this simple woman stating how she had succumbed to the Devil in a rage following the loss of a pair of shoes. She then attended diabolical assemblies where she was recruited by a black Devil who promised her all the money she should want, committed anal intercourse with her ('in the back like animals') and made her renounce God. She danced and sang at the meeting and was given a stick with a box of grease which when rubbed, would carry her anywhere she wanted to go. She acknowledged all the *maleficia* with which she was charged and was beheaded. Did she panic at the charges and agree to them under cross-examination by sophisticated lawyers who put words into her mouth? Did she really believe that she had done these things? Certainly, like many other poor women brought up on tales of witches, she appears to have made matters worse for herself by admissions to her inquisitors under torture, and having been drawn into an admission she went on to embellish it under further questioning. [25]

Among those accused of *maleficium* appear healers who dabbled in white magic, and in Germany midwives or the *Kindbetthelferinnen* (childbed helpers) of larger villages constitute a significant minority (four out of eighteen cases at Augsburg between 1625 and the end of the century). [26] In Britain healers constituted a small percentage of the accused, but in Lorraine, for example, the villages would seem to have been replete with 'healers' who during a witch panic could find themselves the target of accusations. That said, there is no reason to suppose that the use of charms and potions diminished over the period. The ideal of the church was that prayer and approved medicine should be the recourse of the despairing and that the will of God could not be changed or modified except by individual prayer. Protestantism in particular admitted no alternative to a personal plea to God: Catholicism at least offered the intercession of saints, the use of reliquaries and holy water and the magic of the host. Under such circumstances, popular recourse to 'white' magic was scarcely diminished and the gaoler of Canterbury who released a woman accused of white witchcraft in the 1640s on the grounds that she had done more good than the combined efforts of doctor and parson is perhaps indicative of popular sentiment.

Of the German lying-in maids who found themselves before the courts in Augsburg the case of Anna Ebeler perhaps includes all the ingredients which led to a prosecution and death. She was in her sixties and had helped in the birth of many children until accused of poisoning a parturient mother who became delirious (indicating to a twentieth-century mind the symptoms of puerperal fever), but was coherent enough to make a denunciation before expiring. When the tale was told other women who had employed Anna came forward, claiming that their milk had dried up and their child had starved to death; another baby had broken out in pustules or blisters and his brother also fell sick and died; yet another had died with a piteous skin disease and the mother's menstruation had stopped. Anna was tortured and made the standard narrative confession.

It is easy to see in the accusations the terrible apprehensions women had in childbed and the shattering impact of child loss. The arbitrariness of parturition and the failure to produce milk, the lack of understanding of the ravages of venereal disease on the child or of undernourishment leading to rickets (producing a bent child), are all reflected in the denunciations. Someone was to blame for the disaster and a scapegoat is at hand: the old woman present at the delivery.

If the old and poor dominate the records, they are not alone, particularly in eastern France and Germany. A further, though far less numerous, type of person was the young, poor and largely uneducated teenage girl. Some such women could be depicted as 'simple', of low intelligence. They had absorbed stories of witchery from childhood onwards, and when they were accused, they perhaps believed they had intended harm to a victim. Regina Bartholomew of Augsburg in 1670, at the age of 21, claimed the Devil whom she had met for the last five years in a tavern was her lover and her father. He took the form of a nobleman in silken hose and the two enjoyed sausage, roast pork and beer together. For his love she had forsworn God and the Trinity and signed a seven-year pact. These astonishing revelations were made, not as a result of accusations – for her neighbours merely thought the girl strange and a bit touched – but as the result of her own confession in the midst of a case concerning her threat to kill a young woman about to marry one of her father's lodgers.

Regina's case history was that of a young girl, sexually abused by an older man in her early teens, abandoned by her mother who had had an adulterous affair with Regina's cousin, been banished from the town for scandalous behaviour and died of drink. Regina took her mother's place, did the drudgery around the house and fell in love with one of the lodgers, who did not return her affections but brought his young bride to the house and fondled her in front of Regina. Regina believed herself both to have been given and to have administered love potions. She was clearly deeply unhappy, unloved by parent, rejected by the object of her fancy and passionately jealous of the girl who had taken what she deemed to be her place in his affections. At her initial appearance before the judge she threw out random accusations implicating all the men in her life – especially her father. She even added threats of suicide (in a society which believed this a deep sin), but it was her account of a meeting with the Devil which ultimately led the judges of Augsburg to administer torture or threats of torture. This led to the admission that she had bought a yellow powder from the apothecary to poison her father by mixing it in his soup at the Devil's instruction.

By her sixth interrogation she had confessed to attempted arson, to trying also to poison the bride of the cruel young man, and of having 'ridden the beasts' at Groggingen, causing them to sicken and die.

None of these stories had any shred of evidence to back them up. The neighbours were puzzled; even the shepherds of Groggingen could only attest to healthy living cattle. Her father said that he had always found his daughter a bit strange. However, he did not deny the possibility that she was a witch, nor that she evinced an unnatural hatred of him. He abandoned her, in short, to her accusers. Between Regina and her interrogators, men of greater education and sophistication than herself, was a complicated relationship. They put questions and followed up leads she gave them. At first frenzied imagination led her into confessions and the creation of scenes in the courtroon which may have satisfied a need to vent the pent-up rage within her. They helped frame and shape her responses. Her strangeness made possession by the Devil seem plausible. Her alleged proclivity to resort to poison – viewed as a female crime – made her a potential social menace and her rejection of paternal authority represented by her judges perhaps rendered her most troubling of all. Regina was a woman no man would speak for in a city where women were denied the right to live alone.[27]

Some European societies were more confident of their ability to deal with the witch than others and were prepared to commit informal acts of violence against them to reduce their influence. Hence Andrew Camp, suspecting Goodwife Bailey of having bewitched his children in 1661, dragged the woman out of her house, bruising her back, 'and when he had her so under him his wife came out and said she would claw her eyes out of her head and her tongue out of her mouth and she called her a damned . . . old witch'.[28] It was popularly believed that if an injured party could draw blood out of a witch then her curse was lifted, and there are many cases of individuals sticking thorns, needles, bodkins, and knives into suspected witches before they turned to the judicial process. Perhaps, as they saw it, they were taking the solution into their own hands. It could, after all, be a costly business to take a witch to court, particularly if you lost. Yet such activities suggest that the British witch was deemed a far less powerful person than her French or Basque counterpart. French villagers feared that such intervention might only bring down the Devil's wrath upon them. When the Church read out *Monitoires*, warnings that those who knew of a witch and did not report her would be excommunicated, villages frequently tried to prevent the reading lest any listening witch should cause hail to fall. The greater frequency of summer hail in hilly and mountainous regions of continental Europe gave the putative witch an edge over her British counterpart in the range of immediate disasters she could allegedly summon to fall upon an individual or an entire community. Even in prison it was assumed that the Devil still had access to his followers and that the witch who still pleaded her innocence was abetted by her master.

Any attempt to create a standard model witch disintegrates during witch panics or when there were mass denunciations by the 'possessed'. On such occasions, the social origins and the sex of witches could change. Witch-hunts could be officially conducted in Catholic countries on the Continent by the Inquisition itself, by its appointed delegates, or by diviners – cunning men who alleged they knew how to recognize a witch and in some instances had a monetary interest in leading a successful prosecution. Such diviners, however, were treading snared ground. Neither the Inquisition nor civil authorities welcomed their intervention and many in France found themselves punished by a spell in the galleys: in a few instances they were even accorded the death penalty. A hunt could provoke a panic, a belief that everyone dwelt surrounded by witches ready to direct their evil intentions towards property and children. At such a time there was no need for a curse to activate an accusation: a look or the existence of a personal vendetta might be sufficient. Allegations of possession might precede the panic. Parents would anxiously interrogate their children and watch for 'signs' of possession. Tantrums or impetuous gestures such as flinging a holy book to the floor or blasphemous utterances could be explained by circumstances beyond a child's control. Childhood fantasies and dreams, fostered no doubt by fantastic tales and rumours of ever-present witchery, fuelled the endeavour. Once 'possession' had been established, the child or individual was made a great fuss of until exorcism had banished the evil spirit from the body. The 'possessed' individual could, however, before or after exorcism, incriminate neighbours or even relatives in alleged diabolical practices.

A witch-hunt conducted by a judge, de Lancre, backed by the parlement of Bordeaux in 1609 seems to have started the panic in the Basque country which led to claims of witchery on a large scale implicating more than 3000 villagers. These massive panics appear to have been set in train by a young maidservant new to the area who told tales of mountains full of witches and diabolic covens. A wholesale manufacture of witches of all ages and both sexes occurred, the product of panic fantasies, infantile fear and imagination enhanced by confessions extracted under torture or with the threat of torture. The Spanish Inquisition when presented with large-scale events of this nature usually gave mild punishments or released the accused. On this particular occasion, Salazar y Frias, the witches' advocate, represented a growing number of churchmen and civil officials, lawyers and judges, who, as the seventeenth century progressed, began to question not the existence of a power for evil but whether those actually accused of *maleficium* or heresy were truly in contact with that power. They were shrewd enough to perceive that inquisitorial techniques and professional witch-hunters created witches.[29]

The problem was how to arrest or modify the groundswell of denunciations from below which the religious and secular establishment had themselves set in train. While there existed a body of legislation to cope with the witch, they could not withhold judgement in the face of insistent village testimony. Both the French parlements and British judges, however, progressively abandoned a commitment to witchcraft prosecution, largely because they mistrusted the accusers, before the enactment of the legislation removing the crime of witchcraft from the statute book. The Spanish Inquisition strove to stem the momentum of denunciations and the Inquisition itself in north Italy purged the witch-hunters by charging them with the crime of which they had accused others. Such an exercise was largely designed to give the church central control of what it perceived to be a fabricated witch flow. By the end of the seventeenth century the growth of rationalism among the educated classes, who counted both judges and ecclesiastics among their number, also encouraged the abandonment of witchcraft persecution, though this ran counter to popular desires. Throughout, the momentum of persecution was sustained from below.

The question of who denounced the witch has evoked much debate. The accusers were both men and women, but women were fervent denouncers, perhaps particularly if they believed the witch responsible for the death of a child. Indeed, in the English cases after 1590, women predominate.[30] Moreover, they would appear to have clung to such beliefs longer than did men. Methodism was a woman's faith and one which held on to a physical Devil and the witch as his agent into the nineteenth century. The female accusers belong to the same, or virtually the same, socio-economic grouping as the accused. They too often survive by 'an economy of expedients' and in some cases saw the alleged witch as a poacher on their territory, threatening their precarious livelihood or taking an unfair share of the frail charitable or other pickings of the village. In this respect the accusation of Jean Sprot against Janet MacMurdoch was entirely typical. Jean Sprot was in this instance the offender: she stole from Janet, but threw her weight behind accusations made against her. When Janet said she was a witch, no charges were brought against her because Jean had already aligned herself with the accusers.

In singling out as the perpetrator of *maleficium* a particular type of woman, the old, the widow, the deformed, deaf, one-eyed, toothless, the woman in isolation, the one whose limited earning power and consequent poverty had made her a social liability for the community, the most tragic aspects of the female predicament were converted into a potential capital offence. These women came before the courts because of their dependence on the community, their weakness, not their self-sufficiency. They were those in the habit of going 'from house to house and door to door for a potfull of milk, yeast, drink, pottage or some such relief without which they could hardly live'.[31] In doing so they put themselves at terrible risk.

CHAPTER TEN

―――――◄○►―――――

Obedient to Thy Will

Spend much time in church . . . the rest of the day commit
to spiritual causes such as attending the School of Christian
Doctrine to teach the little girls. Then visit the sick and
poor women of the parish . . . then find a quiet church
for prayer. Join a charitable congregation for women . . .
on feast days do not frequent the piazzas and busy streets or
waste time in useless visits.

PALEOTTI, SERMON ON MARRIAGE, 1580

FOR THE reformers of both camps, the work of purification of
belief and practice did not end with an attack on vestigial
paganism or on sexual sin. The goal was a Christian society
characterized by doctrinal orthodoxy and unfaltering obedience to
God's authority as interpreted by the church of the particular
confession. Scripture and in the Catholic case the traditional beliefs
of the church were to be put to work with a new vigour. The letter of
the commandments was re-examined, not least with reference to such
prescriptions as 'Honour thy father and thy mother' which was given
by both sides a wider interpretation to mean obedience to all
hierarchies and the obligation of those in authority to deal in a just
manner with those under their control. The enormity of sin was
driven home and the aberrant made conscious of their faults had to
bear the weighty burden of guilt until God's pardon had been obtained.
The hard path to salvation was outlined with exceptional clarity.
Popular pastimes were scrutinized and came under prohibitions in
a movement aptly labelled by Peter Burke 'the triumph of Lent'– a
triumph of very limited extent. In one form or another, through
sermons, printed texts or pictures, a battle was waged for the minds
and bodies of the masses in order to promote the well-being of the soul.

Neither the reformers nor the human material which they sought to mould started with minds which were *tabulae rasae*. The religion of the early modern world both before and after the Catholic and Protestant Reformations was essentially of a contractual nature: 'Dear God, I am doing *this* on the clear understanding that you too will abide by the rules and respond *thus*.' The hold of the clergy over the people was their claim to know those rules because the church of their persuasion was the repository of divine truth. They also knew how to trade on the fear of eternal damnation and even the temporary hell of purgatory. The pre-Reformation church in the main coexisted with ignorance and pagan practice in which the rules had become obscured or entangled in a confused popular credulity. The church itself had exploited this cred- ulity through the sale of pardons and indulgences, which allowed those with money to buy exemption from purgatory, through false miracles such as the Blood of Hailes (allegedly ever fresh but in fact regularly renewed by the monks) to bolster the tourist traffic, and by blatant flouting of the rules of personal conduct by those in the highest authority – behaviour which was to survive the efforts of both sets of reformers. What was needed was for the church to put itself in order, to serve as example and then to bring the flock whose untutored faith it had abused with it into a new purity. Then, after reforming itself, the job of the newly informed clergy was to impart orthodoxy and the right view of salvation. However, it started from the knowledge of an existing bed- rock of faith.[1]

Along with this foundation of faith, the religion of the peoples of Europe was strongly permeated by an entire pattern of life stretching from the moment of baptism to that of death. Religion shaped the week and the season. It provided sociability and diversion. For women, it was virtually the only focal point of their lives outside the house and the working environment. No society south of the Loire allowed respectable women into the social life of the hostelry and even north of that important line, it was not usually a place for women except perhaps at fairs or on public holidays provided they were in the right company. The well and the washplace, where such existed, and yet more the market were each in their way a part of the working week of ordinary women, but the church belonged to the leisured moments of life, to Sundays, religious festivals and the great ceremonies of life and death which had a public expression. Many of the festivals were marked by special meals: Cattern cake for Saint Catherine's day; Simnel cake for

Easter; pancakes on Shrove Tuesday as a preparation for the Lenten fast
and a multitude of local specialities to mark Epiphany or the end of
Lent. There were the rituals of cleaning and dressing one's family on
Sundays and festivals. For many Mediterranean women, above the poorest levels of society, participating in the Mass was the only public outing
of the day or week. Festivals, kermesses, took everyone out of doors.
Women not only transmitted and helped to shape these rituals, but
depended on them for much appreciated contact with the wider family
and friends.

Religion and entertainment were intertwined. Indeed, there was an
entire panoply of spectacles performed by alleged 'living saints',[2] who
claimed mystical experiences and paraded stigmata and never-healing
wounds or claimed they never ate or were sustained only by the wafer
of the host. Many of these people were women and they adopted a
lifestyle associated with certain saints.

Although the Roman church had, throughout its existence, demonstrated a gloomy view of womanhood in general, it recognized sanctity
in some. As the calendar stood in 1500 there were about three male
saints to every woman. The female saint fell into a number of very
predictable and chronologically differentiated types. In the days of the
early church there had been martyrs and those who challenged evil by
miraculous means. Saint Margaret, who cut herself out of the stomach
of a dragon with a crucifix, was still actively venerated as the patron
saint of childbed. There followed medieval abbesses and queens conspicuous for the foundation of monasteries and churches or hospitals.
From the thirteenth century onwards, however, sanctity moved downwards in the social scale. Quite lowly, illiterate women whose lives
were marked by extreme fasting, their virgin status and sometimes by
mystical trances, visionary experiences, holy writings and above all by
the appearance on their bodies of stigmata or never-healing wounds,
appear in the calendar. The most outstanding of these mystics who also
helped the sick and the poor was Saint Catherine of Siena (1347-80).
Through her writings, dictated because she was illiterate, recounting
her visions and ecstasies she became one of the great spiritual leaders
of the later Middle Ages and a model for emulation.

As well as the few who were later canonized, there were many more
who had reputations as 'Holy Maids', or as they have been subsequently
dubbed 'living saints', who persuaded their communities that they were
endowed with special favours from God. They gained local and indeed

some international fame on the grounds that they lived without food, could fall into trances and have visions, bore marks of God's favour such as wounds which never healed, or could prophesy. Some were tertiaries, that is women who did not have the means or the intent to enter a convent but were devoted to a religious life and were loosely attached to the Dominican and Franciscan orders who were supposed to control them and see that they did not run to excess. They seem to have been particularly common in Italy, where they were drawn from high as well as low social levels. The Spanish and Portuguese *beata* is cast in the same image. She was a holy woman and a tertiary, but usually very poor, who begged her bread and helped those even poorer than herself by sharing with them all she had. She might, or might not, demonstrate certain characteristics associated with the mystic – babbling or raving and claiming she had had a vision or a conversation with a member of the holy family – and she might seek to raise the spiritual level of her village. As long as she did not get too powerful the local authorities, including the parish priest, would tolerate her activities. Later, when the Counter-Reformation was more fully advanced, she would not be allowed to continue for very long before being pronounced by the authorities a *delusa*, usually a discrediting process rather than one which led to burning at the stake.[3]

In Portugal about half and in Spain something under a third of those who came before the Inquisition between the sixteenth and the eighteenth centuries were women and, setting aside the *conversas* (New Christians indicted for clinging to Judaic practices), they fell into this *beata/delusa* category. Such a woman was Maria Vaz from Evora in the Alentejo, who in 1597, confident in her status as a respected local *beata*, shouted out in the cathedral where all were gathered for Mass: 'In the name of the Father, Son and Holy Spirit, God sends me that I should say that within three months the prelates and the clergy must die by iron, fire and blood.' When her confessor fell ill she told him he must die. He promptly did so and the locals were very impressed. The Lisbon Inquisitors opined that she should be punished for falsely claiming divine revelations. However, they did not believe the Devil to be involved and she does not seem to have got more than a short prison sentence.[4]

Some of the *beatas* and 'living saints' who claimed to be nourished by communion wafers were obviously anorexic, some were secret eaters and confidence tricksters. The episodes in which both male and female pretenders to sanctity were involved tax the modern imagination to the full. Take Magdalen Beutlerin di Kenzigen, a former Poor Clare who claimed visions of the infant Jesus and whose last really public act was to prophesy her own death on a determined day in 1430. A large crowd gathered for the event, to take place in church, the spectators including church dignitaries from Freiburg and Strasbourg. For ten days previously she had eaten nothing and was already in a trance, but at the appointed hour she came to her senses and declared that God had proclaimed a miracle to prevent her death. If the masses were persuaded, the authorities doubted, but three years later she was still claiming visions of being baptized with the blood of the Lamb of God and over the next twenty years periodically performed with trances and prophecies before an enthralled crowd.[5]

Perhaps more important than sociability and entertainment, however, was the business of solace in religion. There existed a popular pantheon of so-called saints and holy women whose help could be solicited, for example, to comfort a wronged wife. Of these, the most noteworthy to survive the hand of the Counter-Reformation was the cult of Saint Rita of Cascia, saint of healing and suffering but also of the battered wife, who held out a promise of delivery to the victim. In twentieth-century Italy her cult still outstripped that of the Virgin herself.[6] In addition, religion provided hope and a measure of comfort for the suffering in face of personal and collective disaster. *A peste fame et bello libera nos domine*, the oft reiterated medieval prayer requesting protection from plague, famine and war, still had relevance. In societies which lived in fear, where crop failure, epidemic disease and attendant social dislocation induced by poverty were real and imminent threats, the church was in the business of solace and succour. The arbitrariness of such phenomena, in particular that of personal illness, helped to strengthen the hold. One had to live in hope and hope was part of the package.

While the importance of hope, solace and succour should not be underestimated, nor should the appreciation that adherence to the rules might bring an ultimate reward. Breaking the rules would almost certainly bring eternal punishment and this belief was a significant element in popular mentalities. When the reformers went to work they started from faith, they exploited fear and they promised hope. The populace was told to trust the reformers with their souls, give obedience and salvation would follow.

The main intellectual debates of the sixteenth and most of the seventeenth centuries pivoted on interpretations of Scripture and questions of religious allegiance, and a chasm opened up in Europe separating those who continued to look to Rome and to the traditions of the church as prime authorities from those who rejected the authority of the papacy in favour of a Protestant confession. The breach which began with the actions of a German Augustinian canon, Martin Luther, in time splintered further and there emerged Zwinglians, Calvinists who in turn divided creating congregations committed to a particular and sometimes distinct interpretation of the Bible. Such were Anabaptists, Moravians, Quakers, Methodists, to name merely a few of those subdivisions which grew almost exponentially before the end of the period, each commanding different allegiances, different congregations. States in the process of tighter formation adopted a particular confession and endorsed its interpretation by outlawing others.

The desire for state uniformity in matters of religion intermingled with dynastic ambitions and allegiances and fuelled political conflict. In Spain, Portugal, and Italy the Catholic church received no serious challenge from Protestantism; France experienced serious conflict in the sixteenth century when Protestant influences from Switzerland penetrated the Rhône valley before percolating into northern France and the west. This conflict was in part resolved by an uneasy Catholic dominance leaving the Protestant communities exposed and Protestantism in the role of a fortress faith to be further undermined and ousted in 1687 by the Revocation of the Edict of Nantes. This stormy mixed experience made the French record very distinctive. In the other camp were parts of Germany, Holland, Scandinavia and Britain. In Germany princely commitment and the endorsement of Protestantism by several cities established Lutheranism, but it soon rubbed shoulders with differing Protestant groups and sects. In the Netherlands religious change was closely linked with nationalism and the throwing off of Spanish rule. In Scotland, Calvinism was closely linked with the rejection of an unpopular French connection. The southern Netherlands and Ireland defined themselves as Catholic, but whereas in the first case foreign politics endorsed that choice and helped sustain Catholic orthodoxy, the English as overlords of Ireland sought to crush what was discerned as a threat to Protestant hegemony in mainland Britain and in so doing cemented a relationship between Irish nationalism and Catholicism. The early modern period was also that in which some European nations were reaching out to the conquest of new empires which posed new religious challenges. The Spanish embarked upon the christianization of South America, a triumph for Catholicism, while a century later the sectarian refugees of Protestant Europe streamed into North America.

Religion, politicized and aggressive, gave the early modern period much of its dynamic and caught up in the turbulence were the lives of ordinary people as well as of princes and clerics. For almost two centuries, the grip of religion tightened over the populace. Religious change and the fiery discussions which arose in sermon, print and tract found their way into the humblest parish as zealous missionaries and preachers sought to proselytize or churchmen struggled to maintain orthodoxy. Repressive forces were extended to weed out heresy. Reformation and Counter-Reformation touched the lives of individuals and communities on a scale never before achieved.

Indifference to change was possible: immunity to even a measure of change could be more difficult. With the Reformation and the Counter-Reformation, the writing of history extends to a consideration of the responses of the masses in a way reserved for peasant revolts in earlier periods. Not surprisingly, since women constituted half of any congregation and religion was a part of the warp and woof of their everyday lives and the system of values to which they subscribed, it is possible to discern a distinctive female presence in and response to many of the changes.[7] Neither camp neglected to turn its attention to women, though both assumed that the real battle was for the minds of men and that women would then follow. The annals of the past assume a dynamic gender dimension. Women of all kinds, rich and poor, old and young, disciples of change or resolute adherents to old ways, appear, individually or in groups, to bear witness to personal or community concerns.

In some respects the goals of the two dominant orthodoxies, Catholic and Protestant, are remarkable for their similarity. Both stood for a clearly defined moral order based on chastity, fortitude and obedience to God's teaching as expressed in Scripture. If the Protestants posited a holy household, the Catholics worked to promote the model of the holy family. Both enjoined women to accept their subservient role but deplored passivity in the face of sin. Women had souls and were capable of sin and error. The Catholic faith urged upon women the courage to confess and so to speak out their faith. The Protestant confessions put the holy word, in the form of the Bible, into their hands. For both camps, the religious comportment of women was interpreted as a kind of marker. Women epitomized the ignorant and the superstitious, the sexually lax and the profane. The behaviour of women could then serve as a condemnation of, or as a recommendation for, a particular confession. Raving, undisciplined, wandering, chanting, immodest women who stepped out of the place laid down for them in the books of Genesis and Timothy were seen as evidence of the failure of that creed to conform to God's will. Religious reform involved both sexes, but it focused particularly on chastity and obedience – and who should be more chaste or more obedient than the female? They were, in short, to be brought into line. In a more positive light, both the Protestant and the Catholic reformers embraced the notion of good works and created a space for women in which they might perform them. Whatever the confession, the main enemy was seen as ignorance. For Protestants the way forward was the teaching of both sexes to know the word of God through the Bible. For Catholics knowledge expounded by the priest through catechitical instruction was at the heart of reform. However, as well as similarities in the goals there were differences and those differences were variously expressed according to national, social and often class contexts.

The questions which have to be asked are, what differences did the changes and turmoil make in the lives of women as individuals or as groups? What were the choices which confronted women under changing circumstances? How did the Catholic and the Protestant experiences differ and what were the consequences for women from the changes involved? Which women, and where were they touched the most profoundly? How did they react? Did they follow their husbands or were they themselves in some instances the engineers of change? To what extent were they defenders or instigators of a fortress faith? What was the common ground between the protagonists? These necessary questions are daunting because they demand generalizations about a range of experiences which differed according to geographical location, social class and in many cases personal commitment and decisions. Indeed, there are few aspects of life which can be described without reference to the impact of the Reformation and of the Counter-Reformation.

The immediate impact of the Council of Trent on the lives of women in countries which continued to accept the authority of Rome was felt in the religious houses when they were placed on the agenda in 1563. For some women the regular religious life served as the only alternative to marriage. All towns and cities had a convent of some kind and the great ones could have a dozen or more. At the beginning of our period, when all countries were still attached to Rome, the incidence of such houses was highest in Italy, France, Germany, the Netherlands and Spain. Against the payment of a dowry far less than the sum needful to establish them in marriage, more than a third of the female children of the aristocracy and the patriciates entered, whether willingly or not, from the age of about fourteen on a way of life ostensibly dedicated to prayer and reflection. The nunnery attracted a lot of funding in these countries throughout the Renaissance.

The church insisted on enclosure for women. They were to be preserved separate from the world *tamquam vere mortua* (as if they were dead). Beyond learning – for there were several book-lined cells – such women seemed to have little to do and no social vocation. An attempt made in the thirteenth century to establish the Poor Clares, female Franciscans who might wander around the city begging their bread and that of the poor and dedicate themselves to caring for the unfortunate, had been modified by the reforms of Saint Colette and by the beginning of the fifteenth century strict enclosure was the rule.

Whatever the letter of the law, however, the social realities of being an 'enclosed' nun in early sixteenth-century Italy were very dependent upon the house and order chosen. These institutions were an integral part of family strategic planning for the children of the aristocracy, which may explain a rather perfunctory commitment in some houses to anything approaching strict discipline. Not only were many of the houses centres of learning for women, the cells 'booklined' and very comfortably furnished by the girl's family, but close family links were permitted. Entrance into a particular house could assume the aspect of a family reunion and ties were far from severed with the family that remained in the world.[8] Indeed, before Trent, in some houses annual holidays were permitted when the nuns could go home for a few weeks. There was little restriction on family visits to the convent and 'family cells' were built and furnished for daughters which became on death the property of the convent, but usually passed to a relative or a spiritual daughter within the community. These institutions offered an alternative family structure which perhaps suited many of the women who entered.

The history of the nun has been written by reference to three stereotypes: the pious and holy; the reluctant victim of family strategy; and the 'deviant' interested in lesbian or sado-masochistic behaviour. If all these types existed, and the presence of the last has perhaps been exaggerated thanks to Diderot, the norm may well have been the moderately pious if not fervent aristocratic girl, convent-educated since the age of five, who joined other members of her family and thus eluded the terrors of childbed and the unknown in marriage. If in any way academically inclined, she could within the convent walls indulge this taste to the full. If musical, she could probably also practise her gifts. Bolognese convents in particular seem to have been noted for the high quality of the music they commissioned, which they sometimes performed publicly. Or the nuns themselves were composers, some of the first women to be so. There were sophisticated theatrical performances where the nuns dressed up to perform their parts. Many convents kept a chronicle (the earliest in Germany) to record important events in the life of the house and some went further, permitting the nun who kept the record to name and describe not only incoming novices but visitors and events and the social life of the institution. The first writings by women of saints' lives and stories of holy women who were their foundresses, as well as spiritual reflections, came from these institutions.[9]

Protestantism attacked the convent as unnatural and as a seat of unnatural activity. Luther in particular denied it a place in the godly society where God solemnized the first marriage and made the bearing of children every woman's path to salvation. However, chastity and the opportunity to live an institutional life of celibacy was maintained as a high ideal of the Catholic church. The convent must survive, but it must do so in purified form. The work of the Council of Trent therefore included an attempt to tighten up convent practices. Apart from the Poor Clares, whose standards were strict and whose cloister was a barrier to the outside world, enclosure was too loosely interpreted and must now be more rigorously respected. Public entertainments must cease and there must also be, via the bishop and his officials, a closer scrutiny of this kind of activity within the convent. The coming and going of the nun into the outside world must be terminated and the grille rendered less permeable.

How successful was this attempt? Certainly the generality of women's houses found themselves more restricted in their contact with the outside world, and where the spirit of Trent was quickly put into effect, as at Bologna under the reforming hand of Paleotti, the response was strident.

The nuns of the Monastery of Santi Naborre e Felice in Bologna . . .
express to Your Holiness with all humility their miseries and misfortunes

that, notwithstanding that most of them were shut up in this place by their relatives against their wills, for all that they have borne it with considerable patience, and during a time in which they have been so tormented with various statutes and orders that they no longer have the strength to endure it . . . Now most recently, besides having removed the organ from here, the doctor has been denied them, so that nobody except their father and mother can see and speak with them. Their old servants who were accustomed to serve them in the convent cannot speak to any nun . . . Wherefore we fear that, being deprived with such strictness and abandoned by everyone, we have only hell, in this world and the next. [10]

Paleotti's successors were more tolerant of entertainments provided enclosure was respected.

The history of any particular monastic or religious order needs separate consideration. The Carmelites, who felt the reforming hand of Saint Teresa of Avila in 1567, were persuaded to adopt a newly rigorous life involving considerable physical discomfort and mortification of the flesh and the promise of complete withdrawal from the world. Saint Teresa, who had been called upon by her confessor to resist her visions as the work of the Devil, became convinced of the rectitude of the way of life she planned as a means of securing the salvation of the women who entered. She met opposition from the women who were already in place, and the ecclesiastical hierarchy who thought she was demanding too much and would deter potential donors to the institution. She drew some very fine lines. Excessive fasting and sleep deprivation could convert the pious nun into the false mystic. Whilst extolling deprivation, it must be carefully controlled. She told this cautionary tale of a Cistercian:

There was a nun . . . who by dint of fasting and discipline became so weak that every time she took communion or became inflamed with devotion, fell to the ground and lay there for eight or nine hours, and she and everyone else assumed it was rapture . . . The fame of her raptures was spreading through the town: I was dismayed to hear it, because the Lord wanted me to understand what it really was, and I was afraid the whole affair would turn out badly . . . I told her confessor that I understood what it was and that it was a waste of time, not rapture but weakness. I told him to have her give up fasting and discipline, and seek some distractions. She was obedient and did as she was told. As soon as she gained strength she forgot completely about raptures.[11]

The Carmelites asked for little in dowries and hence drew in girls from a wide social spectrum. In spite of the rigours of the life and its nominal seclusion, they expanded considerably and the expansion process itself profoundly modified the lifestyle of the individual women. This was partly because the monarchy in the person of Philip II saw this order as a tool of politics and encouraged it to spread through France, the southern Netherlands and Germany as well as in Latin America. It may be that the order was regarded as intrinsically Spanish, the product of a proven saintly mystic, and the impeccability of its rigorous credentials was never called into question. To put a daughter in the Carmelites was then a political statement, one of allegiance to a country and its cultural creations. When the spiritual daughter of Saint Teresa, Ana de Jesús, found herself at the head of a small group of nuns crossing France and establishing themselves in half a dozen houses in the Netherlands, life was certainly not enclosed. The sisters were on the road and hardly allowed to settle before they had to move on and begin another foundation. Patronized heavily by the Regent of the Netherlands, who went to the foundation not only for worship but to converse with the mother of the house and to introduce aristocratic families who might help in the expansion process, the group of founding nuns were frequently denied the peace they sought. Although recruitment from the local aristocracy was steady, the life as the institution settled itself was perhaps too demanding in terms of fasting and penance to be an effective substitute for the easier life of the established aristocratic house.[12]

For many aristocratic institutions which managed to evade the over-intrusive hand of a reforming bishop, life could continue much as before, though with more respect given to the rules of enclosure. It is possible to discern minor changes, such as the more rigorous separation of widows and virgins, a decline in the number of public entertainments and a reduction in the number of servants; but on the whole, Reverend Mother or Abbess remained largely untroubled by bishops in her internal management. Although holy women outside the convent make frequent mention of the father confessor in their writings, on this point the convent chronicles are for the most part silent.

What perhaps helped to ensure the largely unchanged nature of these institutions was the need of aristocratic families for a place to settle their unmarried daughters. The same women from the same back-grounds lived essentially the same lives within their walls. A major problem of these houses in Spain in the seventeenth century was the failure of families to pay the full amount of the dowry. Many convents allowed payment to be made in instalments, but once the woman had taken her full vows it could be impossible to send her away. Attempts at litigation could drag on for years. The recruitment to these houses largely sustained itself until the late eighteenth century though in France and parts of Italy numbers had already fallen.[13] In effect, and taken overall, the Tridentine reforms sustained for the next 130 years or so the numbers of women in religion.

The volume of published work of many different kinds emanating from these institutions expanded very considerably as the Jesuits and mission priests encouraged the writing of lives of saints and holy women for distribution to the parishes they visited. However, there were more noteworthy compositions. For example, some remarkable historians are to be found in Italian convents in the seventeenth century.[14] One such, Angelica Baitelli (1588–1650), a Benedictine of Brescia, first involved herself in a history of the founder of her convent whose origins dated back to the eighth century, *Vita Martirio e Morte di S. Giulia Cartaginese Crocefissa*. This work transcended the purely hagiographic, drawing upon charters and histories of early Lombardy, and it was followed by *Annali Historici dell'Edificatione Erettione e Dotatione del Serenissimo Monasterio di S. Salvatore, e S. Giulia di Brescia*. It draws upon a massive archive of the convent, registers and charters, privileges and donations, benefactors who counted in their ranks emperors, princes and dukes who had given land, privileges and relics in exchange for prayers and intercessions by the nuns. She carefully transcribed, translated and analysed ancient Latin texts and drew on the collective memory of the community. The sisters themselves are traced over the centuries and the prestige of the families from which they were drawn, and hence the significance of their political connections, is made apparent. Angelica was making a cogent statement on behalf of the entire community in troubled political times when Brescia had passed under the tutelage of Venice. At the same time her brother Ludovico was engaged in a defence of the privileges of the Brescian nobility which, unlike the work of his sister, was never published. Nevertheless, both were concerned with family business, a work of political affirmation of the aristocratic élites from which they came, and of their way of life.[15]

Some nuns in these aristocratic institutions corresponded with the great and the famous to whom they were related and thus could promote the interests of other family members and exercise a degree of political influence. The papal nuncio in Venice was perfectly explicit on this subject, though Venice in the sixteenth and seventeenth centuries was remarkable for its politics and intellectual life and should not be taken to represent the rest of Italy.[16]

A couple of decades after Angelica Baitelli, in the Benedictine convent of Sant'Anna in Castello, Venice, Arcangela Tarabotti (1604–52) was to write a series of tracts and letters which earn her a place among Europe's seventeenth-century literary feminists. A nun without vocation, in the sense that she was not imbued with a burning spiritual flame, she was nevertheless able to construct for herself a lifestyle which permitted her to think and write about the condition of women in the convent and women in their relationship to men. She was the author of six works published during her lifetime, though official permission for the most contentious of these was delayed almost until her death: the title, *Inferno monacale* (the convent as hell), explains why. Another of her works, *Semplicità ingannata* (deceitful simplicity) published posthumously in 1654 under a pseudonym, was also very critical of the way in which the convent was used. On the other hand *Paradiso monacale*, published in 1643, was a consideration of the terms under which life in the convent could be paradise. Her other works were: *Antisatira in riposta al 'Lusso donnesco'* which ran into two editions (1644 and 1646) and which defended women against the charge of greed and luxury in almost Veblenesque terms; *Che le donne siano della spetie degli huomini. Difesa delle donne* (Women the same species as men. A defence of women, 1651), a theological and philosophical disquisition on the minds and souls of women; *Lettere familiari e di complimento* (Familiar and complimentary letters, 1650) revealed the extent to which Tarabotti was a part of the Venetian literary world although living within an 'enclosed' order.[17]

She was endowed with a very powerful analytical mind but also one capable of descriptive power. The banned *Inferno monacale* begins with a swingeing indictment of the dowry system within aristocratic families which determines the fate of all the children. She describes how the daughter elected for marriage is garbed and bejewelled and taught aristocratic manners – her skin feels silk – while those designed for the convent are deprived – their skin feels rough wool. Thus sacrificed to dynastic interests a cloak of hypocrisy covers her entry to convent life. She must dissimulate, hide her feelings, suppress her true self. The church bears a large measure of blame. It is guilty of false teaching which hallows this hypocritical exercise.

The work is the more powerful if we turn to her *Paradiso monacale*. The convent was transformed into paradise for the woman who had a measure of spirituality. Above all, she must *want* to become a nun, the girl herself must make the choice. If Arcangela Tarabotti's work has a leitmotif it is the denial of choice to women and the restriction of free will to the male sex. Her vocabulary is that of the Enlightenment which has yet to take place. The convent is hell when free will is excluded.

Tarabotti is a far more cogent critic of the convent than Diderot. She allows for differences in temperament and sees nothing unnatural in women wanting to live together. Significantly, perhaps, though a 'forced' nun she herself never sought to leave. Although the convent clearly irked her it provided her with the conditions to write and think. In the world outside she might not have had the opportunity for either. Perhaps she laboured in the knowledge that she had nowhere else to go. It is also perhaps significant that while Venice's most illustrious female poet was a courtesan, Veronica Franco, living on immoral earnings, her most illustrious female polemicist was a nun, living on her convent.

Yet in Tarabotti's lifetime changes were taking place in the religious life for women which had not been envisaged by the reformers who sat at the Council of Trent. They were to have a very profound effect on the history of the Roman Catholic Church in general and the lives of groups of women in particular. The origin of change lay in Italy, but the grip of the male ecclesiastical establishment and the constraints upon women in Mediterranean society meant that development was to be curbed in that country and to reach its full flowering in France.

In 1535 in Brescia, Angela Merici, a Franciscan tertiary who had devoted herself to the care of the sick and the education of poor girls, joined with a number of women of like spirit to dedicate themselves to this work under the patronage of Saint Ursula, and hence the group became known as the Ursulines.[18] The sisters took no formal public vows, wore lay clothes and lived in their own homes. Their numbers grew at a pace which was alarming for the church, which could not adjust to the idea of large numbers of unenclosed and mobile religious sisters. The women in question had stepped into a very decided 'space', that is, social work and education, and they were to become over the next two hundred years the most considerable, and indeed prestigious, teaching order for women of the Roman Catholic Church. They were approved by Pope Paul III in 1544; community life and simple vows were introduced in 1572 by Carlo Borromeo. The order moved into France and expanded under the encouragement of laywomen such as Madame de Sainte Beuve, becoming an important weapon against the spread of Protestantism; after the Edict of Nantes (1598) girls from aristocratic Protestant families were, at the command of the monarchy, sent to the Ursulines to be educated and, it was hoped, brought back to the faith. However, in 1612 strict enclosure was enforced and a modified rule of Saint Augustine was imposed upon the houses which had been established. By 1715 there were at least 300 Ursuline houses in France.

The example of the Ursulines invites reflection. The gap which Angela Merici and her companions had endeavoured to fill was one which some churchmen, among them certain Jesuits, were increasingly to recognize: the need for specialist personnel to perform vital tasks for Christian society. Trent had failed to identify these needs with any specificity, but the more churchmen involved themselves with the moral and social needs of their flock, the stronger became their perception of the vast amount of social work waiting to be done. Even before Trent, in Italy confraternities and associations to help the needy and afflicted, to raise dowry funds and preserve the honour of young women, had been growing and attracting funding. However, there remained gaps to be filled and the great civic endeavours in Italy were not emulated elsewhere. Ignorance could only be fought through education, and what overworked priest could give himself to the teaching of young children? The sick and the poor needed help. Could they be ignored by a church which declared itself committed to the precepts of Jesus Christ? The institutions designed to rescue fallen women needed someone to do the job. An overseas empire in Canada or Latin America was growing. If generations of Catholics were to be created from native populations, who was going to do it? Those who thought about these questions were pushed to an unavoidable answer: women.

That answer, though clear, was however problematic. It demanded changing those who were intended to be passive and whose reputation depended on their restriction to a specific enclosed locale into women of action and flexibility. It is no small matter to cross the Atlantic and venture into the unknown. The need for such a transformation was perceived by a few noteworthy men in the sixteenth century and by a larger number in the seventeenth. They arrived at the conclusion in stages. The first, and that widely promoted by the sixteenth-century church, was to find such women in lay society. The new model was a Christian matron who embraced humility and good works and devoted herself to the wellbeing of those less fortunate than herself.

Father confessors often played a key part. An understanding of this personage and his role in the post-Tridentine world is critical to understanding how the Catholic church sought to control the minds and behaviour of women, perhaps in particular women of some education and wealth whose energies and resources could be used by the church. The parish priest, who was progressively throughout the seventeenth century likely to be seminary trained, and the possessor of manuals indicating how he should proceed in the confessional, urged upon the women of his flock the need to bare their souls. He was made aware that his role as confessor was among his highest spiritual duties and any fall in standards was something the reformers laboured to eradicate. The Inquisition was an important means whereby women who found themselves subjected to immoral advances from the priest in the confessional could report him and secure redress if they could prove their case. The hundreds of cases that came before the Portuguese Inquisition in particular suggest both that women were increasingly prepared to report such activities but also that some priests (particularly friars) continued to abuse the relationship.[19]

In spite of the errant priest, the confessional experience was seized upon by many women. It was soon explicitly recognized by the church that they needed little encouragement and in many ways, as is now urged by Italian historians, regular confession may have helped women to some knowledge of themselves and shaped their capacities for thought.[20]

In encouraging the act of confession, in shaping questions and giving counsel, the influence of the confessor should not be underestimated. The friars had been instrumental in the development of woman as 'mystic' (true or false) to such an extent that Vives actually recommended that widows should keep away from them. Saint Teresa condemned confessors who led women into believing they had visions when in all probability they were hungry. Now, in the late sixteenth century and gaining momentum with the seventeenth, the confessors par excellence

were the Jesuits and many of them laboured to construct a new version
of holiness. This was a version which did not necessarily achieve sainthood or public renown but one which was an unmistakable route to
pleasing God. The new model was to replace the older notion of the
saintly woman as mystic. A concern of the Catholic reformers was to
convey the message that God appeared and spoke to very few and that
what many of those claimed as divine conversation was the work of the
Devil. Although Saint Teresa of Avila (1515–82) was canonized in
1622 and her mystical credentials were impeccable, progressive churchmen were in search of something else, in particular, humility adorned
by good works.

It is worth examining the only female saint created by Pope Paul V
(1605–21), Francesca Romana. The pontiff was extremely cautious in
his election of models. The only male saint he made was Carlo Borromeo,
Tridentine reformer and the saint of plague-ridden Milan, a practical
as well as a deeply spiritual man. Francesca (1384–1440) was canonized
in 1608: the time lag after her death is to be noted. A woman of the
Roman nobility, she was married at the age of thirteen to Lorenzo
de Ponziani and became an exemplary wife and mother. While never
neglecting her wifely duties, she and her sister-in-law began to minister
to the poor. After the death of two of her children, in 1425 she founded
a society of devout women under the rule of Saint Benedict but without
taking vows. Some revelations and prophetic utterances were attributed
to her and in her lifetime given great prominence, but they were played
down in the letters recommending her canonization. She was also
credited with effecting cures through her prayers. Her most persistent
vision was in fact one of a guardian angel, a concept which the Jesuits
were keen to promote. She dressed in harsh wool. Her day was divided
into parts in which she organized the household, prayed long and fervently in her room and visited hospitals and the church, where she
prayed in particular for the repentance of sinners. Entertainments and
feasts never intruded upon her routine and jewels were sold for the
poor. Her main characteristic was her humility. Her appearance was
that of servant, not mistress, and she carried bread for distribution to
the hungry which was reputed never to run out. Francesca Romana had
all the attributes desired for women by the church in her times: ascetic,
obedient, a good wife and mother, dedicated to prayer and charity,
preferring humility over high status, she was a holy matron working
with the permission of husband and family or in virtuous widowhood

to remedy social problems, a perfect example of Christian solidarity and one who went beyond the role of wife to become a civic mother figure.[21]

The Jesuits, and they were not alone, put themselves behind the new version of the holy woman not only in the confessional but in publications. Several lives of holy women, who were not to be serious candidates for sainthood but who presented an example for other women, emerged from their pens. Those women who came to the confessional with claims of having heard voices or having received divine directions were instructed to write down their experiences. These holy autobiographies were probably intended to serve several purposes. First they could be discussed by the woman herself with her confessor and the direction of divine will could be ascertained. He would then channel the instructions to specific ends. The acts of writing and discussion could be a kind of control by the priest to ensure that the woman was not teetering over into dangerous irrationalities. Most of all, perhaps, accounts of spiritual experiences, of a consciousness of acting according to the will of God, followed by those of practical work in furtherance of God's will, could make inspirational reading for the literate and the wealthy woman with time on her hands.

The genre can best be demonstrated by example. Alberto Alberti, the Jesuit, committed to paper the life of Margherita Coloma, a Spanish noblewoman whose husband was the governor of Cremona and then castellan of Milan. A devout woman, particularly devoted to the rosary, she was to interest herself in the work afoot in Milan to rescue women from prostitution – the Convertite of Saint Pelagia. Unable to walk without compromising herself along streets where lewd women disported themselves, she used her carriage, attended by flunkeys in livery, and, dressed as the aristocrat she was, picked up young prostitutes from the street and deposited them at the Convertite. Alberti is stressing how someone, without abandoning the distinction of rank but rather using it to go where middle-class women could not go, and surrounded by the proper protection, can do a practical job. Margherita was of course an exemplary wife and her husband did not impede her holy work. She had visions connected to the presence of a directing guardian angel. She died consumed with penitence for the sins of her life (which appear to have been nonexistent) in 1648.[22]

In 1722 a French priest edited the life of a holy woman, Elisabeth Strouven of Maastricht, active in the 1620s and 1630s. She had been enjoined by her spiritual directors to write down her experiences, a task which she found distinctly uncomfortable. Elisabeth confessed to divine prompts which were edited out of her published autobiography in the eighteenth century when such experiences were becoming increasingly suspect. Orphaned while small, she first gave her energies to the foundation of a boarding school for young children. Although she later left this work and committed herself to prayer, her charitable work – and she had no financial resources of her own – was boundless. Elisabeth had in the course of her work three father confessors. The first was a Jesuit, but she left him for unspecified reasons and sought out two Franciscans in succession. One of the Franciscans told her he would like to be her pupil and placed her in the role of *madre divina*, a not uncommon phenomenon in fifteenth- and sixteenth-century Italy and even in Spain where Philip IV had a nun as confessor. The practice was a recognition of special holiness in the woman, but it also demonstrated that the man was seeking to establish his total humility in the eyes of God by obedience to a woman. Not only her confessor but two other priests submitted themselves to Elisabeth on such terms and she found them a constant source of embarrassment. One of the priests was an ascetic faster and when pressed to eat threw himself at Elisabeth's feet to ask if he must do this. She writes:

> I thought that I would burst. Yes, I think it is a wonder that I did not die out of fear and anxiety, when I was in the presence of people with these two men or even one of them . . . I could not think otherwise than that I would be the laughing stock of all the world and that finally I would be thrown into jail and would be disgraced in the eyes of the world.[23]

The *madre divina* was a less common figure in the southern Netherlands than in Italy and the area where Elisabeth lived was sensitive to Protestant criticism of the excesses of Catholicism. Moreover the role was suspect to many Catholic thinkers, including Dominicans and Jesuits. However, Elisabeth survived, shook off the two priests and under divine prompting founded a convent. Frequently ill, she accepted her maladies as God's will and used them as part of her prompts system: 'If I recover, this . . . will be the Lord's will.' She provides a telling instance of the kind of woman in society for whom the church was searching.[24]

The confessor priest knew the women under his direction. He knew who had money, who had time, who had energy and who had spirituality and all these attributes did not necessarily appear in the same person. He could, however, act as a co-ordinating force. From their early days, the Jesuits as preachers and teachers learned to direct their energies towards women. In Bologna, for example, a group of very wealthy laywomen put themselves behind the establishment of the order in the city in 1546 by providing funds for their maintenance and for linen and vestments. One, who was childless and controlled her patrimony, left a large sum of money in her will to further the Jesuits' work, which aroused the fury of her family. Saint Ignatius Loyola himself cautioned against accepting money from widows or wealthy women where this could draw anger against the Jesuits and lower them in social esteem. He was, however, to be outstripped by events.[25] The Jesuits promoted a 'heroic' (though not uncontrolled) image of woman to cope with the exigencies of the times, a Judith with a Protestant Holofernes' head in her hands. They also placed great hopes in the Ursulines. Although severely restricted by enclosure in Europe, with Jesuit encouragement they made a considerable push into Canada, under the leadership of the formidable Mère Marie de l'Incarnation. In the fluid political and social environment of the new territory, a country there to be christianized, the notion of enclosure was unofficially modified. Certainly, Mère Marie did not herself go out in search of Indian children, but the convent door was permanently open to receive the children and their mothers. The Jesuits recognized the value of the Ursulines in both teaching and child care and assisted their expansion. Jesuit confessors found them recruits in France among widows and wealthy young women who could find the funding for expansion and who had the necessary spirit of adventure involved in a hazardous trip to Canada. Further than they went, in both the geographical and the professional sense, it was impossible for women in the early seventeenth century to go.

In Europe, the limits of the possible were to be crossed first by Isabel Roser from Barcelona who formed a group of women dedicated to active work, education, helping the poor and the conversion of Protestants – though it is doubtful if she ever met any. Ignatius Loyola was apprehensive about her activities and Pope Paul III refused to recognize her order. Then Mary Ward (1585–1645), an Englishwoman who entered the Poor Clares of St Omer in 1606, conceived the idea of a female religious congregation on the model of the Jesuits, committed to an active apostolate, teaching and conversion. Although she succeeded in establishing houses at Liège, Cologne, and even in Vienna and indeed laid claim, perhaps spuriously, to having founded ten establishments containing five hundred women of different nationalities, she fell foul of the Catholic hierarchy, incurred the epithet 'scandalous' by her behaviour, and was imprisoned for a short time in the Convent of the Poor Clares in Munich while her alleged foundations were closed or dispersed. Mary antagonized everyone as much by the rumours of her activities as by the activities themselves. The Jesuits, who were prepared to let heroic women make their contribution to the reconquest of souls, thought that she might discredit the activities of the Catholic church in areas where it was only tenuously entrenched. In the 1630s she herself acknowledged that she had transgressed the limits of the possible and gained permission from Urban VIII to reorganize her foundations on principles more acceptable to the church. Eventually she returned to England where, at the time of the Civil War, she managed to lay down the foundations of a house near Fountains Abbey in north Yorkshire. Although removed to Micklegate Bar in the city of York, it still exists, but it does not, and never did, reflect the principles of Mary's *Three Discourses* (1617) which demands that heroic woman should be free to play an active part in God's work of reconquest.[26]

Virtually contemporaneous with Mary Ward was Jeanne, baronne de Chantal, who developed perhaps the most renowned spiritual relationship between an aristocratic woman and her confessor, Francis of Sales, then archbishop of Geneva.[27] Widowed after a contented marriage of nine years which produced six children who survived infancy, she embarked on a seven-year 'purgatory' in which she immersed herself in prayer and reflection, reading Saint Ignatius Loyola's *Spiritual Exercises*. She had at that time a Jesuit as confessor, one Father Villars, but was inspired to seek out a new spiritual director and having met Francis of Sales in 1604 decided that he was the one suited to her needs. There grew up between them an intense spiritual bond developed in letters, and discussions and a spiritual odyssey, recorded in her *Mémoires*, took place in which the bishop helped deepen her understanding. The visions she experienced and the divine instructions she received were discussed in detail and gradually she was able to replace meditation and extreme mortification (she branded herself) and to understand what God wanted of her: she was to help the poor and the sick. Her husband's family found this decision scandalous. Notwithstanding their opposition and with the help of Francis she formulated in 1610 the Visitation, a small congregation of women living together on an experimental basis (*par manière d'essai*) without enclosure or excessive physical deprivation and with simple rules. These women wished to live a religious life but also to do useful work in the world. This desire was not acknowledged by the Archbishop of Lyons, who refused to have them in his diocese unless they were enclosed. His hard line may have been dictated by Protestant criticisms of the immorality of gadding women, but it corresponds to the general sentiment in the higher echelons of the European ecclesiastical hierarchy. Notwithstanding the restrictions they established 86 houses in 30 years.

The rules of enclosure forced upon the Ursulines and the Visitandines, technically at least, placed them in much the same category as the women living under strict vows who serviced the great charitable institutions of Italy like the Ospedale degli Innocenti or the various refuges intended for the poor or for penitent prostitutes. These women were doing a great deal of practical work, mostly at an administrative level, leaving the dirty work to lay sisters or servants. Throughout the later Middle Ages and at the beginning of the early modern period such institutions were at their most extensive in Italy, for several reasons. First, that country had considerable municipal funds and charitable initiatives burgeoned following the Council of Trent. Many of these initiatives were directed towards the problems of women within the social system: allocation of municipal dowry funds to poor girls, assistance of fatherless children whose mothers were in difficulties, provision for unemployed women and girls without a roof above their heads 'exposed' to dishonourable circumstances, and the particular problems of prostitutes and beaten wives. In all cases the aim was to tend, succour and provide support and solace with a view to inserting them back in the system as reformed women.

The women involved in these charitable initiatives did not scour the streets for clients. They did not enter the homes of the poor. Those whom they were to help were brought to them and the notion of enclosure could thus be preserved. Inevitably, their endeavours left untouched the poor and disadvantaged of the villages. As a task force, enclosed women were too fettered in their activities. Both Angela Merici and Jeanne de Chantal had been aware of this and had pointed to a possible remedy, the abandonment of enclosure and the ability to be simultaneously in religion and in the world. However, it was not until 1633 that any erosion of the principle of enclosure (*clausura*) began. The women who were to drive a coach and horses through the principle

were French, and their activities were remarkable.[28] These women were
to lay the foundations of a new kind of social Catholicism, a *catholicisme
au féminin*[29] in which women became a professional force of nurses,
teachers and social workers. By 1870 they outstripped the numbers of
male regular and secular clergy combined, and they played a major role
not only in France but through the initiatives of orders such as that of
Saint Joseph in the education and assistance to a new generation of
Catholics in North America, Ireland, England and Africa.

It is probably significant that the women were French. Less than four
years after the papacy had declared that the Ursulines of Paris must live
under a strict rule of enclosure (1629), a wealthy and aristocratic widow,
Louise de Marillac, in close collaboration with her spiritual director
Vincent de Paul, a man who was a legend in his own lifetime and who
had worked to create an active apostolate among the Catholic clergy in
the Lazarists, undertook to train and organize girls and widows to form
an active service to reach out to the rural poor.

Vincent de Paul had come to the conclusion that he would never
find enough women who were good Catholic matrons or women living
in a family to undertake the work required. It was through his efforts
that the great leap was made allowing women to live under simple vows
but without enclosure as the nearest thing to a group of professional
social workers that early modern Europe was to know. Vincent de Paul
had experimented with an attempt to organize married women of the
upper classes into work of parochial welfare (*les dames de la charité*) but
he could not get them to enter the hovels of the poor. Louise de
Marillac's Sisters of Charity, however, were of different stock. They
were specifically instructed:

> Your convent will be the house of the sick, your cell a hired room, your
> chapel the parish church, your cloister the city streets or the hospital
> wards, your enclosure obedience, your grille the fear of God, your veil
> modesty.[30]

Their job was defined as home visitors to the poor and sick in villages
where institutional endeavours were nonexistent, the care of orphans
and foundlings, of the old and frail, of wounded soldiers and the victims
of war or local disasters. In exchange for shelter, food, and the promise
of care and sustenance in old age, they contracted with municipalities
to serve in hospitals for the sick (Hôtels Dieu), and in an institution,

the *hôpital général*, which was the brainchild of Vincent de Paul himself and intended to be a place of refuge for the orphaned, the aged and the handicapped (although this aim was to be distorted by the monarchy in 1724 which tried to make them places of general internment for beggars and vagrants). Such institutions were set up by municipalities and interested ecclesiastics or pious lay persons and they were heavily dependent on the bequests of the faithful, not least widows.

Vincent had friends at court and the difficult years of the mid-seventeenth century made the government receptive to his initiatives. The Sisters of Charity were an instant success. When Louise de Marillac died in 1660, they ran about 70 institutions and existed in small groups in an unspecified number of parishes: by 1700 they served more than 200 institutions, including 70 hospitals, and by 1789, 420 institutions of which 175 were hospitals. When women in religion were counted in a highly random way in 1789, these sisters alone accounted for about 15 per cent of the total.

In every sense they were both in religion and in the world. Until 1642 they resisted all attempts to have vows imposed upon them and when they did so, they were 'simple' vows, renewable on an annual basis, made privately and not entailing life in a cloister. This annually renewable provision may have been what persuaded the Vatican. Or the general acceptability of the Sisters of Charity to the French monarchy, the Jesuits, the French bishops and the clergy who themselves fell under Lazarist (missionary priest) influences may have counted for something. All this occurred in France, a country less subjected to the restrictions current in Mediterranean countries, and was not replicated in Italy or Spain until the nineteenth century. The women involved there were also not adventurous aristocrats but good village girls garbed in grey wool and with a linen headdress characteristic of seventeenth-century Breton women. The complex story behind the abandonment of *clausura* has yet to be fully untangled. However, once the Sisters of Charity had forced the pace, other Frenchwomen followed in conspicuous haste.

Few groups or associations were as numerous as the Sisters of Charity. The closing decades of the reign of Louis XIV saw a rapid proliferation of groups dedicated to a specific function designated by their foundress and given a local name. The Soeurs de Charité de Nevers (1680), the Soeurs de Saint Joseph du Puy (1686), the Soeurs d'Evron (1680), the Présentation de Tours (1684), the Soeurs d'Ernemont at Rouen (1690), the Filles de Saint Charles de Lyon (1714) are but a few. Some mushroomed over the next fifty years although the individual houses remained very small. The Filles de la Sagesse, who were particularly strong in Brittany and were to secure the particular opprobrium of Michelet for their activities during the French Revolution, were founded in 1702 and grew from 118 members in 1759 established in 40 houses to 77 houses and 300 sisters in 1789. These small foundations (about four women to each house) were able to serve a village and the women frequently walked into neighbouring hamlets to help the sick drawn to their attention by the parish priest with whom they worked closely. Another aristocratic widow, Madame Villeneuve, founded the Filles de la Croix (1698) which also had a Breton base. A handful of houses started in the diocese of Saint Brieuc in 1705 spread out to Saint Servan (1725), Le Puy (1735), Craponne (1745). These again were parish visitors. Another group, the Filles de la Sainte Vièrge, also founded by a widow, dedicated themselves to providing retreats for spiritual renewal for women of those social classes which could take a break from domestic chores. They swore simple vows which are not untypical of such female initiatives: 'perpetual chastity, obedience and stability in the house, dedicating my whole life to those of my sex who present themselves to make a retreat'. The phrase 'stabilité dans cette maison' may have been intended to reassure the ecclesiastical establishment that the houses were not run by footloose women tempting other women to stray away from their homes but ones who were seriously committed to good order.[31]

Houses dedicated to a specific social need proliferated. Sometimes if particular need passed (for example, helping the victims of an epidemic), the women diversified their activities. If they did not, recruitment would dry up and the house would close. It looks as if many wealthy widows, often encouraged by their confessors, craved their own foundation, leading to a proliferation of institutions with insecure funding. Every foundress hoped to attract more funding as new recruits joined the endeavour. Clearly the widow, urged in the confessional not to remarry but to dedicate herself to good works, was an important source of funds which the secular clergy, and perhaps the Jesuits in particular, were anxious should be dedicated to charitable initiatives. However, as the eighteenth century advanced, women intent upon a useful life in a religious association tended to opt for institutions which had a proven viability and usefulness over several generations. The rapid growth characteristic of the mid-seventeenth century abated and an era of cautious consolidation took its place, although it was to burst out afresh in the nineteenth century.[32]

Another development in the late seventeenth century was that of *filles associées*, associations of women, who could live singly and be in the world (in every sense except the sexual – they were always committed to chastity). Such groups have left few written records, perhaps because those involved were not women of social standing and many were only semi-literate. Many were widows or older spinsters who had spent years tending parents or working. Undistinguished by a religious habit but garbed in sober widow's dress, they made promises, not vows, and committed themselves in very general terms to the business of succour and solace in the name of the love of Jesus Christ.

One such association existed in the Pays de Velay and was known as the *béates*. It was founded in 1665 by a pious woman of Le Puy, Anne Marie Martel, in association with the bishop who identified specific village needs which came to be progressively, though not exclusively, associated with the lace industry. After a brief training in the city of Le Puy a *béate* would be invited to live in a particular village and perform a number of services. The village had to provide her with a simple dwelling with two rooms, one for her own use and the other to accommodate local people for specified purposes. The house had to be crowned with a bell, for the *béate* was frequently a community time-keeper. The usual routine was for the bell to peal at dawn and for the young children and girls of the village up to about the age of twelve to go to the house. For the very young she provided a virtual crèche service, liberating the child's mother from the prying fingers of the toddler while she made lace at home. The children were taught their catechism and to sing hymns and the girls were instructed in the first stages of lace-making. When the natural light faded, the children went home. Then at dusk the bell sounded again. This time their mothers and the village lace-makers gathered for an evening work session in the *béate*'s cottage. She provided light which was chargeable on her behalf to the community. Candles were placed in reflective globes (again community property). Heating was usually by boxes of charcoal embers which were placed under the feet since an open fire would discolour the lace. However, in the *béate*'s room there was a hearth and on it stood a soup pot into which each of the women placed a few lentils or bread or vegetables to contribute to a late night soup which they all shared. As the women worked, they sang hymns and if the *béate* could read she read to them from the Bible.

At the end of the session the rosary was recited. In these isolated mountain villages it could often be difficult to reach the parish church in bad weather, so on winter Sundays the *béate*'s room was transformed into a place of worship with chants and stories from the Bible. The *béate* was the right hand of the priest, an invaluable auxiliary.

This woman therefore served an economic as well as a religious function. Although she was instructed not to interfere in the economics of the lace trade which was carried out between the lace-maker herself and the *leveuse*, the picker-up who served as agent between the lace-maker and the merchants, she did not hesitate to report sharp practices and her services in maximizing the earning potential of the lace-maker were widely acknowledged. She helped inculcate devotions encouraged by the post-Tridentine church.[33]

The services provided by the *béates* did not end there. The young lace-maker of the villages could not earn very much during the learning period. Like every other country girl she needed a dowry and a way had to be found to convert lace-making, ill remunerated as it was, into a dowry-generating force. The solution was found by the *béates* who ran lace-maker dormitories in the city of Le Puy. The accommodation was rent free and funded by philanthropic donation. If other funds were available some heating was provided, but the girl contributed something for her food which was prepared by the *béate*. She also negotiated the sale of the finished lace and the profits were put by to help the girl save towards her dowry. Again, the context of this activity was a religious one: hard work, long hours, and leisure which was supervised. Small wonder these girls did not figure in the illegitimate pregnancy declarations.

The *béate* did not cost the village anything more than the house she lived in; her food was largely provided by those she helped. Representing for many communities the difference between penury and sufficiency, she is one of the best instances of the spirit of Catholic solidarity, in which the lowly helped the lowlier as well as the aristocratic the poor.

Married and middle-class women were not precluded from loose charitable associations which demanded no vows. Saint Vincent had experimented with the Dames de la Charité and while he found them of much less use than the Sisters of Charity, they had some role to play and continued to have an active existence throughout the period. Women with a social conscience and prepared to give a few hours a week to such work visited needy families. They distributed whatever relief funds the town or village possessed, sometimes no more than once a year. Sometimes a soup kitchen was needed for the children of the poor during periods of high prices, or an annual distribution of cast-off clothing. Daughters often took over the work their mothers had done. For example, in the city of Besançon there existed an institution which provided layettes for poor mothers expecting babies and to give them some assistance in the months after the birth so that they could breastfeed. This particular institution had a continuous history throughout the ancien régime, the Revolution – when it laicized its name – and the nineteenth century. The women involved belonged to the same families and one generation carried on where the last had left off.

The work done by the associations and congregations fell largely under four headings: care of the sick; care of the orphaned and the aged poor; education embracing girls of all social categories and village boys as well; social welfare in many forms, some temporary, some institutionalized.

Among the institutions, the largest were hospitals for the sick poor in the cities and larger towns, the Hôtel Dieu, and the Hôpital Général, which catered for the poor and helpless, the orphaned and the crippled. Taken together there were about 2000 of such institutions by the end of the old regime, varying in size and importance according to the size of the town and the generosity of the founders, and certainly well over 100,000 people were in receipt of care within them.[34]

The Hôtel Dieu was in many instances established in the Middle Ages but overhauled in the seventeenth century when administrators or municipalities contracted with one of the new orders to carry out nursing and day-to-day administration. Boards of governors existed to whom the sisters were accountable for financial management, but over time they assumed more and more control. The first choice towns made of order or congregation was usually the Sisters of Charity unless there was a local alternative. Hence the Soeurs de Saint Charles de Nancy (established 1652), the Soeurs de Saint Thomas de Villeneuve (established 1661), the Soeurs Hospitalières de Saint Joseph du Puy (established 1686 and very strong in the Massif Central) or the Soeurs Chrétiennes de Nevers were a mere few of those who might be called upon to help. There were never enough of them and an examination of the work explains why. The sisters drew up an agreement with the contracting authorities laying down what exactly they would do and what were the conditions of their service. The religious as well as the practical was clearly formulated. The sisters were in the business of doing God's work upon earth and asked, in return for untiring and often unpleasant endeavour, their keep and clothing. When they were infirm they might return to the mother house and the product of their dowries and contributions to the order would sustain them through a respectable old age.

They defined the sphere of their activities precisely so that they could operate effectively within the limits they set themselves. The insane and those suffering from an incurable contagious disease or venereal disorder were not admitted. There was an element of sense in such provisions. Operating on a limited budget, in what were often old buildings unsuited to the care of the mentally ill, and cramped enough to allow contagion to spread rapidly, the sisters had to make choices. Saint Vincent had urged upon the Sisters of Charity that chronic poverty and sickness should be the main determinants of those admitted, but the sisters interpreted this to include any person dependent upon the work of his or her hands who was not generally resident or was a servant in the house of someone else. For example, they took in the migrant labourer on the way to or from work in another region, perhaps suffering from sunstroke or fatigue, or the tubercular servant from the silk indus- try. Such people might not be resourceless so much as in conditions which precluded care and they could make a contribution to their nursing. The old with grievous terminal conditions were also helped. Sick and wounded, but not syphilitic, soldiers were another branch of the clientele for whom the army was prepared to pay. Some of the institutions had to receive, despatch and pay for foundlings, which could prove ruinous as these grew in numbers in the closing decades of the old regime.[35]

Surgeons and doctors, paid fees for their services, decided on what treatment should be accorded to the sick. Care and the administration of medicaments and the tending of wounds were left to the sisters. They also had control of the pharmacy which prepared medicines and this became a source of contention as the medical men laid claim to an increasing body of knowledge. The sisters disposed of a limited pharmacopoeia based on traditional lore and placed much greater empha- sis on rest and nourishment. If economies had to be made on drugs to preserve the supply of beef tea, then they were in little doubt they should be made. In this they encountered hostility from the doctors who believed a strict regime needful. Given the weakened physical state of many of the patients, or the need of those with dysentery for salty fluids to prevent dehydration, it is hard to blame the sisters. On the other hand, they emphatically stood in the way of autopsies and hence what the surgeons believed greater medical knowledge. They had a different view of the sick from the medical men, seeing them as souls in preparation for an afterlife and therefore in need of an intact body – a point of view wholly endorsed by at least 90 per cent of the wider population.[36]

The registers of the Hôtels Dieu are not an unrelieved necrology. About a tenth of all patients died in care. Everything depended of course on why they were admitted in the first place. Large numbers of young men from the army or migrant labourers suffering from exhaustion and sunstroke responded to rest, cleanliness and care. The main problem was always the inflexibility of their revenues which came under particular stress in the eighteenth century as the number of foundlings rose. Patients slept two and three to a bed and the nursing sisters could not be increased beyond the numbers laid down in the contract since their food and lodging had to be guaranteed. Some also found that the municipal administrators served them badly by investing funds in John Law's schemes which, when they failed, plunged them further into debt. This was a problem that they shared with the other brainchild of Saint Vincent de Paul, the Hôpital Général.[37]

Saint Vincent's aim had been to create an institution, served by the Sisters of Charity, which would give shelter to the orphaned, crippled and frail where they would live decently under a communal religious regimen involving work and prayer. Such institutions would be funded out of municipal initiatives, philanthropic donations and concessions from the monarchy in the way of privileges. They were vigorously promoted by the Jesuits, who carried the idea throughout France on their missions. However, the monarchy envisaged the institutions as quasi-prisons which could be used to get lunatics and crippled beggars off the streets. In fact, most of the institutions were much too small to realize the great internment project of the government. Most did not extend their efforts outside caring for the debilitated and paralysed, orphans over the age of seven and sometimes the mildly insane. They were also prepared to accept aged servants paid for by their former masters.

The sisters who ran the Hôpitaux Généraux carried out much the same functions as those who staffed the Hôtels Dieu. They were not merely or even primarily nurses. Many of the internees were foul-mouthed and unruly. Orphaned or foundling girls had to be taught sewing or an industrial skill and boys kept occupied until they were ready for an apprenticeship at the age of fourteen. The crippled and blind could be difficult to move and some had to be hand-fed. Some sisters stipulated in their contracts that they would have some male assistance with problem cases such as old soldiers, and occupied themselves with the spiritual exercises of the women who could be integrated into their own devotional pattern. Whatever the routine in the individual hospitals, the life was one of unremitting toil for the sisters. In addition, they were perpetually under pressure to expand their services in difficult or inflationary conditions.

Their main problem was that the internment of all the poor was an unrealizable goal and the knowledge that society was still plagued with beggars and vagrants caused a decline in new donations. Armchair critics imbued with Enlightenment anticlerical sentiment alleged that the women mismanaged funds and that the institutions (in which they themselves had assuredly never set foot) were dens of idleness and vice sustained by a religion which indulged scroungers. That the institutions did fulfil a need, however, was to be made only too apparent when they were abandoned by the government during the Revolution. For their part the poor complained that the institutions were not large enough to help them and that they helped only the poor of the towns.[38]

The country districts were in fact disadvantaged in the services they received. Sometimes the Sisters of Charity and other local foundations were able to place one of their order in a larger village (2000 inhabitants and more) to perform certain services financed out of a local bequest. In some cases they were guaranteed a modest residence with a small infirmary to tend the sick. Medical services probably had a priority. The sisters dressed wounds and visited the sick in their own homes. Sometimes they helped with a periodic food distribution or one of clothing if such resources were available. They were not substantial money-raisers – they were funded by the contributions of the faithful, which was the whole point of Catholic voluntary charity – but they could solicit alms at the church door and, since they had the official approbation of the parish priest, he could recommend the faithful to be generous.

This kind of sister has left little trace in the records. Often she could not write herself or she was hard stretched with very little time to spare.

There were never enough such women. The Filles du Bon Sauveur of Caen, for example, founded in 1730 by a pious spinster called Anne Leroy, had as a mission the maintenance of *petites écoles* (often only winter schools) to teach poor girls working skills and to visit the sick. They rooted themselves firmly in the region and after being dispersed in 1792 for refusing to accept a confessor who had taken the civil oath of loyalty to the Revolutionary government, they re-formed in 1805, burgeoned anew and came to specialize in teaching the deaf and dumb. Such specialist services survived the onslaught on nuns' education by the Third Republic and in 1965 they still had 15 houses and 475 nuns. Widows were often behind many of these endeavours. Madame du Parc de Jezerdo, for example, a close friend of Madame de Maintenon and every bit as pious, founded in 1699 the Paulines of Tréguier whose purpose was to establish in the villages funds, through private donation, which could be invested in *rentes* and provide a reservoir of help for disadvantaged families, or they made collections at times of high prices to help tide families over.[39]

Education was a priority of many of these initiatives. At the end of the old regime in France it was calculated that just over a third of women and two-thirds of men could write their own names. However, north of a line stretching from St Malo to Geneva the levels were much higher, reaching a peak in Flanders. In part this reflects the distribution of wealth in France, but it also reflects the more active role of the women's orders north of the Loire. Mediterranean women, born into societies more hostile to the idea of women active outside the home, provided fewer recruits to these less formal orders or else those that they did recruit were less committed to literacy, like the *béate* of the Velay.

The educational package offered by the *petites écoles* accentuated literacy less than it did firm catechitical instruction which would allow the pupil to resist heresy. Second came survival skills, that is, spinning, sewing, lace-making and embroidery. Some aimed at more elevated fare. The Ursulines and local orders like the Filles de la Présentation de Senlis, for example, ran exclusive boarding schools and used the fees paid by the wealthy to fund enterprises for poor girls. The girl who was admitted into one of these establishments perhaps had a limited educational fare but received the equivalent of an apprenticeship and, like the product of the English charity school, she could expect a good place in service.

*

By the time of the Revolution roughly one in every 120 Frenchwomen was committed to a life demanding celibacy and chastity, but which involved a clear social purpose. They constituted a professional élite of nurses and teachers. Florence Nightingale was to say that if Britain had had the Sisters of Charity there would have been no need for her efforts. These women, along with those who served the great institutions of the Italian cities, did what they could in the way of solace and succour to make the value system of a Catholic society work by helping the at risk, underprivileged and in some cases abused. This scope for professionalization within the church offered a meaningful and active alternative to marriage which a Mary Astell or other women seeking to maintain a dignified single state within the confines of Protestant society might well have welcomed. The price was the habit and the vow.

The remarkable development of congregations and associations had in no sense been a Tridentine brainchild. Trent was concerned with orthodoxy and the education of Catholics in a purely doctrinal sense. The reform of the priest, and his election as model and purveyor of doctrine and as regulator of the lives of individuals and families through the confessional, was very actively promoted though with the greatest success perhaps in France, northern Italy and the southern Netherlands where a seminary-trained priesthood emerged more strongly than in the Iberian peninsula. Both the Jesuits and the Dominicans were energetically involved in strengthening the drive for purity and orthodoxy. Jesuit priests and the Lazarists made a particular effort to penetrate into the parishes, bringing with them books which were intended to be read aloud or lent for the time of the mission to those who could read for themselves. Such books were predominantly the lives of saints who came from lowly stock, like that of Saint Zita, the servant girl of Lucca, a medieval saint but one whose life was to be widely disseminated throughout Italy and Iberia in the seventeenth century. Zita, whose claim to sanctity was that she had distributed the property of her master to the poor (largely sacks of beans) and found it replaced in the cupboard by God, underwent a conspicuous remodelling. Her obedience to her master and her exemplary character as a hard worker and someone with a special relationship with God was emphasized, lest the thieving servant get the wrong idea.[40] The arrival of a mission in the village was a time of great excitement. It meant a different kind of sermon and new faces as well as stories and reading matter. The Jesuits, the Lazarists and later the Redemptorists went on missions to the parishes with the express intent of raising the level of spirituality and commitment. The usual pattern was to deliver a rousing sermon (of the hell-fire variety) in the hope that this would not only bring back any waverers but would stimulate gifts, offerings and pious works to help the poor and promote the missions. Frequently the two sexes were separated and women given individual attention. The priests appear to have found women particularly receptive. The Jesuit Jacques Darcemalle was thus described on a mission to Brissac in Anjou in 1707:

> He presented to them [women and girls] the enormity of their sins and the abuses that they had made so very often of the blood of Jesus Christ [by taking communion in a state of sin]. He put before them the image of Christ crucified reproaching them for their ingratitude and their perfidy. I would scarcely have believed the effect of this discourse had I not been a witness. They prostrated themselves face downwards on the ground. Some beat their breasts and others their heads upon the stones all crying for forgiveness and pardon from God. They vowed their guilt in the excesses of their grief. They took these excesses so far that the priest feared they would do themselves harm and ordered them to stop groaning so that he could finish his exhortations. But he could not silence them. He had himself to shed tears and to cease his discourse.[41]

This text is interesting in that it points to a residual clinging among the uninformed masses to a form of religious expression which the Jesuits were only too anxious to eliminate but which could still erupt in the eighteenth century, as evinced by the *convulsionnaires* of Saint Médard. (These were women and men who foamed at the mouth and went into trances and claimed themselves in divine possession.) However, it also indicates the power of the emotions to be tapped.

The missions were also events when appeals could be made to local people of substance to give generously to help their work. Specific cults were promoted. None of these was more successful than that of the Rosary promoted by the Dominicans from the fifteenth century along with the cult of Saint Anne, the holy grandmother. Although the cult of the Rosary preceded the Catholic reform it was now widely extended, and its significance is not to be underestimated. It was something that could be undertaken in isolation or in groups without the presence of a priest. To utter a decade of prayers while fingering the beads, and to use them as a prompt for spiritual exercise, the faithful did not need a church and did not need to be literate. It could be the perfect expression of faith when Catholicism was persecuted and churches were barred. It also served women well within the home and during their work. Even in the mid-twentieth century, women untutored in Latin would use the rosary (with its Ten Hail Maries and One Our Father) during the ordinary of the mass.[42]

It has often been stressed that the work of the reformers or the 'triumph of Lent' was to get women out of confraternities and rowdy manifestations of popular worship that took place at night and hence to curtail their activities. Certainly the intention was to exclude women, and hence imputations of lewd behaviour, from processions and public manifestations − though the attempt was not invariably successful − but confraternities dedicated to specific charitable ends directed by women grew very considerably in Italy in the late sixteenth and seventeenth centuries. Some were specifically turned to certain women's problems like prostitution and *malmaritate*, houses of refuge for beaten wives.

In stark contrast to what was going on in the Protestant north, the Catholic church developed the appeal of the visual as a means of colonizing and shaping religious fervour. It was not merely sermons and holy books, but a panoply of visual artefacts in the form of statues, pictures and altarpieces which were used to reinforce the all-important catechitical instruction. The illiterate were embraced in a veritable orgy of colour and form to promote a particular message and were presented with a comforting panoply of identifiable and useful personages, cults and saints who served each in their way to further the Tridentine messages. The images had to be correct and the artist also obedient to the truth as seen by the church. The Holy Family, with the bouncing Counter-Reformation baby and his young mother, the holy grandmother Saint Anne, the attentive and organizing Saint Joseph, drew the masses into a recognizable set of relationships with their deity to help in the business of solace and succour.

Veneration was to be rigidly separated from superstition and certain cults, like those of Saint Joseph, Saint Anne, and Souls in Purgatory, were to be used to inculcate specific values. God the Father, to whom all obedience was due, resided in heaven and with Christ and the Holy Spirit represented the Heavenly Trinity, but on earth, in the words of Saint Francis of Sales, 'Mary, Joseph and the Baby Jesus are an earthly trinity representing in many ways the holy heavenly Trinity.' The main altar or the retable was devoted mainly to the passion or the great scenes from the life of Christ, watched over by God, but in side chapels specific devotions were represented and among these the Virgin and Child, holy motherhood, predominated. The Virgin is universal protectress and rescues souls from purgatory. She prays for all and intercedes and gave Saint Dominic the Rosary to remind all of her intercessionary attributes. Saint Joseph is the good and asexual father, the saint of the good death because he dies surrounded by Mary and Jesus in his home. Saint Anne, promoted in the twelfth century and swingeingly attacked by Luther, was put by the papacy into the universal calendar in 1584. Always popular in the west of France, her cult spread throughout central France and Italy. She is of interest because Mary's role as mother is directed to infant care; that of Saint Anne is to raise a woman fit to be the mother of God. She rather than Mary, therefore, represents long-term working maternity. In popular art in the humblest chapels, she teaches Mary to read, hence inculcating Scripture, and watches over her even in childbed. Mary reflects on her mother, as do all girl children on their mothers. Such imagery endorsed traditional family roles: they were models for situations which everyone might experience and they endorsed the value of what every woman had to do. The statues which appeared in village churches of the Virgin and her mother were often donated by women who were thus drawn into another aspect of Catholic solidarity.[43]

The overall effect of the Catholic reform for women was twofold. First, women were converted into important transmission agents of the Catholic faith within the family. They passed on prayers, rituals and beliefs.[44] Second, they were drawn at all social levels into a complex net of relationships with each other, and with the confessor priest to whom obedience was due and who approved or blamed, issued penances and enforced a system, but who also remonstrated with the cruel or irresponsible husband. Above all, however, the process of acculturation, what they learned at home, in the community, at school, from books and through visual imprinting, conveyed an increasingly strong image of woman in the roles of wife and mother obedient at all levels to husband and priest. In return they were promised eternal rewards. So strong was the imprinting that when, in the eighteenth century, educated men who abhorred the irrationality of religion and the hold it had over the minds of the ignorant began to make their first faltering steps away from Christian beliefs as promulgated by any confession, they were not followed by the women. The different behaviour of women and men is reflected in testaments which, in the case of men, requested fewer masses for the repose of the soul or donations to help the poor or to promote missions and sermons.[45] It would suggest that the process of Catholic renewal, with its emphasis on the family, the special obligations of women, the scope it gave for the rich to assist the poor and for the poor to receive aid, and the entire business of solace and succour for suffering, won women to the cause and converted them into the church's staunchest supporters. Was it because it offered them socialization on respectable terms? Was it that they had not yet been given an alternative of equal comfort? Saint Anne and a Marian girdle for childbed; Saint Rita in the hope of escaping a brutal husband; Saint Denis to watch the child in the cradle. *Holy Mary Mother of God, pray for us sinners now and at the hour of our death, Amen.*

How different was the experience of women under the reforming hand of Protestantism? Clearly what had happened to Catholic women was an attempt to build on religious capital they already possessed and to purify and reaffirm the direction of their faith. What was involved in Protestantism was a severance, in some instances instant, in others gradual. If the two reforms had common goals – discipline, self-control, knowledge of and commitment to the word of God – they also had profound differences in how these goals were to be achieved. Protestantism was also nurtured in an environment of political conflict, frequently one of war and one in which national identity was also closely involved. It also had to depend on the support of princes whose commitment to the new moral rules was far from absolute. The one hundred or more years after Luther nailed his theses to the door of Wittenberg cathedral were ones of intense struggle. There was a thorny period of transition from one dominant faith to another. Moreover, there was not one Protestantism but many. In this confused environment, changes, some of which were abrupt but perhaps more were gradual, occurred in the lives of some groups of women. There were some new initiatives and for some a new source of self-awareness was found.

Perhaps the most conspicuous difference between Catholic and Protestant countries in regard to women was the attitude adopted by reformers towards the convent and indeed to the taking of any kind of religious vows by women. Luther attacked the unnaturalness of the practice, claiming that it held women back from their natural destiny as mothers and the means to salvation promised them in Scripture. In Protestant Germany, the spread of the Reformation was marked initially by the assumption by towns of control over the convents and their property on the grounds that women were incapable of effective administration, and later by a pronouncement that women were to be released from their vows and offered a dowry to allow them to marry. Luther himself was eventually to take a former nun to wife.

This policy was clearer and firmer in principle than it was to be in fact. The solution of matrimony was obviously only available to younger women. Whether members of a large or small community, many women clearly did not want to leave. They were allowed to cluster together to end their days in greatly reduced circumstances, and this policy was also adopted in Sweden under pressure from local families who clearly did not want the return of a maiden aunt on their hands. In some instances, orders were confused and bundled together pell-mell. At Augsburg, for example, the Benedictine nuns of Saint Nicolas were billeted on the Dominican house of Saint Katherine with no recognition of the distinct customs of these two orders. At Nuremberg, Caritas Pirkheimer, sister of the humanist, was among those who refused to go and she dramatized the diaspora of her order. She painted the council's henchmen as 'grim wolves' and staged a tearful farewell as each nun removed her veil. Several altercations occurred between 'sheep daughters' and 'grim wolf' mothers: Katerina Ebner rails against her mother: 'You are a mother of my flesh, but not of my spirit, because you did not give me my soul, I am not obliged to obey you in matters which are against my soul.'

Pirkheimer left a poignant testimony to her reluctance as her order disintegrated about her. In many respects she represents the highest scholarly level attained by a woman in the context of sixteenth-century society. Her *Denkwürdigkeiten* reveals not only a high level of spirituality but of biblical and scholastic knowledge. She was the kind of woman who found convent life ideally suited to her taste.[46] Such women, however, could find it difficult to gain support. They were an easy and immediate target for evangelical fervour and for the reforming zeal of what might be no more than a determined minority. Those houses established in the countryside, and whose corporate wealth included rents and dues which limited peasant exploitation of forest and river, could find themselves under attack in the Peasant Wars which erupted in the mid-1520s. Some of the earliest instances of German village women in protest are found during this conflict, when they attacked the nuns as immoral women who turned their back on God's way of salvation for womankind, the act of child-bearing. This policy of women bringing women to account, demonstrated also in attacks on nuns by townswomen during the French Revolution, was not the only form of participation by women in the peasants' bitter conflict. They acted as providers and distributors of food to the insurgents.[47]

Calvinist Geneva simply expelled all its nuns to the nearest Catholic territory. In Holland the more prestigious houses were phased out while at a less exalted social level some groups, like the Dutch *kloppen* (tertiaries whose name probably means 'castrated person'), forced to try to survive in a hostile environment, were driven underground and strove to keep Catholicism alive by teaching young children their catechism, being sustained by the alms of the faithful.[48] In the space of a lifetime, the regular religious life for women in Protestant Europe was undermined and the nun became a hallmark of papistry. Lyndal Roper has pointed out that the closure of the convent in a Protestant German city by 1540 marked the demise of Catholicism.[49]

The first diaspora is scantily documented. Certainly some societies felt this change less than others. England, for example, had a mere 124 female religious houses in 1534 (compared with 610 male) and they were small and poor. The majority had incomes of about £200 a year. The immediate effect of Protestant infiltration seems to have been a great deal of confusion which took some time to clarify. Protestantism and religious conflict in England was distinctive, for the breach with Rome was not undertaken because of any commitment to Protestant doctrine but for political considerations, Henry VIII's need to achieve both a divorce and royal supremacy over the church. The dissolution of the monasteries and the sale of church lands were acts undertaken at government level, less out of faith than out of covetousness. English monks and nuns were legislated away as the monarch, backed by Parliament, assumed the headship of the church.

At the same time, the infiltration of Protestant ideology from the Continent created in England a core of reformers sincerely committed to reshaping Christianity. The reform of the liturgy, and the endorsement of clerical marriage which took place in the brief reign of Edward VI (1547–53) were expressions of Lutheranism gaining ground, but these advances were checked by Mary (1553–8) and only cautiously and grudgingly did Elizabeth I acquiesce in a reversal. During her reign more advanced religious ideas influenced by Calvinism filtered in from the Continent, but it was not until after her death that a move towards more radical change gathered momentum. The tensions between the Stuart monarchy and a Puritanism entrenched in Parliament rent the middle decades of the seventeenth century. What occurred in England, then, was not a single Reformation but a series interspersed with reversions to old practices. In the course of such changes women appear in many guises, starting with two queens who because of birth were in opposing camps and could to a degree influence the course of events. Women exist both as individuals or in small groups for the promotion of change or they appear in defence of their faith when it moves into 'fortress' status. Certainly there was no single woman to represent all women, outside the prescriptive literature which poured from the printing presses.

Most people at the beginning probably experienced general confusion and were hostile to change. Whatever the general mistrust of Rome and a grasping upper clergy or lax priests, the old religion offered solace just as it did on the Continent. The panoply of sainthood and of devotions attached to the Virgin was found in every parish church. The rites of pregnancy and parturition ceded nothing to continental practice, as the numbers of girdles of female saints lent out to help and comfort women in labour shows. The Abbey of St Werburg in Chester made available a girdle of their patroness 'in great request by lying in women'.[50] There were protective saints, saints to help the sick – including children and cattle. Mary enjoyed more feasts than any saint in the calendar and who and what was worshipped in her name may have been highly gender-specific. She may not have overshadowed Christ but she coexisted with him as an all-suffering mother to represent all mothers. In time the Henrician Reformation was to entail a marked shift away from a religious culture rich in visual artefacts and rituals to something much more austere, a religion of the printed word, not of the image. It was also to strip Mary of her special role.

One of the first indications of any hostility to what was generally afoot manifested itself in Oxford in 1530 when the emissaries of the king came to test the waters among theologians and scholars about the royal divorce. Catherine of Aragon was widely seen as a virtuous and wronged wife and the emissaries were pelted with rubbish by the women of the town. Many clearly felt their own security as wives threatened if

this measure went ahead. Henry was also fundamentally disturbed when
Elizabeth Barton, 'the Holy Maid of Kent', a fine example of one of
those charismatic, raving, religious women who made prophecies in the
midst of trances already described in other European contexts, took a
strong line against the divorce and the threat to the church. In 1533
her prophetic utterances included the grim warning that Henry would
not, if he persisted in his actions, be king for more than six months.
She had to be discredited to maintain public order in a county alarmingly
close to London, and so she was arrested, interrogated and forced to
confess to fraudulent practice in much the same way as the Inquisition
dealt with the *beata/delusa* and Henry VII with the Holy Maid of
Leominster.[51] (The woman in this instance had claimed to live by the
sacrament alone and she presided over the rood loft in the cathedral
until an investigation conducted by Lady Margaret Beaufort revealed
that she was secretly fed by the curate.) The discrediting of the Holy
Maid of Kent left her supporters confused and thereafter they dwelt in
a climate of fear as succeeding opposition movements like the Pilgrimage
of Grace were stifled. The banning of confession by the monarchy was
probably an astute move, stripping the clergy of its hold over individuals. It was not until 1544 that Cranmer replaced the old Latin
liturgy of the saints by the vernacular liturgy in which the saints were
reduced to a minimum (one mention for their intercession) and Our
Lady was scarcely to be found. The justification for change was always
the 'word of God' even if this meant 'the will of man' or 'royal power'
rather than 'Gospel truth'. It was a clever step, however, that the same
injunctions which abolished relics and images ordered every church to
acquire a Bible (1538). At a stroke, holy text became the focal point
of holy commitment.

Reactions to the 'stripping of the altars' are now being pursued and
what seems to be emerging is that a fervent group of iconoclasts went
in for destruction but that in many parishes a large number of statues,
chalices and church ornaments used to house relics were hidden, stowed
away by parishioners who included women. Enough were available for
some restitution under Mary.[52] Who knows what happened to the holy
girdles or to the rituals of childbed?[53]

A study of the early 'weaning process' from one faith to another has
yet to be made on any scale for any country and such an endeavour
must be fraught with difficulties. Not to conform with government
policy was illegal and therefore such activity went on *sub rosa*. Most

pointers exist for Geneva, a small enough territorial entity for authority to have some sway. The Calvinist Consistory Court made a determined attack on popish practices (204 cases between 1542 and 1544) and found women outnumbered men usually on a two to one basis, though in the case of the possession of a rosary the discrepancy was much greater, involving 24 women and only two men. Prayers and devotions to the Virgin and prayers for the dead were also issues where there was a heavy female/male imbalance which could be used to justify the statement that women were more tied to Catholic ritual and practice than were men.[54]

Among the women who embraced the Protestant cause in mid-sixteenth-century England and who were called upon to help maintain that faith during the Marian persecution, a number of literate noble-women and gentlewomen emerge who clearly found in the changes an opportunity to promote the beliefs they had developed in active dis-cussion with scholars, theologians or their families or through reading. When threatened during the reign of Mary, they could shelter behind their social status and their sex. An extreme instance is perhaps afforded by Catherine Willoughby, Dowager Duchess of Suffolk, who during the reign of Henry VIII became the leader of the 'advanced' faction at court. Sheltered from royal wrath by her husband, Charles Brandon, a close friend of the monarch, she employed young preachers of advanced views on their estates, supported them financially and recommended others to her influential friends. She subjected the Catholic faction at the court to constant ribaldry lent edge by her ready if not always subtle wit. She had a small yappy dog which she paraded through the corridors with the name 'Gardiner' strung around its neck (Bishop Gardiner was the leader of the Catholic party) and summoned it whenever a Catholic courtier was in view.

She spearheaded innovation on her husband's extensive Lincolnshire estates and among the preachers she introduced there was Latimer, who became bishop of Worcester in the reign of Henry VIII and martyr under Mary. All government directives abolishing holy days, removing images and relics from churches, destroying shrines and banning 'idol-atrous' practices were speedily implemented. She was insistent in her efforts to stop pilgrimages and untiring and constructive in initiatives to lift the level of instruction of parochial clergy and to provide parish churches with a vernacular Bible. Bishops, vicars, and curates were personally exhorted by her to be diligent in preaching at the parochial level against the usurping authority of the pope and to inculcate in all, but especially the young, the reading of Scripture, the Lord's Prayer, the articles of faith and the Ten Commandments in English. In this way change reached out to a broader social spectrum and was associated with the education of a new generation of Protestant believers. Catherine gave advice to churchmen, rather than receiving it. If she maintained silence in church, she paid preachers who accorded with her views. There was no pontificating authority powerful enough to contain her or command her deference. Protestantism had need of her and Catholicism receded before her as long as King Henry lived.

As a wealthy widow at the age of 34, when her energies seem to have been at their peak, she took as her second husband Richard Bertie, her gentleman usher. In social terms this was an unequal match and tongues wagged. He was, however, a godly man and on these grounds commanded Catherine's respect. He was also someone unlikely to restrain her, a husband to whom obedience was not due. When Mary succeeded to the throne and Protestant divines found themselves in prison, Catherine furnished financial means to relieve the distress of Latimer and Ridley and their associates. In March 1554, Archbishop Gardiner summoned Richard Bertie to London to put to him the necessity of silencing his wife. Doubtless threats were made, though it is doubtful if execution was seriously considered. Between them Gardiner and Bertie decided Catherine must go into exile. What followed cannot really be described as 'flight' so much as a leisurely and indeed ostentatious departure with a retinue of eight servants and innumerable pack horses. From Gravesend the party embarked on a long odyssey which went as far as Poland, where the Catholic King Sigismund Augustus received the duchess warmly. Even then, Catherine did not lose touch with England and, once Elizabeth was established on the throne, she was quick to urge upon her minister Cecil the need to reassert the Protestant faith.[55]

Catherine never suffered more than disappointment for her faith. Martyrdom was not the lot of aristocratic or of gently-born women on either side of the religious divide in either Britain or France. Lady Fane, Joyce Hales (daughter-in-law of Sir James Hales) and the widows of Richard Neville and Walter Manuel were a group active during the Marian persecution who struggled to keep Protestantism alive. Somewhat lower down the social scale, a widow called Alice Warner ran a hostelry in Limehouse which was used as a meeting-place for Protestants whose lives were at risk.[56] Jane Wilkinson and Ann Warup, also widows, visited Cranmer, Hooper, Latimer and Ridley in Oxford jail during the Marian troubles. The heavy preponderance of widows is to be noted: lacking a man to control them, they occupied a twilight zone as far as authority was concerned.

The ill-defined status of widows and of married women acting independently in their husbands' absence can also be seen among households which clung to Catholicism under the Elizabethan recusancy laws. The corpus of this legislation applied only very tangentially to women. Neither Lords nor Commons were prepared to intervene in family government and so disturb the authority of the male head. Hence, even during the interludes of more intense application of these laws such as after the Armada (1588) and the Gunpowder Plot (1605), widows and women whose husbands were frequently absent infringed the spirit of the law flagrantly and virtually without retribution. The arrival of 'priest searchers' in a home was the moment for the mistress of the house to offer food and drink and to persuade the searchers that her husband was absent and that they should not proceed. If the husband was present and a search revealed signs of a priest, then the man was liable for capital punishment.[57]

Between 1588 and 1603 more than 800 English Catholic priests were ordained abroad and were committed to recatholicizing England. When they returned to their native land they were at great risk and had to move from safe house to safe house. Some of these were the homes of simple working women like Alice Tully of Stafford or Ann Lyne, a widow who ran a school in London, or Ann Vorx who sheltered the celebrated priest Garnet for the best part of twenty years. More, however, belonged to gentry families who wished to reach accommodation with the British government and within English society where they were landowners and enjoyed a status confirmed by their historic past. At the same time, they wished to preserve their faith and to do so had to support a forbidden organization. Their ambivalent position was reconciled in two ways: first by giving the adult male householder the outward social role of negotiator and seasonal conformist to Protestantism – the law demanded that the head of the household worship according to the confession of the state once a year – and second by endowing the mistress of the house with the responsibility for the perpetuation of the faith within the family home.[58]

Whenever a faith became a 'fortress faith' it tended to fall into the hands of women because it took place behind locked doors and was dependent upon transmission within the family and household. The Catholic fortress faith of gentry households in sixteenth-century England had the mistress of the house as its pivot. She organized the household's day around a liturgical cycle which included the reading of *vies édifiantes*, imported from the Continent and probably largely written by nuns, which spoke of the tribulations and triumphs of the household committed to spiritual defence. The Jesuits provided in translation their stories of heroic women like Judith and Deborah who were the salvation of the tribes of Israel; the increasing popularity of Judith in print and picture attests to a new significance given to her in the context of an an embattled faith. Some recusant women constructed beautiful private chapels such as those prepared by the Countess of Arundel and Lady Montague for the use of the family and household, where a sanctuary lamp was kept alight to attest to the presence of the Eucharist and the faith of the family. During this difficult period, morning and evening devotions were organized without the presence of a priest. The emphasis was on prayer and meditation in conformity with post-Tridentine teaching. They had, of course, to find a spiritual director and priest to give absolution and communion, and he had to be hidden; sometimes he adopted the role of tutor to their children and was integrated into the household as a dependant. The sheltered priest gave systematic teaching and catechitical instruction to the young. He emphasized that the spiritual duties of women must take precedence over their marital duties and insisted on a version of Catholic motherhood that was a spiritual rock of strength serving the church in exile diligently. Martyrdom was not recommended nor did the women offer it, but wiliness and strategy – the traits of Judith – were applauded. Risk-taking was minimized; but the Catholic noblewoman knew how to manage special events, like Christmas and Easter, when a group of loyal friends might be invited to a sung mass with imported musicians. The family had to be organized to cope with the difficult times. Sons, denied places at Oxford and Cambridge, would make for Louvain and the Catholic continental universities; daughters were often sent to consolidate their faith in convents in Antwerp and France. Family contact therefore depended upon letter-writing and upon news from those who returned or came to the household as guests.[59]

While aristocratic women were on the whole spared reprisals, women of the working classes were more likely to be punished for adherence to the wrong faith at the inappropriate time. They appear on both sides of the confessional divide. In Foxe's *Book of Martyrs*, a critical text in the history of British Protestantism during the Marian persecution, 55 women are numbered among the 275 cases executed – one woman for every five men. The ratio is perhaps typical. Authorities everywhere, including the Spanish Inquisition, were more interested in the nonconformity of men although in particular Spanish auto-da-fé women could reach 40 per cent of the prosecuted Protestants.

Foxe's female martyrs, however, are worthy of note. Only one of them, Anne Askew, was from a 'good family'. The rest are simple, poor and unlettered. These women are used by the martyrologist in two ways. First, they provide instances of the tenacity of the simple and virtuous who have an unclouded vision of the truth because God is able to speak to them through their unsophisticated minds. In this respect Foxe's comments draw upon the ideas of the holy woman rooted in the historic past. Secondly, Foxe uses these women to make the reader ponder at the crassness and turpitude of Mary's henchmen who turn their anger on what Foxe labels 'silly women and infants' – 'silly' in the sense of naïve or innocently uninformed. He details, for example, the case of a woman who went into court with a copy of the Lord's Prayer in the vernacular tucked into her sleeve, an act of innocent folly (or of belief in the magical properties of this particular text?) which was the only evidence summoned to condemn her. Foxe seems to despise the partisans of Rome for concerning themselves with the faith of silly women, while at the same time considering the adherence of these pure and simple devotees an ornament to the Protestant case. Similar 'innocent' lowly women who refused to part company with Rome were prosecuted under Elizabeth for sheltering priests or for idolatrous practices.[60]

The oscillations of the English establishment in supporting the Protestant cause make it difficult to assess whether married women followed their husbands or took independent initiatives as in the case of the Catholic widows with whom we have been concerned. Certainly some married women had chosen an independent path by the reign of Elizabeth (1559–1601). There are many instances of the defence of Puritan preachers and demonstrations against 'popish' clerical garb by female groups.[61] Because of widespread female illiteracy it is almost impossible to discover what the loss of Mary and the saints meant to any individual woman in her lifetime. However, much doctrinal change took place gradually, in contrast to Holland where it was accelerated by iconoclastic riots in the 1550s in which women participated. A representation of Magdalen last appeared on the English stage in 1582 and over the ensuing decades attempts were made through Bible reading, sermons, the witchcraft persecutions and the denigration of the pseudo-mystical, along with the substitution of a more austere morality, to change the character of popular beliefs. It was a slow process with implications for future generations, who were stripped of a visual religious culture but provided with more sermons and more biblical instruction.

If English Protestantism was a slow-growing plant, in parts of Flanders and Germany more radical expressions of religious commitment were taking root as sects multiplied. The most conspicuous site of proliferation was Germany, reflecting the diversity of opinions which jostled for recognition in petty states and cities where religious orthodoxy was the concern of the ruler, but where that ruler could not stop dissent subsuming entire communities. Luther had merely opened debates which Zwingli, Calvin and others were prepared to refine, all claiming Scripture as their mainspring. He had placed clerical marriage on the agenda for debate and the relationship between sexuality and holiness was opened up for discussion. If Luther made an ideal of monogamy and the holy household, where fathers and husbands were obeyed and Christian harmony prevailed, a number of fringe sects claiming inspiration from the word of God moved towards a different interpretation. The 'Dreamers', a group of illiterate peasants from the Erlangen area arrested in 1531, scandalized more conventional believers by claiming (mostly under questioning by torture) that they had divorced and remarried according to 'spiritual rules'. For this sect 'spiritual' marriage meant listening to the word of God which came from within, and justified the putting aside of a morally imperfect relationship and opting, after a period of abstinence, for another union based on divine prompting. The new marriage was the perfect one. What was happening was largely an adulterous exchange within the community. Some of the women, when questioned, alleged that they had taken the initiative for change.[62]

The Dreamers, through their belief in adult not infant baptism, were associated with Anabaptism. The group of Anabaptists in Munster found themselves with a considerable excess of women after an expulsion of some of the male members of their sect from the city. To cope with the unattached women (a law code of 1534 introduced the death penalty

for women who refused to subordinate themselves to a husband) poly-
gamy was introduced. This resolved the scriptural behest that marriage
and procreation were essential for woman's salvation. Denounced as
'rabble' by Luther and subjected to severe persecution, a third of the
final toll of martyrs was composed of women, decried as ignorant,
superstitious and heretical by mainline Protestantism.[63]

The first fifty years of German Protestantism witnessed a number of
prophetesses, direct legatees of the Catholic mystic tradition, and the
emergence of the pastor's wife who laid down a new tradition for the
Protestant matron. Katherina Zell, wife of pastor Mattheus Zell and
the only woman pamphleteer of the Peasants War, sought to justify
and to promote the role of the pastor's wife in the godly community.
She later participated in theological debates in a way more conspicuous
for fervour than for clarity. Among the Schwenkfeldian group in Ulm
(centred upon a Silesian who split with Luther over questions of discipline), Elizabeth Heckler gained a reputation for holiness and learning
and she in fact pronounced Schwenkfeld's funeral oration in 1562,
earning obloquy from the local clergy. More individual names could be
cited,[64] among them Argula von Grumbach, a German noblewoman
who published a defence of a Lutheran preacher and urged the right of
women to speak in church,[65] or Ursula Weyda who in an attack on the
Abbot of Pegua in 1524 also claimed the right to speak out as a daughter
of Joel.[66] However, the dominant messages of the German Reformation
did not leave much scope for the abandonment of traditional roles.

In France, Protestantism which had filtered into the country via
Geneva, stronghold of John Calvin, was to become a fortress faith in
the course of the seventeenth century until almost entirely eradicated
by the Revocation of the Edict of Nantes in 1687. The early history of
French Protestantism is one of a movement down the Rhône artery and
into Haute Languedoc and the Cevennes where it nestled in the barren
hills and created its own particular culture, as well as gaining some
foothold in specific towns and cities. Up to the 1570s there is some
affinity with early development in England. A number of noblewomen
embraced the cause, converted relatives, protected pastors, promoted
policies, financed preachers and clearly found excitement and fulfilment
in forwarding the Protestant cause in the way that Catherine Brandon
had done.[67] When their husbands made peace with the monarchy and
reconverted to Catholicism many of the women clung to their views, and
it became an official part of government policy to place their daughters in

convents run by the Ursulines, in the hope of converting them. Groups
of city women of Lyons in the mid-sixteenth century found a new
involvement in a faith which permitted them to sing hymns and take
a more active role in religious rituals. These were women drawn from
a variety of social groups, including merchants and artisans, and some
were to find themselves isolated by the imprisonment of their husbands.
A number of printers' wives continued business in defence of Protestant
views during these embattled times.[68] Finally, when Protestantism was
increasingly isolated in the hills of the Cevennes, it was not only preserved in the rituals of the home but it was also characterized by prophetesses and mystical ravers, very much a tradition of women's religiosity.
Throughout the seventeenth century most Huguenots tried to keep a
low profile under increasing restriction of their activities. Finally, with
the Revocation of the Edict of Nantes, the great diaspora began.

Britain was not isolated from continental developments. Many of the
British women who fled across the Channel during the Marian persecution were neither lowly nor stupid. Among the 788 emigrants who
have been identified, 125 (a sixth) were women and their presence has
been located in Geneva, Strasbourg and Amsterdam. Of those who went
to Geneva, city of Calvin, the career of Anne Locke is best known and
indeed she has been presented as the paradigm of the godly Tudor
matron.[69] She was a friend of John Knox – a difficult role, one would
have thought, for any woman – who initially encouraged her to come
to Geneva as the 'most perfyt schoole of Chryst'. Calvin himself was far
from blind to the influence women of substance could exercise in their
own countries in promoting Protestant doctrine.[70] Anne Locke's husband, a merchant mercer, was opposed to the move, doubtless because
of his business or a less than absolute commitment to his wife's religion.
Anne, however, knew of other wives who were leaving their husbands
to advance in spiritual excellence and she was away for two years. During
this time, she translated Calvin's sermons on Hezekiah and served as
an informant and distributor of news when Knox returned to Scotland.
In 1559 she returned to London and became the centre of a growing
Puritan group who were deeply critical of Anglican ceremonial and
external pomp such as priestly vestments. When her husband died in
1571 she married Edward Dering, a preacher some ten years her junior
and much poorer. He was quick to ensure the integrity of her estate
and the inheritance of her children by Locke.

Dering was a charismatic preacher and a figure conspicuously akin to the father confessors who were moulding the faith of Catholic gentry women in continental Europe.[71] Anne had to share him with a bevy of ladies of substance who hung on his words: Lady Mary Mildmay, Lady Golding, Mrs Mary Honeywood (of Fuller's *Worthies*), Mrs Barnet of Bray. Mrs Catherine Killigrew, one of the four learned daughters of Sir Anthony Cooke, was a very well-connected lady, sister-in-law to Burghley, who had access to the queen and to Francis Bacon, so that she was instrumental in protecting Dering from any official disapproval of his more advanced sermons. Within five years, however, Dering had died from consumption, and in due course Anne married again, this time Richard Prowse, an Exeter draper, mayor of that city and a member of Parliament in 1584. Although a devout man, he was not of martyr material and during the later years of the sixteenth century, when times were difficult for those of advanced Puritan views, he took his wife to the West Country. Here she again turned to literature, justifying herself for her limited ability *because of her sex* to further the building of God's house and proffering what she called 'a basket of stones' towards this construction in the form of an epistle to Ann, Countess of Warwick, another doughty Puritan woman. The work was intended as an encouragement to the godly in difficult times.

For the Reformation historian Patrick Collinson, Anne Locke exemplifies a type of woman seeking the truth of the gospel and believing herself justified in assuming a modest part in the propagation of her beliefs. Her independent initiatives are not great, though it was no small step to go to Geneva, and she is protected by her status as married woman whose husband acquiesces in her behaviour. But she represents in England a first generation of women who gradually redefine the role of a woman and her right to think for herself; she demonstrates a stage in the formation of self-consciousness and shows her belief in her right to determine her own spiritual path to salvation. Her personal life is beyond reproach and she gains in impregnability because she cannot be dimissed as trivial.

Anne Locke is also an early example of a woman writer of a kind that was to become more common after the outbreak of the English Civil War in 1640. Up to that year, women's writings had accounted for a very small proportion of the volume of printed works, but thereafter they experienced a quite astonishing increase. Most of the works were religious and reflect the issues of the times. A large percentage, however, constituted a new genre for women, recording their spiritual experiences. Some were intended for publication (reworked, autobiographical memoirs), but others were not (most diaries). Much of this writing was akin in intent to the accounts recorded by Catholic women on the insistence of their confessor, but with one important difference: the Englishwomen were acting as individuals without anyone to control what they committed to paper. In 1656, John Beadle published a manual for diary keeping as a spiritual examination, but many Englishwomen, mostly drawn from the gentry and upper mercantile classes, were already at work.

The spiritual diary was often a blend of memoirs, meditations, lists of providences and special favours from God, family and community records and miscellaneous memoranda. While some used the diary as a means of retailing their spiritual odyssey, others used it as a means of coping with everyday life. Some clearly found that the exercise helped to reconcile them to a difficult husband, pecuniary problems or loss of infants. Lady Anne Clifford frequently thanked God for taking her side against her unloving husband. Elizabeth Freke actually called her diary 'Som few remembrances of my misfortuns which have attended me in my unhappy life since I were marryed'. When any of these works were published, editors tended to edit out the personal details in favour of the meditations.[72]

Anne Locke, apart from the short period spent in Geneva, had been able to contain her views within Puritan society in England even if they were discouraged by the government. Over the next fifty years others emerged of a more radical disposition and separatist churches proliferated, counting a high proportion of women among their congregations. The first decades of the seventeenth century saw the emergence of Brownists, Independents, Baptists, Millenarians, Familists (members of the Family of Love), Seekers, Ranters. They shared a common belief that the national church contained ungodly elements and that separation, perhaps complete self-government of individually constituted religious bodies, was the only way to create a pure and spiritually regenerated church. For some of the groups this satisfaction could only be sought in exile.[73]

The land that received them was Holland and this is in itself of immense significance. When it came to asserting their equality in church and before God, a segment of Dutchwomen were the first to cross an important threshold among European women. There is no simple explanation for this. Holland was the cradle of humanism; a mercantile economy in which the city populations were predominantly female; a society with women whose husbands could often be absent at sea and who had shared with their men the violence and deprivation entailed in the expulsion of the Spaniards; and the Dutch had an increasing tendency to aggressive anti-papistry. For all these reasons, Holland perhaps provided the best environment for a change in the religious status of women. When that small fraction (a few hundred at most) of Englishwomen left home and possibly husband to cross the channel to Holland to follow leaders like Browne and Harrison, they found an active debate about women's role in the church under way. Most of the Englishwomen were illiterate and have not left any written testimony to their response, but what they discovered was that here and there in the Dutch Calvinist church, a few women sometimes held minor offices as deaconesses and that in some they voted on important matters, perhaps including the choice of minister. They do not appear to have been preachers before 1630.[74]

The separatists who returned in the 1640s appeared convinced of their spiritual equality with men and laid claims to speak in church, if not necessarily to preach. In the 1640s and 1650s groups of women became prominent in the actual foundation of churches. Of the twelve who founded the Baptist church at Bedford in 1650, eight were women. At Norwich in 1645, the congregation contained 31 men and 83 women. It also appears that as more women became capable of reading the Bible, they not only wished to teach each other to read but to expound the Scriptures also. Most of the evidence about women preachers refers to Baptists in London and there is also evidence about Baptist activity by women in Kent, Ely, Lincolnshire, Salisbury, Hertfordshire, Yorkshire and Somerset. However, such women were not numerous. The writer of a scurrilous pamphlet in 1641, entitled *A discovery of six women preachers in Middlesex, Kent, Cambridge and Salisbury with a relation of the Names, Manners and Doctrine*, indicates that they only played a marginal role. The terms of the pamphlet are very like the charges made against *beata/delusa* women or the Camisard *inspirées*. They are presented as insane, raving, ignorant and unnatural.[75]

Dorothy Hazzard was a founder of a separate church and her points of view and independence of action can be measured. Her husband was a Bristol grocer and when he died she ran the business, making sure to keep it open on Christmas Day to demonstrate her contempt for superstition. Clearly her reputation for nonconformity was already well established when she met the young minister Matthew Hazzard. They married and he secured the incumbency of St Ewins (1639–62), where Dorothy gave shelter to families leaving for New England and helped devout women during their confinements so that they could avoid churching and infant baptism. These two elements in conventional Anglican practice were deeply troubling to women who had versed themselves in Scripture, for neither could be justified by reference to text. Increasingly, Dorothy had reservations about the Book of Common Prayer and, having wrestled with her conscience, absented herself from her husband's church to found her own. Her immediate associates in the enterprise were a farmer, a butcher, a farrier and a young minister. The opinions of her husband on her initiatives are not recorded, but even if the marriage was 'unquiet' the couple continued to cohabit for thirty years. Her church had a congregation of about 160 and Dorothy chose the minister, a Mr Pennill. When the royalists occupied Bristol in 1643 the church left, returning two years later. Dorothy's role became less central and the returned group met at the house of a Mrs Nethaway, a brewer's wife, who took the initiative to ride into Wales to find a preacher whose reputation was known and approved of by the group. In 1671, the first list of the 160 members of the congregation showed that three-quarters of them were women, and the ageing Mrs Hazzard was still an active and honoured member when she died in 1675.[76]

Another founder of a separatist church was Katherine Chidley, wife of a London haberdasher and herself a seller of stockings. It is not known which church she belonged to, but she is known both to have preached and to have written eloquent and very pugilistic religious tracts. In the first one she took on a critic of the independent churches, one Thomas Edwards. While educated women for a century or more had published translations of religious treatises or words of spiritual comfort, controversy was a new area. Chidley is also known to have disputed publicly with the minister of Stepney as to whether an ecclesiastical building which had been dedicated to a popish saint could ever be used for the reformed service of God. She is believed to have been the founder member of a church at Bury St Edmunds in 1646.

Women of solid commercial stock, Chidley, Hazzard and others like them believed in their inalienable right to choose a religious form that conformed to principles which they endorsed and about which they had thought closely. They did not follow a husband. They were not necessarily drawn to sects which accorded more rights to women, but they do appear most prominently in sects which did so. Above all, such women wanted to have a say in the choice of the preacher. Very few arrogated to themselves the right to preach.[77]

More assertive of their rights were those Leveller women who emerged in the 1640s. This radical sect looked beyond religious change to political equality for all households in England. When the male leaders of the sect were imprisoned, their wives, Elizabeth Lilburne in particular, continued to print pamphlets and propaganda and organized mass petitions before Parliament for the release of their husbands. They were demonstrably committed to a more assertive role for women in their church. 'We will not sit in silence' became a virtual slogan. Denigrated by the House of Commons as 'whores', 'fishwives' and 'unruly women', imprisoned and subjected to immense physical suffering which included the loss of children in prison, Lilburne and her associates stand out in the annals of Englishwomen. They are not simple and untutored, and they expect no miracles to deliver them from prison; they use all the modern tactics of protest, from the press to mass petitions and demonstrations. They know how minds are influenced and how to work the system. They are not in pursuit of political power for themselves, though they believe in the representation of the household through the male head. What is clear is that, for them as for other seventeenth-century English radical women, the most pernicious of the many inequalities which they perceived to exist between the sexes was religious inequality. In an age of faith it was essential to confront God on equal terms.[78]

Of all the religious affiliations which attracted women in the second half of the seventeenth century, that of the Quakers stands out. The Society of Friends was founded by a shoemaker, George Fox, who was quite unequivocal in his assertions of women's rights to preach and predict. He based his claims on Scripture, and in so doing exposed many of the contradictions in that random compilation and showed that by comparing alternative quotations it was possible to see that the ancient assertion of women's inferiority and alleged need to keep silence was a purely arbitrary decision on the part of churchmen. He claimed that the true church was a living organ and not an ancient building and hence took religion out of an environment, 'the steeple house', in which women had been trained to feel at a disadvantage, and placed it in a simple room or 'meeting house'. It became at once domestic and familiar. Stripped of the trappings of a formal church service, the meeting became an event in which people sat in silent contemplation until an inner prompt caused them to share their inspirations. Knowledge and learning outside the Bible were not vital.

His first convert in 1647 was Elizabeth Hooton, a married woman of fifty who turned preacher and began a career of proselytizing which familiarized her with the insides of many of England's prisons. Incarceration, however, did not silence her. Among the numerous conversions that followed Hooton, that of Margaret Fell, the 38-year-old wife of a member of the Long Parliament, mother of seven daughters of whom three became preachers, was to be Fox's most noteworthy. Margaret became the inspiration behind, and the most substantial contributor to, the Fund for the Service of Truth, a pool of money which financed travelling preachers, paid their passage to overseas countries and helped them and their families if they were imprisoned for their faith. Margaret was articulate and persuasive. She wrote to Cromwell four times to try to secure tolerance for Quakers: she petitioned Charles II to secure Fox's release from prison and she explained to the monarch why 700 Quakers had been imprisoned without just cause and should be freed.[79]

Margaret Fell was the first of a number of active and committed women like Jane Waugh, Anne Clayton, Mary Fisher, who brought Quaker doctrines to New England in 1656, Mary Dyer, later hanged in Boston, or Elizabeth Williams, publicly flogged for addressing the undergraduates of Sidney Sussex College, Cambridge. In spite of such persecution, Quakerism was sufficiently developed for 'above seven thousand handmaids of the Lord' to petition fruitlessly in 1659 against the payment of tithes to the Church of England or any other religious body. This was the first public manifestation of a developing coherence among Quaker women which would be confirmed in the 1670s by the first Women's Meetings in London designed to direct their efforts towards philanthropy.

This social work was aimed primarily at the Friends themselves, to provide help to prisoners and to the sick, widowed or fatherless, but it soon gained wider application. The increased incarceration of the Friends under the Clarendon Code enacted in 1661–5, which imposed stringent penalties on all Dissenters, resulted in the designation of particular women to have responsibility for the care of prisoners in particular prisons. Elizabeth Hooton was given the Fleet, Ann Whitehead took on Ludgate, and Anne Travers, Southwark. The last was a widow of property and an employer of women (probably needleworkers). In the 1680s she ran a boarding school for young ladies in Chiswick. Her work in Southwark jail was shared by another propertied widow, Anne Merrick, who became her second in command. The job largely consisted in purchasing meat and broth and 'ordering their servants to bring it them', that is, to the imprisoned Quakers. Regardless of who paid for the service, they certainly administered it and received money from those prisoners who could pay.[80]

The prison visitors could find themselves imprisoned, though men were more likely to be arrested. When Fox died in 1691, he left 50,000 Friends in England (1 per cent of the population and 4 per cent of the female population). Afterwards, however, lacking his charismatic leadership, they declined in number. The sect seemed to ossify in a number of middle-class families whose main hallmarks were their solidity, their austerity, their total sobriety and their social conscience. Counted among such families were the Ackworths, the Howards and the Frys, active in education for the poor, prison reform, slave emancipation, homes for destitute children and colonial mission work. Even when its buoyant appeal for the masses was lost, the philanthropic basis of Quakerism, a woman's religion, was still maintained.[81]

The Quakers had demanded much, perhaps too much, of their followers. Their closing of ranks in the eighteenth century to prevent members from marrying out, and their deliberate clinging to old modes of dress and archaic speech, converted them into social oddities which perhaps undermined their appeal. The austerity of the meeting, the abandonment of all rituals – particularly those surrounding birth, marriage and death – perhaps deterred subsequent generations. The impetus for growth in the eighteenth century passed without doubt to the Methodists. They were less radical, less exigent and they offered a more sociable and very immediately joyous religious expression, lent strength by a charismatic pair of preachers, Wesley and Whitfield. Novelty may have also enhanced the attraction. Methodism offered a survival kit for the average woman in a society in which the obstacles to self-sufficiency were legion. It presented the world as it was rather than as it should be, that is, imperfect in every way. The collected works of Wesley and Whitfield recommend to women the qualities best fitted for a successful negotiation of the existing system. Women are to become wives – no looking outside the conventional order – and men want a particular type of wife, clean, chaste and thrifty. Such a woman is temperate and eschews all alcohol, which epitomizes lack of thrift, loss of control and hence of virtue, and indifference to cleanliness and appearance. The model presents to an aspirant husband an unsullied reputation and the prospect of sufficiency. She holds out to him the virtuous example and hence leads him to forswear self-indulgence and the evils of drink. The couple's unremitting industry and ever vigilant eye on the Devil and his works would permit survival and with God's blessing more. The less fortunate within the congregation should be helped to regain their sufficiency. Work sessions, hymn singing and social occasions may also have helped to enhance the appeal of Methodism for women. In meetings men and women sat apart. Certainly where statistics for chapel attendance exist, women outnumbered men by nineteen to one. Although the hierarchy was male, it was often under female patronage. Wesley thought that preachers should usually be men but could be women. Until 1803, when the main body of Methodists took the decision to restrict preaching to men, women seem to have found a voice in this church. The decision merely provoked more breakaway congregations to form.[82]

As Bossuet noticed, Protestantism from its inception fragmented further. Sects that broke away tended in the early stages to have a large proportion of women,[83] but as they consolidated themselves in the seventeenth century a male direction assumed control. The fragment then subdivided and the breakaways frequently included more women than men. The process then began again.

The English experience has close parallels with Holland. In the early seventeenth century Dutch sects pre-empted those of England and, through the experience of the immigrants, influenced the English ones very considerably in the opportunities they gave for women's participation. These sects never attracted in either country more than a small minority of women. Within Dutch Calvinism a godly, Protestant matron type with authority in the community emerged very conspicuously and such women have been portrayed in a strong visual legacy showing them as regentesses controlling hospitals for the poor and aged and orphanages, or dispensing charity to the sick and needy. They sit solidly and confidently, symbols of a plain godliness and rectitude. We also find in Holland that religion provided the stimulus, as it did in England, for women to commit their godly thoughts to paper.

In 1638, Anna Maria van Schurman (1607–78) produced the *Amica dissertatio inter Annam Mariam Schurman et Andr. Revetum de capacite ingenii muliebris et scientia*, a plea for the right of women to learn languages, philosophy and theology to arrive at greater devotion. She gained an international reputation and her house in Utrecht was visited by the famous and the powerful. She knew both Elizabeth of Bohemia and Christina of Sweden. At the age of sixty she adopted a more austere form of Protestantism under the influence of the Frenchman Labadie, founder of the first fully schismatic body arising out of the Calvinist Reformed church in Holland. This group found a haven first in Amsterdam and then in Altona, with a congregation of three hundred or more, among whom women predominated and Isabella de Moerloose was for a time counted. Clearly the sect appealed to women who wished to construct for themselves both an alternative lifestyle and a 'family' of believers.[84]

One aspect of seventeenth-century Protestantism was the encouragement it gave to literacy, reading first and then writing. Imbued with the desire to read for themselves the word of God, groups of village women in Britain and Holland gathered together to help each other conquer reading skills. Although it has been estimated by David Cressy that by the early seventeenth century only 10 per cent of women could sign their names and by the beginning of the eighteenth century only about a third, these estimates hide a number who could read. The Bible was the road to scriptural knowledge and every person believed that he or she had the right to read the word of God. Although no mass programme of state schooling was to emerge until the nineteenth century, local initiatives and philanthropic efforts had by the beginning of the eighteenth begun to produce a number of charity schools for the daughters of the poor but honest. Such institutions, which burgeoned exponentially in the eighteenth century, existed to give a grounding in morality, but this included literacy. Unlike the French *petites écoles*, which were often of a vocational nature and did not teach writing, these schools began to make inroads into female illiteracy.

The Protestant reform did not offer women any alternative to matrimony, as did the Catholic reform by the quasi-professional institutional life of the religious congregations, nor did it provide solace and succour in quite the same way as the panoply of saints and cults enriched by the Counter-Reformation. It did, however, in some instances give scope for greater female autonomy, particularly in some of the sects or dissenting groups. It also increased the potential for women's initiatives at the administrative level and in the unpaid voluntary work surrounding institutions such as orphanages, hospitals and schools. Nonconformity

engendered prison visitors and moral campaigners. It fostered generations of daughters, wives and mothers with a developed sense of social
obligation to the wider community. The religious *émigrés* who came to
Britain during the French Revolution thought that women's philanthropic work was underdeveloped in comparison with what they had
known in France. However, no less a person than William Wilberforce,
looking back over the eighteenth century, was to write:

> There is no class of persons whose condition has been more improved in
> my experience than that of unmarried women. Formerly, there seemed
> little useful in which they could naturally be busy, but now they may
> always find an object in attending the poor.[85]

Taken overall, and with close regard to the experience of those individuals who left a written testimony, some gained deeper self-awareness
through the act of writing down their thoughts or through discussions
with priest or pastor. Some gained an identity through choosing a new
religious form and stepping out of the orthodox line. Both Reformation
and Counter-Reformation, however, were committed to the traditional
social figuration of the Christo-Judaic inheritance. As long as Europeans
remained the people of a book this tradition could be dented, but it
could not be fundamentally reshaped. Furthermore, and this merits
reflection, as agents of transmission, mothers perpetuated the message
of a patriarchal religion.

CHAPTER ELEVEN

Corresponding Gentlewomen, Shameless Scribblers, Drudges of the Pen and the Emergence of the Critic

A slip in writing is a slip in virtue.
ALONSO DE ANDRADE, 1642

. . . the Age of ingenious and learned ladies; who have
excelled so much in the more elegant branches of literature,
that we need not to hesitate in concluding that the long
agitated dispute between the sexes is at length determined;
and that it is no longer a question, whether woman *is* or
is *not* inferior to man in natural ability, or less capable of
excelling in mental accomplishments.
RALPH GRIFFITHS, MONTHLY REVIEW, NEW SERIES, XXII,
1798, 441

BETWEEN 1500 and 1800 the number of women who seized
the pen and of those who went further and inched into print
multiplied very considerably and the literary forms they chose
diversified. There were several reasons for this growth: it is related to,
and utterly dependent upon, a number of developments which were
themselves interrelated. One was the increase in literacy, which generated a reading public and which itself was a result of improved educational facilities: the school, the governess or simply the literate mother
who taught her children to read. As well as multiplying potential
readers, a growth in literacy also generated authors drawn from a broader
social spectrum.

Another important factor was the evolution of a 'print culture' assuming multiple forms, including newspapers, philosophical treatises and

creative literature ranging from the trivial to the elevated. The two religious reform movements had aimed to make the people of the west 'the people of a book'. The Bible continued to be Europe's best-seller, and religious works, particularly printed sermons, continued at least throughout Protestant Europe to outnumber other forms of publication (though the number of titles printed does not tell anything about the size of print runs). By 1800, in Britain in particular, but evident in all those countries which had shaken off the control of the censor, there had been a print revolution; and if it did not reach down to the lowest levels of the population it certainly brought books within the reach of the artisan family or that of the comfortable farmer. Increasingly, reading for improvement, the central principle of sixteenth-century reformers, gave way to reading for pleasure. In this process Protestant Europe outstripped Catholic.[1]

During the Italian Renaissance, the patrician who owned and had read a hundred books was accounted learned. By the end of the old regime libraries of nobles and professional men could count thousands of volumes. Alongside these large personal libraries were bookshops which hired out books and in England there were lending libraries with annual subscriptions which were well within modest means. Works increasingly crossed national boundaries and were translated, an exercise generating employment as well as a greater degree of awareness among the reading public. As this reading public spread ever downwards, theological works, classical authors and philosophical or medical tomes were outpaced by newer genres including novels, satire, poetry, ephemera like cookery books or fashion, and a developing polemical literature critical of both church and state. The revolution in consumerism, itself including the acquisition of books, was partly fuelled by journals and literature which contributed to the shaping of taste.

Both men and women were readers and writers, but in neither capacity did the two sexes begin or even end the period on equal terms. There was a considerable difference in the amount of education available to each of them and the kind of literature written by men was, in many cases, substantially different from that written by women. In certain genres, notably the novel, books of household management and allied skills, works on women's duties, schoolbooks, and certain kinds of religious works (though not sermons), the presence of the woman writer was by 1800 very marked. In others such as serious history, philosophy, classical studies, or theology their contribution was relatively slender, though far from absent. As for the writing of treatises on law and medicine and those relating to most sciences, the lack of specialist training virtually excluded women. We do not know how many translations were done by women. Most strikingly, by 1800 a few women writers were represented in the corpus of literature issuing a critical challenge to arbitrary government. They questioned the relative status of the two sexes in existing society. Such women writers were not the first literary feminists, but they were the first whose works were printed and read outside a very narrow aristocratic circle.

The history of the woman writer is obviously closely, if not solely, linked to the development of female literacy. In 1500 the ability to read and write at anything more than a fairly basic level was confined to women of high noble birth, some of whom were to be found at specific courts – particularly in Italy – and some in the convents. We may be dealing with under one per cent of the population. Court and convent both provided the time and the opportunity to write and think for those who wished to do so, although these habits were more likely than not to have been acquired at home, in girlhood. Humanist scholars, notably Erasmus, but others such as Sir Thomas More or the influential Juan Luis Vives, recommended learning as a way of keeping noble women virtuous. Significant figures such as Isabella d'Este at the court of Mantua, who became a patron of both artists and scholars, combined the role of hostess and of learned lady.[2] The earliest poetry by female authors circulated in manuscript at court, but by the late sixteenth century the works of a number of poetesses were printed and their authors celebrated in the verse of admirers within their particular civic cultures of Venice, Bologna and Rome.

Christine de Pisan at the French court wrote the first treatise on the limitations which bound a woman's life in her *Livre de la Cité des Femmes* (1405), which was not printed until it appeared in English translation as *The Boke of the Cyte of Ladyes* (1521).[3] Its publication in English perhaps reflected humanist interests at the court of Henry VIII. Margaret Beaufort, mother of Henry VII, was a promoter of scholarship among women and a force of learning in her own right. Such women were remarkable among their contemporaries.

If humanism gently encouraged the aristocratic learned lady, other trends in Renaissance thought were pessimistic, notably the revival of Greek science, as well as the continuing and pervasive insistence on the Old Testament version of womanhood. Contrasting views of the nature of womanhood gave rise to a debate (known in France as the *Querelle des femmes*) joined by a number of learned men and women in defence of the female sex. The manuscripts that were generated have been represented as Renaissance feminism, interpreted to mean criticism of a view of woman as a being morally inferior to man and the attempt to establish the truth that both sexes were full human beings. Those who supported the positive view of womanhood accentuated the power-lessness and the objectification of women, which they attributed to the moral perversion of men who tyrannized over half the human race. Men needed more of the feminine virtue of gentleness and women were enjoined to develop mind and body against male abuse.[4]

In late Renaissance Venice a number of highly literate patrician women declaimed against the constraints imposed upon women by men. They addressed particular issues, above all perhaps the dowry system, which they saw as turning women into victims. For example, Lucrezia Marinelli, the sister of a famous Neoplatonist philosopher and clearly from a scholarly home, produced *La nobiltà e l'eccellenza delle donne co' difetti e mancamenti di gli huomini* (The nobility and excellence of women with the defects and deficiencies of men, 1601). The work lives up to its title: she praises women and criticizes men who abuse the property belonging to their wives. Male profligacy, largely a way of impressing other men, converts wives into beggars. In Neoplatonic vein she chal-lenged Aristotle for his theories about the inadequacies of the moral and physical condition of women as laid out in *De generatione animalium*. She also questioned his objectivity and claimed that he was a misogynist whose difficult relationship with his wife distorted his judgements. She allowed him to have opinions, but these should not be considered immutable laws. Opinions can vary. If women woke from their somnol-ence, men, whose only attribute greater than that of women is their physical strength, would be forced to listen and then their pride would be turned into gentleness. Her work constitutes a trenchant attack on one of the most important classical influences upon the Renaissance.[5]

We have already seen that in Venice in the 1640s, Arcangela Tara-botti attacked the dowry system from within the walls of her convent and deplored the lack of choice in the lives of women due to the greed of men. Virtually contemporaneously with Marinelli, Veronica Franco wrote love poetry. As she was a courtesan, her writing of amorous verse was acceptable as an accomplishment to be praised along with musical and linguistic gifts as well as some knowledge of a classical inheritance.

The courtesan was part of a 'profane', that is non-Christian, culture and no eyebrows were raised if she entered the world of print on explicitly sexual issues. Franco's verse, however, embodied poignant comment on the price a woman paid for mixing with men in public without the ties of matrimony – loss of respectability and dependence upon physical attractiveness which could vanish all too easily with the years. She was quite clear in her mind that her status as courtesan was transitory and that she was as subject to the whims of men as any wife to her husband. Her apparent freedom was false freedom and the ultimate consequence of her life suffering, possibly in poverty. Her poetry is one of protest and above all it is about the powerlessness of women, the leitmotif of Renaissance feminism.

If the Renaissance feminists succeeded in getting into print, which was by no means guaranteed, their reading public was very small indeed, confined to their own circle. The outpourings of the great lady, and still less of the cloistered nun whose works were vetted by her spiritual director, her superior or the bishop, could not generate any widespread consciousness of gender inequality. Furthermore, the huge economic difference separating the courtier and civic élites from townspeople and still more from a largely illiterate peasant society, dedicated to the sovereign imperative of producing enough food to see the family through the year under the harshest of physical circumstances, hardly permitted one group to communicate with the other.

From the mid-seventeenth century onwards, however, in England, Holland and Germany there were some signs of a broadening of the range of women taking up the pen. The spiritual diary became a vehicle for committing thoughts to paper. Indeed it was Holland of the Golden Age that saw the introduction of commercial diaries, with blank pages for daily entries along with astrological and other information, specially intended for women. This development did not necessarily lead to print.[6] Other factors were involved. In England, the relaxation of publishing controls during the Civil War resulted in a tripling of the printers who were after business, creating new opportunities for the writer; for the first time this meant a number of women writing on their own behalf.[7] At the same time, in the Europe of the Counter-Reformation, another kind of literature was also flourishing, saints' lives and spiritual meditations written by women but under the direction of men.

Reading, as opposed to writing, cannot be effectively measured. The two skills may be related, but generally more people could read than were able to write. One man in three and two women in three could not sign their marriage record in Amsterdam in 1630; by 1730 the percentages were 24 per cent of men and 49 per cent of women and by 1780, 15 per cent of men and 36 per cent of women. Amsterdam had particularly large numbers of female rural immigrants and literacy among the native born may have been greater. In Britain the female literacy rate rose (very approximately) from 1 per cent in 1500 to 25 per cent in 1714 and then to 40 per cent by 1750. Generally, it is assumed that on the eve of the Revolution in France about two-thirds of men and a third of women could write, but these figures obscure a considerable difference between north and south. Again very generally, north of the Loire, town-born women of the middle classes and upwards were able to read and write by the middle of the eighteenth century. The highest literacy levels in Europe by the mid-eighteenth century may have been reached in Prussia where schooling was obligatory from 1717. In Spain, Inquisition trials point to a literacy rate among men of about 50 per cent in the first half of the seventeenth century, but we cannot know whether a cross-section of the population is represented and it is assumed that female literacy was very low indeed. Mystifyingly, it is suggested that literacy levels *fell* in the nineteenth century. Generally, whatever inroads were made into lower class illiteracy, women lagged behind men.[8] However, until a certain basic level had been reached, writing for the lower classes remained at the level of the chapbook, which could be purchased to be read aloud to the many. Until a certain literacy level had been crossed there was little point, for example, in writing a book advising maidservants on what to do with the money they had saved before marriage and how to choose the right husband, and expecting to find a market.[9]

The concerns and aims of the woman writer, the language she used and the works produced, for whom and with what response, have commanded the attention of large numbers of feminist literary scholars. Many individual texts have been analysed to permit an entrée into the writer's world and to offer a summary of any kind is perforce reductionist. The concern here is to examine the woman writer as a historical phenomenon and to ask such questions as what might cause certain women to go into print, and under what conditions might they do so? Then we may discern at what point some women writers became explicit critics of the system.

To understand the development of the woman writer and her position in society, we need to consider not merely literacy but the moral ground such a person occupied at the beginning of the seventeenth century and obstacles to her endeavours. Her problems were explicit in every European context. How could a woman expose her thoughts to the world and still retain her reputation? As the Jesuit Alonso de Andrade remarked in 1642, in a phrase that was to render the Catholic woman author conscious of her deeply ambiguous position: 'For a woman, a slip in writing is a slip in virtue.' He compared her to a pilgrim who could very easily degenerate into an itinerant prostitute.[10]

Why should this be so? The holy father was not referring to the mere act of writing. Indeed, father confessors throughout Catholic Europe were at this time advising the more ardent members of their flocks to write down their thoughts and several were then published, often under the name of the priest and heavily edited. Memoirs and diaries intended for personal or family use within the home were generally commended to women as a proper activity for regulating their spiritual lives. Protestantism was committed to reading the Bible, to prayer and to reflections about one's soul which it was perfectly proper to commit to paper. Letter-writing was almost essential and it went outside the family, but only into the hands of friends so it was not explicitly 'public'.[11] Italian nuns were considerable producers of lives of saints who were conspicuous fo. fortitude in holiness. The contentious act, then, was not to write but to cross over from the private thoughts of the spiritual diary, the life of the saint, the family chronicle or the letter to close friends, into print. The journey from pen and ink to typeface was the one that was fraught with perils for a woman's reputation.

Of course, there was no specific set of written rules to prohibit the female sex from publishing its works. The activity was not illegal. We have seen that the reputations of great court or patrician ladies were not sullied by the endeavour, particularly when it took the form of occasional verse. However, these were very isolated and rarefied beings. For the generality, the activity could be presented as immoral, or rather as not quite moral. This attitude in itself needs explanation. To go into print was not necessarily to present a feminist agenda or to criticize the premises upon which society was constructed. Far from it. But for women's writing to remain on the right side of respectability, it must fit certain stereotypes.

Devotional works, like Anne Locke's biblical commentaries or the saints' lives churned out by nuns, were on the whole neutral documents attesting to impeccable uprightness. Women had souls, and spiritual musings were therefore proper to women. So were child-care manuals. The first two of these in the English language were Elizabeth Jocelyne's *The Mother's legacy to her unborne child* (1624) and Dorothy Leigh's book *The Mother's Blessing* which appeared in 1616, ran into several printings before the end of the century, and was a commercial success for her printer. Other areas of acknowledged and respectable expertise for women were the cookery book or the herbal.[12] Hannah Wooley, twice widowed and a maker of medicines as well as the manager of a training school for servants, for example, flourished as an acknowledged authority and writer on domestic crafts. Her works, which may have brought the author a welcome income supplement, included *The Cook's Guide* (1661) and *The Queen-like Closet* (1671), which combined recipes and domestic advice and ran through five editions. These were clearly secular works but in a female field. At virtually the same time in Venice, Lucrezia Romana wrote an important fashion book for noblewomen, with more pictures than text, *Ornamento nobile per ogni gentil matrona dovi si contiene bavari, frisi, d'infinita bellezza* (1620), and Elisabetta Catanea Parasole compiled *Prestiosa gemma delle virtuose donne* (1600) which promoted lace-making using prepared patterns. For women to go into print on other topics was more contentious, because it was to step into a space not regarded as theirs. It was to go public; to break silence; to throw off all pretence at being a little March violet and demand a hearing from a wider audience than one's nearest and dearest in the way that the male author did. This was the nub of the problem: a woman who entered this dubious space drew attention both to herself and to her family. What kind of a woman would run such risks?

At the other end of the writing spectrum from Saint Teresa of Avila, John Knox's friend Mrs Locke, nuns writing holy lives or the history of their order, holy women whose spiritual writings were edited by their father confessor, women offering good advice to women on child care or household management, were some women of distinctly dubious repute who sought fame and gain irrespective of considerations of respectability. Veronica Franco wrote of love with the authority of the courtesan. The playwright Aphra Behn (1640–89), who carries the distinction of probably being the first European woman to make a living from her literary oeuvre, conformed perfectly in every degree to the general view of a writing woman whose morals were frankly questionable. Such a reputation may have helped her into print but it was not one a clergyman's daughter, for example, might envy.

Behn[13] had had an adventurous youth in Surinam, served as a spy in Antwerp in 1666, was imprisoned for debt in 1670 and then set about earning her living as a playwright. Sixteen of her works for the stage were published over the next nineteen years, the permissive court and city life of the Restoration providing her with raw material and contacts. A friend of courtiers of dubious reputation, rakes and bisexuals like the Earl of Rochester and the lawyer John Hoyle, with whom she had a passionate and unhappy affair, her work was fast-paced, explicitly bawdy, bold and witty. She dedicated *The Feign'd Curtezan* to Nell Gwyn, mistress of Charles II; *The History of the Nun* was dedicated to another royal mistress, the bisexual Hortense Mancini; other works extolled the joys of sexuality for both men and women and declared them stultified by the forced marriage which reduced a wife to the role of prostitute. She wrote poems, songs, epitaphs, and she made translations of French works. Her versatility was to become the hallmark of many later commercial writers. She felt keenly her inability to cope with the classics, unless in translation, and defended a woman's right to study science and philosophy. Her epistolary novel *Love Letters between a Nobleman and his Sister*, some 200,000 words long, was published in three instalments between 1684 and 1687 and ran into sixteen editions over the next century. Its success can be imputed to that well-tried recipe, sex and scandal among the great; indeed, it was based on a real-life scandal in which Lord Grey of Werke (Philander in the novel) eloped with his sister-in-law, Lady Henriette Berkeley (Sylvia).

There was no doubt that Aphra Behn was a woman of the world who nailed her colours to the mast in almost every work she wrote. As such, she conformed to a notion of the publishing woman who overstepped the bounds of propriety in search of an income. She showed that women might indeed write and make money but her reputation as a woman and her reputation as a writer were consonant. The problem for many aspirant writing women was how to transcend the limited range of largely devotional writings while holding on to propriety; in particular, how to broach topics which were regarded as a male preserve without, as a woman, being charged with stepping out of line? In the first instance, we might consider the position of the woman who wished to discuss philosophical, religious or polemical subjects even if publication was not the initial intent. The appropriation and discussion of serious learning was something that a number of women, scattered across the nations and emanating from courts, patriciates and scholarly families, deemed important. How could a woman take part in scholarly debate at the highest level?

The right of discussion or understanding must, of course, be separated from the act of publication. Humanism had extolled the learned lady but not the lady writer. Broadly speaking, there were two major ways in which individual women forced an entry into the world of learning and both implied a close association with men. The first was through the salon and the role of the literary hostess or *salonnière*, which implied some wealth. The second road lay through a literary or scholarly relationship, usually by letter, with a man of acknowledged learning: those who followed this path could be termed 'corresponding gentlewomen'. France more than any other country was to see the full flowering of the *salonnière*, though there were significant literary salons in Amsterdam and Venice in the seventeenth century and in Berlin, run largely by Jewish women, in the late eighteenth and nineteenth centuries.[14] The second mode, that of the corresponding gentlewoman, may have as her foundation model Anna Maria van Schurman, and it also knew a conspicuous development in England in the late seventeenth century and into the eighteenth. Both the *salonnière* and the corresponding gentlewoman were in similar business and the *salonnière* in some instances might become a corresponding gentlewoman. Both courses implied self-realization through scholarship but, with some exceptions and speaking very generally, it was the second rather than the first who sought to publish.

The woman who above all created the typology of the *salonnière* was the Marquise de Rambouillet in the late sixteenth century. It is perhaps to be noted that her Italian mother was herself a woman of great intellectual distinction who had given a great deal of attention to the education of her daughter who, married to a French noble, was frankly appalled by the vulgarity of the court of Henri IV. Her own feeble health and later the political disgrace of her husband under Richelieu, caused her to withdraw into her own home where she created a salon as a centre of refinement and culture. The room, which had to include her bed in an alcove, was decorated and fitted with objets d'art, mirrors (an expensive novelty) and furniture including very comfortable armchairs, antique marble, crystal, Chinese porcelain, the whole put together with exquisite taste. Huge windows overlooking a natural garden and iridescent colours gave the ensemble a sense of light. Into this earthly paradise she invited poets and writers and men and women of taste and sensibility, a truly élite gathering, to engage in the new and developing art of conversation. This was no mere exchange of banalities but conformed to imposed norms of civility, modes of address and intellectual content.[15]

What did such an endeavour do for women? Madame de Rambouillet was the patroness of Madame de Scudéry, an early novelist and a woman who never married, isolating herself from the company of men. More significantly, perhaps, Madame de Rambouillet associated the intelligent woman with new standards of refinement and civility, politesse, contrasting the coarseness of male society to the cultured elegance of the salon environment. This was probably her most conspicuous legacy to an ensuing generation of women.

In the second half of the seventeenth century, and perhaps revitalized after the civil wars of the Fronde, the salons multiplied. The most famous were to be those of the précieuses who claimed for themselves learning at the highest level and set their faces against marriage and the domination of men. These were leisured women excited by the full flowering of French culture – Descartes, Pascal, Fénelon and scientific advances. Molière was to mock them twice, in Les Précieuses Ridicules (1659) and Les Femmes Savantes (1672), for substituting the love of knowledge for the love of men. Their concern with language – they gave the word obscène to the French language and refused to use the word aimer for the love of an inanimate object like a piece of fruit – was accompanied by the desire to return to classical concepts which they considered had greater purity and clarity. Had not the ancient Greeks had three separate words for love?[16] The concern with purity of form, language and authenticity is visible in the works of those aristocratic women Marie-Cathérine, baronne d'Aulnoy, and Henriette Julie de Castelnau, comtesse de Murat, who were among the first writers and compilers of fairy tales in the 1690s; Madame d'Aulnoy was also counted among the précieuses. The writing of such tales, which expanded in the eighteenth century, may have been regarded as an acceptable activity for women since they were intended for the young.

Generally, the précieuses did not themselves, with rare exceptions, seek to publish, but they appropriated for women of their class and education the right to learning at the highest level, thereby challenging the notion of woman as a defective intellect. Their conscious distancing from sexual entanglement and their concern that their group should be woman-centred and focused upon female learning mark them off from the great salon hostesses of the eighteenth century. They contributed in no small part, however, to the growing perception of the leisured learned lady as the quintessence of civility and the arbiter of taste.

The salon of the eighteenth century embodied a new set of values. In Dena Goodman's words 'the eighteenth century salon transformed a noble leisure form of social gathering into a serious working space'. In this space there was room for the male philosophic community, but the whole was presided over by a hostess whose role was not to run a school of *civilité* frequented by leisured nobles but to facilitate discourse between nobles and commoners who, in Diderot's opinion, shared the Enlightenment ideal of changing the accepted way of thinking.[17] Enlightenment philosophy questioned not only the premises on which government was currently based and rejected the notions of a divinely ordered universe, but criticized, argued and tested every accepted assumption – except for the status of women in society. (They did, however, 'modernize' the reasons for the perpetuation of this status.) In this heady atmosphere of challenge and dissent a firm direction was needed, lest discussion should degenerate into anarchy. The hostess was a facilitator and provided a congenial institutional base, a comfortable home environment for the philosopher. She was a professional, in so far as she had to plan and organize the social gathering over which she presided on a weekly or a bi-weekly basis and make it a success. That success was measured by the readiness of the great minds to come and to import other luminaries from the republic of letters. Her salon had to be at one and the same time a central clearing house for information and ideas, a structured forum for appropriate discourse conducted with due formality, and a meeting place for great minds. There was no room in this space for the amateur hostess, the dilettante or the woman incapable of imposing a strict discipline.

What sort of women were the *salonnières* and what did they want? The answer may not be quite the same for the entire set of famous hostesses who characterized the Parisian scene in the second half of the eighteenth century. Certainly they were all intelligent, mostly self-educated, women who also had an educational mission and who found fulfilment in shaping the social form of the salon. The Abbé Morellet insisted that Madame de Géoffrin, perhaps the most celebrated of the eighteenth-century *salonnières*, had as her ambition, 'to procure the means to serve men of letters and artists . . . to be useful in bringing them together with men of power and position'.[18] This definition sounds more self-denying than it actually was. Most of the *salonnières* looked upon their activities as a real career, though one without a salary. They needed to be rich and free from economic or other personal commitments which might inhibit their ability to give themselves to the business of opening their houses to the learned. Madame Géoffrin had apprenticed herself to another *salonnière*, Madame Tencin, for twenty years before opening up on her own account. Madame du Deffand assiduously attended the learned gatherings of the Duchesse de Maine before she developed the confidence to begin. Madame Necker gained experience by frequenting the salon of Madame Géoffrin, and Julie de Lespinasse had been Madame du Deffand's companion for the best part of twelve years before she was prevailed upon by a number of *philosophes* to set up on her own. She was one of the least contented *salonnières*, clearly searching for a personal intellectual and emotional fulfilment that she never quite found. Madame de Lambert opened a salon allegedly to cure herself of too much gambling.

Madame Necker perhaps had the mixed motives of advancing the career of her husband and of finding a niche for herself in a society where she was a foreigner. She, however, has left the best record of how a *salonnière* structured her week. The salon had to be a regular event and she chose Friday so as not to clash with Madame de Géoffrin who operated on Mondays and Wednesdays, Julie Lespinasse on Tuesdays, Monsieur and Madame Helvétius on Thursdays and Madame d'Epinay on Saturdays. Between the sessions the *salonnière* prepared the next event. Madame Necker would jot in her diary aides memoires such as 'je parlerai à Chastellux de la *Félicité publique* et d'*Agathe*, à Mme d'Angiviller sur l'amour . . . Relouer M. Thomas sur son poème de Jumonville'.[19]

Of all the *salonnières*, Madame d'Epinay probably had the most conscious literary ambitions of her own. Her personal life was messy – a loveless marriage which also left her with syphilis, a number of tumultuous love affairs, one with Friedrich Grimm, and two illegitimate children. She was to set herself to become a *femme de lettres* and use all the literary forms available to the age: essays, epistolary novels, dialogues, articles and correspondence. Letters were critical to the *philosophes* of the republic of letters because they broadened the range and possibilities of the discourse outside the salons and conquered geographical space. Certainly the voluminous correspondence between Madame d'Epinay and Galiani was intended to be published.[20] Monarchs themselves, including Frederick the Great of Prussia and Catherine the Great of Russia, corresponded with certain *salonnières* as well as with individual philosophers, demonstrating their commitment to modernity and progress. In Catherine's case, a westward-looking female monarch had to be a learned lady if only by correspondence. Manuscripts could also be circulated and commentaries made by post. The *salonnière* was a critical element in a network of communications. To be a *femme de mérite* in this world real intelligence was needed, but one which did not detract from the sovereign imperative of the dissemination and elaboration of the ideals of the male philosophers.

It would be very difficult to say what the *salonnières* did for a broader section of women than their own very limited constituency. Theirs was a voyage of personal fulfilment, but they also demanded, and largely if not invariably got, esteem from the men whose interests were served by the salons. The philosophers who surrounded them had views on womanhood which were in the main deeply conservative, although given a more modern ring by the use of the word 'natural' in place of the earlier assertion of a God-ordained pattern. The French Enlightenment was profoundly anti-clerical and insisted that the Roman Catholic Church perpetuated falsehoods to keep man in bondage. The philosophers jettisoned notions of a divine will and replaced them by a belief in natural laws which governed the universe and lay at the basis of human behaviour. In trying to discern a 'natural' woman, the most distinguished minds of the century – Rousseau, Diderot, D'Holbach – strove to apply modern thinking, but in so doing frequently reiterated old and gloomy views on the nature of womanhood.

Diderot, for example, admitted that women were thrice victimized, first by defective education, second by the pains of childbearing and third by unsympathetic legal systems, but claimed that their nature was fundamentally different from that of men and was intimately linked to the process of reproduction which constituted woman's destiny and fulfilment. He urged an understanding of woman's violent and frequently irrational emotions, her lust after sexual and reproductive fulfilment, and he lumped female emotions, reproductive systems and religious fanaticism together as a product of the natural defects of composition. In his novel *La Religieuse* (which circulated in manuscript in the salons), Suzanne is the victim of parental greed which pushes her into the convent, making her a victim in turn of her bodily urges and the unnatural physical lusts of the artificial society around her. The salvation he proposes is that of a male protector – though the one he provides cannot solve all her problems. The narrative is riddled with inconsistencies and improbabilities, not least Suzanne's belief that she is capable of earning a living from her needlework which will maintain her free and independent in the outside world: perhaps it was fortunate for Diderot that the book was not available to the illiterate working masses. Above all, for him, as the *Supplément au Voyage de Bougainville* shows, women were intrinsically savages; the veneer of civilization remained skin deep and he firmly believed that they needed to be trained to respect convention as a means of control but also as the way to contentment.[21]

A large body of scholarship on women in Enlightenment thought demonstrates the degree to which distinguished French male minds refused to accord full rationality to women and endorsed submission to the male head of household.[22] Rousseau thought it better that Sophie, the wife of his ideal citizen Emile, should not read books at all, at least before marriage. He despised the *salonnières* as women who neglected wifely duty and stepped outside their natural position. The air the *salonnières* breathed was, therefore, deeply conventional as far as the ordering of the sexes was concerned.

The small literary salon which gathered around the sister poetesses Anna and Tesselschade Visscher in Amsterdam in the 1630s[23] was composed of both men and women. The much larger gatherings of the 'bluestockings' in eighteenth-century London, which included Hester Chapone and Hester Thrale (later Piozzi), Elizabeth Montagu and Elizabeth Carter, were female managed, but they seem to have had relatively smooth relationships with major male literary figures, even Samuel Johnson.[24] The bluestocking ladies transcended the *salonnières* in that they very actively promoted women's writing. They were mostly writers themselves and carefully nurtured networks promoting serious works by women. They were perhaps a development of the corresponding gentlewomen, and several fitted into this category themselves.

The corresponding gentlewomen who emerged in the second half of the seventeenth century were intelligent and informed ladies who corresponded and were associated with male scholars and who, often with their assistance, then published their work. Anna Maria van Schurman, who has already been mentioned, was educated to a high level by her father and a Dutch theologian, Gisbert Voet, whose lectures at the university she attended, discreetly concealed from the male students by a curtain. She conducted a correspondence with many intellectuals of the day, including Descartes, Gassendi and Constantijn Huygens, and with significant political figures like Christina of Sweden and Elizabeth of Bohemia, who openly admired her and was herself counted amongst Descartes' many correspondents. A woman of considerable and varied talents, known as 'the learned and most noble virgin' of Utrecht, able to write verse in Latin and Greek and dedicated to inner truth rather than fame, she published disquisitions and works marked by moral and metaphysical reasoning, but on marrying the Pietist Labadie she retired from writing to contemplate inner truths. Before this spiritual retreat she published in the 1630s a work in Latin, translated into English in 1659 as *The Learned Maid, or Whether a Maid may also be a Scholar*. It claimed the right for women to exercise their intellect while recognizing differences in talent and disposable time among women. Grammar, logic, Latin, Greek, Hebrew, mathematics, metaphysics and history were deemed particularly appropriate, but she also claimed the right to knowledge about theology and politics: 'we in no ways yield that our maid should be excluded from the scholastic knowledge or theory of those, especially from the most noble doctrine of politics and civil government'. Furthermore, 'whatsoever perfects and adorns the intellect of Man, that is fit and decent for a Christian Woman'.[25]

The Learned Maid, though perhaps little more radical in its claims for women than what had emanated from Venice fifty years before, was a product of impeccable Protestantism and lent authority by the knowledge that its author consorted with men of letters and was not found wanting in academic skills. This model soon found numerous replications in England after the Restoration. The first English authoress of any extent, 'author of a dozen works in almost as many genres,'[26] was Margaret Cavendish, Duchess of Newcastle (1623–73). Of privileged birth and married to a man thirty years her senior, to whom she was totally devoted (the marriage was childless) and who was also an amateur poet, she explicitly sought fame through literature.

> I confess my ambition is restless and not ordinary, because it would have an extraordinary fame; and since all heroic actions, public employments, powerful governments and eloquent pleadings are denied our sex in this age, or at least would be condemned for want of custom, is the cause I write so much.[27]

Regarded by her friends and critics as odd or eccentric, an impression confirmed by her elaborate dress, she bestowed her works on university libraries and on her acquaintances. She was passionately interested in natural philosophy and arranged to be invited to a meeting of the Royal Society in 1667. Mocked behind her back, but tolerated for her rank and because her husband condoned what she did, she became the leading seventeenth-century advocate of more education for women:

> Women are become like worms, that only live in the dull world of ignorance, winding ourselves sometimes out by the help of some refreshing rain of good education, which seldom is given us, for we are kept like birds in our houses, not suffered to fly abroad to see the several changes of fortune and the various humours ordained and created by nature, and wanting the experience of nature, we must needs want the understanding and knowledge, and so consequently prudence and invention of men.[28]

During the Interregnum, when the theatres were closed, she wrote closet dramas. She also wrote the first autobiography of an Englishwoman, 'A true relation of My Birth, Breeding and Life' (1656), and in 1667 the first biography of a husband by an Englishwoman, *The Life of the Thrice Noble, High and Puissant Prince William Cavendish, Duke, Marquess and Earl of Newcastle*. The work provoked Pepys into describing the duchess as 'a mad, conceited and ridiculous woman' – indeed, reference to Margaret Cavendish as Mad Meg or Mad Madge seems to have been general. What protected her from imputations other than madness was her social standing. Duchesses are a limited group and the manners of the great are not to be compared with the manners of lesser folk. Moreover, all her work confirmed her as a devoted wife and one who also wrote with the permission of her husband. She praised him for his willingness 'to peruse my Works, and Approve of them so well, as to give me leave to Publish them, which is a favour few Husbands would grant their Wives.'[29]

Margaret Cavendish is exceptional in her precocity, but there are elements in her history which make her representative of certain developments among a very limited sector of European élites in the seventeenth century. She was avid for knowledge and she had enough education and confidence to ask questions. Behind her lay a century of religious conflict and about her was active dissension on the nature of government and the essence of civil authority. She also stood on the shoulders of a couple of generations of isolated women who had made cautious ventures into print on appropriate subjects. She operated both in England and France within circles where intellectual discussion took place and she sought to participate. Like Anna Maria van Schurman she corresponded with distinguished intellectuals – Huygens, Hobbes, Joseph Glanvil, Walter Charleton and Henry More – and as such was an early English example of the corresponding gentlewoman then emerging in England and Holland and later in France and Germany.[30]

The traffic in ideas between these ladies and the scholars they addressed was not just one way. Lady Ann Conway, for example, with the full knowledge of her husband, maintained a close intellectual friendship with the philosopher Henry More (who collected her notes and published them after her death) and is held to have had a distinct influence on Leibniz's concept of the Monad. Distinct coteries formed and certain philosophers such as John Norris, the Cambridge Neo-platonist, became known for their preparedness to respond to questioning women. At first glance it is tempting to see these savants as a secular equivalent of the father confessor, directing the spiritual progress of particular women. There was a difference, however. The business of the male scholar was to receive the questions of his woman correspondent, to elucidate points and guide her towards deeper knowledge and hence greater self-realization. The confessor confined himself to a narrow spiritual range and could cut off a line of enquiry if he did not regard it as pertinent to the woman's spiritual progress. Moreover, questioning the man of letters or the philosopher might give some women the confidence to publish their own work, knowing that the association and approval of the scholar would guarantee respectability.

The career of Mary Astell (1666–1731) illustrates the process and also demonstrates how a woman of considerable intellectual merit could proceed from establishing her academic credentials as a corresponding gentlewoman to becoming a critic of the system. In so doing she perhaps wished to reach the woman reader in particular as well as seeking to persuade men.[31]

The daughter of a prosperous Newcastle coal merchant and the niece of Ralph Astell, a graduate in philosophy from Cambridge, Astell is thought to have been educated by her uncle (a bachelor with an unde-manding job as curate in St Nicolas' Cathedral) in philosophy, logic and mathematics. She came to London at the age of 22 and experienced great difficulty in making ends meet. Unlike the aristocratic learned ladies, Mary Astell knew penury and it may have been this that carried her from philosophic speculation on the nature of pain into a clearer criticism of the position of women in society. She carried on a lengthy correspondence with John Norris on the broad topic of the claims of the spirit in relationship to the claims of the flesh and hence how one should respond to the pain meted out by Divine Providence. Norris was so impressed by her that he sought to publish the correspondence and while he was negotiating to do so Astell published *A Serious Proposal to the Ladies* (1694), the two works appearing within the twelvemonth. The correspondence with Norris gave her second work some respectability: because of the association she and her work could not be dismissed out of hand.

A Serious Proposal might be subtitled 'the long-term survival of the single woman', and proposes that those wealthy women who do not intend to marry should use such financial resources as they command in lieu of dowry to finance institutions – Protestant nunneries, no less – to provide residence and education for upper- and middle-class women, and refuges for hunted heiresses and decayed gentlewomen unable to maintain themselves with decorum. The work is about the preservation of dignity and honour for women outside marriage, although it accepts that many of the women who entered such a refuge might subsequently leave it to marry. The improved system proposed by Astell would in the late twentieth century be recognized as 'networking' and fund-raising by women so as to assist each other. The volume was followed by a sequel in 1697 describing the educational fare which would be made available. In particular, it advanced rules for rational thought on the lines laid down by Descartes.

The work was criticized by Bishop Berkeley because the proposed institution looked too much like a Catholic convent. However, his respect for the writer was evident and Astell went on to publish *Some Reflections on Marriage* (1700) in which she analyses the relationship between husband and wife and concludes that tyranny can exist on the one side and slavery on the other. The vocabulary used is significant as it reflects the preoccupation of the early Enlightenment with contract theory as the basis of political power which is justified only by agreement and never permits despotism. A woman's guard against a despot or tyrant is to choose a morally responsible husband.

The moral tone of her works is impeccable. Women are urged to guard against triviality:

> Let us learn to pride ourselves in something more excellent than the invention of a Fashion, and not entertain such a degrading thought of our own worth as to imagine that our Souls were given us only for the service of our Bodies, and that the only improvement we can make of these is to attract the Eyes of Men. [32]

Other works were subsequently to include treatises embodying High Anglican and Tory principles relating to the Civil War, to the clergy and to the Christian religion. Her piety, asceticism and unimpeachable religious and political principles smoothed her path as a writer. Though satirized in *The Tatler*, she was the most profound and expressly feminist polemicist who had yet surfaced in the British Isles. Defoe, Richardson and Steele all refer to or quote her and she secured the support (probably financial as she certainly could not have made a living from these works) of some noteworthy aristocratic learned ladies like Lady Chudleigh and Lady Mary Wortley Montagu. Her plea for networking among women did not in this respect go unheeded.

If Astell wrote to persuade both men and women, she looked to scholarly literature written by men for her material and many of her ideas. She was at the more ambitious end of the spectrum of corresponding gentlewomen, but the genre expanded very considerably in the course of the eighteenth century and secured almost institutionalized form in the correspondence columns of the periodical press, perhaps *The Gentleman's Magazine* in particular.

The evolution of a regular, high quality, affordable periodical press with articles, translations and abridgements of foreign works, news, poems, book reviews and letters is an intrinsic part of the burgeoning of British print culture in the eighteenth century. It led to growth in all literary genres by fostering an awareness of new works which could then be ordered from the bookseller. It paid contributors who wrote articles and it helped the woman poet to get into print as well as promoting the fuller flowering of a broader spectrum of corresponding gentlewomen. Those who wrote to the correspondence columns could air their views not only on the contents of the journal, but on reviews and literary developments. It was in this journal, for example, that Anna Seward (The Swan of Lichfield) took Boswell to task for his biography of

Dr Johnson. She also published poetry here. At the end of her life she prepared and edited a version of her letters, many of which had appeared in the periodical press.[33]

Publishing poetry in a periodical could be an initial step towards recognition as a poet and it could be the way to finding a patron who, if not prepared to subsidize the poet or poetaster, might undertake to raise a subscription list which would finance a publication. Samuel Johnson, for example, over fifteen years, raised contributions for Helen Anna Williams's *Miscellanies in Verse and Prose*, which appeared in 1766. There were 1200 subscribers, of whom many were women, to Elizabeth Carter's *All the Works of Epictetus* which earned for her £1000 and enabled her to devote her life to her bluestocking interests. There are several instances of women whose careers were an odyssey from random appearance in *The Gentleman's Magazine* into collections of verse, and some went on to command a role in London literary society.[34]

Informed journalism in Britain in the early eighteenth century woke up to the fact that women were counted among its readers and writers and that ideas and discussion were not a male monopoly. For example, *The Spectator* (founded March 1711) set out to be deliberately provocative. The editor, Addison, frequently assumed a tone of heavy irony which provoked questions, in much the same way as did Jan Steen's *Dissolute Household*. Consider, for example, the debate on the value of needlework skills which appeared in 1716 and which is intended in part as a satire on the corresponding gentlewoman. Following a letter from an 'aunt', who certainly never existed, bemoaning the decline of such skills among the young, Addison's reply included:

> How memorable would that Matron be, who should have it inscribed upon her Monument, that she Wrought out the whole Bible in Tapestry, and died in good old Age having covered three hundred yards of wall in the Mansion House.

He continued by proposing:

> 1. That no young Virgin whatsoever be allowed to receive the addresses of her first Lover, but in a suit of her own Embroidering. 2. That before every fresh Servant, she be obliged to appear with a new Stomacher at the least. 3. That no one be actually Married, till she hath the Child bed, pillows etc already Stitched, as likewise the Mantle for the boy

quite finished. These laws if I mistake not, would effectually restore the decayed Art of Needlework, and make the Virgins of Great Britain exceedingly Nimble-fingered in their Business. [35]

The correspondence continued with a spurious answer from the Virgins of England pointing out that they could breed quicker than they could sew and that 'Gilt leather recently introduced into the manufactures of England' made an excellent upholstery material while stimulating industry.

Addison's mockery of the art of the needle and of female correspondents, indeed most of his observations on the female sex, are negative, they belittle and could be interpreted as quite overtly misogynistic; notwithstanding, his observations provoke thought when placed in the hands of a woman reader. 'Is this what I am about?' Furthermore, he was capable of nudging both women and men into questioning their standard of values. His observations on virtue, for example, provoke reflection and discussion on the difference in standards applied to men and women:

The great point of honour in men is courage and in women chastity. If a man loses his honour in one encounter, it is not impossible for him to regain it in another; a slip in a woman's honour is irrecoverable. I can give no reason for fixing the point of honour in these two qualities, unless it be that each sex sets the greatest value on the qualification which renders them the most amiable in the eyes of the contrary sex. Had men chosen for themselves, without regard to the opinions of the fair sex, I should believe the choice would have fallen on wisdom or virtue; or had women determined their own point of honour, it is probable that wit or good nature would have carried it against chastity. [36]

In this reasoning, men and women construct each other. What they admire in the opposite sex becomes the most desirable attribute. To the implied question, 'Is this what should be?' no answers are given. *The Spectator* never explicitly steps outside a reiteration of traditional roles for men and women, but as a consciousness-raising exercise about the folly of human reasoning and behaviour it may have played its part.

The editors of *The Spectator* expected that the journal would be read by women and other journals became sensitive to the sensibilities of a female readership. Edward Cave, for example, was quick to ban obscene riddles from the poetry section of *The Gentlemen's Magazine* when complaints revealed to him that lady readers were offended. Clearly such literature, when left around the vicarage or the middle-class house, did not pass unnoticed by the lady of the house and her daughters. By this means, and to an extent which is impossible to calculate, it was possible for serious matter, economics, politics, social observation, book reviews to be made available to a female reading public even before the development of a particular female press.

Such a press existed sporadically from 1693, when John Dunton launched *The Ladies Mercury*, but few of the essays in this direction had a long life. In 1709, Mary de la Rivière Manley began *The Ladies Tatler*, but the enterprise became embroiled in politics and her anti-Whig invectives incurred lawsuits for slander. In 1721, Anne Dodd started the *London Journal*, once again a deeply political endeavour which occasioned legal proceedings for slander. Then Lady Mary Wortley Montagu in 1737 launched *The Nonsense of Common Sense*, a pro-Whig weekly, to which she made anonymous contributions promoting the idea of serious study for women and lamenting triviality and excess in female behaviour. She did not stay long with the initiative and the field was left open for the enterprising Eliza Haywood whose *Female Spectator* (1744–6) took on issues of marriage, morality and philosophy and promoted the idea of learning, to include science, among women. The main theme, however, for Eliza targeted the market, was what to look for in a good husband. Even so, the publication did not sustain its momentum. Finally, Charlotte Lennox edited *The Ladies Monthly* (11 issues, 1760–1), another publication with a moral purpose which the editor claimed did nothing to relieve her penury.[37]

The competition from the established periodical press, and perhaps most of all *The Gentleman's Magazine* which offered such varied fare, may have impeded the development of a female press. Writers wanted their work to appear in periodicals with an established circulation, and the reading public had to be assured that any new periodical offered something different.

By the second decade of the eighteenth century, and increasingly as the century advanced, the corresponding gentlewoman had been joined by 'drudges of the pen' who were overtly committed to making some kind of living from a wide variety of literary endeavours including plays, translations (an industry which deserves more study), journalism,

schoolbooks (a growth sector in Protestant Europe which also merits
further exploration) and the novel. These new cohorts of what might
be called female jobbing writers joined the Grub Street male in seeking
to make a living from the pen from whatever offered itself. Most of the
women involved were not living in London garrets, but it is perhaps
invidious to distinguish between the penury of the men and that of the
women. Both were a heterogenous set, but the women had to cope with
the perceived impropriety of their position in the literary obstacle race.

One area where women made a conspicuous and successful mark was
with the novel, a relatively new genre. An annual checklist of British
fiction for the years 1750–69 shows that women authors produced more
titles than men did in eleven of those years, but that over the entire
period female output was about one-fifth that of men.[38] Moreover, only
by the end of the century had a few pulled themselves into the higher
leagues. The appropriation of this writing form, as a means of expression
and as a source of income, generates many questions. Who were these
women, what were their chances of success, where did they fit on the
spectrum of respectability?

The answers are not straightforward. The numbers of educated spinsters from the gentry and middle classes escalated after 1690, a phenomenon perhaps linked to the increase in the size of the dowry, but there
were also dissatisfied (and some satisfied) wives and widows who wanted
to write and had the time to do so. Penury impelled some, ambition
others (though few would confess to it). Whereas the pioneers of
women's serious writing had been aristocratic or very upper class, the
social backgrounds of women writers now began to vary enormously.
Nothing except the pen unites Frances Burney and Jane Austen, for
example, with Eliza Haywood or Charlotte Lennox or Mary Wollstonecraft. The first two were buttressed by family circumstances and safe-
guarded from dying in poverty even if they did not live in great affluence
or independence. They were able to give themselves to novel writing
unimpeded by real financial anxiety. The second group wrote to live
and the novel was only one of a gamut of literary endeavours intended
to stitch together a livelihood. Wollstonecraft tried virtually all the
jobs that society made available to the educated but penniless – governess, school teacher, companion, author, translator, journalist, novelist,
writer of polemical tracts and travel literature. Others had unsatisfactory
marriages to profligate men or, in widowhood, were in desperate
straits.[39]

The career of Eliza Haywood (1693–1756) spans an interesting transition between the infamous and the respectable. The daughter of a small shopkeeper and the less than happy wife of a Norfolk clergyman, who in 1721 advertised in the *Post Boy* to announce she had left him without his consent, she appeared first on the Dublin stage and then in Drury Lane in a work of her own composition entitled, aptly in the light of her history, *A Wife to be Lett* (1723). During the 1720s she struggled to build up patronage and was reputed to have been mistress to several men and mother of two illegitimate children. Her main works during this decade were concerned with the vulnerability of women in love. She set herself up as a publisher, a shortlived experiment in the 1740s, and thereafter the tone of her novels, accompanied by good conduct books, began to change dramatically: they adopt a sober, moralizing tone in which the triumph of virtue, sexually defined, becomes dominant.[40] This change reflects more than Eliza's considerable adaptability. Although subsequently hailed as 'a moral conversion' (by Clara Reeve in 1785), it seems probable that the energetic and talented Eliza had read and interpreted the signs delivered to the writing world in general by Samuel Richardson's *Pamela*.

Of the magnificent triumvirate of early eighteenth-century novelists, Defoe, Fielding and Richardson, all of whom waxed eloquent on issues of sex and gender, Richardson best grasped what his audience was seeking, even if it is possible that he fell upon it by accident. In *Pamela* (1740), subtitled *Virtue Rewarded*, Richardson made chastity, in this view a uniquely female virtue, the leitmotif of the plot; and the discourse on womanhood took an interesting turn.[41]

No student of versions of womanhood can afford to ignore this early best-seller. Pamela is an upwardly mobile maidservant, saving her wages, speculating on the profits to be garnered from her mistresses' cast-off clothing, constantly improving her reading skills during her free time and her talents at letter-writing by her correspondence to her father, so that her eye is ever 'to her preferment'. When she finds herself assailed by the dishonourable advances of her deceased mistress's son, Mr B., her implacable defence of her virginity drives the seducer into making her an offer of marriage, since he can satisfy his lust on no other terms. Virtue, that is, female chastity, triumphs in the person of Pamela. Mr B. in the first version of the novel appears as an undisguised intended rapist, but is given a few Prince Charming qualities in the second. Even so, he is a less than convincing hero and the 'B' could easily stand for Beast. However, he is redeemed by his recognition of the worth of a good woman.

Richardson found himself with an instant success on his hands. The work went into five editions within a year of publication, was dramatized by George Bennett, and became the first literary work to inspire what is now called merchandizing, itself an indicator of the new consumerism: there were Pamela teasets and Pamela fans. From the viewpoint of the twentieth century it is a sobering thought that the first English literary blockbuster was a paean to female virtue. *Pamela* was translated into Italian, Dutch, German, French, Swedish, Russian, Spanish and Portuguese, with the text modified to suit national particularities. In French, for example, Pamela is given noble ancestry lest *mésalliance* should raise its ugly head. Although this work sold well in France, it was outstripped by Richardson's next work, *Clarissa Harlowe*, in which the heroine starved herself to death rather than marry her rapist and so gave a new dimension to the grandeur of female chastity. Diderot was stunned into effusive admiration for Richardson and *Clarissa* was incorporated into the intellectual baggage of the republic of letters. What was the key to the success of these volumes?

First, the works peddled a woman who was in no way inferior to man — indeed, her purity is contrasted with his bestiality. *Women do not want to read about their ineluctable inferiority*, was perhaps the first lesson to be learned. Man did not seem to mind the presentation of himself as predatory, though Lovelace, Clarissa's rapist, clearly overstepped the bounds and had to die. Woman has become a civilizing agent imposing right standards upon a man. The message is in tune with the spirit of the times. Pamela negotiates a system with consummate success, offering hope of rising to the modest maidservant and showing every woman that an advantageous match can be contrived by a *virgo intacta*. Any parent can approve such behaviour and recommend it to her daughter. Henry Fielding, who produced no heroine to rival Pamela, objected to her moral standards, and in *Shamela* (1741) claimed that Pamela's virtue was fraudulent because not innate. She used it calculatingly.

Let Fielding mock. The values implicit in *Pamela* accorded with the values of a reading public that included increasing numbers of women. The English language adjusted to changes of meaning: words such as virtue, purity, propriety, modesty, delicacy, decency, acquired a purely sexual connotation and 'indelicacy', as a definition of gross behaviour, appeared for the first time in *Pamela*.

Richardson, consciously or not, had hit upon an infallible recipe guaranteed to find a buyer; but he had also shown how a woman novelist could compose without jeopardizing her reputation. That is not to say that difficulties were erased entirely. The use of a male pseudonym or anonymous attribution ('by A Lady'; 'by the author of . . .') reveals that many ensuing authoresses felt deeply ambiguous about their position. Rather it means that a paean to virtue defended against the male assailant whose aims were unambiguously to gratify his carnal desires conforms in every sense to the moral tale, the fable. It did not raise the question of lack of sexual propriety (à la Behn) in the author's life. A slip in writing is a slip in virtue, but if the writing did not slip then logic surely insisted that the author was blameless?

The concentration on what was recognized as feminine sensibility, moral rectitude, sympathy and passivity when not under attack, obviously limited the range of the female sentimental novel and the genre could readily run to vapidity. It did, however, allow women to complain obliquely by drawing attention to the aspects of the system which disadvantaged them and laid them open to the vagaries of husbands and fathers. It also allowed women to proclaim the necessity of a free choice of a morally responsible husband. Perhaps most consequential of all, it allowed women to arrogate to themselves yet further the moral superiority which totally destroyed the lusty, conniving image of women promoted by Restoration drama. Eliza Haywood never made a total transition to passive virtue, but her works after 1740 were increasingly turned in this direction.

Among the dozens of women to try their hand at the genre, Fanny Burney was perhaps the first to show herself capable of creative work of the highest level and ultimately – though she had to wait – to make money at it.[42] She started with several advantages. Her family was gifted and well connected and her father, a reputable author and musician, belonged to the best intellectual circles in the capital, counting Samuel Johnson among his friends. If Fanny Burney was self-educated, it was under the kind of circumstances which nurture the development of the intellect. Her first work, *Evelina* (1778), was written secretly and published anonymously, but when it was a success and the secret got out the pride of her family and friends knew no bounds. She earned a mere £20 for it: the next, *Cecilia* (1782), brought in £250.

Lacking much in the way of a dowry and clearly unattracted by any potential suitor, she reluctantly accepted a post offered by Queen Charlotte as Second Keeper of the Robes which bored her beyond belief. The experience was not wasted, however, and it left her, when she resigned, with a pension of £100 a year: not riches but more than survival. Marriage to an impoverished French émigré in 1793 brought her happiness, if financial problems, doubtless relieved by the publication of *Camilla* (1796), which earned her £2000, and *The Wanderer* (1814), which also sold for £2000 though it disappointed the public. Her journals and memoirs were also published and are a most vital record of London literary life.

Burney's popularity reposed on the high moral tone of her works and on the delicacy of some of the character drawing, as well as the bestowal of the appropriate rewards and punishments for good and evil. Scattered throughout the books are commentaries on the female condition. Without family and fortune, alone and subject to the censorious gaze of the rest of society, one heroine exclaims:

> How insufficient . . . is a female to herself! How utterly dependent upon situation – connections, circumstances! how nameless, how for every fresh springing are her DIFFICULTIES, when she would owe her existence to her own exertions! Her conduct is criticised, not scrutinised; her labours are unhonoured, and her qualifications are but lures to ill will. (*The Wanderer*)[43]

No one ever depicted better than Burney, unless it was Jane Austen, the humiliations a girl without great means could suffer on the dance floor as she was overlooked by potential partners, or how she could be embarrassed before someone she wished to impress by the vulgarity of her relatives.

Her career offers some considerable contrasts with those of others, for example that of Charlotte Lennox, who died in extreme penury and who can in turn be compared and contrasted with Hannah More and Mary Wollstonecraft. Lennox was the daughter of an army officer, born in 1729, and she found some patronage for her first collection of poems (1747) from the Countess of Rockingham and Lady Isabella Finch. The same year, at the age of eighteen, she married an unreliable Scotsman and thereafter had to support both herself and her children. Between 1748 and 1750 she tried the stage, but had no real acting talent, so she returned to the pen. She had some male supporters in the literary world but managed to alienate her patron, Lady Finch, by a crude caricature in her novel *Harriet Stuart*. Richardson and Johnson together rallied to promote her second and most successful novel, *The Female Quixote* (1752), but their attempts to raise subscriptions for further work failed and she was obliged to take to French translations (including the memoirs of two of Louis XIV's mistresses), while producing *Shakespear Illustrated* (3 vols., 1752–3) and another novel *Henrietta* (1758). She received some help from the Duchess of Newcastle while editing *The Ladies Monthly* (1760–1) in the form of a post for her husband and a free apartment in Somerset House. She tried plays and one, *Old City Manners*, an adaptation of *Eastward Hoe* by Jonson, Marston and Chapman, ran long enough in 1775 to secure her a benefit night. Repeated attempts to raise subscriptions for her failed, if Mrs Thrale is to be believed, because of her indecorous manners towards potential patrons, and there were allegations of her lack of personal hygiene. Johnson warned her severely not to expect Sir Joshua Reynolds to solicit his aristocratic sitters on her behalf and rebuked her for writing hurtful letters to her friends. In her last years she received some grants from the newly founded Royal Literary Fund, intended to help struggling or impoverished authors, and died in poverty and acrimony at the age of 75 in 1804. The ability to throw off her albatross of a husband earlier in life might have eased her passage and certainly a little more deference would have helped her to hold on to her patrons.[44]

No woman writer in the eighteenth century was able to equal the fortune of £30,000 left by Hannah More to charities. The child of a schoolmaster, she trained to be a teacher and ran a successful girls' boarding school with her sisters. Compensation for breach of promise by a man twenty years her senior left her with an annuity of £200. Introduced into London society by Frances Reynolds, sister of Sir Joshua, she became the friend of Johnson and Garrick, who were both to be significant in the advancement of her career as poet and playwright, and of Gibbon and Horace Walpole. Prominent among her literary works were plays and compilations for schoolgirls. She explicitly set out to foster 'a regard to religion and virtue in the minds of young persons, and afford them an innocent, and perhaps not altogether unuseful amusement in the exercise of recitation.'[45]

Her devotion to Garrick was expressed in odes and ballads and she also wrote melodramas, one of which Garrick rewrote and which was a huge success. Then in later years she became absorbed in religion, in particular with the Clapham Sect which mingled progressive views with deep political conservatism: a leading figure in the movement to abolish slavery, she also urged the poor to be content with their lot as it was part of a divine plan to earn heavenly bliss by earthly deprivation, and she deplored the questioning of church or civil authority. During this phase, she produced Bible stories in dialogue form which received criticism but sold well – probably again to the girls' education market. Her personal convictions were coincident with those of the book-buying public in general and she enjoyed the status of pundit on every conceivable subject from prayer to politics. Her *Strictures on the Modern System of Education* (1799) sold 19,000 copies and ran into thirteen editions. It condemned the trivial and the emphasis on accomplishments at the expense of the moral, the practical and the cultivation of the understanding of young women. It is probably More's most 'advanced' work. However, no one set themselves more forcefully than she did against Mary Wollstonecraft and the idea of the rights of women. Women had obligations, not rights – to accept their role, subdue their passions and accustom themselves to self-denial.

In acknowledging More's success we are recognizing that conservatism sold better than radicalism and that the best selling quality of all was the exaltation of specific female virtues distinguishing women from men, followed by offering women the opportunity for self-improvement by moral strength and hard work. We should perhaps also recall that More had a nice little annuity to preserve her from any sharp collapses in her literary income.

If More is to be contrasted with Lennox, she also stands out from Wollstonecraft who, as a failed headmistress and unhappy governess, found her toehold in a literary career first through a polemical treatise – *Thoughts on the Education of Daughters* (1786). There followed a happy association with the publisher Joseph Johnson who gave her translation work and reviewing, which appears to have sustained her. He published her first novel, *Mary, A Fiction* (1788), and articles in the *Analytical Review* of which he was the editor. *A Female Reader* (1789), a piece of total pastiche intended for the schoolroom, was followed by more translation work, including Christian Salzmann's *Elements of Morality*, and then *A Vindication of the Rights of Man* (1790) in response to Burke's *Reflections on the Revolution in France*. This work showed how quickly Wollstonecraft could deliver a manuscript to a publisher to carry the debates of the day still further. Next came the work, written in six months, which is accounted a foundation text in modern feminism, *A Vindication of the Rights of Woman* (1792), followed by *A Historical and Moral View of the French Revolution* (1794) and a travelogue, *Letters written during a Short Residence in Sweden, Norway and Denmark* (1796). An unfinished novel, *Maria, or the Wrongs of Woman*, completes her oeuvre.[46]

Viewed as a whole, the Wollstonecraft literary corpus bears many of the hallmarks of a kind of female writer who emerged in the late eighteenth century: translations, reviews, pastiche, works aimed at the expanding market for schoolroom books for growing girls, historical commentary and travellers' observations, eked out by reviews and articles to form some kind of livelihood. The polemical tracts with their fiery and passionate commitment form only a small – if historically the most significant – part of her work. There was no attempt to write plays or poems, no efforts to court the subscriber and no evident patron, though Johnson was a very sympathetic editor. Mary was a political animal, but she was not the first English woman writer to be so, as the history of the female press, and the more recent works on the historian and republican sympathizer Catherine Macaulay, demonstrate.[47] Yet the *Vindication of the Rights of Woman* took female writing into a new phase (if a temporary cul de sac) in that it linked a change in the status of women with radical political change. The work not only insisted that women were made not born, and that a deliberate male conspiracy converted them into trivial and worthless beings, incapable of being fit mothers, wives and widows, but that to give girls the same educational fare as boys, and provide them with career prospects which would allow them to live independently above the poverty line, would produce human beings as rational and as strong as men. To insist on different forms of virtue between man and woman was false and irrational. Far from hampering women in the role of wife and mother, the changes she posited would rejuvenate the nation, destroy tyranny on the domestic front and produce new men and women who could share political power. However clumsy the prose or repetitive the content, this was a liberal Enlightenment tract of the first importance.

Wollstonecraft was no democrat and watched with trepidation the increasing pressure exercised by the Paris sections over the politicians. The complexities of her private life caused her to return to Britain in 1795. A suicide attempt, another never completed novel, *Maria, or The Wrongs of Woman*, marriage and a confinement leading to her death in

1797 ensued. The posthumous revelation by her husband William Godwin of her stance as a freethinker, and of the details of her private life, lovers and illegitimate child, reverberated on her work. The *Vindication* was interpreted as an immoral work by an immoral woman. A slip in virtue was still a slip in writing.

It cannot be demonstrated that Wollstonecraft could claim an extensive female following, though there were clearly many readers of her work and a recent closer examination of the provincial British press suggests that the *Vindication* was debated by groups of women in public meetings before it fell into disrepute. Her work, labelled eccentric even by those who did not brand her as immoral on account of her private life, seems to have met opposition in different quarters. The literary pundits, including Hannah More, the classical scholar Elizabeth Carter, the poet and critic Anna Seward, writing from the cathedral close in Lichfield, all condemned it. Hannah More asserted that women had duties, not rights. Others, like Lady Palmerston, ridiculed the advanced views. For most, perhaps, the work came at a very inopportune moment. Britain was at war with France and, at different social levels, the war effort was mobilizing British women. A radical work expressly dedicated to a French political figure, Talleyrand, in the hope that the Revolution would inaugurate change, transcended the bonds of patriotism. It embedded a woman question in radical political upheaval at a time when the patriotic were intent on preserving the anachronistic, privilege-ridden, corrupt British system. Mary had gone too far too fast. That her work was not imitated, or that some of the claims she made slumbered for decades, need cause no surprise. Other elements such as her appeal for better education on a male model, her denigration of false values and triviality in women remained alive. Fanny Price of *Mansfield Park* may not be a heroine for twentieth-century tastes, but in her clear-sighted notions of the appropriate, and her eschewing of the trivial, she is something of a spiritual legatee of *The Vindication*.

By the end of the eighteenth century in England, then, a distinct, professional female writer had emerged. To what extent was this situation replicated in other European countries?

If France, Germany, Holland, and at further distance Italy, did not experience the same proliferation of women novelists and 'drudges of the pen', each country had some important developments and saw some noteworthy names emerge. The lag is to be explained not only by different literacy rates but by the smaller population of some countries and states – Holland in particular – which did not generate enough profits for the printer. In both Holland and the German states, translations of already successful English works were more commercially viable than new works from native writers.[48] This did, of course, provide work for translators, among whom were certainly women (probably the cheapest source of labour). Most of Europe lacked the same development of a periodical press which could draw attention to the woman writer and her works. An English commentator, Arthur Young, was frankly appalled by the lack of newspapers and journals in provincial France in the late 1780s. Continuing press censorship by the French authorities may also have contributed to a relative underdevelopment of the small printer, willing to take risks with a limited print run. Catholic societies which depended on the convent boarding school would also seem to have had less demand for the kind of schoolroom literature generated by the demands of the governess, and probably relied more heavily on lives of saints and pious works which would keep the young mind fixed on the faith.

By the end of the century, however, names of distinction were accumulating. Madame de Genlis, Madame de Staël, Sophie von La Roche, Caroline Schlegel Schelling, Belle van Zylen, who later took the name Belle de la Charrière, were mostly women from wealthy aristocratic families who did not need to work for a living, but they all gained not merely national but international acclaim and they coexisted with some distinguished women poets and above all with memoir writers. In the seventeenth century memoir writing as a literary genre was essentially confined to the great and the famous or those who had been associated with them.[49] Madame de Motteville, for example, wrote of her observations of Anne of Austria; Madame de la Vallière wrote her memoirs and penitential meditations on the strength of occupying Louis XIV's bed, and even Madame de Maintenon took to print with much the same justification. The Italian Mancini sisters, who also adorned the beds of the famous, had an international audience for their memoirs, written in the late seventeenth century. However, wars, and above all the French Revolution, caused a truly amazing burgeoning of this genre in both France and Germany as highly literate aristocratic ladies, and even some ousted religious women, thought their special experience, whether suffering or adventures, worthy of recounting. The times in which the events were lived took over from the narrator's social standing as the point of interest for the reader.[50]

Florence, Venice and Milan are all known to have had a spasmodic periodical press in the eighteenth century. Giuseffa Cornaldi Caminer in Venice edited in the 1780s *La donna galante ed erudità. Giornale dedicato al bel sesso*. Elisabeth Caminer, a relative, had some success as a journalist in both Venice and Milan. The writing of opera librettos occupied a number of women in Venice, on what basis is not clear, but this work accounts for about half of the 110 titles identified as the work of women in the eighteenth century. Again, this was the perfect domestic work to engage the efforts of a woman with a measure of education and to be compared with the numbers of prints illustrating both musical scores and works to sell to tourists which seem to have been frequently done in Italy by the female members of the printer's family.[51] Etching, engraving, hand colouring of prints, flower paintings and silhouettes were all aspects of this production.

In Germany literacy levels were higher and the demand for books far greater in the Protestant than in the Catholic states. The Leipzig fair was a barometer registering gradual developments in publishing fashion. Over the eighteenth century, it shows a swing away from a press dominated by religious works to one in which belles-lettres and fiction ruled.[52] The part played by the woman reader in these changes was held to be considerable. Several commentators blamed women for the success of the novel and many fulminated against the woman novelist. Adolf von Knigge in *Über den Umgang mit Menschen* (1790), for example, delivered a quite savage invective:

> Amongst the forty or fifty accounted women authors at present in Germany – without counting the legions who do not publish their inanities – there are scarcely half a dozen with superior genius or real vocation.

The career of Caroline Schlegel Schelling, who was to become a highly significant figure in the German Romantic movement, shows how the German authoress, however talented, had to build her reputation gradually. She was responsible for a remarkable translation of the works of Shakespeare into German – the task of years rather than months. It is from Germany that most evidence emanates of the considerable presence of women translators of the works of all kinds, novels, plays and memoirs, mostly by men, that teemed out of England and France. The work was quite well paid and very flexible; it would be interesting to know how it was organized and whether the printers drew on wives and daughters of friends or received suggestions from women anxious for work. What is known is that this kind of work could inspire the translator to become a novelist herself. Therese Huber, for example, was a considerable translator in the closing decades of the eighteenth century – her work included the letters of Madame Roland. While engaged on the translation of a now forgotten work by the then fashionable author Louvet de Couvray, she records:

> I composed an end to *Divorce nécessaire* and wrote with a fluent pen and a rich imagination . . . writing during the nights when I had to watch over my sick husband and sometimes with a child at the breast, I became an author.[53]

This text may reveal a little more than self-discovery. It shows that the work of translation could be rather free and the translator could introduce some modifications. Above all, however, it proclaims: 'I can do it too.' By 1820, Therese Huber could look back on a very active writing career.

The volume of work done in France by women authors, while not as great as that produced in England, had some distinctive attributes. Both Madame de Genlis and Madame de Staël grew up in a salon environment. The French novel, whether in the hands of men or women, reflected the philosophical preoccupations of the day. A dominant theme in the changing political circumstances of the pre-revolutionary period was that of Republican motherhood and bore the imprint of Rousseau's influence and the messages delivered in *Emile, ou de l'éducation* (1762) and *Julie, ou la Nouvelle Héloïse* (1761). *Emile* in particular gripped the female literary imagination with its exaltation of the joys and duties of wifehood and motherhood.

Sophie, who is the wife-to-be of the ideal citizen Emile, is reared to please a man. Whereas Emile may give full vent to his enquiring mind and experience for himself both intellectual and physical pleasure, her upbringing is different and very much controlled by her mother. Kept ignorant, chaste, modest, without artifice but conscious of the need to dress pleasingly and spend time on her person, she is also allowed a little dissimulation, a little cunning in order to secure 'empire' over Emile's heart. It is most important that the ideal citizen should want to return home to his sexy bedroom. Outside the boundaries of the home Sophie has no place. She will nourish (breastfeeding, of course) the next generation of citizens who will be confident in her love. She will replicate herself in her daughters. The boys, having been loved and nurtured, will gradually be handed over to their father or, like Emile, to a tutor to allow their questioning minds free range over every topic until the man emerges, one free from prejudice and from constraint. It is assumed that Sophie, as a child, will naturally reject literacy and mathematics for sewing and tending her dolls, while boys look for more active toys and grasp at learning.

The success of the volume lay without doubt in the positive emphasis it placed on motherhood which became at once a political duty and a personal joy. The breastfeeding mother was told to expect a new and tender relationship with her offspring and her care was seen as the guarantee of the child's wellbeing. Her feminine attributes and those of the tender, loving, companionate wife, cherished by her husband in a home which is 'the cradle of citizens', were claimed as part of a natural order which had been corrupted by civilization but which would emerge in changed political circumstances or through the efforts of individuals.

Both women and men picked up Rousseau's theme of empowering motherhood as the means to the regeneration of the citizen. Madame de Montbart and Madame Roland, as well as Bernardin de Saint Pierre, all stressed that the end of a girl's education was motherhood. Madame de Genlis in *Adèle et Théodore* (1782) modifies some of Rousseau's message by insisting that the same moral values should be applied to the rearing of girls as boys. Artifice should be corrected in both. However, the end of education is to draw out the child's natural qualities and those to be nurtured in a girl were those of mothering. Hence, the little Adèle needs only a rudimentary training in the profound academic study which is Théodore's lot, but she is instructed in domestic and maternal duties. To this end a real small girl is introduced for her to care for so that she may have the direct experience of 'the pleasures of a good mother'. Madame de Genlis does not permit the borrowed child to pass judgement on the success or failure of the care given – she is presumably one of the lower orders. Women were not the only ones to be charmed by the concept of the good mother: Chardin and Greuze produced pictures and prints of the loving little mother practising her talents on her doll. The imagery of domesticity has no more charming visual expression.

France also produced something in the way of a specialized female journalism aimed at a female periodical market.[54] Like its English counterpart it was highly sporadic, but unlike the English version it was forced to dance to suit the censors or fall into difficulty. After a number of ephemeral experiments, the first journal to enjoy a continuous life was the *Journal des Dames* (monthly 1759–78 with a few interruptions). The agenda of the first editor was to drive home to women that their subordination to men was of their own construction as well. It was the price they paid for passivity. Between 1761 and 1775, an important political period corresponding with the Seven Years War and the essays in free trade which tore French political life from top to bottom, the journal was in the hands of three women. The first of these, Madame de Beaumer, had in 1759 tried to launch a journal in The Hague which she hoped would circulate in France, in spite of the disapprobation of the censors. She was a perfect disciple of the Enlightenment and *Lettres curieuses, instructives et amusantes* made a case for social justice, religious tolerance, equality before the law and the like. The journal failed, but her reputation was established as a contentious dissident and, on her return to France, publishers were wary of her. She took over the editorship of the *Journal des Dames* in 1761, probably knowing that it would not be long before she was in trouble with the censor. The content of the journal reflected all her interests and she called women to a consciousness of their social and political potential. The censor, Marin, spoke of her as an offence to public morality and, realizing that she had probably gone too far, and to save the journal, she left for Holland, leaving the editorship to Madame de Maisonneuve. She came from a wealthy background in the world of finance and managed to keep the Duc de Choiseul, minister to the king, on her side and to become a royal pensionary. The price of this support was the abandonment of the truly contentious. While under her name, however, though in effect edited by Mathon de la Cour, the journal began to support the *parlements* against the king, and when they were exiled by the minister Maupeou, the *Journal des Dames* was silenced.

The baronne de Princen, who took the name of Madame de Montanclos, took over in 1774 and transformed the journal into a vehicle for maternity of the kind that would lead to the moral regeneration of the nation. She did, however, advance the more radical notion that careers should be open to those women desirous and capable of exercising them.

Although the financial standing of Madame de Beaumer is unclear,

the other two female editors were women of some wealth. Madame de
Maisonneuve was a widow and therefore in possession of her dowry
resources, while Madame de Montanclos appears to have lived apart
from her second husband and there may have been an agreement between
them which allowed her total freedom of action.[55]

The ferment of the French Revolution produced an airing of women's
questions in pamphlets, prints and petitions. The volume was not considerable, but it gained in strength very rapidly in the capital and some
large cities and a female press emerged of a clearly political quality.
The *Etrennes Nationales des Dames*, for example, published pamphlets
and information it deemed of interest to its readers while stressing how
the events of 1789, the October Days, had proved the courage of women
and their power to effect change. It made political demands for the
greater representation of women both in the National Assembly and in
the Commune of Paris. In January 1790 appeared the *Véritable Ami de
la Reine ou Journal des Dames*. The title is itself interesting because it
takes the queen as the incarnation of all the evils of aristocratic government and society and it points out the particularly despicable role played
by intriguing women in a corrupt court. Now this had been swept
away, and the periodical aimed to change the tone of French political
life by sound advice directed towards women. The way forward for both
women and the nation is republican motherhood.

Between 1790 and 1791 a number of radical women began to petition
for the redress of specific grievances affecting women, asking among
other things for the abolition of the dowry system, better kinds of paid
employment and educational opportunities. Simultaneously in Paris
and the provinces small groups of women formed, demanding fuller
participation of women in political life. Some of these groups were
merely patriotic societies endorsing women's supportive role in political
change and many offered to help in philanthropic initiatives to tide the
poor over the chaos resulting from the government's 'reform' of charitable assistance. In Paris, however, such groups went much further and
resulted in sophisticated political activity by a number of individual
women. Of these the best known is perhaps Olympe de Gouges, who
in 1791 produced *Les Droits de la Femme*, the first real attempt to
formulate a document demanding basic rights for women.[56] It went
further than the *Vindication* of Mary Wollstonecraft in that, emulating
the terse form of the Declaration of the Rights of Man of 1789, it
actually formulated rights which should be specifically guaranteed to

women by reference to a philosophy of natural rights. Only in the late twentieth century are some feminist thinkers returning to the notion of rights based on the difference between men and women, and that acknowledgement of difference should be made by certain fundamental guarantees. The spirit of de Gouges' work is encapsulated in the first principle: 'Woman is born free and lives equal to man in her rights. Social distinctions can be based on the common utility.' The rights of women should include equality with men in the public sphere and in the obligations of citizenship which by logical extension meant the right to fight in defence of the state. However, among guarantees that should be made to women (and these demands reveal de Gouges to be a product of her times) were the right to own property within marriage, a marriage contract designed to prevent a husband from tyrannizing over his wife, protection against seducers and the regulation of prostitution. The justification for demanding citizenship rights for women was that since they could die on the scaffold they were not in fact considered apolitical.

There is a stunning logic to de Gouges' stark script. Along with Wollstonecraft's *Vindication* it brings demands on behalf of women into radical territory.

De Gouges' background was complex. She was an actress and an activist before becoming a writer and indeed it has been suggested that she could not write at all. The formulation of the declaration, however, reveals her to be the product of a print culture. A royalist and a Girondin, she was also to demonstrate that she was no democrat. She was to perish on the scaffold for her political associations in 1793.

Essentially, the Revolution in which a redistribution of political power was at issue had brought de Gouges and Wollstonecraft to becoming not merely critics of the social system but explicit advocates of political intervention to redress injustices. It is for this reason that they occupy a distinctive place in the history of feminism.

CHAPTER TWELVE

The Woman Rioter or the Riotous Woman?

> Man, are you capable of justice? It is a woman putting you
> the question . . .
> OLYMPE DE GOUGES, DECLARATION OF THE RIGHTS OF
> WOMAN, 1791

THE WRITTEN word is a slow agent of change. Its technique
is persuasion. It seeks to take by stealth, by infiltration or by
a gradual sapping of a specific set of beliefs, and is dependent
on its reception in the right places and among the right people at the
right time. Wollstonecraft and even de Gouges threw their texts into
a void. They viewed politicians as the agents of change, and Wollstonecraft, seeing no hope within her native country, put her faith in those
of a foreign power. They both thought that the fluid political conditions
created by the French Revolution would create opportunities for change.

In the early stages of that Revolution a remarkable demonstration
showed that female protest was capable of achieving a specific political
target. The working women of Paris, arguably, put an end to the
political deadlock created by the influence of the court on the king and
rescued the Constituent Assembly from impotence. During the October
Days they brought the king from Versailles to Paris, placing him in
the midst of his people and thus centring political life in the capital.

Wollstonecraft made no allusion to these events in her book. Perhaps
this was purely tactical: she had no wish to raise the spectre of mob
rule in the minds of her British readers. Perhaps the events did not
accord with her arguments about the woman stripped of power? Perhaps
she herself was apprehensive about the role of the uneducated in politics?
The women of her analysis are ready for political power when educated
to the same level as men, not when acting under what could all too
easily be called atavistic responses to bread shortage. The chasm between

the preoccupations of the *Vindication* and those of the women of the October Days reveals more than anything else the problems involved in using womanhood as a category.

The issue presents itself in a slightly different way if the fortunes of Olympe de Gouges in the context of the Revolution are considered. She may have participated in the October Days. She was certainly prepared to use public demonstrations to further her claims for women to citizenship, but her fall was, at least in part, effected by working women, who did not see a citizenship which entailed bearing arms to be of real relevance to them. The mass of women involved themselves in the Revolution not to change the status of women but to protect their own interests, which could also be interpreted as the interests both of their families and of the wider community.

The issues over which women chose to make a public protest tell a great deal about the priorities of lower-class women. (A riotous environment was usually no place for a lady.) Indeed, they are one of the best ways of getting at some of their perceptions. However, class itself is too broad a category of analysis for riot in societies which were predominantly peasant. We need as well to distinguish between town and country and perhaps between the behaviour of generations.

Riot and revolt in the early modern period have secured a lot of attention both from socio-economic and subsequent cultural historians. The first noted the presence of women in bread riots and struggles to secure fair prices for vital food commodities.[1] The second promoted the interpretation of rituals as a means to understanding a culture, and in this approach carnival and riot came under close scrutiny. Natalie Zemon Davis, starting from her work on sixteenth-century religious riots, urged a special reading of the role of women in protest by reference to the complex relationship between carnival and revolt. In early modern society urban revolt often occurred on days of public holiday and festivity when crowds gathered and ritual celebrations were enacted. The rites of carnival often involved the mocking of authority, which in traditional society came in multiple guises: church, seigneur, royal or urban officialdom. Carnival was the time for turning the world upside down. In costume and ritual the ruled became the rulers for a day. Transvestism was joyously permitted for the occasion. The right to mock triumphed, but in the process serious truths might be made manifest and grievances aired. The tone could change from frivolous mockery to resentment and carnival could become protest. In the philosophy of carnival, Davis argued, the unruly woman, a personage defined over the ages as irrational and needing the control of a strong male figure, was transformed by misrule into the incarnation of wisdom: whatever folly she committed in play was interpreted as the only sanity. She was hence a vehicle for change. An impressive range of riots could be cited in which women appeared as inciters, participators and figureheads, ranging from incidents in the French Wars of Religion to eighteenth-century events such as the Whiteboy riots in Ireland where the mythological Queen Maeve was said to be the leader. In the iconography of the French Revolution, Marianne became a figurehead for the overthrow of tyranny.[2]

The use of a female symbol of change perhaps tells more about ideas of womanhood than about why real women involved themselves in riotous behaviour, or under what circumstances they did so, or indeed which women became involved. The concern here is to explain the relationship of different kinds of women to protest, itself a very complex issue, differing very considerably in structure, scale and content over the three centuries under examination. The sixteenth and seventeenth centuries were rent in many countries by civil wars and national struggles, some in the name of religion. In these struggles whole communities were caught up and women were a part of those communities. We have seen, for example, that in the German Peasants' War, which was largely about economic grievances but given an edge by the links between property and the Catholic church, women appear as organizers of supplies to the insurgents and were indeed responsible for violence against women's religious houses.[3] From the siege of Haarlem in 1586 there are pictures of women throwing furniture and seething liquid over the ramparts to deter and with luck blind the Spanish troops.[4] Their role in Masaniello's rising in Naples was equally assertive.[5] In those peasant risings where guerrilla warfare was conducted, rather than pitched battles, the help of women in alerting their menfolk to the movements of the enemy could also be significant. In Mediterranean society, when death was meted out to a person judged to be an enemy of the community, everyone – man, woman and child – could dig in the knife. The execution became the work of the entire community and, unless the instigators were detected, reprisal by authority was impossible. In these kinds of events the community was unanimous and at this very basic level everyone, irrespective of age and sex, was a political actor.[6]

Where the community was at odds within itself, torn, for example, by differing religious commitment, riot, as Natalie Davis has shown, could involve both men and women in defence of their faith. David Underdown has pronounced the seventeenth century the 'century of the riotous Englishwoman'. What he means by this is that there were more recorded riots initiated by women over bread and food supplies which, added to the protests of Leveller women whose husbands were in prison for political and religious dissent, give 'women' a highly activist profile.[7]

Yet the recorded evidence, mostly emanating from the law courts, does not allow us to discern either a consistent presence or a common function for the women involved. Their roles varied and were often influenced by the laws of their country relating to riotous offences, and to community traditions. One problem arises from attempting to distinguish between revolt, riot and the simple demonstration. Revolts, although rare, were on a major scale and could shake entire provinces. Blood would be shed and reprisals by authority could be savage. Riots were localized and rarely lasted more than a day. Most were bloodless, unless authority considered they were getting out of hand and was in a position to respond. In the days of token police forces the presence of the army in the locality could affect the promptness of any intervention; but the riot could be over before the troops arrived, so such action was the exception rather than the rule. Often property was destroyed in the course of urban riots, such as the doors of the Southwark stews. Or, as in the case of bread riots, the commodity in question was distributed at what was considered to be a fair price. The term 'riot' therefore involved endless subcategorization and in any case most riots probably never entered official records. Falling short of riot, but something which could readily assume a riotous dimension, was the demonstration, which could involve no more than a handful of people or several thousands. The problem comes in drawing lines.

One important distinction to be made is the difference between riot in urban and in rural conditions. The town market was a focus of dissent and bread riots (excluding attacks on grain convoys) usually occurred in towns, but they could involve country people as both sellers and outraged buyers. The city generated riots about indirect taxation (excise duties in Britain) and over elections, as well as other disturbances about political factions, like the Orangist revolts in late eighteenth-century Holland, or 'Wilkes and Liberty' in London, or some of the great

Revolutionary *journées*. In villages, grazing riots and other intercom-
munity struggles over the use of water sources, or anti-seigneurial disputes, could break out intermittently or could assume extensive form
and rock a province. The Whiteboy Riots in eighteenth-century Munster
were largely a result of the Church of Ireland's claim to tithe; and in
the Great Fear of 1789, irate French peasants set about destroying the
records, and therefore any entitlements which could be held up in courts
to justify seigneurial taxes and claim peasant debts.

To concentrate on isolating and enumerating riots can give the
impression that they were a frequent occurrence. This was not the
case. Most communities, both villages and towns, over the entire three
centuries under review, *never* as far as is known had recourse to collective
protest and in those whose records show such behaviour to have taken
place, it was either an isolated event or occurred so sporadically that it
escaped entire generations. Certain cities, mostly lying north of the
Loire, might be considered particularly riot-prone. London was perhaps
the most tumultuous city before 1789 but was then outstripped by
Paris.[8] In both these cities riot, for whatever initial cause, could if
sufficiently extensive assume a political dimension because of the physical proximity to government. Most recorded riots occurred in towns
and cities, but this may be related to the nature of the evidence. Disturbances which occurred in remote areas, beyond the immediate knowledge
of the magistrate and the punitive arm of the law, may have burnt
themselves out and left no traces in the records.

Riot was under most circumstances a public offence and in the course
of the eighteenth century both England and France sought to enact
newly stringent legislation with a view to maintaining public order.
The gravity of the offence was usually related to the numbers involved
and to how long the event lasted. In England, for example, the Riot
Act of 1715 (enacted in the midst of Jacobite fears) sanctioned military
intervention to disperse a riotous assembly by force one hour after the
reading of the act. (This may in no small part explain why women were
not present at the end of such an event.) In France, riot (*émeute*) was
made a capital offence in 1731 and could technically begin with five
people, though in practice the authorities would not move against so
few. In Holland, an *oproer* or disturbance or riot probably involved about
twenty people before officials took note.[9]

Clearly, what passed under the name of riot could involve very few
people and it is quite impossible to talk of what was typical. Legal

practice made a time factor very important. Those who were there at the beginning might not be there at the end, and those there at the end were usually those who appeared before the courts. This could be important if women were the inciters of disturbances in reducing their presence in the courts and hence in the records.

Did the law accord any special position to women involved in riot? In Holland the answer seems to have been an unconditional 'yes' and in England and France one which was more modified. Dutch women in the seventeenth century seem to have believed thay had legal immunity whenever they participated in riot. Hence in a religious riot in Rotterdam in 1621: 'Many women walked through the street and yelled in a very unmannerly way, shouting among other things "women can't do anything wrong".' At Akersloot in 1691 a crowd of women went to rescue a bargeman arrested for tax evasion and warned the men, 'not you, let us do it, because we can't be prosecuted'. At Oudkarspel in 1616 a female rescue operation of the same type received encouragement from two men who said 'they should freely attack, that women are not legally answerable for their actions, that no one should hit or strike them'. On the other hand, there may have been a chasm between the letter of the law and practice. Being a woman saved neither Betje Wolfe nor Kat Mussel, two renowned female protesters in the Orangist riots of the late eighteenth century, from imprisonment.[10]

In England and Wales the situation was confused. Southey in 1807 held it a commonplace that 'women are far more likely to be mutinous; they stand less in fear of law, partly from ignorance, partly because they presume upon the privilege of their sex, and therefore in all public tumults they are foremost in violence and ferocity'.[11] What Southey cites as common knowledge, however, was a grey area. Throughout the early modern period there does seem to have been a widespread conviction – there was certainly no explicit corpus of law to confirm it – that a woman could participate in riot without being legally pursued at law. However, authority was not prepared to accept this principle unreservedly. There seems little doubt that the interpretation was generally acceptable to British, French and Dutch judges in the seventeenth century. A justice's book widely used in Essex in the period as a vade mecum to help the judge stated:

If a number of women or children under the age of discretion do flocke together for their own cause, this is none assembly punishable by these

statutes unlesse a man of discretion moved them to assemble for the
doing of some unlawfull act.[12]

As long as the riot was 'spontaneous' rather than evidently planned,
justices were prepared to accept the interpretation, but only as long as
the event was not repeated. For example, two consecutive grain disturbances at Maldon in 1629 were followed by differing reactions. First, a
group of women attacked a ship known to be bearing grain out of the
area (Essex was an important part of the capital's provisioning zone)
before it left the port and the event passed without criminal proceedings.[13] Indeed, local magistrates may have welcomed the attack as a
way of warning local merchants suspected of speculating that trouble
would ensue if they persisted in their greed. The same magistrates,
however, were not prepared to countenance a second 'unspontane-
ous', indeed clearly organized, attack some weeks later. Essex women
rioters were not automatically on safe ground if they repeated their
actions.

In the course of the eighteenth century in Britain, *laissez-faire* economic policies which allowed grain merchants to sell outside official
markets were at first accepted reluctantly by local magistrates, but may
gradually have led to a hardening of attitudes towards women who took
refuge in their sex as privileged in riot. Blackstone, whose *Commentaries
on the laws of England* (1771) expressed what was to be the standard
reading of the law, was insistent that the right to riot was not guaranteed
to women.[14] However, the contents of treatises and codes may have
been slow to permeate the populace and a chasm in beliefs may have
been growing between the lower levels of society and the establishment
by the eighteenth century.

Even magistrates did not necessarily wholeheartedly reject the notion
of differential sentencing policy for the sexes in grain riot. Nevertheless,
they turned more and more against women who could be shown to have
instigated violent behaviour, destroyed property or exceeded the limit
of what was deemed acceptable conduct. Hence the attitude of the judge
towards Hannah Smith of Manchester, where in 1812 she led raids
(plural) by men, women and children on potato carts and shops, and
whose boast was that she could 'raise a crowd in a minute'. The judge
sentenced her to hanging as a highway robber:

to prove that you were one of the most determined enemies to good order, and it is fit to be understood that sex is not entitled to any mitigation of punishment.[15]

One incident might have been excused, but for making upheavals into a commonplace and boasting about it, Hannah Smith went to the gallows.

Something of the same ambiguity reigned in France where, although the letter of the law did not permit special treatment for women, in practice they could gain a great deal in court by sheltering behind their sexual status. Verbal incitement by women either lacking a husband or in the absence of the husband could be passed off as the product of their innate irrationality. The same reason could be put forward to explain why a woman could have been led into error by others. The privileges of sex, meaning the ability of a woman to excuse her action because she had hungry children or was a poor widow, counted for something with magistrates who would issue a warning about not repeating the offence and would then dismiss the accused. For all these reasons, women could, at least on certain occasions,[16] believe they stood a chance of getting away with a riotous offence.

Which kinds of riots and disturbances in the period were likely to involve women and what were their roles likely to be? The evidence suggests some national and regional differences. In Holland, for example, between 1600 and 1650, riots were concerned firstly with taxation and secondly with religious issues. In both women were present if not predominant. Then in the 1690s and 1760s food prices sparked off disturbances which women frequently initiated. Lastly, in the second half of the eighteenth century some took part in Orangist demonstrations, the turmoil surrounding the Dutch revolutions.[17] In England a systematic analysis of known riots shows that most do not make reference to women, but where they do so, food riots top the list followed by commons and grazing riots.[18] The mid-seventeenth century was marked by religious riots in which women were involved and indeed to the fore. The Leveller protests and the petitions organized by women in the 1650s, which had economic as well as political demands, stand out in terms of numbers and planning. Certainly there existed an abundance of issues, both economic and religious, during the decade of the Civil War and Interregnum which aroused popular hostility and were of particular concern to women.

Riot appears to have receded somewhat in Britain towards the end of the seventeenth century. In the 1720s, however, rumours of an extension of indirect taxation provoked rioting in which women participated, though not to the same degree as men. The 1760s and the 1790s also saw in some areas a recrudescence of bread riots. Purely political unrest like the Gordon Riots, which traded on anti-papist sentiment among the working classes, or Wilkite disturbances appear to have been male terrain. At a much humbler level there was female involvement in riots over sailors' pay and against the activities of the recruitment officer.

In France in particular regions, notably the Paris provisioning zone, there is a recurrent record of women's participation in bread riots over two centuries. In the rebellion of the Camisards in the seventeenth century and in the religious riots which led to the re-establishment of Catholic worship in France after 1796 we find a heavy female presence. Some of the riots in question were wholly female in composition. Women also appear in commons and grazing disputes, where such are recorded, and in village confrontations with an oppressor or identified enemy where it was important that everyone in the community should seem to be at one and share the blame for the results. By the eighteenth century such confrontations only occurred in remote areas where exterior law enforcement agencies were weak. Women also appear in cemetery and *monitoire* riots, which could be called quasi-religious actions. The last were riots which occurred when the parish priest threatened an entire community with excommunication if evidence relating to an offence such as a murder was withheld. In a class of their own were the great women's days in the history of the French Revolution, though the October Days had to a degree been prefigured in a massive march of women to Versailles in the winter of 1708–9 to claim a reduction in the price of bread and an end to French involvement in the War of the Spanish Succession. Less influential in their outcome, though very revelatory of the structure and purpose of women's protests, were the women's demonstrations to the Convention in germinal and prairial of the year III (March/April and May/June 1795). Women are not recorded as having a conspicuous presence in the anti-tax protests of 1648, nor in the anti-seigneurial riots of 1789, and they were absent from the storming of the Bastille with one known exception.[19]

Looking over this vast range of involvement at apparently different levels and degrees of intensity, is generalization about women's concerns

32. Jan Steen (1625–79), *The Feast of St. Nicholas*. Little girls love dolls and learn by tending them. In Steen's picture of the St. Nicholas feast there is the hint that the woman is perhaps spoiling her daughter by over indulgence. The scattered shoe as a symbol of disorder is often found in brothel scenes.

How might a woman become a prostitute? Judith Leyster depicts an industrious young woman tempted by a man with money but leaves the response unclear. Usually the fall of the vain woman is presided over by a procuress (woman as avarice) and in time, as the brothel scene indicates, she takes her cut of the profits.

33. Judith Leyster, *The Proposition* (1631).

34. Giovanni Piazzetta (1683–1754), *A Bravo, a Girl and an Old Woman*.

35. Jan Steen (1625–79),
La Mauvaise Compagnie.

36. Francisco de Goya y
Lucientes, *Maja and Celestina
on a balcony* (c.1808–12).

Grien's fleshy witches producing steaming spells and surrounded by human remains and Dürer's flying hag have comic qualities. These images predate the witch persecutions but show an evolved consciousness of witch beliefs.

37. ABOVE: Hans Baldung Grien, *Witches Scene* (*c*.1514).

38. ABOVE LEFT: Albrecht Dürer (1471–1528), *A Witch*.

39. More prosaic and less sexy, the Northamptonshire witches of 1612 set forth with evil intent on a pig converted into a devilish steed.

41. *Les Soeurs de l'Hopital de Geel Soignant des Aliénés* by an unknown artist. Increasingly, the practical work of hospitals, orphanages, relief of the poor, and teaching were interpreted as appropriate female vocational work.

40. Bernini, *Saint Teresa of Avila* (1645–52). Bernini's St Teresa shows a mystical ecstasy akin to orgasm, but even by the time of her canonisation the church was discouraging female claims to mystic experience.

Pietro Longhi gives two witty observations on female piety: their attachment to the confessional and their concern to see their dying male relatives confront their maker with shriven souls.

42. Pietro Longhi, *Confession* (*c*.1770).

43. Pietro Longhi, *Extreme Unction* (*c*.1770).

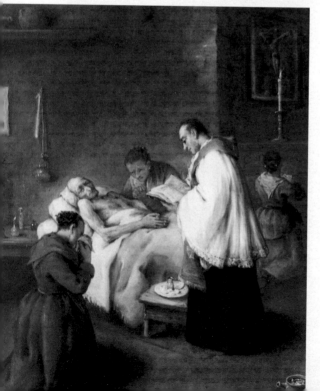

Backer and Hals present positive collective portraits of doughty, authoritative Protestant matrons superintending good works which contrast with the evil procuresses and the witch as hag seen earlier.

44. Frans Hals, *Almshouse Regentesses, Haarlem* (1664).

45. Jacob Backer, *Four Regentesses of the Burgher Orphanage with a Child* (1633–4).

47. Gérard Dou (1613–1675), *Reading the Bible*. The end of the life course. Immense respect for pious old age is revealed in Dou's rendering of a shared moment in the lives of the old couple when the bespectacled wife reads the word of God to her husband.

and roles possible? A number of points stand out. First, women seem to have been primarily involved in economic and religious disturbances, both of which could have a political context. They could act with other women, in the company of men, or merely provide the incitement to revolt, leaving the real action to the men. The numbers involved at any one time are inevitably speculative: most evidence is drawn from criminal records and the police decided who came before the courts. Some women may have been weeded out in the primary stages by magistrates and other officials anxious to reduce the numbers of dependent children who might be left on the parish if penal action were taken against their mothers. Most women appear to be found at the beginning of a disturbance and to fall away as the level of violence rises. Indeed, without going so far as to say that women's role in riot is nonviolent, they seem to have tried to contain the violence in which they might be directly involved. They depend upon threats of what will happen if they are not heard, or they seek to impress a harassed and frequently isolated officialdom by weight of numbers. Women can also, by drawing attention to their plight, attempt to win over the representatives of law and order by simple persuasion. It is clear that they do not expect to find themselves fired upon or stampeded by a cavalry charge. They expect to be viewed as innocent and guileless, as people who do not normally have recourse to such behaviour and who therefore have a right to be heard, and so they go largely unarmed. Or the women give the men a lead, urging them forward with taunts of cowardice and making it clear that they have the courage that the men lack. Where it is obvious that the day will be marked by bloodshed they are conspicuously absent. Their absence from the storming of the Bastille, for example, may have been a deliberate recognition that there was to be a confrontation with troops, and we are explicitly told that the old men and the women and children of the district remained shut up in their houses.[20]

Bread riots were most often marked by a female presence when they occurred in the marketplace itself. Women rarely attacked grain convoys in transit. As purchasers in the market and controllers of the family purse they were price sensitive and equally aware of the quality of the grain or flour they were purchasing. Buying grain or bread or groceries usually meant some bargaining and this could be the prelude to altercation. Furthermore, women who were out on the streets were more likely to pick up rumours and rumours of shortage could be the trigger for panic buying which could in turn cause short-term artificial shortages. Women who witnessed speculative practices and suspected that the merchants were themselves caught up in them could be particularly prompt in their response.[21]

Another generalization possible is that, with few exceptions, women are involved in 'conservative' riots or demonstrations to reimpose an order which suited them better than the one which had replaced it. Such a response might be the result of religious change. Taken overall, there are more recorded women's riots to preserve their faith against the godless than radical action in promotion of change. Or they reacted to what they saw as slights upon the community of women. The first known women's protest in England was in the fifteenth century against Duke Humphrey's attempt to put aside the woman believed to be his wife, and the second was on behalf of the 'wronged' Catherine of Aragon. Queen Caroline would in turn gain female supporters at the end of the period. The women involved in these demonstrations clearly wanted recognition of a wife's security of tenure.[22]

The women involved in riot played on a belief in their innocence and their rectitude in protecting the interests of their families. But they were not naïve and they were dependent upon a specific relationship with the forces of authority. Indeed, riot had its rituals and its own kind of theatre.

As late as the 1770s, despite government commitment to *laissez-faire*, many magistrates and police officials were still basically on the side of the populace rather than the grain merchants whose machinations they mistrusted in times of shortage. When presenting their cases to a higher authority unsympathetic to attempts to impede the freedom of the grain trade, such officials described riots led by women in highly emotional terms. One such was Verdon, *lieutenant de police* at Bergerac in May 1773, who had warned his superiors that the town was 'threatened with disturbance by a revolt and a sedition similar to those which other places in the province have already suffered', and he had to control a nasty confrontation between grain merchants wanting to charge 5 livres the *pognère* (a local measure) and women prepared only to pay 3 livres. He described how a pregnant woman slipped her hand into his and said: 'Monsieur de Verdon, help me, help me. My husband and me and my three children will starve to death if you don't get us corn. I'll stab myself before your very eyes.'

Verdon told his superior that he explained to her that 3 livres would ruin the merchants and that he even offered to lend this woman money, but she refused and said she had no means to repay. The women proceeded to besiege a grain store belonging to a notorious merchant called Gimet. Verdon addressed the ringleaders and they said to him, 'God bless you. We hope you'll give us justice.' He told the women that they were not offering enough to secure a just return to the merchant and he tried to buy off the woman he thought the most intrepid of the rioters by promising her as much free grain as she could carry. However she rejected his offer and by the end of the afternoon, Gimet had been pinned down and his sacks ripped open by the women and sold at their price to all present.

This account is worthy of close examination because it is evidence presented by an official to his superiors. He has failed to prevent a riot ending in *taxation populaire* (the enforced sale of the grain at what the insurgents deem a fair price) and he wants to present himself in the best possible light. He had few police or soldiers to call on to go to the help of Gimet and he could not, whatever his feelings, run the risk of having his forces defeated by an intrepid crowd. His report does not mention how many people were involved, but hints that the crowd was numerous. Verdon speaks only of women: this may represent the true composition of the crowd or he may be attempting to play down the level of violence such a crowd was likely to inflict and his own impotence by insisting on the difficulties involved in dealing roughly with women *some of whom might be pregnant*. He knows that his best chance to maintain face with the community is to buy time, stay on the side of the people and appeal to their inherent notions of fairness. He must also hope that Gimet and his ilk will have received a warning not to let prices rise too high and that the incoming harvest will bring relief. However, he cannot say any of this to his superiors. He therefore presents a poignant story of a pregnant woman and her suffering family, and depicts himself as an intrepid agent in attempts to preserve law and order to the point of attempting to drive a wedge between the ringleaders by buying one off. He will not receive praise for his actions, but he may be able to deflect criticism. If this is a one-off event he has a good chance of succeeding. If not, he will have to make an appeal for more men, either police or troops, to come to his aid. What is also apparent from the events of such a day is that both police official and the women of the crowds knew the rules of the game.[23] These rules would change as police forces became larger and as troops were used with weaponry to quell disturbances, and the changes may have helped to distance women from bread riots after about 1816.

The kind of women who took part differed slightly according to the type of riot. Bread riots involved those women who purchased in the marketplace; political riots a somewhat broader spectrum. Elizabeth Lilburne and the Leveller wives were of very solid artisan status. However, that said, women who were not accustomed to street life did not suddenly pour on to the street to join in. Riots formed in neighbourhoods and on staircases. You rioted with your neighbours, your friends and relatives. A neighbourhood leader or captain sometimes emerged: flags were constructed out of petticoats. Fine clothes were out of place and language was coarse. This was no milieu for a Mary Wollstonecraft. Those village women whose socio-economic status is discernible were also those of modest standing, even during the Counter-Revolution in France when village women rioted for their religion. The rioters were not the priest shelterers.

In Holland twelve out of seventy-six identifiable protesters in political riots between 1784 and 1799 were fishwives and fruit sellers. A memorandum of 1749 proclaimed: 'Musselwives, female hawkers of vegetables and apples . . . are the most dangerous and are those who will come out in revolt.' 'Sovereignty now resides in the fishmarket,' sneered a Frisian nobleman in 1747, while in the midst of the food riots of 1763 at Rotterdam, a monthly periodical ascribed them to fishwives 'who are not the most tractable of people'.[24] Political 'fishwives' also appear in British history, where the notion of market women, coarse and unruly women and politically querulous women became synonymous. The term fishwife was probably used quite indiscriminately to mean any protesting woman, like Elizabeth Lilburne. On the other hand, market women sang and shouted their wares and extemporized political jingles to fit their cries. They were a vociferous bunch, conscious of their right to be outspoken, litigious and used to fending for themselves. The fishwives of eighteenth-century Paris had the right of direct appeal to the Queen of France, Maria Leczinska, and would go in groups to the palace, a tradition which could also have contributed to the decision to march to Versailles.[25]

Another noteworthy aspect of the woman in riot is her relatively advanced age. The age of the typical woman of the Revolutionary *journées* was in the region of fifty and her children were virtually grown up. She was a wage-earner – seamstress, laundress, embroiderer, petty trader, flower or newspaper seller, porter – and sometimes without a man to support her. Many suggestions can be advanced as to why such a woman would involve herself. She had no dependants if she should fall into trouble with the authorities and no job to lose. She was also at the bottom of a vulnerable pile of people, in the same predicament as the elderly protesters of the former Communist Bloc countries of eastern Europe find themselves in the transition to a market economy. These ageing women are stripped of hope, their working energies are receding and inflation has eaten their savings. At the end of their days they have no prospect of a pension as in our societies. Much the same kind of woman, though a decade younger, was found in Dutch riots. Women under twenty-five were rarely present. Most of these in a city might have been engaged in domestic service and servants were rarely found in riot. The average age for participants in food revolts was forty, in religious and political revolts thirty-seven. But instances are found of women over seventy who frequently had a leadership role and may have belonged to protester dynasties.[26]

The English evidence lends itself less easily to generalization. The English poor law was a powerful deterrent to incarcerating the mother of a brood of children and this may have influenced who came before the courts. Though the evidence is scanty, the typical rioter seems to have been between twenty and forty, making her younger than her European counterpart.[27]

An analysis of woman in riot obviously tells us something about gender roles in the community, but what exactly does it tell us and is there evidence of women contesting power with men? Certainly women rioted to protect what they cherished and to bring the notice of authority to the plight of the innocent. They went largely, if not totally, unarmed and to the top if the top could be reached. The law enabled them to shelter behind the notion of the irresponsible and irrational woman, particularly in the absence of their husbands, and this may have allowed the entire community to shelter behind them. Women could rush in where men could not tread, so as rioters they might have been the voice of the community.

As a further consideration, the shame and honour concepts held by these societies may have contributed to endorsing the legitimacy of the woman rioter under certain circumstances. A woman, traditionally, has the right to expect men to protect her. Her earnings are known to be insufficient for an independent life. She depends upon an appreciation of her subordinate status. *L'honneur de la femme est d'être inférieure*, as the French saying ran, needs careful translation. A woman has a right to protection by husband and community. If these fail to provide her needs she is morally entitled to shame them, to bring them to an appreciation of their inadequacy. If she has power it is to inflict shame. In Languedoc it was regarded as dishonourable for a man to bring a woman to court for the theft of food. A woman inadequately provided for by a man occupied a problematic grey area of the law. Bread riots, in reminding authority of the plight of the truly dependent, made manifest the failure of husband and provider and of the structures of society to protect the weak. In urging men to take action and calling them laggards and cowards, the notion of shaming them into action comes once again into account. The women who pre-empt action may find this an empowering experience, if one which only occurs once in a lifetime, but their business is to assert not the power of woman over man but the need for man to be in a position to assume his rightful role as provider. Their appeal is made in some instances away from the patriarchal authority of the home towards the patriarchal authority of the state.

The French Revolution saw riots and protests of very different kinds by women. There were bread riots, political demonstrations and, above all in a village context, religious riots. In all these events, the particular political events of the day either triggered off or influenced the activity and hence they could all be said to be political riots. Many different groups of women were involved and they did not necessarily look to other women for their support. However, most of the protest of the Revolutionary years also demonstrates the traditions of women's riots in the early modern period.[28]

In October 1789, for example, perhaps as many as six thousand women from the working-class districts of Paris, legatees of a tradition of direct action in the marketplace, went to Versailles to demand of the king a reduction in the price of bread. The relationship between the king and the Assembly had reached stalemate over the royal response to the Declaration of the Rights of Man and the Constitution, in which the power of the monarch was conspicuously reduced. The Assembly itself was divided on these issues. Paris reverberated with the story of the Flanders regiment which had allegedly, in the presence of the royal family, trampled the Revolutionary cockade of red, white and blue underfoot and donned black and white ones, the colours of the Bourbons and the Habsburgs. Above all, in spite of the recent harvest which was said to be good, prices in Paris had not yet fallen; perhaps because the peasantry, for the first time, did not have to market their goods to pay their taxes and could wait for higher prices. For the populace the impasse was baffling. Why was nothing happening? The politicians were locked in discussion, but what was this doing for those who had to buy bread?

The solution was to be pre-emptive female action. The police reported hearing criticisms: *les hommes traînent, les hommes sont des lâches . . . nous nous mettrons à la tête des affaires* (the men are holding back . . . the men are cowards . . . we will take over) and then the events unfold.[29]

A dawn assembly of between 800 and 2000 women gathered on 5 October and converged upon the Hôtel de Ville, forced the doors, rushed inside and proceeded to deny entry to any men. The women looked for pikes and cannon and they seized papers and files and prepared to make a huge bonfire of them on the grounds that they contained nothing to help them get bread, the first duty of administrators. They were dissuaded from this action by Maillard, one of the *vainqueurs de la Bastille*, a member of the National Guard and someone they trusted. He agreed to go with them to Versailles to confront the Assembly and the king. The women then split up, some to look for ammunition at the Invalides but many more to round up neighbours and relations so that by the time they kept the general rendezvous at the Place Louis XV their numbers had trebled. It was almost afternoon before they set off for Versailles with eight drummers at their head, and Maillard leading. Lafayette and the National Guard followed several hours later: he was said to be reluctant to go, either because he feared what might happen in the capital in his absence or because he thought that the presence of the Guard might make the women's protest more dangerous. After work groups of men set off and the arms taken by the women may have been for their use. The carrying of arms by women in protest was a new departure and raises questions. Were they intended as symbolic and to show their desperation? There is no evidence that the women knew how to use them or that they had enough ammunition. Or were they intended to lend force to the entire community when women and men gathered together to confront any armed impediments to their plans?

It was late afternoon before the women got to Versailles and, after receiving an initial petition made in highly personal terms about hoarders and speculators in the misery of the people, the Assembly sanctioned a deputation to visit the king around seven. The women chose twelve of their number including, by all accounts, a good-looking seventeen-year-old girl, Louise Chabry, who is said to have mouthed the words 'du pain' and fallen in a breathless faint at the king's feet.

Louis promised to see to it that the city was adequately provisioned and the delegation returned to make its report to the women. The majority were totally dissatisfied. What guarantees had the king offered? Had they got anything in writing? The women were angry. If they went back to Paris now, with so little security, how had their position been improved? Some thought the king's word enough and began the walk back to Paris with Maillard at their head. Confusion now reigned. Some women went back to the Assembly and slept on the benches. Others invaded the Hôtel de la Surintendance to shelter from the driving rain. Inside the Château of Versailles urgent debates on the position of the king were under way. To win over the Assembly to his side, Louis XVI agreed to the Constitution with its limitations on royal sovereignty. The women had achieved a victory for the politicians even at this stage.

By ten o'clock the National Guard had arrived and Lafayette told the king that he could not guarantee his personal safety unless he and his family moved to the capital. The king would not agree. In the small hours the men arrived and in the semi-darkness the mood became much uglier. Some of the crowd broke into the palace and tried to force entry to the queen's bedchamber. In the confrontation, two of the royal bodyguards were killed – but not by women. At this stage of the mêlée, the number of women had conspicuously diminished, though it is at this juncture that we hear for the first time, from royalist accounts, of men dressed up as women. The National Guard intervened and, when order had been restored, the king appeared on the balcony before as many as ten thousand people of whom perhaps only a fifth or less were the original women. He promised bread, but a promise was no longer enough and, overwhelmed by the shouting, agreed to go with his family to Paris.

Michelet was stunned by how much was achieved on this day with minimum violence. There was, of course, nothing inevitable in this outcome. The women had opened up the situation. They had demon- strated how far a large and peaceful march could go, but when their interview with the king was without tangible result or real guarantees, the event had to pass into another phase involving guards and men. Had this further development not occurred, the transfer of the king and the Assembly to Paris might not have been achieved. The *journée* is to be contrasted with the risings of germinal and prairial in the year III when the outcome was quite different and the rioting women were without the support of the politicians.[30]

These insurrections were some of the most bitter and poignant of the entire Revolution. Between them and the October Days lay years in which the working masses of Paris had received a political education in the art of demonstration and petitioning. The outbreak of war caused the immediate and rapid debasement of Revolutionary currency and hence inflation, while simultaneously multiplying the demands of the government for money and men – the sons of the poor – to fight for France. The advance of the Prussians upon Paris and the belief that the people dwelt in the midst of a conspiracy of aristocrats and those who wished to starve the people intensified a growing popular hysteria. After the terrible winter of 1794/5, when bread was in short supply and the black market flourished, when the government had largely abolished measures of price fixation introduced to satisfy Paris and ensure that the purchase of bread was within reach of every working-class family, when amenorrhoea set in among the women of the poor, two risings were organized to demonstrate to the Convention that the people's voices must be heard. The cry was for bread and new elections, putting into effect the Constitution of 1793 (suspended by the Convention in the context of war) in which every man had a vote.[31]

The first of these risings, on 12 germinal (1 April), was an affair involving both men and women, but the organization of the event was in the hands of women. We hear the familiar vocabulary reported as coming from the mouths of women . . . *les hommes sont des lâches* . . . *les hommes traînent* . . . my good-for-nothing husband is standing by and letting his wife and children die from hunger . . .

The people went to the Convention unarmed and shouted for *du pain et la Constitution*. They were told to go home and promised bread. Outside they pillaged and fell into fights with *muscadins*, the name given to middle-class youths who proclaimed themselves anti-terrorist but were themselves young thugs. There may have been as many as ten thousand people present at the beginning of the day, but gradually the numbers diminished as the women in particular disappeared and went home. There was no increase in the supply of bread, and within weeks another rising had occurred, that of 1 prairial (20 May). This *journée* was in essence a last-ditch plea, a women's event terrible in its poignancy. Perhaps the men had lost heart after the events of germinal or perhaps this was seen as the final attempt to make the plight of the people known. The women made a massive round-up of their neigh-bours, in the streets, on the staircases, and went unarmed to the Conven-tion. A certain citoyen Canton, *coiffeur*, who turned up to help with weapons was sent home by *une vendeuse de salades* with the remark: 'anyone who carries arms is a cuckold'.[32]

The politicians responded to this female occupation by instructing the Guard to use whips to disperse them. But whips did not work and the Guard used the butt-ends of bayonets instead. Blood was spilt and the rumour – 'they are killing our women' – got out into the crowd outside. A seething mass of both sexes tried to come to their help, but armed forces had been brought in specially to hold the crowd and this was the prelude to three or four days' fighting that resulted in the disarming of the working-class faubourgs. The popular revolution, of which the working women of Paris were in part the architects, was over.[33]

This rising failed because the initial demonstration was not backed up by forces which could intimidate the Convention. There was no body of politicians prepared to take on the people's cause and forces of repression were to hand. The people themselves did not want to destroy the Convention before new elections were held. It demonstrates how the efficacy of mass, unarmed, female protest, designed to provoke sympathy and initiate change, could be very dependent on other factors to achieve its purpose.

The riots of germinal and prairial, like the October Days of 1789, were obviously much more than bread riots. They were events with a political target designed to ensure the interests of the working class and make their political voice heard, and the women who involved them-selves were working women who were not afraid to be part of a crowd and to take risks. The Revolution was also to witness action of a some-what different character with a different set of participants. These move-ments were designed to gain citizenship for women, and they occupy a significant place in the history of western feminism. Unlike the October Days they were never mass movements, but their existence demonstrates that some women at least had a concept of a society in which the role of women was not passive and where the rights and obligations of citizenship were not confined to one sex.[34]

These views came out of the French Enlightenment and were built above all on the vision of republican motherhood which grew apace in late eighteenth-century France nourished by Rousseau and women writers such as Madame de Genlis and which gathered momentum with the American and French Revolutions. At issue was the birth and perpetuation of civic morality. Republican Rome had been remarkable not merely for its men but for its women – the Roman matron epitomized in Cornelia, mother of the Gracchi, who, when her sons flagged in their remorseless dedication to the state, spurred them on to a personal sacrifice which took their lives. The physical fact of motherhood was not enough. The right kind of motherhood was what was at issue if the republican state was to achieve perfection. In this kind of thinking, motherhood was intertwined with citizenship and the individual woman, whose right to the full realization of her intellectual potential was at stake in the Anglo-Saxon education debate, had little space against the wider social ideal of the generation of citizens. In the reproductive process women had a social role as valuable as any performed by man. They should therefore be recognized as equal to men but different and demanding of special consideration in their status as women, the mothers of citizens.

The only political thinker of any note in France who before 1789 had touched on the issue of political rights, in the sense of voting power, for women was Condorcet. He believed that property was the basis for the franchise and that if women owned land they should have a vote. The subject of women's political role was not even mentioned by the Constituent Assembly. However, the ferment of the Revolution produced an airing of questions relating to women in pamphlets, prints and petitions. The volume was not considerable but it gained in strength very rapidly in the capital and some large cities.[35]

Between 1790 and 1791 a number of radical women began to petition for the redress of specific grievances affecting women and asked among other things for the abolition of the dowry system, better educational opportunities and more pay for women's work. Simultaneously in Paris and certain parts of provincial France (largely the east and the south-west) groups of women drawn largely from the middle classes and many of them the wives of administrators, formed clubs to endorse the supportive role of women for the Revolution and to help in philanthropic initiatives to tide the poor over the dislocation resulting from the government's 'reform' of the system of poor relief. In Paris a number of women of varying backgrounds, but not of the working classes, demanded fuller participation for women in political life and rights of citizenship confirmed by a civic oath. Of these, the former actress Olympe de Gouges, the Liégoise Théroigne de Méricourt, and the Dutch adventuress Etta Palm d'Aelders secured the greatest attention.[36]

Three weeks after the outbreak of war, in the spring of 1792, Théroigne de Méricourt called for the creation of legions of Amazons to defend Paris and the Revolution and insisted that the bearing of arms turned every woman into a citizen. Such initiatives had no official encouragement and, as far as one can tell, next to no popular base. Membership of the women's clubs was small and the majority of the Parisian female population seem to have regarded them as irrelevant. Certainly the issues they addressed were regarded as less than pertinent to the lives of the working populace. If they considered the problem of poverty it was with a view to organizing philanthropy, not controlling the price of bread, and it is not clear that women in general wanted to fight for their country. After all, they had sent their sons to the front. The *clubistes* placed their hopes on the Girondin faction who were overtly hostile to any idea of popular sovereignty. Both de Gouges and de Méricourt (whose fabricated names were scarcely designed to win them a popular following) were acknowledged monarchists, and the increasing association of the monarchy with an unsuccessful war and with treachery following the flight to Varennes did not pass unnoticed.

In May 1793, however, a new club was formed, the Société Républicaine Révolutionnaire, which had a very different agenda and stood a greater chance of winning for itself a popular base among the people of Paris. Formed by real popular militants, Pauline Léon and Claire Lacombe, chocolate maker and actress respectively, and with an immediate membership of about 170, the club stood for fighting grain shortage and inflation, an acceleration of the Terror as a weapon against hoarders and speculators, and a reapplication of the Constitution of 1793 put into limbo by the Convention for the duration of the war. The leaders, Léon and Lacombe − though not necessarily the rest − had links with the *enragés*, far left, popular politicians, and it may have been this which was to cause the Jacobins considerable anxiety.[37]

The leadership was extremely active and very clear in its aims. It was also extremely sophisticated in its methods, using petitioning, heckling from the tribunes of the Convention and street harassment of the Girondin politicians. They organized a group which almost lynched Théroigne de Méricourt, leaving her beaten about the head and humiliated; this public thrashing may have caused the insanity which led to her confinement in the Salpêtrière asylum. The club could claim that it had certainly helped the Jacobins to discredit the Girondins; and Olympe de Gouges went with them to the scaffold.

These victories for the club were not to be sustained. In the next weeks the pressure to accelerate the Terror, to hold fresh elections and to fix prices severely vexed the Jacobin leadership, anxious to consolidate its control. There seems also to have been dissension in the club over the growing association between some of its members and the *enragés* which provoked the resignation of the president. By the end of October 1793 the Jacobins had secured the arrest of the leading *enragés* and had not only closed all women's clubs but also banned women from forming political associations. In suppressing the Société Républicaine Révolutionnaire, which was their main concern, they used the *marchandes de la halle* (market women deeply resentful of *enragé* harassment over the supply and cost of food, and hence no friends of the *clubistes*). The ostensible ground for conflict between them was the club's attempt to force the market women to wear the sans culotte emblem, the revolutionary cockade, obligatory for all citizens. Citizenship was integral to the club's agenda, but the market women declared that it was contrary to their rights as women, because it meant bearing arms and fighting and their duties as mothers of families were different from those of men.[38]

The apparent split in the ranks of women evinced by the opposition between the market women and the club was a real gift to politicians anxious to assert control over street politics. J. P. Amar, speaking in the Convention, excluded women from political activity in a flurry of rhetoric which insisted that 'a woman's honour confines her to the private sphere and precludes her from a struggle with men'. This speech has been deconstructed and decodified and heralded as the foundation text of nineteenth-century woman, banished to the private sphere of the home. This is perhaps to transcend or even to miss its significance.[39] The speech draws on a misogynistic rhetoric as old as the classical world brought up to date by an injection of Rousseau, to whose views many women subscribed. This kind of rhetoric was dredged to the surface whenever those in authority found women's protest inconvenient, or when they wished to postulate the construction of an ideal society. Unruly woman was throughout the period a scapegoat for social evils. The timing of the speech is important, however; the government was pre-empting an alliance between two inconveniences, the *enragés* and the *clubistes*.

A number of other factors need to be taken into account. The club was attacked through women, some of whom may have been the radicals of October 1789, and the club itself was very split. Although it claimed the support of thousands, it is difficult to prove membership of more than a couple of hundred – even if their activism was quite remarkable.[40] Their agenda aimed at popular sovereignty. It is not clear if this meant political rights for women or the rights of the household to be represented. Furthermore, there was no popular demonstration on their behalf and no expressed protest at the banning of women from a separate club life which had never attracted women on a major scale. It is clear that the alliance between citizenship and the right to bear arms may have been a very alienating concept to the bulk of women – even those who were prepared to sit in front of the guillotine and watch the internal conspiracy eliminated before their eyes. Finally, the out-lawing of club politics and the rhetoric about woman in the home did not exclude women from political action. The riots of germinal and prairial bear testimony to their perpetual concern about bread supplies and the representation of the working-class household in politics.

In the aftermath of germinal and prairial, an attempt was made to bring the leaders of the women's protest to court. Before the judges such women might appear submissive, indeed penitent. Dossiers of cases of women on trial reveal that of the 148 arrests of women involved in the prairial rising in Paris, about a quarter had some past record as militants in bread disturbances. Of the 39 whose ages are given the majority were under thirty or over forty-five – women with young children did not involve themselves. Most were wage-earners and about two-thirds could sign their names. As defence they pleaded the sweet-ness and docility of their sex rendered temporarily distraught by the effects of suffering on their families. Or they insisted upon the special vulnerability of their sex in hard times. A few of the right age used the ploy of being menopausal and hence irrational, and so colluded in reinforcing a female stereotype which had traditionally helped exonerate them if they should be brought before the courts. They knew what they were doing. They were not politically naïve and they would do the same thing again in 1812 and 1816. By sheltering behind a stock image, 40 per cent were immediately released and the overwhelming majority of the rest received two-month prison sentences.[41]

*

The history of protest in Paris during the Revolution involves a mixture of the radical and the traditional. Political change was seen in 1789 to open up possibilities that could be used to further, on the one hand, the political aspirations of a de Gouges and, on the other, those of the working masses. Outside the capital, particularly in rural areas, the traditional form of protest was employed to counter radical changes in community and family life imposed from outside.

In much of provincial France, commitment to the Revolution wavered after the heady days of 1789. Away from Paris, in producer France, there existed a large number of people who were first suspicious, and then positively hostile to change. The first to boycott the Revolutionary paper currency and to trigger inflation were peasant women at the markets who refused to hand over basic foodstuffs like milk and vegetables for anything but coin. In the villages traditional religious practice could have a very firm hold; the replacement of the parish priest who refused to take the oath of loyalty to the government and the changes imposed on the church by the legislation of 1790–1 could engender resentment of the intrusion of the government in parish life. At this stage much depended on local commitment to their particular parish priest, which was far from universal. The slump in luxury industries, the deliberate destruction of the old agencies of poor relief in small towns and villages without organizing replacements, price fixing which was clearly opposed to the interests of producing France and also to those of towns which were not a priority in the government's provisioning schemes, and mobilization which demanded the young die for a Revolution to which they and their families were far from committed, created a huge pool of dissidence by late 1792.

In this dissidence, baptized by government officials 'Counter-Revolution', distinct gender roles were to emerge. Young men were draft dodgers, older men held back on the payment of taxes and tried to evade the government's requisitioning schemes. Many village women from 1790 boycotted state priests and subsequently state cults and, if they were distant from prying town officials, organized clandestine masses. They gathered to say the rosary, that convenient expression of a fortress faith, taught the young to pray and kept their children away from state schools. Against change the counter-revolutionary woman of the villages erected tradition.

After 1795, when the hand of government was conspicuously weakened, Paris politicians were to be made aware of protests which were largely female engineered in many provinces, aimed at restoring patterns of regular Catholic worship destroyed during the Terror. These riots were both conservative and adopted traditional forms of female protest using stereotypical ploys. However, they manifested a deep contempt for the workings of Revolutionary officialdom and in many instances lent the tone to evolving village attitudes to the central government and its policies. The Directory was to learn that a regime which cannot command the respect of its women is in trouble.[42]

During the heady days of the Jacobin dictatorship (1793–4) there had been open scorn for what were interpreted as women's practices, which involved adherence to an old religion and its priesthood. When dealing with women, officialdom used a vocabulary of dismissive derivatives – *femelles, femelettes, bigotes, bêtes, moutons, légumineuses, fanatiques* (females, little women, bigots, beasts, sheep, vegetables, fanatics).[43] Indeed, it could be argued that officialdom deliberately made a bid for the minds of men over the issue of religious change by converting the notion of Catholic practice into something only sustained by gullible women. Certainly, in support of this thesis, the Jacobins tolerated at the local level gatherings of women to say the rosary and tried, sometimes with tongue in cheek, to convert statues which had been the focal points of women's cults into patriotic symbols by the imposition of a Phrygian cap on their heads or other symbols of Republican commitment. In some cases they blatantly offended village women by a disrespect manifested both towards them, as women, and to their religion.

In the village of Saint Germain de Laval in the Maconnais in 1795, local Jacobins took a classical nude from a local château and painted a tricolour on her. Having felled as a symbol of obsolete papistry the crucifix which had stood in the village square, they stood the statue in the vacant spot and proclaimed her the goddess of liberty. Days later it began to rain and as the paint started to wash off and to run down her legs, the young guard proclaimed the miracle of the menstruating goddess. The village women, outraged by the tasteless remarks, seized the statue, carried her several miles to the river, washed her and laid her on her side, a purification ceremony which restored her dignity as a female symbol. The next day they broke into the church and reclaimed it for Catholic worship.[44]

This is a striking response to mockery of female dignity and to change imposed in such a way as to slight the women of the community. The balance of shame and honour in the village was destroyed and action by the village women became imperative to restore it. Once restored, it might be hoped that normal or traditional values, in which they were accorded respect, would once again prevail.

Away from civic centres, which were under close scrutiny throughout the Jacobin period, priest sheltering was predominantly the activity of pious and mostly middle-class spinsters and the organization of the clandestine mass was frequently in their hands. After 1796, when the Directory had opened the prison doors and pronounced freedom of worship of all gods or goddesses, but without handing back the parish churches for Catholic worship or permitting mass to be said by any priest who would not take an oath of loyalty to the government, disturbances began on an extensive scale. Village women assumed the initiative by occupying churches and flouting legislation which prohibited exterior manifestations of public worship (mainly the use of bells). They wrested chalices and sacred vessels from unwilling authorities and rescued dissident priests from prison. On these occasions the menfolk stayed behind or gave subsidiary help. Often the riots, depending on the assessed strength of the opposition, were organized and women from other villages were called in. The ostensibly pregnant and the aged were placed in the forefront of attack and then came the older women as ash carriers and stone throwers, the traditional formation.[45]

Village women in fact soon perfected an effective range of oppositional techniques. The first strategy was a simple collective obstinacy in face of prohibitions. An individual flouting the law could easily be isolated and picked off, whereas the entire female population of a village could have much more effect. In this way officialdom could be forced to cede the keys of churches, for example. The second technique was ridicule of an explicitly sexist variety designed to undermine or embarrass pontificating authority when it sought to enforce state cults. The third was openly flouting an official recognized to have little support from guards in his commitment to government policies. The fourth was refusal to budge on issues where female co-operation was needed, as in the case of schooling or attendance at state cults. The fifth was maintaining the old faith through the rosary and teaching the next generation.

When they encountered opposition in the form of rioting, weary local officialdom, whatever the intructions received from Paris, might not put up much resistance. When admitting defeat, such officials might record a somewhat distorted version of events in order not to be accused of cowardice by their superiors who were anxious to maintain the rule of law. They would exaggerate the numbers of women involved from dozens to hundreds and describe an official's suffering as he was thrown to the ground and his clothes torn. Or they would express a reluctance to spill the blood of silly women with children and would describe matters as best resolved by yielding. By 1796 they also knew that if brought to court the women would be dismissed by royalist judges.

Victory was not, of course, inevitable. The rioting women were frequently frustrated by a strategic shifting of imprisoned priests or the disappearance of confiscated chalices. We need to allow constantly for a small overworked force excusing its own inertia and desiring to preserve its face in the community. Nineteenth-century police forces were larger and better equipped, so they were able to be less tolerant of law breakers, whatever their sex. In traditional societies, police forces proceeded more cautiously and on the whole accepted, if reluctantly, that law enforcement reflected the possible not the desirable.

The ultimate aim of the women of the religious riots was the restoration of community solidarity as expressed in communal worship. The women wanted a warm, comforting, personal and familial religion with its own sociability patterns which endorsed the family in its collective celebration of births and marriages and gave the hope of salvation through Christian burial of the dead. This religion, over the centuries, had been structured to provide rites and ritualistic festivals to mark the weeks and the year. The state cults, with their emphasis on reason and liberty, were not only a religious travesty but an irrelevance to the peasant world. Liberty may have been a goddess to replace the old patriarchal God, but she offered nothing in the way of solace and succour. There is nothing rational about the vagaries of life and individual pain and a religion that did not hold out hope to the despairing through prayer and the possibility of change had little to attract them.

The first to seize back Sunday from the Republicans, and to turn their back on the Revolutionary calendar with its dechristianized ten-day week, were peasant women. The first to enter the parish church, even when prohibited by authority from doing so, were village women. Many of them were remarkably indifferent as to who should officiate over their renascent worship provided it was not a priest compromised by having accepted the Revolution. The women looked for non-jurors, those who had not taken an oath of loyalty to the government, and if they could not find such a person, they were content with the services of an educated villager who knew the liturgy and was familiar with the ceremonies, even if he could not, as a layman, administer communion. This circumvention of an officiating priest troubled both the non-juring clergy in exile and those priests who had sworn loyalty to the government and were only too willing to give their services.[46]

What the women wanted was a reversion to normality as they had known it and to the familiar rhythms of parish life. The Revolution had not shaken the bedrock of rural women's faith nor altered their perception of the intrinsic priorities of life, the family, the raising of children, the search for sufficiency, ways of doing. When republican politicians after the Napoleonic coup d'état sought to explain to themselves their failure to capture the minds of the rural masses, some picked out women as the reason for their failure. In particular, they saw the boycotting of state schools and of state religion, the placing of children with former clerics or members of the teaching congregations, as actions which ensured that republicanism was painted to the next generation as the work of the Devil. In this interpretation, the hand that rocked the cradle and guided the child controlled the acculturation process of males as well as females; but it was the moulding of the mind of the female which was the more dangerous because it perpetuated attitudes across generations.[47]

How much truth was there in this interpretation of the failure of the Revolution? The French historian Marcel Marion summarized the reasons for the failure in the following way: 'general demoralization, contempt for human life as illustrated in the events of the Revolution, intense economic crisis, extreme poverty, unemployment and the loss of the habits of work, profound social divisions and the weakness of the forces of repression'.[48] The return to the church was only one manifestation of contempt for government policy.

So why pick on this as the one cause by which to explain the demise of republicanism? First, the republicans were not prepared to blame themselves. It was an uncomfortable fact that republicanism in power had not worked: the economy had collapsed and the politicians had been able neither to reconcile their differences among themselves nor to control the situation. None of this could be admitted, so they fell back on a traditional scapegoat – woman: unruly, irrational and with the power to control the minds of ensuing generations. This monocausal view was particularly convenient because it kept science and rationality on the side of the Republican politicians and raised a familiar rhetorical spectre. Without ever naming her, the figure of Eve was resurrected to explain why man was kept out of earthly paradise. It was an old, old story, one told many times.

CHAPTER THIRTEEN

The Moving Finger?

THE TIME has come to conclude by reviewing or evaluating changes or continuities in the lives of women, distinguished by class and geographical differences, over the long period treated in this book. Such an exercise is not merely daunting but fraught with difficulties. Statistics abound at the end but are lacking at the beginning: a yardstick or the appropriate mathematical means of assessment in the form of equation, linear graph or pie chart is wanting. Where, given the movement of population, the twists and turns and geographical specificity of economic development, the growth of cities, the waxing and waning of religious beliefs at least among élites, the impact of literacy, the growth of consumerism, political shifts which could engender only temporary changes for society as a whole but could colour the experience of entire generations, can the historian find a terra firma to permit of simple generalization? Lacking the comfort of science, denied the possibility of offering empirical data which would justify sweeping statements (such as the 'marginalization' or the 'decline in the status' of women over the period) and thus the ability to make quantitative statements of greater precision than the words 'more' or 'less', where can we begin? Is the only certainty that there is no one woman to represent all women? Are there any threads to help us through the labyrinths of time and place to reach the clearing where a vista opens up?

One path to follow might be that offered by Braudel and to some extent by Tamara Hareven.[1] Braudel proposed that the social historian deal with time by thinking of it in three different ways, the long, the medium and the short term. The first embraced long-term conditions, the limits of the possible extending over centuries. The second would be a medium block of time, perhaps the experience of a generation living through a war or a revolution, a particular trade cycle or the rise and fall of a particular industry (boom and slump), or through the reign of a particular king, or a group of reformers intent on social purification, who pursued particular policies which could have an impact on the lives of groups of people and on individuals, but which did not endure to affect ensuing generations. The third kind of time, the short term, a year, a month, an outbreak of plague, the failure of a harvest which could make the rich much richer and the poor much poorer, could be of significance in the lives of individuals if transitory in the history of communities.

This kind of layering of time is helpful in thinking about women's lives. It promotes a consideration of how the experience of certain generations might differ while the framework of reference remains largely unchanged. Everyone who survived the birth process in the three hundred years considered here was a lifelong hostage to the constraints imposed by economic circumstances and belief patterns and was socialized into a set of values, visions, ways of doing things, dependent on class. While these circumstances, these beliefs, could and largely did transcend the generations, a particular generation or generations could experience disruptions which altered the way they lived. Population growth, such as that which characterized the sixteenth century, was accompanied by inflation and pressure on jobs and could see those women in low-paid employment elbowed out of work they were allowed to do in more prosperous times.[2] The shirtmakers of sixteenth-century Augsburg, for example, were stripped of business by the tailors who during difficult times contested the right of women to produce in this field. Or the guilds assumed a temporary hard line about infractions on their business which they tolerated in easier times. The hard times over, territory would be relinquished as spending resumed and men looked to more profitable work. No man would stay with a job that could be done by a woman, and commanded the level of remuneration of a woman, when he had another option. The contest between the sexes was bitterest when the demand for work far outstripped the supply.

In the context of the sixteenth century, religious reform provided the rhetoric to insist that the proper place for a woman was in the home under patriarchal control. The rhetoric endorsed, in effect, an ordering of society coincident with male claims to jobs. The same period saw, in Protestant Europe, the demise of the nunnery, alongside a hard line towards prostitutes, single mothers, migrant men who abandoned their wives, and those old women designated witches. Or the Inquisition might spearhead a policy in which Jews and heretics were the target. All these were aspects of state and church policy which could affect individuals over a generation or two before such zeal abated.

Wars and revolution in the twentieth century have been motors of change, opening up new avenues for women. In the early modern period, too, groups of women could assume new roles in the context of conflict. We have seen clear signs of this in the German Peasants' War, the Dutch struggle against the Spanish, the French Wars of Religion, all in the sixteenth century, the English Civil War in the seventeenth, and the French Revolution. However, the conflict over, the danger passed, the new roles are generally relinquished even if the experience is there to draw on. The woman warrior, metaphorically speaking, shed her armour and put flowers in her hair.[3] Or she had to seek another outlet for her energies.

Of all these instances of civil upheaval, the French Revolution had an unprecedented impact not merely because the French sought to export their revolution at bayonet point but because of the degree of awareness of events fostered by either the actuality or the threat of invasion, and by newsprint. It can perhaps be argued that the disruption of these years across both occupied and unoccupied Europe had effects which transcended the experience of generations, engendering, at least among some groups of women, a collective memory which would be resurrected in 1848 by the working-class Parisian women who joined the men on the barricades.[4]

For the bulk of Frenchwomen, perhaps 90 per cent, the decade of Revolution (1789–99) was Bad Time, that is, a period in which a familiar status quo was disrupted, and that disruption had a marked effect on the life experience of certain cohorts extending beyond the Revolutionary decade. Inflation followed rapidly on the heels of political change and even worse ensued when, from 1795 onwards, there was a period in which France lacked an effective currency. Inflation hit many different kinds of people. It made nonsense of the maidservant's savings; young men were taken from their communities to go to war and their period of capital accumulation or acquisition of a job skill was conspicuously curtailed. Inflation cut into savings and, most frighteningly of all, it reduced spending on non-essential commodities. That section of the French populace dependent upon textile production, whether on a putting-out basis or in industrial villages or towns, suffered in consequence. For the bottom fifth of the population, those dependent upon some kind of charitable subsidy, the obliteration of Catholic charity without any effective replacement meant real hardship. The charitable initiatives, however inadequate, which followed on the Council of Trent and which were intended to create a society in which the rich gave freely to the poor, were better than nothing. Involved in the system as givers, administrators, receivers were, as we have seen, literally millions of women. For the bottom two-fifths of the population, the Revolution was equated with hunger and dislocation accompanied by unreasonable demands for taxation and personal sacrifice for the state. For the working population of Paris, the experience was more terrible because the Revolution was conceived in hope.[5]

The Revolution witnessed the first highly visible flurry of political activity by groups of women with a discernible feminist agenda, who sought to advance the claims of women, or some part of them, to greater political participation. They used the language of equality, though with a recognition of gender difference, by vaunting the special obligations of Republican motherhood. Divided among themselves and with a shifting and difficult relationship with the market women, they nevertheless constitute a significant 'first', one which must be acknowledged to include the dilemma implicit in the discourse of feminism in its manifold forms throughout history: who can claim to speak for womankind? From this point in time, political upheaval in Europe designed to promote wide-ranging social change can anticipate some participation by small numbers of politically active women who seek to place changes in the status of women on a political agenda. In the medium term, however, they are silenced.

For those at either end of the social spectrum, the very rich and the poor, the decade was one preoccupied with survival. For hundreds of women whose husbands fled the country as émigrés, it was necessary to get a divorce of convenience and so to hold on to the family lands. These were times for female ingenuity, for sheltering behind the image of female helplessness in the face of abandonment, but underneath this cover of frailty were some astute manipulations designed to salvage something of the family wealth. After 1815 these troubles would be retailed, expanded and exaggerated, in print. The writers promote themselves as attempting to preserve normality and continuity in the lives of their children, disguising their anxieties at all costs. They relate with pride how they deceive government agents, hiding the family silver and their jewels or disposing of them to cover costs. Or, like

Madame de la Tour du Pin, they relate extraordinary adventures lest their children should forget.[6]

There are, of course, less exalted histories of survival which have not been transmitted as a continuous elegant and racy narrative but which remain in the pathetic testimonies of unpaid wet-nurses, conspicuous victims of the failure of the state to honour its commitment to the funding of foundling children so that single mothers need not abandon their babies, in the rising numbers of urban prostitutes prepared to sell themselves for a piece of bread, in the necrology of the hospitals, in lawsuits against women who have stolen food or led disturbances in a struggle to keep themselves and their families fed. When women physically assault the representatives of authority who can provide no more sustenance for towns than a delivery of salt fish which already smells foul, or rice which the poor lack the fuel to cook, or Indian corn which they have never seen before and do not know how to prepare, then we can recognize the traditional plight and classical response of ordinary women in conditions of war and revolution. Their job is to protect the family breadbasket.

For the women of the religious orders and congregations, imprisoned, in exile, driven underground, dispersed, these were years of prayer and waiting to revert to 'normality'. Many suffered and many died, but the reduction and martyrization of a particular generation of servants of the poor was followed after the Concordat by an extraordinary and totally unprecedented (even by the standards of the 1660s) growth in female vocations directed towards welfare and teaching services. At the practical level, the social conscience of the nineteenth century is largely in women's hands.[7]

For those in occupied Europe, too, it was Bad Time. Subject to military requisitions and the creaming off of foodstuffs as well as the more notable thefts of art and wealth, survival was again the main concern. For those under threat of invasion, however, across the English Channel, the period was, as Linda Colley has shown, one of some remarkable initiatives at some levels of the population.[8] Patriotic activism among women had never been more extensive. The death of Marie Antoinette, a woman and a mother, provoked not only revulsion articulated even by those like Hannah More who was no lover of the queen, but a cult of heroism, of our brave boys who needed supplying with warm flannel garments, appropriate flags and banners and regimental insignia. In 1798, when rebellion was also afoot in Ireland, many women who could afford to do so contributed so much to the state-sponsored Voluntary Contribution that *The Times* wondered whether a special subscription list for such patriotic women should not be opened. Hannah More and others with less distinguished names boasted of the time they spent raising funds to pay for boots for the military. These public efforts certainly gave some women, those with the time, the energy and the inclination, new organizational experience to set along-side that derived from charitable initiatives.

It may have been an exciting time for them, but for some women, lower down the economic scale, the 1790s were Bad Time, a time of food shortage, of cold (the Thames froze in the winter of 1795–6), of sons and husbands and lovers pressganged into the navy, and even if the girls were attracted by a red coat, some of the wearers never returned or came back mutilated. Their fate left victims behind. Again, there was no single story to tell. Peace came and collectively the poor recon-structed, or failed to reconstruct, a miserable livelihood (as the food riots of 1812 and 1816 were to demonstrate). With peace the female patriots lost the focal point of their endeavours. Upheaval, in short, whatever its thrilling or conversely terrible effects on the lives of indi-viduals, can be followed by a reversion to 'normality', perhaps leaving the traditional status quo shaken, perhaps leaving it strengthened, but without radical modification. On the other hand, it could be argued that women's actions during the Revolutionary decades raised a con-sciousness of their potential for radical involvement. Women's history could well go further in adopting a generational approach or pursuing through diaries, letters and memoirs the legacy of mother to daughter from the Revolutionary decade through the first half of the nineteenth century.[9]

Whatever the ebb and flow of experience as a result of war or economic fluctuations, some structural changes are discernible in the European population over these centuries. However imprecise the statistics, and however regionally different the experience, the European economy expanded over this period and population grew. Viewed as a whole, work opportunities at all levels of the population diversified as govern-ments expanded, imperial ambitions increased, armies and navies and bureaucracies burgeoned; commerce and industry grew as the range of goods extended. At another level, but one capable of modifying the structure of the population to some extent, religious institutions declined in power or lost some of their influence. Religion did not lose its authority in spite of the blows delivered by the Enlightenment and the French Revolution. Indeed, among the rural masses, shattered by the economic disasters of the Revolutionary period, it re-emerged as a source of solace; but its energy was diminished and its capacity to hold on to the poorer sections of the population in the towns was limited, as was its capacity to dictate to governments.

How can the effects of such changes be assessed? One approach might be to imagine a chronological parade and attempt to watch it as it passes, starting round about 1500 and ending three centuries later — we need not be too precise about the year because such an exercise is very impressionistic. Who was there when the procession drew to a close who was not there during the first hundred years and vice versa? Let us begin with the figures missing at the end.

The poor old woman transformed into a witch, the infanticidal mother on the way to the gallows because her baby's lungs had floated in a bucket of water, or because she had failed to register her pregnancy and declare the father and had had her baby alone in suspicious circumstances, the 'possessed' young girl screaming and writhing and orchestrated by her exorcist, the anorexic, raving, 'mystical' nun, those who tortured themselves in the name of religion, the nun facing a forced vocation, the child bride, the girl denied any choice in marriage, the 'cruel' widowed mother forced to abandon her child and leave the marital home in Italy — these are the kinds of figures largely lacking at the end of the period. They belong to history. There are fewer contemplative nuns and monks right across Catholic Europe by the mid-eighteenth century and more women dedicated to social service in schools and hospitals.

There are other striking changes affecting population structure to a greater degree. Agrarian change in fertile grain-growing areas has resulted in large farms, the engrossment of smallholdings, the enclosure of common land, and the conversion of small-scale activities like brewing and cheese-making into large-scale commercial enterprises. As a result there are fewer of these small-scale money-raising initiatives available to farmers' wives. There are also fewer farm servants, at least as a proportion of all female workers, at the end of the period, and at the bottom of the social ladder the most conspicuous increase is in the female, urban service sector. Since the late seventeenth century in Britain, Holland, Germany and France urban domestic service has become feminized and the trend is beginning by the end of the period to be visible in Spain and Italy. The demand comes from middle-class prosperity and the supply is largely, though not exclusively, from the impoverished of the country. The top level of service for women has a secure structure. However, the bottom level of the service sector which comprehended the more long-distance city immigrants (the Irish in London, the north German immigrants to Amsterdam, and so on) spills over into the ranks of prostitution. The number of whores grows with the expansion of the city. Wars, revolutions and upheaval merely accelerate the process.

Among the poor gathered in the cities, there are more free unions perhaps than in the 1650s as the close attention of reforming clerics diminishes. At these levels of society the fragility of the family bond is apparent and the result is that low-earning women can be left to tack together some kind of livelihood from any casual means available, to include prostitution where possible, child abandonment, or public charity or assistance. As a result of demographic growth and regionally specific engrossment of holdings, there are also more families who cannot look to the land for a source of income and many, many more who buttress a minuscule holding by seasonal migration, cottage industry or begging. They live on a series of accumulated expedients. If one resource fails, another must replace it and the family or the individual must restructure their way of life accordingly. This is particularly striking for those dependent upon temporary or seasonal migration.

More people, including women, are on the move and will not die within earshot of the bell that announced their birth. Significant exoduses to the New World are on the horizon, particularly in northern Europe after the famines of 1816 and 1820. In many families the farmer's wife is the farmer for most of the year while he turns casual labourer in the towns. There are more abandoned rural wives as well, waiting for a migrant husband, and concerned Spanish bishops try to force legislation, which turns out to be ineffective, that will oblige the men to return.[10] A situation in which the head of the household disappears, leaving a woman to shift for the family, highlights an interesting paradox. Very often women's labour is described as 'marginal' in the sense that they are not in high status jobs or making a significant contribution to the gross national product. However, looked at more closely, at the bottom of the social scale within the micro-economy of the family, they are absolutely central in ensuring the survival of the members. Indeed, we might offer as a working generalization that the more modest the family, the more essential both the labour and the ingenuity of the womenfolk. They are at the centre of the economy of makeshifts.

There are more women at the end of the parade who depend on industrial work for a livelihood if, in the case of many, only on a part-time domestic basis. If the days of hand-spinning are over, the presence of cottage industry is still very marked. Some farmers' wives may also be lace-makers, commercial spinners with a jenny, makers of gloves or shoes, and still classify themselves as 'farmer's wife' and do the jobs that this entails. For some families in some regions, domestic industry can bring a new prosperity, but for others it can mean exposure to the vicissitudes of consumer demand and to competition. It could keep single women living at home until marriage, hence sparing them not only severance from their family of origin but also the risks and hardships that went with urban migration or living and working in someone else's home. At the bottom of the paid labour pile, the workers who could readily be exploited and laid off when times were bad were women and children. Within any type of production, over time structural changes should be taking place. For example, at the beginning of the period, hand-knitted stockings were the norm and the occasional pair produced in the cottage could be sold or the enterprise could, as in the case of the Jones family cited in Chapter Four, be a full-time activity if need demanded. At the end of the period, stocking frames were taking over much of the business and there were more male stocking knitters. But even if they did own these frames, most stocking knitters in Brittany and Normandy, for example, were still women. A male stocking knitter was often an old man too frail for agricultural work or a fisherman working during inclement seasons.

The precocious industrial development in parts of England in the second decade of the eighteenth century was not only at the expense of areas where spinning had traditionally existed as work for women such as East Anglia; English goods also undercut both French and Spanish cotton production, and the dumping of stocks in the aftermath of the Napoleonic wars prolonged hardship.[11] Since, moreover, in the context of revolution, continental production of luxury goods like silk and velvet dried up under the strains of emigration, inflation and shortages, most continental industrial women workers look distinctly raggy in the 1790s. What is also clear, across Europe, as the statistics compiled by Napoleonic administrators attest, is that there is a considerable reservoir

of women, unmarried in particular but also married, who are looking
for employment, and the unmarried are prepared to move and to accept
low pay if necessary.[12]

Industry has not replaced the dominance of agriculture in the national
economies of Europe and neither are the townswomen in the parade
predominantly textile workers. Setting aside the servants, who constitute the dominant element among the unmarried, the type of work
women do in the towns has not so much changed as expanded. Throughout the period, whether in fifteenth-century York, sixteenth-century
Rome, seventeenth-century Amsterdam, Venice, Seville, London or
Paris, or the innumerable burgeoning towns of the eighteenth century,
women ran taverns, drink shops, *bettole* (little stands in the streets
selling refreshments), *guinguettes* (little outdoor places selling drinks,
particularly on feast days), or they provided pies and sausages and cooked
meals.[13] As the towns expand and demands become more sophisticated
(for chocolate and other confectionery or sweetmeats), or migrant
workers purchase their bowls of soup or stew to take back to their
crowded lodgings or to eat in the street, so this service area grows.
Women are also more remarkable in every branch of the sewing trades
by 1800. They make every item of female dress except for riding habits,
sew lingerie (a very significant element of the consumer revolution),
make shirts and millinery. Most of the women drawn from north-west
Europe are bonneted or hatted by the efforts of other women. They
make shawls and sew sheets and bedlinen, tablecloths and draperies,
fans and bags. They crochet and embroider for underwear and table
linen and make buttons and trimmings of all kinds. They also do other
time-consuming precision work like painting porcelain, silhouettes,
caricatures, or they etch, engrave and colour prints and illustrate music
scores. All this skilled work generated by the extension in consumerism
is low paid and is in the hands of women who have moved in to occupy
a sector outside the ones traditionally occupied by men.

In the towns and cities the power of the guilds has evaporated by
1800, although in Germany they were to survive into the mid-
nineteenth century. Their demise did not see the appearance of the
woman plumber, baker, butcher or watchmaker. Tradition still dictated
who did what and hence the classification of types of work by gender.
The artisan's workshop is still essentially intact in many sectors of skilled
production.

More women in the parade in 1800 can read and write and they have been taught by women. There are now particularly discernible in north-west Europe swarms of ill-paid governesses, schoolteachers and nursery nurses. All these think of themselves as in a different category from the domestic servant, but most depend on residence in the home of the employer.

The business of caring, nursing (as yet unprofessionalized outside the religious orders) and work in lying-in hospitals, in establishments for the relief of the poor and in orphanages, is also in the hands of women. Exception can be made by the end of the period in some large towns for the upper end of the midwifery business appropriated by men in the name of science; even so, most Europeans in 1800 are still brought into the world by women and since there are more establishments dedicated to care, both public and private, more women are paid for doing this kind of work.

In many ways, then, the job profile of women at the end of the period is not conspicuously different from what it was at the beginning – and also from that pertaining in the twentieth century, except that the status of the caring and teaching professions has somewhat, if insufficiently, risen. When in the late eighteenth century women sell their labour in the market, they cook, clean, work in textiles, sew and perform skilled but finicky work, or they teach, tend the sick and cater to the needs of the least privileged members of society. They do in the public sphere of the market what to some degree was done by their ancestors in 1500 without wages in their homes, and the kind of work which they themselves might do at some stage of their lives without wages for their own families. Or they have taken on new work generated by social and economic change, which is deemed appropriate because of its affinity to traditional women's work.

Some have broken new ground. Scattered throughout the parade, starting in the late sixteenth century, are a few women committed to creative activity, for example to painting, writing and the performing arts.

In Italy, women began to appear on stage as actresses in the sixteenth century, but enjoyed dubious repute. Thomas Nashe in 1592 commended the English stage for its moral superiority to the Italian which permitted 'whores' to play women's parts.[14] Then, in the second half of the seventeenth century, we find the emergence of the actress, followed with the half-century by the opera singer and then by the professional dancer. The number of these women is both small and nationally specific and their growth by 1800 is far from remarkable. The English Restoration stage was conspicuous for a number of actresses who may have had some talent but certainly were regarded as being no better than they should be. The path from Nell Gwyn to Mrs Siddons was beaten over the next century. Thereafter, and especially within theatrical families, a number of respectable actresses emerged, but they coexisted with a host of women linked in questionable relationships with the great and the famous. Of these, Dora Jordan is a striking example. Consort of the future king, William IV, and mother of his ten children, she died neglected in Paris. In eighteenth-century France no member of the acting profession, whether male or female, could be buried in hallowed ground. The stage was very particular terrain and the remarkable actress who might hobnob with the aristocracy was still in the eyes of many a woman of dubious morals. The demi-monde of the theatre was in full development in eighteenth-century Paris.[15]

The eighteenth century witnessed the first female international 'stars' on the stage. In 1723 two Italian sopranos, Faustina Bordoni and Francesca Cuzzoni, were paid £2500 and £2000 for a season respectively by London impresarios.[16] (This figure might be compared to the £250 paid to Jane Austen for *Pride and Prejudice*.) Maria Anna de Camargo and Maria Taglioni secured international reputations as ballet dancers promoted by their fathers.

From the sixteenth century, and especially in Italy, a number of gifted women succeeded in establishing themselves as painters. Some, though not all, were the daughters of artists who usually worked within a family workshop. Sofonisba Anguissola (1530–1625), the daughter of a minor noble not a painter, secured the patronage of Philip II, having made a reputation at the court of Milan; Lavinia Fontana (1552–1614) enjoyed the patronage of both Cardinal Paleotti and popes; Artemisia Gentileschi (1552–1614), whose life was made difficult by her domestic relations and financial problems; Judith Leyster, who does not appear to have come of a painting family and who secured entry to the painters' guild of Haarlem: all these are instances of women who surmounted the constraints which inhibited the development of women artists or confined those with talent to flower painting or printmaking within the home. By the end of the period there has been some growth in numbers of flower painters, miniaturists and female portraitists.[17] Were the obstacles encountered by the female painter at the end of the period any less than those at the beginning? Both Angelica Kauffmann and Elisabeth Vigée-Lebrun marketed themselves with conspicuous success, but were careful to respect male territory. Kauffmann's membership of the Royal Academy is indicated merely by her portrait hung on the wall of the room in which the male artists are painted as a group. Vigée-Lebrun made a speciality of painting caring maternity in Rousseauesque mode. The French Revolution and association with an unpopular court converted her into a reluctant exile (though highly successful in career terms) and into one of the first examples of a woman who carried her skill across national boundaries, shed a disagreeable husband and returned from exile to establish herself and her daughter in very solid circumstances.[18]

If the female painter has a shadowy presence in the parade, in contrast with the more flamboyant actress, the most conspicuous growth in the numbers of women in the creative arts is visible in literature. The scribblers and the drudges of the pen now coexist with a clutch of established novelists, some poets and playwrights and those who cater to the varied requirements of a female reading public in terms of fashion and cookery, books of advice and ephemera. A few historians and classical scholars have also joined the parade. The female scholar, however, must tread a cautious path, avoiding political radicalism. Her learning must be confined to neutral matters if she is to avoid the charge of stepping out of line.

The presence of even a slender cohort of creative women suggests a few chinks of possibility for self-realization or gainful employment present at the end which did not exist at the beginning. The fate of Shakespeare's imaginary sister might have still been fraught with seemingly endless difficulties and discomfort had she lived in 1800, but tragedy was not her inevitable lot. Some had already stepped out of line and so she would have been no longer a pioneer.

If this had been a parade of men under review, there would have been visible by 1800 a considerable increase in the numbers of professionals — lawyers, accountants, tax collectors, civil servants, agents of government, officials of Empire, doctors, surgeons (a profession distinctly on the rise). There would have been fewer in holy orders in Catholic Europe in 1800 and the numbers would never recover from the French Revolution, but a fairly steady stream of clergymen's sons in England with assisted places at Oxford and aspirations to a living. All these developing professional sectors were closed to women.

There would also have been more male entrepreneurs in trade, industry and banking. There were more printers and publishers, more book-sellers and more shops, some of which employed both men and women. When a male proprietor died, such a business could pass into the control of the widow and, because there are more such businesses at the end of the period than at the beginning, there are more widows involved. Lending libraries, which did not exist at the beginning of the period, were in the provinces often run by women, though they were not the founders of the important chains. There would also have been more soldiers, and sailors working under terrible conditions.

The male parade might explain some of the anomalies of the female. From the late seventeenth century the numbers of middle- and upper-class spinsters are growing. Educated to a degree, unmarried either through choice or because of the lack of family funding to establish them with the appropriate partner, this growth can be explained by the different opportunities available to men and women. Whereas the opportunities for sons expanded with the growth of empires, armies, navies, the extension of the civil service or the increase in business enterprises, the prospect before a second or third daughter of middle-class origins was the sometimes personally humiliating and invariably low-paid work of companion, governess or housekeeper. A historian dedicated to discerning the motor of change might spend some time on this personage. In the middle-class spinster and the widow struggling to make ends meet we have the raw material of articulated dissent of the nineteenth century, but such a woman is becoming visible in the eighteenth. What she wants is access to the same professional outlets as her brother. She is concerned with inclusion in profitable areas of work to which women have never been admitted.

The visual panoply of the parade cannot tell us what changes occurred in the mentalities of the participants over time. Instead, we might first consider the changes in prescriptive literature, the messages peddled from the pulpit, from books which were read at home and at school – although we should remember that no one can ever assess the potency of good advice.

How different were the images of womankind, versions of woman-hood, promoted in 1800 from those of 1500? At the beginning of the period, prescriptive literature was written by men and most of it was intended to be read either by wealthy women who were literate or to women by the head of the household or the confessor/priest who might then discuss and elaborate on the contents with his audience. Womanhood is refracted through a male prism. The intent is to create a holy household according to Scripture, and the goal is eternal life. The immortality of the soul and the production of a new generation of Christians are at stake. Or the widow is carefully instructed in how to live with God's decision to remove her partner and to keep her eyes turned away from this world to the next. She is lectured upon the need to be an example to the young people in her community by her virtuous withdrawal into the privacy of her home.[19]

To compare Juan Luis Vives' *Institutes of the Christian Religion* (1523) with Dr John Gregory or yet more with Dr James Fordyce's sermons, which so appalled both Mary Wollstonecraft and Jane Austen, is to be conscious of an evolution of a kind. The goal of eternal life, the acceptance of personal suffering and the imminence of Judgement Day, which dominate the approach of the humanist, are to a degree implicit in the later work – certainly religion is still at the heart of the discourse. Female chastity is still the most lauded attribute, but there is an injection of what might be termed consciousness of the expedient which is conspicuously absent from the earlier work. It is a fact of life (and God's will) that women need husbands. They know this and are advised to plan, dissimulate and indulge in a measure of low cunning to get one. Modesty is not praised in its own right. The generous bosom should go concealed not because it incites lust but because it leaves nothing to the imagination. Women can change the behaviour of the most uncouth man because men wish to impress them and avoid giving offence. They hence raise the tone of male company. The virtuous woman can bring the most aberrant of men to heel. In these eighteenth-century texts, men have fallen more perhaps than women have risen. This means there has been some redistribution of virtue. To a degree there has also been some reallocation of intelligence, though women emerge rather with the animal cunning of Rousseau's Sophie than with the lucid rationalism of the male philosopher. Obedience, like many other aspects of the behaviour of women, is allowed to be apparent rather than real. It matters more that a man believes himself to be the arbiter than that he is so, and the wise woman will lead him towards that belief. If Hannah More wrote best-sellers, it was because she extolled the virtue and the intelligence of women who were wise enough to act as examples to men.

This later literature does not envisage the isolated rural property as the locus of the holy household as did Fray Luis de León in *La perfecta casada* (1583). Instead, it locates the individual woman in complex surroundings dependent upon her station in life. In much of this literature in Protestant England no single life model is promoted for every woman. The strategy of the maidservant should be to encourage her intended husband to invest their savings in a nice little shop because she should know that this capital asset might be a buttress in widowhood, but she is not obliged to explain her reasoning to him. She is enjoined not only to be chaste before marriage but also thrifty (echoes of the good housewife of Proverbs 31) and sober. Sobriety refers now less to dress than to the avoidance of alcohol. Her strategies to acquire and manage a husband, given her station in life, clearly differ from those to be adopted by the intended wife of a clergyman or lawyer. The world is immensely complicated and full of snares for the innocent, but it can be negotiated for those with sense (a female attribute). Distraction is not an evil (how could it be so in the world of Bath and Vauxhall Gardens?), but it should not be allowed to run to excess.

The prescriptive literature changed more between 1500 and 1800 in Protestant than in Catholic societies, where, indeed, Vives, Fray Luis de León and Saint Francis of Sales continue to be dominant texts.[20] Moreover, new writers in the late seventeenth and eighteenth centuries seem in Spain and Italy to have been predominantly priests or men in religion. Two Italian Jesuit priests, Paolo Segneri and Antonfrancesco Bellati, for example, were influential writers who distributed old messages about duty and obedience to marital authority. Laymen such as Count Francesco Beretta and the philosopher Muratori, whose advice about the role of the wife and mother appeared dressed in Enlightenment rhetoric and was more sparing of reference to a divine plan, were still concerned with chastity, duty and destiny, accepting one's lot.[21] A few daring thinkers mentioned divorce, but far more insisted upon the sanctity of the family and the maintenance of the chaste and modest woman. A great deal of Italian good advice literature, both religious and lay, worried about the impact of novels on the minds of the innocent and urged careful supervision of female reading.

Even when prescriptive literature was written by a woman for women, it showed similarities to that proffered to the female sex by men. Indeed, the writing of eighteenth-century women has something in common with the moralists of the sixteenth century.

One striking sameness is the emphasis on duty. When Hannah More urged that the purpose of female education should be the development of a sense of duty, and insisted that woman has a natural virtue which impels her to make sacrifices, she dealt in the terms propagated by father confessors in the sixteenth century, although they would have omitted any reference to 'natural virtue': the reader would have been enjoined to overcome her weaknesses. In More's view, women are basically very strong and do not have to combat the weaknesses and proneness to evil conduct that was the lot of a daughter of Eve. Nor do her women have defective intellects. They are sufficiently mentally astute to avoid triviality and they are urged to develop their innate strength and not take refuge in weakness. Every woman should choose a marriage partner wisely and elect the conduct of the virtuous woman. There are no prizes for naïvety either in this world or in heaven.[22]

How we should behave towards our fellow men and women, cautiously laid down in etiquette manuals, has gained in refinement. Speech is more careful and discreet and there is a language of decorum. The home has a predominant place in the literature over the whole period and the mistress of the house is critical to its smooth running throughout, even if, by 1800, at certain social levels the home has gained in appurtenances and many of the functions performed within that home in 1500 are now purchased in the market. The eighteenth century has been credited with the rise of domesticity, argued from commercial growth as reflected in the home (the new consumerism) on the one hand and the celebration of domestic relations within this comfortable, perhaps cloying, environment promoted by the Romantic movement on the other, a vision encapsulated in Greuze's father returning to the bosom of his family, to his smiling wife and his affectionate children. Warmth, comfort and tender emotions are found within this haven of peace. It is also the cradle of citizens and, as ever, of Christians. In 1800 as in 1500, it is held to be the locus of mutual support between husband and wife. Certainly, and even without the cushions and the upholstery, the image of home is of a gentler and less gloomy place than the vision of the Christian home in Becon's *Boke of Matrimony*, where the overwhelming emphasis is on the avoidance of sin and the evils of distraction. The young girl is not now seen as a repository of evil if left to her own devices, even if she is advised to be on her guard and learn how the system works.

The terms of the marriage contract and the sacrament of marriage within the Catholic church remain, of course, intact. In exchange for the powerful offer of love and lifelong support, women promise obedience.

Motherhood, however, has been conspicuously upgraded, not only in works by women but in the writings of men both inside and outside religion. Not only does mother now know best when she follows her natural instincts and places her children's welfare over her own vanity, but she is a nurturer encouraged to enjoy her children rather than watch them closely for signs of the Devil at work. The mother is both example and teacher. The love of children and joy in their progress is generally promoted, as much in the eighteenth-century philosophic treatises concerned with pedagogy as in, for example, Italian Catholic writing where the mother's role is closely allied with the tender care of the Madonna.[23]

Secularization, increasing social sophistication, and a vocabulary paying homage to the sensibility and moral fibre of women, then, have mellowed the tone of prescriptive literature. In some instances arguments based on biology and 'natural law' have gained ground at the expense of Scripture. Holy Writ, with its instances of Eve and threatening visions of the Scarlet Woman of the Book of Revelation, has lost some of its authority, though, outside the writing of French Republicans, far from all. However, and this is significant, medical thought is ready to fill the void and to insist that biology made woman a reproductive vessel and dictated the pace of her life. A woman who stepped outside this 'natural' or normal role was doomed. The case of Théroigne de Méricourt, one of the most conspicuous political female dissidents of the French Revolution, who slipped into lunacy and drew the attention of the medical profession to this unnatural woman, might be cited. She had contracted syphilis from one of her 'protectors' before the Revolution and had had some treatment with mercury. She had been battered about the head by members of the Club Républicaine Révolutionnaire and had spent years in exile and in prison. Now, in her last years in the Salpêtrière, she doused her naked body in dirty, icy water and lived in her own excrement. She attracted the attention of a new generation of doctors studying the mentally ill and appears in their reports as symbol and metaphor not only for the failure of the Revolution but for the woman who assumed an unnatural role.[24] The normal woman would not have chosen thus to step outside a woman's life course.

The version of womanhood drawn upon to condemn those women deemed enemies of the state in Revolutionary France embodied a transference of an old vintage into a new bottle. Marie Antoinette's trial pivots not on her essential perfidy in colluding in the betrayal of France,

but on her abuse of her child: she is an 'unnatural mother'. The pornographic prints of her alleged misconduct (lesbian with the Princesse de
Polignac, adulterous with a variety of enemies of the state), serving at
the same time to present her as a bad wife and Louis XVI as a cuckold
or a dupe, had contrived since 1789 to undermine the image of the
queen as a 'virtuous', that is, chaste and obedient, wife. Like every
woman on trial in the early modern period, a character reference fully
independent of the facts of the case, though in Marie Antoinette's
instance clearly fabricated, served to condemn her.[25] Similarly, Madame
Roland, caught up in the elimination of the Girondins, was presented
as a meddling wife who ruled her husband and through him brought
disaster upon France. In the parlance of the sixteenth century she would
have been described as the partner who wore the trousers, and he who
should have been a lion ceded his claws. Charlotte Corday's trial was
brief but her reputation as the murderer of Marat, the people's idol and
one dear to the working women of Paris, was constructed on the image
of the gullible and ignorant woman, agent of traitors, church and
nobility, Girondins and other enemies of the people. Because of these
traits, which even women acknowledged to be quintessentially female
ones, Corday had been led astray and in so doing had condemned her
sex. Without any mention of her name, Eve lingers in the discourse.

The messages emanating from the moralists, the judges and the
medical men, then, endorsed the traditional role of woman within a
patriarchal family, even though the reasons justifying a woman's role had
been given a different emphasis and in some instances a new vocabulary.
Indeed, it is striking how the old interpretation of sexual difference
could be brought up to date and reinvigorated by more modern infusions
of sentiment and natural law and the beginnings of pyschiatric medicine
insisting on what was normal and what abnormal. If there is a change
in form, the desired purport of the advice is the same.

Criminal and civil law also reflected continuity in a view of woman
as essentially a dependant of man. The easier divorce laws enacted
during the French Revolution and modified by the Napoleonic Code
disappeared when the Roman Catholic Church re-established itself in
France in the opening decades of the nineteenth century, and property
law continued to allow a man the management of the resources a wife
brought into marriage and control of any earnings she made. True,
parity of treatment of the sexes before the criminal law was increasingly
advanced.[26] The agencies of acculturation, particularly those of school,

church and community, peddled essentially the same models of female destiny as those advanced three centuries before. Women's creative writing colluded in this endeavour. Indeed, it could be argued that the greater exposure of a broader spectrum of women to schooling controlled by the church, or by reference to Christian culture, intensified rather than weakened acceptance of the normal, conventional or appropriate role.

Yet the model had always been adapted, renegotiated and tailored to cope with individual circumstances. Lives, as this volume has aimed to demonstrate, were not necessarily fully constructed on the sands of prescription, and within any individual marriage the allegedly standard distribution of decision-making and initiative could vary enormously or be modified to cope with the exigencies of the times. The growing volume of diaries, letters and memoirs produced in the eighteenth century attest to a considerable expansion of horizons for those with money to spare. Books and journals, newspapers and pamphlets opened up issues and vistas and provided food for thought. If much that women wrote for women was trivial, reflecting the demands of the market, there was other matter available as well.[27] More women had some education and though, for most of them, the content fell well short of what was available to their brothers, it gave them some access to information. Such a development was critical in long-term self-formation. Shopping and visits to theatres and gardens, travel to spas and places of distraction like Bath or to the capital cities, was more common. A few wealthy women even had the experience of foreign travel. The improvement in communications made contact with distant friends and relatives easier, and the development of postal services increased the possibilities of social contact. The diaries of the seventeenth century which often speak of intense loneliness and enforced self-absorption gave way to ones attesting to increasing sociability.

Private philanthropic endeavour, for the woman who cared thus to involve herself, burgeoned over the period. The clergyman's wife, the land agent's wife, the wives of professional men and of substantial farmers ran houses where the expectations of a more comfortable lifestyle were immensely extended. The demands on such a wife as manager of larger but still draughty houses dependent upon some servant power, and subject to higher standards of cleanliness and care with little expansion in labour-saving appliances, could still be high. Her life was not necessarily one of visiting cards and exchanged banalities. Indeed, women's writing suggests their lives to be family centred, but increasingly turned to the public world of information, distraction and community service. .

For the middle-class wife or daughter to step outside the home into gainful employment, something impossible at the beginning of the period, was still at the end something which only the most desperate or the most hardy would contemplate. It was the recourse of the impoverished wife with the feckless or sick husband, the widow or the spinster. When the diarist Anna Larpent regretted the dire necessity that made some women look outside the home for financial support, she expressed what was probably a majority view. She pitied those who had to do so from her standpoint as happy wife and mother, one whose time was fully occupied in caring for her children, in shaping their education, in advising her husband in his capacity as theatre censor and in improving her own mind. However, she clearly recognized that all were not as fortunate as she was.[28]

For the bulk of the female populace born of peasant stock, it remained a question of attempting to put something away towards marriage during adolescence and young womanhood or of coming by a skill which made survival possible. If more women than ever before, both in town and country, sought to sell their labour in the market, few could find long-term sufficiency or independence by their own efforts. They saw their main hope lay in a partnership with a man whose higher earning power would see them through the raising of a family and give them some sufficiency in old age. These were time-honoured goals which many would never realize and the vulnerability of those who failed was apparent for all to see. Such failures – and they were many – were paupers, an unenviable state in a world committed to the full flowering of the market economy. Poor relief either topped up family income to a level of minimal survival or catered to the sick, the orphaned, the old and the abandoned, but provided no assistance to the able-bodied outside the family structure. It therefore endorsed traditional roles for both sexes. A family did not ensure security, but without one women were at risk. At the end of the period, as at the beginning, the widow and the woman alone at the lower social levels were dependent on public relief. Moreover, the level of that relief remained the same, neither greater nor less.

More women by 1800 had gone into print as explicit critics of social constraints which bound them, than in earlier periods. They attacked the system where it failed and used to some effect the language of the Enlightenment to deplore marital tyranny and the subjection of woman to man's arbitrary will. Their onslaught should not be seen as making the early modern period one in which womankind teetered on the brink of a great surge of consciousness demanding emancipation; nor should it be assumed that these women envisaged a society in which they would exist in a state of full equality with men. Political power was in the hands of male landed élites and hence denied on any systematic basis to most men. Men did not speak for all men. By the end of the period the limited basis of political power had been challenged by men for men, but this challenge had not got beyond the theoretical stage except for the brief interlude in Jacobin France. To go further and widen the net to include women commanded the explicit adherence of the very few. Critics of the status quo had not evolved an agenda for change beyond better educational facilities for women, as the necessary precursor to any further bid for equality of professional opportunity, and even so modest a request located change in the future. Notwithstanding, it was a first nervous step towards a vision of an alternative ladder of life, one which did not deny a woman's role as wife and mother but held out a little more hope, a little more dignity, a glimpse of self-sufficiency to those who either could not or would not make the standard ascent.

NOTES

<figure>◀◉▶</figure>

INTRODUCTION

1 K. Thomas, 'Shaped by Men and Marzipan', *Observer*, 8 August 1993, 54; a review of G. Duby and M. Perrot eds., *A History of Women in the West*, vol. 3: N. Z. Davis and A. Farge eds., *Renaissance and Enlightenment Paradoxes* (Cambridge, Mass., 1993).

2 Approaches summarized in L. Hunt ed., *The New Cultural History* (Berkeley, 1989), Introduction. 'Culture denotes a historically transmitted pattern of meaning embodied in symbols, a system of inherited conceptions expressed in symbolic forms by means of which men communicate, perpetuate, and develop their knowledge about and attitudes to life': C. Geertz, 'Religion as a cultural system' in M. Benton ed., *Anthropological Approaches to the Study of Religion* (London, 1966), 3.

3 P. Burke, *Popular Culture in Early Modern Europe* (Cambridge, 1978). In both the introduction and opening chapter the possible range of cultural groups is discussed.

4 J. W. Scott, *Gender and the Politics of History* (New York, 1988), has been particularly influential in urging that historical evidence should be read and interpreted with reference to the subjective notions of gender roles held at the time.

5 Italian historiography on women and gender roles has been particularly committed to this technique, e.g. O. Niccoli ed., *Rinascimento al femminile* (Rome/Bari, 1992) and G. Calvi ed., *Barocco al femminile* (Rome/Bari, 1992) bring together a series of mini-biographies to illustrate gender possibilities within a period.

6 F. Braudel, *Civilisation and Capitalism: 15th–18th centuries* (London, 1981), vol. 1.

7 O. Hufton, 'Fernand Braudel', obituary, *Past and Present*, 112 (1986), 208–13, summarizes this work.

8 Defoe's categories are examined by R. W. Malcolmson, *Life and Labour in England 1700–1800* (London, 1981), 11–12.

9 The history of consumption is a growth industry. A. Pardailhé-Galabrun, *The Birth of Intimacy: Private and Domestic Life in Early Modern Paris* (Oxford, 1988); J. Brewer and R. Porter eds., *Consumption and the World of Goods: Consumption and Society in the Eighteenth Century* (London, 1993); M.

Douglas and B. Sherwood, *The World of Goods: Towards an Anthropology of Consumption* (London, 1978); D. Roche, *The People of Paris* (London, 1987) and *The Culture of Clothing: Dress and Fashion in the Ancien Regime* (Cambridge, 1994).

10 Maxine Berg, *The Age of Manufactures 1799–1820* (London, 1985), particularly ch. VI: R. Houston and K. Snell, 'ProtoIndustrialisation, Cottage Industry, Social Change and the Industrial Revolution', *Historical Journal*, 27, 2 (1984); P. Hudson, 'Proto-Industrialization: the Case of the West Riding', *History Workshop Journal*, 12 (1981); P. Kriedte, H. Medick and J. Schlumbohm, *Industrialization before Industrialization* (Cambridge, 1977); J. Rendall, *Women in an Industrializing Society: England 1750–1880* (London, 1990), ch. 1–2.

11 R. Muchembled, *L'Invention de l'homme moderne. Sensibilités, moeurs et comportements collectifs sous l'ancien régime* (Paris, 1988) is the most conspicuous work on this theme but is written without reference to gender difference.

12 Many of Elias's notions of what actually occurred at Versailles could also be questioned. The idea of evolution, rather than its genesis, is what is at stake for most of those who have followed Elias.

13 J. Delumeau, *Catholicism between Luther and Voltaire* (London, 1977); F. Le Brun ed., *Histoire des Catholiques en France du XVe siècle à nos jours* (Paris, 1980); L. Châtelier, *The Europe of the Devout. The Catholic Reformation and the Formation of a New Society* (Cambridge, 1989); B. Plongeron, *Religions et sociétés en Occident, XIV–XXe siècles. Recherches françaises et tendances internationales, 1973–1977* (Paris, 1979).

14 J. Delumeau, *Sin and Fear. The Emergence of a Western Guilt Culture 13th–18th Centuries*, trans. E. Nicholson (New York, 1990).

15 R. Chartier, *The Cultural Uses of Print*, trans. L. Cochrane (Princeton, 1987).

16 J. Delumeau, *Catholicism between Luther and Voltaire*; Le Brun, op. cit., 224–42.

17 L. Stone, *The Family, Sex and Marriage in England, 1500–1800* (London, 1977); for an alternative view where love started among the working classes, see E. Shorter, *The Making of the Modern Family* (London, 1976).

18 P. Ariès, *Centuries of Childhood* (Eng. trans., London, 1962).

19 K. Wrightson, *English Society 1580–1680* (London, 1982), 66–120.

20 L. Pollock, *Forgotten Children: Parent-child relations from 1500–1900* (Cambridge, 1983), particularly 1–67.

21 S. Schama, *The Embarrassment of Riches. An Interpretation of Dutch Culture in the Golden Age* (London, 1987), 496–516.

22 J. Lewis and M. Chaytor, Introduction to A. Clark, *The Working Life of Women in the Seventeenth Century* (London, 1982); A. L. Erickson, Introduction to *ibid.* (London, 1992); and J. Thirsk, Foreword to M. Prior ed., *Women in English Society 1500–1800* (London, 1985), 8–14.

23 Rendall, op. cit., 4–5.

24 Italian historiography has been careful not to assume rises and falls: G. Calvi, 'Dal margine al centro. Soggettività femminile, famiglia, stato moderno in Toscana' in M. Palazzi and A. Scattigno eds., *Discutendo di storia* (Turin, 1991).

25 J. M. Bennett, 'Feminism and History', *Gender and History*, 1 (1989), 251–2 has made a cogent plea for a closer look at 'change'.

I CONSTRUCTING WOMAN

1 The snake as woman seems to have had a particular strength in Florentine Renaissance painting. Paolo Uccello (S. Maria Novella) has a similar 15th-century rendering of Original Sin with a blond temptress. It exists too in the late Middle Ages in Britain: see V. Sekules, 'Women and Art in England in the Thirteenth and Fourteenth Centuries' in J. Alexander and P. Binski eds., *The Age of Chivalry* (London, 1987), 41–2 and the 15th-century glass in St Mary's Fairford, Gloucester. On the influence of Genesis and Scripture in general on views of the sexes: I. Maclean, *The Renaissance Notion of Woman* (Cambridge, 1980), 10–15; P. Bange, G. Dresen, J. M. Noel, 'Who can find a virtuous woman' in *Saints and She Devils, Images of Women in the 15th and 16th Centuries* (English trans., London, 1987), 14; M. Warner, *Alone of all her Sex* (London, 1976), 52–8.

2 S. F. Matthews Grieco, *Ange ou Diablesse. La Représentation de la Femme au XVI siècle* (Paris, 1991), 134–41 and 'The body, appearance and sexuality' in G. Duby and M. Perrot eds., *A History of Women in the West* (5 vols, Cambridge, Mass., 1993), III, 46–84. A. de Montaiglon, *Recueil des poésies françaises des XV et XVI siècles* (Paris, 1869), VII, 287–301.

3 Umberto Baldini and Ornella Casazza, *Capella Brancacci* (Milan, 1990, abridged and trans., 1993), 25; compare the assumption of guilt in the anonymous Irish poem cited by Warner, op. cit., 50: 'I am Eve, the wife of noble Adam; it was I who violated Jesus in the past; it was I who robbed my children of heaven; it is I by right who should have been crucified.'

4 Maclean, op. cit., 6–27; S. E. Ozment, *When Fathers Ruled: Family Life in Reformation Europe* (Cambridge, 1983), 50–80; J. O'Faolain and L. Martinez, *Not in God's Image* (London, 1973), 194–206.

5 Warner, op. cit., *passim*; A. de Cigala ed., *The Imitation of Mary by Saint Thomas à Kempis* (London, 1948); F. Suarez, 'The Dignity and Virginity of the Mother of God' in *The Mysteries of the Life of Christ*, trans. R. O'Brien (Indiana, 1954), 63–5; St Peter Canisius (1521–97), *De Maria Virgine Incomparibili* (Ingolstadt, 1577), 108; N. L'Archevesque, *Les grandeurs sur-éminentes de la très-sainte Vièrge Marie* (Paris, 1638), 485–6; Alonso de Andrade, *Treatise on the Virgin* (1642).

6 Ozment, op. cit., 64–6; E. Muller, 'Humanist Views on Art and Morality' in Bange *et al.*, op. cit., 134–6 and 145; S. Dackermann,

'Chaste, Chased and Chastened. Old Testament Women in Northern Prints',
Harvard University Art Museums Gallery Series, 6 (1993).

7 I Timothy 2:12–15. This critical text (along with Deuteronomy 22:5)
is widely used to exclude women not merely from the priesthood but from
all public affairs. On exceptions not proving rules, see Maclean, op. cit.,
20. On how some English Puritans sought to get round these texts: K.
Thomas, 'Women and the Civil War Sects', *Past and Present*, 13 (1958),
42–62.

8 This is sometimes known as the 'Alphabet of the Good Woman' and
the various interpretations are found in Cornelius a Lapide (1567–1637),
Comentarii in Proverbia Salomonis (Paris, 1633), 517ff.

9 G. Paleotti, *Discorso Intorno alle Imagini Sacre e Profane* (Bologna, 1582;
Latin edn, Ingolstadt, 1594); P. Prodi, 'Ricerche sulla teorica delle arti
figurative nella riforma cattolica' in *Archivio italiano per la storia della pietà*,
4 (1965), 123–212; in contrast, for the Protestant view see D. Freedberg,
'The Hidden God: image and interdiction in the Netherlands in the sixteenth
century', *Art History*, 5 (1982).

10 L. Roper, *The Holy Household. Religion, Morals and Order in Reformation
Augsburg* (Oxford, 1989), 235.

11 H. Hansel, *Die Maria-Magdalena Legende: eine Quellenuntersuchung*
(Bottrop, 1937), 23–52. In 1517 the French humanist Lefèvre d'Etaples
wrote a tract on Mary Magdalen insisting on the distinctness of the episodes
serving to define her and denying that the Magdalen at the foot of the cross
beloved by Christ was the sinner of the earlier stories. Erasmus accepted this.
A. Hufstader, 'Lefèvre d'Etaples and the Magdalen' in *Studies in the Renaissance*,
16 (1969), 31–61. C. Harbison, 'Lucas van Leyden, the Magdalen and the
problem of Secularisation in early 16th century Art', *Oud Holland*, 98
(1984), 124. On the association between the courtesan and Magdalen, M.
Mosco ed., *La Maddalena tra sacro e profano* (Florence/Milan, 1986), 230–2.
On the association between her and the courtesan in France, F. Bardon, 'Le
thème de la Madeleine pénitente au XVIIe siècle en France', *Journal of the
Warburg and Courtauld Institutes*, 31 (1968), 301. S. Haskins, *Mary Magdalen:
myth and metaphor* (London, 1993), 229–96.

12 C. L. Powell, *English Domestic Relations, 1487–1563* (New York,
1917); L. L. Schüking, *The Puritan Family: A Social Study from the Literary
Sources* (London, 1969); K. M. Davies, 'Continuity and Change in Literary
Advice on Marriage' in R. B. Outhwaite ed., *Marriage and Society: Studies in
the Social History of Marriage* (London, 1981), 58–80 and 'The sacred
condition of equality – how original were Puritan doctrines of marriage?',
Social History, 5 (1977), 564.

13 J. L. Vives, *Institutes of the Christian Religion* (original Latin edn 1523)
is at the basis of much writing and has chapters on maids, married women,
widows and a section on the job of the husband. More Italian works seem
to have appeared specifically dedicated to the widow, since the concern to

control the widow after her husband's death was critically bound up with family fortunes (see below). An excellent, though not exhaustive, list of English good conduct works appears in Powell, op. cit., 243–52.

14 J. Casey, *The History of the Family* (Oxford, 1989), 103 interprets this text as a manual for the aristocratic couple, but recent Spanish historiography makes a wider claim: '*La perfecta casada* no es solamente un texto clásico, sino un texto que simboliza magistralmente una ideología y un modo de división del trabajo todavía en vigor en la España de las postrimerías del siglo XX.' (*The Perfect Housewife* is not merely a classic text but one which symbolizes in magisterial fashion an ideology of the division of labour still flourishing in Spain in the last years of the twentieth century.) María Angeles Durán, 'Lectura Económica de Fray Luis de León', Actas de las I Jornadas de Investigación Interdisciplinaria, *Nuevas Perspectivas sobre la Mujer*, Seminario de Estudios de la Mujer de la Universidad Autónoma de Madrid, 1982, 257–73.

15 François de Sales, *Introduction à la vie dévote* (1619), *Veuves*. Multiple translations and re-editions. Still in the 1960s recommended to English and French Catholic women as essential reading.

16 Becon, *Werkes* Part I, f.ccccxxxi, ed. J. Eyre, Parker Society II (1844). Becon was often insistent that the Protestant conception of marriage was superior to that of the 'wicked Bishop of Rome'. *Werkes* Part I, f.cccccixxv.

17 R. C. (Robert Cleaver), *A Godly Form of Householde Government* (London, 1598), at 392 pages the longest good conduct book known to be extant in English.

18 K. M. Davies, 'Continuity and Change in Literary Advice on Marriage' in Outhwaite, op. cit., 70–80 and 'The Sacred Condition of Equality – How Original were Puritan Doctrines of Marriage', *Social History*, 5 (1977), 563–80.

19 O'Faolain and Martinez, op. cit., 195–8 for the essential texts; and Ozment, op. cit.

20 T. Sànchez, *Disputationum de Sancto Matrimonii Sacramento* (1592, repr. 1602); R. Pillorget, *La Tige et le rameau. Familles anglaises et françaises 16–18 siècles* (Paris, 1979), 117–20. Arguments summarized in A. Armengand, *La Famille et l'enfant en France et en Angleterre du XVIe au VIIIe siècle* (Paris, 1975), 41–4. J. L. Flandrin, 'Contraception, mariage et relations amoureuses dans l'Occident chrétien', *Annales, Economies, Sociétés et Civilisations*, 6 (1969), 1370–90 and J. M. Gouesse, 'En Basse Normandie – Le refus de l'enfant au tribunal de la pénitence', *Annales de démographie historique* (1973).

21 Maclean, op. cit., 28–46. Critical Renaissance and early modern texts are Kaspar Hofman's commentary on Galen's *De usu partium corporis* (1625) and Cesare Cremonini's discussion of Aristotle's theories of sex difference in *De calido innato et semine* (1634). The most recent commentary is T. Laqueur, *Making Sex: Body and Gender from the Greeks to Freud* (London, 1990).

22 *The Notebooks of Leonardo da Vinci*, ed. Irma S. Richter (Oxford, 1989), 164.

23 J. Gélis, M. Laget and F. Morel eds., *Entrer dans la vie. Naissances et enfances dans la France traditionelle* (Paris, 1978), 58.

24 L. Lennes, *De gli occulti miracoli, et varii ammaestramenti delle natura* (Venice, 1560); A. Paré, *Des monstres et prodiges*, ed. J. Céard (Geneva, 1971), 60–70; O. Niccoli, 'Menstruum Quasi Monstruum: Parti mostruosi e tabú mestruali nel '500', *Quaderni Storici*, 44 (1980), 402–28, trans. in E. Muir and G. Ruggiero eds., *Sex and Gender in Historical Perspective* (Baltimore, 1990); P. Crawford, 'Attitudes to Menstruation in 17th century England', *Past and Present*, 91 (1987), 47 cites Ezekiel 18:15: 'one of the properties of a good man is not to lie with a menstruous woman'.

25 Crawford, op. cit., 63. This is a translation of a French poem.

26 Muller and Noel, 'Humanist views on art and morality' in Bange *et al.*, op. cit., 140–3, offers an excellent review of Lucretia in northern art.

27 Ozment, op. cit., 69–72.

28 A short list of some Dutch misogynist satire from the 17th century is cited in Schama, op. cit., 668–9. Yet *A Curtaine Lecture* (anon., 1637), 5, felt that Italian literature in particular was the most bitterly anti-woman: 'In turning over the leaves of some both modern and foreign writers, I have met with so many satiricall invectives aimed directly against it (the female sex) and some of them so pathetically bitter, that I am halfe persuaded they forgot themselves to have been borne of mothers.' Cited Powell, op. cit., 163.

29 Schama, op. cit., 392, 484.

30 S. Schama, 'Wives and Wantons: Versions of Womanhood in 17th century Dutch Art', *Oxford Art Journal* (April 1980), 5.

31 J. Wiltenburg, *Disorderly Women and Female Power in the Street Literature of Early Modern Germany* (London, 1992); P. Burke, *Popular Culture in Early Modern Europe* (London, 1978), 65–7; G. Bollême, *La Bibliothèque Bleu: littérature populaire en France* (Paris, 1971); M. Spufford, *Small Books and Pleasant Histories, Popular fiction and its readership in seventeenth-century England* (Cambridge, 1981) and for Spain, E. M. Wilson, *Some Aspects of Spanish Literary History* (Oxford, 1967), 12–19.

32 E. Le Roy Ladurie, *Love, Death and Money in the Pays d'Oc* (English trans., Cambridge, 1982), 1–35.

33 Spufford, op. cit., 59–60, 245–6.

34 *Italian Folktales*, selected and retold by Italo Calvino (New York, 1980), notes, 737. 'Wooden Marian' and 'Orza', who becomes a she-bear, compare with Perrault's *Peau d'âne*. M. Warner, *From the Beast to the Blonde. On Fairy Stories and their Tellers* (London, 1994).

35 J. L. Vives, *Linguae Latinae Exercitatio* (1539, Basle edn, 1555), entry *Domus*, 30–1.

36 Maclean, op. cit., 68–81. W. W. Buckland, *A Textbook of Roman Law* (2nd edn, Cambridge, 1950). R. Pillorget, op. cit., 21–42.

37 M. McKendrick, *Women in Society in Spanish Drama of the Golden Age. A study of the Mujer Varonil* (Cambridge, 1974), 35–7. There are stories, probably utterly exaggerated, of boastful soldiers who 'honourably' murdered their fiancées caught with new lovers. An example of such campfire tales is found in *Memorias de Don Diego Duque de Estrada. Autobiografías de soldados* (XVII), *Biblioteca de autores españoles*, XC, 266–8.

38 K. Thomas, 'The Double Standard', *Journal of the History of Ideas* (1959), 195–216; Y. Castan, *Honnêteté et relations sociales en Languedoc 1715–1780* (Paris, 1974), 162–99. What could be at stake was not simply double standards but different standards. Insulting a man was done differently from insulting a woman. J. A. Sharpe, *Defamation and Sexual Slander in Early Modern England: The Church Courts at York*, Borthwick Papers, 58 (York, 1980) and D. Sabean, *Power in the Blood: Popular Culture and Village Discourse in Early Modern Germany* (Cambridge, 1984).

39 A. L. Erickson, *Women and Property in Early Modern England* (London, 1994); S. Staves, *Married Women's Separate Property in England, 1660–1833* (Oxford, 1989) and J. Greenberg, 'The legal status of the English woman in early eighteenth century common law and equity', *Studies in Eighteenth Century Culture*, 4 (1975), 171–81. S. Moller Okin, 'Patriarchy and Married Women's Property in England: Questions on Some Current Views', *Eighteenth Century Studies*, 17 (1983–4), 121–38; J. Traer, *Marriage and the Family in Eighteenth Century France* (Ithaca, 1980), 22–47; G. Delille, *Famille et propriété dans le royaume de Naples (XV–XIXe siècles)* (Rome/Paris, 1985).

40 J. W. Scott, '"L'ouvrière! Mot impie, sordide . . ." Women Workers in the Discourse of French Political Economy, 1840–1860' in P. Joyce ed., *The Historical Meaning of Work* (Cambridge, 1987), 119–42. J. B. Say, *Traité de l'économie politique* (6th edn, 2 vols., Paris, 1841), 324. These principles are more obliquely laid out in the debates of the *Comité de Mendicité* which met in 1789–91.

41 The term 'law of unequal exchange' is more usually applied to the discussion of development economies but can profitably be used to examine the relative status and value of men's and women's labour in the market.

42 On the ladder of life as one of the commonest means of depicting gender roles widely available in cheap prints to the masses, K. Hazelzet, 'De levenstrap als les voor jong en oud', *In de jonkheid gaan*, 10–11 (1989), 680–96; P. Joeriszen, 'Die Lebensalter des Menschen. Bildprogramm und Bildform im Jahrhundert der Reformation' in (catalogue) *Die Lebenstreppe. Bilder der Menschlichen Lebensalter* (Kleef, Städtisches MuseumHaus Koekboek, 1983–4). It is also discussed in *Emancipatie Emancipation Emanzipation* (Ausstellung des Goethes Instituts, Munich, 1980). H. Wunder, *'Er ist die Sonn', sie ist der Mond'. Frauen in der frühen Neuzeit* (Munich, 1992), 33–55 uses this image as a key to a vision of the purpose of life.

2   THE STRATEGIC PLAN: MARRIAGE AS GOAL

1 The bibliography on marriage and the family is enormous. Among those sources most used here are: J. L. Flanders, *Families in Former Times: Kinship, Household and Sexuality* (Cambridge, 1979); R. Houlbrouke, *The English Family, 1450–1700* (London, 1984); A. Macfarlane, *Marriage and Love in England, 1300–1840* (Oxford, 1986); M. Mitterauer and R. Sider, *The European Family: Patriarchy and Partnership from the Middle Ages to the Present* (Oxford, 1982); R. van Dülmen, *Kultur und Alltag in der früher Neuzeit* (Munich, 1990); J. Casey, *The History of the Family* (Oxford, 1989); R. Pillorget, *La tige et le rameau* (Paris, 1979); G. Delille, *Famille et propriété dans le royaume de Naples (XV–XIXe siècles)* (Rome/Paris, 1985); M. Barbagli and D. Kertzer eds., *Storia della famiglia italiana* (Bologna, 1992).

2 W. Cobbett, *The Cottage Economy* (1821) is a monument to the notion of farmer/farmer's wife complementarity.

3 L. Roper, *The Holy Household. Religion, Morals and Order in Reformation Augsburg* (Oxford, 1989), 27–55.

4 R. Latham ed., *Diary of Samuel Pepys*, IV, 159.

5 G. Delille, 'Consanguinité proche en Italie du XVIe au XIXe siècle', in *Epouser au plus proche. Inceste, prohibitions et stratégies matrimoniales autour de la Méditerranée* (Paris, 1994).

6 Macfarlane, op. cit., 259; K. Wrightson, *English Society 1580–1680* (London, 1982) 70–1; Pillorget, op. cit., 43–80.

7 H. J. Habbakkuk, 'Marriage Settlements in the Eighteenth Century', *Transactions of the Royal Historical Society*, 4th series, 32 (1950); G. Chaussinand-Nogaret, *La noblesse au XVIIIe siècle* (Paris, 1976), 160; Casey, op. cit., 76–7.

8 J. L. Sánchez Lora, *Mujeres, conventos y formas de la religiosidad barroca* (Madrid, 1988), 131–8. Olivares, the statesman, had also (unsuccessfully) tried restriction in 1573. Casey, op. cit., 83.

9 A. Armengaud, *La famille et l'enfant en France et en Angleterre du XVI au XVIIIe siècles: aspects démographiques* (Paris, 1975), 60; P. C. Otto, *Daughters of the British Aristocracy and their Marriages in the Eighteenth and Nineteenth Century, with Particular Reference to the Scottish Peerage* (PhD, Stanford, 1964); T. H. Hollingworth, *The Demography of the British Peerage, Population Studies* 8: Supplement (1964); Cl. Levi and L. Henry, 'Ducs et pairs sous l'ancien régime, caractéristique démographique d'une caste', *Population*, 15 (1960), 807–30.

10 V. Hunecke, 'Kindbett oder Kloster, Lebenswege venezianischer Patrizierinnen im 17. und 18. Jahrhunderts', *Geschichte und Gesellschaft*, 18 (1992), 446–76: E. Cattaneo, 'Le monacazioni forzate fra Cinque e Seicento' in U. Colombo ed., *Vita e processo di suor Virginia Maria de Leyva monaca di Monza* (Milan, 1985), 145–95; D. E. Zannetti, *La demografia del patriziato milanese nei secoli XVII, XVIII, XIX* (Rome, 1972), 83 shows that in Milan

after 1650 female celibacy fell from 75% to 13%. The remarriage of widows virtually dried up; the number of men marrying was fairly constant.

11 B. Harris, 'A New Look at the Reformation, Aristocratic Women and Nunneries 1450–1540', *Journal of British Studies*, 32 (1993), 89–113.

12 Pillorget, op. cit., 94. When Trent insisted on the paramountcy of the religious service and made the exchange of money secondary, disputes over unpaid dowries in Languedoc became remarkably bitter and the woman in question was regarded as an incomplete member of the house, to be treated like a beggar. N. Castan, *Les Criminels de Languedoc. Les exigences d'ordre et les voies du ressentiment dans une société prérévolutionnaire* (Toulouse, 1984), 182–6 and J. Casey, 'Household disputes and the law in early modern Andalusia' in J. Bossy ed., *Disputes and Settlements: Law and Human Relations in the West* (Cambridge, 1983), 193. On the significance of the contrast between societies where dowry was and where it was not a *sine qua non* of matrimony, see Casey, op. cit., 78–9. Where the family did help to raise dowry funds, they had a greater stake in the marriage. Sabean, *Property, Production and Family in Neckarhausen* (Cambridge, 1990), 183–246 on relative input of husband and wife into rural German marriage.

13 Sabean, *ibid.*, 238–9 argues that, if anything, more attention is given to marital funds (his, hers and theirs) at the end of the eighteenth century than earlier. In contrast, many English maidservants have little cash at the end of the eighteenth century, but perhaps have more in clothes and textiles. I am indebted to Dr John Styles of the Victoria and Albert Museum for this information.

14 I am indebted to Professor Samuel Cohn for drawing this shift to my attention; L. Ciammitti, 'La dote come rendita. Note sull'assistenza a Bologna nei secoli XVI–XVIII' in *Forme e soggetti dell'intervento assistenziale in una città di antico regime* (Bologna, 1986), and 'Quanto costa essere normali? La dote del Conservatorio femminile di S. Maria del Barracano (1630–1680)', *Quaderni Storici*, 53 (1983).

15 Macfarlane, op. cit., 277–90; B. Hill, *Women, Work and Sexual Politics in Eighteenth Century England* (Oxford, 1989), 186–91.

16 O. Hufton, 'Women, Work and Family in Eighteenth Century France', *French Historical Studies* (1975); A. Kussmaul, *Servants in Husbandry in Early Modern England* (Cambridge, 1981), 76; J. Hecht, *The Domestic Servant Class in Eighteenth Century England* (London, 1956), 13–25. H. Wunder, 'Zur Stellung der Frau ins Arbeitsleben und in der Gesellschaft des 15.–18. Jahrhunderts', *Geschichtsdidaktik* (1981), 239–51.

17 Quarter Sessions, Rutland, 1563/1. Infractions and paying more were punished by fines. Hence 'presentment of an Eppleby yeoman for agreeing to give his dairymaid £2.10 3d per annum which was more than he ought to give or she ought to accept' (Quarter Sessions, Beedall, Yorks 1680/1).

18 William Ellis, *The Modern Husbandman* (8 vols., London, 1750), vol.5, 92.

19 K. W. Nicholls, 'Irishwomen and Property in the Sixteenth Century' in M. MacCurtain and M. O'Dowd eds., *Women in Early Modern Ireland* (Edinburgh, 1991), 24–6. An average dowry in Castilian villages in the late 1500s was a donkey and four or five cows. D. E. Vassberg, 'The Status of Widows in late sixteenth-century rural Castille', in J. Henderson and R. Wall eds., *Poor Women and Children in the European Past* (London, 1994), 181.

20 J. Hecht, op. cit., 27–8; K. L. McCutcheon, 'Yorkshire Fairs and Markets to the End of the Eighteenth Century', *Thoresby Society Publications*, 1940, xxxix, 158.

21 W. Marshall, *The Rural Economy of the West of England* (2 vols., 1796), vol.I, 109; Hill, op. cit., 72–3.

22 On lace-making the bibliography is mixed in quality, with more emphasis on techniques than people. A good account of these techniques and of shifts in fashion is S. Levey, *Lace: A History* (London, 1983), 21–77; Mrs Bury Palliser, *A History of Lace* (London, 1864) contains some surprising details; see also P. Earnshaw, *A Dictionary of Lace* (Princes Risborough, 1982). Honiton lace was heavily protected against foreign competition by the British government: P. Sharpe, 'A Womanly Accomplishment: Lace Making and Work Culture in England', unpublished paper given at the European University Institute, October 1992. H. Yallop has an unpublished PhD thesis (Exeter) on the Honiton industry.

23 O. Hufton, 'Women, Work and Marriage in Eighteenth Century France' in R. B. Outhwaite ed., *Marriage and Society* (London, 1981), 193. These observations are based on death registers from the local *hôpitaux*. Most long-distance migrants in France came from south of the Loire and excepting the Paris draw (largely of women from Normandy and Picardy and the east) the flow was towards the Mediterranean littoral.

24 L. C. van de Pol, 'The Lure of the Big City: Female Migration to Amsterdam' and M. Carlson, 'A Trojan Horse of Worldliness. Maidservants in the burgher household of Rotterdam at the end of the seventeenth century' in E. Kloek, N. Teeuwen and M. Huisman eds., *Women of the Golden Age* (Hilversum, 1994). M. Jongejans, 'Dienstboden in de Zeeuwse steden 1650–1800', *Spiegel Historiae*, 19 (1984), 214–21. For migrations to Seville, K. Perry, *Gender and Disorder in Early Modern Seville* (Princeton, 1990), 4–5. On the movement into Swiss cities, see D. Rippermann, 'Weibliche Schattenarbeit im Spätmittelalter', *Schweizerische Zeitschrift für Geschichte*, 34 (1984), 332–45 and G. Jacobsen, 'Female Migration and the Late Medieval Town' in G. Jaritz and G. Muller eds., *Migration in der Feudalgesellschaft* (Frankfurt, 1988), 43–55.

25 Hecht, op. cit., 33.

26 *Ibid.* The tax, imposed in the context of war, was a guinea per male servant. Masters were taxed for their servants in France from 1695 in the *Capitation*. The phenomenon of feminization was remarkable by the mid-17th century in both Britain and the Netherlands.

27 For the hierarchy of service see not only Hecht, op. cit., 35–71 but D. George, *London Life in the Late Eighteenth Century* (London, 1966), 119–20; S. Maza, *Servants and Masters in Eighteenth Century France* (Princeton, 1983), 25–106; M. Girouard, *Life in the English Country House* (London, 1978).

28 G. Vigarello, *Concepts of Cleanliness. Changing attitudes in France since the Middle Ages* (Cambridge, 1988), 21–8, 58–69.

29 Linen becomes a surface material along with lace and the contrast of the black garment and the white embellishment becomes a feature of portraiture from Italy to Antwerp and into the northern Netherlands. L. Godard de Donville, *Signification de la mode sous Louis XIII* (Aix en Provence, 1978), 208. Velàzquez incurred problems with a young noblewoman of Zaragoza who refused to accept her portrait because he had not taken sufficient trouble in painting the lace of her collar which was 'puntas de Flandes muy finas'. *Bulletin of the Needle and Bobbin Club*, 14 (New York, 1930), 40–4.

30 C. Davidson, *A Woman's Work is Never Done. A History of Housework in the British Isles 1650–1950* (London, 1982) is the most serious study of housework; for laundry see 136–64.

31 A. Heasel, *Servants book of Knowledge* (London, 1773), 55. This author recommended 'choosing a woman of age and experience, well acquainted with the world and who [had] either kept house herself, or been long in the service of others' (57).

32 C. Johnston, 'Flashes from Domestic Life Long Ago', *Irish News*, 18 October 1961.

33 Trusler, *London Adviser* (1786), 48; Sir John Fielding, *London Chronicle* (1758), 111, 327c. Servants also advertised themselves. This practice spread into continental Europe during the 18th century.

34 Elizabeth Shackleton, a member of the Lancashire gentry, saw 29 maids pass through her house and leave in a single year. This may have been exceptional. A. Vickery, 'Women and the World of Goods: a Lancashire consumer and her possessions, 1751–81' in J. Brewer and R. Porter ed., *Consumption and the World of Goods: consumption and society in the eighteenth century* (London, 1993), 274–304.

35 *Morning Post*, 7 March 1777, no. 1366, 3A. Advertisement for instructing aspirant ladies' maids in hairdressing: 'To Young Women that wait upon Ladies. The Advertiser hereby informs them that they may be taught to dress Ladies' Hair upon reasonable terms. In a short time she will make them fit for places where Hair-dressing is required'.

36 C. Sarasúa, *Criados, nodrizas y amos: el servicio doméstico en la formación del mercado de trabajo madrileño, 1758–1868* (Madrid, 1994).

37 M. Garden, *Lyon et les Lyonnais au XVIIIe siècle* (Paris, 1974), 55–79, 149–50.

38 J. K. J. Thompson, *Clermont de Lodève 1633–1789* (Cambridge, 1982). Fluctuations in the prosperity of a Languedocan cloth-making town. This

industry was also 'put out' into the countryside: 92–4, 119, 205–7, 239–40.

39 A. Arsac, *La dentelle au Puy des origines à nos jours* (Le Puy, 1975), 24.

40 D. Levine, *Family Formation in an Age of Nascent Capitalism* (London, 1977); K. Wrightson and D. Levine, *The Making of an Industrial Society, Whickham 1560–1765* (Oxford, 1991); G. Gulickson, *Spinners and Weavers of Auffray* (Cambridge, 1986); J. Kaplow, *Elbeuf during the Revolutionary Period* (Baltimore, 1963); H. Medick, 'The Proto-Industrial Family Economy', *Social History* (1976).

41 Roper, op. cit, 27–49; C. Friedrichs, *Urban Society in an Age of War: Nordlingen 1580–1720* (Princeton, 1979).

42 L. Mottu Weber, 'Apprentissage et économie genévoise au début du XVIIIe siècle', *Revue Suisse d'Histoire*, 20 (1970), 341. On conflicts between women and the guilds in Switzerland over an extensive period, D. Rippmann and K. Simon Muscheid, 'Weibliche Lebensformen und Arbeitszusammenhänge im Spätmittelalter und in der frühen Neuzeit', in M. Othenin-Girard, A. Grossenreiter and S. Trautweiler eds., *Frauen und Offentlichkeit. Beiträge der 6. schweizerischen Historikerinnentagung* (Zurich, 1991), 63–76.

43 M. Prior, 'Women and the Urban Economy: Oxford 1500–1800' in M. Prior ed., *Women in English Society 1500–1800* (London, 1985), 110–14.

44 J. F. Pound ed., *The Norwich Census of the Poor, 1570*, Norfolk Record Society 40 (1971), *passim*.

45 Archives Départementales Rhône F 302. Such *carnets* are only very occasionally found in hospital records. Sometimes the sums were registered by a notarial act at the end of the woman's employment, e.g. G. Bouchard, *Le village immobile. Sennely en Sologne au XVIIIe siècle* (Paris, 1972), 253.

46 C. S. Davies, *The Agricultural History of Cheshire, 1750–1850*, Chetham Society, 3rd series, X (1960), 80.

3   FINDING A PARTNER, OR QUESTIONS OF CHOICE

1 K. Hazelnet, 'De levenstrap als les voor jong en oud', *In de jonkheid gaan*, 10–11 (1989), 680–3 for a commentary on and an ongoing history of this image; also *The Changing History of Women* (prepd. R. O'Day, Open University, Unit 7), 30.

2 S. Hanley, 'Engendering the State: Family Formation and State Building in Early Modern France', *French Historical Studies*, 16, 1 (1989).

3 A. Farge and M. Foucault, *Le désordre des familles. Lettres de Cachet à Paris au XVIIIe siècle* (Paris, 1982) is an excellent study drawing out the many ways in which the *lettre de cachet* could be used.

4 V. Brodsky Elliott, 'Single Women in the London Marriage Market: Age, Status and Mobility, 1598–1619' and O. Hufton, 'Women, Work

and Marriage in Eighteenth Century France' in R. B. Outhwaite ed., *Marriage and Society: Studies in the Social History of Marriage* (London, 1981). Where women were resident in their own villages, the *curé* could always work to achieve concord between children and parents if dissidence existed.

5 J. Casey, *The History of the Family* (Oxford, 1989), 93–9; J. Gaudemet, 'Legislation canonique et attitudes seculières a l'égard du lien matrimonial au XVIe siècle', *Dix-septième siècle* (1974), 102–3; P. Rasi, 'L'applicazione delle norme del Concilio di Trento in materia matrimoniale', *Studi di storia e diritto in onore di A. Solmi* (Milan, 1941); D. Lombardi, 'State and Church intervention in marriage disputes in 16th and 17th century Florence' (unpublished paper delivered to the Pentofillo group, November 1993). In Italy clandestine marriage, though frowned upon by authority, was never totally banned.

6 S. Teresa of Avila, *Libro de las Fundaciones* (c.1575; Buenos Aires, 1951), 62. She praised a family facing extinction which permitted a daughter to enter the cloister, 'for they would sooner have them lay up wealth and patrimony in that fortunate realm which has no end' (61).

7 Case cited by Casey, op. cit., 108.

8 *Ibid.*, 109–10; compare R. Pillorget, *La Tige et le rameau* (Paris, 1979), 38–9.

9 J. Locke, *Two Treatises of Government*, ed. P. Laslett (Cambridge, 1990); J. Rendall, *The Origins of Modern Feminism. Women in Britain, France and the United States, 1780–1860* (London, 1985), 10–13; M. A. Butler, 'Early Roots of Feminism: John Locke and the Attack on Patriarchy' in M. L. Shanley and C. Pateman eds., *Feminist Interpretations and Political Theory* (Cambridge, 1991), 74–93; M. L. Shanley, 'Marriage Contract and Social Contract in Seventeenth Century English Political Thought', *Western Political Quarterly*, 32 (March 1979), 79–91.

10 A. Behn, *The Ten Pleasures of Marriage* (Navarre Society, 1922), 224–5; Cara W. Robertson, *Relative Choices. Choice of Marriage Partner in some Eighteenth-Century Novels* (D.Phil. thesis, Oxford, 1994) makes a careful study of this issue in both novels and didactic English literature.

11 Caroline Michaelis, Letter to Louise Gotter, 12 January 1781, cited M-C. Hoock-Demarle, *La Femme au temps de Goethe* (Paris, 1987), 38.

12 Dr John Gregory, *A Father's Legacy to his Daughters* (1774); Dr Fordyce, *Sermons to Young Women* are attacked by Mary Wollstonecraft, *A Vindication of the Rights of Woman* (London, 1792; Everyman edn, 1992), 100–8.

13 J. L. Flandrin, *Familles, parenté, maison, sexualité dans l'ancienne société* (Paris, 1976) argues for greater flexibility in England than France. S. H. Mendelson, 'Debate: the weightiest business: marriage in an upper-gentry family in seventeenth century England', *Past and Present*, 85 (1979), 130. A. C. Carter, 'Marriage Counselling in the early seventeenth century: England and the Netherlands compared' in J. van Dorsten ed., *Ten Studies in Anglo-Dutch Relations* (Leiden/London, 1974), 105. To be contrasted with

the Italian marital vade mecum, L. B. Alberti, *The Family in Renaissance Florence*, trans. R. N. Watkins (Columbia, S.C., 1969). The French and Italian models have more in common with each other than they do with Britain and the Netherlands.

14 A. Macfarlane, op. cit., 257–8; Pillorget, op. cit., 111; T. H. Hollingsworth, 'The Demography of the British Peerage', *Population Studies*, 8, Supplement (1964); D. Thomas, 'The Social Origins of Marriage Partners of the British Peerage in the Eighteenth and Nineteenth Centuries', *Population Studies*, 26, 99–111.

15 Hamilton Archives RH 39/1. For parallel cases, see A. P. W. Malcolmson, *The Pursuit of the Heiress. Aristocratic Marriage in Ireland, 1750–1820* (Antrim, 1982), 4.

16 M. Slater, 'The weightiest business: marriage in an upper-gentry family in seventeenth century England', *Past and Present*, 72 (1976), 24–54.

17 Power bases were constructed through matrimony by all rulers and aristocracies and even the pope as is indicated by Paul III's marriages of his nieces: G. Alciati, *I papi costruttori* (Rome, 1990), 84.

18 Cited Pillorget, op. cit., 111.

19 P. Goubert, *Mazarin* (Paris, 1990), 483–92.

20 A. Muhlstein, *Les femmes et le pouvoir. Une relecture de Saint-Simon* (Paris, 1976); Saint-Simon, *Mémoires* (Paris, 1879 and 1930) (43 vols), I, 220–6.

21 G. Chaussinand-Nogaret, *La Noblesse au XVIII siècle* (Paris, 1976), 163–79.

22 In the words of Saint-Simon, 'les femmes perdent ou rétablissent les maisons par leur humeur ou leur bonne conduite' (II. 889) and there are other instances of 'humours' affecting marriage partners (II. 373). The early novel as written by women frequently pivoted on the chance of a beauty catching a rich man's eye. Hence the proverbs warning against physical favour.

23 In Chaussinand-Nogaret's pertinent summary: *l'idéale c'est le juste milieu entre le mariage raisonnable et le mariage d'agrément* (ideally a compromise between reason and acceptability); op. cit., 164.

24 C. Lougee, *Le Paradis des Femmes. Women, Salons and Social Stratification in Seventeenth Century France* (Princeton, 1976).

25 *Memoirs of Madame de la Tour du Pin*, trans. F. Harcourt (London, 1969), 53–65.

26 Chaussinand-Nogaret, op. cit., 165–6.

27 *Ibid.*, 169–70. Lucy Dillon was to write, 'Marriages are made in heaven' (*Memoirs*, 53), a strange interpretation to our ears of the complex negotiations which ended in her marriage. The saying was generally used to suggest that God was the decision-maker in whatever circumstances confronted mankind and that if you had behaved responsibly and had done

what you reasonably could to ascertain the character of your spouse, then resignation to God's will was the only possible attitude.

28 R. Forster, *Merchants, Landlords, Magistrates, The Depont Family in Eighteenth Century France* (Baltimore, 1980), 30–1, 123.

29 My remarks in parentheses used in the quotation from Arch. Dep. H. Garonne 4J. Mme de Cadillac to Mme de Riquet, 31 August 1746, cited R. Forster, *The Nobility of Toulouse in the Eighteenth Century* (Baltimore, 1960), 131. In the Toulousain it was customary for only one noble daughter to marry; *ibid.*, 130.

30 B. Harris, 'Women and Politics in Early Tudor England', *Historical Journal*, 33, 2 (1990), 261–2.

31 Alberti, op. cit., 115.

32 Saint-Simon, *Mémoires*, II, 889 gives some striking examples of groups of women combining to contrive the right matches for daughters, nieces, or even sisters. On the complex interventions of relatives in marriage negotiations in Ireland, see A. P. W. Malcolmson, *The Pursuit of the Heiress, Aristocratic Marriage in Ireland 1750–1820* (Antrim, 1982); see also Forster, op. cit., 130.

33 Incident related by L. Stone, *The Family, Sex, and Marriage in England 1500–1800* (London, 1977), 182.

34 *Great Diurnal of Nicholas Blundell I*, Record Society of Lancashire and Cheshire, 110 (1968), 4.

35 Schama, *The Embarrassment of Riches. An Interpretation of Dutch Culture in the Golden Age* (London, 1988), 441–2; in modification, F. Koorn, 'Vrijen en partnerkeuze in Twente in de 18de eeuw', *In de jonkheid gaan* 10 (1989), 697–706. D. Haks, *Huwelijk en gezin in Holland in de 17de en 18de eeuw* (Assen, 1982).

36 Cited by K. Nicholls, 'Irishwomen and Property in the Sixteenth Century' in MacCurtain and O'Dowd, *Women in Early Modern Ireland* (Edinburgh, 1991), 25.

37 O. Hufton, *The Poor of Eighteenth-Century France* (Oxford, 1974), 84–6 and *passim*. How many returned is always impossible to ascertain. G. Jacobsen, 'Female Migration and the late medieval town', in G. Javitz and G. Müller eds., *Migration in der Feudalgesellschaft* (Frankfurt, 1988), 46–7.

38 Cited V. Brodsky Elliott, 'The London Marriage Market' in Outhwaite, op. cit., 97.

39 *Ibid.*, 90–1.

40 Scepticism about beauty and marital felicity abounds in all languages. See the proverb collection in J. L. Flandrin, *Amours Paysannes* (Paris, 1975), 89–90; M. Ségalen, 'Le mariage, l'amour et les femmes dans les proverbes français', *Ethnologie Française* (1976); A. de Cock, *Spreekwoorden en Zegswijzen over de Vrouwen die Liefode en het Huwelijk* (Ghent, 1911); *The Oxford Dictionary of English Proverbs* ed. F. P. Wilson (1970), entries Beauty, Woman, etc.

41 L. Ferrante, 'La sexualité en tant que ressource. Des femmes devant

le For archiépiscopal de Bologne (XVIIe siècle)', *Déviance et Société*, 11 (1987), 41–66; M. Fubini-Leuzzi, 'Appunti per lo studio delle doti granducali in Toscana', *Ricerche Storiche*, 20 (1990), 345.

42 Cited Bouchard, op. cit., 326–7.

43 Wrightson, *English Society 1580–1680* (London, 1982), 76.

44 'Most busy are the people in these gatherings [i.e. *Spinnstuben*] when a girl in the village plans to marry. Here the girls arrange among themselves how much flax each will contribute in order to make a gift called the *Brautrocken*, to the bride. If the girl marries outside the village, then the *Brautrocken* is to be seen at the top of the bridal wagon with ribbons streaming from it. Everyone watches when such a wagon passes by. From the size of the *Brautrocken* everyone can conclude how much the bride is esteemed by the corps of girls.' H. Medick, 'Village spinning bees: sexual culture and free time amongst rural youth in early modern Germany' in H. Medick and D. Sabean eds., *Interest and Emotion, Essays in the study of family and kinship* (Cambridge, 1988), 332–3.

45 E. Shorter, *The Making of the Modern Family* (New York, 1975), 130–3.

46 Schama, op. cit., 439.

47 L. Dresen-Coenders, 'Een boeren cultur', *Jougd en samenleving* 19 (1989), 628–44.

48 O. Hufton, 'Women, Work and Marriage in Eighteenth Century France' in Outhwaite, op. cit., 201; J. P. Gutton, *La sociabilité villageoise dans l'ancienne France* (Paris, 1979), 244–5; Shorter, op. cit., 137–8.

49 Hufton, loc. cit., and M. C. Phan, *Les amours illégitimes. Histoires de séduction en Languedoc 1676–1786* (Paris, 1986), 74–7.

50 On the ebb and flow of English illegitimacy rates, see Wrightson, op. cit., 84–6. The turn of the sixteenth and seventeenth centuries saw a peak and thereafter a decline to rise again in the eighteenth: P. Laslett, K. Oosterveen and R. M. Smith eds., *Bastardy and its Comparative History* (London, 1980), 71–217. Comparative material for France, *ibid.*, 249–64 and A. Lottin, 'Naissances illégitimes et filles-mères à Lille au 18e siècle', *Revue d'histoire moderne et contemporaine*, avril–juin 1970. M. Ingram, *Church Courts, Sex and Marriage in England 1570–1640* (Cambridge, 1987), 229.

51 M. Mitterauer and R. Sieder, *The European Family* (Oxford, 1982), 64–6.

52 Schama, op. cit., 445.

53 R. B. Litchfield, 'Demographic characteristics of Florentine patrician families, sixteenth to nineteenth centuries', *Journal of Economic History*, 29 (1969), 191ff.

4 ON BEING A WIFE

1 J. Surgant, *Manuale curatorum predicandi prebens modu* (Basle, 1503), cited with commentary by L. Roper, *The Holy Household. Religion, Morals and Order in Reformation Augsburg* (Oxford, 1989), 133; also M. Schröter, 'Wo

Zwei zusammenkommen in rechter Ehe', *Sozio- und pyschogene genetische Studien über Eheschliessungsurgänge vom 12. bis 15. Jahrhundert* (Frankfurt, 1985). On the offering of rings by the family to a new bride to symbolize her entry to a new kin group, C. Klapisch Zuber, *The Griselda complex. Women, Family and Ritual in Renaissance Italy* (Chicago, 1985), 231.

2 L. Roper, 'Going to church and street. Weddings in Reformation Augsburg', *Past and Present*, 106 (1985), 62–101.

3 *Reminiscences of a Gentlewoman of the Last Century. Letters of Catherine Hutton*, ed. Catherine Hutton Beale (1891), 125.

4 A. Macfarlane, *Marriage and Love in England, 1300–1840* (London, 1986), 271. P. Allerston, *The trade in second-hand clothes and fabrics in sixteenth and early seventeenth century Venice* (PhD thesis, European University Institute).

5 *Memoirs of Madame de la Tour du Pin*, 66–70.

6 Roper, *The Holy Household*, 136–47.

7 E. Le Roy Ladurie, *Love, Death and Money in the Pays d'Oc* (Cambridge, 1982), 1–35. On the usual gluttony of the peasant wedding, G. Duby and A. Wallon eds., *Histoire de la France Rurale* (Paris, 1975), vol. 2, 499–550.

8 E. Arenal and S. Schlau eds., *Untold Sisters: Hispanic Nuns in their own works* (Albuquerque, 1985).

9 There was no standard rule. Rural Tuscany had anything up to 45% multi-generational households, but perhaps nearer a norm of 20%. The demographic studies involved are summarized in M. Mitterauer and R. Sieder, *The European Family* (Oxford, 1982), 30.

10 J. Casey, 'Household Disputes and the Law in Early Modern Andalusia' in J. Bossy ed., *Law and Human Relations in the West* (Cambridge, 1983), 200–1; G. Ruggiero, *The Boundaries of Eros: Sex Crime and Sexuality in Renaissance Venice* (Oxford, 1983), 59.

11 João de Pina-Cabral, *Sons of Adam, Daughters of Eve, The Peasant World View of the Alto Minho* (Oxford, 1986), 74.

12 The word itself emerges in 20th-century America, but the notion of woman as the complement of man, that which makes the total, is used in both Catholic and Protestant good conduct literature.

13 B. Harris, 'Women and Politics in Early Tudor England', *Historical Journal*, 33, 2 (1990), 266 and *passim*.

14 *Ibid.*, 272.

15 For general developments in the role of lady in waiting, see A. Somerset, *Ladies in Waiting from the Tudors to the Present Day* (London, 1984).

16 *Ibid.*, 203. In her time Sarah Churchill was Groom of the Stole, Mistress of the Robes, Keeper of the Privy Purse (in charge of the money the queen spent on gambling, charity and rewards to servants). Her two daughters were also made ladies of the bedchamber at £1000 per year. If the political power of the posts declined, this was still useful money.

17 Anka Muhlstein, *Les femmes et le pouvoir: une relecture de Saint-Simon* (Paris, 1976), 63–74.

18 R. Pillorget, *La tige et le rameau* (Paris, 1979), 53.

19 *Ibid.*, 30.

20 B. Schofield ed., *The Knyvett Letters, 1620–1644*, Norfolk Record Society, vol. 20 (1949), 110.

21 J. Loftis ed., *Memoirs of Anne, Lady Halket and Anne, Lady Fanshawe* (Oxford, 1981), 114.

22 C. Durston, *The Family in the English Revolution* (Oxford, 1989), particularly 89–109.

23 M. O'Dowd, 'Women and War in Ireland in the 1640s' in MacCurtain and O'Dowd eds., *Women in Early Modern Ireland* (Edinburgh, 1991), 92–3; and J. Gilbert ed., *The History of the Irish Confederation and the War in Ireland* (1641–9) (7 vols., Dublin, 1882–91), vol.2, 69–73.

24 J. Vidalenc, *Les émigrés français* (Caen, 1963).

25 D. Higgs, *Nobles in nineteenth century France: the practice of inegalitarianism* (Baltimore, 1987), particularly 70–129.

26 Lady Llanover ed., *The Autobiography and Correspondence of Mary Granville, Mrs Delaney* (London, 1861), *passim*; and A. Vickery, 'Women and the World of Goods: a Lancashire consumer and her possessions, 1751–81' in J. Brewer and R. Porter eds., *Consumption and the World of Goods* (London, 1993), 274–304.

27 For a commentary and bibliography on de Maes' painting, see catalogue, *Masters of Seventeenth Century Dutch Genre Painting* (London/ Philadelphia, 1984), 241, I.

28 M. Hyde, *The Thrales of Streatham Park* (Cambridge, 1977), 17.

29 S. Ozment, *Magdalena and Balthasar. An intimate portrait of life in sixteenth century Europe* (New York, 1986).

30 M. Prior, 'Reviled and crucified marriages: the position of Tudor bishops' wives' in M. Prior ed., *Women in English Society 1500–1760* (London, 1985), 118–49.

31 M. Watt, *The Clergyman's Wife* (London, 1945) offers a series of essays as a point of departure.

32 J. Pudney, *John Wesley and his World* (London, 1978), 7–14. A good biography of Susannah Wesley remains to be written.

33 Duby and Wallon, op. cit., 2, 481.

34 D. Sabean, *Property, Production and Family in Neckarhausen 1700–1870* (Cambridge, 1990), ch.4, Patterns of Marital Conflict.

35 W. Howitt, *Rural Life of England* (1840), 105.

36 *Report of the Society for Bettering the Condition and Increasing the Comforts of the Poor* (5 vols., 1798–1808), vol.5, 84–9. Cited Hill, *Women, Work and Sexual Politics in Eighteenth Century England* (Oxford, 1989), 43–4.

37 Water carrying, in villages especially, could be very time-consuming and streams, springs and wells could dry up in summer, forcing recourse to

water sources at greater distance for domestic and farm use. On the problem in England (slight in comparison with Mediterranean countries) see C. Davidson, *A Woman's Work is Never Done* (London, 1982), 7–33.

38 M. Bouloiseau, 'Aspects sociaux de la crise cotonnière dans les campagnes rouennaises en 1788–9', *Actes du 82e congrès des Sociétés savantes* (Caen/Rouen, 1956), 414; P. Deyon, 'Le Mouvement de la production textile à Amiens', *Revue du Nord*, 44 (1962), 201–11; J. Kaplow, *Elbeuf during the Revolutionary Period* (Baltimore, 1964), 39–51; G. Gulickson, *Spinners and Weavers of Auffray* (Cambridge, 1986), *passim*.

39 Cited by Davidson, op. cit., 187.

40 M. Bouloiseau, 'Aspects sociaux de la crise cotonnière', 414–16.

41 Hufton, *The Poor of Eighteenth Century France* (Oxford, 1974), 69–106.

42 Archives Départementales Puy de Dôme (1220–1).

43 A. Young, *A Tour in Ireland with general observations on the present state of that kingdom, made in the years 1776, 1777 & 1788*, ed. C. Maxwell (Cambridge, 1925). Wherever he went, i.e. France, Italy, Spain and throughout England, Young commented on the sexual division of labour.

44 Archives Départementales Hérault C563. Hôpital général de Saint Joseph de la Grave à Toulouse. Etats.

45 I am indebted to Carmen Sarasúa García of the European University Institute for passing on these details to me.

46 Roper, *The Holy Household*, first two chapters; M. Wiesner, *Working Women in Reformation Germany* (New Brunswick, 1986); E. W. Monter, 'Women in Calvinist Geneva', *Signs*, 6 (1980), 189–289; M. Prior, 'Women and the Urban Economy: Oxford 1500–1800' in Prior, op. cit.; M. E. Perry, *Gender and Disorder in Early Modern Seville* (Princeton, 1990).

47 These early censuses are largely conserved in French municipal archives. Those of Bayeux appear in Bayeux F., *Etats de Population, au IV, au VII*. Censuses chronically under-record the casual work of women.

48 Inferences drawn from censuses.

49 G. D. Sussmann, *Selling Mothers' Milk: the Wetnursing Business in France 1715–1914* (Urbana, 1982) is based on registers which record the employment of the father.

50 Much guild history is reconstructed from lawsuits or municipal rulings which perforce show the guild at the moment of attempting to tighten up on infringements. A good specimen case of sporadic penalization of a woman who was clearly a persistent offender is found in M. Wiesner, 'Spinning Out Capital: Women's Work in the Early Modern Germany' in R. Bridenthal, C. Koonz and S. Stuard eds., *Becoming Visible, Women in European History* (Boston, 1987), 237.

51 D. Roche, *Journal de ma Vie. Jacques-Louis Ménétra, Compagnon Vitrier au 18e siècle* (Paris, 1982), *passim*; R. Darnton, *The Great Cat Massacre* (London, 1985), 79–104.

52 Prior, 'Women and the Urban Economy . . .'

53 S. Kaplan, *Provisioning Paris* (Ithaca, 1984), 189, 321–9.

54 M. Garden, *Lyon et les lyonnais au XVIIIe siècle* (Paris, 1974), 216.

55 *Ibid.*, 85–139.

56 M. McNeil, *The Life and Times of Mary McCracken, 1770–1866* (Dublin, 1960), 57. She had a small muslin business.

57 I. Cameron, *Crime and repression in the Auvergne and the Guyenne 1720–1790* (Cambridge, 1981), 31–2; R. Williams, *Policing Crime in Berkshire in the Eighteenth Century* (PhD thesis, Reading, 1986). Joanna Innes, Somerville College, Oxford, informs me this was standard practice in England.

58 Hufton, op. cit., 260–1. In Italy only poorer cloths were disposed of by women.

59 J. Kaplow, 'Sur la population flottante de Paris à la fin de l'ancien régime', *Annales Historiques de la Révolution française* (1976), 6.

60 B. Pullan, *Rich and Poor in Renaissance Venice* (Oxford, 1971), 382; and M. Benabou, *La Prostitution et la Police des Moeurs au XVIIIe siècle* (Paris, 1987), 314.

61 Cited Duby and Wallon, op. cit., 2, 500.

5   PARENTHOOD

1 Curé de Comboux, near Sallanches, 1733; cited Y. Knibiehler and C. Fouquet, *Histoire des Mères du Moyen Age à nos jours* (Paris, 1980), 48.

2 E. Le Roy Ladurie, 'L'Aiguillette', *Europe* (1974), 134–6, trans. S. Reynolds in *The Mind and Method of the Historian* (London, 1981), 84–96; J. Gélis, M. Laget and M. F. Morel eds., *Entrer dans la vie. Naissances et enfances dans la France traditionelle* (Paris, 1978), 56–61; Knibiehler and Fouquet, op. cit., 40.

3 H. Roodenburg, 'The Autobiography of Isabella de Moerloose: Sex, childrearing and popular belief in Seventeenth Century Holland', *Journal of Social History*, 18 (1985), 518, 528–32.

4 Knibiehler and Fouquet, op. cit., 51; other fertility rites such as sitting on bags of corn were common in parts of Mediterranean Europe. J. Gélis, *A History of Childbirth* (Oxford, 1991), 22–5, 28–31.

5 The use of dust and herbs combines the magical and the medicinal in cogent form. Prone figures of parturient virgins, particularly common in Central France in the late Middle Ages, may have been used particularly as objects of veneration and pilgrimage but also to make potions. They hardly survive the Counter-Reformation.

6 M. Peyrache, *Un sanctuaire de la fécondité en Haute Provence: Notre Dame des Oeufs* (Aix, nd). On special pilgrimages, Gélis, op. cit., 17.

7 H. Delahaye, *Les légendes hagiographiques* (1905), 222–34. Generally, attention shifted away from Margaret in the seventeenth century to the Virgin and a Virgin's girdle was placed on the parturient woman to help her.

8 R. Houlbrouke, *The English Family, 1450–1700* (London, 1984), 129.

9 A. McLaren, *Reproductive Rituals: the perception of fertility in England from the sixteenth to the nineteenth century* (London, 1984), 76.

10 M. Laget, 'La naissance aux siècles classiques', *Annales, Economies, Sociétés et Civilisations* (1977), 958–92; F. Mauriceau, *Traité des maladies des femmes grosses et de celles qui sont accouchées* (Paris, 1668); L. Bourgeois, *Observations sur la stérilité, perte du fruit, fécondité, accouchements* (Paris, 1609), vol.II. Bourgeois, as a midwife to monarchy, was an important authority.

11 A. Paré, *Sur monstres et prodiges* (1583) and H. Roodenburg, 'The maternal imagination: the fears of pregnant women in seventeenth-century Holland', *Journal of Social History* (1988), 701–16; K. Park and L. Daston, 'Unnatural conceptions: the study of monsters in sixteenth and seventeenth-century France and England', *Past and Present*, 92 (1981), 20–54.

12 Abbé Thiers, *Traité des superstitions*, cited Knibiehler and Fouquet, op. cit., 53.

13 More instances in S. H. Mendelson, 'Stuart women's diaries' in M. Prior ed., *Women in English Society 1500–1800* (London, 1985), 196–7.

14 A. Thornton, *Autobiography*, ed. C. Jackson, Surtees Society LXII (1875), 95.

15 R. K. Marshall, *Virgins and Viragos: a history of women in Scotland from 1080–1980* (Chicago, 1983), 109–11 cites this and related cases.

16 British Library Add. Mss 27351–6. Warwick, Diary, 24 August 1667, cited Mendelson, 'Stuart women's diaries', 197.

17 *Dévotions particulières pour les femmes enceintes* (1665), 21. As far as I know, a parallel English prayer does not exist, but a 17th-century work, J. Taylor, *The Rule and Exercise of Holy Dying* (London, 1901 edn), 327, includes 'A prayer to be said in the case of a sudden surprise by death as by a mortal wound or evil accidents in childbirth, when the forms and solemnities and preparation cannot be used.'

18 The introduction by H. Marland, *The Art of Midwifery. Early Modern Midwives in Europe* (London, 1993) and the collected essays are landmarks in the reappraisal of the midwife. From *c.*1750 French surgical schools had models with moving parts of the uterus and pieces of skeleton to teach the male midwife. Until the lessons of the Dame du Coudray there was no such 'training' generally available for women. Other essential work includes J. Gélis, 'L'accouchement au XVIIIe siècle; pratiques traditionnelles et contrôle médicale', *Ethnologie Française* (1976); 'La formation des accoucheurs et des sages femmes au XVIIe et XVIIIe siècles', *Annales de démographie historique* (1977); 'Sages femmes et accoucheurs. L'obstétrique populaire aux XVIIe et XVIIIe siècles', *Annales, Economies, Sociétés et Civilisations* (1977); and *The History of Childbirth*, 112–62. See also J. Donnison, *Midwives and Medical Men. A history of interprofessional rivalries and women's rights* (London, 1977); C. Pancino, *Il bambino e l'acqua sporca. Storia dell'assistenza al parto, dalle mammane alle ostetriche (secoli XVI–XIX)* (Milan, 1984).

19 M. J. van Lieburg ed., *Mother and Child Were Saved. The memoirs (1693–1745) of the Frisian midwife Catharina Schrader* (Amsterdam, 1984). For commentary see W. Frijhoff, 'Vrouw Schraders beroepsjornaal: overwegingen bijeen publikatie over arbeidspraktijk in het veileden', *Tijdschrift voor Geschiedenis der Natuur wetenschappen Wiskunde en Techniek*, 8 (1985), 27–38; H. Marland, 'The "burgerlijke" midwife: the *stadsvroedvrouw* of eighteenth century Holland' in Marland, op. cit., 192–213.

20 Angot de Lespeyronnière, *La Lucine, ou la femme en couches* 7e satire (Paris, 1610).

21 On the myths and rituals associated with the placenta, see Gélis, *History of Childbirth*, 162–72.

22 Houlbrouke, op. cit., 131.

23 Delumeau, *Sin and Fear. The Emergence of a Western Guilt Culture 13th–18th Centuries* (New York, 1990), 272–3; J. Gélis, 'De la mort à la vie, les sanctuaires à répit', *Ethnologie Française*, 2 (1981), 3, 211–44 and 'Miracles et médecine aux siècles classiques: le corp médical et le retour temporaire à la vie des enfants morts à la naissance', *Historical Reflexions* (Ontario, 1982).

24 Thiers, *Traité des superstitions* (1743), vol.2, 58–65. M. Vloberg, 'Les réanimations d'enfants mort-nés dans les sanctuaires dits "à répit" de la Vierge' in *Sanctuaires et Pèlerinages* (Paris, 1960). Church hostility manifested itself in official *ordonnances*: 'Nous défendons à tous les fidèles de ce diocèse, sous peine d'excommunication, de déterrer de porter leurs enfants morts sans baptême à la Chapelle de Notre-Dame du Laux ou ailleurs, sous prétexte qu'il s'y fait des miracles et que ces enfants ressuscitant pour un instant, reçoivent le baptême.' Ordonnance Synodale du diocèse de Grenoble, 1687.

25 Bodleian Ms. Rawl D1262–3. Bathurst Diary, 13.

26 N. Llewellyn, *The Art of Death* (London, 1991), 47–8.

27 *The private diarie of Elizabeth Viscountess Mordaunt* (Duncairn, 1856), 14–15.

28 L. Bourgeois, *Le récit véritable de la naissance de messeigneurs et dames les enfants de la France* (Paris, 1624), 177.

29 Edward Hall ed., *Miss Weeton: Journal of a Governess* (London, 1939), vol.2. The first chapters pivot on the different valorization (and the consequences in expectations) of a girl and a boy child. A thorough study based on English clergymen's diaries of the life trajectory of the two sexes would be very valuable.

30 Ambroise Paré: 'Les brunes sont de tempérament plus chaude que les blanches, partant la chaleur digère et cuit mieux l'aliment dont le lait est rendu beaucoup meilleur.' *De la génération*, cited Knibiehler and Fouquet, op. cit., 90–3; Houlbrouke, op. cit., 133–4; D. MacLaren, 'Marital fertility and lactation 1570–1720' in Prior, op. cit., 128–9; V. Fildes, *Wet nursing. A history from antiquity to the present* (Oxford, 1988). On the size and shape of breasts, anon., *The nurse's guide* (1729), 29–35 and works summarized in R. Trumbach, *The Rise of the Egalitarian Family* (London, 1978), 199–200.

31 Houlbrouke, op. cit., 133; F. Le Brun, *La vie conjugale sous l'ancien régime* (Paris, 1975), 128; S Schama, *The Embarrassment of Riches* (London, 1987), 540; C. Klapisch-Zuber, 'Blood parents and milk parents. Wet nursing in Florence 1300–1500', *Women, Family and Ritual in Renaissance Italy* (Chicago, 1985), 132–64.

32 J. Cats, *Moeder, Houwelijck*, 391, cited Schama, op. cit., 538.

33 Some of this literature is discussed in P. Ariès, *Centuries of Childhood* (London, 1976); Dorothy Leigh, *The mother's blessing: or the godly counsaile of a gentle woman* (1616; republished in 1618, 1621, 1627, 1629, 1630, 1633, 1634, 1636, 1640, 1656, 1663, 1667, 1674) bears witness to a demand for such work in Britain, but I have not located a similar work in another European context. B. Berry, 'The first English paediatricians and Tudor attitudes towards childhood', *Journal of the History of Ideas*, 35 (1974), 561–77.

34 Blankaart, *Verhandelinge van de Ziekten der Kinderen* (Amsterdam, 1684), 2–8. On the social standing of wet-nurses, MacLaren, 'Marital fertility . . .', 29–30. On the Paris *bureau de placement*, Sussman, *Selling Mothers' Milk: The Wetnursing Business in France, 1715–1914* (Urbana, 1982). On the poverty of Spanish wet-nurses to foundlings, J. Sherwood, *Poverty in Eighteenth Century Spain* (Toronto, 1988), 67–8, and in France, O. Hufton, *The Poor of Eighteenth-Century France* (Oxford, 1974), 342–3.

35 Hufton, op. cit., 334–49.

36 A. F. Prost de Royer, *Mémoire sur la conservation des enfants* (Lyons, 1778). This observer worked with a small sample drawn from two villages.

37 *Journal de Jean Héroard sur l'enfance de Louis XIII* (Paris, 1868).

38 The crust was known as *le chapeau*; Gélis, Laget and Morel, op. cit., 120; Schama, op. cit., 536.

39 *Livre de raison de la famille Froissard-Broissia. Mémoires de la société d'émulation du Jura*, 4e série (2 vols., 1886), 44–8; D. MacLaren, 'Marital fertility . . .', 22–53; L. Pollock, *A Lasting Relationship, parents and children over three centuries* (London, 1987), 65.

40 J. Locke, 'Some thoughts concerning education' (1690) in *The Works of John Locke* (new edn, 10 vols., London, 1823), vol.IX, 26–7. 'Plenty of open air, exercise and sleep; plain diet, no wine or strong drink and very little or no physic; not too warm and straight clothing; especially the head and feet kept cold, and the feet often used to cold water and exposed to wet.'

41 The perils of the farm cottage for the toddling child and of the farmyard and the well, described in B. A. Hanawalt, 'Child rearing among the lower classes of late medieval England', *Journal of Interdisciplinary History*, 8 (1977), 8–21, still pertained.

42 Murillo's ragged children are also on occasion deloused by an older woman, perhaps grandmother e.g. *Domestic Toilet* (Munich, Alte Pinakothek).

43 R. Schofield and E. A. Wrigley, 'Infant and child mortality in England

in the late Tudor and early Stuart period' in C. Webster ed., *Health,
Medicine and Mortality in the 16th Century* (Cambridge, 1979), 9–60; J.
Dupâquier, *La population française aux XVIIe et XVIIIe siècles* (Paris, 1979), 63,
estimates 3% die at birth, 11–12% in the first week: approximately 6000
out of 10,000 children reach the age of 10.

44 E. Badinter, *The Myth of Motherhood* (London, 1981), *passim*.

45 L. Pollock, *Forgotten Children: Parent-child relationships from 1500–1900*
(Cambridge, 1983) constitutes the most sensible critique of existing
literature. Houlbrouke, op. cit., 150–1; Schama, op. cit., 481–545 claims
that love of children was integral to the Dutch in the seventeenth century.
A. Th. van Deursen, *Plain Lives in a Golden Age. Popular Culture, Religion
and Society in Seventeenth Century Holland* (Cambridge, 1991), 96–115, is a less
positive but certainly not pessimistic view.

46 J. Henderson and R. Wall eds., *Poor Women and Children in the European
Past* (London, 1994) includes several essays and a critical introduction on the
issue of abandonment with considerable emphasis on Italy. An important
collection of the Ecole Française de Rome, *Enfance abandonnée et société en
Europe* (Rome/Paris, 1991), shows how divergent local practices of admissions
to hospitals and different traditions of coping with poverty modify an over-
hasty generalization linking abandonment with family strategy.

47 Houlbrouke, op. cit., 150.

48 S. Ozment, *Magdalena and Balthasar. An intimate portrait of life in
sixteenth century Europe* (New York, 1986), 89–101. For a similar Dutch
example, R. Dekker, 'Problemen rond opvoeding en onderwijs in de 17 eeuw
in het dagboek van Constaintijn Huygens jr.', *In de jonkheid gaan, Jeugd en
samenleving*, 9 (1989), 708–17.

49 Roodenburg, 'The autobiography of Isabella de Moerloose', 520–2.

50 Jeremy Taylor (1600), cited D. Edwards, *Christian England* (London,
1991), vol.2, 363.

51 Schama, op. cit., 508. Rousseau's recommendation that a girl should
be given dolls was echoed by both Chardin and Greuze.

52 Summarized in Roodenburg, op. cit., 523–4.

53 The response of the church was to provide the guardian angel whose
devotion was actively sponsored by the Jesuits.

54 *The life of Glückel of Hameln, 1646–1724, written by herself*, trans. and
ed. Beth-Zion Abrahams (New York, 1963).

55 R. O'Day, *Education and Society, 1500–1800: social foundations of
education in early modern Britain* (London, 1982).

56 R. Chartier, D. Julia and M. Compère, *L'éducation en France du XVIe
au XVIIIe siècles* (Paris, 1976); G. Cholvy, 'Une école des pauvres au début
du 19e siècle "pieuses filles" béates ou soeurs des campagnes' in D. Baker
and P. J. Harrigan eds., *The Making of Frenchmen: current directions in the
history of education in France 1679–1979* (Waterloo, 1980); B. Grosperrin,
Les petites écoles sous l'ancien régime (Rennes, 1984).

6 WIDOWHOOD

1 The statistical basis for a study of widowhood can be found in E. A. Wrigley and R. Schofield, *The Population History of England, 1541–1871* (London, 1981), 258–63 and J. Dupâquier, *La population française au XVIIe et XVIIIe siècles* (Paris, 1979), 60f. On the widow in literature see C. Carlton, 'The Widow's Tale: Male Myths and Female Reality', *Albion*, X (1978), 118–29: E. Mignon, *Crabbed Age and Youth. The Old Men and Women in the Restoration Comedy of Manners* (Durham, N.C., 1947). An excellent bibliography in R. Malcolmson, *Life and Labour in England 1700–1800* (London, 1981), 176, n.53. *Memorie*, 18 (1986), Special Issue *Donne senza uomini*. R. Wall, 'Women Alone in English Society', *Annales de Démographie Historique* (1981). J. Henderson and R. Wall, *Poor Women and Children in the European Past* (London, 1994) contains valuable information and different approaches.

2 London in particular seems to have had an active remarriage market for young widows in the sixteenth and perhaps early seventeenth century, but in the eighteenth century opportunities receded; see J. Boulton, 'London Widowhood revisited: the decline of frequent remarriage in the seventeenth and early eighteenth centuries', *Continuity and Change*, 5 (1990). This may be typical of the large cities of north-western Europe. On the issue of remarriage, see the collected essays in J. Dupâquier ed., *Marriage and Remarriage in the Populations of the Past* (London, 1981), in particular S. Akerman, 'The Importance of Remarriage in the XVII and XVIII centuries', 163–75 and M. Ségalen, 'Mentalité populaire et remariage en Europe occidentale', 69–72.

3 Case cited by V. Brodsky, 'Widows in Late Elizabethan London. Remarriage, Economic Opportunity and Family Orientations' in L. Bonfield, R. M. Smith and K. Wrightson eds., *The World We Have Gained* (Oxford, 1986), 126–7.

4 D. Gaunt and O. Löfgren, 'Remarriage in the Nordic Countries' in Dupâquier, *Marriage and Remarriage*, 49–60.

5 C. Corsini, 'Why is re-marriage a male affair? Some evidence from Tuscan villages during the eighteenth century', *ibid.*, 385–96.

6 S. O. Súilleabháin, *Irish Wake Amusements* (Cork, 1969). Both Catholic and Irish Protestant clergy complained, 146ff.

7 Among the best of these must be S. Richardson, 'Letter from a Gentleman, Strenuously Expostulating with an Old Rich Widow, about to Marry a Very Young Gay Gentleman', *Familiar Letters on Important Occasions* (London, 1741), 90.

8 G. Zarri, 'Monasteri femminili e città (secoli XV–XVIII)', *Storia d'Italia, Annali*, vol.9 (Turin, 1986), 359–429.

9 B. Diefendorf, *Paris City Councillors in the Sixteenth Century. The Politics of Patrimony* (Princeton, 1983), 279–97 and 'Widowhood and Remarriage

in Sixteenth-Century Paris', *Journal of Family History* (Winter 1982), 379–80. J. Hardwicke, 'Widowhood and Patriarchy in Seventeenth Century France', *Journal of Social History* (Fall 1992), 134–5. On the body of legislation, S. Hanley, 'Engendering the State: Family Formation and State Building in Early Modern France', *French Historical Studies*, 16, no.1 (Spring 1989).

10 Isambert, *Recueil Général des anciennes lois françaises depuis l'an 420 jusqu'à la Révolution* (Paris, 1822–33), vol.14, 36. M. Bordeaux, 'Droit et femmes seules. Les pièces de la discrimination' in *Madame ou Mademoiselle? Itinéraires de la solitude féminine, 18e–20e siècles* (Paris, 1984).

11 Hardwicke, 'Widowhood and Patriarchy', 132.

12 S. M. Wyntjes, 'Survivors and Status: Widowhood and Family in the Early Modern Netherlands', *Journal of Family History* (Winter 1982).

13 N. Tamassia, *Il testamento del marito* (Bologna, 1905); L. Cantini, *Legislazione toscana raccolta e illustrata* (Florence, 1800–08), vol.VII, 42–5; C. Klapisch Zuber, '"The Cruel Mother". Maternity, Widowhood and Dowry in Florence in the Fourteenth and Fifteenth Centuries' in *Women, Family and Ritual in Renaissance Italy* (Chicago, 1985), 117–32.

14 G. Calvi, 'Dal margine al centro. Soggettività femminile, famiglia, stato moderna in Toscana' in M. Palazzi and A. Scattigno eds., *Discutendo di Storia* (Turin, 1991), 103–15; and G. Calvi, *Il contratto morale. Madri e figli nella Toscana moderna* (Rome/Bari, 1994).

15 M. Spufford, *Contrasting Communities* (Cambridge, 1974), 113.

16 *Ibid.*, 117.

17 *Ibid.*, 163.

18 Gaunt and Löfgren, 'Remarriage in the Nordic Countries', 52–5.

19 A. L. Erickson, *Women and Property in Early Modern England* (London, 1993), 153–6 estimates that a quarter of Englishmen leaving wills left negative equity.

20 Mary Granvill (Mrs Delaney), *Autobiography and Correspondence* (London, 1861), 109: 'As to my fortune, it was very *mediocre* but it was *at my own command*. Some uneasiness attended it at first, the case of most widows, but I gave myself little anxiety about it' (my italics).

21 G. Calvi, 'Maddalena Nerli and Cosimo Tornabuoni: A Couple's Narrative of Family History in Early Modern Florence', *Renaissance Quarterly* (1992), 336.

22 Wyntjes, 'Survivors and Status', 401.

23 Cited by R. K. Marshall, *Virgins and Viragos: a history of women in Scotland from 1080–1980* (Chicago, 1983), 146.

24 Wyntjes, 'Survivors and Status', 403.

25 R. Pillorget, *La tige et le rameau* (Paris, 1979), 105–6 also gives French equivalents. The practice of widow/daughter marriages by negotiators to widower/heir also exists in Italy from the aristocracy down to the middle classes.

26 J. Collins, 'The Economic Role of Women in Seventeenth Century France', *French Historical Studies*, 16, no. 2 (1989).

27 Johnson's *Rambler* cited with commentary in E. Fussell, *The English Countryman* (London, 1953, 1981), 115–16.

28 O. Hufton, 'Women Without Men: Widows and Spinsters in Britain and France in the Eighteenth Century', *Journal of Family History*, 9, 4 (1984), 361–2. For Augsburg in the 16th century up to 20% of households could be headed by widows: L. Roper, *The Holy Household. Religion, Morals and Order in Reformation Augsburg* (Oxford, 1989), 50; in 16th-century Seville perhaps more: Perry, *Gender and Disorder in Early Modern Seville* (Princeton, 1990), 4, 172–5; M. d'Amelia, 'Scatole cinesi: Vedove e donne sole in una società d'ancien régime', *Memoria*, 18 (1986), 66.

29 D. E. Vassberg, 'The status of widows in sixteenth-century rural Castille' in Henderson and Wall, op. cit., 180–195 gives examples of villages where *all* the widows are needy.

30 Abingdon, 31 March 1785 (Berkshire Record Office. Quarter Session Roll 1785, 205).

31 M. Prior, 'Women and the Urban Economy: Oxford 1500–1800' in Prior op. cit., 98, 103–9; M. Chaytor, 'Household and Kinship: Ryton in the late 16th and early 17th centuries', *History Workshop*, 10 (1980), 43–4.

32 S. Wright, 'Churmaids, Huswyfes and Hucksters, The Employment of Women in Tudor and Stuart Salisbury' in L. Charles and L. Duffin ed., *Women and Work in Pre-industrial England* (London, 1985), 114–16; Prior, 'Women and the Urban Economy', 109–10; Roper, *The Holy Household*, 149–55; M. Wiesner, *Working Women in Renaissance Germany* (New Brunswick, 1986), 157–63; M. Palazzi, 'Abitare da sole. Donne capofamiglia alla fine del Settecento', *Memorie*, 18 (1986), 50–1; Perry, op. cit., 17.

33 Roper, *The Holy Household*, 50.

34 Wiesner, op cit., 113–14.

35 Roper, loc. cit.

36 Wiesner, op. cit., 118; cf. complaints against women hawkers in Seville: Perry, op. cit., 20; and in 17th-century Oxford: Prior, 'Women and the Urban Economy', op. cit., 111.

37 H. Wunder, 'Zur Stellung der Frau im Arbeitsleben und in der Gesellschaft des 15.–18. Jahrhunderts', *Geschichtsdidaktik*, 3 (1981), 239–52.

38 Prior, 'Women and the Urban Economy', 113.

39 d'Amelia, 'Scatoli cinesi', 72–9.

40 *Ibid.*, 70. Compare Bologna: M. Palazzi, 'Abitare da sole', 49–50.

41 L. A. Clarkson and E. M. Crawford, 'Life after Death; Widows in Carrick-on-Suir 1799' in MacCurtain and O'Dowd eds., *Women in Early Modern Ireland* (Edinburgh, 1991), 236–51.

42 *Ibid.*, 247, and L. A. Clarkson, 'Household and Family Structure in Armagh', *Local Population Studies*, 20 (Spring 1978), 14–31.

43 Andres Navagero, *Viaje a España* (Valencia, 1951), 57.

44 Perry, op. cit., 15–16.

45 See L. Ferrante, 'La sexualité en tant que ressource des femmes devant le For archiépiscopal de Bologne', *Déviance et Société*, 2 (1987), 1, 48–9, on how living on work from one loom meant penury.

46 B. A. Todd, 'The remarrying widow: a stereotype reconsidered' in Prior, op. cit., 78–9.

47 Henderson and Wall, op. cit., 18–19 and in the same volume, T. Sokoll, 'The household position of elderly widows in poverty. Evidence from two English communities in the late eighteenth and nineteenth centuries', 207–24.

48 Of the widows living in Lichfield described by Wall, 60% live with children and the majority with daughters, 'Women Alone . . .', 314, and even more in Rome, d'Amélia, op. cit., 68–70; Perry, op. cit., 172–5.

49 Ferrante, 'La sexualité en tant que ressource', 47.

50 M. Carbonell i Esteller, *Pobresa i estratégies de supervivenca á Barcelona ála segona meitat del S. XCIII* (PhD thesis, Barcelona, 1993), 72.

51 S. Cavallo, 'Nozioni di povertà e assistenza a Torino nella seconda mettà del Settecento', European University Institute Working Paper, 1986; Carbonell i Esteller, op. cit., 85–6; J. E. Smith, 'Widowhood and Ageing in Traditional English Society', *Ageing and Society* (1984), 4.

7 OF DIFFERENCE, OF SHAME AND OF ABUSE

1 For generalizations on spinsterhood: L. Henry and J. Houdaille, 'Célibat et âge au mariage aux XVIIIe et XIXe siècles en France, 1. Célibat définitif', *Population*, 33 (1978), 32–83; S. Cott Watkins, 'Spinsters', *Journal of Family History*, 9 (1984), 310–25.

2 For a résumé of known statistical work on spinsterhood: O. Hufton, 'Women without men: widows and spinsters in Britain and France in the eighteenth century', *Journal of Family History*, 9 (1984), 357.

3 P. Otto, *Daughters of the British aristocracy and their marriages in the eighteenth and nineteenth centuries with particular reference to the Scottish peerage* (PhD, Stanford, 1974), 283; T. H. Hollingsworth, 'The demography of the British peerage', *Population Studies*, 8 Supplement (1964); L. Henry and C. Levy, 'Ducs et pairs sous l'ancien régime', *Population*, 15 (1960), 807–30.

4 V. Hunecke, 'Kindbett oder Kloster: Lebenswege venezianischer Patrizierinnen im 17. und 18. Jahrhundert', *Geschichte und Gesellschaft. Zeitschrift für Historische Sozialwissenschaft*, 18 (1992), 446–51; R. B. Litchfield, 'Demographic Characteristics of Florentine Patrician Families, Sixteenth to Nineteenth centuries', *Journal of Economic History*, 29 (1969), 197; D. E. Zanetti, *La demografia del patriziato milanese nei secoli XVII, XVIII, XIX* (Pavia, 1972), 83.

5 K. Rogers, *Feminism in Eighteenth Century England* (Urbana, 1982) includes as appendices a number of mini-biographies revealing a large presence of clergymen's daughters.

6 M. Garden, *Lyon et les lyonnais au XVIIIe siècle* (Paris, 1974), 162.

7 C. Johnston, 'Flashes from domestic life long ago', *Irish News*, 18 October 1961.

8 It should be noted that women in religion represented only a small fraction of the aggregate number of spinsters even in Italian society.

9 On this issue generally: R. Dekker and L. van de Pol, *The Tradition of Female Transvestism in Early Modern Europe* (London, 1989); L. Friedli, '"Passing women". A study of gender boundaries in the eighteenth century' in G. S. Rousseau and R. Porter eds., *Sexual Underworlds of the Enlightenment* (Manchester, 1987), 234–60; T. van der Meer, 'Tribades on trial', *Journal of the History of Sexuality*, 1 (1991), n.3.

10 Dekker and van de Pol, op. cit., 5–19; J. Grand Cartaret, *La femme en culotte* (Paris, 1899); C. J. S. Thompson, *Mysteries of Sex: women who posed as men and men who impersonated women* (London, 1938); F. L. Kersteman, *De Bredasche Heldinne*, ed. R. Dekker, G. J. Johannes and L. van de Pol (Hilversum, 1988).

11 *De delictis et poenis*, cited by J. Brown, *Immodest Acts: the life of a lesbian nun in Renaissance Italy* (New York, 1986), 17–19.

12 Dekker and van de Pol, op. cit., 56–7.

13 B. Erickson, 'A lesbian execution in Germany, 1721', *Journal of Homosexuality*, 6 (1980–1), 27–40.

14 Brown, *Immodest Acts*, is as yet the only full-scale study of such a personage. One partner was said only to consent when she was in a trance and because she thought her ecstasy occasioned by a guardian angel.

15 L. Faderman, *Scotch Verdict* (New York, 1983), 87.

16 A. Lottin, *La désunion du couple sous l'ancien régime: l'example du Nord* (Paris, 1975); R. Houlbrooke, *Church Courts and the People during the English Reformation 1520–1570* (Oxford, 1979); M. Ingram, *Church Courts, Sex and Marriage in England 1570–1640* (Cambridge, 1987); T. Saffley, *Let no man put asunder. The control of marriage in the German southwest: a comparative study* (Kirksville, Mo., 1983).

17 W. Monter, 'The consistory of Geneva, 1559–1569', *Bibliothèque d'humanisme et Renaissance: travaux et documents*, 38 (1976), 467–84.

18 R. K. Marshall, *Virgins and Viragos. A History of Women in Scotland from 1080–1980* (Chicago, 1983), 97.

19 L. Stone, *The Road to Divorce, England 1530–1987* (Oxford, 1990), 231 and *passim*, and *Uncertain Unions and Broken Lives* (Oxford, 1991).

20 Stone, *The Road to Divorce*, 144.

21 G. Zarri, 'Ginevra Gozzadini dall'armi, "gentildonna bolognese" (1520/27–1567)' in O. Niccoli ed., *Rinascimento al femminile* (Rome/Bari, 1991), 133.

22 M. Foucault, 'La vie des hommes infâmes', *Cahiers du chemin*, 29 (January 1977), 12.

23 A. E. Simpson, 'Vulnerability and the age of female consent: legal innovation and its effect on prosecutions for rape in eighteenth century London' in Rousseau and Porter, op. cit., 181–205; J. Sharpe, *Crime in Seventeenth Century England* (Cambridge, 1985), 63–4.

24 E. Bristow, *Vice and Vigilance; purity movements in Britain since 1700* (Dublin, 1977), 60.

25 Sharpe, op. cit., 64.

26 M. Hale, *Pleas of the Crown* (London, 1800), vol. 1, 634.

27 N. Castan, *Les criminels de Languedoc. Les exigeances d'ordre et les voies du ressentiment dans une société prérévolutionnaire* (Toulouse, 1984), 304. A. Mackay has noted the same reluctance in early modern Andalusia.

28 G. Ruggiero, *The Boundaries of Eros. Sex, crime and sexuality in Renaissance Venice* (Oxford, 1985), 89–108.

29 Castan, op. cit., 304.

30 J. E. Walsh, *Rakes and Ruffians. The underworld of Georgian Dublin* (Dublin, 1977 edn), 32–45.

31 The case is related in Walsh, op. cit., 36–40. The girls in question were fourteen and fifteen.

32 Lottin, op. cit., 172.

33 *Ibid.*, 64.

34 Ingram, op. cit., 286.

35 *Ibid.*, 287–91.

36 R. van Dülmen, *Frauen vor Gericht. Kindesmord in der frühen Neuzeit* (Frankfurt/M, 1991); S. Faber, 'Kindermoord in Amsterdam', *Bijdragen en Medelingen betreffende de Geschiedenis der Nederlanden*, 93 (1978), 224–40; R. Malcolmson, 'Infanticide in the eighteenth century' in J. S. Cockburn ed., *Crime in England 1550–1800* (London, 1977); Castan, op. cit., 309.

37 van Dülmen, op. cit., 51–65 would seem to suggest that the second half of the seventeenth century saw higher levels in specific urban courts and that these were sustained until into the third decade of the eighteenth century. The levels remain, however, very low. Sharpe, op. cit., 134–6; J. Beattie, *Crime and the Courts in England 1660–1800* (Oxford, 1986).

38 A.D. Ile et Vilaine, C154 (Rennes, 1721).

39 O. Hufton, *The Poor of Eighteenth Century France* (Oxford, 1974), 321–4.

40 Cited in K. Wrightson, 'Infanticide in early seventeenth century England', *Local Population Studies*, 15 (1975), 10–22.

41 Sharpe, op. cit., 135.

42 Malcolmson, op. cit., 198; all 46 women tried at the Old Bailey were acquitted largely on the grounds that they had made preparations for the child.

43 R. Leboutte, 'L'infanticide dans l'est de la Belgique aux XVIIe–XIXe

siècles: une réalité', *Annales de Démographie Historique* (Paris, 1983), 163–92; and 'Offence against family order: infanticide in Belgium from the fifteenth through the early twentieth centuries', *Journal of the History of Sexuality*, 2 (1992), 159–85.

44 Malcolmson, op. cit., 202–3; Castan, op. cit., 310; Faber, op. cit., 238–40; van Dülmen, op. cit., 823.

45 van Dülmen, op. cit., 84.

46 T. Blaupoin Varlez and M. Bourbon Young, 'Recherches sur la délinquance en Flandres 1714–1750', Microfiche Audir (1971), 1; and A. Lottin, 'Naissances illégitimes et filles-mères à Lille au XVIIIe siècle', *Revue d'histoire moderne et contemporaine*, 17 (1970), 318.

47 Lottin, *La désunion du couple*, 75.

48 *Ibid.*, 78–9.

49 Case cited in A. Farge, *La vie fragile. Violence, pouvoirs et solidarités à Paris au XVIIe siècle* (Paris, 1992), 23–4.

50 L. Ferrante, 'La sexualité en tant que ressource des femmes devant le For archiépiscopal de Bologne', *Déviance et Société*, 2 (1987), 41–66.

51 P. Darmon, *Le tribunal de l'impuissance. Virilité et défaillances conjugales dans l'ancienne France* (Paris, 1979), provides some random examples of such cases; Saffley, op. cit., 135.

52 Lottin, *La désunion du couple*, 139.

53 *Ibid.*, 140.

54 H. de Boniface, *Arrêts notables de la cour du parlement de Provence* (Paris, 1670), 370, cites the case of Suzanne Auquier who described how her elderly husband used his thumbs and lay on top of her for nights on end, causing her pain but never having an erection.

55 Lottin, op. cit., 118.

56 *Ibid.*, 119, 129.

57 *Ibid.*, 118–19.

58 *Ibid.*, 121.

59 *Ibid.* Some of the cases are truly tragic: 'Bernard Dewailly est dans notre village dans un cabaret avec tous les habits de sa femme, sans doute qu'il les mange et qu'il les boit' (Bernard Dewailly is in a tavern in our village with all his wife's clothes, doubtless to eat and drink them) (108).

60 *Ibid.*, 119.

61 *Ibid.*

62 *Ibid.*, 120.

63 *Ibid.*, 128.

64 A. Farge and A. Zysberg, 'Les théâtres de la violence à Paris au XVIIIe siècle', *Annales, Economies, Sociétés et Civilisations*, 34 (1979), 984–1015: and with M. Foucault, *Le désordre des familles. Lettres de cachet des archives de la Bastille* (Paris, 1982).

65 Farge and Foucault, op. cit., 67–75.

66 D. Sabean, *Property, production and family in Neckarhausen 1700–1870* (Cambridge, 1990), ch. 4, Patterns of marital conflict. The pattern is very similar to that in Geneva where prompt action was the order of the day. J. R. Watt, 'Women and the Consistory in Calvin's Geneva', *Sixteenth Century Journal*, 14 (1993), 427–37.

67 Sabean, op. cit., 135–6.

68 Ingram, op. cit., 200–5.

69 K. Bawn, *Social protest, popular disturbances and public order in Dorset 1780–1838* (PhD, Reading, 1984), 100–17.

70 L. Gowring, 'Language, power and the law: women's slander litigation in early modern London' in J. Kermode and G. Walker eds., *Women, Crime and the Courts in Early Modern England* (London, 1994).

71 Stone, *The Road to Divorce*, 247.

72 *Ibid.*, 231–2.

73 J. Casey, 'Household disputes and the law in early modern Andalusia' in J. Bossy ed., *Disputes and Settlements: law and human relations in the West* (Cambridge, 1983), 196.

74 Beattie, op. cit., 97; and N. Castan, 'La criminalité familiale dans le ressort du parlement de Toulouse 1690–1730', *Cahiers des annales* 33 (1971), 136.

75 On the dowry as a cause of dispute, Castan, *Les criminels*, 182–6; Casey, op. cit., 193.

76 Arch. Mun. Castelsarrazin, Registre 1783, supplied by Professor D. Higgs.

77 R. Phillips, *Family Breakdown in late eighteenth century France* (Oxford, 1981); D. Dessertine, *Divorcer à Lyon sous la Révolution et l'Empire* (Lyon, 1991).

78 R. Gough, *The History of Myddle* ed. D. Hay (London, 1981), 124.

79 *Ibid.*, 159.

80 *Ibid.*, 197–8.

81 *Ibid.*, 198.

82 *Ibid.*, 199.

83 *Ibid.*, 201.

84 *Ibid.*, 173.

85 *Ibid.*, 148–50.

8 KEPT MISTRESSES AND COMMON STRUMPETS

1 W. Monter, *Frontiers of Heresy. The Spanish Inquisition from the Basque lands to Sicily* (Cambridge, 1990), 47; J. Contreras, *El Santo Oficio de la Inquisición en Galicia 1560–1700* (Madrid, 1982), 554–80.

2 J. Rossiaud, 'Prostitution, Jeunesse et Société', *Annales, Economies, Sociétés et Civilisations*, 2 (1976), 289–336; L. Otis, *Prostitution in Medieval*

Society. The History of an Urban Institution in Languedoc (Chicago, 1985); R. Trexler, 'La Prostitution florentine au XVe siècle: patronages et clientèles', AESC (1981), 983–1015.

3 Francisco Farfán, Tres libros contra el pecado de la simple fornicación: donde se averigua, que la torpeza entre solteros es pecado mortal, según ley divina, natural y humana; y se responde a los engaños de los que dizen que no es pecado (Three books against the sin of simple fornication: in which it is argued that unchastity between the unmarried is a mortal sin according to divine, natural and human law; and replies to those falsehoods saying that it is not a sin) (Salamanca, 1585), 730; E. Rodríguez Solís, Historia de la prostitución en España y América (Madrid, 1921), ch.1–2; M. Perry, Gender and Disorder in Early Modern Seville (Princeton, 1990), 187.

4 G. Gieger, Die Reichsstadt Ulm vor der Reformation (Ulm, 1971), 173ff.; discussed in L. Roper, The Holy Household. Religion, Morals and Order in Reformation Augsburg (Oxford, 1987), 100, 102.

5 M. González Jiménez, El Concejo de Carmona (Seville, nd), 192–5. The letter is cited in full in fn.30, p. 194. The rules imposed by the Bishop of Winchester are posted on the walls of the Clink Museum in Southwark; B. Schuster, 'Frauenhandel und Frauenhäuser im 15. und 16. Jahrhundert', Vierteljahrschrift für Sozial und Wirtschaftsgeschichte, 78 (1991), 172–89, suggests some municipal brothels were closed before the Reformation perhaps because they were not financially successful; F. Irsigter and A. Lassotta, Bettler und Gaukler. Dirnen und Henker Aussenseiter in einer mittelälterlichen Stadt. Köln 1300–1600 (Cologne, 1984). Here the municipal brothel was closed in 1591 (192–3).

6 B. Pullan, Rich and Poor in Renaissance Venice (Oxford, 1971), 380–94.

7 E. Panofsky, 'Sacred and Profane Love', Studies in Iconology: Humanistic Themes in the Art of the Renaissance (Oxford, 1939).

8 G. Masson, Courtesans of the Italian Renaissance (London, 1975) and L. Lawner, Lives of the Courtesans: Portraits of the Renaissance (New York, 1987) draw a picture of the courtesan which is not endorsed by Franco's poetry: e.g. the courtesans 'were also in a curious way the precursors of modern women: they were independent, by their beauty and wit they earned their living, and they were mistresses of their own fate' (Masson, 168). Franco's verse argues quite the opposite: M. Rosenthal, 'Veronica Franco's Terze Rime: the Venetian Courtesan's Defense', Renaissance Quarterly, Summer 1989; and 'Venetian women writers and their discontents' in J. Grantham Turner ed., Sexuality and Gender in Early Modern Europe (Cambridge, 1993), 114–18 is a crystalline synopsis of Franco's position based on her Lettere famigliari a diversi (Venice, 1580); and A. Zorzi, Cortigiana veneziana: Veronica Franco e i suoi poeti (Milan, 1986). See also A. Barzaghi, Donne o cortigiane? La prostituzione a Venezia (Verona, 1980). C. Santore, 'Inventory of a courtesan's possessions', Renaissance Quarterly, 41 (1988) provides valuable evidence on what a successful woman could acquire in goods.

9 Roper, op. cit., 89–131; I am indebted to L. C. van de Pol for information from her magisterial thesis, *Het Amsterdam Hoerdom. Vrouwen en Prostitutie in een vroegmoderne stedilijke samenleving*. Amsterdam 1650–1750 (Erasmus, Rotterdam). Some of it is summarized in L. van de Pol, 'Prostitutie en de Amsterdamse burgerij' in P. te Boekhorst, P. Burke and W. Frijhoff eds., *Culture en maatschappij in Nederland 1500–1800* (Heerlen, 1992), 179–218; P. Schuster, *Das Frauenhaus. Städtische Bordelle in Deutschland 1350 bis 1600* (Paderborn, 1992), 189–200 lists the closing of the municipal brothels in Protestant cities, but also (200) shows that at Überlingen where they remained open the brothel-keeper had to swear no Lutheran prostitutes would be used.

10 L. Ferrante, 'La Sexualité en tant que ressource des femmes devant le For archiépiscopal de Bologne', *Déviance et Société*, 2 (1987), 41–66; S. Cohen, *The Evolution of Women's Asylums since 1500. From refuges for ex-prostitutes to shelters for battered women* (New York, 1992); B. Pullan, op. cit., 390–4.

11 A. R. Henderson, *Female Prostitution in London 1730–1830* (PhD thesis, London, 1992), 232.

12 Cited Pullan, op. cit., 382. On the German procuress in the same period, L. Roper, 'Mothers of Debauchery: Procuresses in Sixteenth Century Augsburg', *German History*, 6 (1988), 1–19.

13 Luther's sympathy had its limits: *Martin Luther: Selections from his writings*, ed. J. Dillenberger (New York, 1961), 483; L. van de Pol, 'Vrouwencriminaliteit in Amsterdam in de tweede helft van de 17e eeuw', *Tijdschrift voor Criminologie*, 29 (1987), 148–55; Roper, *The Holy Household*, 114–15; L. Roper, 'Discipline and Respectability: Prostitution and Reformation in Augsburg', *History Workshop*, 19 (1985), 3–28; Schuster, op. cit., 172–89 etc. See also note 9 above.

14 Houghton Library, Harvard. *An Enquiry whether a general practise of Virtue tends to the Wealth or Poverty, Benefit or Disadvantage of a People* (anon., 1725), 146. See also T. C. Curtis and W. Speck, 'The Societies for the Reformation of Manners: A Case Study in the Theory and Practise of Moral Reform', *Literature and History*, 3 (1976), 45–64.

15 J. Orne ed., *The Night Walker or Evening Rambles in Search after Lewd Women with the Conferences Held with them* etc. (1696), 16.

16 B. Mandeville, *A Modest Defense of Public Stews* (1724), Augustan Reprint Society, 162 (1973). Mandeville thought a hundred brothels would be sufficient for London's needs.

17 Pullan, op. cit., 380–94.

18 Perry, op. cit., 120.

19 A. Domínguez Ortiz, 'Vida y obras del Padre Pedro de León', *Archivo Hispalense*, ser. 2 (1967), 167. The holy father carried out a ministry to the prostitutes of Seville's brothels.

20 S. Cohen, *The Convertite and the Malmaritate. Women's Institutions*,

Prostitution and the Family in Counter Reformation Florence (University Microfilms, Ann Arbor 1980), 76–126.

21 Pullan, op. cit., 380–94 and C. Black, *Italian Confraternities in the 16th Century* (Cambridge, 1989), *passim*. L. Ferrante, 'L'Onore ritrovato. Donne nella Casa del Soccorso di S. Paolo a Bologna (sec. XVI–XVII)', *Quaderni Storici*, 53 (August 1983), 499–527.

22 Perry, op. cit., 67–141.

23 Ferrante, 'La Sexualité . . .' 41–66 and 'Pro mercede carnale . . . il giusto prezzo rivendicato in tribunale', *Memoria*, 17 (1986) 42–58.

24 Arch. Dépt. Haute Garonne M27 and O. Hufton, *The Poor of Eighteenth Century France* (Oxford, 1974), 308.

25 The statistical basis is extremely slender as only a very small proportion came before the courts. Henderson, op. cit., 59–68.

26 For the plethora of terms in German see Ivan Bloch, *Die Prostitution* (Berlin, 1912), opening chapter.

27 Archives Nationales Y12830, Le Noir to the Commissaires, 16 November 1788.

28 This and the following references to Paris are taken from E. M. Benabou, *La Prostitution et la Police des Moeurs au XVIIIe siècle* (Paris, 1987).

29 Henderson, op. cit., 40–52. A similar breakdown appears in L. van de Pol's analysis, but there are *more* maidservants in the 18th century, a sign of the immiseration at the bottom end of that job.

30 References taken from van de Pol, *Het Amsterdam Hoerdom*.

31 Houghton Library, Harvard University, *The Plan of the Magdalen House for the Reception of Penitent Prostitutes By order of the Governors* (London, 1758), 18; it reflects J. Hanway, *Thoughts on the Plan for a Magdalen House* (1758) and S. Welch, *A Proposal to Render effectual a Plan to remove the nuisance of common prostitutes from the streets of this Metropolis* (1758).

32 L. Roper, 'Discipline and Respectability: Prostitution and the Reformation in Augsburg', *History Workshop*, 19 (1985), 3–28.

33 Pullan, op. cit., 382. P. Larivaille, *La vie quotidienne des courtisanes en Italie au temps de la Renaissance* (Paris, 1975). These women were not courtesans but prostitutes.

34 R. Bassani and F. Bellini, *Caravaggio assassino. La carriera di un 'valenthuomo' fazioso nella Roma della Controriforma* (Rome, 1994), chapters III and IV demonstrates both the upper and lower end of the prostitute range.

35 I am indebted to Professor Angus Mackay of the University of Edinburgh for these references and translations of Delgado, *La Lozana Andaluza* (1528).

9 WOMEN AND THE DEVIL

1 L. Roper, 'Magic and the Theology of the Body: Exorcism in Sixteenth Century Augsburg' in C. Zika ed., *No Gods Except Me. Orthodoxy and Religious Practice in Europe 1200–1600* (Melbourne, 1991), 84–113.

2 *Ibid.*, 90–1. Each religious order would seem to have had a different way of attempting exorcism. L. Febvre, 'Sorcellerie Sottise ou Révolution Mentale', *Annales*, 3 (1948), 405; S. Clark, 'Protestant Demonology: Sin, Superstition and Society (*c.*1520–*c.*1630)' in B. Ankarloo and G. Henningsen ed., *Early Modern European Witchcraft: Centres and Peripheries* (Oxford, 1990); G. Levi, *Inheriting Power: The Story of an Exorcist* (trans. L. Cochrane, London, 1988).

3 J. P. Donnelly, 'Peter Canisius' in J. Raitt ed., *Shapers of Religious Traditions in Germany, Switzerland and Poland, 1560–1600* (New Haven, 1981). Notwithstanding Loyola's scepticism on exorcism, Canisius was highly respected. O. Braunsberger, *Beati Petri Canisii, Societatis Jesu, Epistolae et Acta* (8 vols., Freiburg, 1901) demonstrates the weight of his influence.

4 S. Ferber, 'The Demonic Possession of Marthe Brossier, France 1598–1600' in Zika op. cit., 59–83. The case in Lorraine where both witchery and Protestantism were concerned in C. Pfister, 'Nicolas Rémy et la sorcellerie en Lorraine', *Revue Historique* (1907) gives an excellent idea of the theatrical quality of the spectacle of successive exorcisms.

5 G. Henningsen, *The Witches' Advocate: Basque Witchcraft and the Spanish Inquisition 1609–1614* (Reno, Nev., 1980); C. Holmes, 'Women: Witnesses and Witches', *Past and Present*, 140 (1993), 59 gives a good case of release from her possession of Jane Throckmorton (Leicester, 1616) when the accused witch confessed.

6 The bibliography of the witch persecutions is huge (see pp. 607–8). Many new approaches have been developed and are still emerging, and considerable differences between the north European and Mediterranean patterns have been discerned. Landmarks in examining the witch-as-woman question have been C. Merchant, *The Death of Nature: Women, Ecology and the Scientific Revolution* (New York, 1980) and L. Roper, 'Oedipus and the Devil' in *Oedipus and the Devil, Witchcraft, Sexuality and Religion in Early Modern Europe* (London, 1994).

7 Roper, *Oedipus and the Devil*; R. Muchembled, 'The Witches of Cambrésis' in J. Obelkevich ed., *Religion and the People 800–1700* (London, 1979), 221–76. Micro-history has been at its best when dealing with the witch. See also K. Thomas, *Religion and the Decline of Magic* (London, 1971), 301–32.

8 C. Larner, 'The Age of Faith' in *Witchcraft and Religion: The Politics of Popular Belief* (Oxford, 1984); M. Harris, *Cows, Pigs, Wars and Witches* (London, 1974); M. O'Neil, 'Magical healing, love magic and the Inquisition in late sixteenth century Modena' in S. Haliczer, *Inquisition and Society in Early Modern Europe* (London, 1987), 88–114.

9 Thomas, op. cit., 518–19; A. Macfarlane, *Witchcraft in Tudor and Stuart England* (London, 1970), 67.

10 In Essex, about 85% of those accused between 1560 and 1680 were women (270 cases); in the Nord (France) 82% of 288 cases from mid-14th

to 17th centuries; the same in Germany (Baden-Württemberg) and Basel; in other Swiss cantons about 78%.

11 I am indebted to Dr Richard Williams for this information. On the history of the witch in Normandy, J. Favret-Saada, *Deadly Words: Witchcraft in the Bocage* (Cambridge, 1980).

12 L. C. Hults, 'Baldung and the Witches of Freiburg: The Evidence of Images', *Journal of Interdisciplinary History*, 18, 2 (1987), 249–76.

13 Intellectuals could, of course, read it in Latin, and many of these were churchmen who subsequently wrote treatises in English, e.g. H. Holland, *A Treatise against Witchcraft* (Cambridge, 1590); Hults, 'Baldung and the Witches', 250–2; C. Zika, 'The Devil's Hoodwink: Seeing and Believing in the World of Sixteenth Century Witchcraft' in Zika, op. cit., 153–98. Continental witch trials were frequently translated into many European languages and circulated, e.g. L. Lavater, *Of Ghostes and Spirites* (trans. 1572). In the southern Netherlands the *Disquisitionum Magicarum* (1599) by the Jesuit Martinus Dilrio was influential and based heavily on the *Malleus*.

14 Thomas, op. cit., 525–7.

15 C. Ginzberg, *The Night Battles* (London, 1983) is dedicated to examining how professional witch denouncers could be silenced. Salazar, the defender of witches studied by Henningsen in *The Witches' Advocate*, is committed to a reduction in denunciations. In Britain the juries had to be convinced of an accused person's innocence, and judges could intervene to bring this about when they feared they were convicting on inadequate evidence: *The Most True and Wonderfull Narration of Two Women Bewitched in Yorkshire* (anon., 1658), 4. But as Judge North complained to the Secretary of State in 1682: 'we cannot reprieve them without appearing to deny the very being of witches, which . . . is contrary to law'. Ewen C. Estrange, *Witch Hunting and Witch Trials* (London, 1929), ii, 373.

16 Thomas, op. cit., 633–5; R. Muchembled, *La Sorcière au Village* (Paris, 1979), 187.

17 T. Ady, *A Candle in the Dark: or A Treatise Concerning the Nature of Witches and Witchcraft* (1656), 114.

18 For the Netherlands a general impression based on M. Gijswijt Hofstra and W. Frijhoff eds., *Nederland betoverd: toverij en hekserij de veertiende tot in de twintigste eeuw* (Amsterdam, 1987).

19 R. Scot, *Discoverie of Witchcraft* (1584) has as a major theme opposition to the persecution of harmless old women. He believed that all witches could be placed in one of four categories: the innocent accused out of malice; the deluded who were ignorant and bullied into believing themselves witches but who were totally incapable of harming anyone; the malevolent who used poison not supernatural means to injure; imposters who falsely strove to convince gullible country folk they could heal diseases or find lost goods or manipulate fate. Against the last two categories scriptural condemnation was made. In his lifetime Scot's views were those of a minority.

20 Views on the menstruating woman whose touch causes corn to wither, dough to fail to rise, etc. is also called upon and incorporated into renderings of the witch. P. Shuttle and P. Redgrove, *The Wise Wound* (London, 1978), 221–2. 'When a country wench cannot get her butter to come she says a witch is in her churn', J. Selden, *Table Talk* (nd), 98. Cripples could also be targeted: 'beware of all persons that have default of members naturally, as of foot, hand, eye or other member, one that is crippled': *The Compost of Ptolomeus* (?1600) cited Thomas, op. cit., 677, and 'the old woman with a wrinkled face, a furr'd brow, a hairy lip, a gobbler tooth, a squint eye, a squeaking voice or a scolding tongue': John Gaule, *Select Cases of Conscience touching Witches* (1646), 4–5. 'The bodies of aged persons are impure, which, when they wax cankered in malice, they use their very breath and their sight, being apt for contagion, and by the Devil whetted for such purposes, to the vexation and the destruction of others. For if they which are troubled with the disease of the eyes called *opthalmia* do infect others that look earnestly upon them, is it any marvel that these wicked creatures, having bothe bodies and minds in a higher degree corrupted, should work both these and greater mischiefs.' W. Fulbecke, *A Parallele or Conference of the Civil Law, the Canon Law, and the Common Law* (1618), 97, cited Thomas, op. cit., 553. The fear of a monstrous birth provoked by seeing a cripple can thus be extended. The cripple becomes a deliberate agent of the Devil. The old and ugly are obvious sources of evil. E. Bever, 'Old Age and Witchcraft in Early Modern Europe' in P. Stearns ed., *Old Age in Pre-Industrial Society* (New York, 1982), 150–90. The letters of Philip II (8 November 1595) say that old decrepit women are the commonest witches: R. Muchembled, op. cit., 134–6; J. Bailbé, 'Le Thème de la vieille femme dans la poésie satirique du XVIe et du début du XVIIe siècle', *Bibliothèque d'Humanisme et Renaissance* (1964), 98–119.

21 C. Larner, *Enemies of God* (Oxford, 1983), 99–100. 'Poor Old People, when they are abused by the insulting petulancy of others, being unable to right themselves either at law or at combat, for want of money and strength of body, do oftentimes vent the passion of their discontented soul in threats and curses.' J. Wagstaffe, *The Question of Witchcraft Debated* (1669), 64.

22 H. Roodenburg, 'The Autobiography of Isabella de Moerloose: Sex, childrearing and popular belief in seventeenth century Holland', *Journal of Social History*, 18 (1985), 518–20.

23 Larner, op. cit., 120–5.

24 *Ibid.* and Muchembled, op. cit., 165–6 both insist on the fear of the more affluent in a village of the poor, but that the poor could rally behind each other.

25 Case cited, among others, in Muchembled, op. cit., 85–106.

26 Roper, 'Witchcraft and fantasy in early modern Germany' in *Oedipus and the Devil*, 199–225.

27 Roper, 'Oedipus and the Devil', 226–48.

28 Cases cited by Thomas, op. cit., 633–4.

29 Henningsen, op. cit.

30 On the debates on woman as denouncer, C. Holmes, op. cit. 45–78.
J. Sharpe, 'Women, witchcraft and the legal process', in J. Kermode and
G. Walker eds., *Women, Crime and the Courts in Early Modern England*
(London, 1994), emphasizes the readiness of women to use the courts. The
battle with the accused witch thus became face to face confrontation in the
courts rather than the 'night battles' described by Ginzberg at Friuli between
witches and a force of men elected by the angels to combat them while others
slept.

31 Scot, op. cit., I, 111.

10   OBEDIENT TO THY WILL

1 J. Delumeau, *Catholicism between Luther and Voltaire* (Cambridge, 1977)
and *Sin and Fear. The Emergence of a Western Guilt Culture* (New York, 1990);
L. Châtellier, *The Europe of the Devout: The Catholic Reformation and the
Formation of a New Society* (Cambridge, 1989); F. Le Brun ed., *Histoire des
Catholiques en France du XVe siècle à nos jours* (Toulouse, 1980); L. Scaraffia
and G. Zarri eds., *Donne e fede* (Rome/Bari, 1994) are the contextual framework
of this chapter.

2 G. Zarri, *Le sante vive. Profezie di corte e devozione femminile tra '400 e
'500* (Turin, 1990); and ed., *Finzione e santità tra medioevo ed età moderna* (Turin,
1991). On the influence of Catherine of Siena on this model, see A. Volpato,
'Tra sante profetesse e santi dottori Caterina da Siena' in E. Schulte van
Kessel ed., *Women and Men in Spiritual Culture XIV–XVII Centuries* (The
Hague, 1986), 149–61.

3 J. Bilinkoff, 'A Spanish Prophetess and her patrons: the case of Maria
de Santo Domingo', *Sixteenth Century Journal*, 23 (1992), 21–34; F. Pons,
Misticos, beatas e alumbrados (Valencia, 1991); J. Ameland, 'Monjas y beatas
en la Cataluña Moderna' in J. Ameland and M. Nash, *Historia y genero: las
mujeres en la Europa Moderna y Contemporanea* (Valencia, 1990).

4 D. Higgs, 'Inquisition, Gender and Genealogy in Seventeenth Century
Portugal', *Portuguese Studies Review*, 2 (1993), 17.

5 Zarri, *Finzione e santità*, 67–8.

6 L. Scaraffia, *La Santa degli impossibili: vicende e significati della devozione a
Santa Rita* (Turin, 1990). Her canonization process alludes to her not merely
as the saint of 'suffering' (unspecified) but accredits cures to her. Her cult
grew very considerably after the French occupations of 1805. On trends in
sanctity, see A. Vauchez, *La sainteté en Occident aux derniers siècles du Moyen
Age d'après les procès de canonisation et les documents hagiographiques* (Rome,
1981). C. Leonardi, 'Santità delle donne' in G. Pozzi and C. Leonardi eds.,
Scrittici mistiche italiane (Genoa, 1988), 43–57. G. Barone, M. Caffiero and

F. S. Barcellona, *Modelli di santità e modelli di comportamento* (Turin, 1994).
S. F. Matthews Grieco, 'Modelli di santità femminile nell'Italia del
Rinascimento e della Controriforma', in Scaraffia and Zarri eds., *Donne e fede*,
303–26.

7 An excellent bibliography of specialist articles in English on women
and the Reformation can be found in M. Wiesner, *Women and Gender in Early
Modern Europe* (Cambridge, 1993), 213–17. S. Marshall ed., *Women in
Reformation and Counter-Reformation Europe: Public and Private Worlds*
(Bloomington, 1989); E. Kloek, 'De Reformatie als thema van
vrouwenstudies, Een histories debat over goed en Kwaad', *Jaarboek voor
Vrouwengeschiedenis*, 4 (1983), 106–49. A comprehensive bibliography for
women and religion in Italy is in Scaraffia and Zarri, op. cit., 531–49.

8 On family relations and the convent, G. Zarri, 'Monasteri femminili e
città (secoli XV–XVIII)' in *Storia d'Italia*, *Annali*, 9 (Turin, 1986),
359–429 and 'Le Istituzioni dell'educazione femminile' in *Le sedi della cultura
nell'Emilia Romagna*, vol.5, *I secoli moderni, Le istituzioni e il pensiero* (Milan,
1987), 85–109; G. Greco, 'Monasteri femminili e patriziato a Pisa
1530–1630 "in" Città italiane del '500 tra riforma e controriforma', *Atti del
Convegno Internazionale di Studi di Lucca* (Lucca, 1988), 313–39.

9 On the pre-Tridentine convent as a site for entertainment, C. A. Monson
ed., *The Crannied Wall. Women, Religion and the Arts in Early Modern Europe*
(Ann Arbor, 1992), 3–5 and 'Music in the Nunneries of Bologna in the
Midst of the Counter Reformation', 191–209; J. Bowers, 'The Emergence
of Women Composers in Italy, 1566–1700' in J. Bowers and J. Tick ed.,
Women Making Music (Urbana, 1986), 116–67.

10 Archivio Segreto Vaticano, Sacra Congregazione dei vescove e regolari,
1586. Trans. and cited by Monson, op. cit., 2–3.

11 *Book of Foundations* (1573), cited by A. Weber, 'Saint Teresa,
Demonologist' in A. Cruz and M. Perry ed., *Culture and Control in Counter
Reformation Spain* (Minneapolis, 1992), 180; on Saint Teresa and her context,
J. Bilinkoff, *The Avila of Saint Teresa* (Ithaca, 1989) and A. Weber, *Teresa of
Avila and the Rhetoric of Femininity* (Princeton, 1990).

12 J. L. Sánchez Lora, *Mujeres, conventos y formas de la religiosidad barroca*
(Madrid, 1988), 139–256 on convent reform in Spain.

13 V. Hunecke, 'Kindbett oder Kloster: Lebenswege venezianischer
Patrizierinnen im 17. und 18. Jahrhundert', *Geschichte und Gesellschaft.
Zeitschrift für Historische Sozialwissenschaft*, 18 (1992), 453. On the decline in
numbers of contemplative women in France, O. Hufton and F. Tallett,
'Communities of Women, the Religious Life and Public Service in Eighteenth
Century France' in M. Boxer and J. Quataert eds., *Connecting Spheres. Women
in the Western World 1500 to the Present* (Oxford, 1987).

14 N. Z. Davis, 'Gender and Genre: Women as Historical Writers,
1400–1820' in P. Labalme ed., *Beyond their Sex. Learned Women of the European
Past* (New York, 1980), 153–82.

15 S. Evangelisti, 'Angelica Baitelli, la Storica', in G. Calvi ed., *Barocco al femminile* (Rome/Bari, 1992), 71–95. Baitelli, of course, was not the first nun to write a history of her order and nuns' chronicles go back to the Middle Ages, but her use and checking of source material is totally professional.

16 P. Labalme, 'Women's Roles in Early Modern Venice', in Labalme, op. cit., 149, n.37.

17 F. Medioli, *L "Inferno monacale" di Arcangela Tarabotti* (Turin, 1990), introduction 9–15 and G. C. Odorisio, *Donna e società nel Seicento. Lucrezia Marinelli e Arcangela Tarabotti* (Rome, 1979).

18 P. Caramon, *St Angela* (London, 1963). She was not canonized until 1807: L. Mariani, E. Tarolli and M. Seynaeve, *Angela Merici. Contributo per una biografia* (Milan, 1986). Delumeau, *Le Catholicisme*, 70: M. de Chantal-Gueudre, *Histoire de l'ordre des Ursulines en France* (Paris, 1957–63).

19 Arch. Nat. Lisbon. Inquisition 29 vols. (1640–1802) *Sollicitantes* (Lxa. Liv 745–771); Inquisition Coimbra 34 vols. (1611–1795); Inquisition Evora 22 vols. (1632–1810). I am indebted to David Higgs for this information. Spanish denunciations are less numerous, but cases such as that of Maria Palomino who claimed sexual relationships with a series of confessors over about ten years and those against other *sollicitantes* (48% Friars, 6.3% Dominicans, 3.9% Jesuits) are revealed in S. Haliczer, *Inquisition and Society in the Kingdom of Valencia 1478–1834* (Oxford, 1990), 326–9. The author makes apparent the difficulties of women in proving their cases against the priests, but it may well be that the church was concerned above all to call a halt to their amorous activities rather than actually punish them. The drive to educate the priesthood was more developed in France and Italy than in Iberia.

20 W. Boer, 'Note sull'introduzione del confessionale, sopratutto in Italia', *Quaderni Storici*, 77 (91), 543–72; R. Guarnieri, '"Nec domina nec ancilla, sed socia." Tre casi di direzione spirituale tra Cinque e Seicento' in Schulte van Kessel, op. cit., 111–32 and G. Paolin, 'Confessione e confessori al femminile: monache e direttore spirituali in ambito veneto tra '600 e '700' in Zarri, *Finzione*, 366–411. Delumeau, *Sin and Fear*, ch.17: The Difficulty of Obligatory Confession, 463–79. J. Delumeau ed., *La Première Communion. Quatre Siècles d'Histoire* (Paris, 1987) on the significance of first communion as rite of passage.

21 There is an enormous bibliography on this saint found in M. Tagliabue, 'Francesca Romana nella storiografia', in G. Picasso ed., *Una santa tutta romana: Saggi e ricerche nel VI centenario della nascita dei Ponziani (1384–1984)* (Monte Oliveto Maggiore, 1984), 199–264. The phrase 'civic mother figure' is found in G. Boanas and L. Roper, 'Feminine Piety in Fifteenth Century Rome: Santa Francesca Romana' in J. Obelkevich and L. Roper eds., *Discipline of Faith* (London, 1987), 182; G. Barone, 'La canonizzazione di Francesca Romana: la riproposta di un modello agiografico medievale' in Zarri, *Finzione*, 264–79 maintains that this canonization is a bridge between the

550 THE PROSPECT BEFORE HER

mystical type of sanctity, as she had claimed some prophetic visions, and the therapeutic saint as well as the devout social worker. She is a saint for all seasons.

22 G. Signorotto, 'Gesuiti, carismatici e beate nella Milano del primo Seicento' in Zarri, *Finzione*, 188–9.

23 F. Koorn, 'Elisabeth Strouven, La donna religiosa' in Calvi, *Barocco al femminile*, 127–52. Vaquero, *La mujer fuerte* (1618) as confessor of Maria Vela, a Carmelite, published her biography accentuating her battle with the Devil by prayer and sacrifice and ignoring her descriptions of favours from God which dominate her autobiography. See Bilinkoff, op. cit., 197–8.

24 M. Firpo, 'Paola Antonia Negri, Monaca Angelica 1508–1555' in O. Niccoli ed., *Rinascimento al femminile* (Rome/Bari, 1991), 35–82.

25 G. Zarri, 'Ginevra Gozzodini dall'Armi, gentildonna bolognese (1520/27–1567)' in Niccoli, op. cit., 119–42; H. Rahner, *St Ignatius Loyola: Letters to Women* (London, 1960).

26 M. Rowlands, 'Recusant women 1560–1640' in M. Prior ed., *Women in English Society 1500–1800* (London, 1985), 169–70. The old work by M. C. Chambers, *Life of Mary Ward* (2 vols., 1882–7) still remains important.

27 A. Scattigno, 'Jeanne de Chantal, la fondatrice' in Calvi, *Barocco al femminile*, 153–90. R. Devos, 'La correspondance de Jeanne de Chantal; son intérêt au point de vue de l'histoire sociale des mentalités', *Actes du Congrès des Sociétés Savantes de la province de Savoie* (Chambéry, 1972). J. Delumeau, *Sin and Fear*, 292. E. Rapley, *The Dévotes. Women and the Church in Seventeenth Century France* (Montreal, 1990) is an excellent study tracing the developments in France.

28 E. Rapley explains this by the private nature of the vows. O. Hufton and M. MacCurtain feel something should be attributed to the fact that they were annually renewable.

29 The phrase is that of Claude Langlois, *Le catholicisme au féminin: les congrégations françaises à supérieure générale au XIXe siècle* (Paris, 1984); J. Calvet, *Saint Vincent de Paul* (Paris, 1949), *Louise de Marillac par elle-même* (Paris, 1958), O. Hufton and F. Tallett, 'Communities of Women, the Religious Life and Public Service in Eighteenth Century France' in Boxer and Quataert, op. cit., 77; Rapley, op. cit., *passim*.

30 Archives Nationales S6160 to 6180 (*Fondations*).

31 A history of most of the congregations remains to be written. See Rapley, op. cit., 235–7. P. Coste, *Les Filles de Charité: L'Institut de 1617 à 1800* (Paris, 1913); C. Jones, 'The Daughters of Charity in the Hôtel Dieu Saint Eloi in Montpellier before the French Revolution' and 'The Daughters of Charity in Hospitals from Louis XIII to Louis Philippe' in *The Charitable Imperative. Hospitals and Nursing in Ancien Régime and Revolutionary France* (London, 1989), 122–62; F. Groult, *Une Congrégation salésienne: Les soeurs de Saint Joseph du Puy en Velay* (Le Puy, 1930); A. Le Moigne Kipffel, *Les Filles*

de Sagesse (Paris, 1947); A. Portefaix, *Les Religieuses de la Miséricorde de Billom 1786–1867* (Clermont-Ferrand, 1967); M. Vacher, *'Des régulières' dans le siècle: les soeurs de Saint Joseph du Père Médaille aux XVII et XVIII siècles* (Clermont-Ferrand, 1991). M. C. Dinet-Lecomte, 'Implantation et Rayonnement des Congrégations Hospitalières dans le Sud de la France aux XVIIe et XVIIIe siècles', *Annales du Midi*, 104 (1992), 19–42 also gives an excellent bibliography.

32 O. Hufton, *Women and the Limits of Citizenship in the French Revolution* (Toronto, 1992), 146–8; Langlois, op. cit.; Y. Turin, *Femmes et Religieuses au XIXe siècle* (Paris, 1989); H. M. Mills, *Women and Catholicism in Provincial France c.1800–c.1850, Franche Comté in National Context* (D.Phil., Oxford, 1994).

33 Hufton and Tallett, 'Communities of Women', 83.

34 O. Hufton, *The Poor of Eighteenth Century France* (Oxford, 1973), 139–59; C. Jones, *Charity and 'Bienfaisance': The Treatment of the Poor in the Montpellier Region, 1740–1815* (Cambridge, 1982).

35 C. Jones, *The Charitable Imperative*, 48–86.

36 O. Hufton, *Bayeux in the Late 18th Century* (Oxford, 1967), 97.

37 O. Hufton, *The Poor*, 156–8.

38 These are the complaints in the *cahiers* of 1789.

39 O. Hufton, *Women and the Limits*, 146–7.

40 R. Sarti, 'Obediente e fedele. Note sull'istruzione morale e religiosa di servi e serve tra Cinque e Settecento', *Annali dell'Istituto Storico Italogermanico in Trento*, xvii (1991), 113–15 and 'Zita, serva e santa. Un modello da imitare?' in Barone, Caffiero and Barcellona, op. cit., 307–59.

41 Cited in Le Brun, op. cit., 174–5.

42 P. McNulty remembers her grandmother, an Irish immigrant in Salford, did this in the 1940s and certainly it still occurred in Ireland in the 1950s.

43 A. Pardeilhé Galabrun, *Rétables baroques de Bretagne et spiritualité du XVIIe siècle. Etude Sémiologique et Religieuse* (Paris, 1972); Michèle Nemard, *Mille Rétables dans l'ancien diocèse du Mans. Essai sur les mentalités religieuses des XVIIe et XVIIIe siècles* (Paris, 1977) broach these issues. Luisa Accati, 'Simboli maschile e simboli femminile nella devozione alla Madonna della controriforma: appunti per una discussione' in Schulte van Kessel, op. cit., 35–43. S. F. Matthews Grieco, 'Modelli di santità'.

44 This role as transmission agent is recognized and developed in J. Delumeau, *La Religion de ma mère* (Paris, 1992) and J. N. Vuarnet, *Le Dieu des femmes* (Paris, 1989).

45 M. Vovelle, *Piété baroque et déchristianisation en Provence au XVIIIe siècle* (Paris, 1973) and J. Quéniart, *Les Hommes, L'Eglise et Dieu dans la France du XVIIIe siècle* (Paris, 1978), 282–306.

46 'Denkwürdigkeiten der Caritas Pirkheimer (aus den Jahren 1524–1528)' in J. Pfanner ed., *Caritas Pirkheimer, Quellensammlung*, 2

(Landshut, 1962), 79–84. For a very evocative commentary on the diaspora, see L. Roper, 'Was there a crisis in Gender Relations in Sixteenth Century Germany?' in M. Hagenmaier and S. Holtz, *Crisis in Early Modern Europe* (Berlin/New York, 1992).

47 H. Wunder, *'Er ist die Sonn', sie ist der Mond'. Frauen in der frühen Neuzeit* (Munich, 1992), 236–7 and supporting bibliography. M. Kobelt-Groch, 'Von "armen frouwen" und "bosen wibern". Frauen im Bauernkrieg zwischen Anpassung und Auflehnung', *Archiv für Reformationsgeschichte*, 79 (1988), 103–37.

48 E. Theissing, *Over Klopjes en Kwezels* (Utrecht/Nijmegen, 1935) and E. Schulte van Kessel, 'Virgins and Mothers between Heaven and Earth' in G. Duby and M. Perrot eds., *A History of Women in the West* (Cambridge, Mass., 1993), vol.3, 162–3.

49 Roper, *The Holy Household*, 211.

50 R. Rex, *Henry VIII and the English Reformation* (London, 1993), 83 includes a number of examples. See also E. Duffy, *The Stripping of the Altars. Traditional religion in England, 1400–1580* (London, 1992), particularly 11–52, 155–206.

51 Rex, op. cit., 18–19.

52 Duffy, op. cit., 524–64.

53 It would seem that Henry VIII secured for Ann Boleyn an eaglestone to be worn on the right wrist. This may have been an attempt to replace the religious girdle with something else with magical qualities. Sir Thomas Browne in 1688 asked 'whether the aetates or eaglestone hath that eminent property to promote delivery or abortion respectively, applied to lower or upward parts of the body', *Enquiries into Vulgar and Common Errors* (1688), 115.

54 A. Roget, *Histoire du peuple de Genève depuis la Réforme jusqu'à l'Escalade* (Geneva, 1873), ii, 24ff. and J. Watt, 'Women and the Consistory in Calvin's Geneva', *Sixteenth Century Journal*, 24 (1993), 433ff.

55 C. Goff, *A Woman of the Tudor Age* (London, 1930), 118–90, 219–24. S. J. Gunn, *Charles Brandon, Duke of Suffolk, c.1485–1545* (Oxford, 1988), 198. She waited until her husband died to take sides openly.

56 A. G. Dickens, *The English Reformation* (Glasgow, 1964), 375.

57 M. Rowlands, 'Recusant Women 1560–1640', in Prior, op. cit., 157–8.

58 *Ibid*, 158–9 and J. C. H. Aveling, 'Catholic Households in Yorkshire 1580–1603', *Northern History*, xvi (1980).

59 For the wider Catholic context, J. Bossy, *English Catholic Community 1570–1850* (London, 1975) and J. C. H. Aveling, *The Handle and the Axe* (London, 1976).

60 *Foxe's Book of Martyrs*, ed. abridged G. A. Williamson (London, 1956), 278, 322, 328–9, 335, 363, 365, 369. 'Opportunities' for martyrdom are explored in C. Levin, 'Women in the *Book of Martyrs* as models of behaviour

in Tudor England', *International Journal of Women's Studies*, 4 (1981), 196–207; E. Macek, 'The Emergence of a feminine spirituality in the *Book of Martyrs*', *Sixteenth Century Journal*, 19 (1988), 62–80.

61 P. Collinson, 'The People and the Pope's Attire', *The Elizabethan Puritan Movement* (London, 1967), 92–3.

62 L. Roper, 'Sexual utopianism in the German Reformation' in *Oedipus and the Devil*, 79–106.

63 There is a huge bibliography on Anabaptism. J. Klassen, 'Women and the Family among Dutch Anabaptist Martyrs', *Mennonite Quarterly Review*, 60 (1986), 548–71 gives an introduction; and see W. Harrison, 'The role of women in Anabaptist thought and practice: the Hutterite experience of the sixteenth and seventeenth centuries', *Sixteenth Century Journal*, 23 (1992), 49–70.

64 See Wunder, op. cit., 237–9.

65 Ludwig Rabus, *Historien der heyligen Ausserwolten Gottes Zeugen, Bekennern und Martyrem* (1557).

66 P. Russell, *Lay Theology in the Reformation: Popular Pamphleteers in Southwest Germany 1521–1525* (Cambridge, 1986), 203.

67 N. Roelker, 'The appeal of Calvinism to French noblewomen in the sixteenth century', *Journal of Interdisciplinary History*, 2 (1972), 391–418.

68 N. Z. Davis, 'City women and religious change', in *Society and Culture in Early Modern France* (Stanford, 1975), 65–96.

69 P. Collinson, 'The role of Women in the English Reformation illustrated by the life and friendships of Anne Locke' in *Godly People, Essays on English Protestantism and Puritanism* (London, 1983), 273–88.

70 R. V. Schnucker, 'Calvin's Letters to Women. The Courting of Ladies in High Places', *Sixteenth Century Journal*, 13 (1972), 71.

71 P. Collinson, 'A Mirror of Elizabethan Puritanism; the Life and Letters of "Godly Master Dering"' in *Godly People*, 317–18 gives more details of his relationships – very like those of a father confessor but conducted by letter – with some distinguished women.

72 Cited by S. H. Mendelson, 'Stuart Women's Diaries and occasional memories' in Prior, op. cit., 192–3.

73 K. Thomas, 'Women and the Civil War Sects', *Past and Present*, 13 (1958) reprinted in *Crisis in Europe 1560–1660* (London, 1965), 321–3; E. Morgan Williams, 'Women Preachers in the Civil War', *Journal of Modern History*, 1 (1929), 561–9.

74 Thomas, op. cit., 324 and S. Marshall, 'Women and religious choices in the sixteenth century Netherlands', *Archives for Reformation History*, 75 (1984), 276–89.

75 *Women and Literature of the Seventeenth Century*. An annotated bibliography based on Wing's Short Catalogue compiled by Hilda L. Smith and Susan Cardinale (Westport, Conn., 1990), see part II, Works for and about women, 125–301.

76 C. Cross, '"He Goats Before the Flocks". A note on the part played by women in the founding of some Civil War Churches', in G. J. Cuming and D. Baker eds., *Popular Belief and Practice: Studies in Church History*, viii (Cambridge, 1972), 195–202.

77 *Ibid.*, and K. Chidley, *The Justification of the Independent Churches of Christ* (London, 1641).

78 P. Higgins, 'The Reactions of Women, with special reference to women petitioners' in B. Manning ed., *Politics, Religion and the English Civil War* (London, 1973), 179–224; D. Ludlow, 'Shaking patriarchy's foundations: sectarian women in England, 1641–1700' in R. Greaves, *Triumph over Silence, Women in Protestant History* (Westport, Conn., 1985), 93–123.

79 M. R. Brailsford, *Quaker Women* (London, 1915); M. Fell, *Women's speaking justified* (London, 1667); A. Lloyd, *Quaker Social History* (London, 1950), 107–19.

80 E. Manners, *Elizabeth Hooton, First Quaker Woman Preacher (1600–1672)* (London, 1914).

81 Brailsford, op. cit., *passim*; and P. Mack, 'Teaching about gender and spirituality in early English Quakerism', *Women's Studies*, 19 (1991), 223–38.

82 A. Armstrong, *The Church of England, the Methodists and Society 1700–1850* (London, 1973).

83 L. Romier, *Le Royaume de Catherine de Medici; la France à la veille des Guerres de Religion* (reprint Geneva, 1978), 234–40. 'Plus on étudie les commencements de la Réforme dans les provinces, plus l'action féminine y apparaît considérable . . . C'était le plus souvent par les femmes, mères et épouses, que la Réforme gagnait les familles de l'aristocratie et du peuple.' N. Z. Davis, 'City Women and Religious Change' in *Society and Culture in Early Modern France* (Stanford, 1965), 65–96.

84 J. Irwin, 'Anna Maria van Schurman: From Feminism to Pietism', *Church History*, 46 (1977), 48–62; Mirjiam de Baar, 'De Betrokkenheid van vrouwen bij het huisgezin van Jean de Labadie 1669–1732', *Jaarboek voor Vrouwengeschiedenis* (1987), 11–43.

85 M. Jaeger, *Before Victoria: changing standards and behaviour, 1787–1837* (London, 1956), 37.

11   CORRESPONDING GENTLEWOMEN, SHAMELESS SCRIBBLERS

1 R. Chartier, 'Les Pratiques de l'écrit' in P. Ariès and G. Duby eds., *Histoire de la Vie Privée* (Paris, 1987), vol. III, 130–1 summarizes the knowledge of growth in the possession of books.

2 R. M. San Juan, 'The Court Lady's Dilemma. Isabella d'Este and Art Collecting in the Renaissance', *Oxford Art Journal*, 14 (1991).

3 This book was obviously not a commercial venture but it may have

been a great talking-point in court circles. On the use of standard myths by Christine de Pisan so as to bring out alternative messages, see M. Warner, *Managing Monsters: Six Myths of Our Time* (London, 1994), ch.1.

4 C. Jordan, *Renaissance Feminism. Literary Texts and Political Models* (Ithaca, 1990), 1–64 is an excellent account of the ways in which this writing can be accounted feminist and also of the terms of the debate. I. Maclean, *Woman Triumphant: Feminism in French Literature 1610–52* (Oxford, 1977) remains the most thorough and sophisticated analysis of the French debate.

5 Jordan, op. cit., 267–8.

6 R. Dekker, 'Dat mijn lieven kinderen weten zouden. Egodocumenten in Nederland van de Zestiende tot de Negentiende Eeuw', *Opossum*, 8 (1993), 5–22 traces developments in the use of diaries by women.

7 J. Brewer, 'Authors, publishers and the fabrication of literary culture' in J. Raven, N. Tadmore and H. Small eds., *The Practice and Representation of Reading in Britain: Essays in History and Literature* (Cambridge, 1995). On the growth of the woman writer and the diversification of her interests at the end of the Stuart period: S. H. Mendelson, *The Mental World of Stuart Women* (Brighton, 1987), opening chapter.

8 R. A. Houston, *Literacy in Early Modern Europe* (London, 1988), particularly 134–7; D. Cressy, *Literacy and the Social Order* (Cambridge, 1980); J. P. Anglin, 'The expansion of literacy: opportunities for the study of the three Rs in the London diocese of Elizabeth I', *Guildhall Studies in London History* (London, 1980), 3, 63–74; F. Furet and M. Ozouf, *Reading and Writing. Literacy in France from Calvin to Jules Ferry* (Cambridge, 1982); R. Chartier, D. Julia and M. Compère, *Education en France du XVIe au XVIIIe siècles* (Paris, 1976); E. François, *Alphabetisierung in Deutschland und Frankreich im Zeitalter der französischen Revolution* (Frankfurt, 1989); F. Lopez, 'Lisants et lecteurs en Espagne au XIIIe siècle' in *Livre et lecture en Espagne et en France sous l'ancien régime*, Colloque de la Casa de Velázquez (Paris, 1981), 146.

9 Supplying employers' Christmas gifts and good-conduct prizes for charity schools may have been the way the writer and printer made a profit, but the reader of works like these, published copiously in the eighteenth century, had to be the servant herself.

10 *Porque de romera a ramera hay poquissima distancia* (From pilgrim to prostitute there is but little distance), Alonso de Andrade, *Treatise on the Virgin*, (1642) quoted and commented on by J. C. Baroja, *Las formas complejas de la vida religiosa: religión, sociedad y carácter en la España de los siglos XVI y XVII* (Madrid, 1978), 190.

11 The correspondence of perhaps the most significant letter-writer of the seventeenth century, Madame de Sévigné, was allegedly read by all the French court. Letter-writing was admired as an art and model letters intended for copying or for reflection embodying appropriate modes of address made their appearance in the seventeenth century.

12 P. Crawford, 'Women's published writings 1600–1700' in M. Prior ed., *Women in English Society 1500–1800* (London, 1985), 211–82 includes an important checklist.

13 J. Todd, *A Dictionary of British and American Writers 1660–1800* (Totowa, NJ, 1981), 43–4; Maureen Duffy, *The Passionate Shepherdess: Aphra Behn, 1640–1689* (London, 1977); R. Gilder, 'Aphra Behn. England's First Professional Woman Playwright' in *Enter the Actress. The First Women in Theatre* (Boston, 1931), 173–201; N. Cotton, *Women Playwrights in England (1363–1750)* (Louisburg, Nova Scotia, 1980); Mendelson, op. cit.

14 G. D. Hertze, *Jewish High Society in Old Regime Berlin* (New Haven, 1988), 10–21; J. Georgelin, *Venise au siècle des lumières* (Paris/La Haye, 1978); M-C. Hoock-Demarle, *La Femme au temps de Goethe* (Paris, 1987).

15 E. Magne, *Voiture et l'Hôtel de Rambouillet: les origines, 1597–1600* (Paris, 1929); I. Maclean, *Women Triumphant. Feminism in French Literature 1610–1652* (Oxford, 1978), excellent bibliography. C. Delong, 'From conversation to creation', in Duby and Perrot eds., *A History of Women in the West*, III, 395–419.

16 R. Lathvillière, *La Préciosité, étude historique et linguistique* (Paris, 1966); C. C. Lougee, *Le Paradis des Femmes. Women, Salons and Social Stratification in Seventeenth Century France* (Princeton, 1976); M. Magende, *La Politesse mondaine et les théories de l'honnêteté en France au XVIIe siècle, de 1600–1660* (Paris, 1925); P. Ariès and G. Duby eds., *Histoire de la Vie Privée*, vol.III, particularly chapter by J. Revel, 'Les Usages de la Civilité', 165–209.

17 D. Goodman, 'Filial Rebellion in the Salon. Madame Géoffrin and her daughter', *French Historical Studies* (1989) and 'Public Sphere and Private Life: towards a synthesis of current approaches to Old Régime France', *History and Theory*, 6 (1992); above all, her 'Enlightenment Salons: The Convergence of Female and Philosophic Ambitions', *Eighteenth Century Studies* (1989), 332–60.

18 A. Morellet, *Eloges de Madame Géoffrin, contemporaine de Madame du Deffand* (Paris, 1812), v–vi.

19 Cited by Delong, 'From conversation to creation', 418.

20 F. Steegmuller, *A Woman, a Man, and Two Kingdoms: The Story of Madame d'Epinay and the Abbé Galiani* (New York, 1992); *Ferdinando Galiani, Louise d'Epinay Correspondence*, ed. G. Dulac and D. Maggetti, vol.I, 1769–70 (Paris, 1992); R. P. Weinreb, *Eagle in a Gauze Cage: Louise d'Epinay, femme de lettres* (New York, 1992). B. Craveri, *Madame du Deffand and her World* (London, 1994). The responses and sheer malice of the *philosophes* towards the hostess are manifest in this volume, as well as the latter's commitment to form.

21 Diderot, 'Sur les femmes' and 'Supplément au voyage de Bougainville', *Oeuvres Complètes* (Paris, 1875–7), vol.2. His views on women are examined critically in R. Niklaus, 'Diderot and Women and Eva Jacobs', 'Diderot and

the Education of Girls' in Jacobs *et al.* ed., *Women and Society in Eighteenth Century France* (London, 1979); A. M. Wilson, 'Treated like imbecile children' in P. Fritz and R. Morton eds., *Women in the Eighteenth Century* (Toronto, 1976); Adriana Sfargo, 'La Représentation de la femme chez Diderot', *Studies on Voltaire and the Eighteenth Century*, 193 (1980), 1893–9.

22 The most comprehensive remains P. Hoffmann, *La femme dans la pensée des lumières* (Paris, 1977); and see J. Rendall, *The Origins of Modern Feminism: Women in Britain, France and the United States 1780–1860* (London, 1985), 7–32.

23 S. Schama, *The Embarrassment of Riches. An Interpretation of Dutch Culture in the Golden Age* (London, 1987), 408–9.

24 The best condensed commentary with suggestions for further research on the bluestockings is found in Todd, op. cit., 10–11 and also S. H. Myers, *The Blue-Stocking Circle: Women, Friendship and the Life of the Mind in Eighteenth Century England* (Oxford, 1990); E. G. Bodeck, 'Salonnière and Blue Stockings: Educated Obsolescence and Germinating Feminism', *Feminist Studies*, 3 (1976), 185–99 contrasts the approaches to women's creative writing of the two groups.

25 A. M. van Schurman, *The Learned Maid* (London, 1659), 15.

26 Cited Todd, op. cit., 230; A. Haynes, 'The First Great Lady: Margaret, Duchess of Newcastle', *History Today*, 26 (November 1976) and the older H. T. E. Perry, *The First Duchess of Newcastle and Her Husband as Figures in Literary History* (1918, repr. New York, 1968); Mendelson, op. cit., uses the duchess along with Behn and the Countess of Warwick to represent the range of Englishwomen's writing in the late 17th century.

27 Cited Todd, op. cit., 231.

28 M. Cavendish, *Philosophical and Physical Opinions* (1655), Letter 'To the Two Most Famous Universities of England'.

29 Cited Todd, op. cit., 231. He for his part wrote for the epitaph on her tomb in Westminster Abbey: 'a wise, witty and learned lady, which her many books do well testify; she was with her lord all the time of his banishment and miseries, and when he came home never parted from him in his solitary retirements.' In 1676 he published a collection of letters and poems written in praise of the duchess.

30 On corresponding gentlewomen, R. Perry, 'Radical Doubt and the Liberation of Women', *Eighteenth Century Studies* (1985), 276–7 and M. Reynolds, *The Learned Lady in England 1650–1760* (1920, repr. Gloucester, Mass., 1964). Van Schurman corresponded with British learned ladies.

31 B. Hill ed. and introduction, *The First English Feminist. Reflections on Marriage and Other Writings by Mary Astell* (New York, 1986); R. Perry, *The Celebrated Mary Astell. An Early English Feminist* (Chicago, 1986) and S. F. Matthews Grieco, 'Mary Astell, L'educatrice femminista' in Calvi ed., *Barocco al femminile* (Rome/Bari, 1992), 219–62; J. K. Kinnaird, 'Mary Astell and the Conservative Contribution to English Feminism', *Journal of*

British Studies, 19 (1979); H. Smith, *Reason's Disciplines. Seventeenth Century English Feminists* (Chicago, 1982).

32 M. Astell, *Some Reflections on Marriage Occasion'd by the Duke and Duchess of Mazarine's Case; which is also Consider'd* (1700); followed by *Reflections on Marriage The Third Edition to Which is Added a Preface in Answer to some Objections* (1706).

33 *The Gentleman's Magazine* needs further exploration as a stepping-stone for the woman writer and a way of being heard (even if she never set foot out of Lichfield); J. Hunter, 'The 18th century Englishwoman according to the *Gentleman's Magazine*' in Fritz and Morton, op. cit., 73–88 makes some use of the source.

34 The small biographies given by R. Lonsdale, *Eighteenth Century Women Poets* (Oxford, 1989) are excellent and allow an appreciation of how the female poet constructed a livelihood and established a reputation. The importance of the subscriber, to include groups of women subscribers, leaps out. (See, e.g., 254, 256, 392, 413, 482 etc.)

35 R. Parker, *The Subversive Stitch. Embroidery and the Making of the Feminine* (London, 1984), 114 gives a fuller version of this extract and takes the view that Addison is deriding the needlewoman.

36 Addison, *Spectator*, Saturday 23rd June 1711.

37 A. Aldburgham, *Women in Print. Writing Women and Women's Magazines from the Restoration to the Accession of Victoria* (London, 1972) and K. Rogers, *Feminism in Eighteenth Century England* (Urbana, 1982); J. Hodges, 'The Female Spectator, a courtesy Periodical' in R. P. Bond ed., *Studies in the Early English Periodical* (Chapel Hill, 1957), 151–82; J. E. Hunter, 'The Ladies Magazine and the History of the Eighteenth Century Englishwoman' in D. H. Bond and W. Reynolds McLeod ed., *Newsletters to Newspapers: Eighteenth Century Journalism* (Morganstown, Va., 1977), 103–17.

38 J. Raven, *British Fiction 1750–1770. A chronological check-list of Prose Fiction printed in Britain and Ireland* (London, 1987), 18–19 gives the necessary figures: Eliza Haywood, Charlotte Lennox and Frances Brooke were the most popular women novelists of these years.

39 Lonsdale's biographies in *Women Poets* note the matrimonial problems of the woman author tersely but graphically, also Todd, op cit.; Rogers, op. cit., Appendix with mini-biographies, also allows some breakdown of types to be made.

40 Todd, op. cit., 157–60; Raven, op. cit., 17; J. Spencer, *The Rise of the Woman Novelist* (Oxford, 1986), 147–55; the fullest treatment remains G. F. Whicher, *The Life and Romances of Mrs Eliza Haywood* (New York, 1915).

41 I. Watt, 'The New Woman: Samuel Richardson's *Pamela*' in R. L. Coser ed., *The Family: Its Structure and Functions* (New York, 1964), 267–89; K. M. Rogers, 'Sensitive Feminism vs Conventional Sympathy: Richardson

and Fielding on Women', *Novel*, 9 (1976), 256–70; S. Staves, 'British Seduced Maidens', *Eighteenth Century Studies*, 14 (1980–1), 109–34.

42 Spencer, op. cit., 95–8; Todd, op. cit., 64–7, where Katherine Rogers writes: 'Too often she turned from the vivid rendition of life's surface and the humorous social satire she did so well to shallow conventional moralising or pathos and passion based on nothing deeper than theatrical rhetoric.'

43 Defective education is also to blame for the woman's predicament. 'Difficulties' was the common Burney euphemism for the female predicament of insufficient money, schooling and social status. S. Staves, 'Evelina or Female Difficulties', *Modern Philology*, 73 (1976), 368–81; K. Straub, *Fanny Burney and Feminine Strategy* (Lexington, 1987).

44 Lonsdale, op. cit., 219–21.

45 H. More, *The Search after Happiness* (1773), a pastoral drama for young ladies; Todd, op. cit., 224–7; C. M. Yonge, *Hannah More* (London, 1888) testifies to the persistence of her high reputation.

46 M. Wollstonecraft, *A Vindication of the Rights of Woman* (1792) has gone into at least twelve editions: the most recent, B. Taylor ed. (London, 1992), has a very perceptive introduction; C. Tomalin, *The Life and Death of Mary Wollstonecraft* (London, 1974) is perhaps the most objective of the biographies, and see J. Todd, *Mary Wollstonecraft: an annotated Bibliography* (New York, 1976). The reception of *The Vindication*, if initially 'respectful' (Tomalin, 108–9), was mixed, and there were many satires e.g. *The Rights of Boys and Girls* (anon).

47 B. Hill, *The Republican Virago. The Life and Times of Catherine Macaulay* (Oxford, 1992). Macaulay's *Letters on Education with observations on religious subjects* (1790) had a huge influence on Wollstonecraft. B. Taylor, 'Mary Wollstonecraft and the wild wish of early feminism', *History Workshop*, 33 (1992), 197–220 puts her ideas in context.

48 R. Dekker, 'Dat mijn lieven kinderen . . .', 5 looks at the problems facing those seeking to go into print in early modern Holland. M-C. Hoock-Demarle, 'Reading and writing in Germany' in Duby and Perrot, op. cit., IV, 145–61.

49 J. M. Goulemot, 'Les Pratiques littéraires ou la publicité du privé', in Ariès and Duby, op. cit., III, 391–2.

50 M-C. Hoock-Demarle, *La Rage d'écrire. Les femmes allemandes face à la Révolution française (1790–1815)* (Aix en Provence, 1990); *Les femmes de la Révolution Française. A Bibliography compiled by S. Blanc* (Paris, 1989), 14–30.

51 L. Pizzocaro, *Le revista femminile a Firenze, Venezia, Milano* (Thesis, Milan, 1981–2); Berengo, *Giornali veneziani del settecento*, 571–9; Georgelin, op. cit., and E. Ravoux-Rallo, *La femme à Venise au temps de Casanove* (Paris, 1984); L. Guerci, *La sposa obbediente. Donna e matrimonio nella discussione d'Italia del Settecento* (Turin, 1988), 231–5.

52 Statistics summarized in M-C. Hoock-Demarle, 'Reading and writing in Germany', 147–8.

53 Therese Forster Huber, *Memoires* (1803), cited *Allgemeine deutsche Biographie*, entry Huber.

54 N. Gelbart, *Feminine and Opposition Journalism in Old Régime France: le Journal des Dames* (Berkeley, 1987).

55 N. Gelbart, 'The *Journal des Dames* and its Female Editors: Politics, Censorship and Feminism in the Old Régime Press' in J. R. Censor and J. D. Popkin eds., *Press and Politics in Pre-Revolutionary France* (Berkeley, 1987).

56 J. W. Scott, *French Feminists claim the Rights of Man: Olympe de Gouges in the French Revolution* (St Louis, 1991) and 'French feminists and the Rights of "Man", Olympe de Gouges' declarations', *History Workshop*, 28 (1989).

12   THE WOMAN RIOTER OR THE RIOTOUS WOMAN?

1 E. P. Thompson, 'The Moral Economy of the English Crowd in the Eighteenth Century', *Past and Present*, 50 (1972), 115 and G. Rudé, *The Crowd in the French Revolution* (Oxford, 1959) were probably the most influential of these works in that they opened up the field.

2 N. Z. Davis, *Society and Culture in Early Modern France* (London, 1975), especially 'Women on Top'; S. Desan, 'Crowds, Community and Ritual in the Work of E. P. Thompson and Natalie Davis', in L. Hunt ed., *The New Cultural History* (London, 1989), 47–71.

3 On their roles in this conflict, see M. Kobelt-Groch, *Aufsässige Töchter Gottes. Frauen im Bauernkrieg und in den Tauferbewegungen* (Frankfurt, 1993).

4 S. Schama, *The Embarrassment of Riches. An Interpretation of Dutch Culture in the Golden Age* (London, 1987), 88. The heroine leader was a matron, Kenau Hasselaer.

5 P. Burke, 'The Virgin of the Carmine and the revolt of the Masaniello', *Past and Present* (1983), 3–21.

6 Y. Berce, *Révoltes et Révolutions dans l'Europe moderne, XVIe–XVIIIe siècles* (Paris, 1980).

7 D. Underdown, *Revel, Riot and Rebellion. Popular Politics and Culture in England, 1603–1660* (Oxford, 1985), 211.

8 G. Rudé, *London and Paris in the Eighteenth Century* (London, 1979) compares and contrasts the crowds and rioters of the capitals.

9 R. Dekker, *Holland in beroering: oproeren in de 17de den 18de eeuw* (Baarn, 1982), 8–11.

10 *Ibid.*, 57.

11 These remarks and others of like purport are cited in Thompson, op. cit., 116.

12 W. Lambarde, *Eirnacha or the Office of Justice of the Peace in foure books*

(London, 1619), 180; M. Dalton, *The Country Justice, containing the practise of the Justices of the peace out of their sessions* (London, 1662), 205.

13 J. Walter, 'Grain riots and popular attitudes to the law' in J. Brewer and J. Styles eds., *An Ungovernable People. The English and their law in the 17th and 18th centuries* (London, 1980), 47–84.

14 W. Blackstone, *Commentaries on the laws of England* (1771), Book IV, Of Public Wrongs.

15 Cited in J. Bohstedt, 'Gender, Household and Community Politics: Women in English Riots 1790–1810', *Past and Present*, 120 (1988), 104.

16 Y. Castan, *Honnêteté et relations sociales en Languedoc aux 17e et 18e siècles* (Paris, 1974), 477 notes that it was regarded as dishonourable to pursue a poor woman at justice for stealing bread.

17 R. Dekker, 'Women in Revolt. Collective protest and its social base in Holland', *Theory and Society*, 16 (1987), 337–62 and 'Revolutionaire en contrarevolutionaire vrouwen in Nederland, 1780–1800', *Tijdschrift voor Geschiedenis*, 102 (1989), 545–63; W. P. te Brake, R. Dekker, L. van de Pol, 'Women and Political Culture in the Dutch Revolutions' in H. Applewhite and D. Levy eds., *Women and Politics in the Age of the Democratic Revolution* (Ann Arbor, 1990), 109–47.

18 R. Houlbrooke, 'Women's social life and common action in England from the fifteenth century to the eve of the Civil War', *Continuity and Change*, 1 (1986), 171–89.

19 C. Lucas, 'The Crowd in the French Revolution Revisited', *Journal of Modern History*, 61 (1988), 421–57.

20 J. Flammermont ed., *La Journée du 14 juillet 1789: fragment de mémoires inédits de L. G. Pitra* (Paris, 1892), 13, 22.

21 I. Cameron, *Crime and its Repression in the Auvergne and the Guyenne* (Cambridge, 1984).

22 On the Queen Caroline affair, see L. Colley, *Britons. Forging the Nation 1707–1837* (Yale, 1992), 265.

23 Case taken from Archives Départementales Dordogne, B.648.

24 Dekker, *Holland in beroering*, 56; *Nederlandse jaarboeken*, 1763, 376.

25 O. Hufton, *Women and the Limits of Citizenship in the French Revolution* (Toronto, 1992), 15.

26 Dekker, *Holland in beroering*, 55.

27 M. Thomis and J. Grimmett, *Women in Protest 1800–1850* (London, 1982), 65–80.

28 The full range of protest is pursued in Hufton, op. cit., particularly ch.2 and 3; and for Paris, D. Godineau, *Citoyennes Tricoteuses: Les Femmes du Peuple à Paris pendant la Révolution française* (Aix, 1988).

29 D. Leclerq, *Les Journées d'Octobre* (Paris, 1924); A. Mathiez, 'Etude critique des journées des 5 et 6 octobre 1789', *Revue historique*, 19, 241–81 and 'Les Femmes de la Révolution', *Annales Revolutionnaires* (1908), 203–5.

Most accounts of these events lean on the *Procédure criminelle instructe au Châtelet de Paris sur la dénonciation des faits arrivés à Versailles dans la journée du Octobre 1789* (Paris, 1790), which was an attempt by the Constituent Assembly to placate Louis XVI.

30 Godineau, op. cit., 319–42 and R. C. Cobb and G. Rudé, 'Le Dernier Mouvement Populaire de la Révolution française. Les Journées de germinal et prairial l'an III', *Revue Historique*, 214 (1955), 250–81.

31 The cry was *du pain et la constitution*. For the working-class population bread and politics were indistinguishable, because only with responsible government would the people be fed.

32 Archives Nationales F7 4582.

33 4 Prairial an III legislation followed, threatening groups of more than five women with arrest.

34 H. Applewhite and D. Levy, *Women and Politics in the Age of the Democratic Revolution* (Michigan, 1990) and A. Rosa, *Citoyennes: Les femmes et la Révolution Française* (Paris, 1988).

35 Condorcet, *Essai, sur la constitution et des fonctions des Assemblées Provinciales* (1788) in *Oeuvres de Condorcet* (Paris, 1847), vol.8. On this work in context, see J. Rendall, *The Origins of Modern Feminism: Women in Britain, France and the United States, 1780–1860* (London, 1985).

36 O. Hufton, 'Women in Revolution', *Past and Present* (1971), 90–5; M. de Villiers, *Histoire des Clubs des Femmes et des Légions d'Amazones, 1793, 1848, 1871* (Paris, 1910); E. Roudinesco, *Théroigne de Méricourt: Une femme mélancolique sous la Révolution* (Paris, 1989); J. Vega, 'Feminist republican, Etta Palm-Aelders on justice, virtue and men', *History of European Ideas*, 10 (1989), 333–53 and 'Etta Palm, *Une Hollandaise à Paris*' in W. Frijhoff and R. Dekker eds., *Le Voyage Révolutionnaire* (Hilversum, 1991), 49–59.

37 M. Cerati, *Le Club des Citoyennes Républicaines Révolutionnaire* (Paris, 1966), 86–8; Hufton, *Women and the Limits of Citizenship*, 32–4.

38 R. B. Rose, *The Enragés: Socialists of the French Revolution* (Melbourne, 1966) and *Women and the French Revolution: The Political Activity of Parisian Women 1789–1794*, University of Tasmania Occasional Papers 5 (1976), 10.

39 J. P. Amar in the Convention, session of 9 brumaire year 2, *Moniteur Universel*, xviii, 1/11/1793, E. Badinter, *Qu'est-ce que c'est d'une femme* (Paris, 1989). Rose, op. cit., 63, and A. Soboul, 'Une épisode des luttes populaires en septembre 1793; la guerre des cocardes', *Annales Historiques de la Révolution Française* (1961), 52–5.

40 Cerati, op. cit., discusses numbers.

41 Godineau, op. cit., 337–40.

42 Hufton, *Women and the Limits of Citizenship*, 92–142 and 'The Reconstruction of a Church 1796–1801' in G. Lewis and C. Lucas eds., *Beyond the Terror* (Cambridge, 1981), 21–53. S. Desan, *Reclaiming the Sacred: Lay Religion and Popular Politics in Revolutionary France* (Ithaca, 1991).

43 Cited by Hufton, *Women and the Limits of Citizenship*, 98–9 and M. Vovelle, *La Révolution contre l'Eglise* (Paris, 1989), 221–6.

44 Archives Départementales Rhône 42L61. Saint Germain de Laval.

45 M. de Roux, *Histoire de la Révolution à Poitiers et dans la Vienne* (Lyon, 1952), 251 and G. Lefebvre, *Les Paysans du Nord* (Bari, 1959), 874.

46 Hufton, 'The Reconstruction of a Church', 38–44.

47 The republican Portal spelt out this view in Archives Départementales Haute Loire L371. J. Michelet reiterates the theme in *The Women of the French Revolution* (English trans., Philadelphia, 1855) and T. Zeldin demonstrates its persistence in 'The Conflict of Moralities, Confession, Sin and Pleasure in the 19th Century', in *Conflicts in French Society: Anticlericalism, Education and Morals in the Nineteenth Century* (London, 1970).

48 M. Marion, *Le Brigandage pendant la Révolution* (Paris, 1934), opening chapter.

13   THE MOVING FINGER?

1 F. Braudel, *Civilisation and Capitalism: 15th–18th centuries* (London, 1981), vol. 1 is based on the *longue durée*; T. Hareven, *Family Time and Industrial Time* (Cambridge, 1982) and *Transitions: The Family and Life Course in Historical Perspective* (New York, 1978) raise possibilities for a more complex consideration of women and their life experience and trajectories within an imposed time frame.

2 Although litigation between guilds and women who trespass on guild restrictions is a vital source for women's history in early modern towns (see above, Chapter 6; L. Roper, *The Holy Household. Religion, Morals and Order in Reformation Augsburg* [Oxford, 1989], 40–9; M. Wiesner, *Working Women in Reformation Germany* [New Brunswick, 1986], 155–7), a long-term view is needed to integrate demographic factors and industrial performance (boom and slump) into the picture. This does not eliminate the notion of guild 'control' over women's practices, but it makes comparison between easier and difficult times possible and recognizes the guild structure as geographically confined.

3 Maxine Hong Kingston tells this as an old Chinese story, but it also has resonances in the European folk-tale tradition. Hence Polly Oliver or the literary tradition cited above (Chapter 7) of women temporarily filling men's roles to cope with particular exigencies.

4 Both Victor Hugo and Marc Bloch posited generational influence in this respect (grandparents over children) and more particularly in the election of Bonaparte in 1849 to quell the wild men of Paris. French history (of men) has gone further in the generational approach than any other; e.g. A. B. Spitzer, *The Generation of 1820* (Princeton, 1987), although dedicated to political formation, raises some issues which women's historiography could well adopt.

5 O. Hufton, *Bayeux in the Late Eighteenth Century* (Oxford, 1967), 224–5 and *Women and the Limits of Citizenship in the French Revolution* (Toronto, 1992), *passim*; R. C. Cobb, *Terreur et Substances, 1793–1795* (Paris, 1964). The experience of Paris differed because between late 1793 and 1794 prices were fixed. Hopes were dashed when a return to a more *laissez-faire* economy occurred.

6 An introduction insisting on the preservation of the family memory as the reason for writing memoirs is found in most noblewomen's writings of the 19th century. I am indebted to Professor David Higgs for confirming my impression.

7 C. Langlois, *Le Catholicisme au féminin: les congrégations françaises à supérieure générale au XIXe siècle* (Paris, 1984). In spite of the monumental nature of this book, many of these congregations, their funding and forms, merit individual study.

8 L. Colley, *Britons. Forging the Nation 1707–1837* (Yale, 1992), 250–4.

9 *Ibid.*, 250–1, argues that political action was transforming the roles of some upper-class women. Implicitly the work raises the issue of what did these mothers hand on to the next generation? A. Vickery, 'Golden Age to Separate Spheres? A Review of the Categories and Chronology of English Women's History', *Historical Journal* (1993), makes a commonsense plea for not assuming increased bondage for 19th-century women but to review the evidence of ego documents (memoirs, journals, etc.). Generational history is only possible by reference to such sources.

10 C. Sarasúa García of the EUI drew my attention to these efforts and to the plight of the farmer's wife abandoned on the holding who was now the only family support.

11 The good times of one set of women could be the hard times of another. J. Rendall, *Women in an Industrialising Society: England 1750–1880* (London, 1990), ch.1–2 and M. Berg, *The Age of Manufactures, 1779–1820* (London, 1985), ch.6. On continental slump and its impact on women and children, M. Bouloiseau, 'Aspects sociaux de la crise cotonnière dans les campagnes rouennaises en 1788–9', *Actes du 81e Congrès des Sociétés savantes, Caen-Rouen* (1956), 403–8.

12 S. Woolf and J. M. Delgado, *La Economia Española al final del Antiguo Regimen* (Madrid, 1982), III, 99–169. The Napoleonic wars and trade embargoes made the situation worse.

13 We can arrive at these conclusions by simply using such urban listings and censuses as exist, but census-taking only began in the late eighteenth century and invariably under-recorded the role of married women in the labour market. Useful works: P. Earle, 'The female labour market in London in the late seventeenth and early eighteenth centuries', *Economic History Review*, 10, 2 (1989), 328–52; C. Middleton, 'Women's labour and the transition to pre-industrial capitalism' in L. Charles and L. Duffin eds., *Women and Work in pre-industrial England* (London, 1985), 181–206; J. B.

Bennett, 'History that stands still: women's work in the European past',
Feminist Studies, 14, 2 (1988); V. Stolcke, 'Las mujeres y el trabajo',
Materiales, 12 (1978), 45–68. S. Woolf ed., *Domestic Strategies: work and
family in France and Italy, 1600–1800* (Cambridge, 1991); P. M. Klep
ed., *Vrouwen in het Verleden, 17e–20e euw. Economie, politiek, volkshuisvesting,
cultuur en bibliografie* (Amsterdam, 1987). Lotte van de Pol's work on the
Confessieboek of Amsterdam demonstrates that over the eighteenth century
many small industries declined in the city and more women went into maid
service.

14 T. Nashe, 'Pierce Penniless His Supplication to the Devil' in *The Works
of Thomas Nashe*, ed. R. B. Mckerrow (4 vols., Oxford, 1958), I, 215.

15 A. Fraser, 'The Actress as Honey-Pot' in *The Weaker Vessel* (London,
1984) and J. Pearson, 'Women in the Theater, 1660–1737' in *The
Prostituted Muse: Images of Women and Women Dramatists, 1642–1737* (New
York, 1988), 25–41; C. Tomalin, *Mrs Jordan's Profession: the story of a great
actress and a future king* (London, 1994); on the Parisian demi-monde, E.
Benabou, *La Prostitution et la police des moeurs au XVIIIe siècle* (Paris, 1988),
34–5.

16 *Lord Hervey and his Friends, 1726–38*, ed. *Earl of Silchester (London,
1950), 18–19.*

17 G. Greer, *The Obstacle Race* (London, 1979); R. Parker and G. Pollock,
Old Mistresses: Women, Art and Ideology (London, 1981); L. Nochlin and A.
Sutherland Harris, *Women Artists, 1500–1950* (New York, 1976), which
has an excellent bibliography and mini-biographies; W. Chadwick, *Women,
Art and Society* (London, 1989); E. Tufts, *Our Hidden Heritage: Five Centuries
of Women Artists* (New York, 1974) are stimulating overviews based on studies
existing at the time but perhaps now being modified or developed by new
document-based work. I. S. Perlingieri, *Sofonisba Anguissola* (New York,
1992); M. Garrard, *Artemisia Gentileschi: The Image of the Female Hero in
Baroque Art* (Princeton, 1989); C. P. Murphy, 'Lavinia Fontana: the making
of a woman artist' in E. Kloek *et al.* eds., *Women of the Golden Age* (Hilversum,
1994).

18 E. Vigée-Lebrun, *Mémoires* (3 vols., Paris, 1835–7).

19 L. Guerci, *La sposa obbediente. Donna e matrimonio nella discussione d'Italia
del settecento* (Turin, 1988) is one of the few studies which attempts to depict
continuities as well as developments in eighteenth-century prescriptive
literature. F. Childs, *Prescriptions for manners in English courtesy literature and
their social implications 1690–1760* (PhD thesis, Oxford, 1984) suggests a
change in tone from gloom to idealism in 1700, but points out the
oscillations between the angel and Eve in the past. An excellent short-term
study, M. Legates, 'The cult of womanhood in eighteenth century thought',
Eighteenth Century Studies, 1 (1976), 21–39 dwells on continuities but insists
on an intensification of domestic rhetoric.

20 These three works appear in most European languages and in Catholic

societies continue to run into multiple editions. Vives also had weight in England, but was later outstripped by Puritan literature aiming at a broader social spectrum and hence disappears.

21 Guerci, op. cit., 17–58. The Jesuits, virtually from their inception, targeted women.

22 More's success is astounding: her work usually ran into multiple editions, however lukewarm her critics. A serious study of More and her context remains to be done. She cannot be written off as a mere conservative because in decrying accomplishments and pleading for the nurturing of understanding she is quite radical.

23 Women's writing such as that of Dorothy Leigh (see Chapter 5, n.33) may have led to some of the softening in specific national contexts. P. Crawford, 'The Construction and Experience of Maternity in Seventeenth Century England' in V. Fildes ed., *Women as Mothers in Pre-Industrial England: Essays in memory of Dorothy MacLaren* (London, 1990), 3–38; the enjoyment of the child in Dutch iconography reflects but also spreads a sense of caring motherhood: Schama, op. cit., 531–43. Some bibliographical suggestions for Italy, Guerci, op. cit., 162; Rousseau's romanticism and the cult of Republican motherhood are obviously important and given visual expression in women's painting as evinced by Vigée-Lebrun and still more by Marguerite Gérard.

24 E. Roudinesco, *Théroigne de Méricourt: Une femme mélancolique sous la Révolution* (Paris, 1989), concluding chapter. S. Schama, *Citizens* (London, 1989) concludes the volume with the 'abnormality' of this revolutionary victim.

25 L. Hunt, *The Family Romance of the French Revolution* (London, 1992), 96–7.

26 The legal position of the Frenchwoman in the nineteenth century is, if anything, 'improved' in comparison with customary and Roman law codes of the old regime; however, the effects of parity of treatment vis à vis sentencing policy need to be examined more closely. Infanticide would appear to have been almost a non-crime for women in 19th-century France.

27 Vickery, 'Golden Age to Separate Spheres'; N. Tadmore, 'Household reading and eighteenth century novels' in J. Raven, N. Tadmore and H. Small eds., *The practise and representation of reading in Britain: essays in history and literature* (Cambridge, 1995). In Italy there were entire series of introductory works to serious subjects to help women further or merely to give them some basic information, e.g. F. Algarotti, *Newtonismo per le dame* (Venice, 1737) and *La filosofia per le dame* (3 vols., Venice, 1777); G. Compagnoni, *Chimica per le dame* (Venice, 1792).

28 J. Brewer, 'Anna Larpent: representing the reader', in Raven, Tadmore and Small, op. cit. Anna Larpent's multi-volume diary is in the Huntington Library HM 31201.

BIBLIOGRAPHICAL ESSAY

———◄○►———

The bibliography in a work of this kind cannot lay claim to being exhaustive or even to give more than an approximation of the works consulted. The field is a growth area and new monographs appear on the shelves every week or so in every major European language. The principles adopted in what follows reflect a two-fold intent: first to help the readers to find out more about issues which are their concern and second to point to sources which were particularly valuable in writing this book. The volume of work done by English-speaking scholars about England outstrips in quantity that done on other areas because the field has been developed more rapidly in England and the US than elsewhere. It was, however, never the intent to make this work a series of national histories but one of comparisons and contrasts, so that while the bulk of the bibliography is in English, and where an English work exists on a non-English topic it is usually cited, works in the major European languages also appear for those who would like to find out more and be conscious of trends in European thinking.

THE SOCIO-ECONOMIC BACKGROUND

F. Braudel, *Civilisation and Capitalism* (3 vols., London, 1981)

P. Ariès and G. Duby, *A History of Private Life*, trans. A. Goldhammer (5 vols., Cambridge, Mass., 1987–91)

J. de Vries, *The Economy of Europe in an Age of Crisis, 1600–1750* (London, 1963)

B. H. Slicher van Bath, *The Agrarian History of Western Europe, AD 500–1850* (London, 1963)

Among national socio-economic histories

K. Wrightson, *English Society 1580–1680* (London, 1982)

R. W. Malcolmson, *Life and Labour in England, 1700–1800* (London, 1981)

A. J. Sharpe, *Early Modern England: A Social History* (London, 1988)

R. Porter, *English Society in the Eighteenth Century* (London, 1982)

J. Thirsk ed., *The Agrarian History of England and Wales, 1500–1750* (Cambridge, 1990)

G. Duby and A. Wallon eds., *Histoire de la France Rurale*, vol.2, under the direction of E. Le Roy Ladurie, *L'âge classique*, 1340–1789 (Paris, 1973)

A. Th. van Deursen, *Plain Lives in a Golden Age. Popular Culture, Religion and Society in Seventeenth Century Holland* (Cambridge, 1991)

S. Schama, *The Embarrassment of Riches. An Interpretation of Dutch Culture in the Golden Age* (New York/London, 1988)

R. van Dülmen ed., *Armut, Liebe, Ehre* (Frankfurt/M, 1988)

R. van Dülmen ed., *Arbeit, Frömmigkeit und Eigensinn* (Frankfurt/M, 1990)

D. W. Sabean, *Property, Production and Family in Neckarhausen 1700–1870* (Cambridge, 1990)

A. Dominguez Ortiz, *The Golden Age of Spain, 1516–1659* (London, 1971)

On the growth of towns and cities

J. de Vries, *European Urbanisation, 1500–1800* (London, 1984)

P. Corfield, *The Impact of English Towns 1700–1800* (Oxford, 1982)

G. Duby ed., *Histoire de la France Urbaine* (Paris, 1980–85)

R. Porter, *A Social History of London* (London, 1994)

D. George, *London Life in the Eighteenth Century* (London, 1925)

D. Garrioch, *Neighbourhood and Community in Paris 1740–90* (Cambridge, 1986)

M. Garden, *Lyon et les Lyonnais au XVIIIe siècle* (Paris, 1974)

On the precariousness of human life

A. Appleby, *Famine in Tudor and Stuart England* (Liverpool, 1978)

R. B. Outhwaite, 'Dearth and government intervention in English grain markets, 1590–1700', *Economic History Review*, 2nd series, 34 (1981)

J. Henderson and R. Wall eds., *Poor Women and Children in the European Past* (London, 1994)

O. Hufton, *The Poor of Eighteenth Century France* (Oxford, 1974)

P. Goubert, *Beauvais et le Beauvaisis* (Paris, 1962)

On growing consumption

M. Douglas and B. Sherwood, *The World of Goods: Towards an Anthropology of Consumption* (London, 1978)

J. Brewer and R. Porter, *Consumption and the World of Goods: Consumption and Society in the Eighteenth Century* (London, 1993) Contains a considerable range of essays and bibliographical information.

D. Roche, *The People of Paris: An Essay in Popular Culture in the Eighteenth Century*, trans. Marie Evans (London/New York, 1987)

D. Roche, *The Culture of Clothing: Dress and Fashion in the Ancien Regime* (Cambridge, 1994)

A. Pardailhé Galabrun, *The Birth of Intimacy: Private and Domestic Life in Early Modern Paris* (Oxford, 1991)

On cultural change

G. Vigarello, *Concepts of Cleanliness: Changing Attitudes in France since the Middle Ages* (Cambridge, 1988)

N. Elias, *The Civilising Process* (New York edn, 1978)

R. Muchembled, *L'Invention de l'Homme Moderne. Sensibilités, moeurs et comportements collectifs sous l'ancien régime* (Paris, 1988)

J. Delumeau, *Sin and Fear: The Emergence of a Western Guilt Culture 13th–18th Centuries*, trans. E. Nicholson (New York, 1990)

R. Chartier, *The Cultural Uses of Print*, trans. L. Cochrane (Princeton, 1987)

GENERAL HISTORIES OF WOMEN

G. Duby and M. Perrot eds., *A History of Women* (Cambridge, Mass., 1992), vol.3, N. Z. Davis and A. Farge eds., *Renaissance and Enlightenment Paradoxes*, a collection of largely Francocentric essays. The Dutch and Spanish editions have excellent bibliographical essays on these countries.

B. S. Anderson and J. P. Zinsser, *A History of Their Own. Women in Europe from Prehistory to the Present* (2 vols., New York, 1988), is a miracle of compression but covers the early modern period rather scantily.

M. E. Wiesner, *Women and Gender in Early Modern Europe* (Cambridge, 1993)

R. Bridenthal, C. Koonz and S. Stuard eds., *Becoming Visible. Women In European History* (2nd edn, Boston, 1987). A pioneer work, but the updating did not do justice to works in languages other than English.

H. Wunder, *'Er ist die Sonn', sie ist der Mond'. Frauen in der frühen Neuzeit* (Munich, 1992). An interesting interpretation embodying recent work on Germany and north-western Europe but not the Mediterranean. It has a very extensive bibliography especially on works in German and is a starting point for the history of German women.

BIBLIOGRAPHIES AND BIBLIOGRAPHICAL COMMENTARIES

L. and M. Frey and J. Schneider, *Women in Western European History. A Select Chronological, Geographical and Topical Bibliography from Antiquity to the French Revolution* (London, 1982, supplement 1986)

M. E. Wiesner, *Women in the Sixteenth Century: A Bibliography* (St Louis, 1983)

H. L. Smith and S. Cardinale, *Women and the Literature of the Seventeenth Century. An annotated bibliography based on Wing's short title catalogue* (Westport, Conn., 1990)

B. Kanner ed., *The Women of England from Anglo-Saxon times to the present* (Hamden, Conn., 1979)

AMONG NATIONAL SPECIALIST STUDIES

S. D. Amussen, *An Ordered Society: Gender and Class in Early Modern England* (Oxford, 1988)

M. George ed., *Women in the First Capitalist Society: Experiences in Seventeenth Century England* (Urbana, 1988)

A. Lawrence, *Women in England 1500–1760* (London, 1994)

M. Prior ed., *Women in English Society 1500–1800* (London, 1985)

D. Stenton, *The English Woman in History* (London, 1957)

R. Thompson, *Women in Stuart England and America: A Comparative Study* (London, 1974)

R. K. Marshall, *Virgins and Viragos. A History of Women in Scotland from 1080–1980* (Chicago, 1983)

M. O'Dowd and M. MacCurtain eds., *Women in Early Modern Ireland* (Edinburgh, 1991)

E. Barriot-Salvadore, *Les Femmes dans la Société Française de la Renaissance* (Geneva, 1990)

N. Z. Davis, *Society and Culture in Early Modern France* (Stanford, Conn., 1975)

M. King, *Women of the Renaissance* (Chicago, 1981)

C. Klapisch Zuber, *Women, Family and Ritual in Renaissance Italy*, trans. L. Cochrane (Chicago, 1985)

E. Ravoux-Rallo, *La femme à Venise au temps de Casanove* (Paris, 1984)

A. Kuhn *et al.*, *Frauen in der Geschichte* (5 vols., Dusseldorf, 1982–5)

L. Roper, *The Holy Household. Religion, Morals and Order in Reformation Augsburg* (Oxford, 1989)

M. Wiesner, *Working Women in Renaissance Germany* (New Brunswick, 1986)

M. Perry, *Gender and Disorder in Early Modern Seville* (Princeton, 1990)

MICROHISTORIES

O. Niccoli ed., *Rinascimento al femminile* (Rome/Bari, 1992); G. Calvi ed., *Barocco al femminile* (Rome/Bari, 1992). Two excellent collections of short biographies designed to show the experience of different kinds of women.

N. Z. Davis, *The Return of Martin Guerre* (Cambridge, Mass., 1983)

WOMEN AND CHANGE

Economic Change

A. Clark, *The Working Life of Women in the Seventeenth Century* (London, 1919; new edn 1982 by Jane Lewis and M. Chaytor and 1992 by L. A. Erickson). Both later editions have thoughtful prefaces modifying this influential volume.

J. Rendall, *Women in an Industrialising Society: England 1750–1860* (London, 1990)

M. Berg, *The Age of Manufactures, 1799–1820* (London, 1985)

R. Houston and K. Snell, 'Proto industrialization, cottage industry, social change and the industrial revolution', *Historical Journal*, 27, 2 (1984)

P. Hudson, 'Proto-industrialization: the case of the West Riding', *History Workshop Journal*, 12 (1981)

P. Kriedte, H. Medick and J. Schlumbohm, *Industrialization before Industrialization* (Cambridge, 1977)

Debates on the chronology and nature of change, feminism and gender

J. Bennett, 'Feminism and history', *Gender and History* (1989)

J. Bennett, 'Medieval women, modern women: across the great divide' in D. Aers ed., *Culture and History 1350–1600. Essays on English Communities, Identities and Writing* (London, 1992)

J. Bennett, 'Women's history: a study in continuity and change', *Women's History Review*, 2 (1993)

B. Hill, 'Women's history: a study in change, continuity or standing still?', *Women's History Review*, 2 (1993)

J. W. Scott, *Gender and the Politics of History* (New York, 1988). A very stimulating collection which remains perhaps the focal point of discussion.

M. Perrot ed., *Writing Women's History* (Oxford, 1992), which in its French title asked the question 'Is it possible to write women's history?' includes a set of essays raising some thought-provoking questions about the purpose, intent and limitations of women's history.

L. Stone, 'Only women', *New York Review of Books*, 11 April 1985. Sets down ten commandments for the writing of women's history relating to continuity and change and basic assumptions which need respect.

M. Palazzi and A. Scattigno eds., *Discutendo di storia* (Turin, 1991). Shows a differing sensitivity among Italian women historians as to continuity and changes in their history.

G. Pommata, 'Storia particulare e storia universale: in margine ad alcuni manuali di storia delle donne', *Quaderni storici*, 74 (1990)

A. Vickery, 'From golden age to separate spheres. A review of the categories and chronology of English women's history', *Historical Journal* 36 (1993)

The interest generated in women and gender history has led to the creation of a number of journals: *Signs, Gender and History, Pénélope, Memorie, Jaarboek voor Vrouwengeschiedenis*.

Journals dedicated to economic, social and family history have also included articles at the cutting edge of historical scholarship. Among them: *History Workshop Journal, Economic History Review, Social History, Continuity and Change, Journal of Interdisciplinary History, Journal of Family History, Annales de Démographie Historique, Annales, Economies, Sociétés et Civilisations, Quaderni Storici*, as well as some local and regional periodicals such as *Local Population Studies* or the *Annales du Midi*.

CONSTRUCTING WOMAN

Approaches, ideas, discourses

I. Maclean, *The Renaissance Notion of Woman: A Study in the Fortunes of Scholasticism and Medical Science in European Intellectual Life* (Cambridge, 1980)

S. F. Matthews Grieco, *Ange ou Diablesse: la Représentation de la Femme au XVIe siècle* (Paris, 1991)

P. Bange, G. Dresen and J. M. Noel eds., *Saints and She Devils: Images of Women in the Fifteenth and Sixteenth Centuries* (Eng. trans., London, 1987)

J. O'Faolain and L. Martínez, *Not in God's Image* (London, 1973). An early compilation of documents which remains a classic.

M. Ferguson, M. Quilligan and N. Vickers eds., *Rewriting the Renaissance: The Discourses of Sexual Difference in Early Modern Europe* (Chicago, 1986)

V. Bullough, *The Subordinate Sex: A History of Attitudes towards Women* (Urbana, 1973)

The influence of scripture and religious belief

K. E. Börresen ed., *Images of God and Gender Models in the Judaeo Christian Tradition* (Oslo, 1990)

E. Pagels, *Adam, Eve and the Serpent* (New York, 1988)

R. Ruether and E. McLaughlin eds., *Women of Spirit: Female Leadership in the Jewish and Christian Traditions* (New York, 1979)

M. Warner, *Alone of All her Sex. The Myth and the Cult of the Virgin Mary* (London, 1976)

S. Haskins, *Mary Magdalen: Myth and Metaphor* (London, 1993)

The catalogue of the important exhibition on the Magdalen held in Florence in 1986, *La Maddalena tra sacro e profano*, M. Mosco ed. (Florence/Milan, 1986) and the essays accompanying the pictures remain valuable.

On differing Protestant and Catholic approaches to the Magdalen:

C. Harbison, 'Lucas van Leyden, the Magdalen and the problem of secularisation in early sixteenth century art', *Oud Holland*, 98 (1984)

F. Bardon, 'Le thème de la Madeleine pénitente au XVIIe siècle en France', *Journal of the Warburg and Courtauld Institutes*, 31 (1968)

Good conduct literature

There is no substitute for consulting some of the original texts such as:

L. B. Alberti, *The Family in Renaissance Florence*, trans. R. N. Watkins (Columbia, S.C., 1969)

F. de Sales, *Introduction to the Devout Life* (countless editions)

Becon, *Werkes*, Parker Society (1844)

Commentaries

J. K. Yost, 'Changing attitudes towards married life in civic and Christian humanists', *American Society for Reformation Research*, Occasional Papers, 1 (1977)

M. Todd, *Christian Humanism and the Puritan Social Order* (Cambridge, 1987)

J. Dempsey Douglass, *Women, Freedom and Calvin* (Philadelphia, 1985)

K. M. Davies, 'Continuity and change in literary advice on marriage,' R. B. Outhwaite ed., *Marriage and Society: Studies in the Social History of Marriage* (London, 1981)

C. Levin, 'Advice on women's behaviour in three Tudor homilies', *International Journal of Women's Studies*, 6 (1983)

K. M. Davies, 'The sacred condition of equality: how original were Puritan doctrines of marriage?', *Social History*, 5 (1977)

E. Novi Chavarria, 'Ideologia e comportamenti familiari nei predicatori italiani tra Cinque e Settecento: tematiche e modelli', *Rivista Storica Italiana*, C, 3 (1988)

F. Daenens, 'Superiore perché inferiore: il paradosso della superiorità della donna in alcuni trattati italiani del Cinquecento' in V. Gentili ed., *Trasgressione tragica e norma domestica: esemplari di tipologie femminili dalla letteratura europea* (Rome, 1983)

G. Conti Odorisio, *Donna e società nel Seicento: Lucrezia Marinelli e Arcangela Tarabotti* (Rome, 1979)

L. Guerci, *La sposa obbediente: donne e matrimonio nella discussione dell' Italia del Settecento* (Turin, 1986)

F. Watson, *Vives and the Renaissance Education of Women* (London, 1912)

M. P. Fleischer, '"Are Women Human?" The debate of 1595 between Valens Acidalius and Simon Gediccus', *Sixteenth Century Journal*, 12 (1981)

J. M. Noel, 'Education morale des filles et des garçons dans les Pays Bas au 16e siècle: deux manuels pedagogiques', in E. Schulte van Kessel ed.,

Women and Men in Spiritual Culture, XIV–XVII Centuries. A meeting of South and North (The Hague, 1986)

S. Ozment, *When Fathers Ruled: Family Life in Reformation Europe* (Cambridge, 1985) is largely constructed on predicative literature.

The female body

P. Ariès and A. Bejin eds., *Western Sexuality: Practice and Precept in Past and Present*, trans. A. Forster (Oxford, 1985)

M. Foucault, *The History of Sexuality*, trans. R. Hurley (New York, 1985)

T. Laqueur, *Making Sex: Body and Gender from the Greeks to Freud* (London, 1990)

M. C. Horowitz, 'Aristotle and women', *Journal of the History of Biology* 9 (1979)

L. Scheibinger, *The Mind has no Sex? Women in the Origins of Modern Science* (Cambridge, 1989)

L. Scheibinger, 'Skeletons in the closet: the first illustrations of the female skeleton in eighteenth century anatomy', in C. Gallagher and T. Laqueur eds., *The Making of the Modern Body* (Berkeley, 1987)

I. Veith, *Hysteria, the History of a Disease* (Chicago, 1965)

E. Berriot-Salvadore, *Images de la femme dans la médecine du XVIe au début du XVIIe siècle* (Montpellier, 1979)

R. C. Punnett, 'Ovists and animalculists', *The American Naturalist*, 62 (1928)

F. J. Cole, *Early Theories of Sexual Generation* (Oxford, 1930)

S. R. Roe, *Matter, Life and Generation: Eighteenth Century Embryology and the Haller-Wolff Debate* (Cambridge, 1981)

L. Jordanova, *Sexual Visions: Images of Gender in Science and Medicine between the Eighteenth and Twentieth Centuries* (Madison, Wis., 1989)

P. Crawford, 'Attitudes to menstruation in seventeenth-century England', *Past and Present*, 91 (1981)

O. Niccoli, 'Menstruum Quasi Monstruum: Parti mostruosi e tabú mestruali nel '500', *Quaderni Storici* 44 (1980), trans. in E. Muir and G. Ruggiero, *Sex and Gender in Historical Perspective* (Baltimore, 1990)

J. Astruc, *Traité des maladies des femmes* (Paris, 1761)

J. Astruc, *A Treatise of Venereal Disease* (repr. New York, 1985)

Aristotle's Masterpiece Completed (several editions, that used London, 1684)

C. Merchant, *The Death of Nature: Women, Ecology and the Scientific Revolution* (London, 1980)

P. G. Bouce ed., *Sexuality in Eighteenth Century Britain* (Manchester, 1982)

Text and image

C. Belsey, *The Subject of Tragedy: Identity and Difference in Renaissance Drama* (London, 1985)

S. Carlson, *Women and Comedy: Rewriting the British Theatrical Tradition* (Ann Arbor, 1990)

L. Woodbridge, *Women and the English Renaissance: Literature and the nature of womankind. 1549–1620* (Urbana, 1984)

J. G. Turner ed., *Sexuality and Gender in Early Modern Europe* (Cambridge, 1993)

K. Roger, *The Troublesome Helpmate: A History of Misogyny in Literature* (Seattle, 1966)

J. L. Klein ed., *Daughters, Wives and Widows: Writings by Men about Women and Marriage in England. 1500–1640* (Urbana, 1992)

F. L. Utley, *The Crooked Rib: An Analytical Index to the Argument About Women in English and Scots Literature to the end of the year 1568* (Columbus, Ohio, 1944)

L. Jardine, *Still Harping on Daughters: Women and Drama in the Age of Shakespeare* (Sussex, 1983)

M. Lazard, *Images littéraires de la femme à la Renaissance* (Paris, 1985)

I. Maclean, *Women Triumphant: Feminism in French Literature, 1610–1652* (Oxford, 1977)

J. Emelina, *Les Valets et les servantes dans le théâtre comique en France de 1610 à 1700* (Grenoble, 1975)

S. Schama, 'Wives and Wantons: Versions of Womanhood in 17th Century Dutch Art', *Oxford Art Journal* (April 1980)

M. McKendrick, *Women in Society in Spanish Drama of the Golden Age: A Study of the Mujer Varonil* (Cambridge, 1974)

C. V. Aubrun, 'L'espagnole du XVe au XVIIe siècle' in P. Grimal ed., *Histoire Mondiale de la femme*, vol.2 (Paris, 1965)

A. Mas, *La caricature de la femme, du mariage et de l'amour dans l'oeuvre de Quevado* (Paris, 1957)

Popular literature

M. Spufford, *Small Books and Pleasant Histories: Popular Fiction and its Readership in Seventeenth Century England* (Cambridge, 1981)

G. Bollême, *La Bibliothèque Bleu: littérature populaire en France* (Paris, 1971)

A. Farge, *Le Miroir des femmes* (Paris, 1982). A set of extracts from the chapbooks of the *Bibliothèque Bleu*

E. Le Roy Ladurie, *Love, Death and Money in the Pays d'Oc* (Cambridge, 1982)

J. Wiltenburg, *Disorderly Women and Female Power in the Street Literature of Early Modern Germany* (London, 1992)

In legal theory

K. V. Thomas, 'The double standard', *Journal of the History of Ideas* (1959)

Y. Castan, *Honnêteté et relations sociales en Languedoc 1715–1780* (Paris, 1974)

D. Sabean, *Power in the Blood: Popular Culture and Village Discourse in Early Modern Germany* (Cambridge, 1984)

In civil law

A. L. Erickson, *Women and Property in Early Modern England* (London, 1993)

P. Hogreve, 'Legal rights of Tudor women and their circumvention by men and women', *Sixteenth Century Journal* 3 (1972)

S. Staves, *Married Women's Separate Property in England, 1660–1833* (Oxford, 1989)

J. Greenberg, 'The legal status of the English woman in early eighteenth century common law and equity', *Studies in Eighteenth Century Culture*, 4 (1975)

S. Moller Okin, 'Patriarchy and married women's property in England: questions on some current views', *Eighteenth Century Studies*, 17 (1983–4)

S. Hanley, 'Engendering the state: family formation and state building in early modern France', *French Historical Studies* (1980)

W. Gibson, *Women in Seventeenth Century France* (New York, 1989)

S. Traer, *Marriage and the Family in Eighteenth Century France* (Ithaca, 1980)

W. Bosch, 'Le statut de la femme dans les anciens pays bas septentriaux' in *La Femme. Recueils de la Société Jean Bodin*, 12 (1962)

P. Ungari, *Storia del diritto di famiglia in Italia* (Bologna, 1974)

T. Kuehn, *Law, Family and Women: Towards a legal anthropology of Renaissance Italy* (Chicago, 1991)

L. A. Sponsler, 'The status of married women under the legal system of Spain', *Journal of Legal History*, 3 (1982)

Women and wills

C. Cross, 'Northern women in the early modern period: the female testators of Hull and Leeds 1520–1650', *Yorkshire Archaeological Journal*, 59 (1987)

M. Prior, 'Wives and wills 1558–1700' in J. Chartres and D. Hey eds., *English Rural Society 1500–1800: Essays in honour of Joan Thirsk* (Cambridge, 1990)

M. Vovelle, *Piété baroque et déchristianisation* (Paris, 1974)

G. Zarri, 'Ginevra Gozzadini dall'armi "gentildonna bolognese" (1520/27–67)' in O. Niccoli ed., *Rinascimento al femminile* (Rome/Bari, 1991)

G. Calvi, *Il contratto morale: madri e figli nella Toscana moderna* (Rome/Bari, 1994)

See also Courtship and marriage; Dowries, jointures and settlements; Widowhood; Difference, shame and abuse

In economic thought

A. Kessler Harris, 'The just price, the free market and the value of women' in A. Kessler Harris ed., *A Woman's Wage: Historical Meanings and Social Consequences* (Lexington, 1990). One of the few studies which broaches this critical issue.

J. W. Scott, '"L'ouvrière! Mot impie, sordide . . .". Women workers in the discourse of French political economy, 1840–1860' in P. Joyce, *The Historical Meaning of Work* (Cambridge, 1987)

In political thought

C. Jordan, 'Women's rule in sixteenth century British political thought', *Renaissance Quarterly* 40 (1987)

J. B. Elstain, *Public Man, Private Woman: Women in Social and Political Thought* (Princeton, 1981)

THE STRATEGIC PLAN AND BEING A WIFE

There is a considerable overlap between work patterns, family history and marriage strategies, rendering categorization very blurred. The issues need to be considered as interlinked.

The topic of women and work has been treated in different ways to include how women divided up their working lives: the female labour market; agricultural work; women in industry; town or area studies looking across a variety of activities; individual activities including relationships with guilds.

Life cycle experience

G. Mayhew, 'Life cycle service and the family unit in early modern Rye', *Continuity and Change* 6 (1991)

O. Hufton, 'Women and the family economy in eighteenth century France', *French Historical Studies* 9 (1975)

H. Wunder, 'Zur Stellung der Frau im Arbeitsleben und in der Gesellschaft des 15.–18. Jahrhunderts. Eine Skizze', *Geschichtsdidaktik* 6 (1981). A good bibliography of this author's studies of women's work appears in her *'Er ist die Sonn', sie ist der Mond'. Frauen in der frühen Neuzeit* (Munich, 1992).

D. Rippmann and K. Simon-Muscheid, 'Weibliche Lebensformen und

Arbeitszusammenhänge im Spätmittelalter und in der frühen Neuzeit. Methoden, Ansätze und Postulate', in M. Othenin-Girard ed., *Frauen und Öffentlichkeit. Beiträge der 6 schweizerischen Historikerinnentagung* (Zurich, 1991)

The labour market

K. Honeyman and J. Goodman, 'Women's work, gender conflict and labour markets in Europe, 1500–1900', *Economic History Review*, 44 (1991)

P. Earle, 'The female labour market in London in the late seventeenth and eighteenth centuries', *Economic History Review*, 42 (1989)

C. Middleton, 'The familiar fate of the *famulae*: gender divisions in the history of wage labour' in R. E. Pahl ed., *On Work* (Oxford, 1988)

W. Thwaites, 'Women in the market place: Oxfordshire *c*.1690–1800', *Midland History*, 9 (1984)

Agricultural work

A. Kussmaul, *Servants in Husbandry in Early Modern England* (Cambridge, 1990)

M. Roberts, 'Sickles and scythes: women's work and men's work at harvest time', *History Workshop*, 7 (1979)

P. King, 'Customary rights and women's earnings: the importance of gleaning to the labouring poor 1750–1850', *Economic History Review*, 44 (1991)

M. Ségalen, *Love and Power in the Peasant Family: Rural France in the Nineteenth Century*, trans. S. Matthews (Oxford, 1983). There are many continuities from the earlier period.

D. Sabean, *Property, Production and Family in Neckarhausen 1700–1870* (Cambridge, 1990)

B. Bergren, 'The female peasant and the male peasant: division of labour in traditional Norway', *Ethnologia Scandinavia* (1984)

Industrial work

M. Berg, 'What difference did women's work make to the industrial revolution', *History Workshop Journal*, 35 (1993)

W. H. Crawford, 'Women in the domestic linen industry' in M. MacCurtain and M. O'Dowd eds., *Women in Early Modern Ireland* (Edinburgh, 1991)

M. Garden, *Lyon et les lyonnais au XVIIIe siècle* (Paris, 1974)

G. Gulickson, *Spinners and Weavers of Auffray* (Cambridge, 1986)

S. C. Ogilvie, 'Women and proto-industrialisation in a corporate society: Wurttemberg woollen weaving, 1590–1760' in P. Hudson and W. R. Lee eds., *Women's Work and Family Economy in a Historical Perspective* (Manchester/ New York, 1990)

L. Mottu Weber, *Economie et refuge à Genève au siècle de la réforme: la draperie et la soierie (1540–1630)* (Paris, 1987)

General studies and collections

P. Earle, *The Making of the English Middle Class: Business, Society and Family Life in London, 1660–1730* (London, 1989)

L. Charles and L. Duffin eds., *Women and Work in Pre-industrial England* (London, 1985)

B. Hill, *Women, Work and Sexual Politics in Eighteenth Century England* (Oxford, 1989)

M. Prior, 'Women and the urban economy' in M. Prior ed., *Women in English Society 1500–1800* (London, 1985)

S. Wright, '"Holding up half the sky": women and their occupations in eighteenth century Ludlow', *Midland History*, 14 (1989)

E. W. Monter, 'Women in Calvinist Geneva', *Signs*, 6 (1980)

L. Mottu Weber, 'Les femmes dans la vie économique de Genève, XVI–XVIIe siècles', *Bulletin de la Société d'histoire et d'archéologie de Genève*, 16 (1979)

M. Wiesner, *Working Women in Renaissance Germany* (New Brunswick, 1986)

Urban domestic service

J. Hecht, *The Domestic Servant in Eighteenth Century England* (London, 1956, repr. 1980)

M. K. McIntosh, 'Servants and the household unit in an Elizabethan English community', *Journal of Family History*, 9 (1984)

N. Goose, 'Household size and structure in early Stuart Cambridge', *Social History*, 5 (1980)

D. A. Kent, 'Ubiquitous but invisible. Female domestic servants in mid-eighteenth-century London', *History Workshop*, 28 (1989).

S. Maza, *Servants and Masters in Eighteenth Century France* (Princeton, 1983)

C. Fairchilds, *Domestic Enemies: Servants and their Masters in Old Regime France* (Baltimore, 1984)

M. Carlson, 'A Trojan Horse of worldliness? Maidservants in the burgher household of Rotterdam at the end of the seventeenth century' in E. Kloek, N. Teeuwen and M. Huisman, *Women of the Golden Age* (Hilversum, 1994). Embodies some results of a thesis on *Domestic Service in a changing city economy: Rotterdam, 1680–1780.*

F. Daelmans and K. van Honacker, 'Het Brussels dienstpersoneel in 1796' in *Arbeid in veelvoud. Een huldeboek aan Prof. dr. J. Craeybeckx en Prof. dr. E. Scholliers van di Vrije Universiteit Brussel* (Brussels, 1988)

R. Enhelsing, 'Der Arbeitsmarkt der Dienstboten im 17., 18. und 19. Jahrhundert' in H. Kellenbenz ed., *Wirtschaftspolitik und Arbeitsmarkt* (Munich, 1971)

C. Sarasúa, *Criados, nodrizas y amos: el servicio doméstico en la formación del mercado de trabajo madrileño, 1758–1868* (Madrid, 1994)

Guilds

I. Krausman Ben-Amos, 'Women apprentices in the trades and crafts of early modern Bristol', *Continuity and Change*, 6 (1991)

P. Sharpe, 'Poor children as apprentices in Colyton, 1598–1830', *Continuity and Change*, 6 (1991)

N. Z. Davis, 'Women and the crafts in sixteenth century Lyons' in B. Hanawalt ed., *Women and Work in Pre-industrial Europe* (Bloomington, 1986)

D. M. Hafter, 'Gender formation from a working class viewpoint: the guildswomen in eighteenth century Rouen', *Proceedings of the Annual Meeting of the Western Society for French History*, 16 (1989)

C. M. Truant, 'The guildswomen of Paris: gender, power and sociability in the old regime', *Proceedings of the Annual Meeting of the Western Society for French History*, 15 (1988)

L. Roper, *The Holy Household. Religion, Morals and Order in Reformation Augsburg* (Oxford, 1989) has a great deal to say on working women of Augsburg and their relationship with the guilds.

See also M. Wiesner, *Working Women* . . .

Crafts

P. Glanville and J. Faulds Goldsborough, *Women Silversmiths 1685–1845* (London, 1990)

A. M. Pinz, 'Un aspect de l'économie genevoise du XVIIe siècle: La fabrique de dorure d'Elisabeth Baulacre', *Mélanges en honneur de Paul E. Martin* (Geneva, 1961)

Printing

S. M. Allen, 'Jane Yetsweirt (1541?): claiming her place', *Printing History*, 9 (1987)

Needlework

M. Ginsburg, 'The tailoring and dressmaking trades, 1700–1850', *Costume*, 6 (1972)

Second hand clothing

M. Ginsburg, 'Rags to riches: the second hand clothes trade 1700–1978', *Costume*, 40 (1980)

B. Lemire, 'Consumerism in pre-industrial and early industrial England: the trade in second-hand clothes', *Journal of British Studies*, 27 (1988)

Nursing

R. Dingwall, A. M. Rafferty and C. Webster, *An Introduction to the Social History of Nursing* (London, 1988)

Housework and caring

C. Davidson, *A Woman's Work is Never Done. A History of Housework in the British Isles 1650–1950* (London, 1982)

J. Brown, 'A woman's place was in the home. Women's work in Renaissance Tuscany' in M. Ferguson, M. Quilligan and N. Vickers, *Rewriting the Renaissance: The Discourses of Sexual Difference in Early Modern Europe* (Chicago, 1986)

Casual work

M. Hunt, 'Hawkers, pawlers and mercuries: Women and the London press in the early Enlightenment', *Women and History*, 9 (1984)

The economy of makeshifts

D. Willen, 'Women in the public sphere in early modern England: the case of the urban working poor', *Sixteenth Century Journal*, 19 (1988)

O. Hufton, *The Poor of Eighteenth Century France* (Oxford, 1974), particularly ch.4

R. Wall, 'Some implications of the earnings, income and expenditure patterns of married women in the populations of the past' in J. Henderson and R. Wall eds., *Poor Women and Children in the European Past* (London, 1994)

Histories of the family and marriage

M. Anderson, *Approaches to the History of the Western Family 1500–1914* (London, 1980)

J. Goody, *The Development of the Family and Marriage in Europe* (Cambridge, 1983)

P. Laslett, 'Introduction to the history of the family' in P. Laslett and R. Wall eds., *Household and Family in Past Time* (Cambridge, 1972)

J. Goody, J. Thirsk and E. P. Thompson, *Family and Inheritance: Rural Society in Western Europe 1200–1800* (Cambridge, 1976)

M. Mitterauer and R. Sieder, *The European Family: Patriarchy to Partnership from the Middle Ages to the Present* (Oxford, 1982). Written with a deep knowledge of central Europe.

J. Casey, *The History of the Family* (Oxford, 1989). Emphasis on Mediterranean Europe.

G. Ravis-Giordani, *Femmes et patrimoine dans les sociétés rurales de l'Europe Mediterranéenne* (Paris, 1987)

L. Stone, *The Family, Sex and Marriage in England, 1500–1800* (abridged edn, London, 1979). Particularly revealing for the thesis it posits concerning the changes in aristocratic marriages over this period.

R. Houlbrouke, *The English Family 1450–1700* (London, 1984). A very useful, judicious summary of the bibliography of the English family to this point reinforced by ego documents and legal records.

P. Laslett and R. Wall eds., *Household and Family in Past Time* (Cambridge, 1972)

A. Macfarlane, *Marriage and Love in England: Modes of Reproduction, 1300–1840* (Oxford, 1986)

R. Trumbach, *The Rise of the Egalitarian Family: Aristocratic Kinship and Domestic Relations in Eighteenth Century England* (London, 1978)

J. L. Flandrin, *Families in Former Times: Kinship, Household and Sexuality* (Cambridge, 1979)

A. Collomp, *La Maison du Père: Famille et Village en Haute Provence aux XVIIe et XVIIIe siècles* (Paris, 1983)

F. Le Brun, *La vie conjugale sous l'ancien régime* (Paris, 1975)

R. Pillorget, *La tige et le rameau* (Paris, 1979). An interesting attempt to compare and contrast the English and French record, done with great sensitivity to women.

M. Ségalen, *Love and Power in the Peasant Family* (Oxford, 1983)

G. Delille, *Famille et propriété dans le royaume de Naples (XV–XIXe siècles)* (Paris, 1985)

A. Molho, *Marriage Alliance in Late Medieval Florence* (Princeton, 1994)

M. de Giorgio and C. Klapisch Zuber eds., *Storia del matrimonio* (Rome/Bari, 1995)

F. W. Kent, *Household and Lineage in Renaissance Florence* (Princeton, 1977)

M. Barbagli and D. Kertzer eds., *Storia della famiglia italiana* (Bologna, 1992). Contains important essays on differing classes and regions.

M. A. Visceglia ed., *Signori, patrizi, cavalieri in età moderna* (Rome/Bari, 1992). The essay by R. Ago, 'Giochi di squadra: uomini e donne nelle famiglie nobili del XVII secolo', is particularly revealing.

COURTSHIP AND MARRIAGE

Courtship

Ethnological approaches

J. L. Flandrin, *Amours Paysans* (Paris, 1975)

M. Ségalen, 'Le Mariage, l'amour et les femmes dans les proverbes français', *Ethnologie Française* (1976)

A. de Cock, *Spreekwoorden en Zegswitsen over de Vrouwen die Liefole en het Huwelijk* (Ghent, 1911)

F. P. Wilson ed., *Oxford Dictionary of English Proverbs* (Oxford, 1970) entries Beauty, Woman etc.

Good advice on choice

The good conduct literature (see 'Constructing woman' above) usually embodies advice on marriage which became more frequent when the issue of individual choice became more prominent. It is certainly to the fore in early feminist writings such as Mary Astell (see below) and is a leitmotif of novels written by women. Lack of choice, or the inappropriateness of parental choice, can also be pursued in the comedies of Molière and Carlo Goldoni.

A. C. Carter, 'Marriage counselling in the early seventeenth century: England and the Netherlands compared' in J. van Dorsten, *Ten Studies in Anglo Dutch Relations* (Leiden/London, 1974)

T. C. Hollingsworth, 'The Demography of the British Peerage', *Population Studies*, 8, Supplement (1964)

P. C. Otto, *Daughters of the British Aristocracy and their Marriages in the Eighteenth and Nineteenth Centuries with particular reference to the Scottish Peerage* (PhD Stanford, 1964, Ann Arbor Microfilms)

C. Levy and L. Henry, 'Ducs et pairs sous l'ancien régime: caractéristiques démographiques d'une caste', *Population*, 15 (1960)

J. P. Labatut, *Les ducs et pairs de France au XVIIe siècle* (Paris, 1972)

J. B. Wood, 'Demographic pressure and social mobility among the nobility of early modern France', *Sixteenth Century Journal*, 8 (1977)

J. B. Wood, 'Endogamy and mesalliance: the marriage patterns of the nobility of the Election of Bayeux, 1430–1639', *French Historical Studies*, 10 (1978)

M. Ségalen, *Nuptialité et alliance: Le choix du conjoint dans une commune de l'Eure aux XVIIIe et XIXe siècles* (Paris, 1972)

Dowries, jointures and settlements

J. P. Cooper, 'Patterns of inheritance and settlement by great landowners from the fifteenth to the eighteenth centuries' in J. Goody, J. Thirsk and E. P. Thompson eds., *Family and Inheritance: Rural Society in Western Europe 1200–1800* (Cambridge, 1976)

B. English and J. Saville, *Strict Settlement: A Guide for Historians* (Hull, 1983)

A. L. Erickson, 'Common law versus common practice: the use of marriage settlements in early modern England', *Economic History Review*, 43 (1990)

A. L. Erickson, *Women and Property in Early Modern England* (London, 1993)

H. J. Habbakuk, 'Marriage settlements in the eighteenth century', *Transactions of the Royal Historical Society*, 4th series, 32 (1950). The main contention of this article, that marriage was the means of large estates getting larger, is questioned by C. Clay, 'Marriage, inheritance and the rise of large estates in England, 1660–1815', *Economic History Review*, 2nd series, 21 (1968)

L. Bonfield, *Marriage Settlements 1601–1740* (Cambridge, 1983) claims more division among surviving daughters in the late seventeenth century.

L. Stone, *Family and Fortune: Studies in Aristocratic Finance in the Sixteenth and Seventeenth Centuries* (Oxford, 1973)

S. Staves, *'Our Fortunes are in Your Possession'. Married Women's Separate Property 1660–1830* (Cambridge, 1990)

S. Staves, 'Pin money', *Studies in Eighteenth Century Culture*, 14 (1985)

M. Slater, 'The weightiest business: marriage in an upper gentry family in seventeenth century England', *Past and Present*, 72 (1976)

K. Nicholls, 'Irishwomen and property in the sixteenth century' in M. MacCurtain and M. O'Dowd eds., *Women in Early Modern Ireland* (Edinburgh, 1991)

A. P. W. Malcolmson, *The Pursuit of the Heiress: Aristocratic Marriage in Ireland, 1750–1820* (Belfast, 1982)

In French historiography the dowry is acknowledged as a part of family strategy and hence is considered in histories of the nobility and of particular families, for example:

G. Chaussinand-Nogaret, *La Noblesse au XVIIIe siècle* (Paris, 1976)

J. Meyer, *La Noblesse bretonne au XVIIIe siècle* (2 vols., Paris, 1966)

R. Forster's studies of the eighteenth-century French nobility are particularly informative on the size and importance of dowries and how marriages were brought about: *The Nobility of Toulouse in the Eighteenth Century* (Baltimore, 1960); *Merchants, Landlords, Magistrates: The Depont Family in Eighteenth Century France* (Baltimore, 1980); *The House of Saulx Tavannes* (Baltimore, 1971).

The input of both parties into marriage for other urban classes receives consideration in:

M. Garden, *Lyon et les lyonnais au XVIIIe siècle* (Paris, 1974)

A. Daumard and F. Furet, *Structures et relations sociales à Paris au milieu du XVIIIe siècle* (Paris, 1961)

G. Bouchard, *Le village immobile: Sennely en Sologne au XVIIe et XVIIIe siècles* (Paris, 1972)

For Italy studies are either concerned with the consolidation of clans and lineage patterns or with the dowry institutions of the Renaissance and Counter-Reformation:

C. Casanova, 'Le donne come "risorsa". Le politiche matrimoniale della famiglia Spada (sec. XVI–XVIII)' and R. Ago, 'Donne, doni e public relations tra le famiglie nell'aristocratia romana del XVII secolo' in *La donna nell' economia secc. XIII–XVIII. Atti della 21 settimana di Studi dell' Istituto Internazionale F. Datini di Prato* (Florence, 1990)

S. Chojnacki, 'Dowries and kinsmen in early Renaissance Venice', *Journal of Interdisciplinary History*, 4 (1975)

A. Molho, *Marriage Alliance in Late Medieval Florence* (Princeton, 1994)

H. Gregory, 'Daughters, dowries and the family in fifteenth century Florence', *Rinascimento*, ser.2, 27 (1987)

L. Ciammitti, 'Quanto costa essere normali: la dote nel conservatorio femminile di Santa Maria del Baraccano (1630–1680)', *Quaderni Storici*, 53 (1983)

L. Ferrante, 'L'onore ritrovato: donne nella Casa del Soccorso di S. Paolo a Bologna (sec. XVI–XVII)', *Quaderni Storici*, 53 (1983)

J. Kirshner, 'Pursuing honor while avoiding sin: The Monte delle Doti of Florence', *Quaderni di 'Studi Senese'*, 41 (1978)

J. Kirshner and A. Molho, 'Il monte delle doti a Firenze dalla sua fondazione nel 1425 alla metà del sedicesimo secolo: abozzo di una ricerca', *Ricerche Stotiche*, 10 (1980)

A. Molho, 'Investimenti nel Monte delle Doti di Firenze: un'analisi sociale e geografica', *Quaderni Storici* (1986)

M. Fubini-Leuzzi, 'Appunti per lo studio delle doti granducali in Toscana', *Ricerche Storiche*, 20 (1990)

M. d'Amelia, 'Scatole cinesi: vedove e donne sole in una società d'ancien regime', *Memorie*, 3 (1986)

D. Sabean, *Property, Production and Family in Neckarhausen, 1700–1870* (Cambridge, 1990) gives some very significant tables on the relative input of the spouses into matrimony at the end of the eighteenth century.

Courting rituals

E. Shorter, *The Making of the Modern Family* (New York, 1975)

K. Wrightson, *English Society 1580–1860* (London, 1982), 71–88 gives an excellent summary of English bibliography on this theme.

O. Hufton, 'Women, work and marriage in eighteenth century France' in R. B. Outhwaite ed., *Marriage and Society: Studies in the Social History of Marriage* (London, 1981)

J. P. Gutton, *La Sociabilité villageoise dans l'ancienne France* (Paris, 1979)

H. Medick, 'Village spinning bees: sexual culture and free time amongst rural youth in early modern Germany' in H. Medick and D. Sabean eds.,

Interest and Emotion. Essays in the study of family and kinship (Cambridge, 1988)

Changing legislation and matrimony

J. Gaudemet, *Le mariage en occident: les moeurs et le droit* (Paris, 1987)
A. Esmein, *Le mariage en droit canonique* (Paris, 1891)
E. J. Carlson, 'Marriage reform and the Elizabethan High Commission', *Sixteenth Century Journal*, 21 (1990)
C. Durston, '"Unhallowed wedlocks": the regulation of marriage during the English revolution', *Historical Journal*, 31 (1988)
S. Hanley, 'Family and state in early modern France. The marriage pact' in M. J. Boxer and J. Quataert eds., *Connecting Spheres: Women in the Western World from 1500 to the Present* (New York, 1987)
S. Hanley, 'Engendering the state: family formation and state building in early modern France', *French Historical Studies* 16 (1980)
A. C. Jemolo, *Stato e Chiesa negli scrittori politici italiani del Seicento e del Settecento* (Pompeii, 1972)

Clandestine marriage

B. Gottlieb, 'The meaning of clandestine marriage' in R. Wheaton and T. Hareven eds., *Family and Sexuality in French History* (Philadelphia, 1980)
G. Cozzi, 'Padri, figli e matrimonii clandestini', *La Cultura*, 14 (1976)

Age at marriage and marriage patterns

J. Hajnal, 'European marriage patterns in perspective' in D. V. Glass and D. E. C. Eversley eds., *The Population in History* (Chicago, 1965)
R. B. Outhwaite, 'Age at marriage in England from the late seventeenth to the nineteenth century', *Transactions of the Royal Historical Society*, 23 (1973)
D. MacLaren, 'The Marriage Act of 1653: Its influence on the parish registers', *Population Studies* 28 (1973)

Marriage rituals

J. A. Sharpe, 'Plebeian marriage in Stuart England', *Transactions of the Royal Historical Society*, 5th series, 36 (1986)
A. Burghière, 'Le rituel du mariage en France: pratiques ecclésiastiques et pratiques populaires', *Annales, Economies, Sociétés et Civilisations* 33 (1978)
C. Klapisch-Zuber, 'Zacharie ou le père évincé. Les rites nuptiaux toscans entre Giotto et le Concile de Trente', *Annales Economies, Sociétés et Civilisations* (1979)
L. Roper, 'Going to church and street. Weddings in Reformation Augsburg', *Past and Present* 106 (1985)

The seasonality of marriage

A. Kussmaul, 'Time and space, hoof and grain: the seasonality of marriage in England', *Journal of Interdisciplinary History*, 15 (1984)

D. Cressy, 'The seasonality of marriage in old and new England', *Journal of Interdisciplinary History*, 15 (1984)

Pre-bridal pregnancy

P. E. H. Hair, 'Puritanism and bridal pregnancy: some doubts', *Journal of Interdisciplinary History*, 7 (1977)

See also Illegitimacy

Upper-class wives and their social role

B. J. Harris, 'Marriage and politics in early Tudor England', *Historical Journal* 33 (1990)

P. Wright, 'A change in direction: the ramifications of a female household' in D. Starkey ed., *The English Court from the Wars of the Roses to the English Civil War* (London, 1987)

A. Somerset, *Ladies in Waiting from the Tudors to the Present Day* (London, 1984)

A. Muhlstein, *Les Femmes et le pouvoir: une relecture de Saint Simon* (Paris, 1976)

S. Kolsky, 'Culture and politics in Renaissance Rome: Marco Antonio Altieri's Roman Weddings', *Renaissance Quarterly* (1987)

R. Ago, 'Maria Spada Veralli, la buona moglie' in G. Calvi ed., *Barocco al femminile* (Rome/Bari 1992) demonstrates what a well-connected woman could get for her family from the papal court.

The impact of civil war on family relations

C. Durston, *The Family in the English Revolution* (Oxford, 1989)

A. Fraser, *The Weaker Vessel: A Woman's Lot in the Seventeenth Century* (London, 1984)

M. O'Dowd, 'Women and war in Ireland in the 1640s' in M. MacCurtain and M. O'Dowd, *Women in Early Modern Ireland* (Edinburgh, 1991)

The quality of marriage

For major interpretative texts see Stone, Trumbach, Macfarlane and the works cited above in Histories of the family and marriage

J. R. Gillis, *For Better, For Worse* (Oxford, 1985)

E. P. Thompson, 'Happy families', *New Society*, 8 September 1977; review of Lawrence Stone, *The Family, Sex and Marriage in England, 1500–1800*

G. Q. W. Mueller, 'Inquiry into the state of a divorceless society: domestic relations, law and morals in England from 1660–1857', *University of Pittsburg Law Review*, 18 (1957)

Marriage was not a consistent experience and memoirs and letters reveal only personal perspectives. Among studies based on letters and memoirs, and collections of such documents, found particularly valuable:

B. J. Harris, 'Marriage sixteenth century style: Elisabeth Stafford and the Third Duke of Norfolk', *Journal of Social History* (1982)

A. Macfarlane, *The Family Life of Ralph Josselin, a seventeenth century clergyman: an essay in historical anthropology* (Cambridge, 1970)

M. Slater, *Family Life in the Seventeenth Century: The Verneys of Claydon House* (London, 1984)

S. Tillyard, *Aristocrats: Caroline, Emily, Louisa and Sarah Lennox, 1740–1832* (London, 1994)

La Tour du Pin, Madame, *Memoire*, trans. F. Harcourt (London, 1969)

Saint Simon, Louis de Rouvroy, Duc de, *Mémoires*, ed. A. Cheruel (13 vols., Paris, 1904–6)

A. Muhlstein, *Les Femmes et le pouvoir: Une relecture de Saint Simon* (Paris, 1976)

J. C. Davis, *A Venetian Family and its Fortune, 1500–1900: the Dona and the conservation of their wealth* (Philadelphia, 1975)

G. Calvi, 'Maddalena Nerli and Cosimo Tornabuoni: a couple's narrative of family history in early modern Florence', *Renaissance Quarterly* (1992)

H. Nader, *The Mendoza Family in the Spanish Renaissance 1350–1550* (New Brunswick, 1979)

S. Ozment, *Magdalena and Balthasar: An Intimate Portrait of Life in Sixteenth Century Europe revealed in the letters of a Nuremberg Husband and Wife* (New York, 1986)

H. Roodenburg, 'The Autobiography of Isabella de Moerloose: Sex, childrearing and popular belief in seventeenth century Holland', *Journal of Social History* 18 (1985)

MOTHERHOOD

The immense bibliography on motherhood divides into a number of basic themes leaving considerable gaps. The grand themes are attitudes to pregnancy and childbirth, childbirth as experience (to include a great deal on midwifery and in particular the struggle between the male midwife and female practitioners), breastfeeding, wet-nursing, weaning, advice to parents, children's sickness and mortality, education and the child as consumer. There is relatively little on mother/child relations – distinguished by class, time and place – which is based on sound empirical data, but the exploration of memoirs, letters and diaries kept by women in particular is opening up new vistas. Until further work of this kind has been done, our knowledge of mother/child relationships remains very partial.

Overviews and discussions of approaches

C. Fouquet and Y. Knibiehler, *L'histoire des mères du moyen âge à nos jours* (Paris, 1980). For this period it deals only with France.

P. Ariès, *Centuries of Childhood: A Social History of Family Life*, trans. R. Baldick (New York, 1962). In its day this study raised many interesting questions about the treatment of the child and how this improved over the eighteenth century. It drew heavily on literature and afforded no information whatsoever on motherhood.

J. Plumb, 'The new world of children in the eighteenth century', *Past and Present* 67 (1975). Dealt with the child as consumer but with implications for maternal valorization.

L. Pollock, *A Lasting Relationship: Parents and Children over Three Centuries* (London, 1987)

L. Pollock, *Forgotten Children: Parent-Child Relations from 1500 to 1900* (Cambridge, 1983). Uses diaries and memoirs to show how family relations did not necessarily conform to the literature of good advice produced by doctors and clerics and gives a positive view of motherhood intended to revise black legends.

P. Crawford, 'The construction and the experience of maternity in seventeenth century England' in V. Fildes ed., *Women as Mothers in Pre-Industrial England: Essays in Memory of Dorothy MacLaren* (London, 1990). Heralds a more sensitive approach.

J. Gélis, M. Laget and M. F. Morel eds., *Naissances et enfances dans la France traditionnelle* (Paris, 1978)

See also J. L. Flandrin, *Families in Former Times . . .*; R. Houlbrooke, *The English Family, 1450–1700*; S. Schama, *The Embarrassment of Riches*; A. Th. van Deursen, *Plain Lives in a Golden Age . . .*

Pregnancy

J. Gélis, *History of Childbirth: Fertility, Pregnancy and Birth in Early Modern Europe*, trans. R. Morris (Cambridge, 1991). A truly magnificent piece of work; a master text, in which anthropology and all types of sources are used. It does, however, deal more effectively with France and Mediterranean Europe than with Northern countries.

P. Crawford, 'Attitudes to pregnancy from a woman's spiritual diary, 1687–1688', *Local Population Studies*, 21 (Autumn 1978)

A. McLaren, *A History of Contraception from Antiquity to the Present Day* (Oxford, 1990)

A. McLaren, *Reproductive Rituals. Perceptions of Fertility in Britain from the Sixteenth Century to the Nineteenth Century* (Oxford, 1984)

J. S. Lewis, *In the Family Way. Childbearing in the British Aristocracy, 1760–1860* (New Brunswick, 1986)

Myths and monstrous births

E. Rosselin, *Des Divers Travaux et Enfantements des femmes* (Rouen, 1532)

P. Darmon, *Le mythe de la procréation à l'âge baroque* (Paris, 1981)

H. Roodenberg, 'The maternal imagination: the fears of pregnant women in seventeenth century Holland', *Journal of Social History*, 1988

K. Park and L. Daston, 'Unnatural conceptions: the study of monsters in sixteenth and seventeenth century France and England', *Past and Present*, 92 (1981)

P. G. Bouce, 'Imagination, pregnant women and monsters in eighteenth century England and France' in R. Porter and G. S. Rousseau, *Sexual Worlds of the Enlightenment* (Manchester, 1987)

O. Niccoli, 'Menstruum quasi monstruum' in E. Muir and G. Ruggiero eds., *Sex and Gender in Historical Perspective* (Baltimore, 1990)

D. Wilson, *Signs and Portents. Monstrous Birth from the Middle Ages to the Enlightenment* (London, 1993)

S. A. Seligman, 'Mary Toft. The rabbit breeder', *Medical History* 5 (1961)

R. Manningham, *An exact Diary of what was Observ'd during a close attendance on Mary Toft* (London, 1726)

Midwives and parturition

H. Marland ed., *The Art of Midwifery: Early Modern Midwives in Europe* (London, 1993). An excellent collection of essays in which the debate on male midwives and the attributes of actual midwives from different countries are examined.

A. Eccles, *Obstetrics and Gynecology in Tudor and Stuart England* (London, 1982)

J. Donnison, *Midwives and Medical Men: A History of Interprofessional Rivalries and Women's Rights* (London, 1977)

A. Wilson, 'Ignorant midwives, a rejoinder', *Bulletin of the Society of the Social History of Medicine* 32 (1983)

A. Wilson, 'Participant or patient. Seventeenth century childbirth from the mother's point of view' in R. Porter, *Patients and Practitioners: Lay Perceptions of Medicine in Pre-Industrial Society* (Cambridge, 1985)

A. Wilson, 'The ceremony of childbirth and its interpretation' in V. Fildes ed., *Women as Mothers in pre-Industrial England: Essays in Honour of Dorothy MacLaren* (London, 1990)

A. Wilson, 'The perils of early modern procreation: childbirth with or without fear?', *British Journal for Eighteenth Century Studies* 16 (Spring 1993)

A. Wilson, 'William Hunter and the varieties of man-midwifery' in W. F. Bynum and R. Porter, *William Hunter and the Eighteenth Century Medical World* (Cambridge, 1985)

R. Porter, 'A touch of danger: the man-midwife as sexual predator' in R. Porter and G. S. Rousseau, *Sexual Underworlds of the Enlightenment* (Manchester, 1987)

B. Schorrenberg, 'Is childbirth any place for a woman? The decline of midwifery in eighteenth century England', *Studies in Eighteenth Century Culture*, 10 (1981)

M. Laget, 'La naissance aux siècles classiques', *Annales, Economies, Sociétés et Civilisations* (1977)

J. Gélis, 'L'accouchement au XVIIIe siècle: pratiques traditionnelles et contrôle médicale', *Ethnologie Française* (1976)

J. Gélis, 'La formation des accoucheurs et des sages femmes au XVIIe et XVIIIe siècles', *Annales de Démographie Historique* (1977)

J. Gélis, 'Sages femmes et accoucheurs. L'obstétrique populaire aux XVIIe et XVIIIe siècles', *Annales, Economies, Sociétés et Civilisations* (1977)

C. Pancino, *Il bambino e l'acqua sporca. Storia dell'assistenza al parto dalle mammane alle ostetriche (secoli XVII–XIX)* (Milan, 1984)

N. M. Filippini, 'Levatrici e ostetricianti a Venezia tra Sette e Ottocento', *Quaderni Storici*, 58 (1985)

The testimony of real midwives

L. Bourgeois, dite Boursier, *Observations diverses sur la sterilité, perte de friuct, foecondité, accouchements et maladies des femmes et enfants nouveaux nés* (Paris, 1609, 1626)

Catharina Schrader, *Memoirs* (1693–1745) in M. J. van Lieburg ed., *Mother and Child Were Saved. The Memoirs of the Frisian Midwife Catharina Schrader* (Amsterdam, 1984). For a commentary, W. Frijhoff, 'Vrouw Schraders beroepsjornal: overwegingenbijeen publikatie over arbeidspraktijk in het veileden', *Tijdschrift voor Gechiedenis der Natuur wetenschappen Wiskunde en Techniek* 8 (1985).

J. Sharp, *The midwives book or The whole art of midwifery discovered* (London, 1671)

See also Marland, *The Art of Midwifery* . . .

Maternal mortality

R. Schofield, 'Did the mothers really die? Three centuries of maternal mortality in the world we have lost' in L. Bonfield, R. Smith and K. Wrightson eds., *The World we have Gained: Histories of Population and Population Structure* (Oxford, 1986)

Child mortality

R. Schofield, 'Infant and child mortality in England in the late Tudor and Stuart period' in C. Webster ed., *Health, Medicine and Mortality in the 16th Century* (Cambridge, 1979)

R. E. Jones, 'Infant mortality in rural North Shropshire 1561–1810', *Population Studies*, 30, 305–17; 'Further evidence on the decline of infant mortality in pre-industrial England: North Shropshire, 1561–1810', *Population Studies*, 34, 239–50

F. Le Brun, 'Un nouveau né sur deux', *L'Histoire* numéro special: *Les maladies ont une histoire*, presenté par J. Le Goff and J. C. Sournia (Paris, 1984)

Breastfeeding

V. Fildes, *Breasts, Bottles and Babies: A History of Infant Feeding* (Edinburgh, 1986). The notes to this work give a near-exhaustive list of contemporary printed works on infant and child feeding including wet-nursing.

S. Matthews Grieco, 'Breast feeding, wetnursing, and infant mortality in Europe (1400–1800)' in *Historical Perspectives on Breast Feeding* (Florence, UNICEF, 1991)

P. Crawford, ' "The sucking child": adult attitudes to childcare in the first year of life in seventeenth century England', *Continuity and Change*, 1 (1986), 23–52

D. MacLaren, 'Marital Fertility and Lactation 1520–1720' in M. Prior ed., *Women in English Society 1500–1800* (London, 1985)

Wet-nursing

V. Fildes, *Wet Nursing: A History from Antiquity to the Present* (Oxford, 1988)

G. Sussman, *Selling Mothers' Milk: The Wetnursing Business in France, 1715–1914* (Urbana, 1982)

M. Lindemann, 'Love for hire: the regulation of the wetnursing business in eighteenth century Hamburg', *Journal of Family History*, 6 (1981)

C. Klapisch Zuber, 'Blood parents and milk parents. Wet nursing in Florence 1300–1500', in *Women, Family and Ritual in Renaissance Italy* (Chicago, 1985)

C. Sarasúa, *Criados, nodrizas y amos. El servicio doméstico en la formación del mercado de trabajo madrileño, 1758–1868* (Madrid, 1994)

J. Sherwood, *Poverty in Eighteenth Century Spain* (Toronto, 1988)

S. Cavallo, 'Strategie politiche e familiari intorno al baliatico. Il monopolio dei bambini abbandonati nel Canavese tra Sei e Settecento', *Quaderni Storici* XVIII (1983)

Good advice literature on child-rearing

J. E. Mechling, 'Advice to historians on advice to mothers', *Journal of Social History*, 9 (1975)

A. Ryerson, 'Medical Advice on child rearing 1550–1900', *Harvard Educational Review*, 31 (1961)

B. Berry, 'The first English paediatricians and Tudor attitudes towards childhood', *Journal of the History of Ideas* 35 (1974)

E. Novi Chavarria, 'Ideologia e comportamenti familiari nei predicatori italiani tra Cinque e Settecento. Tematiche e modelli', *Rivista Storica Italiana*, C (1988)

R. Lenz, *Emotion und Affektion in der Familie der frühen Neuzeit, Leichenpredigten als Quelle der historischen Familienforschung* in P. J. Schuler ed., *Die Familie als sozialer und historischer Verband* (Sigmaringen, 1987)

S. Ozment, 'The family in Reformation Germany: the bearing and rearing of children', *Journal of Family History* (1983)

S. Ozment, *When Fathers Ruled: Family Life in Reformation Europe* (Cambridge, 1983)

Childhood

E. Marvick, 'Nature versus nurture: patterns and trends in seventeenth century French child rearing' in L. de Mause ed., *The History of Childhood* (London, 1976)

A. C. Beveridge, 'Childhood and society in eighteenth century Scotland', *New Perspectives on the Politics and Culture of Early Modern Scotland, 1560–1800* (Edinburgh, 1982)

A. Luppe, comte de, *Les jeunes filles dans l'aristocratie et la bourgeoisie à la fin du XVIIIe siècle* (Paris, 1924)

J. B. Ross, 'The middle class child in urban Italy, fourteenth to early sixteenth century' in L. de Mause ed., *The History of Childhood* (1974)

O. Niccoli ed., *Infanzie. Funzioni di un gruppo liminale dal mondo classico all' età moderna* (Florence, 1993)

Studies using personal diaries and letters making special reference to mother/child relationships:

P. Crawford, 'Katharine and Philip Henry and their children: a case study in family ideology', *Transactions of the Lancashire and Cheshire Historical Society*, 134 (1984)

S. H. Mendelson, 'Stuart women's diaries and occasional memoirs' in M. Prior ed., *Women in English Society 1500–1800* (London, 1985)

M. Slater, *Family Life in the Seventeenth Century: The Verneys of Clayden House* (London, 1984)

M. Hyde, *The Thrales of Streatham Park* (London, 1977)

M. Longino Farrel, *Performing Motherhood: The Sévigné Correspondence* (Hanover, 1991)

H. Roodenberg, 'The autobiography of Isabella de Moerloose: Sex, childrearing and popular belief in seventeenth century Holland', *Journal of Social History*, 18 (1985)

S. Ozment, *Magdalena and Balthasar*

B. Z. Abrahams trans. and ed., *The Life of Glückel of Hameln, 1646–1724, written by herself* (New York, 1963)

M. Beer, *Eltern und Kinder des späten Mittelalters in ihren Briefen. Familienleben in der Stadt des Spätmittelalters und der frühen Neuzeit mit besonderer Berücksichtigung Nürnbergs (1400–1550)* (Nuremberg, 1990)

See also Women writers: Literacy and education

Child abandonment

R. C. McClure, *Coram's Children: The London Foundling Hospital in the Eighteenth Century* (New Haven, 1981)

V. Fildes, 'Maternal feelings reassessed: child abandonment and neglect in London and Westminster, 1550–1800' in V. Fildes ed., *Women as Mothers in pre-Industrial England* (London, 1990)

F. Le Brun, 'Naissances illégitimes et abandons d'enfants en Anjou au XVIIIe siècle', *Annales, Economies, Sociétés et Civilisations* (1972)

V. Hunecke, *I Trovatelli di Milano, bambini esposti e famiglie espositrici dal XVII al XIX secolo* (Bologna, 1988)

F. Doriguzzi, 'I messagi dell'abbandono: bambini esposti a Torino nel 700', *Quaderni Storici* XVIII (1983)

The collection of essays *Enfance Abandonnée et société en Europe* (Ecole Française de Rome, Paris/Rome, 1991) is particularly valuable in making clear different family strategies.

Education

R. O'Day, *Education and Society, 1500–1800: social foundations of education in early modern Britain* (London, 1982)

R. Chartier, D. Julia and M. Compere, *L'éducation en France du XVIe au XVIIIe siècles* (Paris, 1976)

B. Grosperrin, *Les petites écoles sous l'ancien régime* (Rennes, 1984)

E. Ravoux-Rallo, *Les religieuses enseignantes, XVIe–XXe siècles* (Angers, 1981)

P. Rousselot, *Histoire de l'éducation des femmes en France* (2 vols., Paris, 1883)

P. Rousselot ed., *La pédagogie feminine extraite des principaux écrivains qui ont traité de l'éducation des femmes depuis le XVIe siècle* (Paris, 1881)

M. Sonnet, *L'éducation des filles au temps des lumières* (Paris, 1987)

K. Arnold, *Kind und Gesellschaft in Mittelalter und Renaissance* (Paderborn, 1980)

C. N. Moore, *The Maiden's Mirror. Reading Matter for German Girls in the Sixteenth and Seventeenth Centuries* (Wiesbaden, 1987)

WIDOWHOOD

Demography

E. A. Wrigley and R. Schofield, *The Population History of England 1541–1871* (London, 1981)

J. Dupâquier, *La Population française au XVIIe et XVIIIe siècles* (Paris, 1979)

D. Herlihy and C. Klapisch Zuber, *Tuscans and their Families: A Study of the Florentine Catasto of 1427* (New Haven, 1985)

Census material yielding information on the distribution of widows appears in:

R. Wall, 'Women alone in English society', *Annales de Demographie Historique* (1981)

L. A. Clarkson, 'Household and family structure in Armagh', *Local Population Studies* 20 (1978)

The widow and remarriage

J. Dupâquier ed., *Marriage and Remarriage in the Populations of the Past* (London, 1981). The essays by S. Akerman, 'The importance of remarriage in the XVII and XVIII centuries', and M. Ségalen, 'Mentalité populaire et remariage en Europe occidentale', are particularly to be noted.

V. Brodsky, 'Widows in late Elizabethan London. Remarriage, economic opportunity and family orientations' in L. Bonfield, R. M. Smith and K. Wrightson eds., *The World We have Gained* (Oxford, 1986)

B. A. Todd, 'The re-marrying wdow: a stereotype reconsidered' in M. Prior, *Women in English Society 1500–1800* (London, 1985)

J. Boulton, 'London widowhood revisited: the decline of female remarriage in the seventeenth and early eighteenth centuries', *Continuity and Change* 5 (1990)

B. Diefendorf, 'Widowhood and remarriage in sixteenth century Paris', *Journal of Family History* (Winter 1982)

A. Bideau, 'A demographic and social analysis of widowhood and remarriage: the example of the Castellany of Thoissy en Dombes (1670–1840)', *Journal of Family History* 5 (1980)

The widow in literature

C. Carlton, 'The widow's tale: male myths and female reality', *Albion*, X (1978)

E. Mignon, *Crabbed Age and Youth. The Old Men and Women in the Restoration Comedy of Manners* (Durham, N.C., 1947)

For specimens of the comic genre of the lusty conniving widow: W. Congreve, *The Way of the World* (1700) for the character of Lady Wishfort; R. B. Sheridan, *The Rivals* (1778); C. Goldoni, *The Artful Widow* (1748).

The widow in good advice literature

J. L. Vives, *Institutes of the Christian Religion* (original Latin edn 1523)

L. Dolce, *Dialogo della istitutione delle donne* (Venice, 1545). Like most works of its kind based on Vives.

G. Trissino, *Epistola de la vita che deve tenere una donna vedova* (Rome, 1703)

The widow, property, law and status

A. L. Erickson, *Women and Property in Early Modern England* (London, 1993)

S. Hanley, 'Engendering the state: family formation and state building in early modern France', *French Historical Studies*, 16 (1980)

M. Bordeaux, 'Droit et femmes seules. Les pièces de la discrimination' in *Madame ou Mademoiselle? Itinéraires de la solitude féminine, 18e–20e siècles* (Paris, 1984)

N. Tamassia, *Il testamento del marito* (Bologna, 1905)

L. Cantini, *Legislazione toscana raccolta e illustrata* (Florence, 1800–08), vol.7

G. Calvi, *Il contratto morale: madri e figli nella Toscana moderna* (Rome/Bari, 1994)

D. E. Vassburg, 'The status of widows in sixteenth century rural Castille' in J. Henderson and R. Wall eds., *Poor Women and Children in the European Past* (London, 1994)

On painting the widow

D. O. Hughes, 'Representing the family: portraits and purposes in early modern Italy' in R. I. Rotberg and T. K. Rabb eds., *Art and History. Images and their meaning* (Cambridge, 1988)

The effects of civil war

G. L. Hudson, 'Negotiating for blood money: war widows and the courts in seventeenth century England' in J. Kermode and G. Walker, *Women, Crime and the Courts in Early Modern England* (London, 1994)

M. O'Dowd, 'The effects of civil war on Ireland in the 1640s' in M. MacCurtain and M. O'Dowd eds., *Women in Early Modern Ireland* (Edinburgh, 1991)

Economic approaches

O. Hufton, 'Women without men: widows and spinsters in Britain and France in the eighteenth century', *Journal of Family History*, 9, 4 (1984)

M. Prior, 'Women and the urban economy: Oxford 1500–1800' in M. Prior ed., *Women in English Society 1500–1800* (London, 1985)

S. Wright, 'Churmaids, huswyfes and hucksters. The employment of women in Tudor and Stuart Salisbury' in L. Charles and L. Duffin eds., *Women and Work in pre-Industrial England* (London, 1985)

L. A. Clarkson and E. M. Crawford, 'Life after death: widows in Carrick on Suir 1799' in M. MacCurtain and M. O'Dowd, *Women in Early Modern Ireland* (Edinburgh, 1991)

B. Diefendorf, *Paris City Councillors in the Sixteenth Century. The Politics of Patrimony* (Princeton, 1983), 279–97

J. Hardwicke, 'Widowhood and patriarchy in seventeenth century France', *Journal of Social History* (Fall 1992)

J. Collins, 'The economic role of women in seventeenth century France', *French Historical Studies* 16, 2 (1989)

R. J. Kalas, 'Noblewomen as managers: widowhood, property rights, and land administration in two sixteenth century French families', *Sixteenth Century Journal* (1992)

S. M. Wyntjes, 'Survivors and status: widowhood and family in the early modern Netherlands', *Journal of Family History* (Winter 1982)

M. d'Amelia, 'Scatole cinesi: vedove e donne sole in una società d'ancien régime', *Memoria* (1986)

G. Calvi, 'Dal margine al centro. Soggettività femminile, famiglia, stato moderno in Toscana (XVI–XVIII secc.)' in M. Palazzi and A. Scattigno eds., *Discutendo di Storia* (Turin, 1991)

G. Calvi, 'Maddalena Nerli and Cosimo Tornabuoni: a couple's narrative of family history in early modern Florence', *Renaissance Quarterly* (1992)

A. Cabibbo, 'La capra, il sale, il sacco. Per una storia della vedovanza femminile tra Cinque e Seicento', *Archivio Storico per la Sicilia Orientale* 85 (1989)

M. Palazzi, 'Abitare da sole: donne capofamiglia alla fine del Settecento', *Memoria*, 18 (1986)

B. Wunder, 'Pfarrwitwenkassen und Beamtewitwenanstalten vom
16.–19. Jahrhunderts. Die Entstehung der staatlichen
Hinterbliebenenversorgung in Deutschland', *Zeitschrift für historische
Forschung*, 12 (1985)
See also L. Roper, *The Holy Household. Religion, Morals and Order in
Reformation Augsburg* (Oxford, 1989), 149–55
M. Wiesner, *Working Women in Renaissance Germany* (Rutgers, 1986),
157–63
H. Wunder, 'Zur Stellung der Frau im Arbeitsleben und in der
Gesellschaft des 15.–18. Jahrhundert', *Geschichtsdidaktik*, 3 (1981)
M. Perry, *Gender and Disorder in Early Modern Seville* (Princeton, 1990)

Widows and old age

M. Pelling, 'Old age, poverty and disability in early modern Norwich.
Work, remarriage and other expedients' in M. Pelling and R. Smith eds.,
Life, Death and the Elderly (London, 1991)
G. A. and I. Gunnlaugsson, 'Transitions into old age: poverty and
retirement possibilities in late eighteenth and early nineteenth century Ireland'
in J. Henderson and R. Wall eds., *Poor Women and Children in the European
Past* (London, 1994)
M. Baulant, 'Un dossier: le person âgé dans la société briarde aux XVIIe
et XVIIIe siècles', *Annales de Demographie Historique* (1985)

DIFFERENCE, SHAME AND ABUSE
Spinsterhood

S. Cott Watkins, 'Spinsters', *Journal of Family History*, 9 (1984)
O. Hufton, 'Women without men: widows and spinsters in Britain and
France in the eighteenth century', *Journal of Family History*, 9 (1984).
Contains a brief critical résumé of demographic work on the issue to that
date.
J. Houdaille, 'Célibat et âge au mariage aux XVIIIe et XIXe siècles en
France. 1. Célibat définitif', *Population*, 33 (1978)
Most work has been done on the aristocracies because they offer a viable
unit for study.
P. Otto, *Daughters of the British Aristocracy and their Marriages in the
Eighteenth and Nineteenth centuries* (PhD Stanford, and University Microfilms,
Ann Arbor, 1974)
T. H. Hollingsworth, 'The demography of the British peerage', *Population
Studies*, 8, Supplement (1965)
L. Henry and C. Levy, 'Ducs et pairs sous l'ancien régime', *Population*,
15 (1960)

R. B. Litchfield, 'Demographic characteristics of Florentine patrician families, sixteenth to nineteenth centuries', *Journal of Economic History* 29 (1969)

D. E. Zanetti, *La demografia del patriziato milanese nei secoli XVII, XVIII, XIX* (Pavia, 1972)

Transvestism and lesbianism

R. Dekker and L. C. van de Pol, *The Tradition of Female Transvestism in Early Modern Europe* (London, 1989)

C. J. S. Thompson, *Mysteries of Sex: women who posed as men and men who impersonated women* (London, 1938)

J. Foster, *Sex Variant Women in Literature* (London, 1958)

J. Wheelwright, *Amazons and Military Maids* (London, 1989)

D. Dugaw, *Warrior Women and Popular Balladry 1650–1850* (Cambridge, 1989)

J. Grand Cartaret, *La femme en culotte* (Paris, 1899)

V. Bullough, *Sexual Variance in Society and History* (Chicago, 1976)

C. Bingham, 'Seventeenth century attitudes towards deviant sex', *Journal of Interdisciplinary History*, 1 (1971)

J. Brown, *Immodest Acts: The Life of a Lesbian Nun in Renaissance Italy* (New York, 1986)

L. Friedli, '"Passing Women". A study of gender boundaries in the eighteenth century', in R. Porter and G. S. Rousseau eds., *Sexual Underworlds of the Enlightenment* (Manchester, 1987)

L. Faderman, *Scotch Verdict* (New York, 1983)

L. Faderman, *Surpassing the Love of Men: Romantic Friendship and Love between Women from the Renaissance to the Present* (New York, 1981)

M. Garber, *Vested Interests: Cross Dressing and Cultural Anxiety* (New York/London, 1991)

B. Erickson, 'A lesbian execution in Germany, 1721', *Journal of Homosexuality*, 6 (1980–1)

F. L. Kersteman, *Bredasche Heldinne*, ed. R. Dekker, G. J. Johannes and L. C. van de Pol (Hilversum, 1988)

Sexual transgressions before the church courts

M. Ingram, *Church Courts, Sex and Marriage in England, 1570–1660* (Cambridge, 1987)

R. Houlbrooke, *Church Courts and the People during the English Reformation 1520–1570* (Oxford, 1979)

P. Rushton, 'Property, power and family networks: the problem of disputed marriage in early modern England', *Journal of Family History*, 11 (1986)

R. Mitchison and L. Leneman, *Sexuality and Social Control: Scotland, 1660–1780* (Oxford, 1989)

A. Lottin, *La désunion du couple sous l'ancien régime: l'exemple du Nord* (Paris, 1975)

P. Darmon, *Le tribunal de l'impuissance: Virilité et défaillances conjugales dans l'ancienne France* (Paris, 1979)

W. Monter, 'The Consistory of Geneva, 1559–1569', *Bibliothèque d'Humanisme et Renaissance: travaux et documents*, 38 (1976)

J. R. Watt, 'Women and the Consistory in Calvin's Geneva', *Sixteenth Century Journal*, 14 (1993)

S. Cavallo and S. Cerutti, 'Onore femminile e controllo sociale della riproduzione in Piemonte tra Sei e Settecento', *Quaderni Storici*, 44 (1980)

T. Saffley, *Let no man put asunder. The control of marriage in the German Southwest: a comparative study*, 1550–1600 (Paris, 1979)

D. Sabean, *Property, production and family in Neckarhausen 1700–1870* (Cambridge, 1990), ch.4

Before lay courts

J. Beattie, *Crime and the Courts in England, 1660–1800* (Oxford, 1986)

J. A. Sharpe, *Crime in Seventeenth Century England: A county study* (Cambridge, 1983)

J. A. Sharpe, *Crime in Early Modern England* (London, 1984)

C. Z. Wiener, 'Sex roles and crime in late Elizabethan Hertfordshire', *Journal of Social History*, 8 (1974–5)

J. Kermode and G. Walker, *Women, Crime and the Courts in Early Modern England* (London, 1994)

J. M. Beattie, 'The criminality of women in eighteenth century England', *Journal of Social History*, 8 (1974–5)

O. Hufton, 'Women and violence in early modern Europe' in F. Dieteren and E. Kloek eds., *Writing Women into History* (Amsterdam, 1990)

N. Castan, *Les Criminels de Languedoc. Les exigences d'ordre et les voies du ressentiment dans une société prérévolutionnaire* (Toulouse, 1984)

Y. Castan, *Honnêteté et relations sociales en Languedoc 1715–1780* (Paris, 1974)

G. Ruggiero, *The Boundaries of Eros: Sex, Crime and Sexuality in Renaissance Venice* (Oxford, 1985)

P. Henry, *Crime, justice et société dans la principauté de Neuchâtel au XVIIIe siècle* (Neuchâtel, 1984)

L. C. van de Pol, 'Vrouwencriminaliteit in de Gouden Eeuw', *Ons Amsterdam* (November 1986)

L. C. van de Pol, 'Vrouwencriminaliteit in Amsterdam in de tweede helft van de 17e eeuw', *Tijdschrift voor Criminologie*, 29 (1987)

Rape

A. E. Simpson, 'Vulnerability and the age of female consent: legal innovation and its effect on prosecutions for rape in eighteenth century London' in R. Porter and G. S. Rousseau eds., *Sexual Underworlds of the Enlightenment* (Manchester, 1987)

L. Ferrante, 'Differenza sociale e differenza sessuale nelle questioni d'onore. Bologna sec. XVII' in G. Fiume ed., *Onore e storia nelle società mediterranea* (Palermo, 1989)

L. Troiano, 'Moralità e confini dell'eros nel Seicento toscano', *Ricerche Storiche*, 17 (1987)

G. Alessi, ' Il gioco degli scambi: seduzione e risarcimento nella casistica cattolica del XVI e XVII secolo', *Quaderni Storici*, 75 (1980)

G. Alessi, *Processo per seduzione: piacere e castigo nella Toscana Leopoldina* (Catania, 1988)

Infanticide

R. Malcolmson, 'Infanticide in the eighteenth century' in J. S. Cockburn ed., *Crime in England 1550–1800* (London, 1977)

P. Hair, 'Notes and Queries: homicide, infanticide and child assault in late Tudor Middlesex', *Local Population Studies* 9 (1972)

K. Wrightson, 'Infanticide in early seventeenth century England', *Local Population Studies*, 15 (1975)

R. van Dülmen, *Frauen vor Gericht. Kindesmord in der frühen Neuzeit* (Frankfurt/M, 1991)

S. Faber, 'Kindermoord in Amsterdam', *Bijdragen en Medelingen betreffende de Geschiedenis der Nederlanden*, 93 (1978)

R. Leboutte, 'L'infanticide dans l'est de la Belgique aux XVIIe–XIXe siècles: une réalité', *Annales de Demographie Historique* (Paris, 1983)

R. Leboutte, 'Offence against family order: infanticide in Belgium from the fifteenth through the early twentieth centuries', *Journal of the History of Sexuality*, 2 (1992)

Illegitimacy

P. Laslett, *Family Life and Illicit Love in Earlier Generations* (Cambridge, 1977)

P. Laslett, K. Oosterveen and R. Smith eds., *Bastardy and its Comparative History* (London, 1980)

B. Meteyard, 'Illegitimacy and marriage in eighteenth century England', *Journal of Interdisciplinary History*, 10, 3 (1980)

A. O'Connor, 'Women in Irish folklore. The testimony regarding Illegitimacy, abortion and Infanticide' in M. MacCurtain and M. O'Dowd eds., *Women in Early Modern Ireland* (Edinburgh, 1991)

A. Lottin, 'Naissances illégitimes et filles-mères à Lille au XVIIIe siècle', *Revue d'histoire moderne et contemporaine*, 17 (1970)

M. C. Phan, *Les amours illégitimes. Histoires de séduction en Languedoc (1676–1786)* (Paris, 1986)

F. Koorn, 'Illegitimiteit en eergevoel. Ongehuwde moeders in Twente in de achtiende eeuw', *Jaarboek voor Vrouwengeshiedenis*, 8 (1987)

Violence, wife-beating, murder

M. Hunt, 'Wife beating, domesticity and women's independence in eighteenth-century London', *Gender and History*, 4 (1992)

A. Farge, *La vie fragile. Violence, pouvoirs et solidarités à Paris au XVIIe siècle* (Paris, 1992)

A. Farge, 'La violence, les femmes et le sang au XVIIIe siècle', *Mentalités* (1988)

A. Farge and S. Zysberg, 'Les théâtres de la violence à Paris au XVIIIe siècle', *Annales, Economies, Sociétés et Civilisations*, 34 (1979)

A. Farge and M. Foucault, *Le désordre des familles. Lettres de cachet des archives de la Bastille* (Paris, 1982)

J. Casey, 'Household disputes and the law in early modern Andalusia' in J. Bossy ed., *Disputes and Settlements: Law and Human Relations in the West* (Cambridge, 1983)

The scold

D. Underdown, 'The taming of the scold: the enforcement of patriarchal authority in early modern England', in A. Fletcher and J. Stevenson eds., *Order and Disorder in Early Modern England* (Cambridge, 1985). This essay, which argues for assertive women being effectively silenced by the ducking stool, is profoundly modified by M. Ingram, 'Scolding women cucked or washed', in J. Kermode and G. Walker, *Women, Crime and the Courts in Early Modern England* (London, 1994)

Defamation

J. A. Sharpe, *Defamation and Sexual Slander in Early Modern England: The Church Courts at York*, Borthwick Papers, 8 (York, 1980)

L. Gowing, 'Gender and the language of insult in early modern London', *History Workshop Journal*, 35 (1993)

L. Gowing, 'Language, power and the law: women's slander litigation in early modern London' in J. Kermode and G. Walker, *Women, Crime and the Courts in Early Modern England* (London, 1994)

A. Gregory, *Slander Accusations and Social Control in late sixteenth and early seventeenth century England with particular reference to Rye (Sussex)* (PhD, University of Sussex, 1984)

T. Meldrum, *Defamation at the Church Courts: Women and Community Control in London, 1700–1745* (MSc thesis, London School of Economics, 1990)

Y. Castan, *Honnêteté et relations sociales en Languedoc 1715–1780* (Paris, 1974)

L. Roper, ' "The common man" the "common good". Reflections on gender and meaning in the Reformation German Commune', *Social History*, 12 (1987)

Divorce

R. Phillips, *Putting Asunder: A History of Divorce in Western Society* (Cambridge, 1989)

L. Stone, *The Road to Divorce. England 1530–1987* (Oxford, 1990)

L. Stone, *Uncertain Unions: Marriage in England 1660–1753* (Oxford, 1991)

L. Stone, *Broken Lives: Separation and Divorce in England 1660–1857* (Oxford, 1993)

R. Phillips, *Family Breakdown in Late Eighteenth Century France* (Oxford, 1981)

D. Dessertine, *Divorcer à Lyon sous la Révolution et l'Empire* (Lyon, 1991)

J. R. Watt, 'Divorce in early modern Neuchâtel, 1547–1806', *Journal of Family History*, 14 (1989)

Microhistories founded on litigation

G. Brucker, *Giovanni and Lusanna: Love and Marriage in Renaissance Florence* (Chicago/London, 1986). In spite of the title, this book is really about shame and honour and breach of promise.

E. Cropper, 'Artemesia Gentileschi, La "pittora"', in G. Calvi ed., *Barocco al femminile* (Rome/Bari, 1992), the famous lawsuit of the Gentileschi against Tassi for rape and breach of promise is also on much the same theme.

N. Z. Davis, *The Return of Martin Guerre* (New York, 1983)

B. Garnot, *Un crime conjugal au 18e siècle: l'affaire boiveau* (Paris, 1991)

PROSTITUTION
General

I. Bloch, *Die Prostitution* (Berlin, 1912)

V. and B. Bullough, *Women and Prostitution: A Social History* (Buffalo, 1987)

F. Henriques, *Prostitution in Europe and the Americas* (New York, 1969)

R. Canosa and I. Collonello, *Storia della prostituzione in Italia* (Rome, 1989)

The Italian courtesan

A. Barzaghi, *Donne o cortigiane? La prostituzione a Venezia: Documenti di costume dal XVI al XVIII secolo* (Verona, 1980)
   Lettere di cortigiane del Rinascimento (Rome, 1990)
R. Ago, *Carriera e clientele nella Roma barocca* (Rome/Bari, 1990)
J. Brown, 'Prosperity or hard times in Renaissance Italy?', *Renaissance Quarterly*, 42 (1989)
E. Cohen and V. Thomans, 'Camilla the go between: the politics of gender in a Roman household', *Continuity and Change*, 4 (1989)
E. Cohen, 'Camilla La Magra: Prostituta Romana', in O. Niccoli ed., *Rinascimento al femminile* (Rome/Bari, 1991)
P. Larivaile, *La vie quotidienne des courtisanes en Italie au temps de la Renaissance* (Paris, 1975)
L. Lawner, *Lives of the Courtesans: Portraits of the Renaissance* (New York, 1986)
L. Lawner ed., *I Modi: The Sixteen Pleasures: An Erotic Album of the Renaissance*, Engravings by Giulio Romano, Marcantonio Raimondi, Sonnets by P. Aretino (Evanston, Illinois, 1988)
G. Masson, *Courtesans of the Italian Renaissance* (London, 1975)
J. Murray, 'Agnolo Firenzuola on female sexuality and women's equality', *Sixteenth Century Journal*, 22 (1991)
R. Bassani and F. Bellini, *Caravaggio assassino. La carriera di un 'valenthuomo' fazioso nella Roma della Controriforma* (Rome, 1994) contains much information on the high and low ends of the profession.
A. Newcombe, 'Courtesans, muses or musicians' in J. Bowers and J. Tick, *Women Making Music. The Western Art Tradition* (Chicago, 1986)
E. Panofsky, 'Sacred and profane love', *Studies in Iconography: Humanistic Themes in the Art of the Renaissance* (Oxford, 1939)
E. Pavan, 'Police des moeurs, société et politique à Venise à la fin du Moyen Age', *Revue Historique* 264 (1988)
M. Rosenthal, 'Veronica Franco's terze rime: the Venetian courtesan's defense', *Renaissance Quarterly* (Summer 1989); and 'Venetian women writers and their discontents' in J. Grantham Turner ed., *Sexuality and Gender in Early Modern Europe* (Cambridge, 1993)
G. Ruggiero, *The Boundaries of Eros* (New York, 1985)
G. Ruggiero, 'Marriage, love, sex and Renaissance civic morality' in Turner, *Sexuality and Gender* . . .
C. Santore, 'Inventory of a courtesan's possessions', *Renaissance Quarterly*, 41 (1988)

R. Trexler, 'La prostitution florentine au XVe siècle. Patronages et clientèles', *Annales, Economies, Sociétés et Civilisations*, 36 (1981)

A. Zorzi, *Cortigiana Veneziana: Veronica Franco e i suoi poeti* (Milan, 1986)

Italian Counter-Reformation initiatives

C. Black, *Italian Confraternities in the 16th Century* (Cambridge, 1989).

S. Cohen, *The Evolution of Women's Asylums since 1500: From Refuges for Ex-Prostitutes to Shelters for Battered Women* (New York, 1992)

S. Cohen, 'Asylums for Women in Counter-Reformation Italy' in S. Marshall ed., *Women in Reformation and Counter-Reformation Europe: Private and Public Worlds* (Bloomington, 1989)

L. Ferrante, 'Honor regained: women in the Casa del Soccorso di San Paolo in sixteenth-century Bologna' in E. Muir and G. Ruggiero eds., *Sex and Gender in Historical Perspective* (Baltimore, 1990)

L. Ferrante, 'La sexualité en tant que ressource des femmes devant le For archiépiscopal de Bologne (XVIIème siècle)', *Déviance et Société* (1987)

L. Ferrante, '"Pro mercede carnali . . ." Il giusto prezzo rivendicato in tribunale', *Memoria. Rivista di Storia delle Donne*, 17 (1986)

B. Pullan, *Rich and Poor in Renaissance Venice* (Oxford, 1971)

In France

L. Otis, *Prostitution in Medieval Society: The History of an Urban Institution in Languedoc* (Chicago, 1985)

J. Rossiaud, *Medieval Prostitution*, trans. L. Cochrane (London, 1988)

J. Rossiaud, 'Prostitution, jeunesse et société dans les villes du sud-est au XVe siècle', *Annales, Economies, Sociétés et Civilisations*, 31 (1976)

E. M. Bénabou, *La prostitution et la police des moeurs au XVIIIe siècle* (Paris, 1987)

C. Jones, 'Prostitution and the ruling class in 18th-century Montpellier', *History Workshop*, 6 (Autumn 1978)

A. Riani, 'Pouvoir et contestations. La prostitution à Marseille au XVIIIe siècle' (Thèse de troisième cycle, Université de Provence, 1982)

In Spain

M. E. Perry, *Gender and Disorder in Early Modern Seville* (Princeton, 1990)

Rodríguez Solís, *Historia de la prostitución en España y América* (Madrid, 1921)

J. Contreras, *El Santo Oficio de la Inquisición en Galicia 1560–1700* (Madrid, 1982)

A. Domínguez Ortiz, 'Vida y obras del Padre Pedro de León', *Archivo Hispalense* ser. 2 (1967)

In England

D. Defoe, *Moll Flanders* (edn London, 1982)

A. R. Henderson, *Female Prostitution in London 1730–1830* (PhD, London, 1992).

B. Mandeville, *A Modest Defense of Public Stews* (1724)

J. Orne, ed., *The Nightwalker or Evening Rambles in Search of Lewd Women with the Conferences Held with Them* etc. (1696)

W. Speck, 'The Societies for the Reformation of Manners: a case study in the theory and practice of moral reform', *Literature and History*, 3 (1976)

R. Trumbach, 'Sex, gender and sexual identity in modern culture: male sodomy and female prostitution in Enlightenment London', *Journal of the History of Sexuality*, 2 (1991)

In Germany

G. Gieger, *Die Reichsstadt Ulm vor der Reformation* (Ulm, 1971)

J. von Grimmelshausen, *Courage, the Adventuress and the False Messiah*, trans. Hans Speier (Princeton, 1964)

L. Roper, 'Discipline and respectability: prostitution and reformation in Augsburg', *History Workshop*, 19 (1985)

L. Roper, 'Mothers of debauchery: procuresses in sixteenth century Augsburg', *German History*, 6 (1988)

F. Irsigler and A. Lassotta, *Bettler und Gaukler. Dirnen und Henker. Aussenseiter in einer mittelälterlichen Stadt. Köln 1300–1600* (Cologne, 1984)

B. Schuster, 'Frauenhandel und Frauenhäuser im 15. und 16. Jahrhunderts', *Vierteljahrschrift für Sozial und Wirtschaftsgeschichte* 78 (1991)

P. Schuster, *Das Frauenhaus. Städtische Bordelle in Deutschland 1350 bis 1600* (Paderborn, 1992)

The Netherlands

L. C. van de Pol, 'Prostititie en de Amsterdamse burgerij' in P. te Boekhorst, P. Burke and W. Frijhoff eds., *Culture en maatschappij in Nederland 1500–1800* (Heerlen, 1992)

L. C. van de Pol, 'Vrouwencriminaliteit in Amsterdam in de tweede helft van de 17e eeuw', *Tijdschrift voor Criminologie* 29 (1987)

L. C. van de Pol, *Het Amsterdam Hoerdom. Vrouwen en Prostitutie in een vroegmoderne stedilijke samenleving. Amsterdam* 1650–1750 (PhD thesis, Erasmus University, Rotterdam)

WOMEN AND THE DEVIL

Possession

S. Clark, 'Protestant demonology: sin, superstition and society (*c*.1520–*c*.1630)' in B. Ankarloo and G. Henningsen eds., *Early Modern European Witchcraft: Centres and Peripheries* (Oxford, 1990)

M. Carmona, *Les diables de Loudun. Sorcellerie et politique sous Richelieu* (Paris, 1988)

M. Certeau, *La fable mystique, XVIe–XVIIe siècles* (Paris, 1982)

M. Certeau, *La Possession de Loudon* (Paris, 1970)

S. Ferber, 'The demonic possession of Marthe Brossier, France 1598–1600' in C. Zika ed., *No Gods Except Me* (Melbourne, 1991)

L. Febvre, 'Sorcellerie: sottise ou révolution mentale', *Annales*, 3 (1948)

C. Pfister, 'Nicolas Rémy et la sorcellerie en Lorraine', *Revue Historique* (1907)

B. Barreiro, *Brujos y astrólogos de la Inquisición de Galicia y el famoso libro de San Cipriano* (1885, repr. Madrid, 1973)

G. Levi, *Inheriting Power: The Story of an Exorcist*, trans. L. Cochrane (London, 1988)

H. C. E. Midelfort, 'The Devil and the German people. Reflections on the popularity of demon possession in 16th century Germany' in S. Ozment ed., *Religion and Culture in Renaissance and Reformation* (Kirksville, Mo., 1989)

General works on magic, witches and witchcraft

B. Ankarloo and G. Henningsen, *Early Modern Witchcraft: centres and peripheries* (Oxford, 1990). Some of the essays, perhaps in particular R. Rowland, '"Fantasticall and Devilishe Persons": European witch beliefs in comparative perspective', address central issues of regional difference.

J. Barry *et al.* eds., *Witchcraft in Early Modern Europe: Studies in Culture and Belief* (Cambridge, 1995)

C. Baroja, *The World of Witches* (London, 1971)

N. Cohn, *Europe's Inner Demons* (London, 1975)

J. Couliano, *Eros and Magic in the Renaissance* (Chicago, 1987)

C. Merchant, *The Death of Nature: Women, Ecology and the Scientific Revolution* (New York, 1980)

R. Kieckhefer, *European Witch Trials: their Foundation in Popular and Learned Culture. 1300–1500* (Berkeley, 1976)

A. Macfarlane, *Witchcraft in Tudor and Stuart England* (London, 1970)

K. Thomas, *Religion and the Decline of Magic* (London, 1971)

C. Larner, *Enemies of God* (Oxford, 1983)

C. Larner, *Witchcraft and Religion: The Politics of Popular Belief* (Oxford, 1984)

R. Briggs, *Communities of Belief: Cultural and Social Tension in Early Modern France* (Oxford, 1989)

R. Mousnier, *Magistrats et Sorciers en France au XVIIIe siècle* (Paris, 1968)

R. Muchembled, *La Sorcière au Village* (Paris, 1979)

E. W. Monter, *Witchcraft in France and Switzerland. The Borderlands during the Reformation* (Ithaca, NY, 1976)

A. Soman, 'Les procès de sorcellerie au Parlement de Paris', *Annales, Economies, Sociétés et Civilisations* (1977)

E. Delcambre, *Le concept de la sorcellerie dans le duché de Lorraine au XVIe et au XVIIe siècles* (3 vols., Nancy, 1948–51)

C. Ginzburg, *Ecstasies: Deciphering the Witches' Sabbath* (New York, 1991)

C. Ginzburg, *The Night Battles: Witchcraft and the Agrarian Cults in the Sixteenth and Seventeenth Centuries* (London, 1983)

R. Martin, *Witchcraft and the Inquisition in Venice, 1559–1650* (Oxford, 1989)

M. O'Neil, 'Magical healing, love magic and the Inquisition in late sixteenth century Modena' in S. Haliczer, *Inquisition and Society in Early Modern Europe* (London, 1987)

G. Henningsen, *The Witches' Advocate: Basque Witchcraft and the Spanish Inquisition 1609–1614* (Reno, Nev., 1980)

H. C. E. Midelfort, *Witch Hunting in South West Germany* (Stanford, 1972)

L. C. Hults, 'Baldung and the Witches of Freiburg: the evidence of images', *Journal of Interdisciplinary History*, 18, 2 (1987)

The witch-as-woman question

B. Ehrenreich, *Witches, Midwives and Nurses: A History of Women Healers* (New York, 1973). This work lacked a sound empirical base to support its generalizations but raised a lot of questions.

A. Barstow, 'On studying witchcraft as women's history: a historiography of the European witch persecutions', *Journal of Feminist Studies in Religion*, 4 (1988)

C. Garrett, 'Women and witches', *Signs* (1977)

C. Honeggar, 'Comment on Garrett's "Women and Witches"', *Signs*, 4 (1979)

J. K. Swales and H. McLachlan, 'Witchcraft and anti-feminism', *Scottish Journal of Sociology*, 4 (1980)

D. Harley, 'Historians as demonologists: the myth of the midwife-witch', *Social History of Medicine*, 3 (1990)

A. Oakley, 'Wise Women and Medicine Men' in J. Mitchel and A. Oakley eds., *The Rights and Wrongs of Women* (Harmondsworth, 1976)

P. Rushton, 'Women, witchcraft and slander in early modern England: cases from the church courts of Durham 1560–1675', *Northern History*, 18 (1982)

C. Holmes, 'Women: witnesses and witches', *Past and Present*, 140 (1993)

J. Sharpe, 'Women, witchcraft and the legal process' in J. Kermode and G. Walker eds., *Women, Crime and the Courts in Early Modern England* (London, 1994)

C. Larner, 'Was witch-hunting woman hunting?', *New Society*, 58 (1981)

C. Larner, 'Witch beliefs and witch-hunting in England and Scotland', *History Today*, 31 (1981)

R. Briggs, 'Women as victims? Witches, judges and the community', *French History*, 5 (1991)

S. Clark, 'The "gendering" of witchcraft in French demonology: misogyny or polarity', *French History*, 5 (1991)

L. Roper, *Oedipus and the Devil. Witchcraft, Sexuality and Religion in Early Modern Europe* (London, 1994). Largely concerned with Germany, a centre of witch beliefs, but raises new and fundamental issues and also criticizes existing historiography on magic.

W. de Blécourt, 'Typen van toverij' in P. te Boekhorst, P. Burke and W. Frijhoff eds., *Cultuur en maatschappij in Nederland 1500–1850* (Heerlen, 1992)

M. Gijswijt-Hofstra, 'Witchcraft in the Northern Netherlands' in Angerman *et al.* eds., *Current Issues in Women's History* (London, 1989)

On the continuation of witch beliefs

J. Favret-Saada, *Deadly Words: Witchcraft in the Bocage* (Cambridge, 1980)

OBEDIENT TO THY WILL

J. Delumeau, *Catholicism between Luther and Voltaire* (Cambridge, 1977)

J. Delumeau, *Sin and Fear. The Emergence of a Western Guilt Culture 13th–18th centuries*, trans E. Nicholson (New York, 1990)

L. Châtelier, *The Europe of the Devout: The Catholic Reformation and the Formation of a New Society* (Cambridge, 1989)

F. Le Brun ed., *Histoire des Catholiques en France du XVe siècle à nos jours* (Toulouse, 1980)

Bibliographies and collections cutting across aspects of women's experience in the Reformation and the Counter-Reformation

J. Irwin, 'Society and the sexes' in S. Ozment ed., *Reformation Europe: A Guide to Research* (St Louis, 1982)

S. Marshall ed., *Women in Reformation and Counter Reformation Europe: Public and Private Worlds* (Bloomington, 1989)

E. Weaver, 'Women and religion in early modern France: a bibliographical essay on the state of the question', *Catholic Historical Review*, 67 (1981)

L. Scaraffia and G. Zarri eds., *Donne e fede* (Rome/Bari, 1994)

E. Schulte van Kessel ed., *Women and Men in Spiritual Culture XIV-XVII Centuries* (The Hague, 1986)

A. Cruz and M. Perry eds., *Culture and Control in Counter Reformation Spain* (Minneapolis, 1992)

E. Kloek, 'De Reformatie als thema van vrouwenstudies: Een histories debat over goed en kwaad', *Jaarboek voor Vrouwengeschiedenis*, 4 (1983)

J. D. Douglass, 'Women and the Continental Reformation' in R. R. Ruether, *Religion and Sexism: Images of Women in the Jewish and Christian Traditions* (New York, 1974)

Convents

M. Rosa, 'La religiosa' in R. Villari ed., *L'uomo barocco* (Rome/Bari, 1991)

J. L. Sánchez Lora, *Mujeres, conventos y formas de la religiosidad barroca* (Madrid, 1988)

Convents and family strategy

G. Greco, 'Monasteri femminili e patriziato a Pisa (1530–1630)' in *Città italiane del '500 tra riforma e controriforma. Atti del convegno internazionale di studi di Lucca* (Lucca, 1983)

V. Hunecke, 'Kindbett oder Kloster: Lebenswege venezianischer Patrizierinnen im 17. und 18. Jahrhundert', *Geschichte und Gesellschaft. Zeitschrift für Historische Sozialwissenschaft*, 18 (1992)

B. Harris, 'A new look at the Reformation: aristocratic women and nunneries, 1450–1540', *Journal of British Studies*, 32 (1993)

Mysticism

J. R. Berrigan, 'Saint Catherine of Bologna: Franciscan mystic', in K. M. Wilson ed., *Women Writers of the Renaissance and Reformation* (Athens, Ga., 1987)

M. G. Bianchi, 'Una "illuminata" del secolo XVII: suor M. Domitilla Galluzzi, cappucina a Pavia', *Bollettino della Società Pavese di Storia patria*, 68 (1971)

F. Pons, *Místicos, beatas y alumbrados* (Valencia, 1991)

J. Ameland, 'Monjas y beatas en la Cataluña moderna' in J. Ameland and M. Nash, *Historia y género: las mujeres en la Europa Moderna y Contemporánea* (Valencia, 1990)

J. Bilinkoff, 'A Spanish prophetess and her patrons: the case of María de Saint Domingo, *Sixteenth Century Journal*, 23 (1992)

J. Bilinkoff, *The Avila of Saint Teresa* (Ithaca, 1989)

The Life of Saint Teresa of Avila by herself (1582), trans. and ed. J. M. Cohen (London, 1957)

Cultural life in the convent

C. Monson, *The Crannied Wall. Women, Religion and the Arts in Early Modern Europe* (Ann Arbor, 1992)

M. L. King, 'Book-lined cells: women and humanism in the early Italian Renaissance' in P. Labalme ed., *Beyond their Sex. Learned Women of the European Past* (London, 1984)

S. Cabibbo, '"Ignoratio Scripturarum, ignoratio Christi est". Tradizione e pratica delle scritture nei testi monastici femminili del XVII secolo', *Rivista Storica Italiana*, 101 (1989)

S. da Campagnola, 'La biblioteca del monastero di S. Anna alla fine del Cinquecento', *Analecta tertii ordinis regularis Sancti Francisci*, 17 (1984)

S. Evangelisti, 'Angelica Baitelli, la storica', in G. Calvi ed., *Barocco al femminile* (Rome/Bari, 1992)

V. Finucci, 'Camilla Faa Gonzaga: the Italian memorialist' in K. M. Wilson and F. Warnke eds., *Women Writers of the Seventeenth Century* (London, 1988)

'Denkwürdigkeiten der Caritas Pirkheimer (aus den Jahren 1524–1528)' in J. Pfanner ed., *Caritas Pirkheimer, Quellensammlung*, 2 (Landshut, 1962)

J. Bowers, 'The emergence of women composers in Italy, 1566–1700' in J. Bowers and J. Tick eds., *Women Making Music* (Urbana, 1986)

E. Weaver, 'Spiritual fun: a study of sixteenth-century Tuscan convent theater' in M. B. Rose ed., *Women in the Middle Ages and Renaissance: Literary and Historical Perspectives* (Syracuse, 1985)

Sexuality

J. C. Brown, *Immodest Acts: The Life of a Lesbian Nun in Renaissance Italy* (Oxford, 1986)

R. Canosa, *Il velo e il cappuccio. Monacazione forzate e sessualità nei conventi femminili in Italia tra '400 e '700* (Rome, 1991)

U. Colombo ed., *Vita e processo di Suor Virginia Maria de Leyva monaca di Monza* (Milan, 1985)

Arcangela Tarabotti

F. Medioli, *L "Inferno monacale" di Arcangela Tarabotti* (Turin, 1990)

G. Conti Odorisio, *Donna e società nel Seicento. Lucrezia Marinelli e Arcangela Tarabotti* (Rome, 1979)

Tridentine reforms and beyond

R. Creytens, 'La riforma dei monasteri femminili dopo i Decreti Tridentini' in *Il Concilio di Trento e la riforma tridentina*, vol. 1 (Rome, 1965)

F. Molinari, 'Visite pastorali dei monasteri femminili di Piacenza nel secolo XVI' in *Il Concilio di Trento e la riforma tridentina*, vol. I (Rome, 1965)

E. Rapley, *The Dévotes: Women and the Church in Seventeenth Century France* (Montreal, 1990)

O. Hufton and F. Tallett, 'Communities of women, the religious life and public service in eighteenth century France' in M. Boxer and J. Quataert eds., *Connecting Spheres. Women in the Western World 1500 to the Present* (Oxford, 1987)

C. Langlois, *Le Catholicisme au feminin: les congrégations françaises à supérieure générale au XIXe siècle* (Paris, 1984)

The Ursulines

M. de Chantal-Gueudre, *Histoire de l'ordre des Ursulines en France* (Paris, 1957–63)

M. A. Jégou, *Les Ursulines du Faubourg St Jacques à Paris, 1607–1662: Origine d'un monastère apostolique* (Paris, 1981)

A. Conrad, *Zwischen Kloster und Welt. Ursulinen und Jesuitinnen in der katholischen Reformbewegung des 16./17. Jahrhunderts* (Mainz, 1991)

The Visitandines

A. Scattigno, 'Jeanne de Chantal, la fondatrice', in G. Calvi ed., *Barocco al femminile* (Rome/Bari, 1991)

R. Devos, 'La correspondance de Jeanne de Chantal; son intérêt au point de vue de l'histoire social des mentalités', *Actes du Congrès des Sociétés savantes de la province de Savoie* (Chambéry, 1972)

The Sisters of Charity (Filles de Charité)

P. Coste, *Les Filles de Charité: L'Institut de 1617 à 1800* (Paris, 1913)

C. Jones, *The Charitable Imperative: Hospitals and Nursing in Ancien Régime and Revolutionary France* (London, 1989)

Other nursing and welfare orders

M. Vacher, *'Des régulières' dans le siècle: les soeurs de Saint Joseph du Père Médaille aux XVIIe et XVIIIe siècles* (Clermont-Ferrand, 1991)

M. C. Dinet-Lecomte, 'Implantation et rayonnement des Congrégations Hospitalières dans le Sud de la France aux XVIIe et XVIIIe siècles', *Annales du Midi*, 104 (1992). Includes an excellent bibliography.

A. Pertefaix, *Les Religieuses de la Miséricorde de Billom 1786–1867* (Clermont-Ferrand, 1967)

O. Robert, 'De la dentelle et des âmes. Les "Demoiselles de l'Instruction" du Puy (XVIIe–XVIIIe siècles)' in J. Delumeau ed., *La Religion de ma mère* (Paris, 1992)

Holiness, sanctity

A. Vauchez, *La sainteté en occident aux derniers siècles du Moyen Age d'après les procès de canonisation et des documents hagiographiques* (Rome, 1981)

C. Leonardi, 'Santità delle donne' in G. Pozzi and C. Leonardi eds., *Scrittici mistiche italiane* (Genoa, 1988)

R. Bell, *Saints and Society. The Two Worlds of Western Christendom 1000–1700* (Chicago, 1982)

R. Bell, *Holy Anorexia* (Chicago, 1985)

C. W. Bynum, *Holy Feast and Holy Fast: The Religious Significance of Food to Medieval Women* (Berkeley, 1987)

Boesch Gajano, *Culto dei santi, istituzioni e classi sociali in età pre-industriale* (Rome, 1984)

G. Zarri, *Le sante vive: profezie e devozione femminile tra '400 e '500* (Turin, 1990)

G. Zarri, *Finzione e santità tra medioevo ed età moderna* (Turin, 1991)

L. Scaraffia, *La santa degli impossibili. Vicende e significati della devozione a Santa Rita* (Turin, 1990)

A. Weber, *Saint Teresa of Avila and the Rhetoric of Femininity* (Princeton, 1992)

D. Latz, *Saint Angela Merici and the Spiritual Currents of the Italian Renaissance* (Lille, 1986)

R. Sarti, 'Zita, serva e santa. Un modello da imitare?' in G. Barone, M. Caffiero and F. S. Barcellona, *Modelli di santità e modelli di comportamento* (Turin, 1994)

Holy women

F. Koorn, 'Elisabeth Strouven, la donna religiosa', in G. Calvi ed., *Barocco al femminile* (Rome/Bari, 1992)

M. Firpo, 'Paola Antonia Negri, monaca Angelica (1508–1555)', in O. Niccoli ed., *Rinascimento al femminile* (Rome/Bari, 1991)

Religious teaching and acculturation

R. Sarti, 'Obediente e fedele. Note sull'istruzione morale e religiosa di servi e serve tra Cinque e Settecento', *Annali dell'Istituto storico italo germanico in Trento*, 17 (1991)

E. Schulte van Kessel, 'Virgins and mothers between heaven and earth' in G. Duby and M. Perrot eds., *A History of Women in the West*, vol.3: N. Z. Davis and A. Farge eds., *Renaissance and Enlightenment Paradoxes* (Cambridge, Mass., 1993)

J. Delumeau, *La Religion de ma mère* (Paris, 1992)

J. N. Vuarnet, *Le Dieu des femmes* (Paris, 1989)

J. Delumeau, *La Première Communion. Quatre siècles d'histoire* (Paris, 1987)

Jesuit influence on women

H. Rahner, *St Ignatius Loyola. Letters to Women* (London, 1960)
G. Zarri, 'Ginevra Gozzadini dall'Armi, Gentildonna Bolognese (1520/27–1567)' in O. Niccoli, ed., *Rinascimento al femminile* (Rome/Bari, 1991)

Mission work

E. Arenal and S. Schlau, *Untold Sisters: Hispanic Nuns in their own works* (Albuquerque, 1989)
D. Deslandres, 'Femmes missionnaires en Nouvelle France' in J. Delumeau ed., *La Religion de ma mère* (Paris, 1992)

Women and the Inquisition

E. W. Monter, 'Women and the Italian Inquisition' in M. B. Rose ed., *Women in the Middle Ages and the Renaissance* (Syracuse, 1985)
J. Martin, 'Out of the shadow: heretical and Catholic women in Renaissance Venice', *Journal of Family History*, 10 (1985)
S. Haliczer, *Inquisition and Society in the Kingdom of Valencia 1478–1834* (Oxford, 1990)
C. Guilhem, 'L'Inquisition et la dévaluation des discours féminins' in B. Bennassar ed., *L'Inquisition Espagnole XV–XIX siècles* (Paris, 1979)
H. Kamen, *Inquisition and Society in Spain in the Sixteenth and Seventeenth Centuries* (London, 1985)
M. Perry, 'Beatas and the Inquisition in early modern Seville' in S. Haliczer ed., *Inquisition and Society in Early Modern Europe* (London, 1987)
D. Higgs, 'Inquisition, gender and genealogy in seventeenth century Portugal', *Portuguese Studies Review*, 2 (1993)

Recusant women

M. Rowlands, 'Recusant women 1560–1640' in M. Prior ed., *Women in English Society 1500–1800* (London, 1985)
J. C. H. Aveling, 'Catholic Households in Yorkshire 1580–1603', *Northern History*, 16 (1980)
J. C. H. Aveling, *The Handle and the Axe* (London, 1976)
S. O'Brien, 'Women of the English Catholic community: nuns and pupils at the Bar Convent, York, 1680–1790', *Monastic Studies*, 1 (nd)

Protestant women

S. Wyntjes, 'Women in the Reformation era' in R. Bridenthal and C. Koonz eds., *Becoming Visible: Women in European History* (Boston, 1977)
J. L. Irwin, *Womanhood in Radical Protestantism* (New York, 1979)

C. J. Blaisdell, 'The matrix of reform: women in the Lutheran and Calvinist movements' in R. L. Greaves ed., *Triumph over Silence: Women in Protestant History* (Westport, Conn., 1985)

M. Carbonnier-Burkard, 'La Réforme en langue de femmes' in J. Delumeau ed., *La Religion de ma mère* (Paris, 1992)

Women and Calvinism

J. D. Douglass, *Women, Freedom and Calvin* (Philadelphia, 1985)

C. J. Blaisdell, 'Calvin's letters to women: the courting of ladies in high places', *Sixteenth Century Journal*, 13 (1982)

C. J. Blaisdell, 'Renée de France between Reform and Counter-Reform', *Archiv für Reformationsgeschichte*, 63 (1972)

N. Z. Davis, 'City women and religious change' in *Society and Culture in Early Modern France* (Stanford, 1979)

N. L. Roelker, *Queen of Navarre, Jeanne d'Albret (1528–1572)* (Cambridge, 1968)

N. L. Roelker, 'The appeal of Calvinism to French noblewomen in the sixteenth century', *Journal of Interdisciplinary History*, 2 (1972)

N. L. Roelker, 'The role of noblewomen in the French Reformation', *Archiv für Reformationsgeschichte*, 63 (1972)

J. Watt, 'Women and the Consistory in Calvin's Geneva', *Sixteenth Century Journal*, 24 (1993)

Women and Anabaptism

J. Klassen, 'Women and the family among Dutch Anabaptist martyrs', *Mennonite Quarterly Review*, 60 (1986)

W. Harrison, 'The role of women in Anabaptist thought and practice: the Hutterite experience of the sixteenth and seventeenth centuries', *Sixteenth Century Journal*, 23 (1992)

M. Kobelt-Groch, 'Why did Petronella leave her husband? Reflections on marital avoidance among the Halberstadt Anabaptists', *Mennonite Quarterly Review*, 62 (1988)

L. Roper, 'Sexual Utopianism and the German Reformation' in Roper, *Oedipus and the Devil*, (London, 1994)

The English Reformation

P. Crawford, *Women and Religion in England, 1500–1720* (London, 1993)

P. Collinson, 'The role of women in the English Reformation illustrated by the life and friendships of Anne Locke' in *Godly People. Essays on English Protestantism and Puritanism* (London, 1983)

C. Levin, 'Women in the *Book of Martyrs* as models of behaviour in Tudor England', *International Journal of Women's Studies*, 4 (1981)

E. Macek, 'The emergence of a feminine spirituality in the *Book of Martyrs*', *Sixteenth Century Journal*, 19 (1988)

Civil War sects

K. Thomas, 'Women and the Civil War sects', *Past and Present*, 13 (1958)

E. Morgan Williams, 'Women preachers in the Civil War', *Journal of Modern History*, 1 (1929)

C. Cross, '"He Goats before the Flocks": a note on the part played by women in the founding of some Civil War churches' in G. J. Cumming and D. Baker eds., *Popular Belief and Practice: Studies in Church History*, 8 (Cambridge, 1972)

A. Laurence, 'A priesthood of she-believers: women and congregations in mid seventeenth century England' in W. Sheils and D. Wood eds., *Women in the Church: Studies in Church History*, 27 (1990)

P. Crawford, 'Historians, women and the Civil War sects, 1640–1660', *Paragon*, 8 (1988)

B. R. Dailey, 'The visitation of Sarah Wight: Holy Carnival and the Revolution of the Saints in Civil War London', *Church History*, 55 (1986)

P. Higgins, 'The reactions of women, with special reference to women petitioners' in B. Manning ed., *Politics, Religion and the English Civil War* (London, 1973)

D. Ludlow, 'Shaking patriarchy's foundations: sectarian women in England, 1541–1700' in R. Greaves ed., *Triumph over Silence. Women in Protestant History* (Westport, Conn., 1985)

The Quakers

M. R. Brailsford, *Quaker Women* (London, 1915). Still the best overview.

E. Manners, *Elizabeth Hooton, First Quaker Woman Preacher 1600–1672* (London, 1914)

P. Mack, 'Teaching about gender and spirituality in early English Quakerism', *Women's Studies*, 19 (1991)

Methodism

J. Walsh, 'Methodism and the mob in the eighteenth century' in G. J. Cumming and D. Baker eds., *Popular Belief and Practice: Studies in Church History*, 8 (1972)

W. F. Smith, 'The women itinerant preachers of early Methodism', *Proceedings of the Wesley History Society*, 28 (1951)

D. M. Valenze, *Prophetic Sons and Daughters: Female Preaching and Popular Religion in Industrial England* (Princeton, 1985). Although mostly outside this period, the continuity between this form of religion and earlier charismatic beliefs is striking.

Reformation in the Netherlands

S. Marshall, 'Women and religious choices in the sixteenth century Netherlands', *Archiv für Reformationsgeschichte*, 75 (1974)

J. Irwin, 'Anna Maria van Schurman: from feminism to Pietism', *Church History*, 46 (1977)

M. de Baar, 'De Betrokkenheid van vrouwen bij het huisgezin van Jean Labadie 1669–1732', *Jaarboek voor Vrouwengeschiedenis* (1987)

Reformation in Germany

L. Roper, *The Holy Household: Religion, Morals and Order in Reformation Augsburg* (Oxford, 1989)

L. Roper, ' "The Common Man", "The Common Good", "Common Women": reflections on gender and meaning in the Reformation German Commune', *Social History*, 12 (1987). See also her collection of essays in *Oedipus and the Devil* (London, 1994)

S. Karant Nunn, 'Continuity and change: some effects of the Reformation on the women of Zwickau', *Sixteenth Century Journal*, 13 (1982)

S. Karant Nunn, 'The transmission of Luther's teachings on women and matrimony: the case of Zwickau', *Archiv für Reformationgeschichte*, 77 (1986)

M. E. Wiesner, 'Women's responses to the Reformation' in R. Po-Chia Hsia, *The German People and the Reformation* (Ithaca, 1988)

P. Veit, 'Les nouvelles Sara, Marthe et Marie: la femme et sa religion à travers les *Leichenpredigten* protestants' in J. Delumeau ed., *La religion de ma mère* (Paris, 1992). Contains an excellent bibliography in German and French on the religious acculturation of women through sermons and schooling throughout the early modern period as well as the preferred forms of both sexes for religious ritual.

WOMEN WRITERS

The volume of work on ideas about women and women writers is enormous because of the obvious overlap between history and literature and the significant focus of feminist theorists on literary texts. What follows is a small sample of the works found most pertinent to the historical development of women and also to ideas about them.

Literacy and education

R. A. Houston, *Literacy in Early Modern Europe* (London, 1988)

D. Cressy, *Literacy and the Social Order* (Cambridge, 1980)

J. P. Anglin, 'The expansion of literacy: opportunities for the study of the three rs in the London diocese of Elizabeth I', *Guildhall Studies in London History* (London, 1980)

F. Furet and M. Ozouf, *Reading and Writing. Literacy in France from Calvin to Jules Ferry* (Cambridge, 1982)

E. François, *Alphabetisierung in Deutschland und Frankreich im Zeitalter der französischen Revolution* (Frankfurt, 1989)

E. François, 'Livre, confession et société urbaine en Allemagne au XVIIIe siècle: l'exemple de Spire', *Revue d'histoire moderne et contemporaine*, 29 (1982)

F. López, 'Lisants et lecteurs en Espagne au XVIIIe siècle', in *Livre et Lecture en Espagne et en France sous l'ancien régime* (Paris, 1981)

Women and education

R. O'Day, *Education and Society, 1500–1800: social foundations of education in early modern Britain* (London, 1982)

R. Chartier, D. Julia and M. Compère, *L'Education en France du XVIe au XVIIIe siècles* (Paris, 1976)

B. Grosperrin, *Les petites écoles sous l'ancien régime* (Rennes, 1984)

E. Ravoux-Rallo, *Les religieuses enseignantes, XVIe–XXe siècles* (Angers, 1981)

M. Sonnet, *L'Education des filles au temps des lumières* (Paris, 1987)

K. Arnold, *Kind und Gesellschaft in Mittelalter und Renaissance* (Paderborn, 1980)

C. N. Moore, *The Maiden's Mirror. Reading Matter for German Girls in the Sixteenth and Seventeenth Centuries* (Wiesbaden, 1987)

Renaissance women writers and early feminist debate

C. Jordan, *Renaissance Feminism. Literary Texts and Political Models* (Ithaca, 1990)

B. Travitsky ed., *The Paradise of Women: Writing by English Women of the Renaissance* (New York, 1989)

E. H. Hageman and J. R. Roberts, 'Recent studies in women writers of Tudor England, 1485–1603', *English Literary Renaissance*, 14 (1984)

I. Maclean, *Woman Triumphant: Feminism in French Literature 1610–52* (Oxford, 1977)

G. Conti Odorisio, *Donna e società nel Seicento. Lucrezia Marinelli e Arcangela Tarabotti* (Rome, 1979)

Women and the Enlightenment

S. Spencer ed., *French Women in the Age of Enlightenment* (Bloomington, 1984)

S. Tomaselli, 'The Enlightenment debate on women', *History Workshop Journal*, 20 (1985)

P. Hoffmann, *La femme dans la pensée des lumières* (Paris, 1977)

J. Rendall, *The Origins of Modern Feminism: Women in Britain, France and the United States 1780–1860* (London, 1985)

E. Jacobs *et al.* eds., *Women and Society in Eighteenth Century France* (London, 1979). A series of essays on Enlightenment thinkers and the woman issue.

A. M. Wilson, 'Treated like imbecile children' in P. Fritz and R. Morton, *Women in the Eighteenth Century* (Toronto, 1976)

A. Sfargo, 'La Représentation de la femme chez Diderot', *Studies on Voltaire and the Eighteenth Century*, 193 (1980)

Memoirs, diaries and correspondence

E. C. Jelinek ed., *The Tradition of Women's Autobiography from Antiquity to the Present* (Boston, 1986)

S. H. Mendelson, 'Stuart Women's diaries and occasional memoirs' in M. Prior ed., *Women in English Society 1500–1800* (London, 1985)

E. Graham ed., *Her Own Life: Autobiographical Writings by Seventeenth Century Englishwomen* (London, 1989)

W. Gibson, *Women in Seventeenth Century France* (London, 1989). Contains an excellent bibliography on women's memoirs.

Madame de Sévigné, *Lettres*, ed. M. Monmerque (14 vols., Paris, 1862–1925). Many selections have been made.

M. L. Farrell, *Performing Motherhood: The Sévigné Correspondence* (Hanover, 1991). Uses the letters to pursue a mother/daughter relationship.

R. Dekker, 'Dat mijn lieven kinderen weten zouden. Egodocumenten in Nederland van Zestiende tot de Negentiende Eeuw', *Opossum*, 8 (1993)

A. Jacobsen Schutte, 'Inquisition and female autobiography: the case of Cecilia Ferazzi' in C. Monson ed., *The Crannied Wall: Women, Religion and the Arts in Early Modern Europe* (Ann Arbor, 1992)

Salons in the 16th and 17th centuries

E. Magne, *Voiture et l'Hôtel de Rambouillet: les origines 1597–1600* (Paris, 1929)

C. Delong, 'From conversation to creation' in G. Duby and M. Perrot eds., *A History of Women in the West*, vol. 3: N. Z. Davis and A. Farge eds., *Renaissance and Enlightenment Paradoxes* (Cambridge, Mass., 1993)

C. Delong, *L'amour au XVIIe siècle* (Paris, 1969), ch. 3

C. Delong, *La vie quotidienne des femmes au Grand Siècle* (Paris, 1984), ch. 4 and bibliography

C. Lougee, *Women, Salons and Social Stratification in Seventeenth Century France* (Princeton, 1976)

R. Lathvillière, *La préciosité, étude historique et linguistique* (Paris, 1966)

M. Magendie, *La politesse mondaine et les théories de l'honnêteté en France au XVIIe siècle* (Paris, 1925)

E. Harth, *Ideology and Culture in Seventeenth Century France* (Ithaca, 1983)

E. Harth, *Cartesian Women: versions and subversions of rational discourse in the old regime* (Ithaca, 1992)

18th century salons

D. Goodman, 'The Enlightenment salons: the convergence of female and philosophic ambitions', *Eighteenth Century Studies* (1989)

D. Goodman, 'Filial rebellion in the salon. Madame Géoffrin and her daughter', *French Historical Studies* (1989)

D. Goodman, 'Public sphere and private life: towards a synthesis of current approaches to Old Regime France', *History and Theory*, 6 (1992)

F. Steegmuller, *A Woman, a Man and Two Kingdoms: The Story of Madame d'Epinay and the Abbé Galiani* (New York, 1992)

G. Dulac and D. Maggetti eds., *Fernando Galiani, Louise d'Epinay, Correspondance, vol. 1 1769–70* (Paris, 1992)

R. P. Weinreb, *Eagle in a Gauze Cage: Louise d'Epinay, femme de lettres* (New York, 1992)

R. P. Weinreb, 'Madame d'Epinay: literary critic for the Correspondance Littéraire', *Studies on Voltaire and the Eighteenth Century*, 304 (1992)

B. Craveri, *Madame du Deffand and her World* (London, 1994). Reveals how the *philosophes* viewed this particular *salonnière*.

G. D. Hertze, *Jewish High Society in Old Regime Berlin* (New Haven, 1988)

M. C. Hoock-Demarle, *La femme au temps de Goethe* (Paris, 1987)

J. Georgelin, *Venise au siècle des lumières* (Paris/La Haye, 1978). Gives some information on Venetian salons.

British women writers in the 17th century

S. Mendelson, *The Mental World of Stuart Women* (Brighton, 1987). A study using three women, the Duchess of Newcastle, Aphra Behn and the Countess of Warwick, as representing different genres and aspects of women's writing.

P. Crawford, 'Women's Published Writings 1600–1700' in M. Prior ed., *Women in English Society*

E. Hobby, *Virtue of Necessity: English Women's Writing, 1649–88* (London, 1988)

J. Todd ed., *A Dictionary of British and American Writers 1660–1800* (Totowa, NJ, 1987). A *vade mecum* for anyone wishing to embark on this field.

A. Goreau, *Reconstructing Aphra: A Social Biography of Aphra Behn* (New York, 1980)

M. Duffy, *The Passionate Shepherdess: Aphra Behn, 1640–1689* (London, 1977)

J. Todd, *The Sign of Angellica: Women, Writing and Fiction, 1660–1800* (London, 1989)

N. Cotton, *Women Playwrights in England* (Louisberg, 1980)

On corresponding gentlewomen

R. Perry, 'Radical doubt and the liberation of women', *Eighteenth Century Studies* (1985)

M. Reynolds, *The Learned Lady in England (1650–1760)* (1920, repr. Gloucester, Mass., 1964)

On Mary Astell

R. Perry, *The Celebrated Mary Astell. An Early English Feminist* (Chicago/London, 1986)

B. Hill ed., *The First English Feminist. Reflections on Marriage and other writings by Mary Astell* (New York, 1986). Has a good introduction on Astell and her context.

S. F. Matthews Grieco, 'Mary Astell, l'educatrice femminista' in G. Calvi ed., *Barocco al femminile* (Rome/Bari, 1992)

J. K. Kinnaird, 'Mary Astell and the Conservative contribution to English feminism', *Journal of British Studies*, 19 (1979)

The bluestockings

S. H. Myers, *The Blue Stocking Circle: Women, Friendship and the Life of the Mind in Eighteenth Century England* (Oxford, 1990). Has a very valuable bibliography transcending the title.

E. G. Bodeck, 'Salonnière and Blue Stockings: educated obsolescence and germinating feminism', *Feminist Studies*, 3 (1976)

R. Halsband, *The Life of Lady Mary Wortley Montagu* (Oxford, 1956)

French women writers

M. Warner, *From the Beast to the Blonde. On Fairy Tales and their Tellers* (London, 1994). Gives a very valuable appreciation of the role of aristocratic women in the late seventeenth century in publishing collections of traditional stories.

J. Hinde Stewart, 'The novelists and the fictions' in S. Spencer ed., *French Women and the Enlightenment* (Bloomington, 1984)

L. K. Horowitz, *Love and Language: a study of the classical French moralist writers* (Columbus, Ohio, 1977)

J. Fabre, *Idées sur le roman de Madame de Lafayette au marquis de Sade* (Paris, 1979)

J. W. Scott, *Madame de Lafayette, a selective critical bibliography* (London, 1974)

R. W. Redhead, *Themes and Images in the fictional works of Madame de Lafayette* (New York, 1990)

C. Venesoen, *Etudes sur la littérature féminine au XVIIe siècle: Mademoiselle*

de Gournay, Mademoiselle de Scudéry, Madame de Villedieu, Madame de Lafayette
(Birmingham, Ala., 1990)

The 18th century novel

In England

J. Raven, *British Fiction 1750–1770*. A chronological check list of prose fiction printed in Britain and Ireland (London, 1987)

K. Rogers, *Feminism in Eighteenth Century England* (Urbana, 1982). Though important, somewhat misnamed; it is about women writers and these were not necessarily feminist.

J. Spencer, *The Rise of the Woman Novelist* (Oxford, 1986)

R. Ballaster, *Seductive Forms: Women's Amatory Fiction from 1684–1740* (Oxford, 1992)

G. J. Barker-Benfield, *The Culture of Sensibility: Sex and Society in the Eighteenth Century English Novel* (Chicago, 1992)

J. A. Boone, *Tradition and Counter Tradition: Love and the Form of Fiction. Women in Culture and Society* (Chicago, 1987)

K. S. Green, *The Courtship Novel, 1740–1820: A Feminised Genre* (Lexington, 1991)

R. Yeazell, *Fictions of Modesty: Women and Courtship in the English Novel* (Chicago, 1991)

M. A. Schofield, *Masking and Unmasking the Female Mind: Disguising Romances in Feminine Fiction, 1713–1799* (London, 1990)

P. M. Spacks, *Imagining a Self: Autobiography and Novel in Eighteenth Century England* (Cambridge, 1976)

J. Todd, *Sensibility: An Introduction* (London, 1986)

J. Todd, *The Sign of Angellica: Women, Writing and Fiction, 1660–1800* (London, 1989)

I. Watt, *The Rise of the Novel. Studies in Defoe, Richardson and Fielding* (London, 1957)

Creative literature drawing upon issues arising from attitudes to, and institutional constraints upon, women

J. Zomchick, *Family and Law in the Eighteenth Century Novel* (Cambridge, 1993)

M. Poovey, 'Fathers and daughters: the trauma of growing up female', *Women and Literature*, 2 (1982)

M. Poovey, *The Proper Lady and the Woman Writer: Ideology as Style in the Works of Mary Wollstonecraft, Jane Austen and Mary Shelley* (Chicago, 1984)

I. Watt, 'The New Woman: Samuel Richardson's *Pamela*' in R. L. Coser ed., *The Family: its Structure and Functions* (New York, 1964)

S. Staves, 'British seduced maidens', *Eighteenth Century Studies*, 14 (1980–81)

Fanny Burney

This writer as well as Jane Austen made a literary career from examining the social obstacles confronting women.

D. D. Devlin, *The Novels and Journals of Fanny Burney* (London, 1990)

K. Straub, *Fanny Burney and Feminine Strategy* (Lexington, 1987)

S. Staves, 'Evelina or Female Difficulties', *Modern Philology*, 73 (1976)

R. M. Cutting, 'Defiant women: the growth of feminism in Fanny Burney's novels', *Studies in English Literature*, 17 (1987)

K. Rogers, *Frances Burney: The World of Female Difficulties* (London, 1990)

The European novel

J. Hinde Stewart, *The Novels of Madame Riccoboni* (Chapel Hill, Va., 1976)

V. Wyndham, *Madame de Genlis; a biography* (London, 1958). A good modern reflective biography of this internationally acclaimed author, who was simultaneously governess to the children of the Duke of Orleans and a very astute promoter of the interests of her family, would be valuable

S. Zantop, *Bitter Healing: German Women Writers 1700–1840* (Lincoln, Nebraska, 1990)

G. Brinker-Gabler ed., *Deutsche Literatur von Frauen* (Munich, 1988)

Women's periodical press

In England

A. Aldburgham, *Women in Print. Writing Women and Women's Magazines from the Restoration to the Accession of Victoria* (London, 1972)

K. Shevelow, *Women and Print Culture: the Construction of Femininity in the Early Periodical* (London, 1989)

J. Hodges, 'The Female Spectator, a courtesy periodical' in R. P. Bond ed., *Studies in the Early English Periodical* (Chapel Hill, Va., 1957)

J. E. Hunter, 'The Ladies Magazine and the History of the eighteenth century Englishwoman' in D. H. Bond and W. Reynolds McLeod eds., *Newsletters to Newspapers: Eighteenth Century Journalism* (Morgantown, Va., 1977)

In France

E. Sullerot, *Histoire de la presse féminine en France, des origines à 1848* (Paris, 1966)

C. Rimbault, 'La presse féminine de langue française au XVIIIe siècle' in *Le journalisme d'ancien régime. Questions et propositions.* Table Rond. CNRS juin 1981 (Lyon, 1982)

N. Gelbart, *Feminine and Opposition Journalism in Old Regime France: Le Journal des Dames* (Berkeley, 1987)

N. Gelbart, 'The *Journal des dames* and its female editors: politics, censorship and feminism in the Old Regime press' in J. R. Censor and J. D.

Popkin eds., *Press and Politics in Pre-Revolutionary France* (Berkeley, 1987)

In Italy

   L. Guerci, *La sposa obbediente. Donna e matrimonio nella discussione dell'Italia del Settecento* (Turin, 1988); lists *tesi di laurea* on the female periodical press in Florence, Venice and Milan (pp. 571–9).

Nonfiction

   M. P. Hannay, *Silent but for the Word: Tudor Women as Patrons, Translators and Writers of Religious Works* (Kent, Ohio, 1985)
   J. R. Brink ed., *Female Scholars: A Tradition of Learned Women before 1800* (Montreal, 1980)
   B. Hill, *The Republican Virago. The Life and Times of Catherine Macaulay* (Oxford, 1992)
   See also Corresponding gentlewomen; Convents: Cultural life

Eighteenth century feminists

Mary Wollstonecraft
   J. Todd, *Mary Wollstonecraft: An Annotated Bibliography* (New York, 1976). Now out of date, given the massive attention to Wollstonecraft, but still the point of departure.
   There are several editions of *A Vindication of the Rights of Woman* of which the most recent, B. Taylor ed. (London, 1992), has a very perceptive introduction; this author has in progress a much awaited study of Wollstonecraft and has published preliminary work in 'Mary Wollstonecraft and the wild wish of early feminism', *History Workshop Journal*, 33 (1992)
   C. Tomalin, *The Life and Death of Mary Wollstonecraft* (London, 1974). Remains a sensitive and objective study.

Olympe de Gouges
   J. W. Scott, 'French feminists and the Rights of "Man". Olympe de Gouges' Declarations', *History Workshop Journal*, 28 (1989)
   O. de Gouges, *Oeuvres*, ed. B. Groult (Paris, 1989)

Other professional work

The actress
   E. Nicholson, 'The Theater' in Duby and Perrot eds., *A History of Women*, vol. 3. An excellent essay which reviews the emergence of the actress in Italy and gradually throughout the rest of western Europe.
   P. H. Highfill, *A Biographical Dictionary of Stage Personnel, London, 1660–1800* (London, 1982). A good reference book.

C. J. Stratman *et al.*, *Restoration and Eighteenth Century Theatre Research: a bibliographical guide 1900–1968* (Carbondale, Ill., 1971)

S. Richards, *The Rise of the English Actress* (New York, 1993)

J. Pearson, 'Women in the Theater, 1660–1737' in *The Prostituted Muse. Images of Women and Western Dramatists, 1642–1737* (New York, 1988). These works give an idea of the early experience of women on the stage and locate them in their society.

C. Tomalin, *Mrs Jordan's Profession* (London, 1994). Written with a good eye for the environment in which the actress operated.

L. Kelly, *The Kemble Era: John Philip Kemble, Sarah Siddons and the London Stage* (London, 1980)

M. Lazard, *Le Théâtre en France au XVIe siècle* (Paris, 1980). Allows an appreciation of the issues but is sparing on the actress.

J. McManners, *Abbés and Actresses: the church and the theatrical profession in eighteenth century France* (Oxford, 1986)

K. McGill, 'Women and performance: the development of improvisation by the sixteenth century commedia dell'arte', *Theatre Journal*, 43 (1991)

The painter

A. Sutherland and L. Nochlin, *Women Artists 1550–1950*, Exhibition Catalogue, Los Angeles Museum of Art (New York, 1977). A remarkable summary of existing scholarship on a range of women painters.

G. Greer, *The Obstacle Race: The Fortunes of Women Painters and their Work* (London, 1979). A scholarly examination of the factors inhibiting the development of women painters with considerable respect for time and place.

G. Pollock and R. Parker, *Old Mistresses: Women, Art and Ideology* (London, 1981)

W. Slatkin, *Women Artists in History from Antiquity to the 20th Century* (Englewood Cliffs, N.J., 1990)

Individual artists

M. D. Garrard, *Artemisia Gentileschi: The Image of the Female Hero in Italian Baroque Art* (Princeton, 1989). Makes many assumptions which have been questioned.

E. Cropper, 'Artemisia Gentileschi la "pittora"' in G. Calvi ed., *Barocco al femminile* (Rome/Bari 1992). Gives an excellent bibliography and measured account of this artist.

I. S. Perlingieri, *Sofonisba Anguissola: The First Great Woman Artist of the Renaissance* (New York, 1992)

Sofonisba Anguissola e le sue sorelle, Exhibition Catalogue (Cremona, 1994)

M. T. Cantaro, *Lavinia Fontana bolognese pittora singolare, 1552–1614* (Milan, 1989). A *catalogue raisonné*.

V. Fortunati ed., *Lavinia Fontana, 1552–1614* (Milan, 1994). A collection of articles, some very loosely tied to the painter.

C. P. Murphy, 'Lavinia Fontana: the making of a woman artist' in E. Kloek, N. Teeuwen and M. Huisman eds., *Women of the Golden Age. An International Debate on Women in Seventeenth Century Holland, England and Italy* (Hilversum, 1994)

Judith Leyster: A Dutch Master and her World (Zwolle/Worcester, Mass., 1993)

A great deal of scope remains for work on seventeenth and eighteenth century women painters and their patrons.

RIOT

In establishing riot as a field for the examination of mentalities and political perceptions the following were influential:

G. Rudé, *The Crowd in the French Revolution* (Oxford, 1959)

E. P. Thompson, 'The moral economy of the English crowd in the eighteenth century', *Past and Present*, 50 (1972)

G. Rudé, *London and Paris in the Eighteenth Century* (London, 1979)

B. Porschnev, *Les soulèvements populaires en France de 1623 à 1648* (Paris, 1963)

R. Pillorget, *Les mouvements insurrectionnels de Provence entre 1596 et 1715* (Paris, 1975). This and other work on French peasant riots is summarized in C. Jouhaud, 'Révoltes et contestations d'ancien régime' in J. Julliard ed., *Histoire de la France. Les conflits* (Paris, 1990).

The debate on women's roles found early expression in N. Z. Davis, 'Women on top' in *Society and Culture in Early Modern France* (London, 1975). This work is discussed in S. Desan, 'Crowds, community and ritual in the work of E. P. Thompson and Nathalie Zemon Davis' in L. Hunt ed., *The New Cultural History* (London, 1989)

Specifically on women and riot

R. Houlbrouke, 'Women's social life and common action in England from the fifteenth century to the eve of the Civil War', *Continuity and Change*, 1 (1986), 171–89

J. Bohstedt, 'Gender, household and community politics: women in English riots 1790–1810', *Past and Present*, 120 (1988). Extrapolates too much about the early modern period from the 19th century.

M. Thomis and J. Grimmett, *Women in Protest 1800–1850* (London, 1982)

R. Dekker, *Holland in beroering: oproeren in de 17de den 18de eeuw* (Baarn, 1982)

R. Dekker, 'Women in revolt. Collective protest and its social base in Holland', *Theory and Society*, 16 (1987)

O. Hufton, 'Aufrüherische Frauen in traditionalen Gesellschaften.

Lebenswege von Frauen im Ancien Regime: England, Frankreich und Holland im 17. und 18. Jahrhunderts', *Geschichte und Gesellschaft*, 18 (1992)

M. Kobelt-Groch, *Aufsässige Tochter Gottes. Frauen im Bauernkrieg und in den Täuferbewegungen* (Frankfurt, 1993)

With significant information on women

D. Underdown, *Revel, Riot and Rebellion. Popular Politics and Culture in England, 1603–1660* (Oxford, 1985)

J. Walter, 'Grain riots and popular attitudes towards the law' in J. Brewer and J. Styles, *An Ungovernable People. The English and their law in the 17th and 18th centuries* (London, 1980)

O. Hufton, 'Social conflict and the grain supply in eighteenth century France' in R. Rotberg and T. K. Rabb eds., *Hunger and History* (Cambridge, 1985)

Women and the French Revolution

There is now a very considerable bibliography on this theme and an up-to-date bibliography can be found in O. Hufton, *Women and the Limits of Citizenship in the French Revolution* (Toronto, 1992). Two sections of this book are dedicated to the analysis of differing types of disturbances involving women.

Overviews
A. Rosa, *Citoyennes: Les Femmes et la Révolution Française* (Paris, 1988)
C. Marand Fouquet, *La Femme au temps de la Révolution* (Paris, 1989)

Among works touching in particular on working class women
D. Godineau, *Citoyennes tricoteuses: les femmes du peuple à Paris pendant la Révolution Française* (Aix, 1988)

D. Godineau, 'Formation d'une mythe contre révolutionnaire: "Les Tricoteuses"', *L'Image de la Révolution: Actes du Congrès Mondiale*, 3 (Oxford, 1989)

O. Hufton, 'Women in Revolution, 1789–96', *Past and Present*, 53 (1971)

S. Petersen, *Die grosse Revolution und die kleine Leute* (Cologne, 1989)

S. Petersen, *Lebensmittelfrage und revolutionäre Politik in Paris, 1792–1793* (Munich, 1979)

S. Petersen, *Marktweiber und Amazones: Frauen in der französischen Revolution* (Cologne, 1989)

R. B. Rose, *The Enragés: Socialists of the French Revolution* (Melbourne, 1966)

R. B. Rose, 'Women and the French Revolution: the political activity of Parisian women 1789–1794', *University of Tasmania Occasional Papers* 5, (1976)

G. Rudé and R. Cobb, 'Le dernier mouvement de la Révolution Française: Les journées de germinal et prairial l'an III', *Revue Historique*, 214 (1955)

Feminism and political activism

J. Abray, 'Feminism in the French Revolution', *American Historical Review*, 80/1 (February 1975)

H. B. Applewhite and D. G. Levy eds., *Women and Politics in the Age of the Democratic Revolution* (Ann Arbor, 1990)

M. Cerati, *Le Club des Citoyennes Républicaines Révolutionnaires* (Paris, 1966)

L. Lacour, *Les Origines du Féminisme Contemporain: trois femmes de la Révolution, Olympe de Gouges, Théroigne de Méricourt, Rose Lacombe* (Paris, 1900)

E. Roudinesco, *Théroigne de Méricourt: une femme mélancolique sous la Révolution* (Paris, 1989)

J. Vega, 'Feminist republican: Etta Palm-Aelders on justice, virtue and men', *History of European Ideas*, 10 (1989)

J. Vega, 'Etta Palm, une Hollandaise à Paris' in W. Frijhoff and R. Dekker eds., *Le voyage révolutionnaire* (Hilversum, 1991)

Religious riots

R. Dupuy, 'Les femmes et la Contre Révolution dans l'Ouest', *Bulletin d'histoire économique et social de la Révolution Française* (1980)

O. Hufton, 'The reconstruction of a church 1796–1801' in G. Lewis and C. Lucas eds., *Beyond the Terror* (Cambridge, 1981)

S. Desan, *Reclaiming the Sacred: Lay Religion and Popular Politics in Revolutionary France* (Ithaca, 1991)

M. Vovelle, *Religion et Révolution. La Déchristianisation de l'an II à Paris* (Paris, 1989)

A. Mathiez, *La Question religieuse sous la Révolution Française* (Paris, 1929)

A. Aulard, *Le Culte de la Raison et de l'Être Suprême 1793–1794. Essai historique* (Paris, 1892)

On women in revolts in the Dutch Republic

W. P. te Brake, R. Dekker, L. C. van de Pol, 'Women and political culture in the Dutch Revolutions' in H. Applewhite and D. Levy eds., *Women and Politics in the Age of the Democratic Revolution* (Ann Arbor, 1990)

INDEX

———◆◆———

The English
A Social History 1066–1945

Christopher Hibbert

'Christopher Hibbert writes so well, and presents a huge amount of material with such skill, that this 900 page volume can be read more quickly and enjoyably than many novels . . . an admirable evocation of the past and a lasting analysis of the English character'
JOHN MORTIMER *Sunday Times*

'From tournaments, pilgrims and kings through to bus conductors and summer holidays, he isolates the changing habits of successive generations. His greatest – and extraordinary – success is to have extracted from this mass of material the exact character of each century he touches' *The Independent*

'Enthralling . . . Barons and peasants, contemporaries of Pepys and Boswell, a people revolutionised by technology – all leap from his pages like figures on a canvas by Lowry . . . How anyone can write as much and as well as Hibbert is a mystery. His big, rich book deserves a place on the shelves of anyone remotely interested in our history'
Mail on Sunday

'A glorious cavalcade of 900 years of life and death, work and play, sex and sensibility amongst the English . . . Christopher Hibbert blends erudition, energy and elegance to perfection . . . Get beyond the myths of history; treat yourself to this feast of a book'
ROY PORTER *The Standard*

'Compiled with flair and skill and with that flair for particularity and even oddity which no historian, "popular" or otherwise, can afford to dispense with' *Times Literary Supplement*

0 586 08471 1

HarperCollins*Publishers*

Patriots and Liberators
Revolution in the Netherlands 1780–1813

Simon Schama

'A rare and magnificent example of total history.'
Richard Cobb, *Times Literary Supplement*

'An outstanding work of historical scholarship . . . Simon Schama writes brilliantly. He can bring a character alive in a sentence . . . This powerful book reads with the ease of a novel. Every page glitters with intelligence and perception. In every way *Patriots and Liberators* is an extraordinary achievement.'
J. H. Plumb

Between 1780 and 1813 the Dutch Republic – a country once rich enough to be called the cash till of Europe and powerful enough to make war with England – was stripped of its colonies, invaded by its enemies, driven to the edge of bankruptcy, and finally reduced to becoming an appendage of the French Empire. Out of these events Simon Schama has constructed a gripping chronicle of revolution and privateering, constitutions and coups, in a tiny nation desperately struggling to stay afloat in the seas of geopolitics. Like his *The Embarrassment of Riches* and *Citizens*, *Patriots and Liberators* combines a mastery of historical sources with an unabashed delight in narrative. The result confirms Schama as one of the most exciting and engaging historians now at work.

'This remarkable book is more than a revision, it is a revelation.'
A. J. P. Taylor, *Observer*

'A dramatic story, full of pathos and true comedy. If any book may be said to inhale without sententiousness the clear, calm and steadying air of a European ideal, this is it.' Michael Ratcliffe, *The Times*

'Schama's book is written in the grand manner, its sweep as impressive as its erudition and the constant brilliance of its style. He gives the Dutch revolution back to the people to whom it belonged – the Dutch.'
Economist

ISBN 0 00 686156 3

The Magus of the North

J.G. Hamman and the
Origins of Modern Irrationalism

Isiah Berlin

Isaiah Berlin is regarded by many as the greatest living historian of ideas. In *The Magus of the North* he unearths with grace and elegance the radical counter-Enlightenment figure J. G. Hamann, the forgotten source of a movement that in the end engulfed the whole of European culture. Born in 1730, Hamann was a solitary and idiosyncratic thinker who lived a life of poverty and neglect in Königsberg in the north of East Prussia. Despite being admired by Herder, Goethe and Kant, he has remained largely unknown outside Germany.

Berlin, with his astonishing capacity to enter the minds of past thinkers, rescues from obscurity this self-styled oracular sage – 'the Magus of the North', as Hamann liked to be called. Hamann, Berlin argues, was profoundly original: the first secular opponent of the Enlightenment, the father of modern European irrationalism, and a crucial forerunner of romanticism and existentialism. Like all Berlin's works, *The Magus of the North* is enlightening, quizzical, passionate and, above all, convincing.

'[*The Magus of the North*] offers us yet another remarkably vivid portrait of an important thinker, in an essay form which Berlin has perfected.'
MARK LILLA, *London Review of Books*

'Isaiah Berlin is one of the most lucid and profound thinkers of our time. Whom he chooses to write about, and why, is no less interesting than what he actually writes.' ELON SALMON, *Yorkshire Post*

'*The Magus of the North* is a delightful surprise . . . The prose flows powerfully, at times torrentially, richly saturated in information and ideas.' MICHAEL ROSEN, *Times Literary Supplement*

0 00 686319 1